HORSE SENSE
FOR THE
NEW MILLENNIUM

HORSE SENSE
FOR THE NEW MILLENNIUM

THE CONSERVATIVE CASE

Wesley Allen Riddle

ISBN: 979-8-89031-806-0 (sc)
ISBN: 979-8-89031-807-7 (hc)
ISBN: 979-8-89031-808-4 (e)
Library of Congress Control Number: 2011913701

THE EWINGS PUBLISHING

One Galleria Blvd., Suite 1900, Metairie, LA 70001
(504) 702-6708

This work is dedicated to

the thinker and thoughtful citizen of these United States.

IMAGES

Interior section page illustration by Gloria T. Riddle-Roe © 2003

TABLE OF CONTENTS

Note 1: See also Index for a complete listing of Articles by Name and Articles by Number.
Note 2: Notation o/a by date indicates publication "on or about."

ACKNOWLEDGEMENTS

I'd like to thank those who made this book possible. It is no easy task to bring one to fruition, or at least a book with substantive content as I hope readers find this one to be. Practically everyone is "matrixed" to the max these days—meaning they do too many things, juggling priorities and tasks constantly. People like to call that multitasking, but it really means they have very little quality time left to give anyone or to any project requiring focus.

I'd like to thank those who did find or make the time. Prosper "Prop" Walker is a fellow West Pointer (Class of 1954) and long-time resident of Belton, Texas. He helped distribute and promote my "Horse Sense" columns for most of the past decade and never asked for anything in return. He did it energetically, in a determined persistent sort of way that is the hallmark of "the Army Way." He did it as he told me, because he believes in the cause of "Faith and Freedom!" and a restoration of the Republic. He did it because we are also best of friends, and for that I am exceedingly grateful. Thank you Prop, and God bless you Sir.

Lisa G. Shockey did the vast majority of work on this manuscript besides the actual writing of the columns, which I'll take credit for (including all errors). She had assistance from her husband Patrick W. Shockey on computer program glitches and some issues involving difficult software codes. Otherwise, Lisa single-handedly accomplished what others tried and failed to do before. She tackled the project head on and refused to let it get bogged down. She kept to schedule, met every deliverable to professional standards. She is truly the most gifted project manager for development of books, manuals and manuscripts I've ever met. Her contribution moreover involved not only technical expertise, but a considerable alacrity with concepts and excellent understanding of the material itself just to be able to organize, categorize and index the work as well as she did. Thank you for bringing out a decade's worth of work in nearly perfect form for publication.

Finally, to thank one's wife could read like an obligatory passage or afterthought. In my case, however, it really is an essential expression from me of the full measure of my gratitude. The book were not possible if others had not helped—for instance, to form the columns into a cohesive manuscript in computer file and then physically. But also, the book were not possible without the one most dear to me, my wife Aida, who sustains what I do every day and loves me whether I've got a book or not. This line is written on the eve of my twenty-fifth wedding anniversary, and I realize that everything we have rests upon a simple fact that we two people fell in love, and also stuck it out 'through thick and thin.' I'm so happy God drew us together and kept us together, and if there is any wisdom found in this book then I know I learned a lot of it from her.

Wes Riddle
Belton, TX
(20 December 2010)

FOREWORD

by Tom Pauken

In 1981, Ronald Reagan entered his first term in office amidst a backdrop of rising unemployment, double-digit inflation, and an oversized government bureaucracy. When discussing the economic challenges he faced at the time, the President quipped, "The status quo, you know, is Latin for 'the mess we're in.'" The President took immediate action to address the problems. He got Congress to pass the Kemp-Roth Job Creation Act to get the private sector moving again. At the same time, in Reagan's first term we reduced discretionary domestic spending by nearly 10% during his first term in office. I am proud to say that we did even better than that at the agency I headed from 1981 to 1985, Action, where we cut spending by 25%. And, the President put a strategy in place to win the Cold War and defeat the "Evil Empire" of the Soviet Union.

Now, three decades later, Americans are anguishing over a new set of problems, resembling those Reagan faced in his first term, but of much larger scale and complexity. As I write this in the second quarter of 2011, current unemployment levels have yet to recover from the national recession that officially began on December 2007. Middle class wages in the private sector remain stagnant. There has been zero private sector job growth nationally over the past decade while the U.S. has lost 5.5 million manufacturing jobs during that same timeframe—that's one-third of our U.S. manufacturing base. The housing market is still adjusting to trend lines preceding the bursting of the subprime mortgage bubble induced by easy monetary policies of the Federal Reserve and credit excesses of the Wall Street crowd. Nearly a quarter of homeowners remain "underwater" as they owe more on their mortgages than their homes are worth. Meanwhile, as Congress wrestles over difficult cuts to programs and benefits, the United States is spending $436 million a day sending its young men and women overseas to fight in two protracted conflicts in the Middle East. Needless to say, for many Main Street Americans, the "status quo" has once again come to resemble *the mess we're in*.

During times of great difficulty, there is a real risk that an ailing society seeking fast relief will fall susceptible to "solutions" that extend government reach at the expense of personal liberty. And it is at these crossroads in history when the conservative voice in politics must be at its clearest and most spirited to ensure that our nation avoids the trap of drifting into a socialist state where the government controls our lives from the cradle to the grave. A government big enough to give us everything we need is powerful enough to take away everything we have. Wesley A. Riddle understands the dangers of an all too powerful government. In the following pages, Riddle offers a lens for interpreting modern political events that is of particular value given the failure of the Washington "political elites" to provide the kind of leadership our nation so badly needs.

While the flawed liberal policies of the Obama administration have made a bad situation worse, the failures of post-Reagan Republicans have made it possible for the most liberal regime in American history to come to power. The presidency of George W. Bush is a prime example of the Republican Party's recent inability to choose capable candidates who place principle before political gain. During Bush's eight years in the White House, federal expenditures grew at an inflation-adjusted rate of over 41 percent compared to the 13.5-percent growth of the economy as a whole. The Bush administration passed the first new entitlement since Lyndon Baines Johnson, an unfunded liability to Medicare that will speed up the date in which that program goes bankrupt. And defense spending for the wars in Iraq and Afghanistan is set to reach $1.29 trillion by the end of 2011.

Clearly, the ideas of Barry Goldwater and Ronald Reagan took a back seat during the two terms Bush was in office, leaving many to wonder: What happened to the conservative principles of Constitutionalism, federalism, limited government, and a foreign policy guided by our national interest?

In my recent book, *Bringing America Home*, I write about the hijacking of the conservative movement by Machiavellian pragmatists and neoconservative ideologues, which squandered the political capital built up over three decades by Goldwater-Reagan conservatives.

Wes Riddle is a Constitutional conservative who understands that the only hope for America's future lies in returning to our nation's founding principles and applying them to the problems facing America today. He understands that we have a road map in the Constitution, and a compass in our Christian principles.

This, in essence, has been the resounding theme of the political writings of Mr. Riddle whose motto is "faith and freedom." Over the past decade, he has enlightened readers of his "Horse Sense" column by applying his expansive academic knowledge of American history into his critiques of modern political events. Riddle's work is informed and shaped by the language of the Framers and he has a special talent for explaining their original intent in light of modern day dilemmas.

In *Horse Sense*, Riddle argues that America's defining principles are not embodied in Roosevelt's New Deal, but rather, are posited in the self-evident truths of Jefferson's Declaration of Independence. He is a man who is concerned about ever-growing government, declining political participation, and the deterioration of moral society. His solutions for bringing America out of "the mess we're in" are basic: faith and freedom, and a little of what he likes to call "*horse sense*." And now, more than ever, are we in need of a good dose of it.

BIOGRAPHICAL SKETCH

of Wesley Allen Riddle

Only forty-nine years old as this book goes to print, Wesley Allen Riddle has already compiled a record that would be deemed remarkable were he twice as old.

A political activist from his youth. A career soldier who helped usher out the Cold War and saw combat in the Middle East. A common-sense philosopher and solid historian. A self-made and successful businessman. An international trainer whose contributions have buttressed America's effort to thwart radical Islamism. A man of demonstrated faith and character. A servant of his community and country. Wes Riddle is a man to take note of.

From humble roots, his life has followed an achievement-driven trajectory. Tracing that trajectory adds yet another vignette to the Great American Story.

Walter Riddle and Gloria Longnecker were the first two members in their respective families to graduate from college. The two met when they were students at the University of Texas in Austin, and married in 1960. Wesley was born a year later.

The marriage lasted only eight years before divorce left Gloria a single parent with two young boys to raise. Combining child support payments with some help from her parents, and holding a number of part-time jobs—switch-board operator, school bus driver, home music teacher—she carved out a middle class existence for her little family in Spring Branch, a suburb on the west side of Houston.

Wes Riddle's early years were the 1960s and 1970s, an era overshadowed by the Cold War and shaken by the counterculture movement. Both had an enduring effect on the youngster. He grew up firmly anti-Communist and discouraged by the unraveling of so many American institutions, particularly the family. He became self-consciously conservative and politically aware at an age when most boys are more typically focused on girls, sports, and cars.

A bright student, he excelled in high school, where, among other honors, he became president of the school's debate team. Reaching out beyond high school, he attended summer speech and debate institutes at Baylor University. His academic strengths and extra-curricular successes brought an appointment to the United States Military Academy. Becoming a cadet at West Point was a natural step for a young man who had come to believe that service in uniform should be an obligation of citizenship.

Wes continued on the path of academic excellence at West Point, winning particular notice in humanities courses. He captained the Academy's debate team and, at graduation in 1983, received the two highest awards for achievement in history. That sterling record propelled him later to pursue graduate studies in Modern History at Oxford University in England, where he garnered still more prestigious awards. He then joined the history faculty at West Point for a three year assignment, during which he taught courses including American Political Tradition. By the time he had completed that tour of duty, Wes had earned a reputation beyond the walls of the Military Academy. Outside lectures and writings established him as an original thinker unafraid to tackle the tougher issues in society. The Heritage Foundation awarded him the Salvatori Fellowship for 1996-97, and the National Humanities Institute named him a permanent Fellow.

Meanwhile, military duties were providing him an unusual breadth of experiences and an expanding array of responsibilities.

Commissioned in the Army's air defense branch, Wes enjoyed early assignments and schooling typical for new second lieutenants. His initial posting was to Hawaii, which proved not only to be professionally rewarding but personally significant. While on a training exercise in the Philippines, he met his future wife, Maria Aida. The two were wed in 1985 in Houston.

His next posting was to Germany, serving with U. S. forces assigned to NATO. This tour, too, brought him an unanticipated bonus. Then Captain Riddle was commanding a PATRIOT missile battery in 1990 when Iraq invaded neighboring Kuwait. His battery was among those units deployed to the desert and committed to combat. Interestingly, Wes found himself a decade later back in the same theater serving for two years as Air Defense Advisor to the State of Kuwait.

His final posting was with III Corps at Fort Hood, Texas, where he was the Chief of the Corps Air Defense Element. He retired as a lieutenant colonel in 2003, rounding out an even twenty years in uniform. He and

Aida chose to make their home in Belton, Texas, a small town not far from Fort Hood.

Immediately upon leaving the Army, Wes entered the political wars. The long-time incumbent in the congressional district that included Fort Hood and Belton—11th Texas—was a Democrat, a career politician whose liberal leanings were the antithesis of Wes' conservative views. Despite having neither money nor name recognition, he decided to enter the 2004 election as a Republican. The outcome of that race will forever remain in the realm of conjecture—for it was never run. Only three months before the primary elections the State of Texas restructured its congressional districts. The incumbent Democrat, whom Wes had hoped to unseat, ended up in another district, while the county containing the Riddle home in Belton was shifted into a district—31st Texas—which had a respected and well-known Republican incumbent. On election day neophyte candidate Wes Riddle carried one county and polled well in all others except the incumbent's home area, but his grass-roots, insurgent campaign designed to defeat a Democrat could not prevail against a fellow Republican. Shrugging his shoulders, he turned his mind to finding employment.

Actually, he and Aida had entered the business world before his retirement from the Army. In 2000 they purchased an historic home in Belton and opened it as a bed-and-breakfast. (That year, also, Wes began to write a weekly column for *The Belton Journal.* Called "Horse Sense," the column has run continuously despite his frequent extended absences in the military and since. Columns from "Horse Sense" form the basis of this book.)

In late 2004 he returned to the Middle East, a region of the world he had come to know rather well during his Army service. After the consuming national tragedy of September 11, 2001, America was attempting to bring stability and democracy to that troubled region, and leaders with his array of experiences could help immensely. Besides, going there was another way to serve. Aida would remain in Belton caring for the family properties.

Wes signed on with Vinnell Arabia, an overseas enterprise of Northrop Grumman working at the behest of the U. S. government to modernize and train armed forces in Saudi Arabia. He was stationed in Riyadh, Saudi Arabia for over five years and performed several management responsibilities, notably with the Office of Force Integration. He was promoted in grade to senior management and finished his service there as manager of the Force Integration Division.

The brief biographical summary recounted above races past several life-altering experiences that, taken together, operated to make Wes Riddle the person he is. Consider only three of them:

The first, in time and perhaps in lasting significance as well, would be the role of religion in his life. His family devoutly followed the tenets of the Christian Science church. They did not drink or smoke or use medicine, relying instead on prayer for healing. Sunday School and church were regular fixtures in his youth, imparting to the inquisitive boy an abiding reliance on faith. He also acquired a personal appreciation of the practical aspects of the First Amendment as it pertained to the rights of religious minorities. Although Aida had been raised as a Roman Catholic, their beliefs did not clash. Religious experiences in the Army tended to be more ecumenical than they were in the general population, which broadened their perspectives. Not long after making Belton their home, Wes and Aida joined the town's First Baptist Church and were publicly baptized. Somewhere along the way, as his religious and philosophical thinking matured, the fundamentals of faith became intertwined with the concept of liberty. "Faith and Freedom!" became Wes Riddle's slogan in the 2004 race for Congress.

Second, entering his teen years Wes underwent a transition tantamount to an Epiphany. The sad spectacle of Watergate, with the image of a President resigning in disgrace, seared itself into his very soul. Government officials in a democracy simply had to function from a base of integrity; they had to be leaders of character. He decided to become engaged in the political process. At that time virtually all political operatives in his area were Democrats, so he went to a meeting of Harris County (Houston) Democrats to learn what he could do. The adults there, not very surprisingly, were patronizingly indifferent to an eighth grader who wanted to discuss serious issues. It happened, though, that one of his mother's music students was the child of a local Republican. Wes approached him. He found that the man not only listened but actually encouraged him to get involved. And get involved he did. While still in junior high school, Wes organized the youngest Teen-Age Republican club in the history of Texas. As he moved into high school he took his club along, but only after successfully lobbying the school board to pressure a reluctant principal to allow it to operate. In 1976 he participated in the Republican National Convention in Kansas City, where he first encountered Ronald Reagan. Reagan's dramatic speech there convinced the boy that both the future of the party and the future of America rested on the shoulders of the California Governor. From that moment he was an avowed Reagan disciple. During his senior year he was named Texas Youth Advisor to Ronald Reagan and Citizens for the Republic. A political flame had been kindled in his heart.

Then, nearly a decade and a half later, while he was studying in England, a stunning tragedy occurred at the compound of a religious cult near Waco, Texas. An armed stand-off ended with dozens, including children, burning to death when federal agents attempted to storm the compound. Keenly following events of the siege, he was shocked—incensed, really—at the government's inept handling of the affair leading up to the terrible conflagration. He saw the awful outcome as an offspring of the unchecked growth and power of the federal government. Even worse, it was evidence in his mind of disrespect for states rights and constitutional prerogative, and showed an appalling disregard for religious and civil liberties. Wes was critical of the elected officials in that area, craven leaders, he believed, who would not take a stand and speak out to avoid the clash. In particular, he thought the U. S. Congressman from that district—being not only a member of the same political party as the President and the Governor at the time, but also the elected federal official closest to the people—had a special responsibility to act. "We should have seen him standing in front of those tanks, like the Chinaman at Tiananmen Square!" he wrote. (Ironically, and perhaps not entirely coincidentally, that was the same career politician he would seek to unseat in the 2004 race.)

His mind was set. Irrevocably. Wes would thereafter devote himself to doing whatever he could to help restore to government the historic values that had made America great. Having been educated at West Point, Oxford, and various Army schools, he had commitments carrying him nearly to the point of retirement. He would therefore finish his time in uniform, retire honorably after a career of military service, and then enter the political arena. Idealistic? Yes, certainly. But that became his plan. Thus it was no surprise to anyone who really knew him that he jumped into the ring as soon as he hung up his uniform.

Dave R. Palmer, Lieutenant General (Ret.)
Historian and Former Superintendent
United States Military Academy

PREFACE

From December 2000 through the first decade of the 21st Century, I wrote nearly 500 weekly columns appearing in *The Belton Journal* and other newspapers and online sites. From these, around half were selected and grouped thematically and are presented in this book. The columns themselves are contemporary; that is to say, they were not written as a look back but rather as they occurred from contemporary thoughts on contemporary events. They are arranged, however, in a way that paints a picture in words and tells the story of a tumultuous and often troubled time. Collectively, they tell of the rush of events in American politics, and they point the way, as a roadmap to the future, towards the possibility of better politics and better policies for the rest of this century. Conservatives of whatever stripe should enjoy the commentary. Others with an interest in politics, as well as students of history and the humanities, should find it interesting and informative—even if this sounds somewhat presumptuous.

I still remember the well-intentioned but very stern lecture I received outside of the Foundation for Economic Education (FEE) in Irvington-on-Hudson, NY, sometime 1996. I had frequented FEE events as an Army officer while on the American history faculty at the United States Military Academy (USMA) at West Point. Professor Hans Sennholz, the Foundation's president at the time, had asked me to submit a few sample columns with the potential (and indeed my firm expectation) that I would soon have a featured spot in the conservative think tank's monthly flagship publication, *The Freeman*. The prospect of having a paid column in such a fine and respected journal excited me tremendously, and I worked hard to produce eight pieces to gain that honor and to expand my livelihood and academic credentials. As I recall, I must have applied all my creative brilliance, because unfortunately I cinched the deal the other way! Professor Sennholz, whom I truly liked and always respected essentially told me I was utterly devoid of discipline since I had written "all over the place"; and worse, I wrote about things for which I had no special expertise or an earned degree, which gave me (to him at least) no credible academic "right" to write about them. Let us say his language and expression contained little in the way of nuance. If I had limited my scope to topics on American economic *history* or the *history* of the American economy, well it would have been okay he said, but oh no—I had provided him with samples ranging literally from world history to American history; from macro economics to ancient and modern philosophy; from religion and metaphysics to culture and current politics! He hated current politics too.

Professor Sennholz was indeed quite "German," and my sample columns that were meant to impress him turned out to be an affront to his traditional and rigorous sensibilities. I came off as being presumptuous, drawing freely as I did from practically all the humanities in my writing. (Ironically, it could have been a relatively easy assignment!). Thankfully as it turned out, I had other essays and reviews that worked out for *The Freeman*, and I did in fact publish all the sample columns I had given to Dr. Sennholz, over the next two years in a quality but short-lived quarterly journal called *The Social Critic*. Indeed, I was surprised one day to receive a very kind and complimentary postcard from Pat Buchanan after he read an issue of *The Social Critic*. Later I was named Fellow at the National Humanities Institute (NHI) in Washington, D.C., which gave some credibility not only to me but also credence to Dr. Sennholz's perception. Clearly I wasn't easily corralled and would tend to borrow my arguments and rationale from various academic disciplines. Quite frankly, I thought then and do still believe that one of the points of being a columnist in the first place is to be able to write about any and everything, and to say those things that otherwise do not fit into neat categories. I admit to seeking connections and to attempting to craft my explanatory narrative in such a way that it hopefully conveys the integral nature of reality and quaint as it may sound, *Truth*.

Then again, it does all come back to basics—master those and sophistication is relatively easy. Principles and values are essential to right reasoning, and this includes knowledge of Scripture and a love and reverence for God. Indeed there is an intellectual tradition of Faith and Freedom that once was ascendant in this country. It actually gave rise to the Constitution and to the Dream of the Republic, and I am grateful that it lives in some iterative fashion amongst a few thinkers and think tanks and with the remnant of folk who live in the Heartland of this nation, wherever that happens to be. I am grateful that its presence is particularly strong in Texas. The political tradition there uniquely stresses federalism and Original Intent. It takes stock of Original Sin and cognizance of the human condition too, the same way it did with the Founders. The Founding Fathers had horse sense enough, and so should we, to forswear and to actively resist the socialist and other experimentations that concentrate power in the hands of men and governments and so extinguish liberty. I hope that you of a like mind may find encouragement to your soul in the pages that follow, and also fuel enough to light a prairie fire of conservatism that engulfs the land.

WESLEY ALLEN RIDDLE

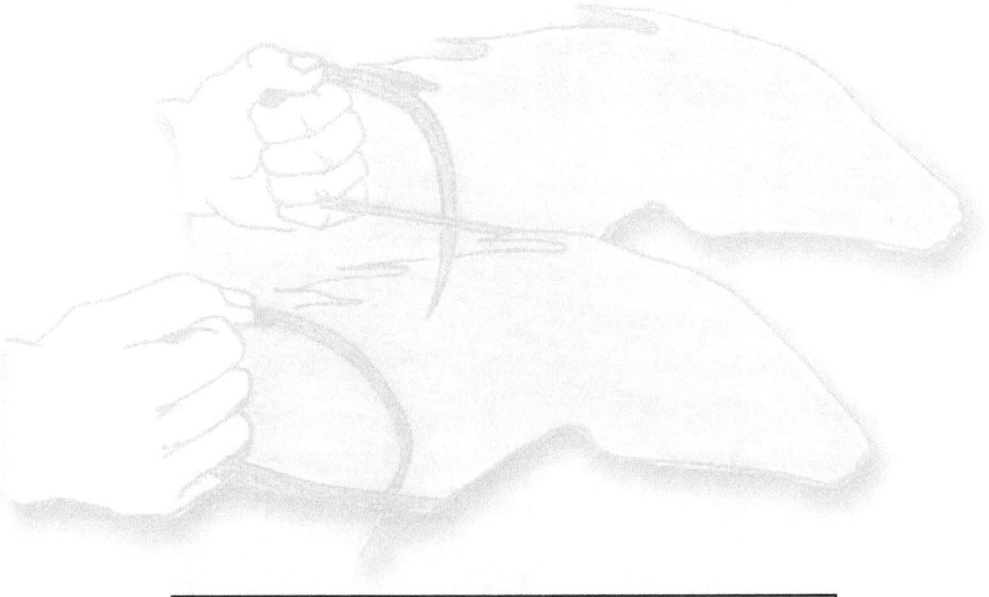

INTRODUCTION

CHAPTER 1

Horse Sense

Horses and Humans Article #028
July 19, 2001

Recently I met a lady who said she'd seen my "Horse Sense" column in *The Belton Journal.* I prepared myself for meaningful, if possibly critical feedback. But then I found out she didn't read the column, because she thought it was about horses! It reminded me of a recent caller, who inquired into the Glen-Riddle Manor B&B. At the end of our conversation, he asked me "By the way, who is Glen?" Of course, glen is a word of Scottish origin meaning valley. When capitalized, it becomes part of the place name (take a look at Scotch Whiskey bottles sometime). Although I assured the lady in Temple this was no column about horses, I do admit this one comes mighty close—it is about horses and humans to be (in-)exact. The paragraphs that follow are written by Herbert Shelley Good (1902-1967), a former director of the Henry George School in Boston. He is author of a yet unpublished private notebook of thoughts, and this piece is from that notebook—having only been carried before by a small magazine in Patchogue, New York, called *Fragments*:

A dictionary defines "horse sense" as "practical common sense," which is very confusing. Any politician, who claims to have any, will assure you that it is not common. The mere fact that a horse doesn't have sense enough to stay away from humans proves that it is not practical either. A horse has to work or run its legs off—and then end up in a glue factory. This is horse sense?

What may be practical to a horse would not necessarily appear to a human being in the same light—except the business of crossing weak bridges. People never give the horse credit for figuring things out, like quicksand and other natural booby traps. It is just "instinct," they say, which goes along with being a horse, like hair, hide, and hoofs.

If humans have any built-in "instinct," they keep it as quiet as possible, or, if they admit it at all, they call it a "hunch"—and use it to pick horses. There is no question that instinct serves animals just as "intuition" serves human beings. Among humans, the female is said to be the intuitive one, and this is probably due to the fact that for several thousand years, woman has not been allowed to know much. If a woman has an idea, which she cannot explain to her educated husband, it is called intuition. No horse ever stopped to explain; it just won't cross a weak bridge. Woman's procedure is somewhat similar.

Now that we men let women learn to read and write, they know more, and intuition is in danger. Woman is losing her advantage over man. It will not be long before intuition will be educated out of existence, woman will be a smarty like a man, and the world will be dependent on the horse to keep us out of trouble.

There is already a very great shortage of horse sense, probably because there are fewer horses. In this scientific age, we find modern horsepower to be the product of physical science; and widespread use of synthetic fertilizers has resulted in an equally widespread unemployment of horses. It is only a question of time before horse sense will be put up in capsules, or cellophane packages, or added to breakfast foods and tooth paste. Looks as if nothing can save the horse and its products—including horse sense—but a dark horse.

Long Live Horse Sense — Article #114
o/a October 26, 2003

Recently I revisited something that no doubt made it through the e-mail gauntlet and died somewhere in the electronic ether. The language I'm using is appropriate, given that the short anonymous piece was called an "Obituary on the death of Common Sense." I remember thinking when I first read it, that it was just too sardonic and dark for my taste. You see, I'm the eternal optimist. Notwithstanding, much of it rings true . . . .

Today we mourn the passing of an old friend, Common Sense. Common Sense lived a long life, but died in the United States from heart failure early in the new millennium. No one really knows how old he was, since his birth records were lost long ago in bureaucratic red tape.

He selflessly devoted his life to service in schools, hospitals, homes, and factories, helping folks get jobs done without fanfare and foolishness. For decades, petty rules, silly laws, and frivolous lawsuits held no power over Common Sense. He was credited with cultivating such valued lessons as to know when to come in out of the rain, why the early bird gets the worm, and that life isn't always fair.

Common Sense lived by simple, sound financial policies (don't spend more than you earn); reliable parenting strategies (the adults are in charge, not the kids); and it's okay to come in second. A veteran of the Industrial Revolution, the Great Depression, and the Technological Revolution, Common Sense survived cultural and educational trends including body piercing, whole language, and new math. But his health declined when he became infected with the "If-it-only-helps-one person-it's-worth-it" virus.

In recent decades, his waning strength proved no match for the ravages of well intentioned but overbearing regulations. He watched in pain as self-seeking lawyers ruled good people. His health rapidly deteriorated when schools endlessly implemented zero tolerance policies. Reports of a six-year-old boy charged with sexual harassment for kissing a classmate, a teen suspended for taking a swig of mouthwash after lunch, and a teacher fired for reprimanding an unruly student only worsened his condition. It declined even further when schools had to get parental consent to administer aspirin to a student but could not inform the parent when a female student was pregnant or wanted an abortion.

Common Sense lost his will to live as churches became businesses, criminals received better treatment than victims, and federal judges stuck their noses in everything from the Pledge of Allegiance to professional sports. When an individual, too stupid to realize that a steaming cup of coffee was hot, was awarded a huge settlement, Common Sense threw in the towel. As the end neared, Common Sense drifted in and out of logic but was kept informed of developments regarding questionable regulations such as those for low flow toilets, rocking chairs, step ladders and auto emissions. Common Sense finally succumbed when, while the United States was fighting a war on terrorism, a federal judge declared the Pledge of Allegiance to be unconstitutional.

Common Sense was preceded in death by his parents, Truth and Trust; his wife, Discretion; his daughter, Responsibility; and his son, Reason. He is survived by two step-siblings: My Rights, and Ima Whiner. Not many attended his funeral because so few realized he was gone.

Fortunately, there are a few reports of a long lost relative, who has been living quietly, out of the way for the past few years. Horse Sense remains in excellent health in mind, body and spirit, and he's been seen visiting small towns and country in Central Texas. He's resolved to name his growing brood after Common Sense and the others of his family who went before.

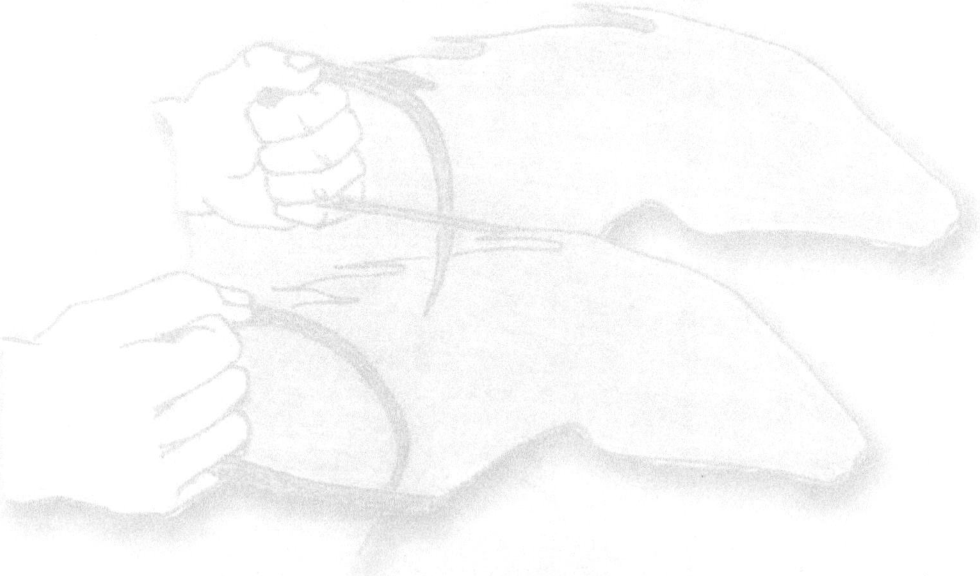

PART ONE: POLITICS

CHAPTER 2

ADMINISTRATION 2000

Election of GW Article #001
Dec. 28, 2000

On the Fourth of July 2000, Governor George W. Bush strode leisurely on Main Street shaking hands. He chose to campaign and to celebrate Independence Day in Belton, and he seemed to genuinely enjoy Belton's famed Fourth of July Parade. My wife and I were in our front yard like many residents, enjoying the weather and the festivities. Since our house is close to the start of the parade route, we probably enjoyed a fresher GW than others at the end of Central. When the Governor came over and shook our hands, I searched for something to say and came out with the thing that hit my mind. I just said, "You're going to be the next President of the United States." Bush started off and got about three steps away, turned right back around again and said, "I hope so." In the way he said it, it was clear to me that this man had the rare quality (for a politician) of sincerity. I felt at the time that if he should really make it, he would be a great president.

Over the course of these last five weeks or more, I've shared the sense of frustration with my fellow Americans about this election. It will stay in my memory as the one that never seemed to end. While Florida and much of the country seemed to be evenly divided, I dare say that GW had solid support in the State of Texas. And while I have respect for other States and for other people's views, I only wish that everyone who uttered a cynical chirp and laughed at the political humor was also someone, who cast an informed ballot at election time and took his civic responsibility seriously the whole year long. I'm afraid that's probably naïve and hopelessly optimistic. But here we are, and the fat lady has finally sung. The easy message to draw is that some election reform is in order, things like better technology and more uniform standards within States for voting. The harder message to discern is for the 43rd President and second son of a president to hold the highest office. Indications are, however, that he's doing it.

Instead of the mantra that's started about the necessity of governing "from the center," I hope George W. Bush will start to govern from the Constitution. His overture speech to the Presidency delivered after Vice President Gore's concession 13 December is encouraging. He evoked Jefferson and Lincoln. He mentioned two important "c" words, compassionate and conservatism. He laid out a broad set of legislative priorities: education; retirement and health security; tax relief; bipartisan foreign policy; and a strong military. From Lincoln, I hope he draws inclusiveness and equal opportunity—a bridging of the racial divide in this country. From Jefferson, however, I hope he stays true to States rights and to the spirit (if not the letter) of Jefferson's Kentucky Resolves. We should also add a bit of the dignity of George Washington to the task at hand. I don't want to see another Waco in my lifetime; but neither do I want to hear rumored, about the sordid degradation and vice of the President. Andrew Jackson called the position Tribune of the People. He's a man after all, who represents you and me.

Bush Tax Plan Article #018
o/a April 06, 2001

To hear the liberals, you'd think we ought to have to justify tax cuts. What's strange is how anyone could get something so entirely "bass ackwards." It is government spending that ought to (*and always*) be justified! To hear the media these days, government creates the wealth and parcels it out to the people. If you "spend" money on tax cuts, you waste it. Hello, is anybody out there? The fact is that government doesn't create wealth—it can't; it can only confiscate it. Individuals through ingenuity and hard work create the wealth, some of which gets taken from them for taxes. Cutting taxes is merely abstaining from taking as much from producers. As Sheldon Richman explains, "money never leaves the hands it originates in, because it never goes to Washington in the first place. Thus, all the talk about how much the Bush-plan will *give* the rich is sheer balderdash. It *gives* nothing to anyone."

Here in America we have become so mired in welfare state thinking, most people approach political issues as though tax revenues are a pot of cash that belongs to the government. Increases in spending are so normal that if someone proposes a smaller increase than planned, it's a budget cut! As Thomas Sowell has pointed out, the historical burden of proof has shifted from politicians to the people, a dangerous situation if you believe as the Founders did, that the power to tax is the power to destroy! Indeed, a government powerful enough to give you everything you want, paid for at taxpayer expense, is a government powerful enough to take everything.

Further, it may be that government is already on the verge of such all-power, because it cannot really be asserted the people have authorized the current tax laws. Richman again: "Tax laws are written in arcane language behind closed doors by a few tenured congressmen and their staffs. Government has myriad devices for mystifying its operations, in order to keep John Q. Citizen at a safe distance. We the people no more authorized the tax-eating monster we live with than we authorized the tornadoes that tore through Arkansas and Mississippi recently." It is not comforting to contemplate that we may have lapsed into a time before the American Revolution. Is the only apparent effect of the American Revolution that we spend our Fourth of July differently?

Possibly somewhere in our collective consciousness, the voice of Patrick Henry whispers. If so, there ought to be some resonance with the president's tax relief plan. Even after paying down on debt held by the public, the government will have 1.8 trillion dollars in excess revenue, a conservative estimate, at the current tax rates between 2002 and 2011. The president wants to reduce income tax rates; double the child-care tax credit; reduce the marriage penalty; expand charitable deductions; phase out the death tax; and extend research and experimentation tax credit. The president is trying to deliver on his campaign promises. As shocking as that is in itself, the irony is that his plan for the most part shouldn't even need to be justified—for in the absence of compelling justification for government spending, tax money should revert to the people who earn it. It is high time we reinstate the Constitutional burden of proof, onto parasitic politicians and their dependents of government largesse—removing it from off the backs of America's breadwinners.

Campaign Finance Reform Article #022
May 31, 2001

A recent essay in *Atlantic Monthly* talked about America's new generation of so-called Organization Kids. They are hard working, civil, and they don't have a problem with authority either. They are inclusive, but they also believe merit should and usually does determine success. The picture was pretty positive, except that the author of the piece took umbrage, that students at prestigious universities were inarticulate when it came to moral reasoning or politics. Seems the rising generation and America's future leaders are so busy and hard working preparing themselves for success, and charting their specific goal-oriented courses to get there, they've plumb forgot about qualitative distinctions—things like what makes a good person or a bad one, and what constitutes a good society, say, from tyranny. Jefferson's dictum, "Eternal vigilance is the price of freedom," gets lost in the busy schedule. One student at Princeton said, "People are too busy to get involved in larger issues." Indeed, the problem besets more than university students—it's a problem with modern life.

Then again, folks are always looking for excuses. There are a million reasons not to go to church on Sunday, but there's a mighty big one to go anyway. There are reasons not to take the kids to soccer or to piano lessons, but the quality of their upbringing (and hence their futures), depends on such things. It seems Americans are always looking for mechanistic ways to take care of politics, because the truth is they just don't want to be bothered with being informed and making choices. So they try to put in term limits, instead of throwing the rascals out at the next election. I used to live in the Seventh Congressional District (Houston), where we had a stellar Congressman. He served for thirty years and only retired this year, but I'd vote him in another thirty if he would serve. Bill Archer became chairman of the House Ways and Means Committee when Republicans became the majority, after years in the political wilderness. He was a consistent and tireless advocate for smaller, more responsive government. When and if you get GW's tax cut this year, think about it. A part of the thanks belongs to a climate of support that took years in the making—a climate that tax-cut, IRS-watchdog Archer helped to foster.

Now there are renewed calls for campaign finance reform. People and powerful media concerns want to place caps on soft money to political parties, the way they did on individual contributions to candidates in 1974.

Ironically, had contributor limits been in place in 1968, Eugene McCarthy could never have gotten his campaign for president off the ground! Large, six-figure contributions from wealthy opponents of the Vietnam War made his campaign feasible. With restrictions in place now, only wealthy people can afford to run for office, because they pay from their own deep pockets. Successful challengers are less likely, because incumbents enjoy name-recognition and other advantages (like free postage). Soft money contributions to political parties grew in response to caps on individual contributions, and that has not been inherently bad. Parties serve as a buffer between candidates and narrower special interests, and the money probably enhanced the sagging importance of major political parties at the expense of some of these. Still, people make calls for campaign finance reform on an erroneous assumption that American politics is corrupt and money is somehow the culprit.

Friends, neighbors, countrymen, please! If politics is corrupt, it is because you are not sufficiently involved. Indeed, the arbitrary $1,000 limit on your First Amendment rights of political participation doesn't help. The Founders did not believe every man should exercise an equal influence in political affairs. Instead, they believed in the equal right of every citizen to participate in the political process. Consider the difference: they rather hoped for more influence by citizens, who actually gave a damn! Reading the paper and watching the news to stay informed is a basic civic responsibility; so is your casting your vote. Beyond that, an overachieving, good-citizenship-award sort of person might even be expected to participate in nuts-and-bolts politics at the grassroots (local precinct or county) level. If you don't know your party preference, check them both out! If you are young, there are the Teen-Age Republicans or Teen-Age Democrats, the College Republicans or College Democrats—and other political groups on campuses as well.

You would be amazed how easy access really is. It is based on the same principle as studying for your SATs to get into college. What you do matters in a free society. It determines whom you meet and what kind of influence you may exert. If you aren't at the rally, you don't meet the candidate. If you don't attend the public meeting, you can't tell him what you think. Except that you *can*—by writing letters, sending faxes or e-mails, etc. In recent election cycles, total direct spending for all congressional races was less than Americans spent on yogurt every year, or the average cost of a movie and popcorn per citizen. We need to eliminate contribution limits, not add more, in order to put government back into the hands of citizens who care. As Gene McCarthy put it years ago, the Founders pledged their "lives, fortunes, and sacred honor." Not their lives, and fortunes up to $1,000.

The Cost of Regulation Article #032
September 6, 2001

Regulations exist to ensure that what people do is done *a certain way*. We don't want people to erect fences, unless they are so high and made of such and such. We don't want folks to be able to add on to their houses, unless the additions blend nicely and meet certain safety standards—for people and for wildlife. We sure don't want someone to invent a craze or gadget that might catch on, unless we determine in advance how the paperwork should be filed, how much it ought to be taxed, who will inspect the item or activity. We don't even want a few folks to work at all, unless we establish licensing requirements first or mandate membership in some organization.

Regulation in general costs individuals and businesses a lot of money to comply. Costs are passed on to consumers, or else taken in the shorts. Of more concern, according to ABC News reporter John Stossel, is the sheer distraction of creative power. The proverbial bar is raised by regulations, i.e., the threshold for achievement goes harder if not exactly higher. Creative impulses can in fact be thwarted, because regulations distract focus, diffuse effort, discourage risk-taking, frustrate intent, and spend a lot of (life)-time. Thus, things that could be simply aren't, because the regulatory environment keeps them from being realized—a new engine or energy source perhaps, new medicine, maybe just a better mousetrap. The reason is that an inducement one place is a disincentive someplace else. Regulatory roadblocks and obstacles, including scrutiny, result in a comparative incentive to do something else or to go somewhere else. The implied message is certainly not one for the budding hero. Rather, regulations choke the best and instruct men and women of initiative to take the easier road, the one most traveled. Regulations don't only depress the economy, they also depress the spirit.

The difference between something regulated and unregulated is in the measure of freedom. Stossel has shrewdly observed that before the fall of communism visitors to Moscow noticed a dead-eyed look in the people. It was not about fear of the secret police, as most Muscovites didn't face intervention by the KBG and certainly not in their daily lives. It was the look people get when they live in an all-bureaucratic state. If you go to Washington, you'll see much the same thing in government agencies.

In order to get a new drug approved today, it costs $500 million and takes ten years. Thousands die waiting on the approved release of drugs that could be available now. Millions die for want of medicines that won't be invented soon enough. The simple alternative in the area of medicine, as elsewhere, would be for the government to serve as an information agency and not as a nanny placement service. Did any of you hire the fed to be your babysitter? Sometimes I wonder who/what the government thinks it is! (It ain't us for sure). Even if we allowed for some (albeit inefficient) government research, information alone would do more to help free people protect themselves than twenty-one warning labels on a stepladder. Indeed, that's where we as a people may have gone wrong: we value other things now more than freedom it seems. "Give me absolute safety or give me death!"

The Clinton years accelerated a trend from the sixties, when he added 500,000 new pages to the Federal Register—a spider web of new little rules for everyone to obey. Notwithstanding the information age growth during the nineties, the US grew into an economic powerhouse in years when the government didn't account for as much of the Gross Domestic Product (GDP). For most of American history, government's share of GDP was five percent or less, but today it's forty percent. Some regulations are necessary, and I don't mean to categorically denounce them all—indeed, some environmental regulations even lack alternative market incentives. But let's get off this regulation kick that stifles innovation. Today Los Angeles has the same economic output as all of Russia. Dallas, Texas outranks the whole country of Thailand, in terms of economic output. That should illustrate plain-as-day this important inverse relationship: between the healthier, wealthier societies of the world and those that are corrupt, bureaucratic, and politically controlled. Freedom should never take a back seat to "the good of the people" divined by government. Tell our babysitter she can go home now; we've suddenly grown up.

America's Republican "Dialectic" Article #097
June 19, 2003

Dialectic is defined as the association or interaction of ideas, forces, arguments, etc., that conflict and compete. The term describes well the American political environment and two-party system. Politically speaking, what provides the parameters or bounds for dialogue to take place and what serves as reference to both sides, is the written Constitution of the United States, as well as the history relating to it. Only once did the dialectic rupture, and that was during the Civil War. Dialogue was suspended and the corresponding two-party system collapsed. People are accustomed to thinking that North and South fought each other, but folks above the Mason-Dixon Line were Yankees and *Republicans*, while those below it were Rebels and Democrats. The Constitution did not serve as common reference again for normal peacetime political dialogue until the end of Reconstruction. Even then it took a century for ideas to exceed geography as the primary determinant of party affiliation. The reason the country resumed organic political union as well as it did is that Northerners and Southerners were also Americans. The Confederate States of America (CSA) Constitution was nearly identical to that of the Union. Hence my view is that the Civil War settled discrete points of disagreement but did not radically alter American political culture, including federalism. Certainly by the late nineteenth century, the republican dialectic had more or less resumed unabated if slightly changed.

Cross-nationally, Americans are still the most Whiggish, classically liberal or libertarian people among the democratic nations. The United States is the only democratic country without an electorally viable socialist party, for instance. Believe it or not, Americans are less supportive of the welfare state than citizens of any other nation. This is because distrust of a strong state was at the core of revolutionary ideology, and this article of faith has continued to influence American political dialogue on all sides. Socialism assumes the need for a powerful state to control the economy and is thus antithetical in key respects to American political tradition. Moreover, equality in America has, until very recently, meant meritocracy; equality before the law; equality of opportunity regardless of social origin; assumed equality before God. Classical liberal values, including high regard for private property, for civil and religious liberty, for limited constitutional government—these have mostly negated the development of class consciousness and have made citizenship a matter of the heart and mind, rather than of ethnicity.

The American republican, ideological dialectic amounts to a range of competing positions within this Whiggish philosophical tradition, which have been restricted by the bounds of a written Constitution. Indeed, extremes frequently represent the strict or loose interpretation of at least *some* articles of the Constitution—for instance, the commerce clause. The Constitution was itself the emanation of older political tradition, just as it was also the fruition of the Revolutionary period, in particular. Americans were clearly the inheritors of a long republican tradition received mostly through the filter or lens of English Whig thought and Country party practice. Always a minority in Great Britain, the English libertarian strain was, for various demographic, historical and environmental reasons, in a majority in colonial America. When the Tories were sent packing in 1776, the United States began political life as a nation of Whigs. This helps to explain America's relatively narrow political spectrum, as well as the unparalleled stability of her political institutions. Newcomers were assimilated into this political tradition. Indeed, adherence to Whiggish political principles was the most important measure of becoming "American." American identity is still preeminently a political one. When Federalists and Anti-Federalists debated ratification of the Constitution, they took sides within this same philosophical tradition.

One important conclusion one gleans from understanding there is a tradition and from knowing that both Federalists and Anti-Federalists were part of it, is that both sides to the ratification debate then become part of the American *Constitutional* tradition. Remember, no anti-Constitutional party emerged in American politics. Anti-Federalists continued to participate, though mostly as strict constructionists. They would eventually become associated with the states' rights cause, as the federal government expanded its role and sectional controversies increased. The same (or clearly derived) Federalist and Anti-Federalist arguments would emerge and reemerge under the various guises of different political parties and movements. Indeed, it is my conclusion that the Federalists and Anti-Federalists and their organized counterparts in the First party system established the ideological dialectic within which political debate has been conducted since and from which policy positions derive their legitimacy. This is true for the Second party system when parties became vehicles of mass appeal and popular participation (instead of just participation by the political elite), as well as for the Third party system after Reconstruction.

Aspects of the Republican "Dialectic" Article #098
June 26, 2003

There are a number of aspects unique to the American republican dialectic—the association or interaction of ideas, forces and arguments that conflict and compete in American politics. These run through American history and through every political party system. The aspects are ideological, which means they can be (and are) part philosophical, part practical, and part cultural. They are aspects of the Founding generation's way of thinking and, despite dramatic cultural changes and some Constitutional distortion, they continue to vitally inform our own way of thinking, as well as most of the terms of political debate. If one examines political party platforms in every party system, one finds variations on these same themes. Indeed, political parties support positions that are largely iterative policy combinations based on aspects of the dialectic. To wit, every major party has considered the following aspects to involve policy matters of the first degree:

a. The quantitative and qualitative extent of democracy in this republic, that is, who is enfranchised and what they may decide. It is a dialectical aspect that pits populism or majoritarianism against a kind of elitism or natural leadership by so-called best men.

b. Qualitative versus quantitative conceptions of American nationalism, that is, constant improvement of the system over time, as opposed to expansion of the given system over space. Either form can be exclusive or inclusive culturally, which makes for particularly interesting variations on both forms of American nationalism.

c. The respective roles of federal and state governments, including the limits and prerogatives of dual federal-state sovereignties. It is a dialectical aspect that pits parochialism and local control against nationalist policy uniformity and centralization of authority. It has been the source of most constitutional controversy, from the nullification crisis in the 1830s to forced busing in the 1970s.

d. The role of the central government in economic matters, that is, the extent of purposeful intervention by the federal government in the form of tariffs, taxes and subsidies to protect or encourage domestic industry; to make internal improvements or to build and maintain the infrastructure; to fund the debt; to encourage entrepreneurship and labor discipline; and arguably, to provide public education. This aspect includes much and has sparked passionate debates over the years concerning the kind of banking system we ought to have, the type of currency, the type of trade policies, etc.

e. The agrarian impulse and ethos in conflict with the commercial or business impulse and ethos. This aspect is largely cultural, but also entails the role of government in furtherance of one at the almost inevitable expense of the other.

Each aspect mentioned relates directly to the limited functions of government in our constitutional republic and, believe you me, there is *plenty* of room within each aspect to disagree. Since 1932, however, one might add to the list *beneficence of the welfare state*. While properly regarded as being outside the American republican dialectic as conceived, it now plays an important part. Indeed, a host of special interests now align with both parties, two sides against the middle-class, in order to redistribute wealth to favored causes and constituents. This aspect is not related to functions of government in the Constitution; rather, it stems from Franklin Roosevelt's Atlantic Charter, an extra-constitutional agreement with Churchill made in 1941 that declared the right to "freedom from want." Domestically, it is justified by progressive-era political assumptions that have no basis in our founding documents or in the ideological origins of the American Revolution. To the extent that it might have implied Constitutional sanction, it would have to be through temporary depression-era and wartime emergency powers. But like the deficit spending that fuels it, the welfare state never wants for emergencies. It moves from one "war" to the next. If a Great Depression or world war is not present to justify extreme measures, a war on poverty or drugs does almost as nicely.

The Two-Party System — Article #099
June 26, 2003

The American republican dialectic corresponds largely to alternating conceptions about the American republic and the direction it should take in given political contexts. The dialectic consists of a free-ranging dialogue between ideas that correspond to relative degrees of conservatism or reform, consolidation or confederation, idealism or pragmatism. These take shape in broad party coalitions representing combinations of competing ideological positions. Further, the dialogue is such, that elements of the dialectic can modernize or drop out—and often trade places between parties. For instance, the "rugged" sense of individualism espoused by Jacksonian Democrats entered later conservative thought, while twentieth-century liberals began promulgating the quintessential Whig doctrine that the good of all should take precedence over the interests of the individual. Jefferson's motto, "the best government is that which governs least," became the credo of later conservatism. Ironically, political parties are not provided for in the Constitution. The Founders actually feared the effects of so-called "factions" and would have preferred government by consensus, which was actually achieved for a short while under George Washington and then again briefly during the Era of Good Feelings. But America's two-party system is at least the next best thing.

The United States has the only polity in the world dominated by two loosely structured coalition parties. Furthermore, the correlation between class and party affiliation in America is weaker than in all other industrial countries. Highly diverse groups come together under the rubric of both the major political parties. Furthermore, notwithstanding the relative infrequency of realignments or even critical elections, constituents of party coalitions can and do shift. For instance, Southerners increasingly voted Republican in the post-World War II era. Blacks were staunch supporters of the Republican party, the party of Lincoln the Great Emancipator, until the Great Depression. Blacks needed New Deal relief more than anyone, and they got it from Franklin Roosevelt and the Democrats. Prior to the Great Depression, the Republican party also included agrarian radicals in the Midwest. The Democratic party garnered most populist support in the 1890s, and the Republican party probably wishes it got less of the same populist support in the 1990s. Although it is possible to identify coalitions of relative "haves" and "have-nots," both parties have remained extraordinarily diverse and heterogeneous. Again I think this proves the inordinate importance ideas have had determining party affiliations in American political context. Europeans look at both major parties and discern little meaningful difference, but in order to understand the distinctions between the major parties, they must refer to the American republican dialectic we have talked about. Then they would see the exceptional political context in which differences must be measured. Differences may still appear to be minor matters to Europeans, who have a much wider operative political spectrum and more narrowly focused parties, but then communists or fascists have not come to power in America. Nor have we had dozens of different governments voted in and out in just so many years, which is the story in a number of European capitals.

The heterogeneity of our two major parties is also enhanced by a primary system that allows antagonistic factions within parties to run against each other. In this way, voters get to choose nominees, even prior to voting for general election candidates. People may also serve on platform committees at various levels, which help define positions supported by primary and general election candidates. The fact that over 500,000 offices are filled in U.S. elections makes public control of the policy-formation process in the United States the most populist in the world. Parties are participation vehicles, practical organizations that serve to further the public's beliefs and to play out the republican ideological dialectic. In addition, the system is never all or nothing. More often than not, the government stays divided and presidents are not reelected. Even when a single party wins big, the party in power is Constitutionally limited as to what it can do. Defeated parties can still win another day. This sounds trite, but in some countries election losers are shot. The checks and balances in the federal government mean that at least one branch will likely mount opposition, even to the big winner. In 1800, Jefferson was swept into office. He controlled the executive and the legislature, but Federalists retained the judiciary. In 1932, Franklin Roosevelt was swept into office. He again controlled the executive and the legislative branches, but Republicans held sway over the courts for a number of years, and this motivated FDR to attempt to pack the Supreme Court. The federalist nature of the country also insures that parties retain *local* strongholds. This is true unless a party gets substantially discredited—such as when too many Federalists actually supported the British in the War of 1812, or when radical sectional philosophies gave compromise a bad name before the Civil War.

History of Two Parties in America — Article #100
July 17, 2003

There have been three American political party systems, at least according to most historians. Some political scientists complicate things by counting changes in coalitions within the Third party system. If they count critical election shifts in 1896, 1932-36, and 1980-94, they could come up with as many as six different party systems. But historians refuse to abandon the Third party system label as long as Republicans fight it out with Democrats. It is not my purpose to examine the intricacies of politics in each party system, but some familiarity is useful and interesting. The parties embody the ideological dialectic and mix and match positions in all the various aspects outlined in previous segments. Realignments happening between party systems jumble constituents and policy positions in ways that prevent strict linear tracing. Tempting as it may be to trace Republicans from Whigs from Federalists or modern Democrats from Jacksonian Democrats from Jeffersonian Democratic-Republicans, parties are more complicated than that. They are more than just "conservative" or "liberal" too. The more conservative of each pair is likely to support some reform measures. No party has ever stood squarely for the status quo in every respect. Parties evince conservative and reform elements at the same time. And by the way, Republicans have as much right to claim Jefferson as their forerunner as do the Democrats. Indeed, modern Republicans resemble Jeffersonian Republicans far more than do New Deal or Great Society Democrats.

The First party system consisted of the Federalists and Jeffersonian Republicans or Democratic-Republicans. The initial alignment occurred between 1796 and 1800 and shattered the consensus George Washington had tenuously held together. Indeed, Hamilton and Jefferson led competing camps from the end of Washington's first term. It was opposition to Federalist economic policies, as well as to the Quasi-War with France and notorious Alien and Sedition Acts that led to permanent schism of the Federalists and to the Jeffersonian political revolution of 1800. Still, Federalists mounted substantial political opposition until they ultimately discredited themselves. During the War of 1812, prominent New England Federalists discussed secession to skirt Madison's embargo, which disproportionately hurt their region. Other Federalists actually aided the British. The public dealt the Federalists a stunning repudiation because of these things, and their party collapsed with the election of 1816. The Hero of New Orleans, Andrew Jackson, would be the one to end the resulting brief consensus called the Era of Good Feelings.

The Jeffersonian Republican party was stressed by Jacksonian democracy. Distinctive wings of the party were discernible by the early 1830s. The more conservative National Republicans let Jackson's followers keep the 'Democratic' identifier. Personalities also entered the picture as various supporters rallied to Henry Clay of Kentucky, John C.

Calhoun of South Carolina, as well as to Andrew Jackson of Tennessee. Calhoun actually supported Clay's efforts to launch the Whig party in opposition to Jackson. Realignment happened between 1836 and 1840 over Jackson's unprecedented concentration of executive authority and over a host of economic issues. But the "revolution" of 1840 that brought Whigs to power for the first time did not last as long as the Jeffersonian revolution had. From the start, the Second American party system of Whigs and Democrats was dogged by sectional issues. Increasingly Northern Democrats and Southern Fire eaters were unable to abide in the same party. Likewise, "Conscience" Whigs and Cotton Whigs were unable to keep ranks in the same party. The Whigs suffered stunning defeat in the election of 1852, but it was the Kansas-Nebraska Act of 1854 that precipitated a six-year process of realignment. The Republican party was the beneficiary of the party system crack-up, and it became the party of the North. Republicans stood for containment of slavery, so when Abe Lincoln was elected in 1860, the South seceded. Civil War and Reconstruction ensued. Obviously, until 1877 there was no normal peacetime party competition. War and military occupation suspended the traditional interplay of the ideological dialectic. Remarkably, however, the Third party system of Republicans and Democrats *did* resume peacetime party competition.

Third Party System Continues Today — Article #101
July 24, 2003

Traditionally, America's political parties had engaged in political dialogue until or unless consensus was achieved. Consensus in a free society was always necessarily short-lived. However, since the Civil War, there has been no period of consensus and no realignments resulting in disappearance of either major party. The Third party system survives, and periods of stalemate or gridlock have replaced the old intervals of consensus. One party or the other finally resolves stalemate by becoming the clear majority party. Republicans dominated national politics after the Civil War and were then faced with a national Democratic resurgence and Gilded Age stalemate. They resolved it when Democrat Grover Cleveland got saddled with the blame for depression and Republicans started to champion progressive reform. From 1896 then, Republicans were the clear majority party—that is, until 1929, after which it was Herbert Hoover and the Republicans' turn to suffer blame for the worst depression in history. FDR came to power in 1932 and cemented his New Deal coalition in 1936. Until the Reagan Revolution and associated "revolution" of 1994, the Democrats were the country's clear majority party.

Today it is unclear whether we have ushered in a new era of Republican dominance or whether we are slipping back into a decade or more of close elections and divided government without clear majority. The appearance of third parties typically signifies coalition shifts and party realignments, at least if the major parties fail to take heed and co-opt third party positions or at least address the issues that give life to third party challenges.

Five key elements make up the conceptual framework of American political tradition: (1) *Religion* heavily influences American political tradition. Not only is the society peculiarly religious, based on Protestant Christian origins and subsequent evangelical revivals, but the political ends of the nation are often touted in religious terms—as if the nation itself pursued a religious ideal and providential mission. (2) The *written Constitution* consists of the nation's founding document and subsequent amendments to the document. It is uniquely American as a departure from the unwritten constitutional tradition in Great Britain. The written form serves as a constant stricture on the government, in terms of what it can and cannot do and also puts great importance on determinations of the Supreme Court, since its interpretation potentially changes the meaning of the written document. (3) *Federalism*—a system of dual sovereignty set up by the Constitution, which represents James Madison's original contribution to political science. Much of the political history of the United States has revolved around the maintenance of dual federal-state prerogative; whereas, our most serious constitutional crises have involved questions relating to it. It serves to provide a vertical balance of power to our political system. (4) The *Republican ideological dialectic* refers to America's relatively narrow political spectrum based on the fact that we were a nation imbued with the Whig or Country party tradition. Ideological limits are generally along original and developmental Federalist and Anti-Federalist philosophical positions, which *both* value private property and limited government. (5) *Political parties* compose our uniquely American two-party system in which both represent broad coalitions generally corresponding to two sides and alternating aspects of the ideological dialectic. As in other democratic countries, the parties also serve as vehicles for political participation. It is ironic, moreover, since the

Founders would have preferred consensus to having long-term, two-party competition.

There may very well be other elements in our political tradition, but these are the main ones. A sixth one I should at least mention has to do with American foreign policy. But while American political tradition may be affected by foreign issues, its primary focus has always been response to domestic concerns. However, the element could be characterized as an "America first" foreign policy that refrains from entangling alliances and which is neutral and noninterventionist in foreign relations, unless security interests are at stake. That should not imply disengagement from the world, nor any number of voluntary economic and cultural exchanges. The military may also play important roles abroad in self-interest or as a tool in the exercise of a just national foreign policy. On the other hand, American political tradition is not altruistic when it comes to the blood of her sons and daughters.

As with Scripture, one finds new insights and fresh aspects the longer one contemplates American political tradition. Certainly it is one of the greatest pleasures one can get. Freedom is, quite simply, exciting. Understanding it fully, however, is a long-term (probably life-long) enterprise. Hence those who study the Founders' handiwork are apt to be struck with a measure of awe at their achievement and to conclude, as they themselves concluded, that divine inspiration played a most beneficent part.

Republican Spending Explosion — Article #138
o/a April 11, 2004

When the Republicans gained control of Congress in 1994, they promised to eliminate the deficit and reduce wasteful spending. For several years, the GOP partly upheld its commitment by modestly curtailing spending growth and balancing the budget. Unfortunately, the balanced budgets of the late 1990s created an "easy money' mindset in Congress, which began a spending spree that continues unabated today. Total federal outlays will rise 29 percent between fiscal years 2001 and 2005 according to the president's fiscal year 2005 budget released in February. Real discretionary spending increases in fiscal years 2002, 2003, and 2004 are three of the five biggest annual increases in the last 40 years. Large spending increases have been the principal cause of the government's return to massive budget deficits.

Although defense spending has increased in response to the war on terrorism, President Bush has made little attempt to restrain non-defense spending to offset the higher Pentagon budget. Non-defense discretionary outlays will increase about 36 percent during President Bush's first term in office. Congress has failed to contain the administration's overspending and has added new spending of its own. Republicans have forfeited any claim of being the fiscally responsible party in Washington.

Looking ahead, Republicans need to rediscover the reforming spirit they brought to Washington after the landmark 1994 congressional elections. Fiscally conservative Democrats should challenge big-spending Republicans and work to cut unneeded programs from both the defense and non-defense parts of the budget. In charge of the White House, Senate, and House of Representatives, Republicans are primarily responsible for the current budget mess, and it is Republicans who have the power to pare back spending to get the federal budget under control once again.

Let's cut through any horse hockey and put the situation squarely: only Lyndon B. Johnson has outspent George W. Bush in history! Johnson spent billions for 'guns and butter'—i.e., for the Viet Nam War and for his Great Society domestic programs. The combination virtually ruined the country's economy and bequeathed to us both double-digit inflation and high unemployment for more than a decade. Today we're spending massively for 'guns and butter' again, and there is no logical reason to believe the result will be less injurious to the long-term health of the nation's economy. The administration likes to blame crisis-level defense and security requirements, but in fact only a portion of the spending increase has been for homeland security in the wake of terrorist attacks September 11, 2001. Much of the tab comes from the expansion of domestic programs, such as No Child Left Behind—a gross and expensive federalization of education. The Bush administration also signed into law the biggest entitlement expansion since the inception of Medicare. It didn't even give itself most-favored nation (best price) negotiating authority with big drug companies for prescription drug coverage. All in all, it was pretty dumb, and Congress went along with it! And let's put the matter squarely again: the president has constitutional authority for the armed forces, ergo (at least indirectly) for much of the "guns" price tag. But Congress is constitutionally responsible for "butter"—actually for all spending, but most explicitly for domestic spending programs. The failure to rein in spending is a failure born mostly by Republican congressmen. It is no excuse to say that they were just playing patsy to or with the president. Congressmen who lack independence of thought *or political action from the president* cannot properly represent their constituents' interests.

The reason we ought to be concerned is that we cannot sustain the current level of spending indefinitely or even for a decade without serious economic and social upheaval. The level of spending may indeed cynically put us through the 2004 election cycle in 'good shape,' and partisan political victory may be a fair compensation for economic wrecking balls. Except, of course, that we're dealing in real lives and fortunes and with dreams and aspirations of the American people that are connected.

Republicans often claim to be the party of smaller government, but on big government spending it is hard to see how a Democratic administration could have been worse than the Bush administration in recent years. A second George W. Bush administration (if there is one) should follow an initial spending freeze with deliberate and conscientious efforts to produce significant reductions in both discretionary and entitlement programs. Failure to do so will produce deep trouble for the economy, and that's the most critical point. Failure to control spending after November elections will also precipitate political woes for the president and Republican Party, as fiscal conservatives seek higher ground.[1]

CHAPTER 3

Election 2004

Voting—Measure of Self-Interest and Patriotism Article #162
o/a September 26, 2004

In the Primary Election March 9th, less than 15% of eligible voters voted in counties around Central Texas; and for the most part, the percentages were equally pitiful in primaries nation-wide. There were precincts in Killeen in which just 4% voted. In the General Election a few weeks from now, only half of eligible voters will likely turn out. An American it seems, will cross the ocean to fight for democracy but won't cross the street to vote in a national election. Thirty-one percent of all Americans 18 and older are not even registered. A previous generation engaged in protest and endured violence to win the vote for young people, whose representation now is worse than all other age groups. They did it so eighteen year-olds couldn't be drafted without some political say-so. Politicians are rumoring a draft again, and they have very little to fear at the ballot box from eighteen year-olds or anyone else. If voter registration drives do pay off and more than 50% show November 2nd, less than 15% still chose the slate of candidates you get to choose from. I'm talking about all races and not just the one for president. Johnny-Come-Lately will mull over Tweedle-Dee and Tweedle-Dum, but it hardly constitutes the level of participation one expects for a thriving democracy—let alone, a great Republic. Ironic really—how we scheduled Iraq's elections and some die trying to pull that one off, while citizens at home hardly vote in our own!

As an historian who studied at Oxford, specializing in American antebellum politics, I'm disappointed in the Republic I came to know through the works of our Founders and keen observers like Alexis de Tocqueville, who reported *circa* 1836 that virtually every able white male went to the polls—and that's when roads weren't too good and conveyances were rough. Of course, universal white manhood suffrage was something new, having caught on gradually after 1820. There was probably still a sense of novelty and excitement associated with voting. And while minorities and women were left out of the electorate, the America of this "Middle Period" was the most democratic in the world, bar none. Voter turnout in those days was routinely 80%.

The trend towards universal suffrage of course continued. Non-Anglo race males were included by the 15th Amendment in 1870; the fairer sex (if I may call her that) was added by the 19th in 1920. Thus it was complete: movement away from a "stake in society" concept to the "one man (meaning one man or one woman)-one vote position that is now taken for granted. Our Founders believed one should have a measurable stake in society (either property ownership or payment of taxes) before you were afforded the right to vote. The right to vote was and is not inalienable—it's an added right that defines our polity. Today we've granted the right to vote to many who do not have a measurable stake in society, at least one that's traditionally understood. Although I've decried a low voter turnout, I must also confess that I am mindful of danger inherent when a democratic people discover the power of 50% + 1; when they fully realize the potential of their votes in a democratic welfare state, in which states rights have been emaciated. Today the federal government has moved well beyond providing a 'safety net' to providing an education, a retirement, prescription drugs and health care, not to mention housing and food stamps. Bottom line: if you're a group without a current stake in society—or perhaps a group with a losing stake or a lesser stake—why not use your vote to press for all the government dole you can get??? The government's power of the gun and bayonet is yours through the ballot box; it is within your power to forcibly redistribute wealth even more effectively. You just have to be active enough to get up off the couch and down to a polling station! Of course if you're a stodgy old conservative and believe in worn out things like private property, self-determination, family values and the rest, and you *don't* want to allow this sort of thing to happen, perhaps you may want to cancel out a socialist couch potato's vote.

Begin a Restoration—Vote your Values Article #163
o/a September 26, 2004

If and when you vote, I hope you will also vote your values. Despite all that's made about George W. Bush's support among Christian evangelicals, the so-called Christian Right, only one in four voted in the 2000 elections.

Of the 59 million evangelical voters who were eligible to vote, 24 million of them were not registered. Only 20 million of the 35 million registered actually went out and voted! With margins as close as they were in 2000, that group alone could dominate the social agenda—they could stop abortion, protect traditional marriage, restore prayer in schools—you name it, if they gave their citizenship and role on earth half the attention they pay getting to Heaven and storing up rewards for the afterlife. I don't mean to be insulting, and I don't mean to presume upon the values you hold. But I know this: there is an awful lot of slack in the electorate—probably on the left and the right. If every veteran, or if every conservative voted, there is little doubt but that elections would produce more promising results. There is something manifestly wrong with a country of nearly 300 million of the smartest, most creative people on the planet—a people who produced the Declaration and Constitution and put the first human being on the moon—there is something manifestly wrong, when it produces Congress after Congress of mediocre men and women, who buy their way through petty patronage and Hollywood smiles. Today when the nation is at war, less than 30% of those in Congress have ever served in uniform. Few have advanced degrees in anything—and few have written anything at all to show a depth of knowledge or understanding. It seems to be enough to say in the right ten second sound bite that you feel somebody else's pain, when in fact the politician hasn't the foggiest idea about the human condition or political vision. Almost no one in government today in this, the twenty-first century (!) is a statesman, say, equivalent to nineteenth century giants like Henry Clay, Daniel Webster, John C. Calhoun, Abraham Lincoln. We have purchased a low bid contract on our House (divided or not), and taken out a second mortgage to boot! We have a $7 trillion national debt and are running the largest annual budget deficit in history. You and I both know that Social Security and Medicare are heading for bankruptcy as 70 million more baby boomers retire; and we do not have the statesmen or the politicians with strength and courage of character enough to even talk about it. Of course, they're not under the same system and it doesn't pay political dividends to raise a hard issue.

In June my political mentor and one of the greatest presidents, Ronald Reagan, passed away. His legacy must ultimately be what those who conscientiously and deliberately pursue his vision will accomplish. That may include you and me, for it falls to this generation to finish the unfinished business. The unfinished business is two-fold. First, you must reclaim the culture—take it back, live according to your lights. Second, we should restore federalism and constitutional government by redressing the imbalance between the state and federal levels of government, so that states operate as intended—as sovereign partners within their respective constitutional orbits. Alas, Tocqueville was fairly pessimistic about our chances. He predicted Americans would lose their liberty—notably through the ballot box, having too much equality. He believed that we would finally trade freedom for the bureaucratic "network of petty, complicated rules that are both minute and uniform, . . . so that in the end . . . [the democratic] nation [becomes] no more than a flock of timid and hardworking animals with the government as its shepherd." The principle of equality, Tocqueville thought, leads Americans to "think of themselves in isolation." That is to say, without superiors or inferiors, every man lives only for himself. Because of their equality, Tocqueville said, "it is . . . always an effort for [Americans] to tear themselves away from their private affairs and pay attention to those of the community; the natural inclination is to leave the only visible and permanent representative of collective interests, that is to say, the state, to look after them."

Too much of this dire prediction rings true, but it does not take into account the more enlightened sense of equality the Founders shared. It is a sense we may yet recapture, as long as there are election days. Namely, a proper recognition of equality demands the preservation of liberty, and the conditions of liberty; in no wise does equality liberate citizens from civic responsibilities. Equality without responsibilities becomes hypocrisy, then license and ultimately tyranny. We have time yet to recover. It took Rome hundreds of years to come undone, but good people—you must take up the serious business of a Restoration of the Republic now.

Make Up Your Own Mind — Articles #164-165
~Part I~ o/a October 10, 2004

If I were to review all the times popular opinion had changed, you would be reading a multi-volume work instead of a column. It is likewise prima facie *the truth*, to point out that the latest scientific evidence is always something new if not entirely different, every time it is referenced. Almost every year—and certainly every ten to twenty-five years, a sea change in so-called 'consensus' opinion emerges or reemerges. In the area of history, consider the textbooks used in high schools and colleges at regular intervals from 1900 to 1920 to 1940 to 1960 to 1980 to 2000. You will learn something very interesting if you read through them as I have—and that is that historical interpretations do change; but the interpretations change well beyond what any research or new discoveries justify, at least by themselves. The limits of our known universe, both past and present, do expand. The confident swings in articles of faith affecting opinion-makers, officialdom and peer groups, however, are much more elastic. They proceed apace like so many bouncing balls without a tune to follow. People who follow these bouncing balls end up hunching and slack-jawed with cramped up necks and loose brain housing groups. It is my conclusion that you are far better off to doubt a professional's opinion much more than your own.

I say it again: you are better off (and freer) to doubt a professional's opinion much more than your own—unless and until compelling evidence and experience suffices to inform your way of thinking and make you change your mind. This is a conservative and prudent approach to knowledge and to what you believe. Always guard the door to your mind as carefully and as dutifully as you would bar the door to your house against the wiles of known thieves and murderers. Never let a thought take lodgment simply because it is popular or new. The latest book on diet or positive thinking or an approach to finance or putting up wallpaper must always take backseat to you. That *you* I'm referring to is the arbiter of your mind, the captain of your soul. Newness is no standard for your approval or acceptance, let alone your fabricating and expanding it into something credible and eventually *status quo*. Popularity runs with Newness, and she is a fickle friend indeed.

Hold out long enough and your opinion will come back into vogue. First you're a so-called retrograde; a few months or years later, you are positively "cutting edge." Keep those fashions in your closet for twenty-five years, and I guarantee they will be all the rage again (even if you can't quite fit them)! Music is no less superior or inferior, when it is performed underground for the first time, behind an iron curtain, or gets played with the golden oldies. The endurance of rhythm and melody and the strength of lyrics; the staying power of color and texture and pattern, quality fabric and careful stitching—these are philosophical components, if you will, of what lay behind music and clothing. They are conceptually permanent, unlike catalogs which show you the latest offerings and selection. If you know the permanent things, you can judge temporal things directly. You can tell when the Emperor has no clothes. You develop confidence in judgment too, such that, you no longer need or seek validation from either peers or experts.

Now follow that logic. Why should you consult almanacs—or soaps or talk shows or talking heads, to know how much of a man or woman you are? I am suggesting there are also philosophical components of material life, and if media helps you discern a few of them fine. But the key is to learn them, or to retrieve them in all probability from earlier instruction and common sense. Attend to the mental, physical, spiritual, social and emotional pillars of one's character. When you know them, you can be a whole and complete person in control of your life—without indulging in self-pity or self-congratulations, and without the voyeuristic detours to "find yourself" on TV. We live in an odd sort of tyranny today, in which the new and modern is presumed to be superior. It is old fashioned to speak of character development. It is passé to say we ought to keep promises and love our families and neighbors. It is Euro-centric and sexist to work hard and to work hard to achieve excellence—in other words, to pattern the divine. And it is a secular humanist heresy to say, "As for me and my house, we serve the Lord." As for me and my house, I guess the reconstructed national consolidated state and academe's minions of puny, control-minded historical revisionists have more work to do. My heroes have always been the Scot, the Rebel and the Cowboy.

~Part II~ o/a October 10, 2004

A democratically derived tyranny now impinges on almost every home, school and community—for anything popular gains the right hand of the state to enforce. Every good idea is presumed good for everyone and must be crammed down everyone's throat. If a modern thing is *scientific*, it may as well be straight from heaven (as if Heaven retained the connotation of authority). For who would dare resist, refute or refrain from anything modern, particularly if it were scientifically derived and popular? That's right; we know not to raise our hands, even if the question presumes we are slaves—slaves who have forgotten or perhaps never knew *American* presuppositions. Namely, that you and I have an unalienable right to be wrong in all opinions whatsoever. We also have the right to be right, or to think we are right.

You and I have the right to act and to live accordingly as well, unless or until we bring harm to someone else or restrict another's freedom by our action. Toleration confers, however, with community standards. Political decisions are reached, and a social environment is produced. If you don't like it bad enough, you fight city hall or vote with your feet. That said, you and I can believe in or reject scientific findings and even *science* itself. You and I can accept or reject medical findings and even *medicine* itself. We don't have to believe in brotherly kindness or the benefits of diversity or globalization either. We don't have to follow the doctor's orders, in other words. The only absolute right there is, is the right to think. And if liberty were regarded the way it should, the right to think and the right to live according to convictions wouldn't be so far apart; belief and conduct would correspond more than they do—or at least be able to legally. Nature and Tradition (which are not the same things) would still serve as presumptive references for the benefit of American society. Of course today, there exists no area which lacks a body of positive law to instruct or entrust to an oracle of expert opinion. Laws and regulations promulgated by government have tied us like so many insects in a spider's web. And rue the day when the benevolence of the state runs out, after the Second Amendment is no longer regarded or the Patriot Act has no review or sunset provision. Despite our wriggling, we have rewritten the edicts of Nature, as well as Tradition and the accumulated wisdom of the past. Capitalism was always a solvent that produced economic and social change; but political boundaries neutralized some of it and prevented the most egregious cultural impacts. The Founders' concept of federalism worked as intended, acting as a social bulwark to unwanted change—enabling voluntary social evolution at the level of the States. Hence, benefits of a large national open market coexisted with social self-determination. Today, however, no corner of the Union is left free of judicially imposed social standards and involuntary social engineering.

Liberty is circumscribed to such a point, that you really have to believe the bunk courts and enforcers tell you to believe, in order to be "law abiding." Political correctness is an attempt to regulate the mind. Be sure you are convincing too, or you jeopardize your future. Perhaps you won't receive a license, or degree or job, a promotion or media coverage. Those who do not perceive the stranglehold we live in today have lost a sense of freedom our Founders fought hard to retain and give Posterity. Our politicians are shadows of statesmen and the great Texas and American patriots who went before.

As a debater in high school, we used to employ arguments on both sides of every resolution—pro and con, affirmative and negative. We would also cite "evidence" from experts to support our various points on whichever side we argued. That's when I learned you can find someone who is supposedly smart to say any and every stupid thing in the world. There are always doctors who disagree on diagnoses and treatments, and there are always disagreeable lawyers period. There are scientific experts, who worry about alien abduction—and they may be metaphysically closer to the truth than we wish to admit. There are also geniuses and other creative spirits, who are obsessive-compulsive, paranoid, mystic, incompetent and downright perverted. Instead of assuming that what you read or hear about is correct, you ought to consider it suspect—assume it is all incorrect! Attribute only a tentative quality to what you learn, especially if it is new or popular. Check it out with your free will, that very personal expert called yourself. Never cede your mind to others concerning diet, fashion, healthcare, politics or especially matters of the soul. It is your mind—start making it up.

Election of 2004: One of the Most Historic and Crucial
o/a October 11, 2004 Article #166

It is my purpose here to lay out a few things regarding elections and to state why the one November 2nd is vitally important. PLEASE VOTE—here's the situation: Political parties have existed as broad coalitions since the days of George Washington. Republicans and Democrats today constitute a Third American Party System comprised basically of two large coalitions. The Republicans are middle-to-right (conservative); the Democrats are middle-to-left (modern liberal). George Washington started the country off without any political parties and governed by consensus. Indeed, the Constitution does not provide for political parties at all. Washington's consensus, however, broke down over disagreement inside his cabinet—especially over Hamilton's financial proposals. Two parties then competed until the end of the War of 1812. Consensus again reigned for a short while under James Monroe in a period known as the 'Era of Good Feelings.' That consensus too broke down around the person and policies of Andrew Jackson during the Age of the Common Man. Two more parties thus competed until both of them cracked under the strain of sectionalism prior to the Civil War. Since that terrible War Between the States, present day party labels have stuck—but a few observations are worth making.

No consensus has ever emerged between the Republicans and the Democrats. Politics is a specialized business these days, and interests of various sorts are literally invested in the two parties. The parties may well come to resemble each other more, but it is hard to imagine a merger or to imagine one of the parties actually disappearing. Ideological consensus is also harder to reach, following the experience of political Reconstruction and military occupation of the South; and because the late nineteenth and twentieth centuries witnessed a number of "isms" infiltrate and modify a traditional American libertarian-republican (or *Whiggish*) political spectrum.

The New Deal under Franklin Delano Roosevelt also represented a most remarkable departure from constitutional parameters prior to 1932. It is as impossible to place that domestic genie in the bottle as it would be to "un-invent" nuclear weapons. Indeed, FDR emulated Germany's Otto von Bismarck, who candidly admitted employing a welfare scheme to force the people of his country into dependency on government. Today both party coalitions use welfare or other give-away programs to produce recipients. Recipients (those who receive benefits) become dependent upon government; and hence, they vote for politicians who protect or increase their share of government largesse. Don't expect a party consensus anytime soon.

Most political observers will say the country is more polarized, more divided than ever before. Instead of consensus, there's gridlock—and stakes are high. The conservative coalition has trended more conservative of late; the liberal coalition has trended more liberal. The cause is the breakdown of federalism, an emaciation of states rights and the federalization of every important issue including issues that involve societal morality. While the situation is unique, in fact since the Civil War there have been similar periods of stalemate marked by refusal to compromise. In place of drastic realignments that replace one or the other political party, there are critical elections or a series of elections which produce a clear shift in the electorate. One party becomes a majority, and the other becomes a minority. Gridlocks are essentially the jockeying for position until something gives. Economic or foreign policy crises provide the "stuff" of critical elections. Between 1896 and 1900 the electorate chose the Republicans of the Gilded Age to lead the country; Democrats were relegated to minority status and the role of loyal opposition. In the South, Democrats nursed bitter resentment but achieved "home rule." Between 1932 and 1936 the electorate moved decisively to the Democrats for leadership, in order to get us through the Great Depression and World War II. Today we are in an unprecedented period of long-term party rivalry that resembles a critical shift. Still the outcome is not obvious, nor preordained. Since 1980 and especially since 1994, conventional wisdom would have it the electorate wants—or at least is flirting with the notion, of replacing Democratic leadership with a Republican majority. Had George W. Bush's term in office been the success it promised to be after 9-11, the critical shift would be complete. As it is, a second term (if there is any) will determine the outcome of this historic political shift that could last some 30 years.

To illustrate the many years of party competition that are relevant in 2004, consider that Democrat John Kerry was a Vietnam era protester taking on a Republican administration under Richard Nixon. His conclusion that Vietnam was a mistake has colored his entire career and view of war. Kerry voted against the wildly popular Gulf War; today he is convinced the more unpopular war in Iraq is like Viet Nam—a "quagmire." The so-called Vietnam Syndrome we thought was over after the Gulf War is back in spades. The efficacy of military intervention is again brought entirely into question. Clearly Kerry would not pull troops out precipitously. Clearly he would do all he could to protect the homeland from terrorism, including approving recommendations of the 9/11 Commission Report. But we are nevertheless at a major policy crossroads in 2004. Bush represents the confidence to win the War on Terrorism, including the war in Iraq. Iraq is to the War on Terrorism as Vietnam was to the Cold War, at least in strategic context. The war in Iraq, however, must be analyzed and weighed in terms that are very different. The desert is not the jungle. Arabs aren't Asians. Radical Islam is not communism or nationalism either. The U.S. volunteer "Army of One" is not the Vietnam era draft army—in personnel or equipment. Our domestic situation is more stable than it was in 1973, and the threat posed by Al Qaeda is arguably graver than anything Hanoi ever represented.

More important by far than the issue of Iraq *per se*, is the implicit issue of national sovereignty that attends all political discussions about Iraq. Kerry would subject American decision-making authority to wage war, not only to congressional authorization, but as a practical matter, to binding and explicit regard for international law and standards imposed by the international community through the United Nations. Bush represents the constitutional position and an assertion of national prerogative which maintains the United States of America requires no permission slip from any nation or nations, institution or law beyond our borders. Coalitions may or may not be wise, but they are never required. The failure of this country since the Cold War to actually declare wars, have gotten us into situations of gray and ambiguity over proper authority and justification for war the Founders never intended and never would have sanctioned. If the Congress had declared war on Iraq, it wouldn't have mattered if weapons of mass destruction were found there or not. British historian Paul Johnson perceives that what is at stake in this election is whether the U.S. should have and will insist upon the means to act alone if and when it deems necessary.

If you were looking for a more historic and crucial election to participate in, I suggest you will not find one for decades. PLEASE VOTE—and also *pray* for our country before and during the coming Election Day: May God bless America and His perfect will be done—Amen.

Post-Election 2004: What Must Be Said Articles #169-171
~Part I~ o/a November 19, 2004

Congratulations—and can I have an Amen?! Red States won, and voter turnout was back where it should be (the most since 1968). The people gave the winner of the presidential race a popular majority this time to go with his electoral win. There can be no more challenge to George W. Bush's legitimacy in office. Not only that, but Republicans can argue they have a mandate to do something. Not only because the voter turnout was strong, but also because Republicans picked up 4 more Senators and increased their margin in the House of Representatives—thanks largely to Texas redistricting. It is the first time since FDR established the Democrat party in a clear majority status that a successful Republican president sees his party pick up seats in both houses of Congress too. It signals, as I suggested before the election, that an historic critical election has taken place; and the importance of 2004 lay with a shift or political realignment in the parties. It doth appear the tectonic plates have slipped into place, and the Republican Party is (at last) the new majority party in the country. This sort of thing has only happened a couple of times previously since the Civil War. And speaking of which, just look at the map! The message is not the divided nature of the electorate, so much as the sectional nature of the divide. The Northeast and Left Coast are isolated and identified for what they are—entire, out of touch societies.

As you would imagine, voters went to the polls with Iraq, terrorism and the economy in mind. But pollsters and talking heads missed the single biggest motivating force for voters this year, namely moral values. Fully one-quarter of all voters voted primarily on their concern over moral values, and 85% of those votes went for George W. Bush. Christians provided the margin of victory to the president in Ohio and throughout the South and heartland of America. They offset the supposed advantage of a larger turnout amongst youth and minorities; indeed, the youth and minority votes did not split as overwhelmingly for John Kerry as cynical political hacks expected. This singular fact speaks well of the American people—Americans don't just vote with the herd. Americans have faith and values deeper than their pocketbook. Americans defy the plastic and pretentious nonsense of star-studded rallies that purport to tell us how we should vote in *real* life.

Iraq has been GW's baby from the beginning. He now has a responsibility to raise the kid or give it up for adoption. We must win this war in Iraq—convincingly in the short-term, to give free elections a chance in January. Marines and Army soldiers have moved swiftly since the election, in order to pacify insurgent strongholds and trouble spots in Fallujah, Mosul, and elsewhere. In the long-term, we must also stay the course: a course towards military victory and eventual disengagement—notwithstanding the uncontestable need for ongoing security assistance to Iraq, probably for years after most troops come home. The president's election victory, however, means that the buck stops with him. He got us into Iraq. He's now got to get us out, or else get us clearly on top.

The next four years will most likely be good for the economy, if the president reins in spending and delivers on his promised Social Security and tax reforms. The Democrats ran an ad this campaign that implied Bush was an ostrich with his head in the sand over Iraq. Yet despite hand wringing over how we got there, Kerry never differentiated future policy in Iraq from what the president is doing now. Moreover, if ever there were an ostrich, it has been Kerry and the liberals on matters of Social Security. Kerry denied the system is going bankrupt and ruled out any drastic reform. The fact is we cannot go indefinitely with only a tweak or two, as Kerry argued. But fortunately Americans perceived the fake. The near term retirement of over seventy million baby boomers will indeed break the back of the present system; reforms must be implemented in the next four years to save Social Security for anybody. The Bush Administration supports a move towards more personal ownership of one's retirement. The likelihood is there would be some minimum level of return guarantee and government insurance to back the system. Moreover, the government will probably approve the private investment vehicle alternatives one may choose. Even with that, it would be a far better cry from what we've got today. I have been and continue to be quite angry and resentful over the government's high-handed thievery of my paycheck over an entire working adult life. Free people should be able to plan, invest, save, risk, succeed or fail without the Nanny State to blame or take credit.

~Part II~ o/a November 19, 2004

Taxes are not only too high, but they are also overcomplicated. A tax code bigger than the Bible is not fit for a free society. GW said he would simplify it, and we can at least wish him luck. There are excellent flat tax and national sales tax proposals out there, but there is also the perfect certainty they will not work. Special interests will insist upon special treatment, subsidies and deductions. Businesses aren't likely to give up cherished business deductions; homeowners will insist on deducting their home mortgage payments. Politicians and lobbies of government bureaucrats won't give up power either, which comes from various tax incentives and disincentives. Nor will they gladly 'kick the habit' to avoid the adrenaline rush that comes from social engineering and behavioral control. The IRS will acquire more responsibilities, not fewer. A national sales tax eliminates the IRS and reduces overall tax burden, only if you simultaneously eliminate federal income tax—but that takes a constitutional amendment to repeal the Sixteenth. Without repeal of the Sixteenth Amendment, Americans would be saddled with both the federal income tax and a national sales tax. They would be crushed more, not less by the burden of taxes. Congress might, however, offer tax-free years for all American workers and also reduce withholding requirements. This would give free people a taste of the real power of their earnings and also reintroduce the pain felt when the tax man cometh again. If people understood the burden of their taxes in stark terms at the end of every year, the country would undergo a tax revolution or a real one. To the extent possible, President Bush should reduce taxes and reduce progressive rates. Of course, both would be pointless if he doesn't control government spending and reduce or hold steady the cost of government.

To change direction of the tax code (and reform Social Security), GW and the Republicans in Congress will have to move swiftly in the early months of next year. "The Second Hundred Days" are likely to be the most important, in terms of domestic policy initiatives in either of Bush's two administrations. Historically it was that way with FDR. Hopefully GW doesn't fritter away his political capital on ill-advised (and politically DOA) measures like illegal alien worker visas. The election of 2004 has brought with it tremendous opportunity and possibility to effect important conservative change. The president must press hard after his second inauguration if he wants a true legacy, something beyond the War in Iraq and political stalemate. The Red States have purchased with their votes a reprieve from national self-destruction, but you and I both know that liberalism (a.k.a. progressivism) is down but not out. You caught a glimpse of the hard edge in John Edward's "concession" remarks. You caught a glimpse of the slippery slope, with Slick Willie's talk of building bridges during the dedication of the William Jefferson Clinton Presidential Library in Little Rock. Democrat lawyers begged Kerry to continue litigation in Ohio and elsewhere. Senator Kerry had the good grace and wisdom not to, but there's speculation he could run again. Demographics are funny things, and Red States are not necessarily the majority forever. Indeed, Red States have their blue areas eating away at their sustenance, just as Chicago swallowed Illinois years ago. Red States have bought a reprieve, nothing more.

The political will of the majority now must find its way to some structural, semi-permanent expression to do any good. We must use the opportunity to reinforce and invigorate federalism, to bolster states rights. That is where federal judges and Supreme Court justices come in. Even if GW solidifies the new Republican majority and it lasts through midterm elections; even if he uses his Second Hundred Days well and moves the country into constructive domestic policy directions; even if he prosecutes the War in Iraq with wisdom and vigor, the Red States are doomed if he does not also successfully nominate and appoint strict constructionists to the bench. The president must move swiftly, resolutely to name men and women who prize the Constitution of Original Intent. Let the States be different—or if liberals insist upon the nationalization of every important issue, including abortion, let Red State morality be imposed on everyone through constitutional amendment.

~Part III~ o/a November 19, 2004

Self-determination is the crux of any meaningful freedom whatever; and we must lift the judicial tyranny that has descended across the land. Let Blue States be blue, in other words; and let Nevada preserve its countryside, side by side with Las Vegas as long as it will. But the Fourteenth Amendment is enforced now throughout the South. So it is time to let the new, New South's Alabama be free to be Alabama, and to deviate from social norms elsewhere on matters besides race if she will. And it goes without saying that Texas will be free period—free to search out and to institute its own destiny! If New York and California would turn the inside plumbing red with the blood of unborn infants, such atrocity must not be made the standard thrust upon the good and righteous people of our Sovereign State. The State Song here is more than a song.

Let us therefore insist upon the constitutional interpretation Democrats feigned over same sex "marriage." Never was there such hypocrisy. The progenitors of modern liberal judicial tyranny sticking up for states rights! Kerry said that States have always decided the issue of what constitutes a marriage. Well, on Election Day November 2nd, they did again. Eleven states resoundingly declared marriage to be between one man and one woman. The people of these states banned same sex marriage, but the political will of the people has again been thwarted by removing the issue in most cases to courts, which are deciding "constitutionality" based upon a living, changing interpretation of what the Constitution means! In the same way, courts have subverted the political will of people in the several states over matters involving State aid, State welfare benefits, State public education, and State health care benefits given to *illegal* aliens.

The madness must simply stop. The president must be as strong as Andrew Jackson in this regard, when Jackson held the power of courts in abeyance. Old Hickory used the co-equal enforcement authority of the Executive Branch to check the Supreme Court (and inferior federal courts), whose legal interpretation flew in the face of the people's express political will. If States will now reassert their rights and the president use his power to facilitate their effort, we can confront an arrogant Judiciary and erect lasting walls to protect Americans from the latest fad and social experiment becoming national law—as well as from the lunacy of one-world village idiots, who would erase national boundary lines and inviolate national sovereignty. To the global village crowd, I would also remind them the Constitution of these United States sets up a dual system of Nation-and-State sovereignty. State boundaries and State sovereignty remain intact, whether or not national policies will compromise the national prerogative.

James Madison explicitly intended federalism to work this way: that a goofy idea in Massachusetts should remain there! If manhood falls out of fashion in West Hollywood, it may nonetheless be sustained in West Texas. Few students today even know Madison is known as the Father of the Constitution. Few politicians pause to reflect the Constitution is what we are supposed to be living under. Moreover, the Constitution as written and ratified and amended serves only the People of these United States. It is a covenant for that purpose. The blood and treasure of our people are invested in the Nation and respective States, that is to say, in ourselves. To hear some these days wax eloquent about the imperative to build global bridges across all conceivable divides, it is apparent they suffer from a perverse notion that American blood and treasure can be diverted through the aegis of the federal government, from service to ourselves and the national interest to the exclusive or conflicting service of other interests—a constitutional absurdity.

If a Supreme Court Justice would cite international or foreign law as precedent for American law, impeachment as a practical matter is imperative. Yet this has been done for the first time in history since GW took office. The people spoke through this last election emphatically, and we must clean up or clean out the Judicial Branch. Judges do not make law; they interpret law. Judges do not overturn the express political will of the people, either of the several States or the Nation.

There are those milksops, of course, who pine for friendship more than good sense or survival. "Can't the Red and Blue States just get along?" The Democrats after losing, in classic style turned to their old standby trick and immediately began calling for reconciliation, telling the president to 'reach across the aisle,' govern from the middle, heal the divide. My response is there in no compromise with evil. Moreover, second place doesn't share the same spot with a gold medal winner in the Olympics or in a political race. Red States must take their spoils while they can, because there is no legitimate trade to make for hard won freedom—and hard won freedom is what this is really about. The stakes were high in the election of 2004 and we won, thank God. Harmony must not be purchased for a velvet-lined pair of handcuffs, an aromatherapy muzzle, or indulgences of any kind. The most precious freedom our big government, Blue State brethren may have forgotten is the freedom to be left alone. Red States demand the freedom to determine our State societies and community environments without their two cents' worth, and most especially unencumbered by judicial fiat contrary to Red State values. Yeah okay, I'll love you Blue Brother if you leave me alone, but I'd just as soon hate you if you don't. Now build a bridge to that!

Timid Conservatism Must End Article #131
o/a February 23, 2004

The 2004 federal budget is more than 22% larger than the 2001 budget—an average annual growth rate of 7-8% for the past 3 years. Even Clinton's budgets increased just 3 to 4%. It is time to get serious about curbing federal spending, instead of scratching everyone's itch or voting for every single good idea and paying for it with deficits.

I spent over 20 years in the military. I joined to do 2 things: to defeat communism; and to enable my fellow citizens to live in freedom while I bore conformity and risk to help defend the country. I was motivated explicitly by Ronald Reagan's vision, and I consider him to be my political mentor. I was his youth advisor for the State of Texas in 1979 before heading off to West Point, and I want to be your congressman now to complete the unfinished business of the Reagan Revolution. For while we won the Cold War, we have not won the domestic one involving the culture and the imbalance that now exists between the state and federal governments. You see culture is a local prerogative; it emanates from families, churches, communities and States. States were meant to be the Union's cradles of culture and laboratories of liberty. They were never intended to be homogeneous provinces or mere appendages of an omnipotent central State. Ronald Reagan wanted and tried to downsize government and empower individuals and States. But the federal government is more of the behemoth today than in 1989—it is an overbearing, overly expensive, intrusive and conforming agent that threatens our very liberty. I left the military to find that so-called civil society resembles a military camp more and more every day. Not only that, people are willingly trading away their freedoms daily—using a majoritarian democracy and the power of a consolidated nation-state-empire to fleece various segments of the population, in order to redistribute wealth to others or to purchase a fleeting sense of security at the expense of liberty itself—Liberty most precious and liberty that's worth dying for. Ladies and Gentlemen, I did not serve 20 years and fight two wars—one cold and one hot—to see my country turn into a nation of people who take orders and serve the collective, or live to execute missions assigned to us by superiors. The military is a wonderful institution. Martial values are extraordinarily valuable—essential for a Republic, but only in the context provided for by our magnificent Constitution.

Ours is a limited government by design. Our Constitution is fixed—its function interpreted according to original intent and not by black-robed legislators, who start to call it a living document so they can infuse it with progressive fads, and call the Founders' document "living" while they call the Ten Commandments dead at the local schoolhouse or the people's courthouses. Ladies and Gentlemen—you and I have inalienable rights. They are natural rights. I believe—and it ought to sound familiar—these rights come from the Creator. The people establish governments to secure the same rights, and the best government is that which governs least. The best government—our government as conceived, has constraints on power: horizontal checks and balances between co-equal branches of the federal government; vertical checks and balances, called federalism, between the federal and state governments.

Today these mechanisms have been subverted. We have a Congress that thinks it can and should literally legislate anything. We have a Judiciary behaving like an Oracle, arrogating to itself the power to invent a "virtual" constitution. We have States behaving like rubber-stamp administrative units, mere wonks of Washington.

Let me tell you something, I believe integrity is the most important thing. It is who you are. Say what you mean, mean what you say—and try to do as you mean and say. I believe in making very few promises but keeping all of them. So there's *gravitas* when I tell you that I will work to repeal the Sixteenth Amendment to the Constitution that gave us the income tax, because the only way we'll ever downsize government is to get control of its purse strings again. I pledge as well, that before voting on any piece of legislation, I will publicly state where and how I have derived the authority for that piece of legislation from the Constitution!

And most of all, I will stand up for Texas—for every county and every individual in District 31. My Fellow Citizens, we still have a 'rendezvous with destiny.' Now let's get to it: vote Wes Riddle for Congress![2]

CHAPTER 4

THE SHIFTING TIDES

The President's Agenda Woes Article #203
o/a July 15, 2005

In general, the president leads his party in setting a political agenda for the country. He tells us what's important, and other things get pushed to the back burners until agenda items are either dealt with, or the political landscape changes. After winning elections, presidents are said to have "political capital" to spend. Indeed, the larger the margin of victory and the clearer certain issues are in the campaign, the more lawmakers feel obliged (or buffaloed) to letting the 'old man' have his way on at least a few things. If the president stumbles politically, especially during his second term, the quicker and more likely it is that he will become a "lame duck"—essentially irrelevant to the political process and to the setting of the agenda. To ward off "lame-duckness," presidents and their staffs try to time, target and limit agenda items, because a victory will breed victory for subsequent agenda items; whereas, an early loss or perceived failure spells trouble for successive items. Experience shows that ambitious domestic and foreign policy agendas are difficult to achieve simultaneously, let alone to afford. Going for guns *and* butter is never a good idea. A setback on the foreign policy front, particularly if it involves war, will almost certainly impinge on what the president can accomplish in terms of domestic policy. Moreover, a relatively discrete list of domestic agenda items is better than a laundry list of a dozen or more things, since short lists focus people's attention and demand serious consideration.

This president is in trouble, in terms of maintaining his lead on the agenda. First of all, he went for guns and butter both; and the war in Iraq, while it may be going well on the battlefield and certainly better than media reports, is going to outlast his presidency. The perception of delay and setbacks, as well as the very real violence and escalating American body count, has plummeted the president's approval rating and boxed him in politically. GW's domestic wish list was as long as his leg to begin with, so really important agenda items such as Social Security have been obscured or easily sidestepped. The sudden retirement of Justice Sandra Day O'Connor from the Supreme Court has thrust a new priority, albeit predictable, into the mix. Add to that the fact the president's chief political strategist, Karl Rove is under fire for CIA information leaks, and you can see the president flapping these days with both arms, sounding more like an AFLAC commercial every day.

Specifically concerning Social Security, the administration mishandled political strategy badly. While personal accounts are popular in every poll, the administration decided to debate solvency instead, exaggerating Social Security's looming financial meltdown. For uncommon candor from the federal government, we can ironically go to page 337 of Bill Clinton's final 2000 budget, the section devoted to Social Security trust funds, which reads: "These funds are not set up to be pension funds, like the funds of private pension plans. They do not consist of real economic assets that can be drawn down in the future to fund benefits. Instead, they are claims on the Treasury that, when redeemed, will have to be financed by raising taxes, borrowing from the public, or reducing benefits or other expenditures. The existence of large trust fund balances, therefore, does not, by itself, have any impact on the Government's ability to pay benefits." So when politicians say not to worry because the trust fund doesn't run out until 2041 (or whenever), they are lying through their teeth or are grossly ignorant—and quite probably both. What should have been an emotional debate about liberty and opportunity, ownership, inheritability and personal financial security, has turned into an accountant's squabble over green-eyeshade issues like solvency dates, transition costs and unfunded liabilities. The administration may yet snatch the victory, but only if the president reasserts his control over the agenda—starting foremost with that new priority thrust to the fore, the naming of Justice O'Connor's successor. The jaws of defeat will snap nearly everything else if GW fails on this test.

President Bush must deliver a conservative, strict constructionist nominee; and he must shepherd his nominee successfully through Senate confirmation hearings. He must choose his nominee according to the values and along the same lines that got him elected. He must, in other words, recur to the terms of his mandate—Red Country and all.

The president has a decisive majority in the Senate, which conservatives have worked long and hard for, for decades. The idea that somehow the president should squander his mandate by nominating someone with unclear conservative credentials because he would be the first Hispanic (a.k.a. Alberto Gonzales), or that he should beat the bush for another nondescript moderate woman like O'Connor to keep the gender ratio unchanged and the ideological balance at a Mexican standoff, is pure ripe horse hockey. As Tim Wildmon, radio host and president of the American Family Association put it recently in an OP-ED, "The bottom line is, Patrick Leahy can hyperventilate on C-SPAN, Diane Feinstein can say the sky is falling, and Ted Kennedy can squeal like a pig; it does not matter. George W. Bush does not need the vote of one Democratic senator to change the face of the Supreme Court. It is up to him. So, Mr. President, the start of a return to judicial sanity in this country depends on you. And as they say in Texas—it's time to dance with the one who brung you." The only thing I'd alter in that assessment is that it does in fact matter—supremely, for the rest of the conservative agenda this term. Otherwise, if it quacks like a duck, it probably is.

Groundwork for Oppression Article #214
o/a September 30, 2005

On the news recently I saw the Republican Governor of Massachusetts, Mitt Romney. He was excited, in good form before the camera, barely able to contain his intent to run for the presidency in 2008. His photogenic appearance was complemented by an intelligent and matter of fact speaking style, which (gratefully) sounded less like a Yankee and more like a Mid-Westerner. Moreover, he had evidently found an issue to resonate nationally, one that garnered him attention—one ironically, often thought of as "right-wing," but just as attractive to liberal supporters in his home state. The thing that brings liberal bedfellows to "right-wing" causes quicker than anything else is the groundwork for oppression. And because of it, we need to take heed. Maybe Republicans will do the dirty work after all, but even if they don't, you can be sure that liberals will use the apparatus the GOP builds, in order to serve a different agenda and to hang us all with the rope we sold or gave away. If American history is any guide, it is a matter of time before political winds change and big government solutions are back in vogue. The fact that self-described "Conservative/conservative" in Congress and the Executive branch have not lived up to the name, and have enlarged the government's scope and power in the years of GW Bush, ought to send a shiver at the thought of self-described "progressives" in their place. Many around these here parts will recall a time before the Reagan Revolution when progressive Republicans were the rule in that party, not the exception. So watch carefully how the parties and the factions within them align, because that can change the nature of your bandwagon. If the Democratic Party had not left the good horse sense, faith and natural conservatism of the Southland, we'd be riding donkeys today instead of elephants.

So just what did Governor Romney say? Only that we ought to wiretap more mosques and conduct surveillance on foreign students, that emergency response ("more fire trucks") as in the case of Katrina, is not enough. We've got to head off events, become proactive and not let political correctness get in the way. Intelligence clearly let us down in Iraq (there were no weapons of mass destruction), so we'd better shift resources to ensure that intelligence doesn't let us down on the home front (read another 9-11 catastrophic event happening while our pants are down). When pressed by the media, however, Romney let political correctness get the better of him. Well, of course the same should apply to wiretapping churches and synagogues. The same surveillance would apply to both legal and illegal immigrants, and the same must apply to domestic terrorists and all such purveyors of hate—those "who teach hatred or might support the violent overthrow of the government." We're not suggesting anything illegal, quoth the Romney, just more of what is currently allowed and going on under the PATRIOT ACT and the U.S. Constitution. In one news source, Romney was actually quoted as saying more of what's allowed "under the Patriot Act *of the Constitution.*" On CNN, Romney drew easy parallels between Muslim extremists and Timothy McVeigh, between 9-11 and Oklahoma City. Now the phenomenon is rife in post-modern American society and politics, and I hope you perceive it too: the evidence that we are no longer thinking as rigorously as our ancestors did. Indeed, we're rapidly losing the ability to think at all. In the particular and convoluted reasoning to which I refer, if you wiretap a Muslim *madrasa*, you will no doubt wiretap the Christian home school next (and I'm not kidding). Romney and his ilk equate all stripes of political violence with terrorism writ large, Al Qaeda with the Irish Republican Army or the Contras, and internal strife in one country with outright external threat to ours.

Sometimes I think the administration and its neoconservative advocates never met an apple that didn't resemble an orange. It's all fruit cocktail to them, and Thomas Jefferson and Martin Luther King, Jr. were terrorists plain and simple. War is especially convenient for politicians anyway and probably always has been, because wars generally prevent people from thinking too hard. They cover up a lot of bad and flimsy arguments with the flag, and drown truth out with Sousa. Hence an open-ended war on terrorism is the perfect thing for laying the groundwork for oppression in America. It still isn't politic four years later to speak of the foreign policy antecedents to 9-11, particularly how the United States played geopolitical chess after the first Gulf War. Likewise, if domestic spies, wiretaps and surveillance activities are equated to soldiers on the ground in Iraq, to the tactics in battle against an enemy, then it is very easy to dismiss domestic grievances and the host of policy antecedents, which give rise to domestic unrest or even to a harsh critique of the status quo. The bait and switch is in place, and the *doublethink* of Leviathan has convinced itself and is trying to convince you too that Oklahoma City (April 19, 1995) is just a terrorist incident and Katrina is a terrorist's equivalent. History is wiped clean, for no mention is made of the siege at Waco (April 19, 1993), or to Ruby Ridge before that. No reference is made to natural rights or to natural disasters, and none allowed to the inherent sinfulness of man according to Western religion. For Government not God is All-in-all, and all belongs to Government. You really gotta love it here in the 'free of the land, brave of the home.' I think it's called *Amerika*.

Government: Let's Super Size It! Article #219
o/a October 20, 2005

You probably recall President Clinton, after conservative Republicans picked up convincing gains during mid-term elections, saying, that "The era of big government is over." Of course, we didn't know just how slick Willie was—for even then, he was triangulating his way to a second term victory. He was right it turns out, however, though not in the way conservatives had hoped. The era of big government was indeed over, so now we just "Super size it" along with the soft drink and Big Mac.

Ten years ago Republicans stood for reducing the size of government. They pledged to eliminate entire agencies. The first House budget passed after the '94 Republican sweep would have ended three (Education,

Energy and Commerce), and over 200 more federal programs were slated for termination. Of the 101 largest programs set to end, however, all but 19 have risen from the dead. The combined budgets of these "living dead" programs have grown by 27 percent after adjusting for inflation. Worse, more than half of this growth has occurred in just the last four years, when the so-called party of smaller government controlled the White House and the Congress. The budgets in GW's first term quickly squandered gains achieved by fiscal conservatives during the Clinton years. The size of the federal government has grown to 20.3% of GDP, which represents a 33% growth in the budget since this Bush took office. That's twice the average growth rate of government under Clinton and more than any president since Lyndon B. Johnson! I'll say Texans like to do it up big. Real big: it's like budgeting for a Whole Other Country. Even if you stripped away defense expenditures and the homeland security increase, Bush beats Johnson in entitlement spending growth.

The sad conclusion is that Republicans did better at controlling spending when they did not control the White House. I would not have believed it ten years ago. I'd heard political scientists wax eloquent about the advantages of divided government, frustrating as it may be, but I said it was horse hockey—just give the Republican party of Ronald Reagan a chance! We'll whittle big government down to size in no time! Of course this is not the Republican Party of Ronald Reagan, let alone of Barry Goldwater. Republican Congresses sent the President consecutive budgets costing $91 billion more than he asked for his first term, but he refused to veto any. GW has resorted to guns-and-butter budgeting. Instead of urging Congress to cut low priority programs to make room for higher priority spending, the administration sanctioned increases in everything. Every president during the past 40 years except Johnson and Carter, has offset increases in defense spending with decreases in non-defense spending, or vice versa. It's something of a common wisdom and horse sense to do that. After all, guns and butters pending historically set in motion hyperinflation and almost wrecked the U.S. economy. It was Democrats, who did it before but not this time.

A recent *Newsweek* article stated categorically that neither Republicans nor Democrats are trying any longer to balance the budget. It's too hard and too unpopular. Congressional Budget Office reports continue to suggest ways to do it, but there's literally no audience. Government programs once created become immortal. The Republican approach is cynical in the extreme, because it is so inconsistent with the party's rhetoric. Even if you control for "mandatory" spending programs like Social Security, Medicare, etc., federal spending has risen 4.8% per year under this president—with no new tax to pay for it (thankfully), but all of it financed with deficit spending. The 2006 budget will likely be $2.6 trillion, with a deficit close to $400 billion. Believe it or not, this kind of deficit spending would be illegal under European monetary rules. Moreover, the spending spree is no anomaly but political strategy at the highest level. According to Karl Rove, it's the way Republicans "seize the mantle of idealism" from Democrats by being for stuff, instead of always against stuff. So we win elections to put off the day of reckoning.

Speaking of which, deficit spending is a dangerous game. Sustained deficit spending not only draws capital away from the more efficient private sector, but it leaves the broader economy addicted to government stimuli. Should the economy undergo a serious recession in such circumstance, the only tool left to the government is even more deficit spending. That's what happened to Japan, which dug a hole so deep it has taken more than a decade to pull out. A serious recession could happen from too many 9-11s or Hurricane Katrina's in close succession, or an accentuated business cycle. There are also structural problems and a glib over-confidence to be concerned about, which the Federal Reserve Chairman, Alan Greenspan has even uncharacteristically alluded to. There are basically two large mortgage firms left (Freddie Mac and Fannie Mae), having crowded out competition in the $5.5 trillion debt market. If they crash, the entire country's financial structure goes. And while we blissfully ignore the warnings we've heard about Social Security, the mathematical fact is that the outlays envisioned, will not only bankrupt the pension system but could bankrupt the total budget. Meanwhile deficit spending limits our ability to maneuver, and baby boomers continue to retire—a trend that peaks in eight years. But by then, maybe Democrats will be in charge and take the blame for what happens. Great strategy, Karl Rove.

Of Ports and Politics — Article #239
o/a March 03, 2006

It is extraordinarily important, based upon historical experience, for second-term presidents to monitor their processes through 'to the end,' so to speak. They must, in other words, run their second terms as wisely, as conscientiously and as politic, as if they were running for reelection! If they did so, their legacy would no doubt take care of itself. Of course, it would be asking far more than the current crop of politicians in either political party is likely to deliver. It is certainly more than Karl Rove is willing to do for our unfortunate Mr. President, GW. For if the political staff had been on their feet, they would have identified the ports deal controversy first of all, and they would have predicted a political firestorm over Dubai Ports World taking over six of the country's great ports. 'It's academic my Dear Watson.'

Even after the story broke and revealed it had long legs, damage could have been marginalized had the administration explained sooner the important distinction between management and security. That is to say, U.S. ports security always belongs to Americans—armed Americans at that—notwithstanding the ownership of port facility managing firms. Most Americans would get it. Security at American ports is provided by federal, state and local governments, regardless of the nationality of the owners of port management firms. Regardless of who operates the ports, the Coast Guard would still control their physical security. The Customs Service would still control container security. The harbor patrols, port authorities and harbor police all still do their jobs. Indeed, many American ports are now managed, in full or in part by foreign-owned firms, and eighty-percent of the port of L.A. is managed by foreign owned firms. The administration, however, revealed again for the umpteenth time, its penchant for two very sad and maddening characteristics: first, a confusing business-as-usual approach to commercial deals at the same time it rattles sabers and conducts war; and second, a grotesquely high-handed way of dealing with critics and the curious, which amounts to a sentiment like, "I don't owe you an explanation, because I'm the president."

Critics are instantly impugned by administration talking heads for having racist or xenophobic motives. They are accused of harboring doubts perhaps, that brown-skinned Middle Easterners can develop stable democracies on their own; else, they are accused of being afraid and less than completely American, to compete fairly with the good and peace-loving peoples around the world. You would think that a security minded president would speak to collective security arrangements with Dubai and other Gulf Countries and explain the nature of important reciprocal arrangements we have, that are helping us win this War on Terror. But the president is more interested in secrecy. He wants a free rein to do as he pleases, without the corresponding duty to lead the people, by informing and persuading them. It may be true as Secretary of Commerce, Carlos M. Gutierrez, said in Riyadh February 26th, that we all have an interest in defending free, fair and open trade, and promoting a business environment friendly to U.S. commercial interests. It may very well be true that ex-pats abroad generate income stateside, that imports and exports bring jobs home. But really, no one should be surprised by the furor, which erupted on Capitol Hill in connection with the, albeit indirect, acquisition of management leases by Dubai Ports World.

True it was pursuant to that company's acquisition of the venerable British firm Peninsular and Oriental Steam Navigation Company. Contrary to President Bush, who observed how strange it is no one objected to a British firm holding such leases, it is entirely reasonable that we should object—or at least give more scrutiny to the commercial access and tangential security implications of the UAE firm. 'Free and fair are free and fair for all' is very trite and politically correct. It is also very knuckle-headed. How many times this and virtually all the presidents after Monroe, have talked about the "Special Relationship" with Great Britain! That relationship has Department of State sanction and strategic significance and nuclear connotations; it is also recognized, even within the very close context of other NATO allies. We've certainly seen GW cozy up to Tony Blair more than Whomever-the-king-of-UAE-is. Moreover, the fact that I would have less trouble with "Anglo" management of U.S. Ports has less to do with race than it does with institutions, including legal institutions and similar work ethic and business practices; as well as with cultural predilections, including the intolerance of private graft and official corruption. I used to hate it when Al Gore spoke to the Great American Public, because he always sounded like he was talking down to a group of junior high school students. He would stretch his words to make sure you heard how they were pronounced. This president doesn't even deign to talk to us, possibly because he doesn't know how to pronounce his words either.

Reagan Revolution 25 Years Later Article #227
o/a November 18, 2005

Ronald Reagan's Inaugural as 40th president of the United States occurred 25 years ago, on January 20th, 1981. At the time, I was in the audience with my mother, listening intently to the loud speakers some distance away from the West End of the White House. On special leave from West Point, having been a part of Reagan's youth—and no one had excited young people to politics like he had, at least not since Kennedy—I had worked in a volunteer capacity for this day since 1976. Indeed, I had been in the audience too at the Republican National Convention in Kansas City in '76, the youngest one there, my trip having been sponsored by the youth organization for Ford—when Ford won the nomination, and Ronald Reagan stole my heart. I share this with you, in order to convey a sense of the historical, as well as an individual connection to it. Your connection may or may not be as personal, as regards Reagan and his Inauguration, but we all do live in time and are shaped and influenced by the currents of history. At times, we are even privileged to swim against the tide, and maybe to feel the tide as it changes. The Reagan Revolution was a great moment in history, and I am prideful merely to have been alive at the time.

I am mindful, however, that the Reagan Revolution has not been completed, at least not to the full extent, as I understood it then. Now let me state, that there are disagreements within the conservative movement, in terms of just what this Revolution entailed. But I was a student of politics at the time and listened to what Reagan said. I cannot agree that Reagan would have supported the runaway spending in Washington, and the concentration of power in the federal government. He would no doubt have supported the War on Terrorism, possibly even before 9/11. He probably would have supported the invasion of Iraq, although we cannot know how his execution of that war would have differed. In no wise, however, would he have refrained from using his veto to cut out Republican or Democratic pork. It is hard to imagine we could have doubted his intent to nominate conservative judges, especially after an election mandate to do so. He would not have sanctioned the trade of sacred American rights, in a cynically named "Patriot Act"—without sunset provision or oversight—for a parcel of Executive perk and privilege, and the shirk of responsibility to live according to the rule of law, including the organic law of the Constitution. The Reagan Revolution also has not succeeded to the extent of redressing the imbalance of power between the States and federal government, effectively restoring federalism. "New Federalism" was something the modern conservative movement talked about and promised to do, from Goldwater to Nixon to Reagan. Somehow that notion was high-jacked in the '90s by a conservative nationalist and crusading zealotry to keep and hold power, instead of returning it to the people, in order to administer the Welfare State simply "better" than liberals. Conservatives would spend money on better things, in other words, but with the same level and national prerogative of control. Fascism is perhaps better than communism, but if neoconservatives have more or less implemented Reagan's vision abroad (which I'm not prepared without serious caveat to say they have), they have failed in the most miserable fashion to restore self-determination and meaningful freedom to the people at the State and local level.

Self-determination and meaningful freedom at the State and local level does not include Republican sponsorship of a mega-state that subsumes everything to it. It does not sanction the transmogrification of avowedly conservative political platforms to the embrace of extra-constitutional powers, because ends do not justify the means—at least not to free peoples. The "conservative" Congress and President have essentially adapted Franklin Roosevelt's own sleight of hand: speaking in tongues, to convince the American people they need rights not found in the Constitution—the right to a job, to food and to clothing, to medical care and to an education—all guaranteed by the federal government. These things are of course vitally important, necessary for life or the quality of life in fact, but they are the province of free minds, free markets and free men. They are not to be had or sustained from a guaranteed dole out, levied and redistributed as all things are by the federal government, breaking the backs of productive and working citizens. If you want to subsidize education or healthcare, find a constitutional way (through tax deduction, tax credit, or facilitation of choice) to do it. Top-down bureaucratic control of matters that are essentially local or private or both, is not what the Founders had in mind. It isn't what the Reagan Revolution was about either. To paraphrase Larry Arnn, president of Hillsdale College, Michigan, the importance of things like education, food and medicine have been known to practically any fool since the start of civil society. The question is how these things should be provided! The Founders practiced the art of constitutional government, under which government is limited and people have the right to provide for themselves. Under this system one gets more food, more medicine and more education than under bureaucratic rule. One also gets his liberty under the law—which is, as yet, an unfulfilled promise of the Reagan Revolution 25 years later.

Mid-Term Democracy Article #251
o/a June 16, 2006

In November the GOP is sure to lose a number of seats in the biggest anti-incumbent vote since 1994. Of course, the possibility won't sneak up on Republicans the way it did on Democrats back then; and Republican gerrymandering has erected structural defense against typical, mid-term winds of change. Losing power is unlikely for Republicans in either House, unless political backlash comes to resemble Hurricane Katrina force winds; that is to say, unless voters evince only once-a-century intensity of political fury. While possible, it's unlikely. There aren't many contestable seats in this year's election, making it hard for Democrats to net the 15 House seats or 6 Senate seats needed. The wildcard is Iraq, and news from that front will have direct bearing on the election at home. News of the death of Abu Musab Al-Zarqawi, as well as the treasure trove of intelligence recovered recently about Al-Qaeda, may actually turn the tide in Iraq—it surely provides the political cover essential, to start drawing troop levels down before November or to make an announcement to do so next year. There's no question too, that regardless of the physical situation, the tide of information has turned from all bad to, well, much better. From this standpoint, there's only four months to go before the mid-term elections—Republicans only need the hundred yard dash, i.e., a short-run politically speaking. The marathon comes later, and Republicans will worry about the presidential race later. Indeed, they must. Expected Democratic gains in November are most likely going to increase political gridlock, not break it. In all likelihood, this will set the stage for watershed elections in 2008.

Now then: a word or two about the state of our "democracy," much less our Republic. In the U.S. House there are only 30 out of 435 districts that are truly competitive. According to James Bovard in his book, *Attention Deficit Democracy* (Palgrave Macmillan, 2006), the politicians have picked the voters they want, rather than the other way around! Bovard argues that elections now resemble "reverse slave auctions," whereby largely clueless voters select which gang of politicians to control their lives. Hey I've got my favorite gang, and you probably do too, but his point is worth considering. I remember studying U.S. and Southern history. It was fascinating to discover a tremendous variety of conditions and situations possible under nineteenth century slavery. In some places, the institution was far less oppressive than in others. Though always backed by violence or the threat of violence, there was a certain "freedom within slavery" possible, such that, slaves formed a unique culture, had families and practiced religion, even fished and performed the jig. Moreover, in my travels around the world I've discovered freedom in oppressive regimes as well—pockets of private space, as well as practical accommodations between rulers and the ruled, by virtue of power and of interest. A separation of powers principle indeed exists in many countries around the world, not just in so-called democracies. The point I'm making implicitly is that what we now call freedom in this country is to some extent an illusion, or at least it is no more substantive than the practical freedom experienced by slaves, who have no theoretical rights left under a living Constitution, at least none that our masters are bound to respect.

Much of what government does today is done covertly. Covert governments require no accountability; and if they have elections, it is a formality. Does anyone seriously believe the president or Congress actually wants to discuss the war, NSA spying, or prisoners held at Guantanamo? Had they wanted to persuade us at all in the first place, or merely trick us into going along? We consider ourselves free now because almost everyone is entitled to vote, but I sometimes question what we're voting for. Few have the slightest idea of freedom, property rights or the Constitution's limits on state power. According to Bovard, "The less people understand about how government works, the easier it is to get them to focus on promised results rather than actual procedures. Due process becomes a mere phrase, or even a pointless distraction in the pursuit of a Great Protector. This is reflected by the tacit acceptance by many Americans that an election victory entitles a politician to 'do what he thinks right.'" Thomas Jefferson thought that politicians had to be bound down by the chains of the Constitution. He never once placed his faith in guaranteed rights on the momentary whim of fifty-one percent, or the bare majority of a minority who bothered to vote. Our democracy today resembles the inhabitants of George Orwell's *1984* more than the independent-minded and resolute individuals, who fought for liberty and established an American Republic 230 years ago. Mid-term elections in 2006 bode no serious philosophic change, only a shift in the crop of rascals in Washington. People are sadly content with the general outlines of a welfare-warfare state, and while the election of 2008 is bound to be "watershed," "what for" remains to be seen.

Illiberal Democracy — Article #252
o/a June 16, 2006

Modern political discourse treats democracy as if it were the same thing as liberty. Whereas Liberty was the highest political end in American tradition, we have come to speak almost entirely about democracy and hardly a whit about liberty. Of course, what we're after is not a system where anything goes if and when the majority decides. What we want is rule of law, as well as protections of our life, property and civil rights, and the freedom to go about peaceful business without assault or being harassed. Then we shall talk of majority rule! After the rule of law is established, the political process should indeed open up, as it did in America, but to imagine that "all we need is free elections" is to fundamentally misconceive the problem of democratic development. It is to confuse political end with one possible means of achieving it. To speak of "democratization" as something worthy in and of itself, is to put the cart before the horse without one lick of horse sense. A political system in which everyone has a vote and a voice is one thing, but it is worse than nothing if it is not first and primarily a system in which the most important matters aren't subject to a vote at all. Liberty and democracy are not the same things, and frequently democracy is quite illiberal from the standpoint of rights in the American tradition. That's true at home, and even more true abroad. Furthermore, to run American foreign policy based on the aim to "democratize" the world is stupid plain and simple, and it is very often inconsistent with the national interest, which ought to come first in matters of foreign policy.

Often I've heard the president say that "Democracies are peaceful countries," and I'm left to wonder what bozo taught him that. Even if the rationale were halfway correct, we don't possess unlimited resources or power to transform the world at will. To abandon balance of power, deterrence and punitive action in favor of a scheme to recast political cultures of broad regions around the world is foolhardy. We also do not possess the moral right to do so, if you believe might does not make right. I'm not talking about defending our way of life from attack; I'm talking about an overt crusade to impose democratic ideology worldwide, which by the way, amounts to serious corruption of the republican ideals that gave birth to our country. Anyway, the fact is that the rationale isn't correct at all, even if we did manage somehow to force-feed the world. Germany was a democracy when it was a primary instigator of World War I. Italy was democratic when it joined the entente to wrest South Tyrol from Austria. Japan was democratic before militarists took over, while it was yet still embarked on an aggressive course during the 1930s. There were many 19th-century colonial conquests by democratic European powers. There was a Mexican-American War, a Spanish-American War and a War Between the States, all between largely "democratic" countries. The latter was entirely a democratic matter over interpretations of democratic instruments. No perfect democracy exists, because no perfect peoples exist. Ergo, there is simply no logical way to conclude that democracies, let alone representative governments, will necessarily remain peaceful with each other or with anyone else.

Now here's the real rub. Look at what democracy gets you in the Middle East. Hamas wins the election in Palestinian territories, and the U.S. is reduced to preventing legitimate wire transfers of funds through international banks to a duly elected regime. We look to the rest of the world as if we support elections only when and if they turn out the way we want. Every analysis done also indicates that as Turkey, Pakistan, Lebanon, and Kuwait become more democratic, the more Islamist and potentially extreme they become. They are likely, in other words, to do things contrary to our national interest, the more they take our foreign policy seriously and actually institute the democratic reforms we suggest. Further, consider the excellent strategic relationship we have with the Kingdom of Saudi Arabia. If Saudi Arabia were to become a democracy tomorrow, do you seriously believe it would support American interests as well as its king does today? To suggest that it would, is to be an ostrich in a seriously overcrowded cow pasture. Unfortunately in foreign policy, carelessness and confusion—whether brought about by well intended well wishing or not, often leads to tragedy. There is no substitute for sober, self-interested calculation concerning our relations with other countries and other regions of the world. The Constitution posits legitimate power from the American people to the Government, in order to serve Americans according to its terms. It is no altruistic document, according to which Americans die for the sake of bringing democracy or anything else to the rest of the world.

Mechanics of Consolidation Articles #259-260
~Part I~ o/a July 13, 2006

Consolidation of power at the national level has occurred, and that is historic fact. Just why it is, is something more difficult to tell. I remember in graduate school at Oxford expressing a certain naïve measure of wonderment, that what the Founders intended did not come to pass and indeed went badly wrong in some respects. One of my professors with a Harvard background merely smiled, without explanation but with apparent glee. He was a proponent of consolidation you see, and he knew that proponents of liberty were on the losing side of history thus far. There are evil professors making muck of minds and placing their stamp, yea mark, upon the careers of young academics, and writing the textbooks and determining acceptable "consensus" amongst those who depend upon them for their Ph. D's. I tell you this, having been there in the Ivy League; I tell you this to sound a trumpet—there's more than one global war going on! Some are wars between nations, twixt civilizations, but the biggest war of all is always spiritual—and its close cousin, the war of ideas. Simple really, this war of ideas: it is between those who would control, and those who would set free.

I know now more than I did, some of the history that isn't always taught. One place to begin is in the Senate. That august body was meant to be an institutional safeguard against consolidation. Indeed, the Founders expected it to serve as guardian of States' reserved powers. The reason may come as some surprise to you. It is because the Founders intended Senators to be selected by State legislatures. Senators would therefore be direct representatives of the States, within the Legislative branch of the national government. That was indeed law according to the Constitution, before adoption of the Seventeenth Amendment in 1913. Like the federal income tax, passed by the Sixteenth Amendment in 1913 also, popular election of U.S. Senators is the product of the Progressive Era, which transformed the nation even more than the War Between the States did, at least if taken in isolation. The Progressive Era, so far as the Constitution is concerned, represents a departure from republicanism and institutionalized safeguarding of dual-sovereignty; it represents a corresponding triumph for national party politics and blind faith in democracy. One has to wonder why the Founders would have worked so hard at the Constitutional Convention, if all that were needed were elections and the people's choice.

Next there is the very strange gravitation of all issues and concerns to the national level, something that continues to this day as if towards a black hole. What were clearly intra-state activities, to be regulated by local officials, have all fallen in Congress's purview of delegated powers.

Congress has express power to punish only a handful of acts, such as piracy, crimes on the high seas, treason, and counterfeiting according to the Constitution. The number of crimes punishable by the federal government did increase after Appomattox, but it did not skyrocket until recent years. Over forty percent of federal crimes were enacted since 1970. The reason, which may not come as quite the surprise, is political. Senators and congressmen found that law-and-order platforms are winners at the ballot box. Tough-on-crime conservative politicians found liberal colleagues to be cuddly bed partners too. The fact remains, however, the people of the several States never delegated a generalized "law and order" power to the federal government. Of course congressmen are want to find it, like a catcher in the rye. So broad in fact is Congress's interpretation of the Commerce Power, that other enumerated powers are superfluous. The regulation of interstate commerce has become akin to a general police power, such that, if anything could affect the national economy, Congress can regulate. Of course that's a crazy, unconstitutional assertion, because my friends will all tell you my backyard barbeque no doubt threatens a series of establishments! (Be that as it may,) commerce in the Founders' day was understood to be, well, uh "commerce." That is, *commercial* intercourse, i.e., exchange of one thing for another, the interchange of something, trade or the trafficking of goods. Commerce was not, as Congress and the Supreme Court now interprets, a synonym for every "gainful activity," "economic activity," "agriculture" and "manufacturing" activity. James Madison noted that the object of the power to regulate interstate commerce was "the relief of the States which import and export through other States." In other words, the Founders wanted to remove internal trade barriers and create a national free-trade zone. Ironically, the freedom they sought to give us has, through the politician's turn of phrase and sinister Constitutional reinterpretation, become the source of much internal regulation, constituting an unlimited grant of legislative power. Today any activity that tangentially affects the economy, or could affect the economy if hypothetically, a lot of people engaged in it, is fair game for regulation—and quite possibly, another platform for winning votes. (Yippee).[3]

~Part II~ o/a July 13, 2006

As I said, consolidation of power at the national level has occurred, and that is a historic fact. Just why it is, however, is an interesting process. Not only has the Commerce Clause been subverted through a Constitutional reinterpretation that has no textual basis, so has the Congress's spending power. Congress uses the Commerce Clause to regulate almost everything conceivable, but it uses its spending power to make sure its regulations hurt enough to stick. Congress claims spending power, as part of the General Welfare Clause, but it uses it in such a way as to reach outside the scope of its delegated authority. For instance, Congress taxes citizens of the several States and then offers the money back to States, but with certain strings attached to the "federal funds." On the face of it, the federal government engages in an extortion racket, which subverts dual sovereignty, federalism and the Original Intent of the Founding Fathers. So the federal government will not grant federal highway funds, unless States adopt specific blood alcohol content standards for drunk driving, or perhaps certain speed limits, or seatbelt laws, or helmet laws, etc., etc. Moreover, prevailing Supreme Court precedent permits Congress to attach myriad strings to almost all its federal spending. In 1987, the Supreme Court upheld a congressional enactment of law that withholds transportation funds from States that don't have 21 defined as the minimum drinking age. In a virtually incomprehensible finding, the Court in *South Dakota* v. *Dole* held that, "the power of Congress to authorize expenditure of public moneys for public purposes is not limited by the direct grants of legislative power found in the Constitution." Come again? They might as well have said the Constitution isn't binding, or that if you're slick enough to find a way around it, you can exceed delegated authority. Not only is the aforementioned use of spending power a gross Constitutional violation of the States' reserved powers, the use is morally offensive and as stupid as it was during the Viet Nam era, when it applied only in some States—and when young men marched to war unable to vote for or against the congressmen who sent them there! You can get married and go to war okay, die and leave a widow and children; just don't let me catch you raising a glass to the ladies, or toasting your president at the Army Birthday bash—at least not with real wine. (Muslims of course forbid the evil substance too).

The structure and history of the Constitution do place limits on congressional spending power, regardless. In his Virginia Resolutions, James Madison explained the historic basis for the General Welfare Clause, its language having been "copied from the very limited grant of powers" out of the former Articles of Confederation. He continued in his Report of 1800 that the language was used in the Constitution, to ensure that no general grant of power could be construed, or that the language be used to allow Congress to escape its limited enumeration of powers! (So much for plain language and history). Even that pales, however, next to the overreach by the Supreme Court through the Fourteenth Amendment. The Supreme Court uses the Fourteenth Amendment as a vehicle for increasing the power of federal courts and restricting reserved powers of the States even further. The original purpose of the Amendment was to improve the lot of former slaves. The Court has taken phrases like "due process" and "equal protection" out of context and applied them in ways that impose the personal views of judges on the nation. Both Alexander Hamilton and Chief Justice John Marshall both recognized explicitly that the Bill of Rights was not applicable to the States, and Hamilton opined that the term "due process" was a technical term that applied to courts of justice and not to acts of the legislatures. But in 1937, the Court issued a new doctrine of "incorporation," again without textual basis, which used the Due Process Clause of the Fourteenth Amendment to incorporate the Bill of Rights into that Clause, such that, the Court now enforces in States its own notion of rights belonging to citizens, based upon the first Eight Amendments. Of course, the first Ten Amendments were passed historically, as strictures on the Federal Government alone. To now have the Federal Government in charge of interpreting the whole Bill of Rights and using the enforcement provision of a single Amendment (the Fourteenth) to enforce that interpretation, is putting the fox in charge of the henhouse. One might say the troll under the bridge is now charging the toll.

In 1996 the Supreme Court found another creative way to restrict States, this time utilizing the Equal Protection Clause out of the Fourteenth Amendment. The Court struck down the Virginia Military Institute's all-male admissions policy. For 150 years, VMI operated as a single-gender, state-supported school. Whether the policy ever was, or continues to be wise, is a different matter than whether the policy raises constitutional questions. The matter of policy wisdom belongs to the people of the several States and their elected legislatures. Education has until the past ten years, been regarded as falling entirely within the reserved powers of the States, the use of the Fourteenth Amendment to remedy specific violations based on race, notwithstanding. Education is no longer in the States' exclusive domain, however, and there really is nothing left. The States are rendered administrative subdivisions of the national government, consolidation complete. Yet when I look upon the Texas sky, I see blue from horizon to horizon; and I thank my God that I was born where the sky at least still beckons men and women, to become what they can be. We are not as free as we once were; but Praise the Lord, there is some measure of freedom left—indeed, more than much of the world will ever enjoy. Moreover, I have faith that it is the essential measure required, in order to redeem the time and take back what was lost. It is enough for what must be done, and accepting this, we start as we should: being truly grateful—grateful enough to be disquieted, grateful enough to join with the contest, and to reverse the mechanics of consolidation.[4]

After the Thumping — Article #272
o/a November 17, 2006

On November 7th, voters nationwide gave the Republican Party a "thumping" according to President Bush. Although a thrashing might be more accurate, I suppose a thumping will do—or should. For those of us concerned about flagging voter turnout, we should at least be heartened. The turnout was well above that of recent midterm elections, in some races motivating 60 to 70 % of registered voters to participate. While the margins of victory from race to race were not spectacular between Republicans and Democrats, the cumulative effect of Democratic victories in case after case certainly was, and the undeniable conclusion is that there was a national wave that washed across the political scene in 2006—and it was a Democratic wave. Analysis reveals that whereas, some Republicans switched sides in the General Election or stayed home; and whereas, the Democrat Party's Get Out The Vote (GOTV) phase of its campaign was more successful than in recent years, the margins of victory (10% or less) came from Independent voters. These same voters who broke for Republicans 50-50 in 2004 went 2 to 1 against them in 2006. Moreover, fully one-third of white Evangelical Christians (core of the so-called 'rightwing religious base' of the Republican Party) voted for Democrats.

After the thumping, Republicans had lost the House and the Senate. Democrats picked up 29 seats in the House for a majority in that chamber; and 6 Senate seats for a 51-49 majority there. This was clearly not a very good election day for Republicans. They were supposed to have a "firewall" in the Senate—no way they would lose it. To lose the Senate, why they would have to lose practically everything under any contest, including staunchly Republican "Red States" like Montana and Virginia! Republican West; Republican Southland: standard bearers of the Grand Old Party. Yet it happened. In addition, Democrats picked up 6 Governorships for a 28-22 "advantage" in states, which means less now than later when you're gauging likely outcomes in the 2008 presidential race. Political analyst Mark Shields opined that the election was not a Democratic victory so much as a Republican defeat. Howard Dean, Democrat Party chairman, explained what happened in similar terms. Grinning from ear to ear, he explained the president had helped Democrats "a lot."

Issues affecting the votes varied. Perhaps the biggest surprise was that corruption and ethics topped the list for many going to the polls, even more than terrorism or the war in Iraq. Of course war was on everyone's mind too, and no one claimed to be pleased with the current situation. One of the most encouraging notes I received before the election was from a fellow conservative attempting to motivate the Republican base, advising everyone to just "hold your nose and vote All Republican." I figured things weren't going to go too well, if that was the best we could do. Indeed, Democrats deserve a little credit. They didn't trot out the Ted Kennedy model, at least not in prime time. Liberal and conservative labels got a little mixed up if you ask me. John Kerry's pitiful "botched joke" gave us all cause for a guffaw, but anyone with a lick of sense knew it was never intended to insult the troops. People can be forgiven for catching media clips and losing context, but the president knew better and still played it for coarse political advantage.

Maybe that's all that was left. Indeed, I was amazed how vapid and vacuous had become the rhetoric from self-styled conservatives facing moderates for the first time in years. If God and guns were removed from the panoply of political discussion, Republicans seemed lost, possessing no original or thoughtful idea on virtually anything else. Howard Dean got this much right: part of their problem was that they were conjoined with the president! And sadly, he really could have used the oversight and constructive criticism from within his party for a long time—he needed it in fact, but never got it. Instead, the president bought into fallacious neoconservative foreign policy assumptions and most in Congress followed merrily along. The president continued to combine the wars in Iraq and on terrorism as if they were the same things, without drawing distinctions, without offering meaningful explanation, without detailed strategic discussion; and he got a bye from his party that the people refused to give Republican candidates. Worst of all, the president said it was cool to be a Big Government Conservative, especially in time of war, and Republicans tripped over themselves to get "with it." Since 2004, Republican government has resembled the animals at the end of *Animal Farm*, looking and acting like the people they replaced; or in this case, Republicans dancing around and behaving like Democrats. After twelve years (1994-2006) of Congressional domination, Republicans proved they could spend more for guns and butter at the same time than LBJ. Instead of inflation, they just added debt. Republicans proved they could govern as arrogantly as FDR and Nixon put together, flippantly dismissing dissent and criticism, failing to address valid concerns with current policies, as well as concern over issues not being addressed, such as immigration. Always, always, however, considering a self-ascribed holy cause to be the Republicans' inoculation from legal or constitutional strictures, and even from meddlesome, unpatriotic questioning.

In addition, this government's management competence came under question after Katrina, and quite frankly remains there. If the government were competent, for instance, Defense Secretary Donald Rumsfeld would have left easily, in good graces after the 2004 elections, and not after the thumping. Certainly by summer this year he should have gone, when it was clear how the war was going, clear we needed "fresh eyes" in terms of strategy, clear even as to how the outlines of this election were shaping up. Robert Gates replacing Rumsfeld helps put realism back into American foreign policy and clears the way for a course correction in both the wars on terrorism and in Iraq. Likewise, the Baker-Hamilton Iraq Study Group's ongoing work, as well as the Democrats' choice of Steny Hoyer (MD) over John Murtha (PA) as their new Majority Leader, bodes well for serious reassessment, for prudence and bipartisanship in the road ahead out of a difficult and challenging situation. For many of us, I'm sure it was hard to take the thumping; but it was even harder perhaps, to realize for the first time in twelve years, that the good of the nation does not always follow the political fortunes of a single political party.

Getting Back to Progress Article #286
o/a March 02, 2007

Legal controversies during the Progressive and New Deal Eras sorted themselves out in favor of expanded government power, but there is no constitutional reason why they may not be revisited and hopefully settled again differently. Conservative opinion favoring a respect for precedent (meaning the accumulated wisdom of the past), which counts on that for protection against the use of arbitrary power, is mistaken when arbitrary power actually becomes enshrined. Moreover, the assumption that something new or modern is innately better is out of place in matters of politics. Although science sometimes follows a path of linear advancement, the same cannot be said of the law where insights and mistakes tend to recur. To the extent that traditional classical liberal ideas of constitutional government have been compromised or abandoned, we can and must still bring them back. The exigencies of rapid industrialization, war and the Great Depression must be seen for what they were. Exceptions should prove rather than remove the rule. Further, as we have institutionalized protections and procedures to deal with some of the emergencies in history, we ought to recur again forcefully to a classical liberal synthesis—to private property, freedom of contract, limited government, low levels of taxation and regulation, federalism, and to the sovereign reserved powers of states. (This synthesis would, by the way, restrict eminent domain only to public use upon payment of just compensation).

The constitution keeps its presumption and confers whatever legitimacy there is to the law. If erroneous precedent has intervened, the error is illegitimate and must be overturned. Notwithstanding, Rome wasn't built in a day and can't be undone in one either! The behemoth government we have today has extensive reliance interests attached to it. It cannot be dismantled quickly, even partially, without grievous harm to somebody. Nevertheless, the peaceful acceptance of illegitimate change temporarily, is not the same as acceptance of precedent into constitutional law, on which the change is based. A reigning constitutional regime can be changed and indeed changed again! From a political standpoint, progress might be a forward or a backwards exercise. Otherwise, the doctrine of "separate-but-equal" announced in *Plessy v. Ferguson* (1896) would never have been overturned in *Brown v. Board of Education* (1954). The same may be asserted concerning *Roe v. Wade* (1973), which shall be overturned.

In 1964 Barry Goldwater lost his bid for president in part because of a perception that he was hostile to Social Security. It wasn't until the 1980s, however, that House Speaker Tip O'Neill coined the phrase "third rail of American politics" and made discussion of changes to the system so poisonous politically. Social Security may yet become a voluntary system.

It may well have been already, except for the War on Terrorism and getting bogged down in Iraq. The political arena is certainly not closed to further deliberations concerning the proper understanding of our constitutional system or roles of the three independent branches within it. Civil rights progress for minorities aside, much in the pre-New Deal constitutional legal order was superior to what followed, and it bears scrutiny. Reversals in the older order arguably entered mistakes into our constitutional system, which today cry for redress, particularly regarding federalism and individual rights. The Progressive view of social progress, which triumphed *circa* 1937, equated active government with good government; and political pressure prompted the Supreme Court to invent a constitutional theory to go along with the Progressives' political worldview. The theory applied faux empiricism and scientific certainty to law where it shouldn't have. It took the concept of scientific linear advancement and attributed it to what federal regulation could bring to national economic planning. In so doing, it stripped the states of reserved powers, as these applied to regulation of economic activity. Moreover, Congress began regulating the economy to a far greater degree, pursuant to its newly discovered authority. Likewise, the theory held that nothing outweighed "public interest," not personal liberties nor privileges enjoyed by individuals, hence these could be sacrificed—regulated by the federal government, particularly to further economic reform aims. The difference in constitutional regime proved to be a seismic shift, which led to rapid growth in the size and power of the federal government, though the government was no longer "federal" in character at all.[5]

Progressive Overreach and Loss of Rights — Article #288
o/a March 09, 2007

In 2005 the Supreme Court decided *Kelo v. City of New London*, a case decision that has given rise to considerable public outrage. Essentially the Supreme Court decided that the city of New London, Connecticut could take someone's home for general economic development purposes. The concept of government's "eminent domain" is based upon the "Takings Clause" of the Fifth Amendment: "Nor shall private property be taken for public use, without just compensation." Of course, the underlying assumption has been that there is a compelling public use at stake in back of any seizure of private property—if so, then due process and just compensation would follow. The *Kelo* decision, however, resulted in the

Supreme Court's supporting a government taking of private property for private use, i.e., to give to another private party—not a public use at all. The public interest or purpose, as it were, was only that an existing homestead was less advantageous to economic development and tax base than something else! Public use was redefined to mean a public purpose. Public purpose meant that if a local tax collector collected more money by the taking of property by government and its sale to a different private owner, it was deemed public use and perfectly constitutional. The ruling may have shocked some citizens out of slumber, but it is just the latest example of government overreach and shrinking rights in a post-Progressive Constitutional regime that dates back to *circa* 1937.

Progressives have been giving the government more and more power through judicial reinterpretation of the Constitution for decades. No longer using Original Intent or intent of lawmakers; not using the authoritative text; not using common law or custom either—but rather, using their position and their power to rewrite key provisions of the Constitution to suit their taste and their socialist intellectual predilections. As Richard Epstein concludes in his study on the subject, Progressive Judges have been "determined that their vision of the managed economy should take precedence in all areas of life." Progressive Justices have sacrificed an expansive view of individual liberty and a correspondingly restrictive view of the state's police power. They have turned presumption of liberty into presumption of control; and individual rights into government rights. They have redefined words (like use to purpose); gone well beyond natural law boundaries; and dispensed with the strictures inherent in an older classical liberal synthesis. Under the Progressive regime, it was logical and compelling in *Kelo* that the importance of private property should pale compared with the interest of a city or state to plan its economy. And you may have thought that we operated in a capitalist, free market environment based on, among other things, a private property order! Well, not so fast . . . .

It was this same sort of sleight of hand we see clearly displayed in *Kelo* that enlarged the power of the federal government through the Commerce Clause before. The Commerce Clause allows Congress to regulate commerce with foreign Nations, among the several States, and with Indian tribes (Article I, Section 8, clause 3). The assumption was that while Congress could and probably would regulate interstate commerce, it could not reach commerce that was strictly intrastate. Commerce occurring within the boundaries of a state remained that state's purview. Only when Progressives redefined commerce to mean all economic activities and then all activities having an impact on the economy, did the full depth and reach of Progressive reform so-called, become apparent. The initial expansion of power over the economy took place with the railroads, Progressives applying federal regulation to purely interior traffic in the transportation grid in 1914. Since then, and particularly since the New Deal, the Court has expanded the jurisdiction of federal regulation from transportation to food distribution and to every other imaginable economic activity. After thoroughly redefining the word commerce, federal directives were made concerning maximum work hours, child labor, minimum wages, unionization and the like. The upshot has been the deliberate unmaking of a structural separation that existed in the Constitution between local and national regulation. Further, Progressive Courts have deprived our country of competitive federalism, James Madison's notion that states might approach their problems and situations differently, experimentally—it was their right of dual sovereignty to be able to do so—even the economic ones.[6]

What's Left and What's Right? Articles #289-290
~Part I~ o/a March 16, 2007

For most folks, terms like Left/liberal and Right/conservative are easily confused and generally hard to fathom. Unless you pay attention to politics and engage in a political discussion from time to time, the taxonomy means little. Nonetheless, when you do you'll find the terminology helpful though imperfect. The original designations for Left and Right were coined at the initial stages of the French Revolution in 1789. Proponents of the aristocracy, i.e., conservatives wanting to conserve tradition, literally sat on the right side of the National Assembly; proponents of a new kind of France, i.e., liberals wanting to radically change the system, sat on the left. For a brief moment, the designations were crystal clear—Right, Left, Conservative and Liberal. The labels have been helpful since then in their relative context, but waters do muddy a great deal. For instance, conservatives and liberals differ widely depending on what country you're in. Conservatives in the United States try to *conserve* traditions that are quite a bit different from the ones conservatives in China or Somalia want to keep. Moreover, after a long interval of time and particularly if there is a change in regime, the labels can switch. A conservative in China would have once supported the Emperor, and communists would have been "on the Left." Today China has taken up free market reforms, so a conservative might be someone who wants the old communist planned economy back.

Liberals in the United States generally seek change (or should) within the constitutional framework, as opposed to starting from scratch, like Russian communists after the fall of the Czar. Americans should be quick to note the practical similarities between a far Right regime (ex: Nazis) and a far Left one (ex: Stalinists). Either way the people get a raw deal! In American politics, conservatives and liberals are situated in the middle between extremes and they thankfully agree on a lot more things than Rightists and Leftists of most other countries. That's probably why the terminology here evokes so little loyalty from very many people, except for a small but important class of politicos, who are ideologically driven, whose identity is bound up with this or that political movement.

Although taking place before the French Revolution, we can apply the concept of Left and Right backwards to the American Revolution too: Left/liberals seeking change versus Right/conservatives trying to conserve, preserve or maintain a status quo. Until the United States separated from Great Britain we were a part of the British Empire ruled by a monarchy. Rightists in that context would have wanted to keep the Colonies intact with the Mother Country. Loyalists and Tories and supporters of King George III therefore were conservative or "on the Right." Rebels, Whigs and Patriots—all our heroes of the Revolution were liberals by definition. Indeed, the way the word liberal was first used as an adjective in the nineteenth century connoted a generous spirit or broad-mindedness. In the American context politically, liberal normally meant you were seeking a reform of some type. As I said, however, regime change can effect a switching of labels, and that's what happened after the New Deal when the Great Depression and World War II finally ended.

The conservative movement in American politics is a post-World War II phenomenon. It has had broad popular support and also a crop of intellectuals to lead it (indeed competing crops). Because the New Deal's constitutional regime change brought about unprecedented regulation of the economy and an attendant growth in big government, conservatives began promoting the very same things considered liberal just a few years before. In other words, conservatives found they wanted to *conserve* much of the older liberal regime (pre-1937). In a very similar way, so-called ultraconservatives today might (and some do) stand for nearly the exact same things "classical liberals" stood for, the ilk of Washington, Madison and Jefferson.

Today's peculiar political definition of conservatism is mostly the achievement of the Reagan years. According to Phyllis Schlafly, by the end of Reagan's two administrations it meant sticking with "unchanging principles based on the Constitution the way it was written, the Judeo-Christian moral code, limited government, victory over Communism, American sovereignty, military superiority, lower taxes, less government regulation, private enterprise," and even a sense of optimism about our country. The liberal label took a tumble in popularity around the same time, as it became associated with government solutions for almost everything, mismanagement of the economy, and a dangerous weakness towards Communism and foreign threats.

~Part II~ o/a March 16, 2007

It is no wonder the end of the Cold War (an international bipolar regime of sorts) started to shake up political labels again. Victory in the Cold War took away a major defining aspect of conservatism and along with it, a host of military and foreign policy related issues no longer resulted in unanimity on the Right. The end of the Cold War also gave liberals a reprieve, particularly with the return of economic prosperity and the advent of the information age and a global economy. You might think conservatives would be more cohesive and organized today than they are. After all, there are always more liberal reform directions to go in, and theoretically there is just one heritage and a few identifiable traditions to defend. That's why liberal parties get most of the bad rap for incessant squabbles. Lately, however, the conservative movement finds itself in special disarray, reminiscent of the Democratic Party of the Sixties. There's a tremendous debate on the Right about what went wrong and what is necessary to define the "next" brand of conservatism. Although there are particular circumstances producing this problem for the conservative movement, the situation was predictable if not altogether inevitable. For decades the conservative movement operated in and thus affected both of the major political parties in this country. After the Reagan Revolution, however, it became increasingly identified with the Republican Party. Of course, since political parties are vehicles for electoral success primarily, when movements based upon ideas become identified with one or the other political party, they tend to lose steam or worse, find their central tenets and cherished principles compromised for the sake of political expediency. For a long time conservatives enjoyed Republicans' electoral successes with at least a partial success of their ideas. The war in Iraq, however, has opened up fissures in their coalition, and a host of inconsistent policies misnamed "conservative" by the Bush Administration has stymied the movement outright.

If ideological movements can and do use political parties, political parties and administrations also use ideological labels when they think it helps them sell their policies—compromised tenets and principles, or no! The buzz today amongst conservatives is about a small cadre of intellectuals within the conservative movement called neoconservatives, who were once constructive (or at least they did less damage) while we were engaged in the Cold War. Since 9/11, however, they led the administration into war with Iraq. Further, the "neocons" are so hawkish in the War on Terror that some would prosecute war on the entire Muslim world. They are at the forefront of saber rattling towards Iran, even though our military is overcommitted and stretched thin. A traditional or "paleoconservative" objects to changing foreign policy emphasis away from national security and protecting America's vital interests to that of democratizing the entire planet. A traditional American conservative supports attempts at brokering peace, not using war unnecessarily as an instrument for foreign policy. Phyllis Schlafly completes the list of other things the Bush Administration has stood for, alien to conservatism defined during the Reagan years: "nation-building overseas, highly concentrated executive power, federal control of education, big increases in social entitlements, massive increases in legal and illegal immigration, forcing American workers to compete with low-wage foreigners (under deceptive enticements such as free trade and global economy), and subordinating U.S. sovereignty to a North American community with open borders."

Now you could be one of those, like most Americans, who thinks we should try to get away from polarizing political labels and maybe from ideology altogether. Your point is well taken to this extent. At the end of the day, it may not matter if there's "big" government or "small" government or whether it is a conservative or liberal thing to be for one or the other—just so long as it's a "smart" government (and I would add *constitutional* government), i.e., having enough of the right kind of government to get the right job done. Ideology is fine, even important, but so is pragmatism and common sense. Ideology shouldn't obscure facts or preclude someone from entertaining other viewpoints and alternative approaches. Ideology should facilitate thinking, not substitute for it. That goes for whether you are liberal or conservative, no matter what's Left and what's Right.

CHAPTER 5

Getting Back to the Roots of Conservatism

Goldwater Again Article #291
o/a March 30, 2007

Even though he lost to Lyndon B. Johnson in 1964 by a landslide, Arizona Senator, Barry Goldwater's presidential bid was an auspicious moment—a major turning point in politics of the twentieth century. It was the first time a presidential candidate of the post-World War II conservative movement got a hearing on national stage. Without Goldwater, it is likely there would have been no Reagan or George (Herbert Walker) Bush administrations. Goldwater contributed much of the philosophy, having written a best-selling book *The Conscience of a Conservative* in 1960, and his campaign of 1964 contributed essential political infrastructure that would deepen and grow and indeed triumph, helping to bring about the Reagan Revolution of 1980. His policy positions and electoral strategies (emphasizing Western and Southern constituencies) became standard fare in Republican politics afterwards.

In hindsight therefore, political loss can be a gain. That applies whether you are Left or Right, but this is a story of the Right. According to J. William Middendorf II, Goldwater's campaign treasurer, the defeat in 1964 left behind a cadre of millions of true believers and a loyal base of future convention delegates and activists. Moreover, in the very next election, the 1966 midterm, the Republican Party that had been so badly beaten for the presidency and in Congress gained 700 seats in state legislatures, 8 governorships, 47 seats in the House, and 3 in the Senate. Nixon was nominated in 1968 with the decisive support of Goldwater leaders and supporters, but the support was more utilitarian than ideological and quite frankly, in gratitude for Nixon's practical and tireless help giving speeches and raising money on the campaign trail in 1964 for Goldwater. Goldwater supporters were later chagrined that the "conservative" mantle ever fell to Nixon, because his policies diverged in key respects from what they wanted. Further, Nixon steadfastly refused to subordinate the liberal Rockefeller wing or "Country Club" Republicans within the party. Consider the persistence of the liberal wing's support within the Republican Party as late as 1976. After Vice President Spiro Agnew resigned, House Speaker Gerald Ford took his place. When Nixon resigned and Gerald Ford became president, Ford chose Nelson Rockefeller to be his Vice President!

The groundwork laid in 1964 took years and several election cycles to leaven the whole loaf as it were. The Republican Party, and particularly the conservative movement as it relates to the Republican Party, are at a crossroads today reminiscent of 1964. The search is on for another Barry Goldwater. Now partisans will surely grimace and say they would rather have another Ronald Reagan—after all, he won while Barry Goldwater went down in flames. The reason political circumstance resembles 1964, however, is there is such a dearth of ideas now on the Right, and the Reagan formulation is mostly spent. Moreover, the neoconservatives have made a wreck of the conservative message. There is a desperate need to rearticulate conservatism for the first half of the twenty-first century the way Goldwater did for the last four decades of the twentieth. Anyway, whoever runs has to believe he can win. His or her supporters must believe it too. And at the end of the day, maybe they can. The context now is different, and the distance may not be so great.

The kind of clarity and originality of thought of a Barry Goldwater, however, is absent from leading candidates on the Right. There's certainly no Republican "Obama" with star quality and charisma. There's only one candidate with the intelligence and ideological depth of a "Hillary" on the Right—and that's Ron Paul (TX-District 14), who announced his candidacy for president in March. Incidentally, if Hillary scares you, it is precisely because you know she's sharp. High-school senior Hillary Rodham was a Goldwater Girl in 1964 and went on to head the Young Republicans at Wellesley! Her political preferences took a left turn after that. Her marriage to Bill Clinton may have been a practical political alliance of sorts too (and I'm not the first to assert it). At any rate, political historians agree the centrist administrations of President Bill Clinton (it's all relative) were hardly possible, had it not been for Barry Goldwater's effect on political dialogue and the conservative Republicans' threat to a once solid Democratic South.

Ron Paul's success may depend on results of the Texas G.O.P. "Straw Poll" to be held in Fort Worth's Convention Center August 31st-September 1st this year. As many as 20,000 activists are expected to participate, and a win could produce momentum for him nationally. An M.D. and specialist in obstetrics/gynecology, Ron Paul has delivered more than 4,000 babies. His pro-life stance is based on what medical science tells him, as well as what the Constitution says—essentially leaving abortion and most other issues to states to decide. In 1976, Paul was one of only four Republican congressmen to endorse Ronald Reagan for president. He is more than capable of reenergizing a dispirited conservative base of the Republican Party with his message of limited and constitutional government, and traditional foreign policy based upon U.S. interests. He has an exemplary record in office too, having never once voted to raise taxes! Detractors may call him "Dr. No," but his political message in an era of run-away debt, and nation building-run amuck and a so-called "living" constitution, have resonance. Ron Paul could become "Goldwater Again" for the Republican Party, in the very best of ways. Imagine what a clear voice for constitutional conservatism might accomplish in 2008 and beyond.

Ghost of Campaigns Past: Goldwater, 1964 Article #292
o/a March 30, 2007

Arizona Senator Barry Goldwater lost to Lyndon B. Johnson in 1964 by a landslide. Goldwater carried just six states: Alabama, Arizona, Georgia, Louisiana, Mississippi and South Carolina. The popular vote was 42 million for Johnson and 27 million for Goldwater—Johnson winning 64 to 36%. Robert Novak wrote that the "bullet that killed Jack Kennedy [November 1963] also struck Barry Goldwater." Indeed, while Barry Goldwater did well in the South based on conservative philosophy, he obviously didn't win Texas or some other Southern states—not least of all, because the bullet that killed Kennedy did put in "the first citizen of a Confederate state to occupy the White House since Andrew Johnson." LBJ had campaigned for reelection to the Texas Senate in 1960 on an anti-civil-rights platform, simultaneously running for vice president on a pro-civil-rights (Kennedy) platform. Goldwater's record was also mixed but more solidly pro-civil-rights and consistent, but issues had been eclipsed by the fact LBJ was Southern.

To the extent that issues won or lost Goldwater the election elsewhere, the Kennedy assassination also figured in. For a while, rumors and speculation abounded that the "radical right" was involved somehow in Kennedy's murder. Of course, the communist connection is more plausible given the Cuban Missile Crisis, and anyway, we all have our favorite conspiracy theories. The unfortunate fact is that Barry Goldwater was smeared with the "radical right" and "extremist" label by the Rockefeller machine. The Republican primary fight was nasty, and Democrats picked up on everything the liberal wing of the Republican Party led by Nelson Rockefeller (NY) and William Scranton (PA) contrived against Barry Goldwater. It was this political experience that led Ronald Reagan a few years later to assert the Republicans' so-called Eleventh Commandment, i.e., "Thou shalt not speak ill of another Republican." It actually meant that Republicans would have to control their vitriol and mudslinging in primaries unless they wanted to get hit over the head with the same thing during a general election. Also clearly, if things get out of control and feelings are genuinely hurt, you can't pull your party back together in a way you need to, in order to win elections against the other party. The Eleventh Commandment remains good advice today, for all sides involved in political debate and competition.

Of course, Goldwater had his own penchant for giving himself problems and allowing political rivals to stereotype him. While discussing a possible Goldwater campaign, Kennedy told reporter Ben Bradlee, "People will start asking him questions, and he's so damn quick on the trigger that he will answer them. And when he does, it will be all over." At a dinner speech in New York to the Economic Club, Goldwater said, "The fact is that most people who have no skills have no education for the same reason—low intelligence or ambition." His candor sometimes lacked political finesse to say the least! Even campaign confidants begged him not to answer questions unless he had thought them through first—but he usually felt compelled to answer anyway. When he did think things through, he sometimes got strategy badly wrong. For instance, after being tarred an extremist by the Rockefeller wing, and needing their acquiescence in his nomination, as well as peace in the party for a bigger election ahead, Goldwater rubbed extremism in everyone's faces. At his nomination acceptance speech, he uttered some of the most famous and maligned words in American political history: "I would remind you that extremism in the defense of liberty is no vice. And let me remind you also that moderation in the pursuit of justice is no virtue." The words may have been true, and certainly they are eloquent in their way. Political science professor Henry Jaffa wrote them for him to say. Thomas Paine said virtually the same thing in his masterpiece *The Rights of Man* (1791). So did Cicero, circa 100 B.C. But the lines were impolitic in the context of just having won a raucous primary against folks calling him extremist.

Goldwater also made a mess on nuclear weapons, such that a lot of people thought he was going to give authority to use them to every Major in the U.S. Army. Goldwater confused people on the issue of Social Security too, until Ronald Reagan explained it beautifully in perhaps the best TV speech of any campaign called, "A Time for Choosing." Coming as it did one week before the general election, the speech was too late to save Goldwater, though it launched Reagan's political career. The first "Reagan for President" club was established soon after, and Reagan was elected governor of California in 1966. Goldwater did in fact enjoy a late and significant swing of support. Three times more voters shifted their August preference from LBJ to Goldwater as switched from Goldwater to LBJ; and twice as many August undecided voters voted for Goldwater in November as voted for LBJ. If the election had been held in April, a number of political measures and trends indicate Goldwater may have won. Of course, campaigns have an ending (or are supposed to), and elections take place on dates certain. What remains after are ghosts of campaigns past, and hopefully a few lessons learned.[7]

Follow Jefferson and Reagan Article #054
February 28, 2002

There are a lot of people who talk about Jefferson and Jefferson's philosophy, who don't have the slightest idea about his vision. His vision of an extended agrarian Republic, comprised mostly of independent yeomen, seems as close and familiar today as the nearest galaxy. Something similar might be said concerning Ronald Reagan, and I suppose it is inevitable that great men and presidents will be misinterpreted or rendered in politically convenient ways. I have personally heard Ronald Reagan on many occasions extol the virtues, as well as the constitutional imperative, of States rights. Yet the most aggressive nationalist and big government advocates now use Ronald Reagan as their patron saint—to endorse big government spending and imperial design! As if the context of Cold War and stagflation and political opposition were identical today. Of course they are not, and it takes some horse sense (in this case, understanding intent and sharing his vision) to enable us to move forward on what Reagan began—or indeed, on what Jefferson accomplished in very different historical context.

Simply stated, Ronald Reagan started to roll back the welfare state and to reassert the sovereignty of States in their proper constitutional orbit. He challenged a century of modern liberalism—from Reconstruction to Progressivism to World Wars, topped off by the New Deal and Great Society. Reagan's message resonated with the people, because he clearly articulated the vision he—and we—shared with the Founders. His understanding of original intent led him to seek a paring back of the federal government and the restoration of real *federalism*—the vertical balance of power based on countervailing responsibility in the Constitution, between the States and the Federal Government.

In his draft of the Kentucky Resolutions of 1798, Thomas Jefferson declared, "Free government is founded in jealousy, and not in confidence; it is jealousy, and not confidence which prescribes limited constitutions, to bind down those whom we are obliged to trust with power." According to professor of law and history David N. Mayer, Jefferson's strong conviction was that the Constitution had "fixed the limits" of political power. In Jefferson's view, cumulative accretion of power to the levels wielded by the federal government today was not allowed, at least not without radical amendment of the Constitution. The essence of Jefferson's theory can be found in his remark, that "In questions of power, then, let no more be heard of confidence in man, but bind him down from mischief by the chains of the Constitution." In his day, Jefferson depended on the strong reaction of an informed voting public, to roll back excesses in areas of foreign policy and economy that ultra-Federalists had steered through all three branches of government. Today the dirty little secret, known to pollsters and political hacks, is that there's hardly an informed voting public around that isn't lethargic. Even if we argue that apathy is less since September of last year, few Americans are knowledgeable about political issues or even about their own government institutions. Skillful politicians and powerful media interests use polls to play upon the public and to lay the groundwork for so-called direct democracy—"mobocracy," according to Matthew Robinson in his new book about media's political impact.

What's happening now is the exact opposite of deliberative democracy. The "eternal vigilance" of the people has come up lacking. Laziness perhaps has enabled our process to become corrupted. So much so, that according to Richard Reeb, Jr., a political science and philosophy professor in California, we have essentially bypassed "limited government, separation of powers, federalism, and [the] economic and religious diversity that made popular government possible for the first time in human history." Jefferson moved power back to the States, and he also successfully acquired land that outran (for a time) the consolidation of power and centralizing tendency in Washington. Reagan strove for something akin to Jefferson, albeit without a Louisiana Purchase. Reagan gave us the opportunity to take back our rightful Constitutional portion of power, by ending the Cold War and by empowering us economically through tax cuts and decreased regulation. Although he changed political assumptions and gave us a fighting chance, we are not winning in the wake of Reagan the way republicans won in the wake of Jefferson. Today there is a black hole in the American political universe, and Washington threatens to crush us. Tyranny, however well intentioned, must end. States must begin to insist upon their Constitutional prerogative, if we should ever hope to restore the Union. We are no less patriotic or American for saying this, no less committed to the people's freedom and the Founder's vision, nor "rebels" for saying we shall 'pledge to each other our Lives, our Fortunes, and our sacred Honor' to achieve this end.

On Principle Ron Paul is Best Choice in Texas Republican Primary

o/a February 08, 2008 Article #334

The Republican Party holds its Primary election in the State of Texas on 4 March 2008. Three points I wish to convey: First and foremost, please vote. Second, after weighing sound criteria (ex: character, competence, platform and philosophy), come to a conscientious decision concerning the candidates running. Third, do not let gamesmanship spoil your vote! If you vote on principle, you may conclude as I have that Ron Paul is the best choice for president.

Those accustomed to this column may be surprised at my endorsement. They will naturally understand their civic duty to vote, and they may agree with the hard criteria on which to base their informed decision. Nevertheless, a lot of otherwise consistent Horse Sense readers may fall prey to a strange kind of gamesmanship, which negates their ability to reason and even mocks their civic duty. What I'm referring to is a stratagem of second-guessing: "Since Ron Paul can't win, I won't vote for him." Of course, it goes without saying there's a Catch-22 involved. If you won't vote for him, he certainly can't win. But the opposite construction of thought, i.e., he can't win so I won't vote for him, is illogical. It's actually an argument used time and again to fool you, and to get you to support somebody's Establishment or status quo.

In 1976 the second-guess argument won the day against Ronald Reagan. Ford was nominated, but Carter was elected president. Reagan was unelectable and Ford supposedly wasn't, notwithstanding the fact that 'In your heart you *knew* he was right!' (Incidentally, Goldwater was afflicted during primary season by the same sort of thing, but the reasons for general election defeat have more to do with party rancor and dirty tricks by Democrats). Point being: Reason told us to vote for Reagan, but gamesmanship told us not to. It took hyperinflation and U.S. military retreat around the globe to shake us awake, and to make us see the travesty of the argument in the first instance. Maybe Reagan was unelectable in 1976, maybe he wasn't. What was it about the argument, however, that altered my conviction? Nothing. Then as now, it was only a political sleight of hand by those, who prefer the Republican nominee be less conservative.

The Republican establishment as it were, might surprise you. It prefers a standard bearer that is less of a stickler than Ron Paul for the Constitution or for separation of powers—far less the advocate of Original Intent or consistency with the Founders' vision concerning anything. We have Democracy now and very little Republic left—the establishment says get used to it. Most people want big government to serve the national majority. It is more efficient that way, and more beholden to special interests who fill our trough. Surely we shouldn't be inconvenienced by the will of separate majorities in little sovereign things called States! Federalism is the constitutional model of dual sovereignty, charming but hopelessly passé. How could we possibly follow the Constitution and use political power in Washington to do what we want? Answer: You probably couldn't if Ron Paul were elected president.

The Republican Party is more hierarchical than the Democrat Party, and Republicans are supposed to follow the elders. Democrats Hillary Clinton and Barack Obama have issued their clarion calls for Progressivism to define the next eight years and perhaps the Twenty-First Century. Instead of joining this fight with a clarion call to Liberty and to Restoration of the Republic, the elders tell us to go soft in order to get "our man" elected. Choose McCain (!) since Romney has faltered. Bush/Cheney neoconservatives actually supported Romney first. They said Mike Huckabee was the spoiler for Mitt Romney, but why is Huckabee still in the race and Romney not? I guess Huckabee's supporters didn't fall for the feint—and good for them; now fully 25% of the GOP has gotten uppity (Paul and Huckabee both). The Republican establishment is worried, because it likes these contingents to carry water and leave policy to the big boys on Wall Street. Forget the Constitution. The Alamo is another Lost Cause. Grow up and make money, and don't dare question at whose expense or why.

On principle, Ron Paul is the best choice. He is right on issues, even where uncertainty surrounds the Rev. Huckabee. The ex-pastor's compassion towards illegal aliens is understandable on a human level and has proper place in religious ministry and individual Christian conduct. In the present crisis, however, there's been far too much of *Newspeak* about compassionate conservatism. Compassion, like Barack's "Hope" is hardly a plan or good public policy. Secure borders are the imperative, as well as sane immigration levels. Ron Paul has taken the most criticism in the area of foreign policy—specifically on the war in Iraq, which he opposed and opposes. The criticism, however, is moot. The war in Iraq is over, whether the president knows it or not. Bush is a lame Peking duck, and the next president will have to withdraw and/or reestablish strategic lines outside Iraq.

Ron Paul recognizes the fact that 'we are where we are,' and we have his assurance that he would act prudentially in the interest of *American* troops and *American* security. I have yet to understand why any voter would knowingly vote for a president prone to launch and conduct wars indefinitely without the sanction of Congressional declaration—particularly when there is no emergency or vital enemy threat. We are fighting phantoms now. At very least, we have a luxury to take more considered approaches involving diplomatic maneuver and specifically targeted military action. Conservatives should rediscover their traditional philosophy, which cautions against unnecessary entangling alliances whether for defense or spreading democracy; and which counsels strongly against wars except as last resort, because war causes accretion of power in government and corresponding loss of civil liberty in society.

People seem to get it with sports but not at all with politics! The New England Patriots should have won the Super Bowl. Statistics and all the experts said so. New York should have just stayed home, never taken the field and bowed to the inevitable. Of course, that's not how reality played out. Most folks intuitively realize that whatever the odds, games are played by real and committed players; real and committed fans support both sides. Unlikely things happen in almost every ballgame and anyway, who is to say what's unlikely after any given snap? New York wasn't second-guessing its right to win, even if a few fans hedged their bets. The dynamics of championships and home games are such they are always unique. Timing, lucky breaks, and heart all play a part in it, and "Giant" upsets are possible in politics as well as sports. If your favorite team is eliminated in the play-off, only then do you move to the next best possible choice available. You would never think to pick the Giants or Pats while Dallas is in the game! Sandra Crosnoe of Associated Conservatives of America wrote recently, "A vote of principle is truly never wasted. Please don't let anyone convince you otherwise." Amen to that—I'm voting for Ron Paul.

CHAPTER 6

Character and Politics

Politics of Character — Article #021

May 24, 2001

It has always been a mystery to me how some folks could think character does not matter—or rather, that it doesn't matter enough to demand particularly high standards of our elected officials. It was the ancient Greek philosopher Plato, who instructed us that character was *the* defining qualification for a ruling class. Now a recent study by the Institute for Advanced Studies in Culture at the University of Virginia sheds light on America's strange ambivalence. "The Politics of Character" survey was based on 1,200 telephone interviews drawn from a national probability sample representative of the adult civilian population, eighteen years and older, living in private households in the United States. The survey has a sampling error of plus or minus 3 percent. Basically, the study found that most people do think character is important (90%), but the same people aren't exactly sure what constitutes character or how it remotely relates to politics or to public policy. Character is popular, but the concept is bereft of content! The study found our country's commitment to character is pretty shallow—and probably inertial, a function of our history.

Indeed, character and conviction were once conjoined and esteemed. The Founders were adamant about character's importance. Christian faith and traditional Western values supplied its content. No one doubted that people should and would choose leaders of character, and that good representatives are indispensable to good government. George Washington said, "Virtue or morality is a necessary spring of popular government." Thomas Jefferson said, "A degeneracy in these is a canker which soon eats to the heart of [a republic's] laws and constitution." Alexis de Tocqueville wondered how America should escape destruction, "if the moral tie is not strengthened in proportion as the political tie is relaxed." And James Madison, Father of the Constitution and author of its most famed checks and balances said, if there be no virtue among us, "we are in a wretched situation. No theoretical checks—no form of Government, can render us secure. To suppose that any form of Government will secure liberty or happiness without any form of virtue in the people, is a chimerical idea."

The architects of this Republic knew the importance of character and the high moral qualities that comprised it. Taken together, this was a basic article of democratic faith. Today's democratic faith is laced with confusion and contradiction. The majority of Americans believe that "all views of what is good are equally valid" (72% agree) and that "everything is beautiful—it is all a matter of how you look at it" (69% agree). On the other hand, the majority (77%) also believes "we would all be better off if we could live by the same basic moral guidelines." By wide margins, the majority believes that both "obeying those in positions of authority" (92%) and "following your own conscience" (81%) are important to character. They also believe "sacrificing your own interests for the good of others" (88%) and "protecting your own interests" (88%) to be important to character. Likewise, the majority believes that "sticking to one's principles no matter what" (95%) and "enjoying yourself" (92%) are essential. Similar contradictions continue, when respondents are asked about specific moral issues. In terms of holding officials accountable, just 46% insist the president (a high symbolic representative of the people) needs the same virtue as the people, in order to govern effectively. Americans have become rather indiscriminate it seems, and that's not fuzzy math—it's fuzzy thinking.

Two Patriots Article #339
o/a March 28, 2008

The spectacle of the presidential race on the Democrat side, as well as two recent and highly publicized falls from grace by public officials, in New York State and Detroit, Michigan, makes me think of other historic rivalries and the difference character makes. It is in the current context that history informs, and possibly warns. Rivalries and competition are generally positive unless they get too personal. Character in the final analysis means more for the country than courage, convictions or experience.

There is not a man or woman in politics who has not at least unintentionally made enemies, or who has not done things objectively or subjectively let us say, not quite so good. If one learns from mistakes and refrains from intentionally making enemies, then one minimizes personal opposition—and personal opposition is far more dangerous than issue or philosophical opposition. Eventually, the garnering and nurturing of loyal support offsets and effectively defends against the barbs, remarks and maneuverings of opponents and can even win converts, except for those with the most vehement personal hatreds or vendettas. It may be true what they say: friends come and go, but enemies accumulate.

Benedict Arnold had a penchant for collecting enemies, whether in his native Connecticut or wherever he traveled. He would either physically intimidate his rivals or personally humiliate them, often in public. It may also be true what they say about 'what goes around comes around,' and how small the world really is. Even today when there are 300 million people in these United States, it isn't very wise to burn your bridges unnecessarily (you may need to cross over again, seek employment from an old boss, etc.). Imagine mucking around when there were only 3 million people at the time of our nation's founding! Not to mention, your circle gets awfully small when you're engaged in a patriots' struggle with the Sons of Liberty; leading military campaigns; smuggling goods shipboard; trying to conduct business. Indeed, all of us in practical terms create far smaller circles for ourselves than what the latest census indicates.

George Washington had a temper but worked hard his whole life to control it. He walked with humility, not lacking in prowess or confidence, but rather out of respect for others and out of respect for the cause, which he deemed larger than himself. Washington had a number of rivals, but it is unlikely any of them hated him. Both Arnold and Washington experienced unhappy circumstances growing up, consisting of serious financial reversals, untimely deaths, and family dysfunction. In early adulthood, both experienced failure. Both would become successful, self-made men. Both were skilled and courageous at their work (Washington-surveyor and farmer; Arnold-seaman and druggist) and had a penchant for the military art. Arnold's drive, however, may have been a deep-seated resentment built up over years; whereas, Washington's drive seems to have been almost entirely positive not negative.

Life made Arnold bitter, whereas it made Washington better. In the French and Indian War, Washington suffered defeat at Fort Necessity and participated in a disastrous expedition against Fort Duquesne. In politics, he lost his first bid running for the House of Burgesses in Virginia. Of course, he would later win even more consequential battles and even bigger political races. What is remarkable is the way in which Washington remained civil and extraordinarily self-controlled and exhibited a servant's heart to his men and to his chosen country. Arnold suffered military defeat in Canada, despite heroic effort. He also continued to nurse wholly selfish grievances, which silenced his future triumphs. He became a well-deserved hero of the Revolution, taking a leading role in the decisive Saratoga Campaign. Americans remember him for his treachery, however, because he sold his integrity to betray his countrymen. For military daring, he was once compared to Hannibal; for character we compare him now to Judas.[8]

Character Then and Now Article #344
o/a April 18, 2008

In a previous column, referring to the presidential candidates, I averred that character in the final analysis means more to us, i.e., to the welfare and benefit of the country than courage, convictions or experience. The opinion is borne out in the purpose of West Point, which from the year 1802 has existed to produce leaders who would possess *character*. Of course there are other things a person must have to be good at leadership or to be good at anything, but the presumption is at the academy as well as in the finest literature, that character is most essential and determines the measure of a man or woman whatever else their failings. Hence we may want to examine character more closely than mere common usage of the word.

According to historian and retired Army general Dave Palmer, for all the symmetries and similarities between George Washington and Benedict Arnold, it was strength of character that separated them and made all the difference. After having been one of the American Revolution's greatest heroes, Arnold nearly caused the Revolution to fail in 1780 by undercutting defensive preparations at West Point and attempting to transfer plans of the fort to British who were planning for an attack. Fortunately the spy carrying those plans was caught. Washington personally took charge of reinforcing West Point and foiling British strategy at the very last moment.

This close call, counter-intuitively braced Americans' resolve until victory was achieved at Yorktown.

Today as in antiquity character is what matters first, foremost and last. Moreover, the analytical framework employed by the ancient Greeks is every bit as good as any you might find in a modern textbook (provided we still taught about character!); accordingly, character may be thought of as the sum of four synergetic virtues: fortitude, temperance, prudence, and justice. Palmer provides us with definitions. *Fortitude* is strength of mind, along with the physical and moral courage to persevere in the face of adversity. *Temperance* is self-discipline to control passions and appetites. *Prudence* is practical wisdom and the ability to make the right choice in specific situations. *Justice* is fairness, honesty, lawfulness, and keeping promises. By Palmer's reckoning, Arnold scored positive for one virtue (fortitude), mixed in one of them (prudence), decidedly negative on two counts (temperance and justice). The Greeks thought these four virtues had to be kept in balance to have good character. Arnold gets no cigar for character therefore, and in Monopoly parlance he doesn't even pass "GO."

Educators and moral philosophers continue to modify the formulation and explain it differently in modern terms. For institutions like West Point, leaders of character are leaders who know the difference between right and wrong and have the moral courage to act accordingly, i.e., to choose the harder right instead of the easier wrong. They have what Union general Joshua Chamberlain described as "a firm and seasoned substance of the soul," which is actually how Chamberlain defined the word character. The word is deceptively simple, however, hinging as it does on momentous and value-laden things like right and wrong. No wonder few institutions bother to teach it in a post-modern age in which right and wrong have become so relative, so confused.

Palmer says Benedict Arnold knew the difference between right and wrong in a legal sense, but that the legality of something was purely incidental. Indeed, many Patriots weighed and had to weigh the legality of matters strictly speaking against the interests of the Revolution, the Rights of Man, and a qualitative rationale for violent secession from Great Britain. Their mental calculus, however, was value-based not selfish. To them the Revolution was animated by values, which defined the harder right. Arnold gave up and gave in at some point, most historians agreeing that it was sometime after sustaining a terrible leg wound at Saratoga. Whether a physical wound can change the soul of a man is a fascinating and relevant question, what with so many veterans these days returning with injuries and others in all walks of life having to deal with the effects of disease or accident. There is little doubt that misfortune, particularly serious injuries present a person with challenges—not all of which are physical. Arnold decided to sell his soul for 20,000 pounds sterling, but his life showed a disturbing pattern throughout. Palmer concludes that for Arnold, "right" was always whatever was good for Arnold. "Wrong" was whatever was bad for him personally. "Instead of substance, Arnold had an emptiness at the center." He that hath an ear let him hear.[9]

The Edwards Catastrophe   Article #360
o/a August 15, 2008

U.S. Senator John Edwards (D-NC) has taken a precipitous and very public fall since it was revealed that allegations of a love affair two years ago were actually true, despite his lies on camera about the story, ostensibly so he could run unhindered for president. There are layers of compost too on the topsoil. To start with, the callous compartmentalization, as his wife Elizabeth battled with cancer in technical remission perhaps during the affair. Not to mention the attractiveness that a younger, healthful, energetic and adoring staffer must have had to the man; and the attraction that power, success, drive and vision have always had on the opposite sex and those negotiating an uphill climb. Easy to succumb to temptation of the eyes, but not the awful conceit! The conceit is that what no one sees is necessarily hidden from God and from man. An atheist worries about only half the equation to start with, that is whether man will find out; whereas, a man of faith may lose second thoughts over God's omniscience in the heat of passion or blind overconfidence. Edwards offers the self-diagnosis of narcissism.

Worse is the metaphysical lapse that says no matter what one does, it makes no consequential difference anyway, either to one's ambition or to character (as if that mattered). A liar once becomes a liar, true—but only if someone else knows about it. Secrets can smooth out the rough edges. Greek tragedy meets now with modern psychodrama, considering the three living children Edwards has with his wife Elizabeth, and what conflicted emotions and embarrassment they must feel. How ironically this compares with the potential lovechild Edwards may have with the other woman—what it means for families on both sides, and for the child who learns the truth and knows the unfortunate limits imposed by various shades of love, fairly or not. Values and institutions and responsibilities intersect when parentage is involved, and for Edwards (and anyone who observes), the picture of his family and the sanctity of marriage in general, are never what they were in the camera of the mind once before a lens cracked.

It seems trite by comparison, but what also of the peculiar blend of political and spousal partnerships he and Elizabeth worked so hard at and achieved: something beautiful, something practical, and practically ideal—trumped by the fallibility and weakness of a man! The Lord has a wicked sense of humor sometimes. The question remaining is both irksome and urgent; namely, what relation, if any, is there of the life and love and contributions made *before the fall*, i.e., the things that once were, to what crawls out from the ashes? As if we could know (and we can't), just what gets lost and what becomes new, what is forgiven and what redeems a personal catastrophe of such magnitude.

Almost inconsequential to the entire episode is the incredible wealth, the millions of dollars Edwards enjoys, and how little joy it brings him now. Jesus said, unto them and to us, ". . . Take heed, and beware of covetousness: for a man's life consisteth not in the abundance of the things which he possesseth" (Luke 12: 15). Edwards gambled and lost, or else he did what he did unthinkingly, or self-righteously. He *sinned* (as uncomfortable as we are with the concept), but he also subordinated truth to ambition, a variation on the age-old theme that the ends eventually justify the means. Everything would be okay, if he just became president and his wife the first lady! Forgiveness, even self-forgiveness might come easier, and at that level of personal success it were a mere indulgence in the 'Church of Edwards.' If so, it is a terrible and tragic miscalculation. The president is only there four to eight years in office and has to live with himself both before and critically in most cases, afterwards. How empty would be the life consumed by ambition, whether or not the ambition is achieved, if life isn't on the level. All the fictional biographies and autobiography notwithstanding, it really is how you play the game that counts and not the score. Whether rich or poor, black or white, politician or proletariat, Romans 14:12 reminds us of the obligation of every living soul: "So then every one of us shall give account of himself to God."

The impact of the Edwards catastrophe on the Democrat Party is probably negligible, and it is unlikely to be a factor in the upcoming elections. Elections hardly matter, compared to the gravity of what we have witnessed. It reminds us that some of the worst things that can happen, things that create the most misery and despair are not necessarily illegal. Indeed, some would call them "victimless" in a classic sense. Morality, however, remains altogether relevant in a free society. The most important decisions we make, and the things that regulate our quality of life more than anything else, have little to do with government. People have an inalienable right to be free—that is the presumption and how they are born. Which is another way of saying they also have the right to be wrong, even to be immoral. A free society is not necessarily a good society, but then that remains the ancient challenge of free peoples everywhere, to learn and to put into practice what is good; to persuade others to pursue their better lights; and to remind them that goodness and virtue are ultimately the surest guarantors and protection of freedom. Moreover, even as people suffer from the consequences of their own actions (as suffering and death are the wages of sin), we have a Christian obligation and human duty to love them and make things better if we can.

Corruption Articles #321-323

~Part I~ o/a October 13, 2007

Since 2005, evidence of corruption in the American system of government involving lobbyists and members of Congress has spilled out and damaged public trust in the political system. Obviously it is only the latest round of corruption to gain public attention. Before that it was all about business corporations and the accounting scandals of late 2001 and 2002. In one sense, revelation and expected cleanup is testament to our economic and political systems, which do generally police their own albeit imperfectly. Indeed, it is the latest round of corruption that worries me most. The level of secrecy in government is considerably higher than it was prior to the War on Terror and even during periods of war under different administrations. In one sense, private dealings in business may invite corrupt bargains, but the price mechanism and other economic forces in the free economy tend to offset and correct these. Not so with the public sector and operatives involving the state and legal structure.

Quite frankly, I'm also disappointed. Corruption has long been the hallmark of developing countries, statist regimes, or at least very different cultures than our own. It is rife in Latin America, Asia, the Middle East, as well as southern and eastern Europe. The relative lack of corruption in America is based on cultural antecedents extending to northern and western Europe, as well as institutional ones and most especially the *rule of law* from Great Britain. We seem now to have joined the other club. But for those of us who value a culture of integrity, as well as transparency in a political system open to redress, it behooves us to examine the phenomenon of corruption and to consider its nature and perhaps to suggest ways of reducing it. Corruption necessarily weakens the rule of law and, as clearly demonstrated around the world, it can become steadily more difficult to control or eradicate. It can also become endemic to the culture, which will be the beginning of the end for this great civilization—or contrariwise, a corrupt state will insulate itself so far from the populace, that government is no longer accountable to them.

The public will no doubt adjust, but the adjustment institutionalizes the problem. That is to say, if you circumvent corruption through some extra-constitutional mechanism then you essentially make corruption work! You add costs or inefficiencies to doing business and to getting things done, while leaving corrupt officials and their clients alone to profit. In China corruption necessitates an entire class of middlemen just to limit the number of payments demanded by different corrupt officials from a single briber; and to some extent, to enforce implicit agreements between the various officials and those corrupt individuals the middlemen represent. Economic analysis by Shan-Jin Wei demonstrates that an increase in the corruption level from that of Singapore, where it is low, to that of Mexico where it is high, is equivalent to raising taxes over twenty percentage points. It is small wonder that so many of the people in Mexico are poor. It should be intuitively obvious that a principal cause of emigration from that and other home countries is corruption.

Corruption like a cancer spreads to take over the body politic; whereas, its insidious nature is seldom known until it is too late—meaning it will require some radical surgery, i.e., political or military revolution in order to fix. Gordon Tullock, the public choice economist, observes that corruption causes the state to take action, "not for its ostensible reason [i.e., the common good], but for the secret reason of private benefit—that is, [it] pretends to favor the public interest but is in fact favoring [a personal interest or] pocketbook." At that stage of disease, you can no longer trust your representatives or public servants, and you cannot believe what they say. One must conjecture, that corruption generally precedes and certainly encourages a conspiracy of one sort or the other.

The Framers of the U.S. Constitution understood the frailties of man's fallen nature, which afflict the public as well as state officials. They were keen to introduce ingenious and somewhat elaborate checks and balances into our system of government, in order to preclude a concentration of power in the hands of a single individual or branch of government. As James Madison observed, men are not angels and they are given to temptations. He and the other Framers presumed an imperative that we must reclaim, i.e., that of watching the watchman. As Lord Acton reminded us, "Power tends to corrupt and absolute power corrupts absolutely." This applies to powerful everywhere—in corporations, religious organizations, private business ventures, etc., wherever people have power without being accountable to those they lead. Nevertheless, private institutional corruption is more difficult to sustain in the long run and symptoms will likely get noticed. The market solution is simple and Darwinian: perish or give in to a takeover. The market mechanism ironically works as a morality check too. This is not the case, however, with public institutional corruption. The best we can do is what the Founders of our country would have wanted: follow the Constitution; reduce a bloated federal bureaucracy; begin to minimize the potential for corruption, by limiting the discretionary powers of the state.[10]

~Part II~ o/a October 14, 2007

Sometimes I contemplate corruption—yikes, not in a positive vein, mind you—rather what it's made of and how to reduce it! Distinctions may seem academic, but there is a difference, say, between corruption and just regular run-of-the-mill crime. Tax evasion is a crime, but not corruption. Now if you bribe the tax-auditor, that's corruption. Running a red light or breaking the speed limit is a crime, but not corruption. Bribing the policeman to avoid getting a ticket definitely is. So now we're getting close to a definition. Corruption amounts to a voluntary transaction between a culprit and the person who is supposed to hold him to an accounting, with the intention of defrauding some third party (in my examples the government). Taking the opposite tack, a person who works for the government and receives large donations from outside the government (without actually working there) could imply obligations to the donor contrary to the duties of that public servant to his constituency or the state. For instance, Rep. William Jefferson (D-Louisiana) is the guy with a $90,000 home freezer. He is accused among other things, of taking millions to broker business deals in Africa. The deals were valuable to somebody, but not necessarily to competing businesses in his district or to foreign policy interests of the United States.

When this kind of thing is widespread, it skews the economy and creates a perverse patronage between office holders and favored beneficiaries. It undermines both the free market and the democratic state, by making some activities artificially profitable regardless of supply and demand, and by interjecting private interest into legitimate security and diplomatic interests of the state. According to economist Osvaldo Schenone and political philosopher Samuel Gregg, "In economic and legal terms, corruption may be defined as the performance of illegal, voluntary transactions between an agent and his customer with a detrimental effect on a principal, whom the agent was legally obliged to serve." The essential evil of corrupt action is the agent's betrayal of his legitimate obligations to his principal—it is indeed the breaking of an implicit and often explicit contract. Corruption is a denial of justice on that basis, not to mention a violation of the Golden Rule.

Thomas Aquinas wrote that justice involves "the enduring and unwavering willingness to give to all other persons what is rightfully theirs." The proper object of justice being the common good, a denial of justice undermines it. It is also easy to see how, in that corruption undermines the basic bonds of trust in society and not only between individuals. Corruption also shatters those bonds of trust between citizens and their political community, including those charged with legal authority. Moreover, corruption entails secrecy injurious to the democratically elected government, since corruption can't stand the light of day and almost inevitably involves deceit.

So why are some people corrupt? One may as well ask why folks do bad things, since from the standpoint of theology corruption is one more form of sin. The answer is as you might expect, deeply philosophical. The phenomenon of sin first appears in the Scripture book of Genesis. Although God created everything good, man's free moral agency gave us a loophole! God made man holy, but men and women abused their liberty from the beginning of human history, choosing to set themselves against God and attain goals apart from Him. Mankind as it were did not want to follow the rules laid down by God; rather, men and women wanted to make up their own rules and define good and evil, right and wrong on their own. Instead of accepting a state of harmony, we essentially chose the school of hard knocks by deciding to live selfishly. Ironically, the root of sin is man's free will, the capacity to sin and be corrupt written into personhood. Schenone and Gregg again: "As paradoxical as it may seem, to acknowledge the reality of sin is to acknowledge the reality of freedom. To ascribe all blame for our personal sins on external factors would amount to denying our freedom as persons." If the cause is interior, however, the effects of corruption don't stay there but enter into the social environment, because man is also a social being. Indeed, every human moral weakness informs the social and political order. Since we have linked the interior man with external culture, however, there is also hope and method for reversal. Even in those societies where corruption seems to be integral, culture is not entirely static. Men and women are not altogether subordinate to their culture, and cultures can and do transform over time, in response to human choice and actions.[11]

~Part III~ o/a October 14, 2007

There are a few sure fire ways of minimizing corruption in society. One distinct method involves individual choices and actions, making the culture give way incrementally to the good things you choose and do (it is more effectual than it sounds, though necessarily a slow process); we should also include with that category the use of contracts between individuals. Another category involves government and equates to those important institutional bulwarks that protect society from corruption, especially private property and the rule of law.

People problems always seem to relate back to, well, people. In society, social problems are the outward manifestation of so many individual ones. Corruption depends on those who choose either to induce an occasion or take an occasion for sin. In addition, corruption is sustained by those unwilling to sacrifice anything to overturn injustice; by those, who are willing to exploit the situation; by those indifferent or lazy; and by those, who rationalize the corruption some way or say the problem is too intractable and certainly not amenable to anything they could do. Therefore the first thing that needs doing in a society to make the social environment unfriendly to corruption, is to build character. It sounds trite, but look at what's been said. If kids are taught to be honest and to do what they know is right; if young men and women are physically and morally courageous; if enough people refuse to sanction any unfair taking of advantage; if they stayed informed, engaged, participatory, energetic; if they work hard and really care about justice; if people are sober, analytical, educated, and feel empowered—I dare say corruption doesn't stand a chance in that society! Of course, the same might be true if pigs could fly. Nevertheless, choose your medicine now and make a few personal New Year's resolutions for the coming year.

Making and honoring contracts is particularly helpful. The philosopher Rocco Buttiglione observed, "The smallest element of the free market is a contract, the encounter of the free will of two human beings." Indeed, through contracts we commit to obligations and acquire responsibilities. We also place limits on the tendency to act out on whim. A contract is a commercial convention and has legal status, but the basis of the exercise is really promise-making and promise-keeping. According to economist Osvaldo Schenone and political philosopher Samuel Gregg, "This willingness to make promises with each other—necessarily precedes the contract. . . . Contracts, thus, enlist our willingness to be truthful and to act upon reasonable promises and commitments.

Of course, the question of whether corruption is minimal or rampant may exceed our scope of influence. Society is bigger than us. A lot depends on how much discretion state officials enjoy in terms of regulating economic and other activities. The more discretion that is involved, the higher potential there is for corruption. It follows that you may want character, including prudence in those persons you support and elect to office. Did I just see a pig fly by? The political process will determine how strong government's institutional bulwarks remain against corruption. The ancient rights of freeborn Englishmen enter in where they entered the Constitution: private property was once so sacrosanct that people could be classified as chattel. The federal government couldn't touch the institution of slavery, because private property rights trumped almost everything else. While there's no need to go that far, the Thirteenth, Fourteenth and Fifteenth Amendments do well enough thank you. Private property promotes economic growth in that it assures everyone involved (and not involved) that the fruit of your effort belongs to you. You bought the car and it's yours—the watch too (even if it is fake). Your home is your castle and so on. Moreover, people can't exchange something unless they own it. Property makes free exchange possible without resorting to force. It also makes us cognizant of the rights of others; in particular, an affront to your neighbor's home or property is probably too close for comfort—it resembles a threat to yours. This is true whether perpetrated by a robber or extorted by a corrupt official.

Finally, the rule of law ensures that individual contracts count for something important and that property rights are respected. Indeed, the rule of law is that indispensable legal framework necessary to minimize corruption by providing for the just resolution of disputes; and the objective fair enforcement of all rules equally regardless of who you are, or whom you happen to know. Otherwise, the strongest and meanest group or individual wins every time. Think about it the next time you have to serve jury duty, what it would be like if decisions made by the courts and judiciary were arbitrary and inconsistent—sold to the highest bidder or subject to the whim of those in power. There are places in the world like that. Pray it does not happen here. Edmund Burke said, "The only thing necessary for the triumph of evil is for good men to do nothing." That's where character enters in.[12]

Leadership and How — Article #130
o/a February 16, 2004

I was asked to address leadership experiences that led up to where I am today—the implication that I'm successful and worthy of emulation, the idea being that some of my experiences may bear out in your lives if you pattern yourself accordingly. Not only do I think the topic is good, but I think the implications are valid. It's a shame that history no longer emphasizes biography. That was the theory behind biography as well—study great men and great women, and you might just become one!

Okay, Here goes. I'm going to give you a short biography: what's distilled on a paper. Then I'll wax some philosophically to explain what it means. *Wesley Allen Riddle* was born and raised in Houston, Texas. He went to Northbrook High School and then to the United States Military Academy at West Point, NY (class of 1983). He spent twenty years in the U.S. Army and, at the time of his retirement, Lieutenant Colonel Riddle served at Fort Hood on III Corps Staff as the Chief of the Air Defense Element (ADE). Previous assignments include both stateside and overseas tours in Europe and the Pacific. Awards and decorations include the Legion of Merit, the Bronze Star Medal and Defense Meritorious Service Medal.

During the Gulf War, he commanded a Patriot Missile battery that shot incoming SCUD missiles in northern Saudi Arabia. From August 2000 to August 2002, he worked at the Office of Military Cooperation-Kuwait, U.S. Embassy, as Air Defense Advisor to the State of Kuwait. Wes obtained his Master of Philosophy degree in Modern History from Oxford University in 1993 where he graduated with Distinction, after which he taught Advanced American History and American Political Tradition for three years at West Point. He was awarded a Salvatori Fellowship by The Heritage Foundation for 1996-97 and is widely published in the academic and opinion press on matters of American history and political theory. He is Fellow at the National Humanities Institute in Washington, D.C., Adjunct Scholar with the Ludwig von Mises Institute, and Policy Advisor to the Virginia-based Future of Freedom Foundation. He is best known locally for his weekly conservative column in Central Texas area newspapers called "Horse Sense." He and his wife Aida own and operate the Glen-Riddle Manor Bed and Breakfast in Belton, which they have closed for the duration of Wes's campaign to win Republican nomination for the U.S. Congressional District 31 seat.

That's the record, the resume and "bio." It represents concerted effort and application of all my strength and smarts for what I pray is only half my life. It also implies a lot behind me too—family and friends, bosses and subordinates, and even the infrastructure of school, church and government and the ethos of accomplishment we enjoy in this country. The bio tells what; it does not address how—and that's what you need to know. So let's talk turkey: the Bible says you've got 70 years to live your life if you're lucky and get the full measure of life in years. Of course, today you can count on 80 at a reasonable, healthy life expectancy. Anything over 70 is still gravy! So if you segment your life into 4 twenty-year periods, you see where I'm headed with this. You guys are almost done with the first quarter! I've just finished the second quarter and am charging into the third! If you reason that the first quarter is preparation: childhood and education and the fourth is retirement—time hopefully to savor, to reflect, to play with the grandkids, and to do so in some physical comfort because you saved and prepared for retirement—you see you've got two quarters in the middle. They are different and distinct, but that's basically marrying and raising your family; it is you're your working life, accomplishment of career goals, your contribution and highest level of productivity given to gross domestic product (GDP).

Why do I tell you this? Because YOU MUST START TO THINK IN TIME. There's only a limited amount of it. If you never did or accomplished anything between the ages of 20 and 60, you're still going to be 80 years old—if you're lucky. Sometimes that's a good thing that time passes, because experiences along the way are sometimes unpleasant. But whether pleasant or ecstatic, "Time stands still for no man." Thinking in time is characteristic, by the way, of Western man. Some cultures—those which have stood still in history and remained underdeveloped or taken a collectivist and minimalist approach, have thought not in straight lines, i.e., from goal to goal, but circularly. "The Circle of Life" is a romantic notion. In some metaphysical sense, the "circle" may be unbroken. Maybe it is self-satisfying—certainly it is easier—to vegetate under a fig tree or to lose yourself and lose all track of time in a dream-state, high on something or lost in some distraction or addiction. But you still only have your allotted time, and you run the risk of waking up momentarily, say, at 40—and many people have done this: to find they didn't finish their education, they didn't apply themselves at their career, they didn't marry or start a family. "Time stands still for no man."

Why do I tell you this? Because YOU MUST START THINKING RESPONSIBLY. Be sober and take a considered approach to life. The world will tell you otherwise; it is only too glad to pull you in to a million webs and devices of man and nature.

Now, I hope you don't find this talk depressing. It shouldn't be. For on the one hand, tears are never too far from the surface because of the nature of our material condition: we are finite and temporal. That is to say, we don't live forever and we don't see but a speck in time and place at every given moment. But knowing this is also empowering and confers considerable judgment on the people who get it. Why? Because you will compensate, and you will take life seriously; and you will strike out with purpose and not waver. You may compensate for what's behind by becoming historically minded: learn history—your country's, your State's, yours and your family's history. The Founders believed that history was the general framework for all human knowledge. Compensate for what's ahead by thinking philosophically and following a good moral guide. The Bible is more than sufficient. The example of Jesus and others like George Washington will serve very well. You take life seriously by living it—understanding life is a gift to you and you are a gift to Life. Discern your purpose from your higher self, pursue your purpose with all your gusto. Develop and explore your potential and all your sensibilities.

Why do I tell you this? SO YOU WILL BECOME A WELL-ROUNDED PERSON AND A GOOD CITIZEN IN THE VERY BEST CONNOTATION OF THE WORD. A citizen is whole, complete, individual, and still serves a higher purpose and calling. The Greeks called it the Golden Mean. Many of our Founders were called Renaissance Men, because they did exactly that—learned and tried their hand at music, math, religion and science; they led active lives as thinkers and doers and engaged in life with passion—they knew grief and trial and tribulation, as well as love and joy and the elation of victory. Their lives fit them to be our leaders and heroes, and the same can be said of you in modern context—live the lives that will fit you to become the leaders of the Twenty-First Century and the heroes for centuries to come.[13]

On Political Debate and Political Action Article #458
o/a July 04, 2010

Sometimes it just isn't worth the effort. Oh one can try to convince the other side, assuming they haven't clam-shut their minds entirely. At best it will be a lot of work, but increasingly two sides in American politics seem to be from different cultures entirely—if not from different planets. They mostly talk past each other, not really to one another. No one strives for consensus, because consensus no longer involves statesmanlike compromise over details or method, but rather fundamental matters of conviction and principle. Glenn Beck tried to reach out (sort of) through his book, *Arguing with Idiots* (2009). Mark Olsen and Thomas Rexroth do perhaps the best job possible trying to convert nincompoops out there with a new fiction book called *Animal Colony* (2010), a modern rendition of George Orwell's classic. Reading it, grade school students certainly and quite possibly a few indoctrinated adults, may come to understand why socialism is a terrible idea. And while outreach programs and community education initiatives are fine, all that has to wait until after the election November 2nd. If Republicans are handing out Abe Lincoln pamphlets now to the African-American community, well, they're idiots and need more than just a couple good reads.

The political class has failed the American people—both parties. Many Christians are indeed hypocrites, or apathetic, or both these days. Those who do get theirs, so to speak, forget the struggle of their own climb, as well as whom actually enabled their ascent. Main Street supports Wall Street; and people raised the government in Washington, D.C., albeit the American people are always searching for a mechanistic device to replace the eternal vigilance required. Every election is theoretically a "term limit" after all, and some of the same people at rallies won't even bother to vote, much less get involved in politics this campaign season—now just over three months left, with the U.S. Congress and the Texas House at stake, and indeed our country.

Although progressives refuse to believe it, many conservatives were highly critical of George W. Bush and did not save their caustic ammo just for Obama Days. The establishment GOP, however, was hijacked by the so-called neoconservative faction. So while vocal critics of President Obama were arguably more passive when Bush was in office, their voices are not now as silenced by a Republican machine or incumbent Republican administration. Unfortunately the battle for the GOP is not quite over, and neoconservatives still hold sway—which is why so much (though not all) of the Tea Party movement is fueled by disaffected conservative Republicans.

Things are not inevitable. No History is. It depends on what you do. In politics action counts for more than debate at election time (and if you hadn't taken notice yet, election time is upon us). The rationalist deterministic mantra that defines modernity in only a certain way is a total crock. The complexity of our society does not justify violation of the Bill of Rights, or violation of States rights and federalism, or indeed the general loss of freedom we are experiencing. Moreover, ours is not the mental calculus of most Europeans—i.e., what do I get for my tax money? In some instances, Europeans see trade-offs in terms of money for services and they conclude it isn't that bad. It might not be so far removed from crony capitalism either. Of course, Americans aren't supposed to trade their taxes and hence their freedom, for a bunch of cradle-to-grave social services, at least not according to Original Intent or the enumerated powers in the Constitution. Americans are not supposed to be "socialist" in other words; albeit, they have been trending that way ever since the Progressive Era and New Deal.

The modern and somewhat resurgent progressive impulse has placed Obama in power, but only after a perceived failed, neoconservative administration. We do need problem solvers and competent people in government to tackle the hard problems. Only they ought to be restricted to constitutional activities! One of the reasons the government is so inept at crisis management, is that it is doing everything else but. The world is not a rosy picture, never was and probably never will be. Someone's particular problem or special need does not place a government coerced responsibility or legal obligation on a freeman or freewoman to go fix and solve it. One shouldn't have to pay for someone else's stupidity, mistakes or bad luck either. We can talk moral suasion, and I'm all for family, church and charitable assistance. I also believe in the power of free enterprise and of mutually beneficial exchanges to make things better over time for most people. My acknowledgment of the real world we live in, in other words, does not lead me to the conclusion that freedom is ever a wrongheaded idea or that it should take a back seat to many things.

In a recent speech, the Chairman of the Texas Workforce Commission, Tom Pauken addressed a 2010 high school graduating class: "Our nation is desperately in need of good leaders. America faces a more serious set of challenges than any time in my life, including our most serious national recession since the Great Depression . . . . This is a time of high levels of unemployment and the hollowing out of our U.S. manufacturing base. (Even here in Texas, where we have lower unemployment than any other large labor market state in the nation, we too have been hard hit by this nasty national recession). Your generation will be the most adversely affected if we don't put in place policies to get our economy moving again. It is not inevitable that unemployment remains persistently high, or that our U.S. manufacturing base continues to deteriorate. Americans—and Texans, in particular—have always risen to the occasion whenever our nation faced serious challenges before; and we can do so again if we have the political will and civic courage to make bold decisions for the long term good of the country."

Now here's what I think too: that ours could be—I said *could be*, the next 'greatest generation.' But don't underestimate the degree of effort required. The good Lord rarely sets up His victory along a primrose path. Freedom has never been free—no, not for Israelites and certainly not for us Americans. The road ahead the next few years is arduous, even risky, but we have every talent we'll need to win, survive and prosper and to pull this country through, *on Election Day* and beyond.

CHAPTER 7

Election 2008: Conservatives Trying to Hold On

Shades of 2008: Battle Lines on Faith — Article #299
o/a May 02, 2007

One evening in early May, I caught Christopher Hitchens on a television program discussing his new book, *God is Not Great: How Religion Poisons Everything* (Grand Central Publishing, 2007). Hitchens is the ultra-contrarious liberal pundit, acerbic and witty—whom I should think becomes the life or death of the party, depending on the mood he's in and how much he's had to drink. His political commentary is entertaining, even when you disagree with him. The point of his latest book is to forcefully state a case against religion. He sets out to show how religion is an accomplice of every bad thing: ignorance, guilt, slavery, genocide, racism and tyranny; as well as the enemy of nearly everything that's good, including all healthy human sexuality, ethics, science, rationality and (by implication) single malt scotch. In discussion, Hitchens explained how faith needed to go away, because faith is the position in thought of least evidence. Hence, Hitchens found it inexplicable that faith and people who have it, are afforded in many quarters some measure of respect and even a measure of presumptive legitimacy. He stated categorically that he wants to change this; indeed, the world would be better off without religion. For without religion, the hatred of the birth canal shall cease! And man and woman and all things in between shall be at last free. Free at last to have fun, to make love and not babies, to be entirely rational—blinded only as it were, by science.

Hitchens' book of course is not the first broadside by an atheist to come out in recent years. God has got some awful bad press lately, including Sam Harris' *The End of Faith* (2005) and Richard Dawkins' *The God Delusion* (2006). What is most interesting is that we seem to be in the midst of a full-fledged counteroffensive in the world of ideas against people of faith. Since the late Seventies at least, a Fourth Awakening has been in progress, good news that has yielded its share of beneficial political and social consequences. But ready or not, here comes the counterreformation. Unfortunately for Christians and conservatives, they have not consolidated their political gains nor restored the culture. The Supreme Court has not been firmly placed back into a constitutionalist's corner. The Republican Party and most conservative hopes are in a weak position headed into the 2008 election cycle. While mainstream Democrats are unlikely to badmouth religion and faith, a significant stratum within the Democratic Party's liberal base has already begun. Moreover, there is a long-term agenda behind their noise. Hitchens himself does not merely refute religion but seeks to demonize it. According to a reviewer, Bruce DeSilva from Associated Press, arguments employed in *God is Not Great* aren't new either though exceptionally well said. The tone is unlikely to change minds, and the title practically ensures nobody will read the book unless he agrees with it already. Hitchens is, pardon the pun, preaching to the choir—so why write the book? The answer is that enemies of religion and faith are digging in for a long night's battle, which is clearly on the horizon. Christians need to take note and begin taking appropriate action.

Having transformed the Constitution into a "living" document, all that is needed is sufficient political power on the Left to rid America of its heritage, including a strong American Judeo-Christian heritage of faith. "In God We Trust" is a statement of faith. Our national motto is quintessentially faith-based. Hitchens, an Englishman, scorns anyone foolish enough to accept this proposition, or indeed any other idea, on faith. His argument aims straight at the heart of American national identity: its ethos of ordered liberty; of one Nation under God; of an optimism born of faith and based on Scripture; of Natural Law and even annual Thanksgiving; of the Blessings of Liberty and unalienable Rights endowed by our Creator. It is not for small potatoes this salvo's been fired: it is for souls. Hitchens' book is the latest in a series that demonstrates the high-stakes ideological struggle ongoing in our culture, on the periphery of the political arena biding its time. Pundits are talking about how the presidential campaign of 2008 has begun so early; how debates are being held; how unprecedented levels of money are infusing the political camps and campaign coffers of individual candidates; and how most people aren't paying any attention. H.L. Mencken called the 'average Joe' a boob, and a lot of people I know hardly know their right from wrong, much less their political right from political left. Admittedly, it takes a little effort as well as faith to know these things and not be a total boob. (It's your prerogative). At the end of the day, you're free to take sides, to sit on the fence or be completely oblivious. Whatever happens, however, elections will be held and decisions made for the future course of the nation. When battle lines get drawn on faith, the world may never be the same.

Which Candidate to Support Article #331
o/a February 01, 2008

The American people may have lost the ability to make very good political decisions. Perhaps it was a gift of Providence they have simply squandered, along with so many others. At any rate, it isn't a failure in aggregate of which I speak—elect this president or that, it has happened many times before that people make mistakes or get fooled once (maybe twice after four years). Rather, the inability to which I refer afflicts both major political parties from the core primary constituencies through to broad coalitions of party band wagoneers. People are less politically able perhaps, now because they are so savvy. We have loads of information and the breadth of wall-to-wall media coverage, yet we never develop a corresponding depth of understanding!

Most people can't give you a decent definition of liberal or conservative, even if they're quite sure they don't like the other one. Talk about the Constitution or federalism and dual sovereignty, it is 'sleepy time.' People have long since sacrificed their independence and political conviction to pseudo-democratic forms of infancy—never believing very much, looking for happiness on the cheap without investing in relationships and institutions that make happiness possible; never learning, much less capturing the Founders' vision for liberty in a Republic; and worse, never even standing on their own two feet as responsible and free people.

Instead we want Big Brother to do it all, more and quicker, and that's why we love the politicians' promises so much. The more he/she promises, the more we are inclined to vote for him/her. So ask yourself, how are you making your decision, on what basis are you rendering it? How to select the man or woman, black or white to lead this great and erstwhile good nation is a question of signal moment. Make it more than a popularity contest please.

In terms of suggested framework, let me offer three points for consideration, which may aid in personal judgment concerning candidates running for office: first, the basis of character; second, an assessment of competence; and third, the philosophy and corresponding policy prescriptions he or she offers, i.e., the platform. To do well in all three categories is a pretty tall order, and quite frankly no one is perfect. In terms of character, however, with all things being equal (or not), you probably ought to prefer someone who doesn't lie frequently, at least on the big stuff while looking you in the eye; and someone who wouldn't steal you blind just because they could pass the law and do it; and someone who generally respects rule of law and conventional morality, who doesn't believe ends justify the means or Olympic gold is worth steroids if you never get caught. In other words, you look for someone who won't lie, cheat or steal. Beyond that very high bar these days, you might also want someone who evinces a teensy weensy bit of loyalty, long-term, even in a pickle or tempted—loyalty to country, to spouse, and to you.

Competence is harder. You might have to look at a candidate's resume and background. Start by insisting the candidate have one! And don't misjudge experience for competence—lots of people have experience holding jobs they never do very well in. Moreover, a job is not a job is not a job—any more than every college course is like any other. How hard, how complex were positions held and the work they entailed? Did the roles involve leadership, innovation and overcoming obstacles? How many people did a candidate lead; what was his style; did the group achieve its goals or develop a process for continuous improvement that led a little closer? I know this sounds difficult. Freedom is tough sometimes, and the price of freedom high. Your effort is worth it though, and far preferable to the risk that's borne and to arduous conditions of fatigue and pain extant at frontlines throughout the world. For yours is a civic duty, while others sustain the military burden that stems directly from your political choice!

Most talk about the candidates involves ideas, and certainly ideas matter. Policy prescriptions are important, presuming a candidate possesses character sufficient to keep promises. Guiding philosophy needs to be taken into account, because not every problem is long-lived, and other problems are too complex for easy solution. It is amazing how priorities on political agendas have shifted. Inflation used to be the rage but isn't these days. Depending on economic conditions, unemployment or mortgages get high priority. Depending on test scores and national competitiveness so might education. If they aren't going bankrupt, Social Security and Medicare will lie on the third rail. Depending on border security, immigration won't always be a hot potato. Crime in cities goes up or down. If States decided abortion policy rather than the Supreme Court, you'd be amazed at how quickly the issue would recede (and political polarization too).

Environment and health care are big issues today for good reason. Almost nobody cares about the race into space anymore, even if they should. Nuclear energy sounds better than fossil fuels when the case was opposite a few years ago. Lots of energy alternatives sound better now than foreign oil, given prices at the pump and places rife with conflict. You get the idea—platforms are largely transitory. That's why you want to know not only what a candidate perceives to be current challenges and what he would do, but also what propensities the candidate has based upon philosophy (ideology if you prefer): government vs. private solutions, regulation vs. deregulation; what defense posture; what kind of foreign policy; what kind of planet; international new world order vs. national sovereignty; friendly towards public expressions of faith, or not. After doing your part judging on the basis of this criteria, I hope you won't find a no-win situation or come to the unsettling conclusion involving a lesser of two evils. No bets here, however.

Republican Party Lost Its Way by Abandoning Conservatives
o/a February 08, 2008 Article #333

The Election of 2008 will probably continue a precipitous turn away from the Republican Party, which began with the election cycle two years before. The irony is that while Republicans lost in 2006, their ideas did not. The cumulative effect of the past eight years has been to profoundly prejudice the American people against the GOP, but for policies its conservative base never did propound. Instead of vouchers and parental choice, Republican legislative initiative in 2001 amounted to the federal takeover of education. No Child Left Behind is a massive federal program with testing mandates, which by the way has failed to raise test scores and at any rate is unconstitutional. The solution was borrowed from Democrats and is now an albatross around the Republican Party's neck.

Medicare Part D is another example of Republicans cross-dressing as Democrats. *The Christian Science Monitor* called it a 'political stroke worthy of Bill Clinton!' The move to expand prescription drug coverage under Medicare cost hundreds of billions of dollars and could easily have targeted a very small sector of the seniors who may have needed it. Instead the Republican plan amounted to a vast federal entitlement program. It moved 3.8 million seniors with workable private prescription drug plans to the government's plan and into bureaucratic nightmare. Republicans abandoned market solutions to confront the health care challenge, so Democrats built on the argument and are calling for more government spending because Republicans did not go far enough.

In August 2005 President Bush signed a $286 billion transportation bill with 6,371 pork projects in it, which added $24 billion to the cost. Moreover, the transportation bill is just the most notable—all thirteen appropriations bills have brimmed with pet pig for a while. Republican congressmen, most of whom are pledged to smaller government, supported 15 times the number of earmarks in 2005 than they did in 1996! Congress was so inept it couldn't summon the political will to transfer funds from a Bridge to Nowhere in Alaska to rebuild bridges damaged by Hurricane Katrina in Louisiana.

Then Bush teamed up with Ted Kennedy and John McCain to produce the McCain-Kennedy illegal alien amnesty bill. Call it what you like, "comprehensive immigration reform" or whatever. A combined Republican-Democrat conservative grassroots effort defeated the bill last summer. Republican presidential front-runner, John McCain says he heard the people loud and clear, i.e., people want border security first. Okay, but if he thinks all he needs is a border fence *before* he legalizes twelve million newcomers he's got another think coming. More than six years after 9/11 the Republican president and Congress have failed on national security to this extent: they failed to secure the borders. Instead, they dicker with half measures to transfer jobs from working class Americans to illegal aliens; and to overburden local and state level health, welfare, education and protection services—mandating unconstitutionally that Americans provide these services to people who have no legitimate claim on anything paid for with taxpayers' money.

With the arguable exception of immigration, on the face of it the Republican Party has lost its way by not being true to itself—i.e., not being true to its core set of principles and conservative beliefs that have defined the party since 1980. Moreover, Reagan's Attorney General, Ed Meese oversaw the 1986 amnesty plan. He states that an explicit lesson learned from the attempt made then, is that amnesty does not work. Further, if you remember, NAFTA was supposed to foster economic development in Mexico thus removing an incentive or "push factor" that caused emigration. The argument proved to be pure horse hockey. We're 'globalized' now more than ever and Mexico is more developed, but the problem with illegal immigration is worse. Meese is convinced that Ronald Reagan would never in the present day context repeat the same mistake! The Republican Party has goose-stepped to the tune of Aye Macarena for eight years and seems surprised that the conservative base is fed up with it.[14]

Truth for Change Article #338
o/a March 21, 2008

Truth is a thing you imagine or perceive, but very hard to reach. It is elusive to the touch and comprehension, like the sunrise or sunset. Truth is also different and unique at every instant you view it, and no less concrete or phenomenal for being difficult to describe. Truth is the quality of being in accordance with experience, facts or reality; and how hard it is: hard indeed to know, impossible to capture completely—essential to pursue. Like the proper role of government, what with self-evident *truths* laying a foundation for our system, establishing the very rationale for independence and existence of these United States: 'that all men are created equal, that they are endowed by their Creator with certain unalienable Rights, that among these are Life, Liberty and the pursuit of Happiness;' and more. If there are no truths, if there is no Truth—then nothing matters or everything matters, but no self-definition is possible and there is no political sovereignty worthy of respect or loyalty from its people. Government that does not respect the truth becomes a liar.

Enter change, clearly essential to the notion of progress. Everyone wants change these days, implicit to which is the expectation of something better. Note the caveat in calls for change. It isn't change for the worse that we want—of course not. It would not be progress or moving forward as it were. So here's an important qualification for all those running a mad dash for the cliff this year. As John Foster Dulles said, "A capacity to change is indispensable. Equally indispensable is the capacity to hold fast to that which is good." Progress very often involves working out inconsistencies within our tradition, not throwing it all away. We don't throw the proverbial baby out with the bath water in other words. American tradition includes private property, free markets, individual liberty, freedom of conscience, as well as the self-determination of communities and states to determine how to live within the bounds of *liberal* institutions—now surely there is something here worthy to *conserve*, i.e., worthy *not* to change.

Hence change is subordinate to any number of things, including truth and the proper role of government—to things in accordance with experience, facts and reality! Those who would depose the natural order by denying there is one, or who would make change itself the order of the day, are by definition liars and perhaps fools or both. No freeman or freewoman ever remained free by giving in to that sort of order. Change is a quicksand if you have anything at all worthy to conserve. Even so-called have-nots have things they would conserve: if not a home or family or job now, then the opportunity to have them in the future and always, always to dream big. Political charlatans play on present discontents, proposing change as a temporary salve at the inevitable expense of the future. The charlatan of change bakes bread of seed corn, robs Peter to pay Paul if necessary, and leaves the grandchildren to grub. Constitutional processes are set up to prevent that kind of change, but only if they are respected and observed.

Government activism in general is a bad idea, especially unchecked, passionate or *compassionate*. Exceptions prove the rule. A majority of Americans have shared this presumption throughout our history, because they recognized that a constitutional republican tradition is worthy to conserve and that a broad expanse of liberty is also worthy to conserve, even if it isn't quite as easy or secure as living in a cage with three squares provided free each day and a water hose spray to clean out your gunk. In political contests positing various reforms, conservatives have usually argued as the defense attorney might, and sometimes as a devil's advocate. Since George W. Bush, however, conservatives have largely abandoned this role according to political historian Jonah Goldberg. Defenders are either out to lunch or embarked on some other quest, not to say hopelessly marginalized. Which leaves the nation's political house ripe for a wrecking ball in the 2008 election cycle, and come January if change artists get their mandate to do damage. Goldberg writes: "Liberals therefore control the argument without either explaining where they want to end up or having to account for where they've been. They've succeeded where the fascist intellectuals ultimately failed, making passion and activism the measure of political virtue, and motives more important than facts." Ergo, change threatens to overwhelm the truth, self-evident or otherwise, unless someone steps into the breach or liberals just happen to self-implode.

The Palin Factor Article #364
o/a September 12, 2008

Just when a lot of Republicans thought it was over—or that it didn't matter much, John McCain has reenergized them in a most astonishing manner. He has given hope to the conservative base by choosing an unlikely running mate for the Vice Presidential spot, Alaska Governor Sarah Palin. Her cultural and religious conservative roots are matters of record. She has also made a leap most politicians these days don't seem capable of, and that's the one from mouth to hands and feet, i.e., from words to reform *action*. Voters need to demand this from their politicians. It doesn't matter how high sounding the rhetoric, unless the actions match. Indeed, actions must be commensurate with words, or else the full measure of integrity is lost. That's why most conservatives are happy, at least happy *enough* to vote for this ticket now. Finally. It was not a foregone conclusion, even if certain cynical political strategists thought it was.

The leftwing will also imagine that the country has been governed by conservatives for eight years, and that conservative policies have therefore failed. The truth is that conservative talkers failed the Republican Party and the American people. So-called conservative representatives sent to Washington to change government—to make it less intrusive and more accountable, were transformed by the system instead. They joined the proverbial club! They failed in their oversight responsibility, and they spent like drunken sailors. They also figured out how to fool the people at election time. Many have even used the Global War on Terror as a platform and excuse for talking tough, while literally ignoring everything else. Little wonder why the economy, as well as energy, healthcare, education and immigration situations are in such a mess.

There is no one who thinks we don't need change, and no one but no one wants a third Bush term! Pay cuts and unemployment are not the kind of change we want, however, so it really does matter whom to elect in November. Socialized medicine and tax increases are not what most people want by way of change. Open borders are unacceptable, and if we don't fix those soon a populist groundswell may yet precipitate political realignment. If we're serious about energy independence and being good stewards of the environment, then domestic drilling and nuclear energy are at least part of the mix necessary to achieve them, since God still helps those who help themselves! Weak-kneed, "Carteresque" foreign policy—vicarious action through talk, talk, talking with assorted lunatics—would prove a disaster, diminishing American security rather than restoring credibility with the rest of the world.

Ironically, as long as McCain had no running mate, his longevity in Washington and years of experience worked against him. Moreover, it was unclear which direction this maverick would take the Party of Ronald Reagan. If he had chosen Senator Joe Lieberman (D/I-Connecticut), it would have been all over. The choice of Palin now makes it possible that McCain may win the Presidency. The spike in polls that followed their unprecedented "his and her" nominations at the Republican National Convention, have made the presidential race a dead heat with momentum on the side of Republicans for the first time. Given the lackluster primary season and McCain's run from behind for the GOP nomination, this race constitutes one of the most impressive dark horse candidacies in history should McCain win. It would also constitute a passing of the torch to a new generation of conservative leaders, as well as major change and new direction for America. Not exactly what Ted Kennedy had in mind when he endorsed Barack H. Obama!

Batons have passed on both sides of the political aisle in this relay dash to the finish line, for change as yet to be determined. Sarah Palin is a serious reformer for *conservative* change. She is much more ideologically consistent than John McCain is. What McCain did by choosing her, is to put a stamp on the direction of the Republican Party into the future. The direction may yet define Twenty-First Century politics in America. Panic gripped liberal bloggers and pundits immediately after they found out McCain had chosen Governor Palin. A woman (the nerve of those Republicans)! Not only that, but Sarah Palin is a leader; and a pro-life mother of five, who apparently doesn't hate men or the concept of family, or the institution of marriage either. Her oldest son deployed to Iraq with the Infantry. She says she's proud of him, and all the fine men and women who serve their country in uniform. Governor Palin also likes guns and believes in the Second Amendment (she even shot a moose for crying out loud). Her husband Todd is First Gentleman of the State of Alaska, but still seems comfortable with his masculinity (weird, huh?). He's four-time champion of the Iron Dog—the world's longest (2,000 miles) and toughest snow machine race, a commercial fisherman, and a production operator in the oil fields on Alaska's North Slope. Of course political vitriol quickly followed, with fierce personal attacks on Palin's family and on her faith, proving again that it doesn't matter how much lipstick you put on a liberal.

McCain-Palin and the Era of Restoration Article #365
o/a September 19

Political historians have observed that a liberal or "progressive" direction seems inherent in Western-style democratic processes evinced over time. That is to say, change happens and moves forward in a left leaning reform direction. Even when conservatives come to power, they regress as it were just one step for every two steps taken. The next reformer takes two steps forward, and the next conservative takes one step back. If the Republic is lost, it is therefore lost forever.

Of course, this description is somewhat prejudiced since many of the same historians theorize what they are hoping for. They don't take careful stock of evidence when liberalization gets reversed, and they overlook the longer view of history that shows any and everything is indeed possible. Philosophers of history say nothing is inevitable, but practicing historians constantly work out their case studies to show the opposite. So-called historical consensus is always against the traditionalist's arguments. Free will is hardly acknowledged in the historical profession to move in a direction other than the New Deal or Diversity, whatever that is.

Politics is the art of the possible, however, according to Otto Von Bismarck. And if so, this should give heart and cause as much to conservatives as anyone else. It is certainly possible to dream of freedom again. It is possible to study the Constitution too, to interpret and apply it more strictly, and to recapture the Founders' worldview even if altered to the modern context. It is possible to restore the Republic in other words.

Even the empirical example of the Progressive Era in history serves notice that an Era of Restoration can and might be on its way.

Senator John McCain and Governor Sarah Palin provide America with an historic opportunity. They have been dubbed as mavericks by journalists, because the reform impulse they represent tends in a different, i.e., rightward direction. That is to say, the change they represent would point our historical course to Restoration in key respects and so reverse the otherwise "inevitable" trend towards serfdom. Whether you interpret America's direction now as a drift or slide or slouching towards Gomorrah, there is near unanimity that things aren't well—indeed, that the things government should do either haven't been pursued or that the attempts to do them have fallen far short. I refer now to basics: a platform the Government should always be "for"—Prosperity, Peace and Freedom.

These are the things America has been known for before. They are things we have experienced and things that should be recaptured. If and when restored, they must be actively maintained. It takes a government comprised of dedicated, professional and patriotic people to serve and to bring these things to fruition. It takes smart, hard-working civil servants, as well as men and women of integrity to serve in elective and appointed positions. Prosperity, peace and freedom are not the stuff of something new and neo-progressive but of something old and enduring, the permanent things our Constitution gives us the ability to keep if we would follow it. The kind of service required from our leaders now calls for character and competence, not charisma. It requires a vision of the tried and true, not a vindication from Oprah Winfrey.

The free market needs oversight not repudiation. Taxes ought *not* to be an instrument of social engineering or class warfare at home, nor should they be an impediment to American business success abroad. Peace moreover should be won and reinstated through strength and with honor, rather than through fatigue or weakness. An Era of Restoration from McCain-Palin would potentially bring some good things back to the future: national sovereignty, including border security and a foreign policy based upon U.S. interests; accountability and transparency of government by and for the people, not beholden to special interests that subvert law and financial institutions; and the U.S. Constitution including federalism, according to which the people of the several states may pursue different policies, social objectives and methods of solving unique problems.

It is not far-fetched to suggest in the Election of 2008 that Sarah Palin could come to resemble Teddy Roosevelt, who was also nominated to be vice president before ascending to the presidency. Both Palin and Roosevelt were reform-oriented governors before being picked for second spot, and both determined to root out corruption and special privilege. Indeed, the nature of the Progressive Era is such that it began with cities (Palin was a reform mayor) and then spread to states. It was propelled by the middle class's insistence that its mores and social norms be respected, counter to a direction laid out by entrenched and acquisitive interests representing the status quo. National policies were informed comparatively late by virtue of McKinley-Roosevelt's win in 1896 and Roosevelt's succession to office.

The issues, personalities and imperatives of reform today are different, but the example illustrates the resilience and hope embedded in our American system of government, according to which the American people, if sufficiently determined, can change or reverse course by picking Washington outsiders to lead them. Reform will resemble the long-awaited Era of Restoration whenever we begin to apply local, common sense solutions and populist standards of decency from the American Heartland. It is time to end the elite and corrupt business-as-usual politics entrenched inside the Beltway and in both political parties. It is time to place the prosperity, peace and freedom of the country first and foremost, and to end this sad mockery of the Founders' great Republic.

Foreign Policy Challenges Face the Next President — Article #366
o/a October 02, 2008

The biggest thing in the news and on people's minds lately, and understandably, has been the credit crunch and implicitly the extent to which it threatens financial institutions and poses a threat to economic wellbeing in the country and indeed around the world. Boys and girls on Wall Street screwed up, and their mistakes trickle down a lot quicker than the obscene profits do. Effects could be stagflation, unemployment, not to mention declining value of stock, which affects so many savings and investment vehicles like mutual funds or retirement accounts. Wall Street is tied to Main Street in other words. Bad bank loans might mean someone misses payroll and someone else gets laid off. The Treasury Secretary and Fed Chairman used the last ounce of credibility left to this administration and sounded an alarm the sky was falling. They looked visibly rattled during testimony, so much so the Congress actually moved to do something. Amazing.

Wise, unwise or indifferent Congress acted to rescue private interests with public money and to socialize the economy further. Government is convinced now it can repeal the business cycle and prevent ever having another recession, at least a deep one (Government does everything else so well. Why worry). Precisely. The next president, whomever he is, is going to have unprecedented problems to manage, economically speaking. Ditto in terms of foreign policy. Moreover, the linkage between the economy and foreign affairs has perhaps never been as star-crossed. It takes money backed by more than debt to run an empire, hold enemies at bay and help out friends. That's in a good year. Whether or not you are embroiled in Iraq and Afghanistan, or faced with a subversive adversary like Iran or an outwardly resurgent hegemonic hopeful like Russia. Risk is better played on board games than on banks and battlefields.

The list of problems facing the next president will be large. Moreover, the country is moving from one policy phase to another. The situation in Iraq has turned around since 2006 and is all but won, if by winning we mean sufficiently stabilized. Soon U.S. concerns and foreign policy debate won't be all about Iraq, but rather on how best to responsibly downsize forces in Iraq to face mounting challenges elsewhere, including in Afghanistan, with resources that are admittedly stretched thin. If we are smart we'll invest some slack in a strategic reserve of forces, i.e., not to commit all our troops but to give ourselves flexibility, just in case things go south in Pakistan or we're faced with events in the former Soviet Union like the recent conflict in Georgia (to say nothing of domestic hurricanes).

The next president will confront difficult situations with Iran, as well as with Russia. The two are not equal, however, as the threat Russia poses far exceeds anything Iran can do. One very important strategic challenge involves keeping Russia from successfully reaching out to Iran and Iran from accepting strategic accommodation and/or cooperation with Russia. We ought to work hard to achieve a more stable understanding with Iran if possible. We need Iran to stop hurting our interest in Iraq and start helping it in Afghanistan; after all, there's no love lost between Iran and the Taliban, any more than with Saddam Hussein. Both Iraq and Afghanistan border Iran too, which given U.S. troop presence in those countries, should give pause to consider a perception of threat posed by us—particularly if we believe they are part of an 'axis of evil.' Even if by hard work and bargaining we win Iranian cooperation, we won't win the war in Afghanistan without closing down sanctuary and supply lines entering in from Pakistan, which constitute the Vietnam equivalent of the Ho Chi Minh Trail.

The president also needs to close the book on Al Qaeda and stop exploiting that threat for political purposes and for concentrating power in Washington. It is as easy and as hard as declaring victory and moving to other foreign policy challenges. The fact is that Al Qaeda is decimated and hasn't been successful in attacks in the United States since 2001 or in Europe since 2005. That doesn't mean Islamist terrorism won't be around for a long time, but it does mean the war on terrorism is down to swatting fleas and watching for larvae to grow. There are successful models to employ moreover, which do not involve wholesale occupation of foreign countries. We need Turkey's cooperation more vis-à-vis a resurgent Russia (Georgia borders on Turkey), than we need stoke worries over Iraqi 'Kurdistan' (which also borders Turkey).

Talk about change. Americans want change. This is a so-called change election. Both Republicans and Democrats spout about change, and it's a campaign slogan for at least one major party candidate. But change in foreign affairs as the term indicates, follows events that aren't altogether in domestic hands. Many of the most important issues from 2009 to 2013 can't even be imagined today any more than 9/11 was foreseen during the election of 2000. Any more than Truman knew Korea would dominate his second term or JFK expected the Cuban Missile Crisis to happen or knew it would define his presidency. In 1976 Carter didn't imagine his presidency would or could be wrecked by an Iranian revolution deposing the Shah and American hostages being taken. George H.W. Bush didn't expect to preside over the collapse of communism either. The point is that it isn't all about the economy stupid.

Ultimately voters will judge which of the candidates has the character and competence needed to lead and to make right decisions in a very challenging, geopolitical landscape. Clearly soldiers on the front have their duties. Public servants also have theirs, from the postman to the fireman to the policeman to the teacher. We don't think of it nearly enough, but while the freeman, freewoman and citizen have arguably few of what are termed duties per se, the one that stands out in peace and in war, in boom or in bust is the duty to vote. It is the duty as it were, to determine who takes the helm and steers a course through known and choppy water and perhaps through a few spans uncharted.[15]

Economy and Politics: Foregone Conclusions Article #367
o/a October 08, 2008

For most of my adult life, banks and lending institutions have been engaged in an aggressive effort to retrain Americans, trying to get them to "lighten up" on their innate value of thrift and just accept the credit card or whatever EZ Credit line they "qualify" for. It's the late-twentieth and twenty-first centuries Information Age, and a brave new economy to boot with no end in sight to growth, especially with the (inevitable—don't try to resist) advent of globalization. New tools enable you to be the modern man or superwoman and realize your potential. It is practically self-actualizing. And if it's new and easy to get, you know it's good. Take the loan; and here, have another.

Everyone should be able to purchase nice clothes, and good food, and fun things when they want them. A credit card helps. Nine credit cards help more. Everyone also needs transportation in today's mobile society, so the car loan is a necessity. Two car loans are more convenient for the working family couple or partnership of today. Everyone should, it goes without saying have a house, because it's the American Dream and everyone should achieve all dreams hopefully on their own private time schedules. It's your right too if you're a low-income minority, especially if you have little prospect for steady or rising income in the future.

Marketing efforts and sheer persistence have certainly paid off, though not necessarily in the positive economic vein. Presumption against debt, however, has gone the way of the horse and buggy, or at least gone the way of your dad's Oldsmobile he shortsightedly paid for with hard-earned cash. People seem genuinely shocked by the credit crisis we're experiencing: how things could go so wrong, as quickly; or that bottom lines matter to more than the abstract. Nevertheless, we shouldn't worry since most people are still pretty much resigned to the fact they will never be totally debt free, which is another way of saying they will never ever be totally *free* until they die. The American people are still a fit species to saddle and ride for greed and gain well into the future.

The challenge is to figure out what the technical glitch was that occurred, and fix that. The financial calculus made by investors should have taken all the stuff into account. I mean mortgage lenders, according to the magic of the marketplace should have figured in their percentage losses and escalating defaults and made sure to jack rates up accordingly on everyone else. Granted, it's hard to quantify the government's capacity to bail out; albeit, its willingness to do so is by now a foregone conclusion. It really is all the most unfortunate academic failure. Don't confuse the situation with moral failure or responsibility. The people are never to credit or to blame, either for personal spending habits or for the filtrated talent they elect to lead them.

Things that don't matter still don't. Take the stress on people—Joe Six-pack, the hockey moms, a few professional elites so-called—all facing their respective mountains of bills each month. That is someone else's calculus. Am I my brother's keeper? Never. Or take the gradually diminishing resources that a family has to live on month after month, after month after year. Multiply that by millions of households. It really isn't a considerate part of macroeconomic equations or public policy, as tempting as it might be to think about it once in a blue moon. What matters is that enough people are willing to go on and to continue to work and to pay; work and pay; perchance and increasingly likely, to divorce; to remarry and divorce; and to have children and finally to die in due time. The beautiful circle of life continues to make money; and future returns, if taken in aggregate justify the inherent risk of isolated or plurality loans cases.

Moreover, it really doesn't make sense to blame politicians either. The leading presidential contender, who by now is another foregone conclusion, had the best of intentions and that's the most American voters ever require. Instead of suspending his campaign, he was cool and got style points. Concretely, however, in the 1990s he helped low-income people in Chicago get the loans they deserved so they could move into houses. As a lawyer and volunteer on behalf of civic-minded groups, he helped pressure banks and lending institutions from unfairly redlining so-called bad credit risks, or people who just happen not to have any money. His efforts contributed directly towards the grand collective goal that many hardworking community organizers and liberal congressmen have, to put more than a chicken in every pot, but rather everyone in a house they can't afford.

Lending institutions responded to the threat of litigation after legislation in 1995 (Clinton) strengthened the Community Reinvestment

Act of 1977 (Carter), and they also ultimately responded to greed for more and more transaction fees, because it was clear that government chartered organizations would back them. Flexible lending programs mushroomed, which included 100 percent financing, no check of credit scores, and income for loan qualification without requiring documentation. After all, you don't need documentation to be in the country, to collect welfare or even to vote—after 9/11, the Justice Department found eight of the nineteen hijackers were registered to vote. Not sure if they had sub-prime mortgage loans, but they could have and definitely deserved them.

Fannie Mae's commitment to low-income loans rose from just $1 billion in 1992 to $80 billion by 1999, and upwards of $600 billion by 2003. Freddie Mac's story is the same. The two bought an increasing share of risky sub-prime securities too, which started unhinging over a year ago. Both institutions were underwritten by the government, which effectively socialized risk, privatized profit and guaranteed the taxpayer bailout. Anyway, our man on the move has pledged to break with failed economic policies of the past if they happened in the last eight years. You do the math.

Black Vote: A Mind is a Terrible Thing to Waste Article #368
o/a October 15, 2008

Free people must judge or ultimately they are not free, and freedom is prior to other values—at least that was the faith of our Founders. That is to say, it is best certainly to be free *and* right and we ought to strive to be so, but it is better far to be free *than* right. Moreover, it takes a relatively smart citizenry to be able to relate, explain and judge tomatoes, much less two or more political candidates! Granted the identification and relation of A to B is often a perception of fact but as we've learned with politicians, looks can be deceiving. Then getting past that if you can, to explain something about A and B is more difficult, as this deals with aspects that can be ambiguous—where they're from, what type are they, what are the similarities and differences? To judge A and B, to say which is actually better, well, that takes decision if not conviction, and also involves a little moral courage in the case of choosing leaders.

It doesn't matter if judgment involves opinion or subjective elements. The determination of judgment rests upon values and/or criteria, and they can be those that are arguably fair, sophisticated, lawful, objective, measurable, and even "correct" in a policy sense. Every professional is forced to analyze this way in their line of work, but somehow consumers—even political consumers, are often the last to do so. If taken broadly and applied to politics, to history, science, medicine or art, it sounds radical. Indeed the concept of freedom is quite radical. Imagine: the idea that we ought to make up our own minds, rather than the master, or the hive, or private passionate impulses! Imagine: the idea that in a democratic republic, we ought to make up our own minds deliberately, regardless of what experts say even if we end up agreeing with them. Only you can assess your needs and beliefs. Only you are properly regarded as the arbiter of your own mind, if ever you should be called a freeman or freewoman. A mind is a terrible thing to waste, and so is your vote.

Now what does it say if a racial group votes overwhelmingly one way in election after election? (The same if one gender votes that way, which they don't). Maybe nothing. Maybe everything. After the War Between the States, blacks voted overwhelmingly Republican, since it was President Lincoln who pronounced the Emancipation Proclamation as a war time measure. It was the Republican Party during Reconstruction that passed civil rights legislation and enforced those measures and largely forced favorable changes to the Constitution with the 13th, 14th, and 15th Amendments, before military occupation of the South ended. The strong affiliation with Republicans continued for African-Americans until the 1930s. Franklin Roosevelt and his New Deal programs appealed strongly to blacks, but then much of the country also swung Democrat during the Great Depression. From 1936 to 1960, Democrats never did worse than 60 percent of the black vote. Which is to say, one-third to forty percent of blacks still voted the other way.

Since 1964, Democrats have never got less than 80 percent of the black vote. Today a Democrat expects to get over 90 percent no matter who the nominee is! By contrast to the New Deal era moreover, the country did not become more Democratic. Until recently it became much more Republican. This has resulted in a strange sort of political segregation for blacks, all the more curious since it happened after the time when Congress passed the Civil Rights Act of 1964 and Voting Rights Act of 1965 and thus extended full political rights to them. The most common explanation for this incongruity is that the Republican Party was stigmatized with the label of racist within the African-American community after 1964. Not only had Democrats sponsored favorable legislation during America's "Second

Reconstruction," many Dixiecrats and avowed segregationists bolted the Democrat Party and some became Republican. Voting patterns amongst whites, however, have shown more diversity than amongst blacks, in terms of their support for independents, third parties and/or changing allegiance between the two major parties—as indeed the times have changed, and changed again. Even the so-called Bradley Effect is in decline. Named for the black candidate Tom Bradley, who ran for California governor in 1982 but lost, the phenomenon refers to white voters telling pollsters one thing because they don't want to appear prejudiced, then voting a different way in the booth.

Bradley had a nine-point lead going into the election but lost by a point. Other elections have shown a "Bradley Effect" too, but since 1990 the percentage has been on the wane, and in 2006 there were five statewide races with black candidates for U.S. Senate or governor where the polls got it right every time. This would seem to bode well for Obama's nine-point plus lead in the presidential race. Black voter turnout reached all time highs in the 2008 Democrat primaries, and blacks supported Obama by margins often exceeding 97 percent against a field of other candidates. There is no other group in America that votes so lopsided. In terms of the upcoming general election, it seems futile but somehow important to suggest to conscientious and thoughtful African-American voters, that the stigma of voting Republican is hardly justified—not on the basis of racism anyway. Notwithstanding, there may be good reasons for both white and black voters to repudiate the policies of George W. Bush and to consider whether they apply to the McCain-Palin ticket. For all concerned, the only votes that will count are the ones cast on Election Day.

In Search of Ethics Before the Election Article #369
o/a October 10, 2008

Few would dispute that our country is confronted with huge challenges. Right now we are mired in wars, and the government is trying to stave off the onset of a financial collapse. There are whispers of a possible depression. Indeed, the financial crisis will certainly dominate the first year of the next administration, whomever wins—driving almost everything else off the political agenda awhile. Notwithstanding, the country needs a strategy to secure energy independence; and programmatic approaches to increase health care access, and get medical costs down. We still must address the disrepair and inexcusable lack of investment in various infrastructures. And we need to overhaul and invest in education or risk falling from world leader status economically. Wherever you look for guidance or problem solving, you find instead examples of cheating, fraud and deception, not to mention bad judgment.

Parents moreover face numerous outside forces that threaten the moral and physical wellbeing of their families. The tenor of society is disjointed, as parents, businesses, educational, religious, and political leaders, and the average Joe have their sensibilities rubbed raw, and their intelligence, morals, and characters bombarded daily by harmful solvents. Dr. Katherine Vessenes says that the "mirrored image of our society is not one that we can brag about. It is clear that we must elevate ourselves above the lying, cheating and abuse so readily accepted in our society." Ultimately the nation is only as strong as the people who live in it, run its schools and businesses, raise its children.

Dr. Rushworth Kidder adds that we can't expect to survive the 21st century with the ethics of the last one. Values are more than just the right thing to do. For upon them, the success and possibly survival of our society, depends. As the only global superpower with a democratic-republican political system and capitalistic free enterprise economic system, we are still regarded as the leader of the free world. Without the moral authority and trust it engenders, however, we may lose our position of leadership in the world. Events over the last eight years have already begun to place our position of leadership in jeopardy. In the worst case, despite our superpower status we could face the real possibility of destroying ourselves from within, a potential that should not be dismissed lightly. There are enough rifts in American society it could look like Shiites and Sunnis in Iraq under the right circumstances. It behooves Americans thus to consider what holds Americans together in society and as one nation.

The answer is that regardless of our various religions, races and ethnic backgrounds, we do tend to share a common set of values. These are not imposed but rather shared and probably acculturated, and this is borne out in surveys. The values Americans most frequently profess are: honesty, respect, responsibility, freedom, fairness, love, service and loyalty. The same or similar themes are expressed whenever Americans are asked to define their values. So the problem isn't misguided values per se. The problem is with the serious disconnect between those values we profess, and the behavior we demonstrate. Dr. Len Marrella writes, "For whatever reason, the self-discipline, courage, and the commitment required to forge the connection between values and behavior" have gone missing.

Most people know what is right and even have a latent goodness inside of themselves, but many people are more concerned about appearing to be honorable than with being honorable or conducting themselves accordingly. They are more interested in style as it were, than substance. Socrates said, "The shortest and surest way to live with honor in the world is to be in reality what we would appear to be. All human virtues increase and strengthen themselves by the practice and experience of them." The bottom line is there has been a moral meltdown and the trend line is still on a downward slope. Today it isn't enough to know what is right if you fail to follow through and actually do it. This aspect needs to be relearned.

In his book. (2001), Dr. Marrella warns that, "When you combine deteriorating ethics with the leverage that modern technology provides, you have a situation wherein a few unethical people can do a considerable amount of harm to all of the rest of us. So we need to pay attention to the ethos and moral fiber that we carry into the 21st century. Now is the time to pay attention to the problem." His warning nearly eight years ago could not have been more prescient, but it went unheeded in key respects by the government and by Wall Street. There is much now especially, that needs be done in this fast-paced, changing, and technology-driven world of ours. Americans are up to the task no doubt, but meeting the challenges we face will take an awful lot of character at every level—starting at the highest office in the land and percolating throughout the bodies social, economic and politic.

Ideology of Liberty — Article #370
o/a October 31, 2008

In the late campaign, many stupid things were said on all sides. I suppose that's normal in American politics, but some undeserving things were accorded the mantle of common wisdom by the media and political analysts. For instance, that we're too polarized as a nation and ergo, that's why civility is lacking and Congress can't lead itself out of a wet paper bag; and we're too divided *according to ideology*, so thinking is to blame and a new way of thinking must transcend the old. If only politicians were less ideological the story goes, then they should be more practical in problem solving. If political parties adhered less to certain ideologies, then they should rise above petty little selfish interests and begin to govern effectively for the common good. The critique is like eye candy of rainbows floating on water, where light passes through the prism of a pretty oil slick. It belies the dunce of democratic majorities and special interest lackeys, who lack an understanding of political philosophy, political science and language, whilst they mouth words and feel quite smart.

The reason is polarization can have many causes, not the least of which is the concentration of power in Washington. Some people have asked why I ran for U.S. Congress before, and not for a county or state position first. My answer is grounded in the unfortunate reality that Austin can do almost nothing when the federal government has arrogated to itself power to make every decision and the authority to enforce every decision beyond checks and balances or separation of powers; in spite of the text of the Constitution, and the Original Intent of the Founders; and notwithstanding the Ninth and Tenth Amendments, or quaint federalist constructs in American political tradition involving dual sovereignty. Today we face the political prospect of restoring constitutional government and decentralizing power from within at the source of power or not at all.

The impressive police and military might of the present empire will not be assailed from without, nor confronted or avoided from within without a corresponding political change. There is hope for change from where power lies, however, if and when the people effect their representation; that is, if and when they will elect representatives grounded in the ideas and ideology of Liberty. This means they will get busy, informed and serious about voting for men and women who are committed to free markets and free minds, and to the government that governs least, i.e., according to the strictures of the Constitution. This means they will themselves respect again the historic, textual, ideational reality of the Constitution—and that instrument as the organic law of the Land. It means they will not stand down their effort after this election, as no patriot ever stands down completely knowing the price of freedom is eternal vigilance.

The situation in Washington today is a huge and daunting challenge, an American equivalent to bringing down the Soviet Union. It cannot be done with improvised explosives, but rather only with ideas. Now if the people are too far-gone as it were, the fact the political system may still open to change is of little consequence and no avail. We vote and hope there will be enough people like us to make any difference. Else we settle for the placid answers and easy solutions so many politicians parrot and spout; and follow those rainbows floating on water, to the pots of fool's gold nested firmly at the bottom of seas of tyranny and oppression.

Should we elect politicians to restore lost Liberty? If this sounds like a riddle, then it is because we have lost a basic American tenet and popular understanding about the workings and nature of power and power's cousin, politics. Namely, individuals and communities empowered by freedom can do just about anything, but there are serious limitations to what politics can accomplish and also what politicians plausibly and legitimately may promise under the Constitution. We need our politicians to do and to try to do less than what they are doing now, but it takes men and women of character and intelligence, and statesmen to do the less, and to discern and accomplish what is needed well. To paraphrase P.J. O'Rourke, barbarians are at the gates and are besieged by worshippers of big government. The quote is an oblique reference to the historic sack of Rome, but also metaphorically to the loss of Western Civilization occurring today. By implication, it foreshadows the onset of darkness and new Dark Ages. The barbarian perpetrators are those who have lost faith in themselves and the people, and the American Republic. They attribute instead all power, omniscience, glory and honor to national state planning and central government. After the last election, you might call it a bipartisan consensus. It seems we are all socialists now.

The truth is that we have become far too comfortable with state regulation of speech and expression, of business and the economy, of schools, churches, boy scouts, factories, airlines, fraternities, state and local government entities. As Mark Steyn describes it, we're conditioned to the idea of regulating freedom in the interest of social harmony so-called, indeed to such a degree that we use the legal system to circumscribe debate and criminalize vigilance. The great world historian Arnold Toynbee wrote, "Civilizations die from suicide, not murder" and it is clear Americans have a most peculiar death wish on many levels. For those who choose to wriggle in their death grip and pray without ceasing for supernatural intervention unto the end, we ought also to cry out "No" as often as we can—being altogether less socially harmonious and cooperative with our own destruction, and parting ways with errors in common wisdom repeated so often that you start to believe it. 'Do not go gentle into that Good Night!' The worst ideology of all is the one that says resistance is futile. We ought to stop sending the oligarchs to Washington and elect true representatives who believe in Liberty. The door to freedom is not yet closed, even as darkness falls.

McCain's Loss Republicans' Gain Article #371
o/a November 07, 2008

Senator John McCain ran a good race in a year that, by all accounts and historic markers, was going to be for the Democrats. When the economy tanked, there was no hope left in numbers. Having said that, his accomplishment as a campaigner was quite remarkable for his having been an agent of Republican disunity through much of the race and for years before. Everyone knows McCain was the dead last choice for a nominee in Texas, and the base still rallied to him! His choice of Governor Palin helped, as did the emerging and stark contrast to the Democrat opponent. Today voters set aside their lingering questions of patriotism, about origins, Marxist ideology and plain bad associations, to give the president-elect our benefit of doubt, well earned and deserved. The electoral landslide and corresponding gains in Congress are such that they give him a political mandate if indeed any president should have one. Moreover, Obama said that he hears the voices of those who did not elect him, that he will be their president too. Expectations and hope are coming from all directions. Virtually everyone wishes him well and to tell the truth, it might just be the best thing for Republicans.

Obama is already being called the black Kennedy. That means a lot to liberals in this country: a personification of hope, a promise of equal justice, and the spreading of wealth around. His triumph is akin to Reagan in key respects. Only a few years after Watergate, President Carter had become so unpopular in office that it gave rise to the Reagan Revolution. President George W. Bush's tenure, his second term in particular, were so unpopular it gave rise to an Obama Revolution. If Obama doesn't overplay his mandate or try to enact extreme radical policies, he could very well consolidate the Democratic majority for twenty years to come—and diffuse potential political backlash. Meantime, Republicans will have time to think, as well as for inevitable political infighting. They are going to seek internal scapegoats and factions to blame for defeat. The ins will be outs, and the Republican Party that emerges four years from now is likely to be different in important respects from what went into the 2008 election cycle.

Not only will it not resemble the neoconservative faction leading Bush to ruin, it is doubtful it will resemble McCain very much either. Remember McCain came to national prominence as a "maverick" Republican, meaning he championed controversial causes and policies affronting many parts of the Republican coalition. Indeed, he was one of two GOP senators, who voted against the 2001 Bush tax cuts and one of three who opposed reductions in 2003. Senator McCain co-authored legislation for extensive regulations related to the environment. In 2001 he and Senators Ted Kennedy and John Edwards introduced the Patient's Bill of Rights that included expensive mandates for health coverage. Overall the Senator from Arizona has shown little respect for the free market and had little appeal to economic conservatives. Social and religious conservatives too, who remember the 2000 primaries warmed up to him even less, remembering that he called them "agents of intolerance" and suggested their religious leaders had no place in American politics. McCain also co-sponsored the McCain-Feingold campaign finance law, which passed over the opposition of 80 percent of congressional Republicans! The reason is that law was designed to restrict political speech of groups at the core of the Republican Party coalition: the National Rifle Association, as well as anti-abortion organizations and businesses. Few in the Republican Party on the right will mourn McCain's loss this past November 4th.

A prominent McCain sympathizer, *The New York Times'* David Brooks, had predicted a President McCain would change not only the nation but also the GOP. He felt people and groups who worked for the Reagan victories and also 1994 Republican return to power would find themselves exiled. McCain's loss has given them a new lease as it were. McCain styled himself a maverick, whose appeal to independents and Democrats this season would make up lost GOP votes. Except for pressure from the base and strong advice to sidestep outright political suicide, his inclination had actually been to choose his close friend Senator Joe Lieberman of Connecticut, a former Democrat to be his running mate! Independents and Democrats this year wanted change, however, and sixty percent of independents voted for Obama.

McCain wasn't about change, and the voters saw through the smoke and mirrors. Senator McCain was just as much a hawk on Iraq as President Bush. Of course the irony is that the military surge worked so well there were no U.S. casualties for the entire month before the election. The issue receded entirely from people's minds. The economy took its place, and

McCain had as much principled opposition to government spending as President Bush, which is to say none at all. McCain never did answer Obama's query: "Name one economic policy of President Bush you weren't for!" McCain differed from the status quo only in his willingness to tax more. Indeed, McCain was the standard bearer of big-government conservatism: taxing and spending us into the drink at home and crusading stupidly for democracy in foreign lands, while reinvigorating the imperial presidency that brought Republicans low once before during the Nixon Era. This kind of faux conservatism deserved electoral defeat to match its abject political failure. The situation is grim short-term for Republicans, but the election defeat also opens a sorely needed debate about the principles of the Republican Party.[16]

Creeping Coup Article #372
o/a November 14, 2008

Something happened along the way to the American mind, and quite frankly it isn't working well the way it used to. Americans today aren't half the speculative or political philosophers their grandparents once were. They don't sit on the porch as much, and they certainly don't share opinions with family and friends in a constructive way that invites feedback or a counter tirade. They don't read newspapers much either, or pass them around with or without editorial comment. The pastimes and concerns such habits represent have all but been pushed aside by busy lives and quasi-meaningless competing priorities. Increasingly, the capability to do so has lapsed for the want of practice.

Radio and TV shows talk a lot but without discussing anything, and politicians speechify to no end without real debate. Public education has all but ceased to teach the communicative and intellectual skills needed for critical analysis on which deliberative democracy is thought to rely.

Our opinions are no longer formed from the bottom up as it were, or even from side to side but from the top down. The Party, the Government, and the Media tell us what spin to believe in; and we no longer possess the filter of our own minds to commit to what we boldly call the truth, our truth even if it is a perception. The change is important, because it unhinges our past and supportive culture from the running of constitutional government. It is important to the whole country moreover, because it allows what professor of politics at Catholic University of America, Dr. Claes Ryn observes, is "a creeping coup d'état from within."

The old American idea of government was likened closely to the Golden Rule "to love thy neighbor." Its modus morality placed primary emphasis on individuals controlling their passions, fighting personal demons, leading considered and disciplined lives. Liberty depended on as much, since it made for strong communities and minimized the need for overarching government. In the early 19th Century, Alexis de Tocqueville recounted the tremendous reluctance on the part of Americans to give up any power over their lives to distant authorities, whether church or state.

The written Constitution has always rested on foundations unwritten, even upon the character of the American people, upon the quality of received inheritance: the religious, moral, intellectual, cultural and social habits and beliefs of the people. As these have changed, we should not be surprised that constitutional government no longer runs the way it once did, or that checks and balances no longer preclude accretions of power unheard of in the days of the Republic's Founders. Ryn: "The moral momentum behind the old decentralized society weakened. Today strong, centralized Federal power seems to more and more Americans not merely acceptable but desirable . . . Americans say increasingly to government: 'Act for us!'"

Americans no longer run their own government, the government runs them. We know longer tell the government how much tax we're willing to give, but rather the government informs us how much of our earnings we're allowed to keep. In the name of social good, in the name of fairness, in the name of crisis or necessity—anything but in the name of Freedom! Americans are detached from their historically unique, even exceptional tradition of constitutionalism with its deep cultural roots. Allegiance has shifted from something real and achievable to plastic abstractions and universal rationalist principles, more akin to the French Revolution than to the American. History and concrete experience once taught us the importance of self-restraint, as well as the importance of restraint on government power. Today we celebrate the unitary power of the modern president in spite of the checks and balances of the Constitution designed to restrain that power. Indeed, we search for an American Caesar to rid us of all our problems and to fix every hurt.

According to Ryn, "We are living through the progressive dismantling of America's proudest political achievement" as we watch the Constitution die. Strict constructionists, even if the people should elect them to office, will find it nigh impossible to resurrect the constitutional edifice, much less perpetuate a system of government shorn from its moral-ethical and other culture that gave it birth. "Restoring American constitutionalism would presuppose some kind of resurgence of that old culture . . . [Americans] would have to rearrange their priorities and start acting differently, placing more emphasis on family, private groups and local communities. They would have to want to take back much of the power ceded to politicians."[17]

Inaugeration of Change Article #383
o/a January 30, 2009

With the ascendance of Barack Obama to the presidency at noon on January 20th, 2009 a new era certainly ushered in. His supporters and enthusiasts are certain that change is here, and the mantra goes that it is a "Change You Can Believe In." Perhaps it should be stated more accurately, as "Change—You Better Believe It!" From a conservative and Republican standpoint, there is no denying the watershed in politics. Prescriptions involving free markets, tax cuts and deregulation are embattled, deemed no longer to apply. Moreover, "You [had] better *believe* it" connotes the psychological, not to say psychotic nature of change many of Obama's supporters seek—a change of your mind. A mind is never terribly wasted if it is brainwashed and used. *Believe* in change: from individual to collective responsibility; from private to public welfare; from any and everybody's initiative to vast government ownership and activism. *Believe* in change: from majority and regional affiliations to guilt; from old normal to the new left out, if you aren't diverse enough; from familiar cultural patterns to the latest import. Yes we can.

Political historians and longtime politicos will recognize swings of the pendulum. It happens. Politics, like economics tends to be cyclical. On the other hand, President Obama and the Democrats now seek to repeal the business cycle, forbid unemployment and recession through bailout after bailout as well as eternal prime pumping of the economy with dollars hot off the press. Theoretically a tire shouldn't deflate no matter how many holes are in it, so long as you pump it hard and fast enough with ever increasing volumes of gas. Lord we get our quantity from the politicians. President Obama and the Democrats may also seek to repeal the political cycle. If Obama is successful, he knows he could potentially consolidate Democratic majorities for at least twenty years. Moreover, political developments may not be entirely cyclical if history is forgot or retold well enough, and if constitutional parameters completely disappear—which they will, if they are never mentioned. One is tempted to say his oath didn't matter, neither one of them in fact. For no amount of government spending exceeds this president's political capital for the moment.

Of course in any sort of open competition there will be another party, indeed more than one to contend with sainted progress so-called. In the two-party system we have, such as it is, Republicans will have a say even from the wilderness. Ironically, contrary to laying blame entirely on George W. Bush and the last eight years, Republicans lost the last election due to their success in part. By that I mean that third parties have always had the air let out by the two big parties co-opting their positions. Likewise, when a big party finds itself in a minority or at a stalemate vis-à-vis the other one, it turns the table by selectively co-opting the tone, style or substance of the other. Obama is big on tone and absolutely exquisite for style. He looks and acts more presidential than poor GW ever did. Obama can also read a script and appear to answer thoughtfully, something that at least one Yale graduate never mastered even with lots of practice. The jury's still out in terms of change in policy, however, and so far it appears the president is notable for following careful process—a little light on specific ideas newly minted or otherwise, with almost no ideological rudder.

Regardless, look at his Inaugural rhetoric: a vision of America's greatness (a.k.a. Shining City on a Hill); a public nod to faith, even if Muslims and nonbelievers were inclusively embraced (closer to Faith-based initiative than clinging to religion); patriotic support for the military, with or without a lapel pin (sounded like Ronald Reagan or George W. Bush); strength in foreign policy (no Jimmy Carter here); and considerable emphasis on values 'that are old' like nurturing children, work and being responsible (Family Values, conservatism with a small "c"). People yearned for a change, and they got it. The methodology, however, was Obama's charismatic appeal and classic political response, in effect to co-opt important elements out of the Republicans' portfolio in order to produce the new Democratic majority.

There is no doubt it will be harder now for Republicans to get elected, especially nationally for some four years or more, because the political landscape has changed. Republicans are going to have to sound different and sound off differently. They can't sound the same or mouth the old lines, or they'll rightfully be accused of sounding just like Obama. It is up to conservatives and Republicans and others to reformulate their message, indeed if there's going to be a notable or effective opposition at all. They need to make a serious effort and take the necessary time to reorganize, plan and strategize; and to rearm and refit, as it were in military parlance. Better not take too much time, however. Could be 'A hard rain's a-gonna fall' in the words of Bob Dylan. "There are some who question the scale of our ambitions, who suggest that our system cannot tolerate too many big plans," the 44th president said at his Inauguration. "Starting today, we . . . begin again the work of *remaking America*."

CHAPTER 8

THE POLITICAL TWO-STEP/MISSTEPS

Life of the Party Article #385
o/a February 13, 2009

Both parties in America's unofficial "two-party system" are large, constantly morphing national coalitions comprised of individuals and interests forming vehicles for political participation. Political parties facilitate policymaking and governance of course, but they by and large nominate and run the candidates whom people choose from to elect. Elected officials in turn become our Government, constitutional or otherwise, wise as not. They also become de facto leaders of the party that got them there.

Political parties are also porous things, and any individual so inclined is able to join, leave and try some other brand, or decide to come back again. Many do it all the time, depending on whom which candidates are, and on what the party platforms say. Of course those platform documents are imperfect and never binding, but imperfect as they are they do attempt to codify the ideational basis of a party, at least for the season. One does have to ask, however, just what it means to be a lifelong Republican or Democrat, considering how different either given party has been, and will be again over the course of a typical lifespan. This leaves many citizens saying with perfectly good conscience that, "I don't vote for the party, I vote for the man or woman" or "I didn't leave my party, my party left me." Neither of the two major parties it turns out has the proverbial corner on better character or better solutions.

Then again times change, history moves on, and situations alter. This leads the likes of Rush Limbaugh to ask as he did in remarks at the Hillsdale College Churchill Dinner in Washington, D.C., "Do conservatives [and in this case the more conservative party or Republicans] need to get beyond Reagan?" His answer might be predictable, but not for reasons one may think based on liberal stereotype of the talk-show host. Limbaugh concludes "there is no *pragmatic* reason today for conservatives to abandon the *ideas* [emphasis mine] of Reagan." Then he proceeds to pick one idea from out of many that Reagan used to talk about, one that may yet form a kernel of some future Republican Party majority. He admits Reagan anti-communism lost relevance in the post-Cold War world, and supply side economics is spent in the current environment. Notwithstanding, Limbaugh says Reagan argued and history has shown "that America does best when it is true to its *original idea* [emphasis mine]. It does best when its people are left free to work in their individual self-interest—not meant in the sense of being selfish, but in the sense that they are left free to work to improve their own lives and the lives of their families, and for the good of their communities and of the nation at large."

He tells Republicans to seek a reformulation along old lines about individual liberty and freedom. He further defines what the Party should be by negative reference to what it should not be. That is, he says there is no such thing as "big-government conservatism," thereby castigating the neoconservative wing and most of eight years of economic and regulatory policy under George W. Bush. Limbaugh is trying to breathe new life into the GOP by redirecting its energies, its younger candidates and its platform to the cause of limited government. Whether states rights and federalism are a prominent part of this "original idea" to which he alludes is implied, though less clear. We are nevertheless witnessing a classic morphing process ongoing inside a national party that went through significant electoral defeat in 2008.

Indeed, various stripes of conservatism and libertarianism are coalescing within the Republican Party towards the firm fixed idea of limited government, Founders-style. The Ron Paul movement has broken way out of bounds from the growing fan club built around a single individual to a nascent political movement called Campaign For Liberty built upon specific and well-developed *Pauline* ideas. While C4L affects both political parties, its impetus is likely to force advocates out of the party advocating new and bigger New Deal approaches to the party that intelligently mounts opposition. Of course it remains to be seen if that will be Republican Party. After all, the last major political party and national coalition to disappear in American politics was the Whig Party. Whigs ostensibly comprised the conservative party of their time too, at least before 1854. While it is generally conceded the rising Republican Party in the North was a beneficiary of the Whigs' demise, Whigs also reinforced the constitutional and cultural conservatism of the South.

It is possible that conservative voices are the most likely to abandon liberalizing coalitions, as opposed to liberal voices saying goodbye to conservative ones. If for no other reason than that change is usually most pronounced in liberal coalitions, and liberal positions are more tolerant of the quantitative and qualitative gaps from whatever the new now is to whatever is conceived as the nation's "original idea." Conservatives don't normally brook the distance but instead keep returning.

Political Consensus Article #387
o/a February 27, 2009

Consensus is interesting, particularly when it comes to large and complex organizations and societies, as must be the case in politics. The idea that a political sovereignty moreover, whether a state or the entire country, could actually govern from the standpoint of general opinion and common agreement on anything—much less most things, this smacks one as being either absurd or hopelessly naïve. It is perhaps more likely to happen if it were a paternalistic island kingdom somewhere. Tonga is one thing, but a republic this size, or democracy rife with radical and free-floating individuals presumptuous enough to believe they rule themselves well, that's another. Yet this is the vision one hears enunciated, serious or not, concerning President Obama and his hope for governing the nation: the era of partisan bickering is over, the post-partisan era has begun. Baloney.

In point of fact, the Founders started that way too. There is absolutely no mention of political parties in the Constitution. It doesn't provide for one, two or a hundred political parties. It doesn't provide for any. If today purports to be the post-partisan era, theirs was pre-partisan. If we are trying to get beyond all of the bickering, the Founders were trying before the worst even got started. Consensus was always their hope, even if it were not their realistic expectation. The Founders believed it possible to govern with a virtual unanimity, but they were wont to admit it seemed very unlikely. George Washington was the one man whom all sides loved. His policies had few detractors in that most fledgling period of our history. Of course differences emerged over the course of his two terms in office, over economic and foreign policy, and limits on authority vested by the

Constitution. The short consensus gave way to rival factions, and yes to some pretty rancorous partisan bickering. Nevertheless, for years factions that rose up would eventually subside and give way, albeit to short periods of political consensus. The Era of Good Feelings after the War of 1812 is the most prominent and indeed aptly named example of such. It was no less real, even if Monroe's presidency belied fundamental transformations that led to sectional rivalry and deep animosity.

One imagines we could recreate the Era of Good Feelings today, say, after a War on Terror—using all the technological advantages at our disposal, and every element of national power. The president can hold teleconferences everyone, while people text their suggestions and opinions on how he is doing. Websites will tally results on-line, and feedback is but an email away. One wonders why we haven't gotten rid of the old Electoral College yet and those bothersome, messy state sovereignties too. Consensus can be measured as one mass electronic response to the power of the Bully Pulpit, confirmed too when approval ratings peg high enough during the speech. Elections four years from now are the people's only veto. In the meantime, organization is key to a new consensus.

If the administration is organized enough, the country is like a big cozy boardroom, with decisions implemented through the staff. The President and his cabinet, the President and Congress form partnerships and achieve synergy; after all, people do love their boss at the level of corporate headquarters. They respect him, and sometimes even like him. The fact is that he can withhold some of your paycheck, and this convinces some people to go the extra distance, even when their hearts aren't into the challenge. The Constitution well, is an incidental thing, more words of text on an old page far removed. People don't really read much anymore anyway, or understand what they read when they do. They don't listen very well either, or understand what they hear. We might blame it on public education but then again, the meaning of words is mostly fuzzy in or out of the public schools. No one holds anyone else accountable for what is said, least of all the person doing the talking; and it's hard to take a liar to task when you never understood the meaning of what he said—the meaning inherent in the words he spoke, or the textual definition of words in context. Perjury becomes tricky business, and there are many contracts nobody understands and implicitly, quite a few people running around who agreed to something who aren't quite sure what. Political consensus is an agreement like that amongst many.

Granted, it's good to hear someone speaking in complete sentences, who evinces serious thought and sophistication about the economy and foreign policy. Thank you President Obama for that. But getting back to words, as you certainly do have a way with them, what exactly did you mean in your speech before the joint session of Congress on 24 February? You said you *told* "mayors and governors across the country, that they will be held accountable by me [the president] and the American people for every dollar they spend," and you said you "appointed a proven and aggressive Inspector General to ferret out any and all cases of waste and fraud." That must be the proverbial stick and not a bad technique. It took Governor Rick Perry one day to come to his senses after a redoubtable rhetorical performance. Just one day after talking about the dangers of accepting stimulus funds, he wrote the president saying, "We (Texans) will accept the funds." It might be considered a carrot, except that there is something more than meets the eye to the Bully Pulpit when resistance to it exerts such irresistible political pressure to conform to word from the top. Never mind that state governors never were and never are "accountable" to the president of the United States or to all the people, but only to the people of the sovereign states who elected them. Dangling stimulus funds turns out to be another political stick of sorts—a form of extortion: if you want any of your state's money back, take it with strings attached.

What exactly did you mean, Mr. President, when you said the banks would be held accountable by the federal government, not only for taxpayer assistance voluntarily accepted by them, but also for times "when we learn that a major bank has serious problems . . . ."? Or when you decide, however you do that, to "force the necessary adjustments . . . ."? So the president asked Congress to join him "in doing whatever proves necessary." Talk about an open-ended commitment, not to war but to power. It makes sense only if you believe, as President Obama does, that "Government/government" has the leading role in "laying the foundation for our common prosperity." Quitting high school is out of the question, because you wouldn't want to quit on your country, now would you?

U.S. Government Quitting on Itself — Article #388
o/a March 06, 2009

These are anxious times, teetering on a proverbial edge towards dreamlike fall to something and somewhere else. President Obama has frequently characterized this as a "critical moment," and I do tend to agree. The difference is that I do not want to teeter us off into an abyss of socialism, but rather to roll us back gently from it. American history hasn't been so bad after all, and freemen and free markets have never substantially failed and have certainly never quit this country, no matter what else may have gone wrong. On the contrary, it is the country's Government that appears ready to quit on itself, but this would be a singular tragedy with irreversible consequences for the world.

According to Professor Donald Kagan of Yale, historian and subject matter expert on Western Civilization, all law and indeed every constitution rests ultimately on force. If the citizen will pause to think about it, he knows it is true even for ours. It is only by granting a monopoly or near monopoly on the use of force, normally through the aegis of government, that civilized and orderly, and indeed *modern* life is made possible. That's what the president and congressmen, policemen and soldiers in our system, are all about. Nevertheless from the standpoint of justice not all regimes are alike or equal.

A tyrant will make laws, maybe even some good ones. He will induce stability and room perhaps for the favored few or favored class to thrive. The majority who mind their corners may even find in them a modicum of freedom, or at least comfort there.

"Stay out of politics" is a wise saying in many parts of the world where strong leaders rule and a single party controls things. If one does this, he may live longer and prosper more on crumbs. In general, however, based on the most ancient American criterion of freedom, only those constitutions that rest on the freely expressed consent of the people, responsibly its citizens are legitimate.

Today as in the time of Socrates in Athens, citizens are free to question the law and to try and change it by legal means, free indeed to leave their country without penalty if they find it offensive. In the meantime we have a moral obligation to peace and to obey the law, however little we may like it. To the point, at least, according to the Declaration of Independence, when Government becomes destructive of the ends to which it has been justly established. This is the point at which the Government quits itself, and the people in order to remain free must alter or abolish their Government and institute a new one.

It is similar to the idea of changing political affiliations when and if the party you belonged to radically changes its platform in key respects.

You didn't leave that party, but rather the party left you; and likewise, it is possible though more difficult and rare for the Government to so debase the Constitution and its founding traditions that it may no longer be truly called the Government of the United States of America.

There will be turbulent markets. The market has had negative returns in 23 of the last 82 years. If you're 50 years old, you've lived through 9 recessions (it's not called a business *cycle* for nothing). Moreover, the process of globalization, which is ongoing, has over the past 20 years ushered in seismic changes to the economic landscape worldwide. That being said, Government as such ought to remain consistent to its purpose and its core animating principles. The same rights it secures according to the Constitution are the rights that must be secured in good times and in bad. Indeed, the stronger the challenge facing us, the more have the people counted on leaders in the Government to serve with integrity and be that steady anchor and not to throw everything to the whirlwind. That's why we have elections as scheduled, in peace and in war. That's why taxation without representation is never allowed and always a call to arms.

If King George III in effect justified the American Revolution for having "combined with others to subject us to a jurisdiction foreign to our constitution, and unacknowledged by our laws; giving his Assent to their Acts of pretended Legislation . . ." then presumably the Chief Executive who does the same today runs the same risk. Borrowing terminology Star Parker has used, president Obama seems intent on moving everyone onto Uncle Sam's Plantation. I'm sure Uncle Sam will be a benevolent master, but while we have the choice we may think twice. Parker writes, "Americans can accept Barack Obama's invitation to move onto the plantation. Or they can choose personal responsibility and freedom."

In point of fact, the American people can choose much else besides—and they have the political tradition of doing so whenever the Government quits on itself. Yet citizens shouldn't have to, when as Kagan explains, they want and "they need leaders who understand that individual freedom, self-government, and equality before the law are of the highest value . . . . And they especially need leaders with the talents to persuade their impatient citizens that these political institutions are the necessary first foundation for a decent regime and a good life for all." The exigency of the moment, critical or otherwise, demands no less.

The Way We Were — Article #433
o/a December 10, 2009

People need a sense of who they are, in order to look out for their interests and those whom they serve. If it doesn't really matter, or if one is simply unable to distinguish preferences, then money from a paycheck, resources, opportunities, public and private benefits, as well as physical security may as well go to someone or anyone else. Typically when one goes shopping at the grocery store, he or she brings the food home. Whether one thinks about it or not, one acts out on a clear preference and moral imperative. If a man goes shopping but then takes the food and pearls over to his mistress, instead of to his wife and children, he commits something of a fraud and terrible betrayal. It is a responsibility and altogether appropriate as such, to favor those whom we love and especially those who may depend upon us because of our love and duty incumbent. A country is not exactly the same thing as family, but we typically do call upon our leaders to prefer their own and to know the difference.

One year into this current administration, we seem to be moving headlong into a storm and also losing our sense of being American. From an historic standpoint, the sense of being American involves what is called American *exceptionalism*, a feeling and philosophy of being uniquely blessed by Providence and having a special place on His green earth—as well as a definite role or mission to fulfill, in becoming an example for mankind and womankind to see. The example moreover entails something else besides material wealth or technological and military prowess. It is supposed to be an example of Liberty and Virtue entwined, enabling what the Pilgrim Fathers called 'a shining city on a hill' to emerge (itself a Biblical allusion). Symbolically the torch of Lady Liberty was never intended to be a beacon drawing things out of the darkness to our shores, but rather a lamp radiating light into the dark recesses of the world, where other people inhabit—an example for the rest of the world to follow.

To pursue this model, however, we would have to recognize a difference between "them" and us, a simple distinction of place, station and affiliation, not moral worth. Somehow we have got things crisscrossed of late, and our light as a nation dims because of it. When asked about American exceptionalism on visits abroad last year, the American president answered that we Americans think we are exceptional, just like the British and Greeks and peoples of 189 other countries do. In other words, we are not that special, in any other sense than the most subjective or parochial point of view. Obama has consistently sought to raise us above narrow partisan patriotism, above our clinging to 'guns and religion' and anything else we have traditionally valued. He aims to raise us above our country too, if not above the world, and straight to him. Accordingly, Americans happen to inhabit a place on earth. They happened to establish a free society and create more wealth than others. Americans are, if anything, singularly lucky truth be known to have survived the last few centuries. The United States has a lot to learn and a lot to borrow from others, in order to make it better and make our country a more humane place. America comprises no place or people the president necessarily prefers, if given an objective opportunity.

Last fall Americans were shocked to find schoolchildren being taught songs of praise to Obama in places where Christmas carols are no longer allowed to be sung. In Indonesia the United States Ambassador presents 2-meter-tall statues made in the likeness of a 10-year-old Obama to schoolchildren there. The ceremony and official token convey the administration's "Change" message and fill the children with hope, because as the Mayor of Jakarta puts it, this statue represents childhood spirit and Obama's image "embodies the ideal of a successful child." Americans used to think the Christ Child did. For many generations American parents have told stories to their children about George Washington as a little boy, and his impressive display of honesty, including the time he admitted that it was he who cut down the cherry tree. Americans never made of him a graven image, however, or tried to put him in the place of God. They never dreamt to do it during his lifetime, as Washington never would have allowed it. If you hadn't noticed, however, we live in a post-modern post-Christian world, increasingly also post-American. It hardly seems worth mention, but what passes for post-this and post-that reflects little more than a change of affiliation in your minds. We are being brainwashed pure and simple, our limbs tied by invisible bands of nothing.

So if it matters anymore to be an American, consider this a wakeup call near midnight. Start to draw some distinctions: puppies and hyenas are not the same specie; and baby crocs and lizards look alike only for a season. George Washington and Chaka Zulu were leaders of an entirely different sort too! Now I am all too familiar with the pitfalls of divisive and polarizing thoughts and language, particularly if drawn to extremes or given to racism, and fed to lab rats three times a day for years at a time.

It is not my intention to divide us Americans, but to make all Americans of whatever color and background more self-aware. The world is not a pretty or nice place. Americans are very much the exception far and wide from the rest of the world. If we are still capable of fathoming "intelligent design" or grasping at faith less than the size of a mustard seed, it may dawn upon our minds the Reason why and also why it matters.

Leadership is an amoral term after all. It is about moving people away from where they are toward some new goal set by the leader. The ancient visionary goal was about Life, Liberty and the Pursuit of Happiness, which led Americans once upon a time (and of all the people on earth) to form "a more perfect Union" under the strictures of a marvelous Constitution. The brave Americans way back when knew who the British were, and also the Indians. Above all else they knew who they were.

The West and Who We Are Article #434
o/a December 10, 2009

Some years ago when I ran for office, I found to my surprise that many people, even those who participate in serious discussions and usually vote, don't really understand basic terminology in politics. Many educated and intelligent folk have a fuzzy notion of what it means to be conservative or liberal, right, left or in the middle. The more uncertain they are, the more likely they just say they're independent or undecided. A majority finds it hard to distinguish a party platform from administration policy or political philosophy that lay behind at least some of it. Few venture a guess at connections between faith and freedom; freedom and religion; freedom and capitalism; war and liberty; and more.

An elderly gentleman once asked me how someone could be pro-life and pro-guns at the same time. A little girl during a parade cried for "faith and freedom" like it were candy (she had apparently missed getting hers). It's okay though. Many of those same people are experts in other fields, as well as good and conscientious people who work for a living, take care of their families, and pay taxes. Not only that, but some of them will dabble so much or often in politics, that they will eventually master the art and mystery of answering stupid questions with sufficient political obfuscation to be thought well of. (Everybody hates a politician, but everyone loves the statesman).

Seriously most members of the Great American Public (GAP) are just looking for someone they can trust with the unfortunate details and associated headaches involved with politics. But then, there's the rub: it seems to be a hard thing to find someone these days both competent in terms of what you're looking for, and also trustworthy. Character anyone? Rocky Balboa had character, but we might need a little more than that. The congressman who hid 90,000 bucks of "cold cash" in his freezer may have been pretty smart, but he sure wasn't honest. Teddy Roosevelt used to joke that, "When the roll is called in the Senate, the Senators don't know whether to respond 'present' or 'not guilty.'" A few successful businesspeople, doctors and soldiers are in politics but not very many and not nearly enough.

What the GAP doesn't realize is that it depends upon them to do the recruiting and to even apply for some of those positions that come open, even if it means on-the-job-training (OJT). There's simply no Human Resources (HR) department in the country for political office, and the established political parties are doing a lousy job. The political class has shown itself to be imbecilic or criminal, and this is not a true reflection of who we are. The Founders envisioned a filtration of talent to occur, such that, those who were elected to serve the public would be the best from amongst the public—i.e., a successful planter or businessperson, a respected lawyer or judge, an accomplished surveyor, writer, musician, scientist, plumber, whatever. Today we seem to have left that field to charlatans and charity cases. We have entrusted our present earnings and the wealth of Posterity *on our watch*, to profligate spenders and tax-addicted money hounds.

Folks this needs to stop. The future of our country and possibly the entire West depends upon it. Oh, sorry. You may need to be reminded of what the West is, since Western Civilization, a.k.a. "Civ" courses have been scrapped from the curricula in so many places. So here's a little lesson according to Professor Victor Davis Hanson, Distinguished Fellow in History at Hillsdale College. By the West "we refer to the culture that originated in Greece, spread to Rome, permeated Northern Europe, was incorporated by the Anglo-Saxon tradition, spread through British expansionism, and is associated today primarily with Europe, the United States, and the former commonwealth countries of Britain—as well as, to some extent, nations like Taiwan, Japan, and South Korea, which have incorporated some Western ideas." What are Western ideas? "They include a commitment to constitutional or limited government, freedom of the individual, religious freedom in a sense that precludes religious tyranny, respect for property rights, faith in free markets, and an openness to rationalism or to the explanation of natural phenomena through reason."

The United States is today the chief agent and most successful example of Western Civilization ever, but also nearly the only one left. It is who we are. I say again, the future of our country and possibly the entire West depends upon our being able to change out this awful political class and to fill political vacancies (which may describe most incumbents) with competent men and women of character, who will come out from among the GAP to fill the gap or proverbial breach in the dike. Every election is in fact a new job announcement, and the job is open to anyone who wants to apply. This is where an allusion to Rocky and to boxing may be the right one. Campaigning isn't the typical job interview, and politics isn't for the faint of heart, but neither is scuba diving, driving trucks, or following the south end of northbound cattle. Something about the south end of northbound cattle reminds me of most politicians, but I yield to the distinguished Gentleman or Gentlewoman of the West. Thank you for making the trip.

2010 Debate in GOP Determines Future of the Country
o/a January 28, 2010 Article #435

On January 20, 2010 Massachusetts elected a Republican to the U.S. Senate, indeed to the same seat once held by Democrat "Lion of the Senate" Ted Kennedy—this after exactly one year of failed *Obamanomics*. The special election result amounted to a political earthquake, which shook the Democrat Party, gave the GOP some hope for prospects in November, and validated the populist grassroots nature of the Tea Party movement. On the policy front, Scott Brown's election from the bluest state in New England had national implications: it stopped the healthcare/health insurance reform effort in its tracks, at least temporarily. Nobody but nobody likes the Senate or the House versions of the bill as currently proposed, as they appear loaded with everything but common sense.

One week later, however, the president delivered a surprisingly tough State of the Union Address. In his speech, he lectured the Republicans and bucked up the Democrats, but also rededicated himself and America supposedly to his entire Progressive agenda. Having thrown a 12 to 40 percent budget increase into various government agencies already, he decided that it is time to call for a spending freeze . . . uh, next year. The spending freeze of course won't affect defense, Medicaid/Medicare or Social Security. Moreover, he wants to beat that freeze as it were, by spending hundreds of billions of dollars more for a "Jobs Bill" this year, which really amounts to a second stimulus bill called by another name. He also expressed his intent to end tax cuts put in place by President Bush, at the same time he promises punitive financial measures on banks, which aren't lending very much now as it is.

The logic of all this causes one to scratch his head or else accept the obvious, which is that the measures the president proposes lead to economic ruin; to future generations being saddled—nay, more accurately *bridled* by debt; and to socialist despair and equal poverty for everyone. The president will either go down in history as the most economically devastating the nation has endured since Hoover, or else the people will respond to the political emergency and quite apart from handling any financial crisis, seal his fate in the election of 2012 as a one-term wonder.

Meanwhile the outlines of political debate are taking shape on the Republican side. Two important books will be released this spring, which present the major outlines of intellectual argument for what to do on the right. One or the other approach for the country (or perhaps some hybrid of the two) will guide organized opposition to the administration for the next three years and potentially set the parameters for governance in the future. If as expected the GOP rebounds in 2010 and 2012 and perhaps comes into majority, the importance of the intellectual debate this season becomes clear. Every citizen and certainly every Tea Party activist needs to become conversant in the dialog. Ideas truly do have consequences.

The first book is called *Courage and Consequence* by former top White House Aide Karl Rove. It is a memoir and, as might be expected, provides a vigorous defense of the George W. Bush/Dick Cheney years in office. More importantly, the book serves not only to justify its policies but also to rearticulate and repackage operative neoconservative governing principles and philosophy, which guided that Administration.

The second book is *Bringing America Home: How America Lost Her Way and How We Can Find Our Way Back* (Rockford, Illinois: Chronicles Press, 2010) by Tom Pauken, who served on President Reagan's White House staff and who is currently the Chairman of the Texas Workforce Commission appointed by Governor Perry. As the title reveals, his is a virtual point/counterpoint to Rove. Pauken rejects "Big Government Conservatism" and argues strenuously for return to limited government free market solutions, as well as to strict interpretation of the Constitution including its inherent structure of federalism and states rights. He rearticulates and repackages the traditional or *paleo*conservative governing principles and philosophy.

Rove takes a more elitist "subject matter expert" approach and never shies from implementing optimal solutions using the coercive power of the federal government; whereas, Pauken takes a discernibly grassroots approach, which in effect embraces and potentially co-opts the resurgent populist impulse characteristic of town hall meetings and tea party rallies since Obama tried to socialize America. All around the country in 2010, the Republicans are fighting a critical internal battle for the soul and future of that political party. The populist Jeffersonian type may seem to have an upper hand after the GOP's electoral defeat in 2008, but neoconservatives are fighting an end-run to hold on to the levers of power and continue influence in the Republican Party until they can take advantage of the inevitable disenchantment with Obama. It may be that this debate in 2010 will determine more than anything what Republicans look like in 2012, with critical implications for the future of the country if Obama gets tossed out on his ear.

Big Government Conservatism Is an Oxymoron Article #439
o/a February 26, 2010

So reads the title of the third chapter in Tom Pauken's *Bringing America Home*. Pauken chronicles how Nixon/Ford retreads had begun to reassert influence over the Republican Party during the single term of George Herbert Walker Bush after Ronald Reagan left office. Dominance of a big business, "corporate liberal" elite grew during George W. Bush's two terms in office. Worse, while the elder Bush held by and large to a realistic, balanced, and security-driven approach to international relations, a coterie of former liberal Democrats who joined the Republican Party in the late 1970s literally began running American foreign policy in the aftermath of 9/11. These neoconservatives believed in global democratic revolution, as well as preemptive and indefinite warfare to accomplish that aim.

Many were former Marxists, who transformed their communist paradigm into a similarly utopian vision for imposing democracy everywhere. If one searches for an American precursor, one may fairly conclude that it is Wilsonian. It is therefore true that progressivism had reentered the Republican Party even before the more recent emanations so apparent in the Democrat Party. By the time George W. Bush left office, a Big Government domestic crowd and a Big Government military-expansionist crowd had virtually assured runaway spending and the near financial collapse. President Obama really did inherit a mess, notwithstanding his penchant for making things worse.

The Republican Party is still digging out from shambles, but it was never the conservative principles of Goldwater/Reagan that failed. Pauken opines the Republican Party must reassert basic conservative principles, not only to do well in the next election but in fact to save the country. The past, à la Goldwater and Reagan offer salient policy positions for a course correction, as do recently popular libertarian-conservative expounders of limited government and constitutional conservatism, such as Ron Paul. Paul supporters were instrumental in igniting the Tea Party movement. Paul may even be this generation's Goldwater in terms of being the intellectual progenitor, giving rise to a fresh articulation of conservative principles and to future realization of conservative political ascendancy. How soon that ascendancy happens depends as much on what the Democrats do as Republicans, and also on how bad things get.

Pauken points out what is now widely understood across conservative ranks, that "Federal spending and unfunded federal mandates on state and local governments are completely out of control." He then asks rhetorically, "Is there any hope whatsoever that a true federalist could actually get elected president, reduce the growth of federal spending, and return power to the states, local communities, and the people?" Sadly the question is now unanswerable, because it may depend on what emerges from the shambles of the Republican Party and whether the GOP rediscovers its conservative root. It depends as well, as it always does, on the people—whether they give in to having stirrups at their sides, and saddles cinched to their backs and Big Government riding herd.

According to Pauken, "The Republican Party of Barry Goldwater and Ronald Reagan was a conservative party of limited government. That all changed in the post-Reagan era of Republican politics." During the first eight years this century, Republicans came to embrace big government conservatism, but this had more in common with the New Deal of

Franklin Roosevelt or the Great Society of Lyndon B. Johnson than with the conservative philosophy of Goldwater and Reagan.

Neoconservative Fred Barnes lauded George W. Bush for pursuing conservative ends by traditionally liberal means, a.k.a. activist government. Barnes noted that neoconservative Republicans were favorably disposed towards a conservative welfare state. As Pauken sums it up, "A cynic might suggest that what Barnes was really saying was that there is nothing wrong with big government so long as 'our guys' are in charge." Of course from the standpoint of the economy, big government conservatism still bankrupts the country and stifles recovery. From the standpoint of liberty it matters only by degree, if one master happens to be more benevolent than another. From the standpoint of the Constitution, however, it matters not one whit.

Destruction of American Middle Class Possible Within a Decade
o/a March 05, 2010 Article #440

In his book, *Bringing America Home* Tom Pauken covers many varied topics ranging from the economy and foreign policy, to politics and culture. As the book's sub-title, *How America Lost Her Way and How We Can Find Our Way Back* suggests, it offers a veritable platform for guiding these United States back safely as it were, through crisis and challenges, by implementing a series of common sense and *traditional* conservative policies. One chapter in particular makes the book entirely worthwhile, even if one reads nothing else. Namely, Chapter 5 details the ongoing destruction of the American Middle Class through both poorly devised economic policies and outright failure of political leadership in Washington.

Unlike many on the Republican side, Pauken is not a mouthpiece for big business or the corporate elite. His sentiments are with populist Main Street, admitting what many liberals have sounded from the hills for quite some time, that the rich are indeed getting richer while the Middle Class grows poor. His solution is not a resort to socialism or to government takeover, however, but a return to free market capitalism and to limited constitutional government run in the interest of Americans. Pauken explains that what has caused existential inequality, as well as the hardship on the Middle Class is not free market capitalism but a corrupted form or crony capitalism. It is the self-serving alliance between Big Government and Big Business, and between the corresponding drives for both power and profit.

Pauken is highly critical of the lack of business ethics and humanity evinced by modern American business practice. Some in business at the highest levels of management raid their own corporate assets for personal gain and pass off the wreckage to others. Similar behavior gave rise to the recent housing bubble that burst and to instability in what amounts to a "bubble economy," with originators of loans and mortgages deliberately and sometimes deceitfully evading responsibility for risky financial behavior. The business culture in this respect mirrors a decline in standards of morality throughout the broader culture. For all the obscene bonuses and exploitive practices on Wall Street, however, these do not explain why manufacturing jobs have left or why real income for the Middle Class has shrunk.

According to Pauken, "A central reason for . . . [the] huge trade deficits and the shift of economic power from Main Street to Wall Street is a business tax system that gives private-equity moguls incentives to take such risks with the companies they control." They have an advantage over U.S. company owners who might otherwise run businesses in a conservative fashion. Simply stated, business debt is encouraged because it can be written off on taxes, whereas the 35% corporate tax rate discourages business savings and investment. Except for the U.S., every major trading country in the world provides tax advantages for domestic manufacturers. Information technology companies are outsourcing now at an alarming rate for a similar reason.

Moreover, U.S. goods shipped overseas carry an average added 18% tax burden compared with most foreign competitors, and this keeps trade deficits widening every year. According to Warren Buffet, the trade deficit is possibly of greater worry than the budget deficit or consumer debt burden near-term, because we have to borrow from other countries to finance it. The annual account deficit is now more than $800 billion. The politically chic idea that the U.S. would somehow sustain its quality of life for the Middle Class while giving up its manufacturing base and transforming into the world's premier 'knowledge-based economy' was a sheer fantasy. The competitive global environment and rampant trend towards American outsourcing has gone on unabated and continues, while elective politicians mouth empty promises and defend a principle of "free trade" amidst the uneven playing field and structural disadvantages created by America's own stupid business tax system.

Americans are clinging to their Middle Class status, living paycheck to paycheck, mired in consumer debt and finding it difficult to find good jobs or to work the requisite number of hours needed to pay their bills. Meanwhile Pauken says, "We are passing out money we do not have through a Keynesian stimulus package designed to revive the economy." Moody's has declared the United States runs the risk of losing its triple-A credit rating within a decade if the federal government does not bring soaring levels of spending down. Imagine what this will mean if the U.S. has to finance its debt at dramatically higher interest rates owing to the loss of most favored bond rating status!

In part it was this sobering recognition, which led Jim Bunning (R-KY) to bravely though ineffectually remind his colleagues in the Senate that even unemployment benefits have to be paid for. Lawmakers couldn't find the $10 billion to do so. The annual budget deficit is running $1.35 *trillion* this year, and the national debt topped $12 *trillion* and is set to double in less than ten years—and when it does the U.S. will lose its triple-A credit rating. One economist remarked that America today resembles less the developed economic superpower we have come to think of, and more like something of an emerging market having both a weak currency and huge deficits. America is headed for the perfect economic storm, as well as destruction of its vaunted Middle Class inside the decade unless we reverse track resolutely and swiftly.

National Guard or States Must Halt Mexican Border Reivers
o/a April 01, 2010 Article #444

In Anglo-Scottish history, border reivers were members of families and clans that lived along the border region of northern England and Lowland Scotland and participated in cross-border raids. The historian George MacDonald Fraser tells us that, while young Shakespeare was writing wonderful plays, respective monarchs in both England and Scotland ruled in two mostly secure kingdoms. Their kingdoms were nevertheless separated by a "narrow hill land between . . . dominated by the lance and the sword." The area between kingdoms, i.e., the border region was often violent. Indeed borders tend to separate distinct nations and peoples almost by definition. While political lines now and again might be established in an arbitrary, gray, ambiguous, disputed fashion, in the case of nation-state borders along identifiable geographic features, say, like the Rio Grande River, well it's pretty darn clear in any language.

Political lines separate much more than sovereignty and law, which some still regard as matters of high importance, by the way—they also separate differences involving race, religion, culture, custom, language, worldview and economy. No doubt it's great to vacation south of the border if you're gringo and north of the border if you're Mexican. It's exciting and frequently profitable to conduct business and trade involving mixed labor forces, as well as the import/export of goods and services. Exchange rates at banks allow you to collect and spend your dollars in pesos or your pesos in dollars. The scholar and future historian will marvel from a safe distance, at how energetic and talented both sides of any given border really are!

Yet borders represent lines of demarcation twixt sides involved in competitive interaction, if indeed they interact at all. If left uncontrolled, border regions are tense, uncomfortable places where each side potentially poses a threat to the other. If borders are left unsecured or under-secured, large differences between the sides inevitably lead to violence. A primary purpose of any government is to secure its borders therefore, and it is impossible to overstate the level of gross negligence and malfeasance on the part of the American federal government in terms of insecurity along the U.S.-Mexican border.

Robert Krentz, a third generation Arizona rancher was recently gunned down on his own property by an illegal alien. While the incident touched off renewed calls for National Guard troops to secure the U.S. southern border, few politicians connect the dots or bother to bring up the fact that literally thousands of murders occur each year that are committed by illegal aliens in this country, including some of the most vicious sex crimes. Moreover, overcrowded state and federal prisons are stuffed full of illegals—literally one-third of the entire prison population are illegal aliens. The liberal solution is to abolish borders and legalize "undocumented" immigrants, and then give them Obamacare at taxpayer expense. Liberals say the sweetest stupid things (hey, if the amber waves of grain are set ablaze, at least the night sky looks pretty). Progressives in the administration and Democrat party in Congress are pusillanimous petty tyrants who, like Nero fiddle while American cities burn and ranchers in fly-over country lay dead.

What is needed is the political will now to employ the technology, men and equipment needed to keep illegals out and to use deadly force if necessary. If the federal government will not militarize the border, states can and must take independent action and enlist assistance of local militias and citizen groups if deemed expedient. State borders are every bit as sovereign as federal borders. Failure to take responsibility for action at one level of government is no excuse for another level of government to be as inept. Indeed failure at one level of government, in this case the federal government, may necessitate interposition by states. The use of the National Guard for defense and protection of the state and national borders is not a local law enforcement issue and does not pertain to state internal policing per se, so this could be done by Congress in full respect of the post-Reconstruction Posse Comitatus Act of 1878.

Senator John McCain too has changed his mind on the point, largely because the situation along the border has worsened so badly over the past ten years—and because he faces a conservative primary challenge in his bid for reelection. He did not originally support use of National Guard troops along the border, apparently favoring their extensive use abroad instead, as an active element in the United States armed forces. Since Krentz's murder, however, he has joined Arizona's state governor in a formal request to President Obama for National Guard troops to be stationed in the State of Arizona to defend its border. More reliable conservatives have called for this for years. In his new book *Bringing America Home* (2010), Tom Pauken not only calls for the National Guard to be used in securing borders, he also addresses the importance of rewriting immigration laws to restrict immigration from countries with predominantly Islamic populations. He simply states the obvious, which escapes most federal bureaucrats in Washington, and that is, that "our own national interests should be our highest priority." That's true in foreign policy or domestic policy, and whether or not the Mexican president or Osama bin Laden likes it very much.

States, however, do not have to rely on Congress for protection. For the Founders, the militia arose from the original *posse comitatus*, that is, as constituting the whole people or citizenry—in practical terms, all those who might receive an official message and answer the call; and thus attendant, to constitute a constabulary. The idea of *posse comitatus* embodies the Anglo-American idea that the citizenry is the best enforcer of the law. At state level it may be recurred to whenever the federal government shirks its duty or fails in its responsibility to secure borders. At state level it must be recurred to today, in order to repel invasion and put down border reivers crossing from the south.

Government Spending: Americans on the Titanic Article #447
o/a April 09, 2010

It is amazing how observable circumstances can produce varying opinions about what to do. If two people agree on a problem, they may nevertheless disagree on a prescriptive solution. For instance, author Don Peck says that unemployment and social problems attributable to joblessness are likely to persist for years. I happen to agree that recovery may be slow, and the impact of sustained chronic unemployment is corrosive on society. Peck says we have a civic and moral responsibility to do everything in our power to stop the economic hardship on the unemployed and the underemployed. He believes our bias should be towards doing too much in terms of government stimulus and intervention, rather than too little. He concludes that paying higher taxes in the future involves a "trade worth making." Well, I think he's nuts. Paying the piper may be the least we can do.

The call is also very familiar. Crisis begets extreme measures and the inevitable justification for still more government control and less individual freedom. It sounds impractical and darkly romantic, but I would rather die free by the viaduct, than live as a slave on the expropriated largesse *stolen* by the government from hardworking fellow taxpayers—receiving a government check, living in government quarters, working the government job, going to a government provided doctor. I'm not talking about military life. I've been there, and the context is unique and special and at any rate provided for in the Constitution. What I'm talking about is the inexcusable transformation of civil society into a quasi-military environment. I'm talking about the Imperial Presidency; about the semblance of Parliamentary supremacy coming from a corrupt Congress; about living legislation emanating from the Bench—all in contravention to the will of the People and terms of the United States Constitution. I'm talking about the end of the Republic, if we don't come together and get it right in 2010 and 2012. The rhetoric may sound shrill to you.

Then listen to what the experts are saying. Last month the Congressional Budget Office Director, Douglas Elmendorf said that U.S. fiscal policy, as "a matter of arithmetic" is simply not sustainable.

Further, he said fixing the problem requires fundamental changes not just tinkering at the margins. That's a nice way of saying that revenues aren't even close to keeping up with all the wild spending. Metaphorically if you're paddling a boat, you're about to get swamped by the next wave. Federal Reserve Chairman, Ben Bernanke likewise sounded an alarm over America's growing and unsustainable debt level. He counseled that big changes are needed soon, in order to reduce the deficit—either higher taxes or the reduction in America's most cherished entitlement programs. So we've finally come to this: sacrifice the golden goose, or—as so-called "realistic" liberal ideologues would have it, raise taxes to save our country! Just swallow hard and do your civic duty. If you ask me, that kind of civic duty is a total crock.

The darling answer for many a Progressive is the Value Added Tax (V.A.T). Lots of countries have it. It's a tax on consumption aimed mostly at businesses and it requires a considerable government accounting mechanism. Nevertheless, it is sure to bring in hundreds of billions of dollars more in revenue to the government. The problem is that every country in the world that has enacted the V.A.T. has never achieved one iota of fiscal discipline. Quite the opposite: what they have done instead is to extend their social netting even further, as well as to enlarge the government apparatus. There is absolutely no reason or empirical basis whatsoever to believe the U.S. Congress or President will rein in spending or use the money to pay down debt. There is every reason to believe they will as quickly relapse, like hopeless food addicts at a pastry shop. Metaphorically if we're aboard the Titanic as Elmendorf and Bernanke suggest, despite their warnings we're headed for an iceberg, at least with this crew in charge.

The only hope we have is to radically change government by ousting the political class at the helm—by repealing Congress in 2010 and Obama in 2012. We have to replace Big Brother profligate spenders with frugal accountable servants, who respect the U.S. Constitution and who are willing to stay within the bounds of enumerated constitutional powers. What we need are representatives and elected officials who are not beholden to special interests, men and women of integrity. We dare not vote to raise taxes or enact a V.A.T., because our better judgment tells us that what is missing most of all from government is plain honesty and integrity—higher taxes won't solve anything. Even if they could, we can't trust those politicians who tell us they would use taxes to pay down and keep down the annual deficits or national debt. Our political system is such anyway they can't bind their successors, so every precedent grows the government. New powers to tax inevitably become new powers to destroy American businesses and entrepreneurship. We don't need more would be tyrants to lord over us, but rather we need a few humble spirits to apply the military ethics of hard work and integrity to public office: to say what they mean, mean what they say, and most of all to *act* accordingly.

Subversive Role of Health Care in Progressive Agenda Article #449
o/a April 16, 2010

Progressivism has had episodic success in American history to the general detriment of constitutional government. Moreover, one cannot say it belongs to one political party more than the other, even if progressivism tends to be liberal and the Democrat party more liberal than Republicans. Prominent Republicans have spurred progressivism as much as Democrats. Indeed both major political parties while in the majority overreached the constitutional bounds of government; spent money we did not have; and woefully ignored the insecurity along our southern border. The Tea Party Movement as a political phenomenon attests to the failure of America's Two Party System in modern time.

Notwithstanding, both presidential candidate Hillary Clinton and President Obama invoked progressivism so explicitly, as to make it the Democrats' cause primarily in our immediate political context. President Obama imagines that he will shape American social and political policy in ways as substantive in terms of change, as the Progressive Era, the New Deal, and the Great Society put together. This fourth wave of progressivism, however, if it were to happen, would destroy these United States of America. It is on this basis I assert, that the combined effect of elections in 2010 and 2012 will determine whether we shall continue with the American Dream or give it up and become as European style socialist welfare states. We are in fact past a certain tipping point already, with sixty percent of American households receiving more government benefits and services as measured in dollars, than they pay back in taxes.

The estimates concerning the president's budget show that "net dependency" is actually increasing to around 70 percent. Coupled with the way in which the president has undercut U.S. leadership in space and promised unilaterally not to test nuclear weapons or to even use them if attacked, it is clear he has resigned us to second tier rank in terms of international power, at the same time his unsustainable budget deficits consign us to a third world future in terms of the economy. Health care is particularly essential to this president's misguided and subversive strategy.

Once implemented, i.e., once the government will have subsumed one-sixth of the economy devoted to health care, when this is combined with other public spending the government will have gained control of 50 percent of national production. We will have ceased being primarily a free market functioning economy. We will have achieved the progressive dream and killed the American Dream. When Congressman Phil Hare (D-IL) was questioned about his vote for the health care bill, he spouted out that he simply didn't care about the U.S. Constitution. What he cared for more, were all the poor people without health insurance who were dying! [Gag].

That's the same, largely disingenuous tactic progressives nearly always resort to: urging Americans to forget the hierarchy of a free society, in which the only Higher Law to the U.S. Constitution is God Himself. In the tearful name of universal humanitarian *compassion*, progressives would have you trade the U.S. Constitution or make it a Gumby-like "living" thing, in order to accommodate this or that centralized government program. As if natural sympathy for any real or alleged victim should justify violation of one's sacred oath to uphold and defend the U.S. Constitution! Men and women of more character recall that 'an officer on duty knows no one.'

If the Administration were truly interested in addressing problems with the healthcare system, it would have sought and obtained bipartisan support for rather modest and straightforward improvements. Congress could have ended unfair tax discrimination, whereby people who pay for their own healthcare aren't allowed the same tax deduction benefit as persons who have healthcare provided them by employers. High-risk insurance pools at state level could easily be implemented for those with pre-existing conditions, in order for them to get affordable coverage. Ending health care monopolies and letting people purchase health insurance across state lines would immediately drive costs down, just as it does for car insurance and other services. Establishing transparency in terms of costs and quality of care would empower consumers and provide the impetus for creative free market solutions.

Ah but there's the rub! The Administration and Democrat progressives in Congress are hardly interested in addressing problems with the healthcare system per se. Rather, the Government is interested in progressive policies that will be transformational of the entire system—that is to say, away from the U.S. Constitution and traditional concepts of liberty, towards a different model based on international codes and regimes and notions of freedom reached by the fleeting consensus of democratic majorities. The whole idea of the health care scam is to create another entitlement program and to push net dependency rate beyond a point of no return. The health care bill is so huge, its benefits so alluring, that Obama may yet achieve (*if the healthcare bill cannot be repealed*) his vision of personal grandeur and that of an American people utterly dependent on government benefits for nearly everything important. He will have cemented the welfare state beyond the reach of constitutional conservatives or the free market, forever.[18]

Public Lands Threat to Public Safety — Article #450
o/a April 16, 2010

One thing one discovers from searching old newspapers and website articles is that border violence is hardly something new. It may have gotten worse of late, but there really is no excuse for our government's failure to take effective action prior to this time. The U.S. Government's inaction and incompetence are materially responsible for the death recently of rancher Robert Krenz among others, not only because the Government knows about vulnerabilities in border security and has empirical evidence of violence on U.S. soil, but also because the illegal alien who murdered Krenz found easy entry and exit through U.S. public land. The Mexican gunman entered and subsequently escaped through the San Bernardino National Wildlife Refuge.

The stupidity of all this is mind-boggling, since a large portion of the border with Mexico involves U.S. Public Lands controlled by the Department of the Interior (DOI), and the DOI actually *prevents* the Border Patrol from performing essential security tasks on public lands, in favor of the flora and fauna! One can hike or have a picnic and possibly die from assault by illegals or a criminal drug gang, but the snakes and cactus are to remain quite undisturbed either by the tire tracks or noise created by U.S. Border Patrol vehicles. If and when the Border Patrol determines it is necessary in an emergency to enter public lands and conduct operations, it has to pay millions to the DOI for the privilege to mitigate environmental damage.

Not only does the Federal Government extort money from the States, apparently federal agencies extort large sums of taxpayer money from each other too—regardless of priority of mission. Even after 9/11 the Homeland Security bureaucracy has proven inept at energizing the Executive Administration or Members of Congress, to prevent the various land laws, Wilderness Act, and Endangered Species Act from essentially trumping border security operations. The federal lands along the border—mostly in California, Arizona and New Mexico—equate to over 600 linear miles administered by some 9 different agencies. They offer what amounts to an unpatrolled highway for criminals, smugglers, drug gangs, human traffickers and potential terrorists—some coming all the way from Mexico's unsecured southern border with Guatemala.

During the Cold War, the U.S. Achilles Heel that is our southern border was at least more appreciated. Foreign policy initiatives with South American regimes were designed to enforce internal and border security and keep violent communists and terrorists out of Mexico and the United States. Today an increasing number of South American states have far leftwing regimes and are overtly anti-American. Moreover, drug cartels have gained influence and so have undermined law enforcement measures in South America and Mexico. Our border to put it bluntly is a sieve, and thousands of criminals cross over daily—doing so with impressive armed security of their own, frequently retreating to retrieve more waiting shipments of drugs, guns, and increasingly desperate people.

It has gotten so bad that some criminals don't retreat but are farming vast tracks on public lands far from the border region. Mexican drug gangs have in fact commandeered U.S. public land for growing marijuana, including at the Sequoia National Forest not far from Yosemite's waterfalls. Law enforcement officials have discovered similar hidden farms tied to Mexican drug gangs, on remote public lands in Texas and Nevada, and surprisingly also in Wisconsin and Michigan. Some of these "monster gardens" are cultivated by smuggled immigrants and are also trip-wired with improvised explosives.

The political decay allowing this to happen is not all on the Mexican side. The lack of attention paid to border security and to safety on public lands belies a curious kind of corruption American-style, at the heart of our own vaunted political system. For when one examines the nature of political will—and why we don't seem to evince any when it comes to the border, one has to look not only at the American electorate but also at the organized political parties. The sad fact is that Democrat leaders too often dismiss the harder measures that must be done, because they see immigration—even *illegal* immigration, as a way to build ethnic and economic constituencies to vote for them. Whereas Republican leaders frequently vote contrary to their grassroots supporters, instead to gain favor with corporate contributors who want a steady endless supply of cheap labor. It seems that not only ecology, but also plain old-fashioned political power and money greed, are trumping our border security operations, compromising public safety and endangering the American people on their own public lands.

Corruption of Political Culture and Health Insurance Article #422
o/a October 30, 2009

As political scientist and legal historian Bradley Watson explains in his new book, *Living Constitution, Dying Faith* (2009), the Founders believed in both revealed and rational truths that transcend the temporal moment and time/place of human experience. They fashioned the Constitution in a way that was consistent with Christian worldview and which reinforced Natural Law. When Darwinian theories and spin-offs such as social Darwinism altered the presumptive framework of philosophy during the Progressive Era, this led to changes in jurisprudence and ultimately to unhinging the Constitution. To conceive of the Constitution as "living" is essentially to kill it, because the Constitution was designed to enshrine timeless ideals and to at once fix and limit political processes so as to respect the natural order of things. Today's predominant view is that we have an infinitely interpretable Constitution, which indeed must be interpreted in light of a historically situated, constantly evolving state of reality (i.e., changing notions of the individual and society, as well as governmental responsibilities).

Earlier constitutionalism offered us regimes of limited and dispersed power that served the "laws of nature and nature's God." Today's "evolutionary" approach displaces the eternal verities with the latest flu vaccine as it were, responding to whatever strain of thought happens to appear or get worse this year. The Constitution no longer operates according to historical American political culture, or even to traditional rules and conventions of logic, grammar and rhetoric. The Supreme Court, and to some degree all branches of the federal government have become like Dr. Frankenstein, raising up the Constitution in grotesque and contorted forms quite unlike the Founders' Original Intent or even the intent of subsequent amendments. The legalization of same-sex marriage, Professor Watson argues, is a compelling contemporary manifestation of this.

Recently I was in a discussion about politics with friends at dinner, and it became evident that we were discussing within a historically recognizable framework of reference, plus faith-based assumptions that were quite common once upon a time. We were discussing American politics within the framework of traditional American political culture in other words. At one point we paused, recognizing intuitively that this type of discussion proves more and more unique every day, that it would have sounded strange amidst the contemporary din of political correctness. One of the saddest realizations we uncovered was that many, if not most Americans now view themselves in the context of some group with special rights and needs and a legitimate claim upon the largesse of the federal government. Men and women who run for office are bombarded by constituents, all asking the same question, "What are you going to do for me?" Everyone thinks and acts like a special interest, then wonders why all those earmarks in legislation or the huge budget deficits. Political culture is nearly ruined, and the miracle of the Constitution that rose like the sun is now waning like sunset into darkness.

Unless we start to think, unless we start to relearn a few things, the Republic will entirely end. Folks, we don't have a right to anything but life, liberty and the pursuit of happiness, as well as those rights in the Bill of Rights protected by states or the people, respectively (speech, religion, press, implied privacy, etc.). People have the right to work, not the right to a job necessarily nor to any particular standard of living. People don't have the right to an education either, or to home ownership, or to health care, or to a pension. These things are all good, beneficial and terribly important, but they are the stuff of liberty and pursuit of happiness—they are the means and instrumentalities, not rights. No one should steal from someone else or the taxpayer to provide these things to others. The American Dream might be a home in the suburb and two-car garage, I don't know. Whatever it is, it isn't defined or enshrined by the Constitution, and there's no guarantee you'll get it. There may indeed be national regulatory and tax regimes that facilitate the means and instrumentalities better; and for most of American history people of the several states determined that they should provide for public education. Today, however, we want so much from government and particularly the federal government that we can't seem to think straight.

For instance, we can't remember what insurance is for. Insurance is a system of protection against loss, normally an unexpected loss that significantly alters someone's life or situation. So people ensure private property, perhaps their diamond jewelry and silverware, but generally not five-dollar costume stuff. They ensure their house against fires and floods but generally not a squirrel in the attic. People don't ensure a coat of paint or the other maintenance that goes into owning a house. People absorb the cost of those things or they go without. People also ensure their cars but frequently pay for a dent in the fender to keep premiums from going up. Insurance doesn't cover the flat tire or fair wear and tear of the upholstery. Some insurance policies are more comprehensive and expensive than others. People elect different deductibles, depending on how much risk they want to reduce, and how much convenience they want to add in for a price. Benefits, however, are not the same thing as insurance.

There's really no difference in paying for cold medicine or visit to the doctor, say, from getting a set of windshield wipers or check under the hood. People will absorb the cost of those things too or go without. They may accept risk from time to time (no harm no foul), and also make lifestyle choices that truly are theirs to make and not the government's. They bargain with God and sometimes tempt His favor, but the only thing that's truly a health insurance policy would be something against catastrophic disease or accident. Everything else is a benefits package, and none of it is a right. The federal government is entirely out of bounds mandating health insurance for anybody. The idea amounts to a gross infringement of the people's freedom and their money. Worse, it is a gross misreading of the Constitution. Such legislation is reflective of the corruption of political culture. It is indicative of a people, who have ceased applauding heroes and electing the better sort from among them, who celebrate and advance their incarnate appetites and desires in the name of a changing American Dream at the expense of the Constitution they have forgotten.

Clarion Call to Conservatives Article #407
o/a July 17, 2009

We can argue whether it was real conservatism or faux and mistaken conservatism that lost the last election in November 2008. Regardless, 28 years of a nominally conservative governing philosophy is the proverbial baby that was thrown out with the bath water. Nor is the current crisis only a partisan political thing. The nation's economy is the worst since the Great Depression, such that capitalism and even the whole idea of having free markets are under siege and, with *this* president and the Pelosi Congress, at risk. Nobody has done anything either to solve our porous border situation or to rein in illegal, much less legal immigration. The military is run ragged and not even completely transformed to its new generation of equipment or training. Tens of thousands of veterans will rightly demand long-term care, and now the government talks about 25% cuts in defense spending!

All this, when foreign policy challenges are quite serious: from Mexican instability and drug violence spilling over the border; to North Korea feeling its oats and shooting off missiles (at the same time it implodes under demographic pressure and famine); from a crazy man in Iran resisting pressure for democratic change, to the tough guy in Russia killing off political rivals (both shades of Evil Empire); and always that Red Chinese dragon lying in lurch—silently building its military, becoming an economic powerhouse too; not to mention those bad guys we call terrorists lodged in failed or failing states, searching for safe havens to launch future attacks against our people; and least perhaps but very sad, our European brethren who inherited directly the great Western tradition, now losing all religion and becoming a mere secular shell, submitting blithely to self-loathing and to the sense of inevitable decline.

Almost the only thing we can agree with President Obama about is, well *yes*—this is indeed "a critical moment"! Counter intuitively perhaps, this may also be a most auspicious beginning for the next conservative change making political movement in America. Indeed, it is my strong conviction that it is from this great place, figuratively and geographically nearest to the heart of Texas—it is from this place, that Americans will learn what to do and how they ought to respond to the criticality of this moment. It is from Central Texas conservatism they will be reminded of certain principles and of what it means to be American in key, essential ways. This conviction is born of a faith that we can and will meet the challenges I've mentioned, and any other challenge, if we have the heart; if we give it our all; if we live up to the character of our forebears and invoke the name of the same Almighty, who helped them on behalf of the righteous cause of *Liberty*.

This State whose battle cry is, "Remember the Alamo!" appreciates and understands this better than any other. This place, Bell County, where the Chisholm Trail runs through *knows*. Central Texans have known glory in victory, valor in defeat; they have persisted through tough times, drought, fires and floods. They know if you want to get on with it, sometimes you have to get back up and dust yourself off; and if you want to get from one place to another, you've got to 'get a move on.' Not all trails lead to the same destination, and few are what we'd call totally "Happy Trails." Bluebonnets have a short season, as it were. And yet the trail you embark on will convey you, through time and experience—and the same trail that takes you to a new place, dotted with a few other places along the way, can also take you back on your journey home.

The conservative leads his or her country *home* as it were; or the next best thing, the conservative will pack up the relics, the essential tools, seed corn, keepsakes, brands, favorite recipes, and the family Bible. He or she will stow them safely in the wagon as he heads off to parts yonder or parts unknown. When he gets there, the new home will surely bear a resemblance and continuity with the old, even in the midst of a new environment and more changes to come. In this way, the old remains vital and relevant while still moving forward. And it is not a joyless trek either, because part of the kit involves Texas optimism, as big as the Texas sky.

Texans have a penchant for finding the silver lining, as well as adjusting their own attitudes when necessary—in order to bend nature to the will, and to visualize the prize against any background whatsoever, because they know (to borrow a folk song lyric) that 'everywhere you go, you take the weather with you.' Texans are funny that way because they're cock sure they got the best, no matter what it is or what condition it's in! Their attitude, if you will, is always more than equal to any task. Which is a good thing, because we shall need this quality in spades. Nevertheless, I tell you from a political standpoint, this is ground zero of the next political Revolution, one that rivals the Jeffersonian and Reagan Revolutions—and this is an exceeding great day to be called a Patriot![19]

Andy Barron's Strange Stand against the Evil Tide Article #462
o/a August 08, 2010

Dr. Andy Barron of Belton, Texas is an orthodontist running for Governor in the Great State of Texas. He says the nation is a sitting prey, about to lose the war of "incrementalism." As an orthodontist, he knows how to move teeth around incrementally little by little, so he thinks he recognizes a similar but evil process at work in American politics. He just announced his candidacy in late July. He is definitely not to be mixed up with the New York City councilman and former Black Panther, one *Charles* Barron who announced entry into the gubernatorial race for his state a month earlier. What Charles Barron is to the Democrat Party in New York, however, Andy Barron is to the Republican Party of Texas. Both are sorely tired of "Republicrats" and to that extent, they mirror a very large discontent across the country with both major political parties, as well as an advanced polarization of American politics and the fragmentation of old coalitions whether conservative or liberal.

Andy comes at Republicans from the religious Right; whereas, Charles attacks Democrats from the radical Left. The "Barron" of New York is black and a racist, while the "Barron" of Texas is Anglo, supports the Tea Party movement, and is decidedly not a racist. The latter is inclusive of every race and color, empathically and ideologically, notwithstanding the reference he makes occasionally to "the evil tide" of Socialism happens inadvertently to echo a title of an obscure white racist's autobiography. People of many stripes have, after all, talked and written about rising tides and stemming tides, not to mention bad moons rising for centuries.

Timing as they say, especially in politics is everything, and Andy says "our time has come," by which he means time for serious Christians to take a stand, conscientiously in politics as elsewhere based explicitly on their worldview. In Texas, two-term Governor Rick Perry has already won the Republican Party's nomination, fending off challengers Senator Kay Bailey Hutchison and Debra Medina and avoiding a run-off. Likewise, Bill White soundly beat Farouk Shami for the Democrats' nod, while Kathie Glass beat her opponent Jeff Daiell to earn top spot on the Libertarian Party ticket. That was all back on March 2nd! Moreover, the Green Party of Texas successfully met a May 24th deadline for new parties, submitting more than enough signatures on their petition to qualify for ballot access. Now enter Andy Barron, the Johnny-come-Lately who has to be the largest underdog in the race for Governor ever in the history of the State. Not to worry though, because if his endeavor seems quixotic, the reason he gives for entering the race four months after Primary elections are over is equally compelling: God told him to do it.

As a political phenomenon, Andy Barron offers anecdotal evidence as to the undercurrent of a movement not yet fully self-aware. Witness the thousands of people from various conservative factions and groups, who protested the president's mere visit to Austin August 9th chanting the words, "Hands off Texas!" Andy Barron speaks in similar terms of wanting to save Texas, not necessarily the entire United States—because that may not be possible. Texans are not too keen on raising their taxes or spending a dime, in order to bail out the likes of profligate spender states like California, Illinois or New York. Texans have their own budget challenges ahead to face in their own way. Peggy Noonan in a recent op-ed observed more urgently than she did before in 1994 prior to Republican takeover of Congress, that there is a clear tendency and potential in American politics to extricate political sovereignties from consolidated national government, particularly if the country's national leadership have remained tone deaf for extended periods of time ignoring the people's fundamental concerns and demands.

From time to time my "horse sense" has alluded to the apparent metaphors in life, i.e., to the physical and material happenings which correspond to deeper spiritual reality and meaning. Believers are more accustomed to this unique method of understanding, since the wars we fight in daily life typically have their spiritual dimension. So I was taken by a certain reference Andy Barron made to "the evil tide" of Socialism, indeed as black oil from the BP spill washed ashore on the Gulf Coast. This was similar in fact to comparisons and interpretation of events in something that Dr. Charles Stanley, Pastor of the First Baptist Church of Atlanta, preached July 4th in his sermon. Speaking of "Turning the Tide," a primary focus of that sermon was on the clash between Christianity and Socialism. Dr. Stanley: "We find ourselves as a nation, violating the laws of God and heading in a direction that is going to be disastrous for us, for our children and for the generations that are to come, unless there is a change . . . . There is a tide that has touched our shores and reached the heart of our nation. It is a tide that is bringing with it ideas and philosophies, actions and attitudes, that will ultimately destroy the way of life that you and I have."

Referring to Socialism, Stanley exclaims: "This tide is bringing in [a] control that will attempt to silence the truth, and will attempt to squash the religious devotion and worship of the people of God. There will be a collision with Socialism and the Gospel of Jesus Christ," whereas Christianity, Stanley said, interferes with the spread of Socialism.

On that basis, one may assert that the loss of freedom regarding religious expression and public display of religious symbols, and especially the removal of opening day prayers from the public schools beginning in 1962, were a prerequisite not only to the advance of secularism but also to the accomplishment of the progressives' transformational agenda that leads to a Socialist state. Andy Barron says that our youth are left without foundation. In that context therefore, everything of a policy nature that does not address our relationship with God becomes the treatment of symptoms rather than a cure for disease. He propones matter-of-factly that, if a substantial majority of people in Texas believe that we ought to have prayer in our public schools—which is what he and the polls consistently find—then by God, we ought to institute the same regardless of what a national government says.

His reasoning is also very interesting and something quite a bit more than academic neo-federalist constitutionalism or the Southern impulse towards a strict construction, Original Intent and textual definition. He says that Texas is at the center of resistance to evil these days, and Central Texas is at the Heart. A squeeze, as from a constrictor is coming to Texas, and Texas must brace herself and resist with all her might. Andy Barron speaks of a dream he had, in which he is inside a corral with other people. Its gate is about to be shut, and all the while he sees the enemies of freedom perched to shoot inside and kill the people there, as soon as the gate is securely closed. He says he knows with a certainly, that it is now or never to make our move to escape.

CHAPTER 9

Election 2010: Conservatives Reshaping the Republican Party

Hardcore Conservative Principles Article #405
o/a July 03, 2009

There was this young man who rode a bus to work every day. On the bus he'd always notice a pretty young woman sitting up front. Well the ride lasted about a half an hour, so his mind would typically drift off. He'd wonder what she was like, and he'd think about how they might meet one day and come to know each other better . . . Maybe she'd get on the bus and come sit by him, maybe she'd smile and say hi, and then he'd ask her name. If things went really well she'd probably start saving him a seat by her every day! If she did, they'd no doubt become close. Well, sure as rain one day this pretty young thing did in fact get on the bus later than normal so that the only seat available was right beside him. Just like in his mind, she came on over, smiled and gently said "Hi"—but instead of asking her name, he blurted something out about getting married and how many kids did she want. She left the bus in a hurry.

The moral of this rather awkward story is that you really do have to take your time and proceed by steps, at least if you expect things to turn out well. It's true with life and political coalition building too. While it is important to have a vision and keep your eyes on the prize—you can dream and dream big and say "Yes We Can" till the cows come home, but there's still no substitute for hard work and smart work. What I'm talking about is taking one thing at a time, all things in succession. And one of the first things we have to do as conservatives is to get our act together. It starts by defining what we're about—after which, we may begin to attract a broad coalition and shape policy positions, and also lead the next conservative change making political movement. On 25 May I laid out to the Central Texas Conservatives what I believe to be our hardcore conservative principles. We must advance from these six principles with a resoluteness of purpose and deliberate active work if we are to win back America.

To Restore the Republic meaning we demand a return to representative government. For instance we call our country what it is—a republic and not a democracy, a democratic-*republic* if you must. The national majority does not rule the States or the Nation in fact. Minority rights are never subject to the whim of 50% plus 1. We choose to follow the Founders' Original Intent—their vision of peace and prosperity, virtue and happiness, that of a 'Shining City on a Hill.' To Reinforce adherence to the Constitution, which is to say that words mean something, that the text of the written document itself has a fixed meaning, that while enumerated powers are subject to some interpretation they are also largely defined; and there are constitutional processes for determining how best to interpret the Constitution's meaning. There are political possibilities based upon the separation of powers amongst branches, and also based upon sovereignty inherent in the states. The Constitution moreover has an amendment procedure, and that's the only way to legitimately change constitutional parameters. Reduction of the Constitution by the Supreme Court to a so-called "living" document amounts to a gross malfeasance on the part of judges-turned-legislators.

To Reinvigorate Federalism meaning that we recognize implicitly the compound nature of our Republic, the fact that it is and by design was made to be a Republic of republics to preclude tyranny and magnify the possibilities of Liberty. Federalism lies at the heart of the original constitutional edifice and is a primary contribution from the Father of the Constitution, James Madison. States ceded specific, enumerated powers to the federal government while retaining everything else. The Ninth and Tenth Amendments are explicit in this regard. To Respect the Flag, which affirms our commitment to the Union as conceived by the Founders and discretely altered by constitutional amendment or tribunal of arms. We respect the Flag as that primary symbol of our country and that Republic for which it stands, and the nation amongst all others on earth to which we owe primary allegiance and to which we hold the love of countrymen for our native or adoptive homeland. We respect the Flag also, as symbol of the highest ideals to which men and women can aspire and to which the nation has mostly been true, as it has progressed through history at great sacrifice and expense in blood and treasure. We are proud Patriots, who celebrate also those various symbols of national and regional heritage.

To Rigorously exercise Freedom is our commitment to living according to our lights without hypocrisy and with utmost personal integrity, to do as we say and believe, to attempt in this life to implement what we have planned and visualized and worked so hard to accomplish. This is our political commitment too, to do as our ancestors did by pledging 'our Lives, our Fortunes and our sacred Honor' to the great project before us into which we have enlisted; to walk as freeborn individuals, possessing Rights from Heaven which no man may put asunder or play God to undo, or unduly restrict. Fundamentally this means that we insist upon *self*-determination, in accordance with those natural and freely chosen responsibilities we *should* acknowledge—chiefly those to God and conscience and family; and to our various avocations and social networks; to neighborhood and community; State *and* Nation.

To Remain Steadfast in Faith recognizes the indispensable relation between faith and freedom, whereby they raise and support each other. True faith presupposes a conviction of the heart made freely and without coercion by state or religious authority. Freedom moreover demands that a people exercise self-restraint, the regulation and discipline born of good conscience and drawn to perfect and Higher Law to which man is tenderly and lovingly obliged to choose. We understand that in the order of things, all the Earth is subject to Him and so we trust in the God of our Fathers. Moreover, as Americans we acknowledge the special role the Nation has fulfilled in the advancement of mankind and in the continuous unfolding of Providential Plan.[20]

On Party Politics, Conservatives and Conspiracy — Article #421
o/a October 23, 2009

The political situation in Texas is interesting, given Sen. Kay Bailey Hutchison's decision to challenge Gov. Rick Perry in the next Republican Primary. She has set up a number of dominoes as it were too, as people jockey to run for her seat and significant offices become vacant by various candidates or incumbents for this reason. For Sen. Hutchison to challenge the Governor, well, isn't exactly playing the good Republican, indeed with Texas doing as well as it is. Supporters on both sides argue which is the true conservative, and both have their conservative detractors. At the same time, insurgent conservative-libertarian Debra Medina is affecting the same race. Nationally, Governor Palin made waves by endorsing a conservative third party candidate over the choice of the local GOP in a congressional special election for New York's 23rd District. The Republican nominee angered many conservatives by supporting same-sex marriage and abortion, and this caused some to bolt. All of which is very instructive, in terms of what is happening within the Republican Party.

With the Reagan coalition in tatters and for many, a perceived Socialist in the White House, conservatives are literally pinging off walls. In Texas, Republican moderates dream about broadening the party, but ardent conservatives are committed now to expanding their leadership of the GOP and consolidating political position in the State during 2010, in order to become an important national political base in 2012 for countermovement against the out-and-out socialization of America. It's a meaningful strategy, considering that Texas is the most conservative but also the largest and most prosperous "Red" state—and the only viable bastion of states rights and strict constitutional construction left in this federally overregulated, overtaxed and debt-ridden Union. If conservatives do not defeat themselves, they might just pull it off.

Notice that I said conservatives might pull it off, and not Republicans per se. That's because more and more Americans are coming to the conclusion that both parties are wedded to power and to the self-destructive status quo. More Americans see a need to reinforce national sovereignty and independence from various international regimes that seek to tie us down like so many Lilliputians, and they see the government refusing to do so intent instead on someone else's New World Order. Americans are increasingly demanding the return to representative governance, to sound money, to accountability and transparency, to character in office—honesty and moral courage from the men and women they elect. George Wallace once famously remarked, "There's not a dime's worth of difference between them" (by which he meant the two political parties). There seemed to be for a little while, but his critique cuts now again to the bone.

The truth is that both parties are loose coalitions—one happens to be left leaning, while the other is right leaning. Both contain disparate elements. Ins and Outs compete within both of the coalitions, and electoral defeats normally provide the opportunity for Outs to get back in. Traditional *constitutional* conservatives are still the Outs in the Republican

Party, trying to take over from neoconservatives who decimated it. Both political parties are participatory vehicles primarily. The ideas that animate them juggle around all the time, and predominant strains change over time as the history of political parties shows. Many conservative Democrats and American Party types joined with the Reagan coalition and are still nominally Republican, although many are showing up at tea parties preferring to call themselves Independent. Quite a few are joining the Constitution Party. If conservatives don't succeed in firm capture of the GOP soon, a national third party alternative is more or less assured.

In the interval, conservatives of all stripes should try not to fall into an easy trap of faulting negative reality on other people's conspiracies. If anything, what we experience is a conspiracy of mass irrationality and error stemming from lack of vigilance. The country and economy are far bigger than anyone who presumes to pull strings, whether the Fed or Wall Street or dozens of petty little czars friendly with the president. The good news is that our political system does and will yield to populist political action and particularly to truth in action. Integrity becomes the point of your spear, and there's more in Scripture about putting on the whole armor of God, which is also highly recommended. It is within the power of the American people to reinstate good government during any given election cycle, but the price of freedom is still eternal vigilance as it always has been. If there is a conspiracy, or if there isn't, consider what part of your life and how much effort you are willing to invest in fixing things, in making them better, and in fighting the multi-headed beast called Leviathan.

Bringing America and the Republican Party Home Article #437
o/a February 12, 2010

The conservative party in American politics is still the Republican Party, but there are tremendous differences in terms of which faction may rule the roost from time to time. Tom Pauken in his book, *Bringing America Home,* argues that "Machiavellian pragmatists and neoconservative ideologues" hijacked the Grand Old Party (GOP) and did so by pretending to be Reagan conservatives. Pauken maintains that true conservative principles provide the correct roadmap to solutions for the big problems facing our country. He also argues that they provide the right roadmap back to power for Republicans. This is obviously contrary to Obama's radical presumption, which may have contributed to his overly ambitious domestic agenda and squandering of his first year in office, and that is that Democrats' victory in 2008 meant people now broadly repudiate conservative values and solutions. The rise of the Tea Party movement and sizeable back-to-back defeats of Democrat candidates in 2009 and 2010, unhinge the presumption. On the other hand, Republicans would make a huge mistake believing that the electorate somehow longs for a return to the debt and domestic spending levels, centralized decision-making, or expansive military and foreign policy aims pursued under George W. Bush. The People have turned a corner, and so should the Republican Party.

Notwithstanding past policy mistakes, any real progress in making America great again will require the party in power to address budget and trade deficits. The fiscal conservatism of constituencies in the Republican Party make it more likely Republicans can do this. Moreover, social conservatives in the Republican Party coalition will contribute outside the normal realm of hot-button issues, by helping reassert classic traits of the American character, which Pauken says are needed to fix among other things the economic crisis. For instance, policies are necessary to rebuild the middle class, but the middle class is defined foremost by character traits, and only then by median income. To slow or reverse the growth of government represents an economic imperative to be sure, but also a character imperative—including the willingness of more people to postpone gratification and resist public dependency. Character is thus essential to rejuvenation of the free enterprise system.

Character is clearly needed by people and legislators alike, to responsibly address the unfunded liabilities of our bloated entitlement programs. Recognition of character is needed too, in order to discern that good jobs are not always the so-called white collar ones. Not all good jobs do or should depend upon getting a college education either. The idea that every child should be a four-year, liberal arts or science major is narrow and elitist at its core. The attitude and attendant policies from Washington have helped rob labor of its inherent dignity in America, while helping to decimate the American manufacturing base. Having just one kind of global comparative advantage, say, in information systems, fails the common sense test and is largely responsible for moving American jobs offshore and losing out to foreign competitors. America is big enough and must be big enough for all kinds of work: blue and white collar, manual and managerial, technical and services.

Whether fiscal and/or social conservative, solutions as such will be incomplete—and hence the metaphorical war to *save*, much less to make America great again will be lost, if Republicans (and by extension the majority of Americans) do not also adopt *political* conservatism in terms of how they regard their Constitution. Quite aside from the necessary social morality informed by principles of Christianity, the nation most urgently requires restoration of "constitutional morality." That is to say, the Founders' political culture on which our republican system and Founding Document depends, must regain relevancy in Congress, at the White House, inside the Supreme Court, in town halls and state legislatures across the land. The emphasis on checks and balances, separation of powers, states rights and federalism, must be observed and even relearned, if the country would not devolve into tyranny or to the status of a second-rate, socialist backwater where once freemen and freewomen called home.

Principles of Political War Articles #459-461
~Part I~ o/a July 18, 2010

The people are rising up. Americans are waking up at last to the threat: a leftist elite, bent on fundamentally changing America and making every citizen entirely dependent on the state. The Obama machine driven by a socialist agenda is spending trillions of tax-payer dollars to finance takeover of the American workplace and to stifle personal initiative and community awareness and self-determination. America is built of better stuff, however, namely the principles of private property and individual freedom, and the Resistance has begun.

In May 2009 Californians launched a tax revolt, indeed at a time when their state government's deficit was larger than the budgets of most other states and many countries. State law according to its "Initiative" process required legislators to win a two-thirds referendum of the people before they could raise taxes. Forced to hold special election with multiple ballot Initiatives to raise taxes, California citizens shocked legislators by sending an unmistakable message by margins of 60 percent even in San Francisco: *Taxed Enough Already! No more taxes!*

The "TEA" Party movement quickly spread, gaining steam across the entire nation. David Horowitz calls it "the most innovative, exciting and powerful grassroots force in the history of American conservatism." Today and through the election cycles of 2010 and 2012 it is not only vital to the health of the country, but essential to the survival of America. Consider that on the eve of the 2008 presidential election, Barack Obama proclaimed, "We are five days away from fundamentally transforming America!" Tea Partiers threw themselves into the political breach, so to speak, saying unequivocally "*No*" to Obama's plans to fundamentally alter the federal constitutional Republic and turn it into a socialist state.

The breach is one thing, but politics is really more about sustained effort and long-term commitment to ideas. A particular movement without an effective plan or strategy will not succeed. Therefore it is critical to reacquaint ourselves with some principles of political war. Many political philosophers have characterized politics as warfare by other, presumably peaceful means. Nixon described politics as being part and parcel of an overall spectrum of conflict. Most Americans are naïve politically and unfamiliar with what philosophers and political operatives know about the electoral game played every two to four years. Americans think about politics as some kind of spectator sport or movie show, a passive distraction that doesn't require any of their personal involvement. They mistake the huge personal consequences while sitting in the bleachers or back row of a dark auditorium. They might bemoan results of an election at tax time, but then they turn again to something else entertaining or pressing.

Liberals are morally bankrupt and clueless about policy, but they still win elections because they understand American politics is driven by a dime novel Hollywood romance, with Americans sitting idly by as, you guessed it, *spectators*. According to Horowitz, the story they love to watch is about an underdog—you know, the little guy who goes up against the system and triumphs in the end. It is a story about opportunity and fairness too, and to win the flitting hearts and minds of American voters, you have to tap into emotions evoked by the underdog. America's heroes are cut to a common mold: George Washington, Abraham Lincoln, Davy Crockett, Thomas Edison, Henry Ford, Amelia Earhart, Jackie Robinson, Ronald Reagan or Colin Powell, etc., etc. Always it is about the common man who rises against the odds. Yep, Mr. Smith goes to Washington and make things right! Luke Skywalker saves the planet! Horowitz isn't as cynical perhaps about the narrative. Truth is, practically everyone in America thinks of him or herself as the underdog and aspires to be a hero. The romance in fact resonates with our deepest convictions, as well as faith in freedom and the ability to overcome adversity or to challenge and win against unjust power arrayed against you. It is the American Dream and largely her story—rising to the top through hard work in spite of humble origin.

Until the Tea Parties showed up, the political left wielded this romantic narrative as a political weapon virtually unopposed at election time. In positioning themselves as champions of the underrepresented, neglected and oppressed, leftists manufactured a version of the American story and spread it far and wide through the media and academe. According to Horowitz, the left successfully transformed America's story from "an epic of freedom into a tale of racism, exploitation and domination. In their telling, American history is no longer a narrative of expanding opportunity, of men and women succeeding against the odds. Instead, it is a Marxist Morality Play about the powerful and their victims." Elections have become staged political dramas too, as progressives invariably speak in the name of America's alleged victims—women, children, minorities and the poor.

Conservatives play into the trap, approaching politics like management on every issue, as a mere practical problem that needs to be solved—emphasizing, say, utility of the tax cut, efficiency of a certain program, the optimal method to approach this or that. They talk like businessmen in other words, and while there is nothing wrong with instituting good policies and running things efficiently or turning profit, progressives label them as servants of the rich, oppressors of the weak, defenders of the strong and privileged. Conservatives become the enemies of the people, in the liberal parlance of political warfare. Witness Mario Cuomo at the Democrats' 1996 National Convention: "We need to work as we have never done before between now and November . . . to take the Congress back from Newt Gingrich and the Republicans, because ladies and gentlemen, brothers and sisters, the Republicans are the real threat. They are the real threat to our women. They are the real threat to our children. They are the real threat to clean water, clean air and the rich landscape of America." Ooh, such good spectator sport. Only now it won't wash.[21]

~Part II~ o/a July 18, 2010

Progressives connect emotionally with people at the level of their fears and anxiety. The metaphysical reason for this is that liberals don't really want men and women to stand very tall on their own. They want mankind always dependent on something, most usually on the state or fellow human beings. They themselves fear a self-confident, self-reliant freeman or freewoman. They fear a venturesome spirit and would much rather return to the hole or crawl up under a rock, and have everybody else do the same. Now one may put a better face on government coercion and just say that the liberal and progressive appeal is based on helping underdogs and defending bona fide victims. This resonates well with Americans, who are basically a fair-minded people. Regardless of the motive or psychology you ascribe to a fantastic error, conservatives are nonetheless usually busy defending the real America—its record of success now and in history. The real America is as a land of opportunity and freedom. Almost nobody is properly called oppressed or "an oppressed class." No group has ever flocked as it were to get out of America except arguably chattel slaves and the Old South, but all sorts of people still clamor to get in.

The truth is that no one alive, nor indeed their parents, grandparents or great-grandparents either, were alive during slave times! It has been 47 years since Rev. Martin Luther King, Junior's great "I Have a Dream speech. We have a black president for crying out loud. The institutions are dead that gave us slavery and Jim Crow. The Constitution and laws changed long ago, and the social norms and mores of a majority that once sustained socio-economic prejudice against minorities are overwhelmingly different. One is hard-pressed anymore to find a majority. White means nothing in modern day America. The vestige of slavery is reduced to prejudice in its mildest form; and racism is no longer properly attributable to an inheritance per se, but rather to subjective individual experience in present day context. Received memory is received *media*, hardly a matter of real history. At this juncture in history, misguided efforts to whip up the issues of race in order to kill the last spectral existence of racism are far more likely to intensify aural projections and lead to something else reactive, unintended and substantial. If that happens, it will be the product of modern and gross political folly on the left and not the product of historical inertia, vast right-wing conspiracy, or of majority opinions extant today.

Indeed further attempts to kill the specter can only result in the strangulation death of freedom itself. That is because free people may and should be able to agree or disagree, to associate or disassociate, and even to seek or not seek their own. They may politically congregate and rally too or choose not to, because freedom requires the existence of choice and the ability to choose in every respect. If I don't like blue jeans, then I don't have to wear them. Or maybe I like them, say, in one context or liked them just fine yesterday, but now I prefer something else at church or going to the opera. Quite frankly I've got no idea whatsoever what I'll put on tomorrow. People aren't blue jeans or horses, but the point is valid in terms of selection and the dynamism and free flow of opinions. Freed of historical legacy, we are all individuals again. Therefore we really ought to be appealing to people now on the basis of individuality, their character and the ideas they hold, not on the basis of their racial groupings. The divisive and racially charged rhetoric from the national NAACP of late is unhelpful in this regard. The unsubstantiated attack by liberal politicians and community leaders, and bold innuendo from the left-leaning press against Tea Parties labeling them as racist, is also unhelpful and could backfire in November.

But politics isn't just about reality. If it were, according to David Horowitz, "good principles and good policies would win every time." Rather, in terms of political war, the contest is "about images and symbols and the emotions they evoke, [and] this is a battle that conservatives generally lose. In the romance of the victim as progressives stage it, Republicans and conservatives are always on the side of the bad guys—the powerful, the male, the white and the wealthy . . . . Defending America is readily misrepresented . . . . The left relishes the opportunity to smear patriots as members of the selfish party instead of as defenders of individual freedom." Ann Coulter describes the motto of the left as "Speak loudly and carry a small victim." For Democrats, the romance of the victim stirs supporters and energizes their base. Conservatives are the targeted victimizers. Leftists become champions of the so-called oppressed. Sure hate to say it, but news from the front so far is that the Battle of the Bulge is going to the Nazis!

Learning how to confront the left's strategy, however, will turn the political war around. It requires that Americans become a little more clear-headed and informed, and less crybaby when leftists sing their predictable tearjerkers and blues. Fortunately, as Horowitz explains, "conservatives can use the left-wing attack against them. Contrary to the left's view, America is not a land of victims. It is a highly mobile society, with a citizenry that aspires upwards *through* the system, not against it . . . . [The] most powerful forces obstructing opportunity for poor and minority

Americans, the most powerful forces oppressing them, are progressives, the Democratic Party, and their political creation—the welfare state." Welfare state programs are demonstrably obstacles to the production of wealth and barriers to private opportunity. What is necessary is for conservatives to connect the dots so to speak, to connect their analysis to a political strategy that gives them a decisive edge in battle against the left's propaganda—or if you prefer, the left's purely innocent though misguided interpretation of events. In this way, Horowitz believes we can "neutralize the class, race and gender warfare attacks of the political left" and hopefully rise above such petty, counterproductive and polarizing politics.[22]

~Part III~ o/a July 18, 2010

Here are six principles of political war the left understands much better than most conservatives: 1) Politics is war conducted by other means; 2) Politics is a war of position; 3) In political wars the aggressor usually prevails; 4) Position is defined by fear and hope; 5) The weapons of politics are symbols evoking fear and hope; and 6) Victory lies on the side of the people. Now let's explain them further, one at a time. *Politics is war conducted by other means*: In modern political warfare one doesn't only fight to prevail in argument but to destroy the opponent's ability to argue at all. Conservatives often regard their political combat as a debate before the Oxford Union Society. Theoretically one's winning should depend upon rational and well-articulated arguments. Unfortunately the democratic audience in American politics today is not made up of many Oxford dons, and the modern media environment gives one about 30 seconds to make his point! Even if one were afforded time to develop arguments sufficiently, the undecided voter and millions not paying close attention still won't get it. Careful analysis or policy prescriptions are quickly forgotten in the hurly-burly of everyday life. A certain advantage is afforded to the left, which sidesteps argument altogether, in order to paint conservative debaters as mean-spirited-racist-religious-zealots-in-bed-with-the-filthy-rich. Now quite simply, anyone who sees another this way will not try to listen to his argument. Liberals don't play an attrition game in politics, they shoot to kill. The result is to make conservatives dead politically, a.k.a., Endgame.

Politics is a war of position: There are essentially two sides to every political contest, namely friends and enemies. One can also identify two sides as winners and losers. A political combatant strives to define oneself as "friend" to the largest possible constituencies compatible with his principles. Friends that way become winners. "Others" (i.e., not friends) are simply enemies, and these become the losers. Caution is in order, however, in that American politics takes place in a pluralistic framework. Constituencies are diverse, overlap and are often in conflict. Coalitions are always shifting. Over the course of several election cycles, one's friends might become enemies and vice versa. Two unwritten formal rules in democratic engagement are therefore fairness and tolerance. According to David Horowitz, "If you appear mean-spirited, nasty, or too judgmental, it will make the task easier for your opponent to define you as a threat, and therefore as the enemy." Only nice conservatives win, in other words.

In political warfare, the aggressor usually prevails: Aggression is advantageous precisely because politics is a war of position. Position is defined by the images that stick moreover. By striking first, one defines issues and the adversary. Defining the opposition is indeed the most decisive move in a political war. Other things being equal, whoever is put on the defensive generally winds up on the losing side. Going negative, as it were, increases the risk of being defined as an enemy, but ruling that out is a huge risk. The trick is to be aggressive and selectively negative towards an opponent without being ugly about it.

Position is defined by fear and hope: The twin emotions of politics are fear and hope. Those who provide people with hope become friends; those who inspire fear become enemies. *The weapons of politics are symbols evoking fear and hope*: Conservatives lose a lot of political battles, because they come across as too hard-edged. David Horowitz says a good rule of thumb is to be just the opposite. "You have to convince people you care about them before they'll care about what you have to say. When you do get to speak, don't forget that a sound-bite is all you have. Whatever you have to say, make sure to say it loud and clear. Keep it simple and keep it short . . . . Repeat it often. Get it on television. Radio is good, but with few exceptions, only television reaches a public that is electorally significant. In politics, television is reality."

Leftists always spout the party line. That's because it is short and simple and one message is a sound-bite, whereas many messages become an indecipherable noise. Horowitz again: "The result of many messages is that there is no message. Symbols and sound-bites determine the vote. These are what hit people in the gut before they have time to think. And these are what people remember. Symbols are the impressions that last, and what ultimately defines you. Carefully chosen words and phrases are more important than paragraphs, speeches, party platforms and manifestos. What you project through images is what you are" in effect.

Victory lies on the side of the people: This is our faith, but if conservatives are to win the political war they have to turn their negative images around. They have to turn campaigns into causes also. In the Cold War conservatives had a cause and were elected time and again to defend the nation. The cause of anti-Communism resonated well at every level of American society, and even the poorest citizen understood that freedom was at stake. In a democracy, the cause that fires passions up becomes the cause of the people. As the left has shown before, the idea of justice is a powerful cause and energizes its troops in the political war. Horowitz reminds us that, "Conservatives believe in economic opportunity and individual freedom. The core of [conservative] ideas is freedom and justice for all. If we can make this intelligible to the American electorate, we will become the majority again and stop the socialist juggernaut that [now] threatens our American future."[23]

Election of 2010: Analysis and Prospectus Article #476
o/a November 13, 2010

When the smoke finally cleared, Election Day November 2nd turned out to be about as big as conservatives could have hoped. If expectations soared unrealistically high in some areas (many hoped the GOP might retake the Senate but had to be content flipping six seats), still elsewhere those expectations were exceeded (as with the conservative sweep across the country at state level). Democrats lost control of nineteen state legislative chambers and eleven governorships. In Texas, Republicans expanded their two vote majority in the state house to almost fifty.

Congresswoman Nancy Pelosi may yet serve as Minority Leader in the U.S. House next session, but she is defanged without her Speaker's gavel. Democrats have started to reorganize with or without White House direction, inventing an "Assistant-to-the-Leader" position basically to promote moderation inside the Democrat leadership. Considering that come January 2011 for the first time in more than six decades there will be fewer than two hundred Democrats in the House, it probably isn't such a bad move.

The year 1994 was considered a wave election by Republicans too, but that "revolution" fizzled when President Clinton beat a very fast track back to the center. This time the wave election turned out to be a veritable tsunami—nearly twice as big with Republicans picking up 60 seats in the House. President Obama also seems far less likely to dance a soft shoe; and anyway, the Tea Party contingent of the GOP, which did not exist in 1994, will hardly be impressed. Clinton took everyone's breath away, and even his opponents swooned when he declared 'the Era of Big Government' to be over. It was a lie. Now Tea Partiers and conservative stalwarts know better and won't fall for the line again.

The mid-term election is more akin to the Reagan Revolution of 1980 in terms of its size and its professed ideological purpose. In an article by Lou Cannon appearing in Politics Daily, he attributes four factors to the results of the election in terms of Republican resurgence. Accordingly, "The first [factor] is public dismay with the slow pace of the recovery. The second and related factor is the perceived ineffectiveness of the stimulus and various government bailouts. The third is reaction to Obamacare, which the White House wrongly expected would become popular after it became law . . . . [and the] fourth factor, both effect and cause, is the tea party . . . ." This litany of causal factors is more or less complete and indeed now common wisdom, except that Cannon overly limits his explanation about the tea party in his piece. The Tea Party as such, is more than just a populist reaction to the serious economic downturn. Yes it bears resemblance to other populist backlashes, except this one has a history and a serious accumulation of discontent dating back years even before the tea party movement coalesced in 2009.

The oversight is worth pointing out, because what is behind the Tea Party also offers causal explanation for the Republican tidal wave. The additional factor is correctly identified as a simmering brand of strict Constitutional construction, which has mostly been maligned, shoved aside or overlooked since the 1960s. It is an insistence no less populist but altogether separate. It is a subsurface and traditional inclination of a majority of the American people and is defensive aggressive in its nature, which explains its robust reappearance. Classically it is a response to tyranny or perceived tyranny and is a distinctive conservative lineament of political philosophy very closely aligned, by extrapolation to the Founding Fathers' worldview. Its critique of the current social, economic and political milieu has it that government is indeed too big, and also too powerful, too intrusive, too much "in the way," too overbearing and monitoring, as with Big Brother or the stereotypical Nanny. It is also far too costly of late, and—to the extent that the federal government no longer respects its legal and constitutional bounds, may constitute an impediment to Freedom writ large (which is after all the American project), as well as a physical and moral threat to the People themselves.

A "neo-federalist" wing of the Republican Party with direct Southern and Middle American historical roots has been kept down for years by the GOP establishment and most recently by domination of the neoconservative wing, which reached its zenith of power during the years of George W. Bush. States rights and Tenth Amendment advocates are now demanding their day in the sun, and the intramural strife will be clearly in play as the GOP seeks next year to integrate its newfound friends in the Tea Party, much like swallowing an anaconda.

The Election of 2010 could very well herald a new era of conservative dominance, whatever its eventual stripe. While winning elections is hard work, however, it is only the first step towards what one hopes will be effective governance. Tea Party freshmen are going to Congress for a purpose, but they are going to need continuing grassroots support and a constant store of encouragement and concrete ideas to get anything done over the long haul. The enthusiasm of new Tea Party members in Congress will also eventually have to translate into specific policy actions that really do help "restore the Republic" according to the Constitution and Founders' Intent, if that's what they want to accomplish. Policies and legislation are most definitely required to put Americans back to work and to achieve full and sustained economic recovery—and sooner rather than later, as the Democrats found out. There is also the long and intentionally ignored political imperative that the United States must secure her borders; and then address the sheer magnitude of legal and illegal immigration, ensuring it reaches a reasonable and assimilative level.

The new kids on the block are going to have a lot of work to do. The Tea Party "revolution" could very well fizzle like others before, if they fail to repeal Obamacare or compromise too much with the president on this issue; if they are unable to get government spending under control, or reverse the trend of ballooning national debt. If the Republican Party establishment is seen to subvert the tea party effort, there will almost certainly be a third party alternative for an increasingly large number of disaffected conservative voters inside the GOP's base, and this could portend a potential realignment or collapse of the Third American Party System.

The best thing that could emerge from the Election of 2010 is a new and more conservative consensus, marked by serious bipartisan hard work and honest efforts to address the crisis dynamics in our economy and polity. Another more likely scenario is that we could be looking at two more years of not only divided, but also gridlocked government leading up to the Election of 2012. If this happens of course, what's hot is likely to get hotter and what's a problem is likely to get worse. Arguably only when one of the two major parties (possibly with the help of a strong independent contingent) takes charge of two branches of government (usually the Congress and Executive Branch), does gridlock give way to a period of significant political and economic achievement—the next one presumably stamped by clear conservative branding, but only as it emerges from the Republican dustup.

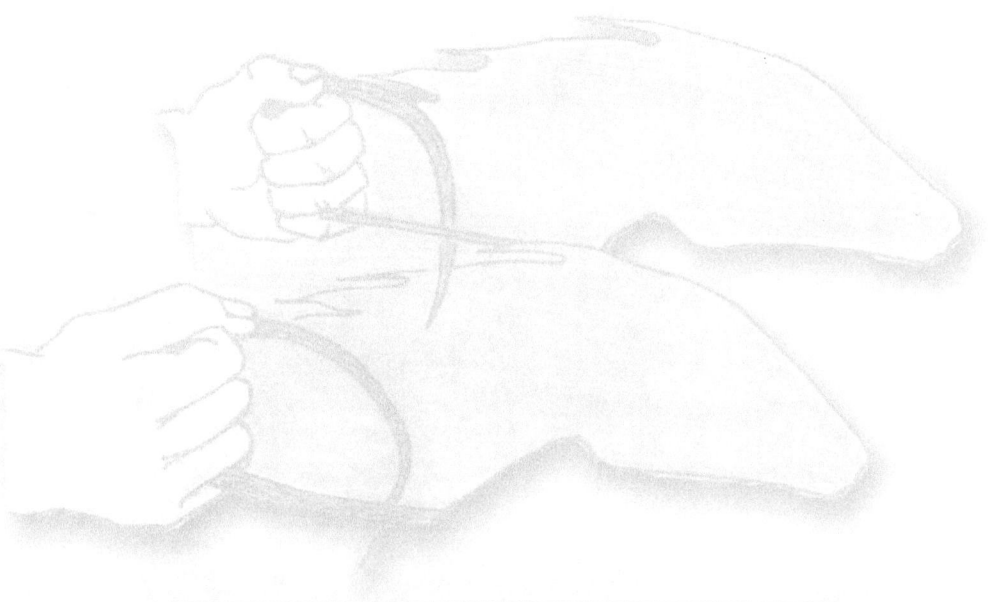

PART TWO: GOVERNMENT

CHAPTER 10

Domestic Policy

Employment Preference Given to Immigrant Aliens over U.S. Citizens
o/a September 25, 2010 Article #469

You may have noticed Ethiopians collecting tolls in Dallas, or Somalis working for the Texas prison system doing contract work. Not African-*Americans*, mind you—we're talking *Africans*. Apparently state agencies hire people on visas and not necessarily the thousands of qualified American citizens who are out of a job in need of work. Preferring aliens over U.S. citizens, particularly in times of economic downturn, is a despicable policy even for Obama's "Amerika." The liberal mantra is that one truly can't find an American to do "that kind" of work in America, no matter what kind of work that is. At the heart of the matter are preference categories, affirmative action for so-called disadvantaged minorities and women, or special categories like handicapped. Employers have to verify that an individual whom they plan to employ or continue to employ in the U.S. is authorized to accept employment, not whether he/she is a citizen—about that, employers frankly don't care.

It is true that no alien may accept employment in the U.S. unless he/she has been *authorized* by the Government, but you see aliens are more equal than the majority of U.S. citizens and that's the rub. Aliens, such as those who were admitted as permanent residents, granted asylum or refugee status, or admitted in work-related nonimmigrant classifications have employment authorization *as a direct result of their immigrations status*. Moreover, other aliens may apply individually for employment authorization. In general, temporary non-immigrant workers will fall into the work category of seasonal agriculture, or else specialty areas like defense, nursing, fashion, athletics and entertainment. Permanent workers fall into one of several categories that represent extraordinary ability, advanced degree, a certain profession, business or skill. There are in fact many ways in which a person may be able to work in the U.S. Approximately 140,000 immigrant visas are available every year for alien permanent worker categories, and there are *millions of permanent resident aliens* already living and working legally now in the United States.

You'll also be happy to know that Congress mandates a Diversity Immigrant Visa Program too, which is administered annually by the Department of State. Section 203(c) of the Immigration and Nationality Act makes 55,000 Diversity Visas (DV) available each year to persons from countries with low rates of immigration. The Department of State conducts a lottery to hand these out, and international registration for one of these babies opens up on October 5th and closes the day after Election Day, November 2nd. These lucky "Lotto" Winners will have preference for hiring when they arrive in the U.S. All of which doesn't sound that terrible, until one considers something else alongside of it. American citizenship places one at a positive disadvantage for employment opportunity, especially if one is white and it involves applying for a government job or government contract. U.S. citizens are actually disadvantaged when it comes to getting a job with the U.S. or State Government in these United States of America!

Whereas a government job now and again may require a security clearance, which could possibly advantage citizenship, most government jobs do not require one. Some preference categories such as for veterans in the State of Texas might also give a citizen the edge. Federal preference categories, however, direct preference in hiring based on minority race/ethnicity, female gender, or disabled status. State agencies across the state follow Federal Guidelines and Federal "law/laws" with respect to the eligibility to work in the U.S. based solely on the U.S. Department of Homeland Security's U.S. Citizenship and Immigration Services (USCIS) policy directives. The USCIS standard is that, as long as an individual completes an I-9 and the agency can verify an individual is legally able to work in the U.S., that state agency (or any private employer) is able to hire them. U.S. Equal Employment Opportunity Commission (EEOC) guidelines with respect to non-discrimination practices further and expressly do *not* have "preference" criteria to hire *American citizens* over someone else, say, who is legally able to work by virtue of permanent legal residency or the VISA that authorizes work in the U.S.!

Virtually every Human Relations (HR) Department in government and quite a few larger businesses parrot the politically correct policy position that, why yes, we certainly do not preference a mere *citizen* but will gladly hire someone with a VISA if that person is the "most qualified candidate" and most especially if that person happens to fall into a minority category. As the U.S. Department of Labor proclaims, "Affirmative action must be taken by covered employers to recruit and advance qualified minorities." Translation: a person who is African and black has a better chance to get jobs under the law and EEOC guidelines than a person who is a U.S. Citizen and happens to be white—for Federal jobs and contracts to be sure, and also for the states and employers who follow the same idiotic rules.

The majority of unemployed and underemployed people fall into that unfortunate category of being both white and citizen, but then a policy of not hiring them first over immigrant aliens is only idiotic if the Government chiefly serves them. Silly Rabbit, you just answered your own stupid question. Consider the full extent of the mess we're in. As stated, employers must verify that an individual whom they plan to employ or continue to employ in the U.S. is authorized to accept employment in the U.S. That's truly amazing, even if it no longer sounds strange, because it wasn't always so. You see, once upon a time Americans enjoyed an existential right to work and a corresponding right to hire virtually unimpeded by government "oversight." The presumption of freedom changed only with the Immigration Reform and Control Act (IRCA) of 1986, which provided terms of the last amnesty for illegal immigrants. In other words, we started enforcing dictatorial terms of hiring, in order to advantage certain legalized and formerly illegal immigrants over newly arriving illegal ones. Of course there shouldn't have been too many of those, since the implicit precondition for amnesty was that we would secure our U.S. borders.

In periods of economic downturn and high unemployment, citizens compete more directly with alien residents and temporary workers for scarce job openings. Some of them will no doubt experience disappointment and anxiety if/when they do not "win" the competition for jobs. Today there are more than four job-seekers for every opening. For any given job, there probably are dozens of applications. Historically periods of economic downturn correlate strongly to increased political nativism and to anti-immigrant sentiment among the native population (majority ethnicity and citizens). Prior to 1965 the political establishment showed a pattern of responding to this, through steps to alleviate the overall numbers of legal immigrants being admitted to the U.S. National origins percentages were applied to aid in the process of assimilation. In many ways, the period we witness today is atypical, because there are many favored categories for hiring that did not exist before the Civil Rights Era. Moreover, we have a much larger problem today with illegal immigration, as well as with illegal hiring and employment.

Under such a circumstance, it would appear prudent to introduce legislation and administrative policy preferences that address the obvious and valid concern, and which recognizes the fact that U.S. Citizens do indeed have greatest stock in our society. The edifice of government is chiefly maintained by the citizen-voter and citizen-taxpayer. The government's obligation to its American *citizens* and the rights that inhere in them under the Constitution exceed that for resident aliens or nonimmigrant workers, foreigners and visitors of every stripe. Preference in hiring should be afforded to the native born and naturalized citizen worker in these United States. Government agencies do not currently discriminate on the basis of citizenship versus non-citizenship, so long as the person is authorized to work in the U.S., but it is time that they should.

Private vs. Public Education — Article #106
o/a August 26, 2003

Just before football season began, I heard a high school coach wax eloquent about his team. There are few things I enjoy more than to hear someone speak clearly about something he or she knows well and dearly loves. Even if I don't know the particular subject or generally care much about it, when I hear someone like the football coach talk, I can't help but pick up useful information and catch a bit of the same enthusiasm. Unfortunately, the coach ended on an unrelated and sour note about how public education was great and private education was bad, and how private education stole resources from public education and was by its very nature "elitist."

Of course, nothing could be farther from the truth. Elite vs. common doesn't even enter into a proper comparison. Public institutions can be elite (service academies) and private institutions can be common, since private institutions set whatever entry requirements they want. The fact is that many private institutions, to include parochial schools, are no-frills and barely scrape by. Home schooling is private too, and surely no one would call it an "elite" institution, although I guess you could say it depends on the family! And since private education generally (though not always) touts better performance among its kids, are we to stigmatize merit and relative success with a loaded term such as "elitist"? I guess a man who plows more land and yields a greater harvest than his neighbor is "elite" by comparison, but I fail to see how the connotation is helpful. Indeed, I see where it reflects both ignorance and envy.

The distinction between public and private has everything to do instead, about the source of funding and about who is in charge. Parents have more say, and teachers have more discretion, in private arrangements. That's not how it used to be—parents and individual teachers had far more say, over discipline, the dress code and curriculum when Beaver and his brother Wally went to public school. The local PTA was empowered. Schools reflected the mores of respective communities then. Which made sense, by the way, since communities paid the property taxes to do the job. Of course, now we delegate parental responsibility away to so many other agents—to government, to teachers' unions, to so-called "professionals." And where performance suffers in public school settings, the result is for private educational alternatives to spring up. Competition puts pressure on the public schools to improve, and they often do. Moreover, as kids leave public schools for private school settings, available money per child increases and the teacher-to-student ratio improves.

A good education should be the aim, and if it is, it hardly seems to matter whether it is achieved by public or private means. There is every reason to believe that private education offers a corrective to failing public systems. In the best of circumstances, public and private alternatives are positively symbiotic. It is also worth pointing out that monopolies are virtually never a good thing, so why would the exception apply in the case of government monopoly over education? To support government monopoly over education is to sustain a dangerous pretense, whereby government controls the mind and what the next generation shall think. A mind is a terrible thing to waste indeed, and a hideous thing to enslave or condition according to modern liberal political correctness. Like football, education is no zero-sum game. If private education is one team and public education another, the losing team today can learn from its character-building experience. If it will, then it may win again the next game or perhaps another season.

Smoking Article #007
February 22, 2001

First of all, let me say that I do not smoke cigarettes. I tend to agree with James I, who wrote in 1604 that tobacco use is "lothsome to the eye, hatefull to the Nose, harmefull to the braine, [and] daungerous to the Lungs." Notwithstanding, I don't agree with modern prohibitionists either, who use government to squeeze the tobacco industry—ostensibly to reduce smoking (*and* to make money too). The spectacle of the Clinton administration pursuing any industry, even tobacco, for "perjury" was almost enough to make me sue the prez for stomach nausea.

Like many federal programs, Medicare/Medicaid induced (or seduced) states into undermining freedom and constitutional processes. After all, states actually pay out less to treat smoking-related illnesses than they save in pension payments and elder care when smokers die prematurely! But because they can recover money for Medicare/Medicaid patients if they can show liability, the incentive is strong to pursue "creative" legal strategies, in order to recoup big bucks from tobacco companies. For decades, states couldn't actually make good, because courts and the law recognized an "assumption of risk" standard. Hey, if you knowingly smoke when you know the risks, you're responsible for the consequences of those risks you assume. So trial lawyers worked with bureaucrats to change laws, actually preventing—if you can believe this—specific kinds of defensive arguments from being used in trial cases dealing with Medicare/Medicaid and tobacco. By stacking the legal deck in state after state, the tobacco industry was finally coerced into making an out of court settlement. The November 1998 settlement made sure that no money went to individuals for real smoking-related illnesses, only that a quarter of a trillion dollars over twenty-five years would help some 46 state budgets and turn a lot of lawyers into multi-millionaires.

The tobacco industry also agreed to erect no billboard ads; to place no ads in buses or taxicabs; to distribute no merchandise emblazoned with tobacco logos; to run no ads that target kids (no more cartoon characters like Joe Camel); and to limit themselves to one sports sponsorship per company. As Georgetown professor Robert Levy points out, we now "protect the speech of the Ku Klux Klan. We protect flag burning under the First Amendment. We protect gangsta rap—which is directly targeted at kids . . . . But if Tiger Woods shows up in a tobacco advertisement on television wearing a Joe Camel tie-tack, we are going to bring the boot of government down on the neck of R.J. Reynolds." Go figure. Anyway, I won't really miss Joe Camel. I always thought the Marlboro man was "cooler." Funny, even as a kid I remember thinking he was cool, but I still didn't smoke. My parents and Sunday school teacher had more influence. Some of my peers smoked—and many of them have quit despite the addictive qualities of tobacco. In fact, forty-five million people have also quit, roughly the same number of people who continue to smoke. Anybody else think that it's time for a National Smoke-IN? Bring the kids.

Social Security — Article #009
March 1, 2001

Now that GW Bush has squeaked into the Presidency, he'll be confronted by hard political opponents and discouraged from making good on his campaign pledges. I'm sure it's because of their humane concerns over popular mandate and bipartisanship, nothing at all to do with political advantage, say, in 2002? Certainly GW is going to meet with fierce opposition over his "risky scheme" to partially privatize Social Security. I just hope he can overcome it. GW's plan would allow workers the choice of diverting 2 percent of their earnings, out of the 12 percent payroll tax, to individual (personally owned) retirement accounts. Seems to me the only risk in that is to politicians. Empowering real people is not something the "pols" like to do. Indeed, the option to shift just 2 percent of the Social Security tax into personal accounts would give young average income workers 40 percent more benefits than Social Security—at just half the average long-term return in the stock market! Something like that could make folks a little uppity, since they'd be less dependent on government. As a historian, I know how we got to this point. I also know how much my grandparents still admire, even love FDR. But I asked my grandfather a few years ago about this "Bum Deal" called Social Security, and he admitted he's resented it. The reason is simple: he knows he could have done better with one-eighth of his wages—for 40 years as a chemist with Dresser Industries, *much* better—than a 1 percent return. Robert

Bartley, editor of *The Wall Street Journal* writes, "An investor choosing stocks with a dartboard would be hard put to do worse."

In fact, Social Security was originally billed as an insurance program. Everyone knows insurance isn't meant to be an investment, but at least it's something substantial. The money you put in confers a property right and guarantee. Social Security benefits are not government guaranteed. All you have are political promises. Politicians long ago turned Social Security into an income redistribution program, by imposing an "earnings limitation" that took back Social Security from those who dared provide for themselves. Fortunately, the Republican Congress recently repealed the earnings limitation. The U.S. Supreme Court, however, has ruled that Social Security is not insurance. The Court has twice ruled that paying Social Security taxes confers no right to benefits. Congress retains ultimate authority to restrict or deny benefits. You don't actually own anything either, because Social Security is a pay-as-you-go system. Working people who contribute pay for today's seniors and rely on the next generation of workers to pay for theirs. Hard to believe, Social Security has no assets. That's why Social Security must go bust, unless it is partially privatized. When the Baby Boom generation retires, the math (fuzzy or otherwise) won't work anymore. After 2029, the contributions currently fixed by law will cover only 75 percent of the payouts. The government's own reports show that payroll taxes would have to be raised by 50 to 100 percent, in order to pay "promised" benefits to today's workers. It's long past time we had a New Deal for Social Security.

Social Security Choice — Article #177
o/a January 16, 2005

President (GW) Bush has staked some hard ground for his second term. Social Security reform leads an ambitious domestic policy agenda. His choice in this regard shows courage and foresight, and he is doing what a leader should—'choosing the harder right instead of the easier wrong.' Indeed, his choice must overcome entrenched and powerful interests to beget more choice for us. And choice is the very stuff of freedom! And yet it amazes me still—how in America—there are nay-sayers, who sacrifice theirs and everyone else's opportunity to do better for the fear that someone somewhere, hypothetically, could do worse. Liberals have choked the freedom of the middle class long enough and condemned too many of our fellow countrymen to impoverishment in old age. A measure of the liberals' perverse philosophy is that they would rather produce a hand-to-mouth retirement for every succeeding generation, rather than allow ownership of retirement dollars for all American citizens and the opportunity to pass that individual wealth on to their children. They would clip the wings of eagles for irrational fear of flying.

Ironically, debate centers on whether a Social Security crisis is at hand. It is true that, depending on the statistic you use, a crisis will happen sooner or simply later. The argument that a crisis looming more than a decade away is trivial or immaterial to leadership is symptomatic of spendthrift, consumption-oriented government—certainly not a deliberative democracy or republic led by statesmen or strategists. Social Security is safe today, but will run deficits in less than 15 years. That's not a very long time to fix the world's biggest government program! Every two-year election cycle we wait to reform Social Security costs an additional $320 billion. Saving Social Security without individual accounts will require a 50 percent increase in Social Security taxes or a 27 percent cut in benefits, period. That's because by 2030 there will be twice as many Americans (some 70 million) of retirement age as there are today. Two American workers will have to put up the taxes to pay every single recipient! In 1950, there were sixteen workers for every retired beneficiary. A survey found eighteen-to-34 year olds believe the existence of UFOs to be more likely than Social Security solvency when they reach retirement (and they would be right).

It is true markets go down as well as up, so the question of risk naturally presents itself. But over the long term, investing is remarkably safe. Over the last 80 years, for instance, private investment in the United States has earned an average annual return of almost 8 percent. This is a period that not only includes the market decline of the last few years, but the Great Depression, World War II, several smaller wars, numerous recessions, and the "stagflation" of the 1970s. We need to remember that with compound interest and stocks held over the life of a typical U.S. worker, the money grows, even if some years the returns on that investment are lower than others. On the other hand, we also know that young workers can expect a return on their Social Security taxes of 2 percent or less (maybe zero). The program over the next 75 years owes more than $26 trillion in benefits that it cannot pay (that's trillion with a "t"). And worse, workers have no legal right to their money! Two Supreme Court cases (*Helvering v. Davis* in 1937 and *Flemming v. Nestor* in 1960) both held that Congress and the president may reduce or even eliminate benefits at any time. The "ownership," such as it is, belongs to government. Congress has already raised Social Security taxes more than 40 times since the program's inception, and it arbitrarily reduces benefits whenever the program gets into trouble. In 1983 Congress raised the retirement age. The full retirement age today is 65 years and four months, but it rises two months every year until (for people born after 1959) the age is 67. The purely political nature of the program places the people's retirement at risk more than anything else. Personal ownership of individual accounts empowers the citizen with a legal right and claim to his or her real assets.

The idea of allowing people to save and invest their Social Security taxes into diversified mutual funds is not new or untried. Chilean reform begun in the 1980s proved so successful to its Social Security system that at least seven other countries in Latin America followed suit with similar success. With less fanfare, Great Britain began changing its Social Security system almost 20 years ago—and now about three-quarters of its workers have individual accounts. Australia adopted a system of individual accounts. So did Poland and Hungary. Even Communist China allows urban workers to save half of their payroll taxes in privately invested, individual accounts. A Zogby poll found 68 percent of American voters support individual accounts too, but big-government liberals persist in frustrating the political will of the people on this and other matters. These liberals are literally worse than Chinese communists when it comes to Social Security choice! Even though the United States has the most sophisticated investment markets in the world, we are falling behind other countries when it comes to providing retirement security. The president knows what a liberal can't fathom—that the American dream is not to suckle at the breast of a nanny state forever. Rather, it is to work, earn and to own—and to consume or pass on a goodly inheritance the way we freely choose.[a]

Environment — Article #010
March 8, 2001

A founder of Greenpeace International, Patrick Moore, said in an interview in the *New Scientist* (December 1999), "The environmental

[a] For more on Social Security Choice, see *www.socialsecurity.org*.

movement abandoned science and logic somewhere in the mid-1980s . . . [P]olitical activists were using environmental rhetoric to cover up agendas that had more to do with class warfare and anti-corporatism than with the actual science . . . ." Obviously, the comment is a generalization. There are many good groups, which care about the environment and don't fall into the unfortunate excesses of the modern environmental movement. But exaggeration and untruths are still employed, often to gain political support for government plans or treaties or assistance to stop so-called looming catastrophes. Never mind public policies combating exaggerated claims dangerously delay the economic and technological developments needed to improve both the lot of human life *and* human stewardship of the environment. In fact, economic development resulting in increased wealth has caused emissions to fall, because development enables citizens to invest more resources into environmental protection. When people take care of basic needs, they naturally move to improving the quality of their environment. Moreover, free economies do a better job than less free economies. The worst polluters in the world were communist controlled, centrally planned states.

The American people do clearly support a clean and safe environment. Yet most do not endorse proposals by many environmental organizations. The reason is that environmental decisions demand choices between oft-competing values; they demand reason and compromise and deliberative democracy at its best. Caution and prudence are in order, not Chicken Little tactics. For most of human history, mankind eked out his life against strongly indifferent and hostile forces of nature. Man's effect on creation was localized, short-lived. The science of ecology dates from the middle of the nineteenth century, when human power began to pose potential threat to the integrity of creation. Early industrialization did pollute cities, air and water. After a difficult transition period, however, industrialization and modern agriculture have enabled worldwide average life expectancy to increase from less than 30 to almost 80 in just 250 years. New technologies have made famine a thing of the past, except where political tyranny or turmoil is the cause. Manual laborers in developed economies have achieved a level of security and sense of dignity unknown before.

An "environmental transition" has enabled nature to begin a comeback too, such that America's forests have recovered now for 50 years and are larger today than 100 years ago. Air and water quality has steadily improved for 25 years. Trade will ensure that developing countries benefit from cleaner technologies and lessons learned quicker than we did, if well-intentioned environmentalists don't reverse the process. Problems remain and challenges are sure to follow, but honest scientific inquiry, rigorous economic thinking, and sound theological reflection—these will lead us to optimal solutions.

The Energy Chicken Article #058
March 21, 2002

As the weather changes, I look forward to the spring and summer—and to paying a lot less for natural gas. That's somewhat of a new twist and something I never thought I'd say. That's because as the cost of natural gas for heating recedes, the cost of electricity for cooling increases. Until the last year or so, I always paid more for air conditioning than I did to stay warm! Alas, how times change. It also reminds me that when I was growing up, the price of beef and chicken were practically the same. So I ate more steaks then, just as I wear more sweaters now. Let me tell you, not all trends amount to progress!

For nearly two decades, natural gas was touted as the clean, cheap alternative to most other fuels—especially to heating oil and to coal. It is still clean, but it sure ain't cheap. Prices began to rise three years ago from a low of around $2.00 per million British thermal units (BTU). Last year, prices in some areas of the country reached $50.00 per million BTU. In Texas, the average monthly bill jumped 50% in 2000-01. The reason bills were (and are still too) high demonstrates the old adage that chickens come home to roost.

The problem had been building for several years actually. For while the federal government encouraged widespread use of natural gas as a substitute for dirtier fuels and was successful (over half of America's homes now use natural gas to heat with), environmental restrictions prohibited most exploration. This is particularly true in known gas-rich areas, such as the Rocky Mountains. With little new exploration, gas producers have been unable to match supply with increasing demand. Moreover, natural gas is now the fuel of choice for power plants that produce electricity.

I have always wondered at the stupidity that hungers but won't eat. It is the same that saps the strength of the US military but sends it everywhere to put out fires and police the world. If you want energy, you have to provide for it. You either import or produce—or invest in something entirely new. That is the simple horse sense we ought to expect from representative government. Instead, we get these wunderkind presidents who squander supplies and pass along problems. Clinton even resorted to depletions in the national Strategic Petroleum Reserve! You can bet the last president takes full credit for the flush of progress and economic boom during his tenure, however temporal, illusory or unsustainable it has proven to be. His failure to have an energy policy (like many other failures) is a big chicken come home to roost. California is a case in point that demonstrates the connection: the most environmentally friendly state—and the most energy strapped. If you shut down nuclear power plants and don't provide alternative sources for the energy, what do you think will happen? Duh.

Utility officials did move to increase supplies, and thankfully the political environment under GW has been conducive to doing so. In 1999 there were 360 rigs drilling for natural gas nationwide. Today there are over 800, and the number is climbing. Ironically, the economic slowdown also reduced demand and retail prices for energy this past winter. Of course, to eliminate our overwhelming dependence on fossil fuels (blamed for greenhouse gases that produce global warming, a REALLY big chicken), the long-term answer for cheap, plentiful, clean energy may lie not only with Natural Gas, but also with alternative sources we have yet to develop. One of the most innovative and comparatively affordable ideas I've heard is to build a power plant on the moon. From there, energy from solar panels could be converted to microwave beam and sent back to earth. Power-producing solar satellites were first suggested in the 1960s, but the lunar power plant makes more sense—Why build a satellite? We already have one.

You Don't Have to Like It Article #201
o/a July 01, 2005

Freedom is fascinating, not least because you really don't have to like what people do with it, in order to love freedom and its possibilities. You don't even have to like the other people, who participate or make freedom what it is! If this sounds uncivil and not sufficiently genteel for your taste, consider only that if you actually *had* to like "it" and everybody, then you wouldn't be free at all. Notice I didn't say that you shouldn't or couldn't—only that you don't or won't have to. And therein lay a key concept, which seems all but missing from a common understanding of freedom in these latter days of political correctness. One misunderstanding is that it is illegal or unconstitutional to be prejudiced or to discriminate. Prejudice is a state of mind—and you can literally think anything you feel. If we had to go to jail for every bad thought, I reckon we'd all serve life sentences. Freedom to think is perhaps the only absolute right, even if you may not like my thoughts (if indeed you know them). Of course, the freedom to discriminate based upon race is not one people are likely to tout. It is a very unpopular freedom and usually morally wrong. Practically speaking, it is also circumscribed by the Fourteenth Amendment and enforcement by the Federal Government, as well as by Court application of the letter and intent of the law to actions by private individuals. You can in fact legally discriminate, except in the workplace or places serving "the public." After all, the First Amendment includes freedom of speech and the right to free association. Implicit is the right to say things people don't like to hear, as well as the freedom *not* to associate. The reasons people have not to associate may be ignorant, capricious and totally subjective. I don't have to like it, and they don't have to like me either.

Toleration is what it is all about. That may sound funny and counterintuitive coming from an avowed conservative, but that's because people don't appreciate freedom or see through the smoke and mirrors of what passes for "diversity." Diversity may or may not exist in fact; it may or may not actually be a good thing, in any given context. I happen to like diversity most of the time—the cosmopolitan flair of big cities and foreign capitals, the exotic ethnic sections of town outside military bases. Diversity must not, however, be a force-fed and predetermined end result. Else we're hardly choosing from a rich menu or living free at all. Not only that, but I may decide that I've had enough diversity for a day. Indeed, besides the qualitative aspects of racial and ethnic diversity, there are valid considerations like economic (short-term or long-term) impact and dislocation; demand on tax supported social services; impacts on language, culture, schools and other institutions; on the mores of the people; whether assimilation is desirable or occurring; and whether the pace of change is appropriate to the time. Toleration isn't supposed to be at one's expense, and it shouldn't presuppose a death wish for those of us who employ a little of it. Indeed, whereas the Constitution protects citizens and confers or protects fewer rights for legal residents and visitors, it doesn't apply at all to those living outside these United States of America—unless you happen to be a U.S. Citizen abroad, in which case the application of the Constitution is not the same either. Point being: you have the legal right to discriminate all day long against Ethiopians or Norwegians to keep them out of this country. Now I didn't say you should, only that you could. You can even make fun of them if you'd like (ever hear a Canadian talk—eh, it's a riot).

Bureaucratic government and majoritarian-democratic society seem intent on making everybody love everybody else, even to the point of making it illegal to police borders or decide certain referenda aimed at controlling or mitigating against *illegal* immigration. The situation amounts to a coercive and coerced brotherly love, based upon a weird internationalist mumbo jumbo, entirely separate from any political tradition or religious heritage. Indeed, it is a secular, godless and unpatriotic impulse, which makes it most akin to outright communist doctrine. It's John Lennon and Big Brother combined! Thomas Jefferson definitely would not relate—either to the applied doctrine of equality, or to the express hostility to states rights, and even to self-determination and national sovereignty. Martin Luther King, Jr., hardly had in mind the global village imperative, when he raised consciousness and awareness to the injustice rife in American society. He did, however, want equal protection under the Constitution and for Christians to live up to their better natures and to their Creed! Of course, you don't have to like it—not then or now. You can even switch sides to get it right, in case you were wondering. At least you are free to do so, despite the fact that the Country of our Forebears is rapidly disappearing. Increasingly, the Republic is perceived like any other ancient civilization, albeit revered; and Sons of Liberty, who helped us win our freedom, lay silent or maybe speaking, drowned by the steady drum of a million stupid people. And if somehow these Sons would rise again, would they be whisked to an undisclosed location? Perhaps held and interrogated at Guantanamo for failing diversity training, or never really developing that requisite heart for Paternal Government and for the 'wretched refuse' lying outside the scope of their Glorious Revolution.

Reflections on Katrina Article #213
o/a September 22, 2005

A couple of weeks ago, I said that an important lesson concerning Hurricane Katrina had to do with infrastructure—its importance to modern society, as well as our responsibility to plan for and provide resources to build it and to keep it maintained properly. True enough, but I think there are other things to learn if we reflect on what we saw in New Orleans after the storm.

It is my sincerest hope, that the people displaced will find opportunity wherever they've been flung, as well as the wherewithal to return home if that is their desire. Many will in fact find better lives elsewhere than home, because the ironic result of displacement can be a change in cycle or break in pattern—cycles and patterns that would otherwise perpetuate poverty and even some bad habits. Moreover, the outreach from communities across this country, particularly faith based initiatives and church sponsorships, will turn the lives of thousands of people around for the better. Positive examples from helpful citizens and those who befriend evacuees will elevate dreams and uplift spirits to the benefit of all. Thousands more people will find in their adversity, strength and aspirations they never knew they had. Thus it could be America is made better, as another great generation gains perspective on values and is steeled for the inevitable future challenges. At least that is a silver lining in the proverbial storm cloud.

The storm cloud over New Orleans, however, bodes ill as a warning to us all. What we saw were the leftovers and underbelly, 25% of a city population who could not or would not evacuate. There were decent and innocent people there, and not everyone in public housing projects is a bad person, but it is also true that a large number of the 25% remaining were from the city's public housing projects. Further, a destructive contingent came from city jails, which were emptied out during the flooding, many of whom used to live in housing projects. As Robert Tracinski has written, Katrina exposed the awful psychological consequences of the welfare state. Normal behavior in crisis was not the norm in New Orleans. Far too many people used the chaos of disaster to prey on their fellow man, to push dead bodies aside as it were, to steal stereos. A huge number evinced an attitude that is not so common in middle class America—an expectation and a lethargy that government would take care of them. If ever there was an example of the rotting, hollowing effect of welfare on people, this was it.

The people's government failed them to be sure, but I remind you it is the people who elected the government. Decades of corrupt government in New Orleans date all the way back to Huey Long. His approach to machine party politics and welfare promises built up a substantial national following, until 1935 when he was cut down in full career by an assassin's bullet. Indeed, Franklin Roosevelt brought similar machine party politics to the national level. The Great Depression provided the exigency and may even have justified a welfare approach temporarily to deal with the crisis, but welfare has continued ever since to produce dependent political constituencies by design. It is mind-boggling, the incompetence of New Orleans' mayor and local government that left 569 buses to flood, which might have carried over 33,350 people to safety! It is virtually inconceivable, the level of indecision and delay of Louisiana's governor to issue evacuation orders or to accept federal help, because her lawyers worried about liability implications! But this is symptomatic of the root cause, which is a patronage system of government built around dependency and socio-economic/ethnic constituencies that support the welfare state, both to their moral detriment and to the tax detriment of everyone else.

The last thing we need is for Washington to decide it needed more power to intervene in local and State affairs. What the nanny state has created in many big cities and places across America, is a class of citizens who are psychologically averse to taking care of their own needs. When government fails to take care of them, that psychology turns to incapacity to react "normally" in expected and appropriate ways. Government and police can only do so much, and in our towns and communities, the laws and peaceful coexistence of us all are maintained by self-reliant and independence minded people. You generally obey the law and live civilly with your neighbor, because you figure that's the right way to live the good life. You work hard and refrain from jeopardizing what you have by acting foolishly. Moreover, you value the rules of the game and understand that how you act is as important as what you get. Those who've been given everything by government and are told they are victims in a society, which owes them a living, have no similar compunction or self-regulating prohibitions on behavior.

New Orleans is going to be rebuilt and rise from the wet ashes. It is far too important to the nation's economy and transport system not to. The largest port in these United States cannot function without a city around it. It is far too historical and culturally important a city too, keenly impacting on the nation's and especially the Southern psyche. But let us make it better than it was please, and start by demolishing public housing projects and replacing the welfare state with a responsibility-ownership-opportunity state that includes everyone.

Lesson of Katrina is About Infrastructure Article #211
o/a September 09, 2005

In the aftermath of Hurricane Katrina, troubling questions remain that will have to be answered. It is almost certain there will be an inquiry of some sort into the slowness and inadequacy of response to this natural—and increasingly it seems, man-made disaster. The federal government no doubt shares some portion of blame, and this was after all, the first big test for that bureaucracy to end all bureaucracies called the Department of Homeland Security. Government organizations do, however, tend to get better at something after being stressed and then with good leadership, coming to grips with their shortcomings. Something tells me the lessons learned from this particular case study will be studied well into the future. Nevertheless, I am inclined to believe the federal government bears less responsibility than levels of government closest to the people whose responsibility it is to lay and execute the plans and to identify where it is they need help from the federal government in a given crisis—those levels of government which are supposed to conduct emergency response and evacuation first of all and enforce the law first and last. In the case of New Orleans and the sovereign State of Louisiana, it most certainly was not their "finest hour." It wasn't the president's finest hour either, when he came to view the devastation and said on at least two occasions that he was there to see things for himself and to tell the good folks in "this part of the world" that help was on its way. It's sad when the president forgets the good folks are *part of this country*. He could have said exactly the same thing in Bangladesh or Thailand. Then again, I know the president has a good heart and isn't exactly known for his exactitude of speech or cleverness in turn of phrase.

The idea that racism caused the crisis is pure horse hockey, which is not to say that racism isn't a residual in society. It most certainly is in white and black America, both North and South. The point is that delay of 48 hours or more simply can't be explained that way. Moreover, the compassionate response in this the proverbial morning after, puts the lie to that thesis. In Texas, nearly a quarter million displaced coastal residents are finding asylum and immediate assistance in Houston, San Antonio, Dallas, and other Texas cities. Thousands of Texas emergency personnel were dispatched to aid in the Louisiana search and rescue effort. Hundreds of churches and civic organizations are giving aid and sponsoring fellow human beings of any and every color, who have simply lost everything. No, the problems that transpired resulted from institutional and organizational failure of the first order, and were also a symptom of our crumbling and neglected infrastructure nationwide. Part of the underlying cause is our mixed up notion of government priorities, which doesn't line up too well with the Constitution or with American political tradition. If the priorities did line up, the president wouldn't mistake Louisiana for Bangladesh; the National Guard wouldn't be in Iraq; police organizations wouldn't buckle; and people would not rush to blame the president for hurricanes or for trouble with city hall and the local bus transit. Moreover, as a former FEMA director said, we might then begin to think at least 15 years ahead in order to address problems like building up levees!

Our ancestors did this in days before we had computers, and they gave us an infrastructure that we inherited, which until the 1990s, was the envy of the world. Today many of the roads, railroads, ports and shipping facilities, power grid, sewers, water treatment facilities and distribution systems, dams, tunnels and bridges are in a sad state of neglect. The people and their representatives in Congress have opted instead for current consumption and the mortgaging of our future with debt, piled upon a mountain of debt. We are not planning ahead or taking care of first things first. The Corps of Engineers, for crying out loud, was slated for a 20% budget cut before this disaster. One of the most enduring lessons from Katrina ought to be how quickly a modern and humane, 21st century city, can be turned into the Third World—replete with desperate and violent men, whenever the infrastructure goes down. Indeed, we are worse off than our ancestors in such an event, for we no longer have families on the farm. Fewer people possess the skills needed for total self-reliance in a survival situation. Urban populations, as opposed to rural or semi-rural folk, starve to death and dehydrate in natural and man-made disasters, unless conscious provision and backup provisions are made, rehearsed, and funded. Modern civilization is, in a sense, more fragile than before, because its roots are not very deep. Of course, on the bright side, we have an ultra modern information superhighway that brings us hundreds of movie channels and good sordid attractions, our favorite streaming music videos, as well as access to the whole worldwide global village. At least it will be easy to tell the *rest* of the Third World when it's over, over here.

A Wise Consistency Article #151
o/a July 11, 2004

A wise consistency is the foundation of a free society. Yet everyone knows, or thinks they know, that consistency is the "hobgoblin of little minds." How many times has Ralph Waldo Emerson been quoted to belittle a consistent philosophy defending freedom? The need to discredit consistency is utterly endemic—in the Congress and in society at large. It may reflect apathy towards thought in general or the imperative to think very hard—or perhaps it is just ignorance, rife, even amongst the so-called educated, concerning history and our founding documents. Indeed, popular wisdom holds that it is most beneficial to be flexible and pragmatic and to reject consistency. If it were not so, then self-criticism would be more than most could handle. Few congressmen would be able to defend their voting records. The comfort level of most politicians in D.C. requires an attitude that, consistency is not only unnecessary but altogether detrimental. For this reason Emerson's views are conveniently cited to justify pragmatism and arbitrary intervention in all legislative endeavors.

Communism was dependent on firm, consistent, and evil beliefs. Authoritarian rule was required to enforce these views, however. Allowing alternative views to exist, as they always do, guarantees philosophic competition. For instance, the views in Hong Kong eventually won out over the old communism of the Chinese mainland. But it can work in the other direction too! If, within the context of a free society, the ideas of socialism are permitted to raise their ugly head, socialism may well replace what we have if we do not consistently and forcefully defend the free market and personal liberty.

It's quite a distortion of Emerson's views to use them as justification for the incoherent and nonsensical policies coming out of Washington today. But, the political benefits of not needing to be consistent are so overwhelming that there's no interest in being philosophically consistent with one's votes or one's beliefs. It is a welcome convenience to be able to support whatever seems best for the moment—or for the congressional district, or one's political party. Therefore, it's quite advantageous to cling to the notion that consistency is a hobgoblin. For this reason, statesmanship in D.C. has come to mean one's willingness to give up one's own personal beliefs in order to serve the greater good—whatever that is. But it is not possible to preserve the rule of law or individual liberty if our convictions are no stronger than this, because something will replace our Republic that was so carefully designed by the Founders. That something is not known, but we can be certain it will be less desirable than what we have.

As for Emerson, he was not even talking about consistency in defending political views that were deemed worthy and correct. Emerson clearly explained the consistency he was criticizing: he was most annoyed by a *foolish* consistency. He attacked bull-headedness, believing that intellectuals should be more open-minded and tolerant of new ideas and discoveries. His attack targeted the flat-earth society types in the world of ideas. New information, he claimed, should always lead to reassessment of previous conclusions. To Emerson, being unwilling to admit an error and consistently defending a mistaken idea, regardless of facts, was indeed a foolish consistency. His reference was to a character trait, not sound logical thinking. It most certainly was not a reference to consistently and precisely following the *oath* to uphold the Constitution of the United States!

It has already been proven that centralized control over education and medicine has done nothing to improve them. But instead of reassessing these programs, more money is actually thrown into the same centralized planning—this is much closer to Emerson‘s foolish consistency than defending liberty and private property in a consistent and forceful manner while strictly obeying the Constitution. Moreover, Emerson‘s greatest concern was the consistency of conformity. Nonconformity and tolerance of others are obviously much more respected in a free society than in a rigidly planned authoritarian society. The truth is that Emerson must be (and is regularly) misquoted, in order to use him against those who defend a free society, cherish and promote diverse opinions, and encourage nonconformity—even the nonconformity of tradition. A wise and consistent defense of liberty is more desperately needed today than at any time in our history. Our foolish and inconsistent policies have brought us to a critical junction, with the American way of life literally at stake! It is the foolish inconsistencies that we must condemn and abandon.

To name a few of these, consider the inconsistency of conservatives who rationalize huge spending increases and the gigantic growth in the size of government and say that deficits no longer matter. Consider those who support free trade through massive international bureaucracies (a.k.a.

NAFTA, WTO, FTAA) to manage tariffs and sanctions in ways, which threaten national sovereignty and serve powerful interests rather than enhancing free trade. Consider the foolish inconsistency inherent in this situation: that cancer patients must come to congressional offices to beg and plead for a waiver to try some new drug or to receive comfort from marijuana raised legally in their own home state; while the DEA actually arrests and imprisons ill patients, because federal laws blatantly preempt state laws.

Few remember that the first federal laws regulating marijuana were written as recently as 1938, which means just a few decades ago our country had much greater respect for individual choices and state regulations in all health matters. Recently it was determined that a drug used to cause an abortion can be available over the counter. However, Ephedra—used by millions for various reasons and found in nature—was made illegal as a result of one death after being misused. Now it will require a prescription and cost many times more; and weight loss by thousands using Ephedra may well have saved many lives. But the real issue is not the medicinal effect of these drugs. At root, the issue is that government policies reflect disturbing moral standards for Reason or Right. The foolish inconsistencies reinforce neither individual freedom and responsibility nor traditional notions of right and wrong. They are at once wicked, as well as coercive.

By far the worst foolish inconsistency we must condemn and abandon is judicial review. Respect for the original intent of the Constitution in federal courts is at an all-time low. Instead of depending on these courts, we must *curtail* courts, which routinely overstep their authority by writing laws, rubber stamping bad legislation, and overruling state laws. Congress must begin now by removing jurisdiction from the courts—and they can do so by a simple majority vote! Let us begin by removing jurisdiction of all First Amendment controversies from all federal courts, including the Supreme Court. Issues dealing with prayer, the Ten Commandments, religious symbols or clothing, and songs, even the issue of abortion, are properly left as a prerogative of the States.[24]

Who Decides — Article #293
o/a April 13, 2007

Hypothetically if you were part of a club comprised of birdwatchers, you might vote on things that determined what the group would do, what programs it would have, what causes it would support, even what the membership should be and whether the purpose of the group should change. Decisions you reach with the other members might lead in several different directions. Should club activities, for instance, embrace conservation of mammals and marine life and not just birds? Should bird catchers and bird owners be admitted to club rolls with the same full voting rights as birdwatchers? This illustration could be made a thousand different ways, and most Americans will implicitly understand exactly what the role of the group is and what their role as a member is, since Americans are after all members of so many different groups from church to PTA to boosters. Americans routinely shop around too; they quit one group, join another, try to reform some place, or just start their own. Political parties are like that, and you can see how a political party changes itself; or rather, how the actions by people in the party changes it over time. So you get new platform planks, new community outreaches, policy initiatives, etc. The ideas involved can be new, old or some of both. In a very similar manner, societies at large change themselves by what's known as voluntary social evolution.

That was indeed the prescription the Founders left us to use. Most figured slavery would go out of fashion eventually, and for decades it appeared that it would. At any rate, there were lots of things about life in Eighteenth and Nineteenth century America the Founders knew could probably be better. The question was how change should proceed and who would call the shots; how rights would be protected and legitimate interests balanced at the same time. The Founding Fathers gave us the Constitution, as well as divided political sovereignty to work out details, including the pace of change and dimensions of our polity. The Constitution gave us parameters and a process to use. We could lead society in many directions according to its terms; or change the governing instrument through amendment according to its terms. Who would decide, however, was determined by who could vote. Those who voted held power over those who couldn't, just as today those who vote hold power over those who don't. James Madison's original contribution to political science amounts to a division of sovereignty between states and federal government. The Constitution divides roles between the two levels too, enumerating certain functions to the federal government and keeping the rest within the purview of states. It means in practice the same voters will choose representatives to two dual levels of government who represent them in each, respectively. So you are actually a member of two different polities, that of the state and that of the federal government. It has worked pretty well but not always.

Violence between the sections North and South during the Civil War suspended normal operation of the Constitution. In a sense it brought the two levels of government into war, but this example stands alone in our entire history. If you concede that African-Americans were thus brought into our polity through the force of violence as a precursor to the 13th, 14th and 15th Amendments, you must also concede that men peacefully submitted to the inclusion of women; that old and mature adults conceded to bringing eighteen year olds into the process; that dominant ethnic groups acceded to the inclusion of Indians and Chinese and others as citizens (which were not always).

Voluntary social evolution is in a very real sense a measure of self-determination; and self-determination is perhaps the single most important measure of freedom for members of the polity. If the sheriff escorts you to carry out your garbage, then you didn't determine to do it by yourself and you were hardly free to do it another day. If Washington withholds highway funds until Texas will or won't do something, then Washington violates the self-determination of Texans plain and simple. Hey, we might have gotten around to it or not, but our choice in the matter was robbed by someone else. The birdwatchers may have decided to help the dolphins as well as birds, but the gardeners' society forced them to water plants also, and astronomers said they had to draw the tails of comets and report on shooting stars. Those who valued their freedom and said that self-determination of a birdwatchers club resides with members of that group alone have since moved on. Texans unfortunately would need a Whole Other Country.

CHAPTER 11

Foreign Policy

Military and NMD — Article #003
January 18, 2001

A lot's been said about the shape of the military. Certainly it was a campaign issue with some resonance. If absentee ballot results are to be believed, folks in the military overwhelmingly agreed with the critique handed the Clinton-Gore Administration: conventional capability has eroded the past eight years; capabilities are overextended; morale is down; and retention is at the lowest level since Vietnam. If you talk to soldiers at Ft. Hood as elsewhere, it's clear they aren't very happy. Moreover, with the economy as good as it is, there's a lot of opportunity elsewhere without the BS that still goes with military life. The prospect of Bush-Cheney (and Powell) has given the military some hope that things will get better. Indeed, I think the problems mentioned above have turned a corner; they can and will be fixed soon enough. There is, however, a bigger strategic problem that goes to the heart of our military dilemma. The single greatest national security failure of the Clinton-Gore Administration has been its policy to leave the people of these United States utterly defenseless against missile attack.

Clinton squandered eight perfectly good years, budget surpluses and all, years in which the U.S. had a narrow window of opportunity immediately after the Cold War to deploy a National Missile Defense (NMD) system or system of systems. He produced a situation of vulnerability now that was nowhere close even four years ago. Now as I read my copy of the Constitution, I find that one of the primary functions of our government is "to provide for the common defense" (Preamble). I don't know if Clinton's copy reads the same way but thought it might, when he at last signed the National Missile Defense Act in July 1999. The act admitted to the growing threat and gave force of law to the NMD program, committing us to fielding when "technologically possible." It is clear in hindsight that the president intended to stall and to concoct technological fairy-tales, in order to give arms control advocates in Congress and the next Administration (he assumed would be Gore's) the chance to scuttle NMD for good and to revitalize the Anti-Ballistic Missile (ABM) Treaty instead. The ABM Treaty was made with the former Soviet Union, a country that doesn't even exist. Our adherence to it is by our grace.

The leader of Russia, Vladimir Putin, recently traveled to Canada to ask the Canadian head of state to help pressure the United States to forego its ABM system. If any country on the face of the earth presumes to tell the United States it cannot protect its own people with defensive weapons, that country is no friend of the United States—whether it's Russia or Canada. The Mutual Assured Destruction (MAD) deterrence theory was mad from the beginning, but it had a modicum of respectability in Cold War context—never mind, that the technology for NMD at the time wasn't feasible, but merely stated an existential fact. Frederick Seitz, former president of the National Academy of Sciences, has testified that we have technical feasibility for NMD today. The only thing we've lacked is political will. GW should deliver on his campaign pledge to change this. The policy of holding the American people at risk and hostage, when means exist for their defense, is categorically immoral and also unconstitutional.

Missile Defense Imperative Article #052
January 31, 2002

Almost exactly one year ago, I wrote that GW should deliver on his campaign pledge to amend or abrogate the Anti-Ballistic Missile (ABM) Treaty, to enable us to test, develop and deploy a missile defense system, or system of systems, for protection of the American homeland. To the President's credit, he has given the Russians a six-month notification of U.S. intent to withdraw from the obsolete 1972 agreement. GW's move is contrary to liberal think tank and media elite opinion, which indeed reinforces my judgment that it is an excellent decision. September 11th should have cemented the case for national missile defense. The roster of rogue nations actively developing long-range missiles that threaten the United States include North Korea, Iran and Iraq. There is every reason to believe such weapons, with their potential to carry nuclear, chemical or biological payloads, are the terrorists' dream-weapons of tomorrow. If

Osama Bin Laden had one September 11th, does anyone doubt he would have used it? Not even our best jet fighters could have kept a single ballistic missile from taking out the White House and the Capitol building at the same time.

The government's primary constitutional duty is always to provide for the common defense. Last year I wrote, "The policy of holding the American people at risk and hostage, when means exist for their defense, is categorically immoral and also unconstitutional." That statement becomes a most urgent dictum, in light of recent events. How can anyone continue to place these United States in the unenviable position of being blackmailed someday by terrorists or by rogue regimes? And wake up sleepy heads! The Russians and Chinese are even supplying our enemies in Iraq, Iran, Libya and North Korea with the ballistic missile technology to do us in. Moreover, although we downplay and publicly assure the Chinese that a defensive umbrella could never defeat its strategic missile strike capability, I'm here to challenge that notion and to ask why not? Red China has at least 20 intercontinental ballistic missiles (ICBMs) aimed at us right now. Our government doesn't have to advertise the effort, but it certainly should understand the imperative to protect us from even such a threat. Again, let us recur to recent events: am I the only one who remembers the Chinese clipping our military aircraft and then detaining American airmen last year? Terrorists bombed Khobar Towers in Saudi Arabia, two U.S. embassies in Africa, and then the USS Cole in Yemen, before we ever decided the terrorists were serious. The consequences of underestimating the threat from China are far more devastating than even the World Trade Center disaster. Make no mistake about it, 9-11 was the result of compound failure in American foreign policy and intelligence for at least a decade.

Brian T. Kennedy, political scientist, historian and editor of *www.missilethreat.com*, asks us to "Imagine a ballistic missile attack on New York or Los Angeles, resulting in the death of three to eight million Americans. Beyond the staggering loss of human life, this would take a devastating political and economic toll. Americans' faith in their government—a government that allowed such an attack—would be shaken to its core. As for the economic shock, consider that damages from the September 11 attack, minor by comparison, are estimated by some economists to be nearly 1.3 trillion dollars, roughly one-fifth of GNP." That's a lot more relevant scenario than global warming disaster, which we have little immediate recourse to offset—notwithstanding prudent steps we can and ought to take. Yet we do have technology now that can begin to offset the ballistic missile threat. American missile defense research has included ground-based, sea-based, and space-based interceptors, as well as air-based and space-based lasers. Each of these systems holds promise, having undergone successful, if limited testing. What's been lacking for at least the eight years prior to GW has been the political will to do the right thing.

Second Thoughts Article #053
January 31, 2002

Second thoughts don't necessarily imply second-guessing. I've been entirely supportive of my country's War on Terrorism. Indeed, I am certifiably committed to pulverizing any and everyone responsible for attacking these United States on September 11th. Nor do I think the military ought to make detainees at Guantanamo Bay, Cuba more comfortable. And that Walker creep can sweep horse hockey behind Fourth of July parades for the rest of his natural life! But I do admit to feeling a bit uneasy, when big government gets bigger because of it and no one even suggests that the trend might reverse itself. The era of big government being over is over, or so it seems. It wasn't convincing when Clinton said big government had had its day in 1995. We thought if Republicans got in there, it just might be. Then war came. Granted, extraordinary times may require extraordinary measures. War came to us first—a despicable and horrendous sucker punch that claimed three thousand lives, rocked the economy, and emotionally affected virtually every American. The psychic connection we all felt with New York and Washington, D.C.—and with each other—was uncanny. Neo-Confederates were no exception, and they have proudly waved the national banner above and alongside the Battle Flag. The United States are become States United from this perspective. Southerners will again fill the ranks of volunteer enlistments in disproportionate numbers, as they have in every war since World War I (in the Gulf War, it was 60 percent). How different is the unity of purpose today, say, from the way things were after Election 2000!

The problem is that wars historically concentrate power and control in the hands of government. When wars end, things rarely revert back. When wartime administrations end, residual authority remains and is often turned to other purposes by politicians. Moreover, the Cold War was one of the most devastating to freedom, because it was so drawn out. Its cumulative impact on politics and society from 1945 to 1991 is still being felt. The War on Terrorism is the first war of a new millennium and one that stands to be as protracted. This prospect should give us pause, especially as the immediate threat recedes. Terrible things might still happen in this war, but we are not locked in a mortal struggle for existence the way we once were with the Soviet Union. The discrete and concrete threat posed by the Taliban regime (to the extent that it provided safe harbor to Al-Qaeda terrorists) has been dispensed with. Mopping up requires concerted international effort for some time remaining, and it is prudent to reinvigorate international intelligence gathering and analysis capability. We ought not, however, trend away from sacred liberties on account of any of it. Attempts to trade liberty for security will likely produce neither.

In December, I flew domestically for the first time since 9-11 to visit relatives for the holidays. The airport security was stringent, and the lines were long. My small screwdriver was taken from me—I'd had it for twenty years, and it fit on a key ring. It was shorter than my car key and more blunt. I didn't want to point that out, afraid they might take my car key too! (The only thing I could not do with the car key that I could with the screwdriver is, well, . . . turn a screw). Military Police, with their M-16s strapped on, were prominent. I wasn't going to argue. Not only that, but had I forgotten to take a shower? Did I shave close enough? Man, I don't want to look like that Shoe-bomber! (No kidding). Later I had a conversation with someone, who said it was just a matter of time before we all had national identity cards, or internal passports. It would be the most effective way to tell immigrants from U.S. nationals! Indeed, more than 100 nations have something like national identity cards already. One multinational company proposes to do even better—it is optimistic owing to the surge of interest in its computer chips that can be implanted in people, to help identify and track them. I heard another American say, "If you have nothing to hide, you shouldn't worry about increased surveillance or answering questions!" I wanted to draw some historical allusion to Jews in Germany in the 1930s, but the deer-in-headlights expression convinced me not to bother.

For the record, I'm not as optimistic if we go down the present path much longer. The best thing to do with war is to win it, and to win it as quickly as practicable. I hope someday not to have to see our fine young MPs patrolling in domestic airports. And I think it's positively stupid for Republicans or Democrats to pick more fights in the world than you have to, especially when they are somebody else's fights. Our service men and women serve proudly and honorably at home and abroad. They do so abroad as America's forward presence and first line of security. Our service men and women accept risk and endure the hardship of military life, sometimes in un-free places quite different from home. They do so constitutionally for our well being, in order to protect the homeland and keep America free.

The lines of modern battle space are drawn differently now by technology and ideology, and homeland security is a bona fide issue. Notwithstanding, as David Theroux wrote recently, "Americans seek security, but not as an end in itself. We seek security to enjoy the blessings of liberty . . . . We must achieve security in a manner consistent with a diverse and open society, individual liberty, and the rule of law." History teaches that this can be exceedingly difficult—in total, world war certainly—but also in prolonged periods of mostly low-intensity conflict, which the War on Terrorism seems to be shaping up to be.

A Question of Executive Power Article #236
o/a February 24, 2006

Sen. Arlan Specter (R-PA) says the president's use of NSA surveillance outside the congressionally established approval process is in "flat violation" of the Foreign Intelligence Surveillance Act or FISA (1978). The only question is whether there are inherent powers in Article II of the Constitution, which somehow supercede that law. Attorney General Alberto Gonzales, quick to defend the president, countered with a peculiar history lesson, stating unequivocally that the presidency has the power to "surveil"—and presidents have used it again and again to conduct the same type of electronic surveillance ever since the Civil War! (Come again?) That's right, Ulysses S. Grant was listening to Horace Greeley's cell phone conversations. It hardly seems helpful to say he would've if he could've, since the powers vested in the president and the technical devices to which they pertain, are certainly no older than the twentieth century. Indeed, it is remarkable to listen to the drivel that escapes the mouth of supposedly educated men, who have our best interests at heart if not quite in mind.

While representing the administration, they seem to leave good learning and common sense behind. Take Ken Mehlman, the articulate chairman of the Republican National Committee (RNC) who, while interviewing with George Stephanopolous, said something similar: "It's been recognized since the Civil War, the president has the authority in war or peacetime to do what he is doing." And Senate Majority Leader, Bill Frist (R-TN), who takes the cake on a number of occasions, opining matter-of-factly that the president under the Constitution, at a time of war, has authority to [fill in the blank with practically anything]. Of course GW Bush frequently sidesteps hard issues, like whether the president has such-and-such power. He simply assumes it and uses it for our safety and benefit ("trust me," I work for the government); and anyway, if there is no show of abuse (hard to tell since it's a secret), then the extraordinary powers granted (Patriot Act) and some that aren't (NSA domestic surveillance) are perfectly fine. Do you want another 9-11? Oh do you, do you? If a loaded gun is pointed at your head, there's no problem with it since you can't prove the trigger's been pulled, and indeed it hasn't yet. So what's your problem? Dick Cheney comes to mind, because a little safety in the hunt might be justified after all.

Now let's set something straight. Some things were codified in the Constitution as a result of the Civil War and some were not. The existence of slavery at the time notwithstanding, the other gross violations of rights on virtually every level during the War Between the States and the unprecedented abuse of power by the Chief Executive at that time are still matters of debate, which demand sober consideration. Perhaps the extraordinary political crisis did demand expediencies unforeseen, neither contemplated by the Constitution—for indeed, it is a fact that the normal operations of the Constitution during the War were suspended. So is our Constitution likewise suspended today? Is that what the president requires to fight Al Qaeda miscreants around the globe? And if Lincoln is redeemed in the light of history, because we know or think we know now that ends justified means in his case, are we to grant the same authority using hindsight in one instance to energize this modern president in an entirely different instance? Shall GW cleave more States in two like Virginia? Shall he suspend habeas corpus also, so there can be no appeal or hearing for wrongful imprisonments by the government? Shall he exile his political opponents and quash dissenting editors by shutting down their presses or banning political cartoons? This really isn't what the Republican Party celebrates at its Lincoln Day dinners, and I'm not sure why all the president's men are so hasty to embrace Lincoln's extra-constitutional powers without half his wit or wisdom. The Constitution allows presidents to wield power, in peacetime and in war, but these powers are delineated in the Constitution. Beyond the scope of clear delineation, some presidents may wield more, but the extent of their effective power is predicated upon convincing the majority of people and States; and acquiring either the sanction or acquiescence from the other independent and co-equal branches of government. The political remedy for gross overreach of power is impeachment. More usual than not, however, ambitious second-term presidents are forced into lame-duckness, and Americans are better off for it.

Conveniently Constitutional — Article #312
o/a August 31, 2007

The United States signs international agreements with other countries, but we don't call them treaties so that we can avoid Senate ratifications as required by the Constitution. In the same way, you probably realize that we fail to declare wars anymore, no matter the length or degree of military commitment. Yet we marvel at the consequences: how we could get in a war on bad intelligence and faulty pretext; how we would manage to prosecute and win like the United States, only to lose national credibility and strategic objectives by performing the aftermath like the United Nations; how politicians should all second guess and point their fingers, as if they bore no responsibility for debate or a decision to go in and stay there—because in fact they shirked that responsibility in the first instance. The two-year anniversary of Hurricane Katrina was August 29th. Yeah we weathered the storm, as it were, but performed the aftermath like a Third World Country. It occurs to me our Congress resembles the hapless Iraqi regime more than we care to imagine!

State legislators have reported that the border of Texas with Mexico has been regularly violated, as armed vehicles cross the Rio Grande to provide security for illegal drug trafficking and whole convoys carrying the poisonous stuff to our youth come across the border. Yet there is hardly the hue and cry one would expect, no not from independent Texans or patriotic Americans, not a peep from the Governor or the President—none like in the days of Pancho Villa, when Blackjack Pershing took out after him into Mexico! And we deign to offer this brand of democracy to the Middle East and the rest of the world, as if they should even want it. Oh give me the Republic instead; or a home where the buffalo roam, instead of senators in airport lavatories. It makes you wonder if there isn't a connection between the inconvenient loss of character displayed by so many of our leaders and representatives today, and the "conveniently constitutional" approach they take to actual governance. The Founders believed that character lay behind not only good statecraft, but also maintenance of the liberties they bequeathed to us.

There is perhaps an inverse lesson to be drawn from experience in Iraq. That is to say, that despite the military success of the surge strategy there has been no progress on the political front there. Indeed, the reason for the surge was to buy a breathing space in terms of security for the Iraqi regime to make political headway. While the security situation on the ground has improved and the rate of American casualties has actually declined, there is less political unity and stability in Iraq than there was before the surge began! It was nearly a foregone conclusion the commander of the Multi-National Force-Iraq, General David Petraeus, as well as and other military brass would testify before Congress and show evidence of military success. It is true, so far as it goes. It should have been almost as certain, however, that the Iraqi regime would score miserably when it came to meeting the political benchmarks set by Congress and the administration. All the talk and "revelations" coming out this month will give politicians of both parties the cover they've been looking for, in order to reduce American troop levels before the next election—all the while declaring victory, or at least the end of a good college try. The inverse lesson to learn is that political rot at home will not stave off the day of reckoning that is sure to come, whether or not we have the most powerful and professional military force in the world—which we do. Moreover, political expedience and political consensus that comes at the expense of constitutional scruples, conceivably jeopardizes military readiness at home and strategic flexibility to face emerging threats abroad. The destruction of constitutional underpinnings is leaving these United States perilously adrift and at risk in the world, neither the Republic we once were, nor quite as yet the competent empire. For the sake of liberty, we can at least be grateful for the latter shortcoming. For the sake of liberty further, we should begin to elect leaders of character next year and into the future, men and women who care about the Constitution whether or not its dictates and procedures are convenient.

CHAPTER 12

Broken Borders, Broken Birthright

Broken Borders, Broken Birthright Articles #358-359
~Part I~ o/a August 08, 2008

We cannot help but have compassion towards those who want to come to America, but neither can we let them wreck the stadium and rush the field! Intentional trespass on our soil by people from other countries is totally unacceptable. It is contrary to the rule of law and to private property rights, as well as to national sovereignty on which the international system depends. It is contrary to dual state and national sovereignties, i.e., to federalism, on which the Constitution of these United States is also based. Illegal immigration presents to Americans—by birthright, as well as Americans by choice who have naturalized, and many more residents who came through legal means—problems of huge magnitude. These problems involve issues that should be the subject of deliberate policy debates and decision-making; instead, the challenges are forced upon the people who are living legally here now, by others selfishly and/or desperately seeking a place, station, economic or social claim against them. Any right or privilege sought illegally comes at the expense of legal birthright and naturalized Americans, because any right or privilege obtainable by someone else, must first come by express grant of the people living legally here now who are part of this polity.

The problems Americans face from illegal immigration are many, and just because they have sometimes been overstated or exaggerated does not excuse or altogether diminish them. Illegal immigration is unjust on its face to the inhabitants of this country, to the extent that illegal outsiders should have no claim on goods and services paid for with taxpayers' money—yet our laws and court decisions currently obligate us to pay for medical care, education and welfare to anyone who happens to cross our borders. Illegal immigration by definition bypasses the normal processes, including precautions for safety such as health screening and criminal background checks; and while it is overstating the case to say that deadly contagions have spread far and wide because of illegal aliens, it is no more just to say that only a handful have died because of it. The same sentiment that would outlaw capital punishment for a miscarriage of justice or the potential of innocents being convicted and executed hypocritically provides a safe-haven for illegals, whose diseases endanger far more people, including children in public schools.

Illegal immigration has long been linked to crime, including violent assaults and murder, assassinations, thefts and robberies. One-third of inmates in federal and state penitentiaries are illegal aliens. Moreover, since 9-11 the very real threat of terrorism from persons entering the country illegally raises the level of concern over isolated violent crime to that of widespread public safety and national security. Seven years after 9-11, however, the borders remain broken. Yet the truth remains, that there can be no homeland security without border security. Each year twenty thousand aliens enter the country illegally from Canada; and three million illegal aliens come in from Mexico! As Texas Governor Rick Perry reported a few months ago, drug cartels use military-trained commandos and transnational gang members routinely to establish armed perimeters on both sides of the southern border during drug and human trafficking operations—ensuring that Texas and federal law enforcement officers are met with deadly force whenever they attempt to interfere. There are *hundreds* of attacks on the U.S. Border Patrol every year. Furthermore, more people from outside the Americas—increasingly from Middle East and Asian countries—attempt to exploit this effective and dangerous conduit into our country.

Notwithstanding the Olympic spirit—according to which athletes from all over the world compete on fair and equal grounds for the gold and for recognition that comes from humanity based upon a superb performance, the 'wretched refuse of teeming shores' in respective countries of this world, have no claim on their medals or an entrance to the games. Moreover, a desperate Mexican has no more claim on legitimate entry to the United States by virtue of his being closer and geographically adjacent, than any desperate Chinese or African—indeed all are equally held at bay;

or rather moved as it were, to apply, in order to legitimize their desire to come in. All for the simple reason that their desire is subject to a grant of admission under the sovereign authority of the American people. We can talk about the prudential level of *legal* immigration too, how and whether it should be based on national and ethnic origins. Whatever your solution, the twelve million *illegal* cases and the millions more streaming across our borders annually stand in the way of as many people from all over the world, with similar or better aspirations and the qualifications to match. These are the other victims, law—abiding immigrants from all over the world, who applied and waited their turn but still can't come in—forced to wait decades, all because a lawbreaker stole their gold and despoiled a laurel crown.

~Part II~ o/a August 08, 2008

The challenge of assimilating too many people too quickly is often dismissed as racism, yet collisions of cultural patterns and norms creates the potential for social violence, and this is readily and empirically provable from our history. There are also understood, though arguable rates of assimilation; whereas, exceeding the rates produces unhealthy and unnecessary conflict and stress in society. The Babylonian confusion in having multiple languages too, as well as the expensive provisions to alleviate the same is similarly dismissed and likewise unnecessary—borne every day by Americans, who speak English and never cast one ballot to speak or do their business in any other. Economists will argue macro and microeconomics, but the local competition for jobs is real and felt, as is the transfer of wealth both within and without the national economy. Moreover, through fraud or physical presence alone, the development of political constituencies occurs, aided by institutions and organizations with special interests and ties to lobbyists. Illegal aliens press informally and formally to be heard and represented, thus reshaping the political landscape through sheer demographic weight.

It is not a prudential compassion to let the soup line invade the kitchen or kill the cook. Moreover, at some stage we have to ask if there isn't a responsibility others have to take care of their own home and countries, not by milking someone else's cow but by raising their own; not by breaking and entering a better place owned by someone else, but by making a better place where they live and doing the work Americans did in their own backyards. The foreign policy of the United States is strange and insipient that serves as an economic and political safety valve to corrupt and tyrannical regimes worldwide, particularly at our own doorstep. Indeed, more immigrants would likely be welcome if immigration were distinct from joining the polity, or laying claim to social services; and if the children of illegal immigrants—and legal immigrants on work status—were not conferred full rights of U.S. citizenship through the accident of birth and an asinine misinterpretation of the 14th Amendment.

One of the biggest magnets for illegal immigration is the policy whereby children of illegal aliens born within the geographical limits of the United States are entitled to U.S. citizenship. The policy is a perversion of American political tradition in that, under the Constitution the premise of citizenship is based on consent of the governed. Citizenship does not exist by nature but is created by law, and according to political science professor Edward Erler, the identification of citizens has always been essential to sovereignty. The Constitution mentions but does not define our citizenship. The first definition entered in 1868 as the result of the 14th Amendment, passed in the immediate aftermath of the War Between the States. The Amendment created dual state and national citizenships, however mandating that state law not abridge the basic rights due according to national citizenship. Familiar language includes: "All persons born or naturalized in the United States, and subject to the jurisdiction thereof are citizens of the United States and of the State wherein they reside."

We have somehow come to believe that anyone born within the geographical limits of the U.S. is automatically subject to its jurisdiction, but this renders the jurisdiction clause superfluous and without force. If this had been the intent the framers of the Amendment, they would have simply said that all persons born or naturalized in the United States are thereby citizens. Indeed, during debates on the Amendment, northern congressmen assured the whole country that while language was intended to make freedmen (freed slaves) and their children citizens, it did not make Indians or their children citizens! Indians were not subject to the same jurisdiction; that is to say, Indians owed allegiance to their tribes. Illinois Senator Lyman Trumbull, chairman of the Senate Judiciary Committee rose to support this view, saying that, "subject to the jurisdiction thereof" meant "not owing allegiance to anybody else and being subject to the complete jurisdiction of the United States." This excluded persons born in the United States who were foreigners, aliens, or who belonged to families of ambassadors and foreign ministers. Senator Jacob Howard of Ohio compared the right of expatriation favorably with the right of citizenship. In other words, jurisdiction was the critical qualifier to right of citizenship, more so than place of birth. It is absurd to think the 14th Amendment confers the boon of American citizenship on the children of illegal aliens, and difficult to fathom how those who defy American law could derive benefit for their children—or that any sovereign nation would allow it. The same confusion has led us to tolerate dual citizenship, when framers of the 14th Amendment specified that citizens must owe their exclusive allegiance to the United States, in order to be included in its jurisdiction. Broken borders and broken birthright are the harbingers of America's decline and eclipse of the American century so-called, unless we stop the madness and begin to reapply horse sense to what is happening.

CHAPTER 13

CONSTITUTION

The Immutable Nature of the Constitution Article #015
March 29, 2001

There's a philosophy about the constitution that's killing it—ironically, by conceiving it as a so-called "living" thing, subject to reinterpretation by society. In our entire history, the view has been ascendant for only the last forty years—a "contribution" largely of Earl Warren's Court. Before that time, judges discerned the meaning of the constitution from what it says, i.e., from its text. They understood the constitution to be a legal document. Though not unaware of popular opinion (nor even unaffected by it), they necessarily gave primacy to the original intent of the Founders, who wrote the constitution, which became the organic law of the land.

Today, instead of garnering enough support from the public to pass laws in accordance with the constitution—or to amend the constitution if need be, advocates influence judges. The judges continually revise their views of the constitution, in order to satisfy "the public." Fixed principles thus no longer guide the High Court's decisions; rather, a poll of the majority does the trick—for any given subject, at any given time. Understanding political history and the Founders' views hardly seems relevant anymore. Indeed, Supreme Court Justice Antonin Scalia (a Reagan nominee) rightly observed the situation "places the meaning of the Bill of Rights in the hands of the very entity against which the Bill of Rights was meant to protect"—namely, a temporal majority as expressed by or through the federal government. Hence, the view of the constitution as "living" renders the verdict of the American Revolution (or the Civil War—or any verdict) moot, because ultimately you make the constitution mean anything you want.

One might reflect on the reason the Founders wrote the constitution down in the first place. After all, the British constitution wasn't (and still isn't) written down. One of the biggest problems with the English system addressed by the Constitutional Convention was the fact that the English constitution was not fixed. It operated on common law assumptions, which enabled it to absorb changing precedent. This "living" approach, over time, gave Parliament its unfettered power by the time of the American Revolution. Every American knows (or ought to know) about the genius of this country's checks and balances. The Founders put in place written, fixed checks and balances to prevent unfettered concentrations of power over time. The States were as important in this regard as the three, co-equal branches of national government. How can checks and balances now work, if the fixed meaning of written words is traded for a modern equivalent of common law—i.e., public opinion, informed or otherwise?

The central government was limited by actual design. The limited function at the center was defined by enumerated powers in the constitution—essentially, a delegation of authority by States and the people to the federal government. In this way, the national government was set up to serve grass roots. Every State already had its bill of rights when the national "Bill of Rights" (first ten amendments) was adopted. Indeed, the language of the Bill of Rights is entirely negative—*precluding* the federal government from doing certain things that infringe upon States or the people. In no wise did the Bill of Rights confer power on the federal government to enforce rights it divines 210 years later, through a living reinterpretation! That would be a prescription for unfettered power, and that's the point Scalia was making—one I hope we all get soon, before it's too late.

Declaration vs. Constitution Article #016
o/a April 06, 2001

The Declaration of Independence (1776) and the Constitution (ratified 1789) are the founding documents of the American Republic, regarded as secular "holy writ." Ironically, however, many Americans confuse the two. It may be too bad, but days are past when school children memorized much of the Declaration and at least the Preamble to the Constitution. Thomas Jefferson wrote the Declaration; whereas, the Constitution took months of work by an entire convention chaired by George Washington.

Thomas Jefferson was serving elsewhere at the time, but he called the Constitutional Convention "an assembly of demigods." It is common to say the Declaration was the promise—the Constitution its fulfillment. The Declaration set out a vision statement of sorts, and the Constitution established a practical means (the apparatus of government) to approach an ideal.

It may seem trivial, but we might ask ourselves what that promise of the Declaration really was—was it, say, equality; or was it, say, independence? Let me give you a hint: it's called the Declaration of *Independence*. The second paragraph of the Declaration begins, "We hold these truths to be self-evident, that all Men are created equal, that they are endowed by their Creator with certain unalienable rights, that among these are Life, Liberty, and the Pursuit of Happiness—That to secure these Rights, Governments are instituted . . . ." Note that it is self-evident men are created equal, but governments are actually instituted to secure the natural rights of life, liberty and pursuit of happiness—not equality. "All men are created equal" is a phrase that was arrogated to greater relative importance by the Civil War—in particular, in Lincoln's famed Gettysburg Address. The context of that day certainly justified attention to the phrase and to the concept of equality, but mischief has occurred through an overemphasis on equality, which has turned into open-ended commitment by the federal government. The phrase in the Declaration is morphed outside of all literal context or history, when the original Constitution and Bill of Rights contains no mention of equality whatever.

In fact, the majority of the Declaration is a laundry list of empirical reasons why we ought to secede from Great Britain. The Declaration in effect proves that King George III was a tyrant; ergo, based on natural law and natural rights philosophy, we could (and should) institute a new Government. Of course, to do that, we had to break away from the Mother Country. The Declaration also lays out generic rationale and criteria, such that, should Washington DC ever become as corrupt and tyrannical as the King of England once was, Americans possess the same right to secede and to institute new government. The precedent set by the War Between the States was simply that secession would not be a peaceful, "Constitutional" process. Rather, secession is revolution by definition—still justified theoretically by the circumstance of oppression in our very own Declaration of Independence!

The Constitution was written after Americans won their independence. It gave vent to Revolutionary aspiration, as well as to prudence learned during and immediately following the Revolution. It applied the lessons learned from government under the interim and problematic Articles of Confederation. Most of the same Revolutionary heroes who fought Redcoats, helped to give us the Constitution—for the express purpose of establishing a better government. They did so in full light and consideration of the Declaration's shining vision. In terms of function as organic law of the land, however, the Declaration pales next to our Constitution. Remember, the Constitution fulfills the promise of *independence*. Not only that, but the Constitution was ratified and the Declaration was not. Today the Declaration still informs our vision of what constitutes good government, but its idealism is subject to the means of the Constitution itself—including the federalist construct, which leaves broad prerogative with the States.

Equality is Over Rated Article #023
June 21, 2001

Someone got me to thinking the other day about this line in the Declaration of Independence, and I wanted to share some of my musings with you. The line is the one everyone knows, or at least thinks they know: "We hold these Truths to be self-evident, that all Men are created equal, that they are endowed by their Creator with certain unalienable Rights, ..." Read the line again. Sometimes I wish Jefferson had chosen a different word to avoid some confusion, but he did the best he could I'm sure. Somehow people have got the line all disjointed about the "equal" business. They turned the adjective form of the word into a noun, so they can talk about "equality." Then they started to claim that "equality" is an unalienable right. But look at the text yet again: notice that while equality is a "self-evident Truth," the next phrase after that qualifies and explains it—men are *equal*, to the extent that God endows them with (presumably the same) unalienable rights. Among these rights is not listed Equality. Rather, men are in equal possession of certain natural, unalienable rights. Men are equal, because—as Jefferson continues—". . . that among these are Life, Liberty, and the Pursuit of Happiness."

Recently the Army decided to give all soldiers black berets. To be an "Army of One," everyone needed to be equal or look that way. Distinctive headgear worn by Rangers or Special Forces amounted to visible signs of elite status. The erroneous assumption is that other soldiers felt slighted or that special insignia is somehow injurious to the morale of everyone else in service. Ironically, the opposite is actually true. Most soldiers are altogether proud of who they are and what they do. They may indeed aspire to something someone else has or does, but that isn't the same thing as envy and it ain't all bad for morale to keep a little fire in the belly. Most don't give a rat's behind what the other guy's specialty is, because they are so busy being professional and "elite" in theirs. In fact, they're happy someone else chose to do their job too, because that makes teamwork so much easier. In the Army, everyone's pulling at the same wagon, so to speak: do your job, I'll do mine—and we all accomplish the mission. I recently had a son-in-law graduate from the "Q" Course, so I'm very proud for him. His accomplishment, symbolized by the distinctive green beret, makes him part of an exclusive group. That's something any and everybody ought to admire. For the life of me, I haven't met anyone in or out of the service, who doesn't understand and admire the symbol and the accomplishment. Even if lots of people start to wear berets, folks will still know the difference.

Now what does this all have to do with the line in the Declaration or the no-right of Equality? I'm getting there, don't rush me. In the book *Killer Angels* about the battle of Gettysburg, there's a great passage by one of the characters—an experienced NCO, who also happens to be Irish. He philosophizes about equality, pointing out correctly that there are no two things equal on the face of the earth. Not even two leaves off of the same tree; no two siblings, no two twins either. We may be created equal, but we aren't even born that way. We inhabit different spaces and different environments, however subtly. We inhabit different overlaps in time, since few are exactly the same age as anyone else. More importantly, however, a different mind actually inhabits each of us. I dare say, we each even have a different soul. We begin to move amongst different friends and have different experiences almost immediately. Why, we even experience the same things differently. We most certainly make different choices and get different results. Random aspects in life too, including sometimes opportunity, knocks at our doors at different times in different ways. Sometimes it's an insistent rap; at other times, it's barely audible. We can't anymore be equal, than we can be the same person.

Poets know that sooner or later all metaphors break down, because equating two unlike things has severe limitations. Yet we try to do this with people all of the time! Worse, we fool ourselves into thinking we have a sanction for the nonsense from our very own Father of the Declaration of Independence. But he understood the words he wrote better than we do. He knew that difference is really a good thing, and he counted on it. That, by the way, is the same thing as saying inequality is a good thing too. Because of inequalities, we can each contribute our own special talent or gifts. We can communicate, interact, exchange, help each other—which is possible, only when there's something to learn, something there special, something to need or be desired in another—even if it is only to make one's own contribution to another's well-being or effort. Markets couldn't even exist if everyone made tiddly-winks or cars or sliced roast beef. There would be no comparative advantage, no division of labor, no competing value! Simply stated, our innate, equal right to "Life, Liberty, and Pursuit of Happiness," which Jefferson attributes to each of us, is altogether contingent on our being innately unequal in every other respect.

Constitution and Civility — Article #031
August 23, 2001

One of several important breakthroughs in political science our Founding Fathers achieved, is the establishment of an entirely new category of law; namely, the Constitution. The Constitution is the nation's highest legal and moral authority—popularly accepted as such. Yet its ratification took place over 200 years ago, amongst a generation long since dead and gone. Charles Kesler, professor of government at Claremont McKenna College, says "Thus for Americans, the *oldest* law is the *highest* law." And he continues to point out how unique this is among nations:

> This is not a normal or an automatic outcome of popular government. Most of the time, republics and the people who move their politics tend to think that if they make a law "A" one day, and a law "B" that contradicts "A" the next day, the newer law supersedes the old. What is unusual about the Constitution is that this rule is completely reversed in respect of it. The oldest law is the most authoritative, and is indeed the only law that "the people" as such have ever passed.

> Other law is statute law, law made by representatives of the people. Thus every other law needs to be adjudged in light of the only law that is genuinely ours, the Constitution.

Clearly, some would prefer that the Constitution evolve and stay up with the times. There is even a modern liberal legal theory that affirms a so-called "living Constitution." This is another way of saying the Constitution means what lawyers and judges say it means.

Besides the Constitution as a category of law, the Founders also bequeathed an aspect of culture, which helped to give the Constitution stability and its impressive longevity. Historically a part of America's democratic culture, the aspect has sadly deteriorated as "living Constitution" theory advances. I'm referring to political civility, the idea that citizens will be civil to one another despite political disagreements. The disagreements are less important than the resolve to remain fellow citizens. Of course, a necessary precondition for this type of civility is that citizens do agree on certain fundamentals, so that disagreements really involve secondary issues. This is possible when the central government remains limited, or when fundamentals are settled at State and local government levels. The War Between the States was a time when folks (rightly and wrongly) disagreed on fundamental issues, which the federal government could not leave to States or localities. With discrete fundamentals settled on the battlefield, we've stayed more or less civil since Reconstruction.

Today I wonder about the Founders' great handiwork. Though altered much, it has survived in large measure. But I worry as civility departs, because government has grown too big and too intrusive in matters belonging outside its scope. I worry as respect for the Constitution itself declines, when citizens fail to distinguish rights from their desires, and political expediency supplants principle. During the last presidential election, people were tempted to say the popular or consolidated national majority (pure democracy) should rule the day—even though the *constitutional* majority entails both democracy and federalism and is the only majority that may govern the United States as a free country. What would George Washington have thought of the spectacle? The first president was quintessentially *both* civil and constitutional, in his personal example and professional conduct. He was also straightforward and literate. The following is taken from his Circular Letter of 14 June 1783, but Washington's words ring true today:

> The foundation of our empire was not laid in the gloomy age of Ignorance and Superstition, but at an Epoch when the rights of mankind were better understood and more clearly defined, than at any former period; the researches of the human mind, after social happiness, have been carried to a great extent; the Treasures of knowledge, acquired through a long succession of years, by the labors of Philosophers, Sages and Legislatures, are laid open for our use, and their collected wisdom may be happily applied in the Establishment of our forms of Government; the free cultivation of Letters, the unbounded extension of Commerce, the progressive refinement of manners, the growing liberality of sentiment, and above all, the pure and benign light of Revelation, have had a meliorating influence on mankind and increased the blessings of Society. At this auspicious period, the United States came into being as a Nation, and if their Citizens should not be completely free and happy, the fault will be entirely their own.

A Compound Republic — Article #042
o/a October 04, 2001

The compound republic—or federal republic based upon federalism—was a unique feature of the Founders' constitutional handiwork. Two levels of government (state and federal) are supposed to check each other against potential abuses of power, the way that three, coequal branches of government do at the national level. Indeed, the federal or compound nature of the Republic amounts to *vertical* check and balance, similar to the horizontal checks and balances produced between legislative, judicial and executive branches, exercising their delegated powers at the top or center of American constitutional government.

The federal structure provides for a separation of powers—dual sovereign orbits of responsibility—between the federal and the state governments. Unfortunately, the Constitution is not explicit, in terms of how to resolve constitutional disputes. Although judicial review has been the primary mechanism for doing so since *Marbury v. Madison*(1803), the result of this method over time has been to strengthen the federal government at the expense of state governments. Of course, the purpose of a vertical check and balance in the first place, is to provide for safe and stable freedom of individuals and communities (themselves comprised of freely associating individuals). The emasculation of vertical check-and-balance and the cumulative increase in power at the federal level, now threatens the freedom of individuals and societies in the various states. Moreover, constitutional reforms are needed to shore up the power of state governments, as well as to protect the system from similar concentrations of power in the future.

According to William A. Niskanen, chairman of the Cato Institute and a former chairman of President Reagan's Council of Economic Advisors, "the necessary change to make the federal government an effective guarantor of individual rights is to restore the federal protection of the privileges and immunities of all citizens, a protection formally guaranteed by the Fourteenth Amendment but eroded by later court decisions." Ironically, this key protection was eroded, even as the Fourteenth Amendment was used to expand federal power in other ways. At the same time, Niskanen says, "the necessary changes to make the state governments an effective guarantor of individual rights are to provide formal constitutional authority (a) for a specified *group* of states to nullify an action by the federal government, . . . and *maybe* (b) for an individual state to secede from the federal union, preferably by two successive votes over some interval and subject to some rule for the allocation of the assets and liabilities of the federal government."

Niskanen's recommendations will no doubt provoke controversy, but it is high time for the debate to begin. We must engage this problem directly concerning the lopsided turn the Republic has taken since the New Deal—away from the sovereign power of states in their proper orbits. States must begin to act as a ballast or counterweight to the insatiable demands and incessant meddling of the federal government, which too often represents the narrow special interests of ideology and private bank accounts, as well as the disloyal subterfuge of internationalist do-gooders. American tradition demands these kinds of constructive recommendations, which build on *The Federalist Papers*, as well as the Kentucky and Virginia Resolves and the Civil War constitutional controversy. Indeed, although post-Civil War constitutional amendments abolished slavery and established national citizenship rights for persons regardless of race, no constitutional amendment ever abolished the right to secession. Moreover, the Declaration of Independence practically enshrines its principle, inherent in natural rights political philosophy.

In *Federalist* No. 28, Alexander Hamilton stated that it was an "axiom" of the American system of government "that the state governments will in all possible contingencies afford complete security against invasions of the public liberty by the national authority." Should the national government prove to be a danger, Hamilton expected the states "at once [to] adopt a regular plan of opposition, in which they can combine all the resources of the community. They can readily communicate with each other in the different states; and unite their common forces for the protection of their common liberty." Likewise, James Madison in *Federalist* No. 51, described how the federal government and the states "will control each other; at the same time each will be controlled by itself." They would simply be aghast at the situation today, for we essentially have a dominant national, unitary government—which also defines its own powers. They would say it is a prescription for tyranny, if not tyranny outright. Hence, if constitutional procedures are not explicitly introduced to resolve the imbalance that now exists, i.e., to enable states the symmetrical ability to control the federal government in its proper orbit, then Niskanen predicts that gross "abuse of constitutional authority . . . can be constrained only by actions that [again] risk civil war."

Theory of America's Founding Articles #065-066
~Part I: Equality and Natural Right~ o/a September 08, 2002

The principles of America's founding amount to a remarkable and radical departure from government, as practiced for centuries prior to the American Revolution. To be sure, a tradition is tied to the theory and to the men responsible. We are, however, quite remarkable as a nation today, because the Founders were indeed radical in their definition of liberty and their uncompromising demand for freedom. The theory of America's founding may be said to be embodied in the Declaration of Independence. If anyone reads it, he or she finds that it is stated rather clearly, not hard to understand unless you're a modern day bureaucrat or store bought politician. What comes as shock and discouragement to many, is the realization that it is no longer the dominant theory in our government or in American politics. A new political theory arose during the Progressive Era, which came to dominate outright during the 1960s.

Popular and powerful today, it has already changed our government and society and now threatens remaining liberty. But let action proceed first from understanding, and to understand what's happened, we should review the theory of America's founding. The material that follows will borrow heavily from work by Thomas G. West and Douglas A. Jeffrey, two eminent historians associated with the Claremont Institute (www.claremont.org) in California.

The ideas or principles that comprise the American theory of government are posited as self-evident truths in the Declaration. They are universal in their application and may be true for men everywhere and for all time, because they are based on the "Laws of Nature and of Nature's God." They are the proper building blocks for human reason in matters of politics. They are themselves inherent in human nature. To be governed accordingly, is to be governed as well as man can be. These conceptual building blocks for righteous government are: Equality, Natural Rights, Consent, Revolution, God and Honor. The Declaration's statement of principles begins: "We hold these truths to be self-evident, that all men are created equal . . . ." Of course, humans are entirely different from each other in terms of their gifts and attributes. The Founders, however, meant to observe that regardless of differences like looks, talents or strength, etc., human beings are all equal in the life and liberty they are born with and deserve to keep. This kind of equality confers on everyone responsibility as well. James Madison explains in *The Federalist* 54 that every human being, but no cow, is held morally accountable for violence committed against others, because every man is free to choose his behavior. Moreover, because of the innate temptation to abuse power (part of human nature), equality as the Founders understood it meant that no one should have inordinate power over others.

Men are therefore equal in their potential towards depravity and cruelty, if entrusted with too much power. Madison observed that men are not angels; if they were, there would be no need for government in the first place. As it is, government should not concentrate too much power in the hands of anyone or any group of people. Note that if you deny personal responsibility or pass it along to someone else or worse, to some drug or psychosis or whatever, you practically lose your basis for equality as understood by the Founders. People re-categorize themselves with cows all the time, and that's just not good horse sense. The Founders expected us to walk on two legs and to get up off all fours—to behave like responsible moral agents, because we are equal in that respect. Only in this way are the great mass of men, to paraphrase Thomas Jefferson, unfit to be saddled, booted and spurred by the favored few.

The Declaration continues that human beings are "endowed by their Creator with certain unalienable rights, that among these are life, liberty, and the pursuit of happiness." A right, according to the Founders, is a claim that a person may rightfully make against someone who would deprive him of what is his own. You own your clothes for instance, and you have a *right* to them. If someone takes them from you, you have a legitimate claim against that person. He or she owes them back—or rather, he or she has a *duty* not to take them in the first place. A *natural* right is a claim to what one rightfully owns by birth, or by way of one's nature as a human being. Natural rights are unalienable, because they cannot be alienated or given away to someone else. A right from this point of view is a duty from another. If you have a right to liberty, I have a duty to respect that right. The Declaration specifically mentions three unalienable rights. No one may rightfully deny us these things. Note the third one mentioned above is the *pursuit* of happiness and not happiness itself. But the Declaration also says these three are "among" our natural rights, so there must be others. Additional natural rights may be gleaned from official documents and writings of the Founding era, and they include the rights of conscience and property, free speech and free press, freedom of religion, and others protected in what became our Constitution's "Bill of Rights."

The Founders would never have said that you have a right to decent housing, health care, recreation, or anything else before you have worked to get them. It is only after you have acquired your property in some legitimate way that your right to own property comes into play. That said, property rights can be seen as part of the right to liberty and the right to pursue happiness. There is also a natural right to work, and property comes into play here too. We own ourselves and our labor by human nature; ergo, we are free to work and to keep the fruits of our labor. The right to earn property, and to keep the property one earns is fundamental to the conception of Natural Rights shared by the Founders. Moreover, the right of religious liberty was not a right to exclude religion from public life. Indeed, the *right* to religious liberty flows from the *duty* that all human beings have towards their Creator. The most basic reason for freedom of religion understood by the Founders, was not to free man from obligation to God or religion, but to free him to perform his duties to God, without obnoxious coercion into modes of worship by fallible human beings in government.

~Part II: Consent, Revolution, God and Honor~ September 9, 2002

Besides Equality and Natural Rights (discussed previously), the ideas or principles that comprise the American theory of government, i.e., the proper conceptual building blocks for righteous government are Consent, Revolution, God and Honor. Consent is needed to form legitimate government. The Declaration of Independence says that to secure the rights of life, liberty and pursuit of happiness, "Governments are instituted among Men, deriving their just powers from the *consent* of the governed." Indeed, people must join to form governments to secure all their natural rights, but governments do not derive unlimited powers to perform that function! Just powers are only those consented to by the people. The Founders believed that a republic was that form of government that best reflected consent, in that, all powers are derived directly or indirectly from the great body of the people" (*The Federalist* 39). I have observed, however, that consent may be measured differently from culture to culture—and not always democratically. Some people in the world don't even value their vote. All I can say is that we Americans possess a political culture and explicit heritage that measures consent exclusively through democratic republican means. Notwithstanding, consent in and of itself is not the sole standard of legitimacy or goodness. The people do not have the right to consent to *unjust* powers. According to Thomas G. West and Douglas A. Jeffrey, the Founders would tell us we cannot rightly consent to powers of government that violate the unalienable rights of individuals. Consider then that the people are not supreme to the standard of Right per se. The standard of Right would be God's province. Democratic majorities may not redefine what is right. The inalienable rights are set for all time by Nature and Nature's God, and they are written and fixed in our founding documents. The Founders would not recognize any such thing as a "living" Constitution. They would impeach half our judges today for suggesting it.

Hence the real challenge of self-government: people must be of such character that they will only give their consent to good and just measures. And this extends to establishing government and to operating it. The Founders essentially took care of establishing a just government with the people of the first generation. They made a "social compact" with fellow citizens, and I would argue that they covenanted not only with each other but with God as their Witness and Gaurantor. But that still leaves the ongoing matter of consent in the operation of government. That's something you should be doing on a regular basis, at least by casting your informed ballot on election day. But no matter what ballot initiative you consent to, you always retain the unalienable right to liberty and may never delegate to the government permanently. In a sense, the government rests on a renewable source of consent, which you give it through participation, acquiescence or peaceful protest.

The right to Revolution naturally follows. West and Jeffrey again: "Government exists to protect natural rights, and government derives its just powers from consent. If it is not doing this, the people should get rid of it and set up a new one. [Indeed], the right to revolution is reflected in the early American conviction that the people have a right to keep and bear arms and to govern themselves in all local matters through local governments close to the people." Of course, the right to revolution doesn't mean it is right or good to overthrow government at the drop of a hat. If government is doing a tolerably good and decent job, you put up with its shortcomings and mistakes. If the system remains open to a redress of grievances, you continue to participate. The Declaration says, "Prudence . . . will dictate that governments . . . should not be changed for light and transient causes." Prudence is what we might also call "horse sense." Revolution is dangerous—it throws men back into the state of nature, where destructive passions and violence may become uncontrolled. For that reason secession is probably the preferential form of revolution, should revolution ever be justified in America.

Additionally, the Founders placed God and Honor ahead of narrow self-interest when they established the government. They commended us to do the same in its ongoing operation. The Declaration says that when a people are subjected to a long train of abuses aiming at absolute despotism, it isn't only their right—"*it is their duty*," to change the government. The duty is higher than one's own personal survival or selfish interest. The Founders' sense of honor taught them that they must be ready to sacrifice their lives and property for the sake of their duty. In order to establish and preserve free government, they pledged their lives, fortunes, and "sacred honor." In the *Declaration of the Causes and Necessity of Their Taking up Arms* (1775), Thomas Jefferson and John Dickinson wrote: "We have counted the cost of this contest, and find nothing so dreadful as voluntary slavery.

Honor, justice, and humanity, forbid us tamely to surrender that freedom which we have received from our gallant ancestors . . . ." It was a notion behind much Southern chivalry before and during the War Between the States, i.e., the Founders' conviction that political slavery and dishonor are worse even than death. As honor is a keen sense of right and wrong, it implies integrity and an adherence to right action or principles above else. In this view, people are legitimately supreme to government when it comes to upholding standards of Right. For standards of Right on earth become a nexus ultimately, where God and the individual meet in man's conscience. Government may not arrogate to itself the legitimate power to speak for any individual at this level of communion or duty. There is no collective conscience and no collective Soul. One person at a time may redefine what is right, if and when government gets it terribly wrong. The inalienable rights are set for all time by Nature and Nature's God. We end then where we started, with the Creator. Indeed, there are four distinct references to God in the Declaration of Independence. To the Founders, separation of church and state was meant to prevent a single religious sect from becoming official religion for the whole country. But the principles of this nation in fact constitute religious doctrine, the Declaration's own theology—with God as author of Law and Source of rights for mankind, eternal and unalienable on earth as it is in Heaven.

Only Fixed Constitution will Protect Freedom Article #091
June 5, 2003

A purely traditional or customary approach to the rule of law does not adequately defend freedom. Rationalist approaches are even less capable, because they lack the element of fixity required by a legal system. A fixed constitution requires reference to substantive principles, from which tradition is derived—reference points anterior to, and controlling upon, the development of pure tradition. These reference points are ultimately religious and axiomatic in nature. In a way, it is the "establishment of religion" that will restore for us the Constitution and secure the Blessings of Liberty that were intended. If we consult the official public record, including legislative transcripts dealing with the First Amendment, there is no other conclusion but that the Supreme Court was woefully (if not willfully) off the mark in its 1962 decision banning prayer in a New York school district.

The latest and most thorough research based on primary sources establishes clearly that the origins of ordinary Americans' values were not in classical republicanism or rational humanism, but in reformed Protestant Christianity. Neither were the elite a lot of skeptics, secularists and "Deists." The vast majority of the Founders were church-going Christians, and none were as hostile to religion as, say, Justice Hugo Black. Excellent work proving this point has been done by M.E. Bradford, W. W. Sweet, and Rene D. Williamson. The Founders' beliefs are important, because they shed light on the intent of the First Amendment. Disestablishment of official churches where it occurred did not equate to modern secularism, nor did the First Amendment injunction preventing the *national* Congress from establishing a religion disallow the states from doing so. Indeed, James Madison's discussions in debates about the First Amendment reveal it was an object of the amendment to prevent *Congress* from threatening the religious diversity of the states, which ranged from established churches to doctrinal requirements of various sorts.

Massachusetts, for instance, had an established church until 1833. Ironically, the First Amendment wording as voted on by the House came from Fisher Ames, conservative from Massachusetts. Wording was compromised in conference committee before sending the amendment on to the Senate for a vote. Roger Sherman and Oliver Ellsworth, stalwart Calvinists from Connecticut, worked on that committee project. At the time, their state had a law that fined anyone 50 shillings for not going to church. One had to be Protestant to serve in the New Hampshire legislature until 1877. Roman Catholics could not hold office in North Carolina until 1835, in New Jersey until 1844. In Maryland, until 1826, one had to be Christian to hold office. As North Carolina "liberalized," it still required public office holders to be Christian until 1868; thereafter, they had to profess a belief in God. Of course, the First Amendment did not prevent the appointment of chaplains or the establishment of Thanksgiving Day at the national level either. In fact, the day after Congress passed the First Amendment and sent it to the states for ratification, the House adopted the resolution calling for *a day of national prayer and thanksgiving* with language thanking God for the "opportunity peacefully to establish a constitutional government . . . ."

Thomas Jefferson's words "wall of separation" have been bandied to support the 1962 High Court decision and other decisions derived from it. The words come from an 1802 letter and are taken totally out of context. Indeed, we have only to look at Jefferson's second inaugural address to find what he really said regarding church and state. Jefferson clearly states that the free exercise of religion is independent of the general government under the Constitution; that is, Jefferson left religion as the Constitution found it, "under the direction or discipline of state or church authorities . . . ." His interpretation squares identically with Madison's rationale and the intent of the First Amendment. The wall of separation, such as it was, was intended to be between the federal government and the states and not between the people and their religion.

The American Whig Party of the last century (and not a few of the Founders) equated the leading principles of the Bible with those of the Constitution, but it has not been my intent to equate the Constitution with religion or religion with the Constitution—only to point out using the example of religion that the intended and fixed nature of the Constitution (and the purpose of its written format) have been subjected to a kind of cumulative violation. And indeed, this fact plays havoc with various aspects of American political tradition. Time has a way of losing what is not fixed by strict construction. A fluid Constitution means the loss of our whole political tradition at some point.

Historical Aspects of Our Amazing Constitution — Article #092

o/a May 09, 2003

Through most of our history the Constitution has been regarded as a kind of secular holy writ. This itself is something unusual for nations, but high regard for the Constitution is for good reason. After all, it represented the Founding generation's republican consensus and their gift to Posterity, the fulfillment of a nine-year Revolutionary struggle and some six years of domestic tribulation that followed. The Constitution of the U.S. embodies the basic law of the land and is the world's oldest written constitution. James Madison is known as the Father of the Constitution, because he led with the initial Virginia Plan that served as the basis for subsequent deliberations. After four hot summer months' work, the Constitution was adopted by the Federal Constitutional Convention in Philadelphia, 17 September 1787, and was then sent by the Continental Congress to the states for ratification.

A two-year ratification debate followed. When the ninth state affirmed ratification, the instrument superseded the problematic Articles of Confederation. George Washington was inaugurated President on 30 April 1789, and Congress met in session for the first time the same day to declare the new Constitution in effect. Washington embodied the remarkable apotheosis that took place behind the Constitution by former Federalists and Anti-Federalists alike (those who campaigned in favor of ratification and those who had opposed it). Of course the Federalist Papers (1787-88), written by Alexander Hamilton, James Madison, and John Jay had allayed many initial concerns about the Constitution by expounding aright its political philosophy. Even more importantly, the Federalists acquiesced to Anti-Federalist demands for a Bill of Rights, that is, to the first ten amendments, which were proposed in 1789 and became part of the Constitution in 1791.

Among the most important features of the Constitution are the horizontal checks and balances that insure independence and autonomy between three equal executive, legislative, and judicial branches of government. Borrowing heavily on Montesquieu, Madison explained the contrivance in Federalist Paper 51 (February 1788), e.g., the interior structure of government whereby "constituent parts . . . by their mutual relations, [become] the means of keeping each other in their proper places." The Founders had no knowledge of a fourth branch of government, written about in political science texts today, called the bureaucracy. Nominally part of the executive branch, it operates outside the interior structure of checks and balances Madison referred to. There were just three original executive departments after all: state, treasury, and war. The fact that the secretaries of each were appointed by the President with the Senate's approval, but were removable by the President alone, was intended to preclude departments from evolving into powerful ministries independent of the chief executive, the way they had done in Great Britain.

Even after Constitutional ratification, the Constitution had to be "filled in." Senator Oliver Ellsworth of Connecticut worked on the creation of the federal judiciary. Alexander Hamilton shaped national monetary policy and worked on creation of a national financial system to manage debt and currency. It was not until after the first decade of the nineteenth century that the constitutional system can be said to have firmly jelled. Furthermore, even after the famous *Marbury* v. *Madison* decision (1803) in which Chief Justice John Marshall affirmed the doctrine of judicial review, each branch still retained equal right and duty to determine constitutionality for itself. For that matter, until after the Civil War, so did each state.

The most important feature of the Constitution (besides perhaps its written form and fixity) is also James Madison's original contribution to the field of political science and the most unique aspect about American constitutional government. Called federalism, it comes as close as there is to an essence of American constitutionality and exceptional political philosophy. The supremacy of Federal laws is limited to those made "in pursuance of the Constitution," and states are in no legal sense subordinate entities to the Federal government. Amendment ratifications, for instance, are dependent upon the consent of three-quarters of state legislatures or conventions. Federalism is, in effect, an ingenious vertical system of checks and balances implemented by the Founders, and the written Constitution is primarily a document in federalism. It was chiefly regarding this "exterior" structure of government to which DeTocqueville referred, when he called the Constitution of the United States "the most perfect . . . that ever existed . . . ." We'll talk more about that next time.

The Health of a Republic — Article #143
o/a May 18, 2004

The term republic had a significant meaning for all early Americans. The form of government secured by the Declaration of Independence, the American Revolution, and the Constitution was unique, requiring strict limitation of government power. Powers that were permitted would be precisely defined and delegated by the people, with all public officials being bound by their oath of office to uphold the Constitution.

The Constitution made it clear that the government was not to interfere with productive nonviolent human energy. This is the key element that has permitted America's great achievements and made America the political and economic envy of the world. We have truly been blessed.

Today, however, the nature of a republic and the current status of our own form of government are of little concern to most Americans. But there is a small minority, ignored by politicians, academics, and the media, who do spend time thinking about the importance of the proper role of government. The comparison of today's government with the one established by our Constitution is a matter worthy of deep discussion for those who concern themselves with the future and look beyond the coming election. Understanding the principles that were used to establish our nation is crucial to its preservation and something we cannot neglect.

In our early history it was understood that a free society embraced both personal civil liberties and economic freedom. During the 20th century, this unified concept of freedom was undermined. Today we have one group talking about economic freedom, while interfering with our personal liberty, and the other group condemning economic liberty, while preaching the need to protect civil liberties. Both groups reject liberty fifty percent of the time. Sadly, there are very few in this country who, today understand and defend liberty in both areas.

Many Americans wonder why Congress pays little attention to the Constitution and are bewildered as to how so much inappropriate legislation gets passed. But the Constitution is not entirely ignored. It is used correctly at times when it's convenient and satisfies a particular goal, but never consistently across the board on all legislation. The Constitution is all too frequently made to say exactly what the authors of special legislation want it to say. That's the modern way: language can be made relative to our times. But without a precise understanding and respect for the supreme law of the land, the Constitution no longer serves as the guide for the rule of law. In its place come the rule of man and special interests.

That's how we have arrived in the 21st century without a clear understanding or belief in the cardinal principles of the Constitution—the separation of powers and the tenets of federalism. Instead, we are rushing toward centralized control. Executive Orders, agency regulations, federal court rulings, and un-ratified international agreements direct our government, economy, and foreign policy.

Congress has truly been reduced in status and importance over the past hundred years. And when the people's voices are heard, it's done indirectly through polling, allowing our leaders to decide how far they can go without stirring up their constituents. This is opposite to what the Constitution was supposed to do: protect the rights of the minority from the abuses of the majority. The majority vote of the powerful and the influential was never meant to rule the people.

In a free society individuals should control their own lives, receiving the benefits and suffering the consequences of their actions. Once the individual becomes a pawn of the state, whether a monarch or a majority that's in charge, a free society can no longer endure. We are dangerously close to that happening in America, even in the midst of plenty and with the appearance of contentment. If individual freedom is carelessly snuffed out, the creative energy needed for productive pursuits will dissipate. Government produces nothing, and in its effort to redistribute wealth, can only destroy it.

Freedom too often is rejected when there is a belief that government largesse will last forever. This is true because it is tough to accept personal responsibility, practice the work ethic, and follow the rules of peaceful coexistence with our fellow man. The temptation is great to accept the notion that everyone can be a beneficiary of the caring state and a winner of the lottery or a class action lawsuit. But history has proven there is never a shortage of authoritarians—benevolent, of course—quite willing to tell others how to live for their own good.

Some of my good friends suggest that it is a waste of time and effort to try to change the direction in which we are going. No one will listen, they argue, and the development of a strong centralized authoritarian government is too far along to reverse the trends of the last century. Why waste time in Congress when so few people care about liberty? The masses, they point out, are interested only in being taken care of, and the elites want to keep receiving the benefits allotted to them through special-interest legislation.

I am not naïve enough to believe the effort to preserve liberty is a cakewalk. But ideas, based on sound and moral principles, do have consequences. Our Founders clearly understood this, knowing they would be successful, even against overwhelming odds. They described this steady confidence, which they shared with each other when hopes were dim, as "divine providence." We face tough odds, but to avoid battle or believe there is a place to escape to someplace else in the world would concede victory to those who endorse authoritarian government. The grand experiment in human liberty must not be abandoned. A renewed hope and understanding of liberty are what we need today.[25]

The Constitution Always — Article #148
o/a June 20, 2004

I recently started teaching U.S. History for Central Texas College at the Ft. Hood campus. Our textbook is *The American Nation* by Carnes and Garraty. It isn't the best or worst textbook out there, but what disturbs me more than passages of political correctness is what passes for truth. "The United States in the 1780s was far from the powerful centralized nation it has since become." Indeed, truth it is which bothers me! Moreover, numerous modern textbooks attribute a fundamental change during the Civil War vaguely linked to the Fourteenth Amendment, which ended the American theory of dual sovereignty. The country launched by the Founders is not the country we live in today. The Constitution no longer applies the way it used to. This country isn't even called a Republic in most political discourse. The Pledge still has it right, but most lawmakers ignorantly refer to our country on and on as a democracy—when the most it is, democratically speaking, is a democratic-*republic*. By all accounts presented in textbooks or mouthed by most politicians of both parties, the American centralized national government we have now, led by Congress, could very well issue another Declaratory Act just as categorical as Parliament's in 1766. Washington, DC could say to us, '*Citizens of the States are inferior . . . We own you.*'

In the *Austin American-Statesman*, a story appeared Sunday, June 20th about Supreme Court Justice Clarence Thomas. The piece was by a *Los Angeles Times* reporter, David G. Savage. The story centered on Clarence Thomas's use of the Constitution of Original Intent, i.e., the 18th Century document to guide his judicial opinions. "Justice's views on the Constitution . . . veer from standard." Again, truth it is which bothers me. By focusing on the words and history of the document as it was written in 1787, there could be "far-reaching" consequences. The piece goes on to conclude that "Constitutional scholars credit Thomas with reviving a historical, if now outdated, view" of the Constitution—in particular, that of the First Amendment regarding religion. You see the original Constitution does not contain a so-called "wall of separation" between church and state governments. A University of Texas law professor says the constitutional viewpoint expounded by Thomas is downright "astonishing." Imagine looking back to 1791 when the Bill of Rights was ratified to discern meaning today! A professor at Notre Dame Law School concedes Thomas is right "as a matter of history" but asserts, "Most people would see it as water under the bridge." God save us when our Constitution has become "water under the bridge." I say the Constitution always!

In 1994 there was an effort by Heritage Foundation to encourage lawmakers to recur to the Constitution whenever they considered legislation. Just have U.S. Congressmen state where and how they derive authority for what they're doing! The effort proved too hard and worse, too confining for what even conservative *nationalists* wanted to do, so the idea was given up. A hopeless minority of Congressmen led by Republican(s). Ron Paul, still run through the exercise, but sticking to the Constitution these days is clearly optional if you represent the national government. It is denied you entirely if you represent a State. Strict construction would have it that the president should have led Congress to a declaration of war before we invaded Iraq. It was a terrible lapse in leadership and vision in my opinion that he did not do so. It would have been easily accomplished with a Republican majority in Congress. The implications, say lawyers and insurance companies, are just too inconvenient. But if he had, Bush would have made short shrift of the second-guessing and jockey for political advantage he now endures from critics of all stripes. These are strange times when logic doesn't even enter in what the government does; when precedent bears so little relation to the modern/post-modern age; when chronology and intent and discrete change as it occurs are disregarded—presumption cast aside for what finite, temporal and *present* men simply will. When will we rediscover and reaffirm that the Founders knew what they were doing? When will we at least admit their Intent, barring constitutional amendment, must be the organic law of the land or it is illegitimate?

Since I am an historian, I will go out on a limb and tell you that Ronald Reagan's legacy is secure—he belongs to the Ages. In the same way, Bill Clinton's legacy (despite his recent book tour) is lost to the Ages because of his awful character and the way he besmirched the high office of the presidency. It were his distractions and dalliances that gave us 9-11. Ronald Reagan fought the Good Fight his whole life, and he just passed you and I the baton! WE are his political and ideological heirs. And it is up to us to see through the completion of his Revolution. At root, the Reagan Revolution foresees a day, when we shall end judicial tyranny in America and reclaim the culture from liberals and from all those who would deprive us of our Godly heritage. His Revolution foresees the day when we shall also revere the Constitution again and restore constitutional government by redressing the imbalance between the state and federal levels of government. It can happen as quickly as the fall of the Berlin Wall, or it may take the last full measure of devotion, when we shall restore the Constitution of our great Republic and make and interpret the laws consistent with the Original Intent of the Founders.

We shall live as free men and free women and Texans again—and we will have self-determination or submit to a new tyranny. Thomas has it right—it is the Constitution *always*! It matters if Liberty still matters. The Reagan Revolution must succeed, or there will be cause for another kind of revolution our Founders understood well also.

The Constitution and the Constellation Article #414
o/a August 28, 2009

When the Constitution went into effect in 1789 it had a meaning inherent in its text, which could be interpreted when necessary by a ready recurrence to the Founders' stated Original Intent. If we choose to describe this as the first or original constitutional regime, we can certainly distinguish a few other subsequent regimes based upon the Amendments applied to it. Essentially, whenever Amendments are made to the Constitution according to its terms, the operative nature of the document changes to greater or lesser degree. Except for discrete changes, the Constitution remains the same, animated by the same Original Intent and historic textual understanding vested in the document. Whereas one may say that every Amendment represents a new regime in the order that it becomes ratified, for all practical purposes political thresholds determine that clumps or groups of Amendments tend to come into play at roughly the same time.

Hence the first Ten Amendments (Bill of Rights) were ratified at exactly the same time. The Thirteenth through the Fifteenth Amendments came within a few years of each other after the War Between the States, mostly codifying existential changes wrought on the battlefield or military occupation. The next four Amendments after that spanned seven years, but are clearly identifiable as part of Progressive Era changes. Two more Amendments came in during the New Deal, and the Twenty-Second is related to the death of the New Deal president while it revalidates a two-term precedent begun by George Washington. Four Amendments are tied to an era of social change during the 1960s. The Twenty-Seventh and final Amendment (1992) is one left over from the early Republic that had simply not been ratified. It is the sole constitutional achievement of an era mostly characterized by conservative political resurgence. This fact belies a huge failure on the part of the post-World War II conservative movement, not only to roll back New Deal political assumptions, but also to reestablish a fealty to the text and Original Intent of the Constitution.

If Amendment alone determined constitutional regimes, things would not be so bad. By way of illustration, the Thirteenth through Fifteenth Amendments did not overturn state sovereignty, states rights or "home rule" for good, bad or otherwise. They did not usher in unending change and reform, even if the Civil War Amendments (so-called) did make fundamental shifts in the nature of the Union. Historically the shifts were not the result of peaceful political process, but they were *exceptions* or additions integrated by virtue of what Grant called a Tribunal of Arms. Fortunately the Union knit back along antebellum lines to a surprising degree. The "Republic" picked up constitutionally speaking, after a hiatus of suspension that probably extended from start of the War through to the end of Reconstruction. It was decades later and not until the Twentieth Century before the Constitution changed peaceably again through an amendment process. During the Progressive Era fundamental changes were introduced and ratified, which gave us among other things, the income tax and woman suffrage.

After the Progressive Era, Amendments to the Constitution are misleading. They do not capture the essence of changing constitutional regimes, because change has occurred outside the Amendment process. Particularly since the New Deal, Amendments have mostly been technical and procedural. Notwithstanding, fundamental shifts in the meaning of the Constitution outside of the text have occurred at an alarming rate and qualitative degree of change. Original Intent was altogether dropped in favor of a "living" interpretation. This living interpretation has made a zombie of the United States Constitution.

The Flag as we know has thirteen stripes, alternating red and white for thirteen original Colonies and the first States to ratify the Constitution. The "union" of the Flag is that portion in the upper inner corner that contains a blue background and constellation of white stars—one star for every State in the Union. This symbology is apt. Note the political Union is comprised of States, but the relation of States one to another and to the whole, comprise the Union. The only visible objects on the Flag represent the States. Fixed stars in combination make up a constellation. Likewise, States that ratify the Constitution comprise a Union or political constellation, and this terminology was common amongst the Founders. In combination, stars in a constellation produce more light than a single star alone. As conceived, the synergy of States combined, economic and otherwise, produces more than a sum of parts.

It may be asserted that the Union exists, even if some stars fall out, burn out or explode. Indeed, the size of the Union itself might be expected to change—whether more objects get caught in the gravity or fly out from their orbits. Nevertheless, the Union does not exert a central pull around which everything else revolves. It is not a solar system—the Nation is not the Sun and States like planets. All the States are stars, and the Union is their grouping or Sign. They are held together in a Union, but their relation against the celestial sphere is through the aegis of the Constitution. It is the Constitution that holds them and defines their relationship to each other and to the whole. The Union might expand (as it has), or contract (in theory or by Tribunal of Arms). Each star, however, is an irreducible object, just as each State is an irreducible political sovereign. *According to its terms*, the Constitution alone defines how States must share, divide and mix their sovereign prerogatives with the federal government. But when the Constitution is dead, States will realign as separate stars into new and different combinations. In so doing, they may yet, ironically, restore the constitutional Union, which for the present seems lost—they might restore that great political constellation, an American Republic, which *meant* what it was called, the United States of America.

The Whole Constitution and Nothing But: A Presumption

o/a April 15, 2005 Article #193

Picture the Constitution shot full of holes. Indeed, it is as if words and passages have been cut out. Certainly the U.S. Constitution as we know it bears little resemblance to the Original. And it is no matter of having been amended, but rather it is a matter of arbitrary decision by Supreme Court judges, upheld and enforced by Executives and Legislatures, who don't know their heads from a hole in the ground. Worse than particulars of interpretation, errors that are inevitable in any human activity, is the sheer abandonment of the presumption of Liberty.

Liberty is a great concept that could use a little more reflective study these days, especially in the Congress. It's the thing Patrick Henry said was more precious than life itself. But presumption is an important concept too, one we too often skim over. The presumption of Liberty is what the courts especially—and all public servants really, should have. Presumption in this regard is what makes you innocent until proven guilty. Presumption is what gives you privacy in your own home. In the absence of some compelling state interest or probable cause for crime, it simply 'ain't nobody else's business!' How you raise your kids is presumed to be your business. Whether you clean your toilet or make up the bed, well you get the idea. I may think you're a slob, but it isn't my place to instruct you on how to do those things. It isn't the government's place either, to instruct us on half the things they "presume" to now. The fact is they really do tell you how big your toilet's water tank should be, and everyone knows it isn't their business and it isn't big enough to boot.

The presumption of Liberty would have it, that whenever the Constitution gives government the authority to act, courts should apply a demanding test. Laws that infringe upon liberty should be presumed invalid, unless the government can show they are the least restrictive means of achieving legitimate objectives. Indeed, the legitimacy of government itself rests on that very notion that government acts to protect the liberty of all. If it doesn't, better to dispense with the government! Only government that protects liberty commands the obligation of a free people to follow its decisions. There can be no moral obligation on the part of a freeman to submit to rule that undermines his status as a freeman; the decision to make you a slave is never a morally binding one, even if you are obliged for the moment to submit in the face of power. Decisions of courts should naturally lead to a maintenance of or expansion of liberty, not towards the restriction of liberty through every subsequent, precedent-setting decision. The loss of freedom and the restricted area of liberty today which is so apparent—in the loss of prerogative in family life, education, health care, and in setting the moral tone and environment of our communities, severely undermines the legitimacy of our government and increasingly makes the breaking of law as morally binding as upholding it should be.

If the drafters of the Constitution had really wanted to protect rights against government encroachment, why didn't they simply list all the ones they meant to protect? The answer is that the list of human rights would be virtually endless. This is where the "lost" Ninth Amendment enters in. It reads, "The enumeration in the Constitution, of certain rights, shall not be construed to deny or disparage others retained by the people." That was meant to prevent the emergence of the kind of "some rights are more important than others" nonsense jurisprudence that we now have. The people are supposed to retain all their rights by a presumed maximization of, a.k.a. presumption of liberty. The right to pray in a school controlled by the local folk, is at least as important as the right of every teenage girl to an abortion—which by the way, is a misconstrued right that wouldn't exist had the federal government not gotten involved where it should not have. Indeed, the federal government has begun a list of rights the Founders wisely omitted, in deference to a much broader presumption of Liberty. Unfortunately, what the federal government leaves out is no longer protected in a system that retains no semblance of balanced power between the States and federal government. Since the federal government controls everything, its omission of specific rights leads to an admission that Congress can and will legislate all the other rights out of existence. It is a sorry state we've come to.

In the federal government's so-called war on drugs, the federal government conducts a full-scale war on the States and the people's rights. The voters of Arizona, California, Alaska, Nevada, Oregon and Washington have all passed medical marijuana initiatives to enable categories of citizens, who are sick and have little hope with standard treatment to control pain associated with their diseases, to use the drug. The federal government prosecutes these cases anyway, indeed with greater zeal, regardless of the territorial and political sovereignty of these States. A similar observation is true concerning State initiatives dealing with illegal aliens. Whether you agree with the policy *decisions* of these State initiatives is not the point. When the federal government pursues legal aims that are contrary to the explicit political will of the people and abandons the Constitution's time-honored and moral presumption of Liberty, these become anew the times that try men's souls—and as for me, 'Give me Liberty or Give me Death.'[26]

The Relation Between Property and Freedom Article #194
o/a April 18, 2005

There is an inseparable connection between the development of private property and freedom in the West. Indeed, perhaps the most glaring example is the delayed and relatively shallow development of private property tradition in Russia. The corresponding history of what is otherwise a European country is almost entirely autocratic. The reason is that property serves as a primary basis for rights, and it is the having of rights, which supports the Rule of Law. Where there is no property and hence little basis for rights, the capricious will of rulers will tend to supplant the law. The most essential ideological dispute between communism and capitalism had to do with just this, that is, with how to deal with and view private property. Communism strove to eliminate it entirely. Aristotle had rightly observed that it isn't private property that is evil, or which causes class or human conflict; rather, it is the *desire* for property—and you can hardly eliminate that. Private property may have its vices, but it leads to fewer quarrels and wars than an ill-conceived notion to try and eradicate it. Indeed, the abolition of private property is an assault upon human nature.

Quite contrary to Marx's assertion that acquisitive feelings and the desire for property result from environment, these are inborn and very close, if you will, to the soul of a human. One of the first words children learn is the word "mine." Seventy-five percent of conflicts among children are over possessions. Like all living creatures, people are acquisitive in order to survive! In the case of human beings, we are acquisitive also, in order to define our space, to discern what matters most and what doesn't, to order priorities and establish values, to derive sense of dignity, self-worth and purpose. The most extreme example of an attempt to eradicate possessiveness was the *kibbutz* in Israel. In those communes children had nothing of their own, not even socks or underwear; everything was shared. The results were terrible. When they grew up, those children could not establish normal human relations with other human beings because to them it was "selfish." They could not fall in love because love involves possessiveness. They could not write poetry because it was not something that the group enjoyed.

Notwithstanding, private property began in ancient Israel. When the Israelis settled in Canaan they apportioned the land among themselves by lot. In Europe, building on a Judeo-Christian heritage, kings were obliged to respect the property of their subjects. Kings ruled but subjects owned. In most of medieval Europe, the kings actually ran the government from their own income—leasing out large estates, collecting rent, and using much of the revenue to run their courts and army. By 1300, however, English kings didn't have enough money to do everything required, which led them to convene a House of Commons to ask their subjects to subsidize the government through taxation. Increasingly power passed from the kings to kings-and-Parliament and then almost entirely to Parliament. This process formed the basis of European and trans-Atlantic liberty: possession of property required government to come to its subjects, ask them for appropriations and grant them power in return. In this way, property rights led to the development of parliamentary institutions and to many other rights.

In Russia the story was different. Russian czars appropriated the totality of the land and granted the land to servitors, mostly military men, under the condition of absolute obedience and loyalty. They could live on the land and use it, and were given serfs to work for them. But only as long as they served the crown—otherwise, the land would be given to someone else. As a result, every subject had to loyally serve the czar for life, and there was very little soil for the spirit of individualism and freedom to grow. The czars never had to seek permission to raise taxes! So the idea of a loyal opposition remained alien and never took root either. The tragedy for Russia and its contemporary backslide into authoritarianism, emphasizes the extent to which private property is vital for liberty and economic progress at home. Although nobody challenges the notion of private property directly in America, property is challenged daily by liberal apologists, who uphold and expand the operation of the welfare state. The welfare state is the enemy of private property and a threat to freedom itself. Today in these United States, the federal, state and local governments together control 35 percent of Gross Domestic Product (GDP). The excessive taxation is dangerous, and enables the government to influence public policy in less than transparent or democratically legitimate ways, telling universities whom to hire and fire for instance. Whenever government enriches itself beyond a sharply defined and limited functional scope of activity, it correspondingly divests citizens of private property and the precious rights of freedom that are attendant to it.[27]

True to the Founders: Two Things They Ask of Us Article #197
o/a June 02, 2005

In the hot summer of 1787, our Founders gathered in Philadelphia for the Constitutional Convention. Thomas Jefferson was our Minister in France, but he called the men at the Convention an "assembly of demigods." Indeed, they were the best and brightest of America, and of the whole world during what was an Age of Enlightenment. The elder statesman at the Constitutional Convention was Benjamin Franklin. He said democracy is two wolves and a lamb voting on what to have for lunch! Franklin was certainly no democrat—and neither were the other Founders, who knew more about political definitions and theory, not to mention the English language than we, and our elected leaders apparently do now. Consider the Pledge of Allegiance—it's to the flag "and to the *Republic* for which it stands." This squares with something else Franklin said, which points to the huge distinction between democracy and a democratic *Republic*. When the Constitutional Convention had ended, an anticipative crowd was gathered outside. A woman asked Franklin directly, as he came out of the building, this question: what form of government have you (the delegates) given us? To which he replied, "A Republic if you can keep it!"

Further, our Founders were very specific in how we should go about 'keeping the Republic.' They wrote at length in letters, essays and sermons. Their worldview is not at all beyond comprehension; it is plain. Original Intent is something we can pick up and recapture, if and when we are sufficiently willing. And if we are willing, there are two things the Founders ask of us: to be a virtuous people and to follow the Constitution. To be a virtuous people is to affirm the truth of the Bible and to apply Judeo-Christian morality in our families and communities, the way the Pilgrim Fathers did 150 years before the Founders. George Washington said organized religion was an "indispensable support" to public virtue, i.e., he believed churches and church life were important. He also said we would never be a happy nation without widespread personal commitment to imitating Christ in our daily walks. That's right, the Father of our Country wasn't 'politically correct' in the least, but he was quite literally correct both politically and philosophically. The rationale for public virtue was that it is necessary for a people to exercise good judgment (in juries, for instance), as well as to have proper discernment, in order to fulfill our democratic responsibility under the Constitution to vote—that is to say, virtue is required for an ability to choose wisely our representatives and president, persons of character from amongst the people to lead.

Of course, the Constitutional Convention and the two-year ratification process by the States afterward, would have been pointless if the Founders' product were never intended; or if the ratified instrument, that along with the Declaration became the organic law of the Land, were some April Fool's joke! The Founders clearly intended Posterity to 'keep the Republic' by following the Constitution they worked so hard to give us—to amend it, if and as necessary according to its terms, but to follow the Constitution always. Duh, and no duh (if only the Congress and the Supreme Court these days believed it, or the people would demand)! The conservative critique over the past 25 years has proven that the modern liberal welfare state, as it now exists in these United States, is unconstitutional according to Original Intent. The terms of amendment have not been kept. The intellectuals on the left have lost the argument, so they have shifted instead. Sen. Hillary Rodham Clinton (D-NY) said in an interview this month that she is opposed to judicial activism (judges legislating from the bench), but then she offered a qualification—*if it 'turns back the clock!'* In an attempt to portray herself as responsible moderate for a presidential bid in 2008, she has positioned herself against unpopular and unconstitutional judicial activism—but only if it is conservative. It is perfectly fine to change the Constitution in 1973 by inserting an inalienable right to have an abortion that the Founders apparently overlooked. It is likewise okay to enforce a single standard nationally, invalidating laws in over forty sovereign States. It is, however, quite unacceptable for a judge to opine that the Supreme Court in *Roe v. Wade* may have made a mistake or overstepped its bounds. The political environment is less conducive to progressive reform after the 2004 elections, so liberals are holding ground. Senator Clinton knows they've done enough damage for the moment—if they can enshrine decades of liberal judicial activism that emaciated States Rights and legislated new and sometimes twisted legal rights without basis in the Constitution or tradition. Opposing conservative judicial activism is not the same thing as following the Constitution, not by a long shot or country mile. In the present predicament, following the Constitution to 'keep the Republic' may very well entail turning the clock back in key respects.[28]

True to the Founders: Now or Maybe Never Article #198
o/a June 09, 2005

It is hard to know where we are in the grand scheme of things. I mean people have been predicting the end of the world since the world began. Some people read the End Times in the news of today, especially since 9-11. And while we ought not live as if we would live forever (since we will not), it isn't wise perhaps to live as if our heads were on the chopping block all the time. That sage and Founder, Ben Franklin, counseled moderation in all things, and indeed, a sober and reasonable perspective doth seem proper in this case. For if we do not have all the time in the world, surely the Lord hath given us enough time to make a difference. But I wonder what it takes for His patience to run thin, or when it is that time has really passed us by. If we can save the Republic in the Eleventh hour but fail to do so, what good is it to wail the second before Midnight?

My Friends, I do not know the answer to that question. Forbid it, God that we should ever find out. I do know, however, that it is later than you think. We live today in that proverbial Eleventh hour, now even as we speak—both in terms of the decline of public virtue and the utter abandonment of our magnificent Constitution. The Founders told us the two things were intimately tied together, that the loss of virtue would undermine the Constitution and the undermining of the Constitution would jeopardize public virtue—that both are required to 'keep the Republic,' that the end of this Republic, should we fail, would be abject tyranny. Illustrations concerning the Eleventh hour abound, much more than I prefer—of course, it means that '*Wisdom cries and understanding puts forth her voice!'* But again to what avail, if judges lead a procession to sell out the country; and Congress and a docile Citizenry sit back to watch the parade?

In the last quarter of 2004, a scholarly journal called *Critical Review* ran an essay that dealt directly with arguments presented in Randy Barnett's book, *Restoring the Lost Constitution—The Presumption of Liberty* (Princeton University, 2004). As the book title should imply, Barnett's case is that the U.S. Constitution—the one found in school textbooks and under glass in Washington, is not the one enforced today by the Supreme Court. Since at least the 1930s, the courts have cuts holes in the original Constitution and its amendments to eliminate parts they don't like. People ask me if it is a conspiracy, and I say it is a conspiracy whenever Stupidity, Arrogance and Power converge. Rather than debunk the case Barnett makes, the *Critical Review* essay by the former clerk for a U.S. appellate-court judge, says there just is no persuasive reason to follow the original Constitution anyway. Further, the essayist opines that most people still assume these United States are governed by the Constitution. "Ironically, however, the very class of persons entrusted with understanding, interpreting, and applying the Constitution—namely, lawyers—regards this common supposition as a polite fiction, if not a noble lie." He concludes that judges should, as in fact they do, turn to sources of authority other than the Constitution in deciding constitutional cases.

There are good points made in the *Critical Review* essay by Austin Bramwell, and there is certainly a valid critique to be made of Barnett's work. But to abandon the Constitution and to hold that up as sound constitutional theory is insane. It is also the sort of sleight of hand that ends nations and civilizations if the people fall for it. If a majority or determining group of power elite ever buys the theory, then all legitimacy goes out of this government. Disturbingly, some of the power elite has bought it. In April 2005, Tim Russert interviewed several Supreme Court Justices on television. Comments made by Sandra Day O'Connor (a Reagan appointee) and Stephen Breyer (a Clinton appointee), were appalling on their face. Breyer: "It's appropriate in some instances to look how other courts have decided similar issues . . . . A year ago, I went to the 10th anniversary of the Supreme Court of South Africa . . . . They might have, with their document—which reads very much like ours—and their judges, who are human beings just like we hope we are, and a society that has certain similarities—as all societies do more—they have a way of working out a problem that's relevant to us, it's worth reading." O'Connor: "Of course we look to foreign law . . . . We have a provision in the Eighth Amendment dealing with cruel and unusual punishment, and saying that's unconstitutional. Now, our ideas of cruel and unusual punishment, . . . have evolved, and our court has said over time that that concept is one that evolves. What's our best way of knowing whether it's evolved? . . . It doesn't hurt to be aware of what other countries have done . . . . It doesn't hurt to know and it's part of the concept of an evolving concept of decency."

To state clearly the obvious, the U.S. Supreme Court ought not to decide U.S. cases, based upon the law or precedent in other nations and international organizations. Moreover, when Supreme Court Justices speak in gibberish, they ought to be removed quickly from the bench, if we are to 'keep the Republic' of our Fathers in this the Eleventh hour.[29]

Constitutions Then and Now — Article #209
o/a August 26, 2005

It has been four years since the attack on our nation September 11th, 2001. Iraqi representatives are now struggling to write a constitution, which they will ultimately have to talk to their people about and then ratify (or reject) through special election. Our Constitution, by way of comparison, was written over 218 years ago and ratified 216 years ago after two years of debate, in the Year of our Lord 1789. The president, in order to give the Iraqi government encouragement, and perhaps to limit U.S. domestic expectations as to the product, said at the Veterans of Foreign Wars convention August 22nd, that "we understand how difficult it is to write a constitution from our history—our Constitution has been amended many times over." The statement hit me like a splash of cold water, and I wonder how many Americans realize what a stupid thing the president said. A conservative president—or at least one whose conservatism embraced strict construction of the Constitution—would never have said such a thing, either by referring to the Constitution in the context of one in Iraq, or by lading it with so many negative and erroneous implications. Moreover, for the president to say it is far worse than someone else, because he is the chief executive of this Constitutional Republic. The implication that our Constitution was deeply flawed from the beginning, or that democratic government necessarily entails frequent amendment to its organic law for a just and stable regime to emerge, is hardly History 101 or Civics 101. Indeed, it is pretty much horse hockey. The historic War Between the States witnessed a de facto suspension in the operation of the original Constitution, and this fact may or may not imply a serious flaw in the original Constitution. But that remains a debate of first order amongst historians and constitutional scholars, and the issues involved are manifold, difficult and nuanced. To flippantly assert that the Constitution was messed up and so was amended a lot of times, is more worthy of a middle school essay than a speech by the president.

In point of fact, we've had 27 amendments. The first ten are known as the Bill of Rights and were essentially agreed to during the ratification process to ensure passage of the Constitution. They went into effect in 1791, virtually in tandem with the main body of the document. So that leaves 17 amendments in 214 years, an average of one every 13 years. The last amendment in 1992 regulates congressional salaries and is something of an anomaly among the rest. Its origin is the early Republic too, but the measure lay dormant until a college student discovered it was procedurally "stuck." The United States in its first 76 years added just two amendments besides the Bill of Rights, and these dealt with technical matters of Judicial reach and operation of the Electoral College. Indeed, most amendments are procedural improvements, not substantive or philosophical. Since George Washington, all presidents adhered to two terms (maximum) in office. Only when Franklin Roosevelt ran until he dropped, did we have to amend the Constitution to reflect what was the political tradition and custom. Middle class values likewise have always been Victorian, as it were, and people moderated drink or shunned it altogether through both suasion and legislation at community, county and state level. Two amendments to the Constitution involve a passing of national prohibition on alcohol and subsequent repeal. One amendment involves when the terms in office begin and end, and when Congress shall assemble; another involves how succession to the office of president occurs in the event of his death. One amendment specifies Electors for the District of Columbia (DC), so it can participate in the selection of president and vice-president. One amendment extends the franchise to women; one prohibits poll taxes in order to vote; and another lowers the voting age to eighteen.

In all the years of our history, we've had only two short periods when several amendments to the Constitution occurred nearly at once. In other words, there are only two periods—an average of once every hundred years—during which it can be argued the Constitution lagged social reform of democratic majorities. The first was during Reconstruction, after the War Between the States. The 13th, 14th and 15th Amendments redefined the rights attendant to a national citizenship and integrated freedmen (former slaves) for the first time into the polity. The second period during the Progressive Era, resulted from the eclectic demands of rapid industrialization, mass immigration and the rise to world power status, and gave us the 16th through 19th Amendments. The 16th provided for the income tax, which proved also to be the wherewithal for big government and the prosecution of modern wars. For all its amendments, however, the U.S. Constitution remains the oldest fundamentally unchanged governing document in the history of the world. It would be good if historians were left to describe the constitutional "regimes" which follow amendments, especially following the periods of Reconstruction and the Progressive Era. Unfortunately, constitutional regime change is also identifiable after the New Deal and again since the Sixties until it has become a kind of constantly moving target. Constitutional change is wrought now, not by amendment but by "living" reinterpretation of the Supreme Court supplemented virtually at will by congressional and executive edict.

Constitutions then and now are difficult instruments to construct and even more difficult to live by and maintain according to the intent of their founders. As the president would have it, it is certainly nice to know that you don't have to get it completely right the first time since you can always amend the instrument. It is by far much better to know you can count on a constitution's meaning, unless and until it is amended.

Constitutional Clarifications Article #212
o/a September 15, 2005

These United States have enjoyed unprecedented liberty, prosperity and stability, in large part because of the Constitution. Moreover, the Constitution was written for the People in clear language intended for a popular audience. Pity we have turned so often to judges and lawyers to tell us what it means, instead of reading and coming to grips with the document itself, as well as with the other key informing documents such as the Declaration of Independence, *The Federalist Papers*, and Washington's First Inaugural Address. The truth is lawyers and judges in the 21st Century are far less likely to know what the Constitution means, because they have ceased to interpret it based on Original Intent and *the law* per se. Nor are they even necessarily steeped in the traditions, mores, beliefs and philosophies of this country—let alone in the honest horse sense of Central Texas or Middle America. In some respects, the future of the Constitution rests on whether the People will ever take it back and begin to think again for themselves.

One of the biggest popular misconceptions about the Constitution is that public policies of which we approve are constitutional and public policies of which we disapprove are not. Gadzooks—the Constitution created an architecture of government designed to limit the abuse of governmental power. But while the Constitution constrains government, it does not seek to replace the representative process! That is to say, governments may and often do carry out unwise public policies without running afoul of the Constitution. Lack of wisdom does not constitute grounds for judges to strike down the law in judicial review, for instance. Redress for unwise public policies come as the product of deliberative democratic debate and at the ballot box, not through judicial correction.

Another popular myth about the Constitution involves the Bill of Rights. The Founders intended that individual rights and liberties would principally be protected by the architecture of the Constitution, i.e., the structure of government set forth in its original seven articles. Three great animating principles of our Constitution are in evidence throughout the structure: the division of powers between the national government and states called *federalism*; separation of powers, according to which co-equal legislative, executive and judicial branches of government have distinct responsibilities, yet are subject to the checks and balances of the other branches; and limited government of a particular sort in which the national government is constrained to exercise only those powers set forth by the Constitution (such as issuing currency, administering immigration laws, running the post office and waging war). Since these principles make it difficult for government to exercise power that would abuse rights, and also limits the impact of abuses, many of the Founders believed the Bill of Rights was unnecessary. Until 1925, the Bill of Rights was not even thought to apply to the states, but only to Congress. Notwithstanding the fact that rights were not always recognized or equally applied to African-Americans, states did not generally infringe upon indispensable freedoms such as speech and religion, mentioned in the Bill of Rights. This is because there was no majority sentiment to do so and because each state had a constitution of its own, which protected similar rights.

Today the Bill of Rights has been construed by the U.S. Supreme Court to apply to the states, creating more uniform and more centralized policy and government. The application to the states is by exception, however, because of what the 10th Amendment makes clear: the federal government can do *nothing* under the Constitution unless it is affirmatively authorized by some provision of the Constitution; whereas, the states can do *anything* under the Constitution unless they are prohibited by some provision of the Constitution. "States' rights" refers to the rights of sovereignty retained by the states under the Constitution. States' rights are those extant, where an examination of the Constitution reveals both that the national government lacks authority to act and nothing prohibits the state governments from acting. Indeed, in our system that's quite a lot. On the other hand, a simple reading of the Constitution will tell you there's no state right to impose barriers on trade coming from another state or to establish a separate foreign policy.

One reason the Constitution, as well as our laws generally, should be interpreted according to the straightforward meaning of language, is to maintain the law as an institution that belongs to all the people, not merely judges and lawyers. Unfortunately what passes for constitutional law study at many colleges and universities is exclusively the study of Supreme Court decisions. While such decisions are important, it is more important to compare what the Supreme Court has said to what the Constitution says. The role of judges is to do justice *under law*, not to impose personal views of right and wrong upon the legal system. The highest example of judicial duty is in effect, to subordinate one's personal will and private views to the law. As Chief Justice John Marshall said 200 years ago, it is the duty of the judge to say what the law *is*, not what it *ought* to be—that's the province of the legislature. It is the duty of the judge, as it were, to give faithful meaning to the words of the lawmaker.

And that leads us to perhaps the biggest misconception about the Constitution, which is that it is a "living" document. Now it is beyond dispute that the principles of the Constitution must be applied to new circumstances over time—the Fourth Amendment on searches and seizures to electronic wiretaps; the First Amendment on freedom of speech to radio and television and the Internet; the interstate commerce clause to automobiles and planes, etc. But that is a very distinct thing from allowing the words and principles themselves to be altered based upon the preferences of individual judges. Our Constitution would become an historical artifact—a genuinely *dead* letter—if its original sense became irrelevant, to be replaced by the views of successive waves of judges intent on "updating" it or adding in contemporary moral theory. That's precisely what the Founders sought to avoid when they instituted a "government of laws, not of men" and gave us a Constitutional Republic.[30]

Room for Freedom Article #217
o/a October 20, 2005

Most folks are familiar with Thomas Jefferson's home at Monticello. It is shown on the back of the old nickel. Jefferson designed it himself, and the dome on top gives his house a distinct and attractive aesthetic quality. For those who have visited the upstairs, however, that room under the dome is less impressive—a bit too squat, hot in the summer and impractical. Some conjecture that Jefferson wanted to put a billiards table there, but he couldn't because the Virginia legislature outlawed gambling and also games like billiards. Jefferson apparently honored the law of his State. The irony is that his "druthers" were almost certainly to have lived in an agrarian republic, in which independent freeholders—a landed middle-and-upper class—would have been free from government interference to pretty much do what they will in their own homes. For while there is no right of privacy per se spelled out in the Constitution, the right has a long history and general favor amongst the people. Of course, in that day there was still the practical freedom to basically ignore the legislature, because they sure weren't going to enforce that measure on every plantation or in every cabin. To do so would have proven impractical, and also hazardous. Moreover, it is far from certain the legislators actually cared to enforce the measure, having expressed the public standard as it were, and having satisfied whatever pressure group did care.

Less than a hundred years later, around 1850, Massachusetts found a legislative zeal for compulsory public education, even though their literacy rate was 98% and would never be as high again. The last holdouts clung to the coast where the Puritans first landed, but the area of practical freedom was shrinking in the North. Barnstable in Cape Cod retained their own schools until finally, the area was overrun by state militia in the 1880s, who then marched the children to state school under guard. One of the great benefits of Northern military occupation and the resulting State Reconstruction governments in the South would be compulsory education. Today at least there is room enough for freedom to have competing systems of education. One and a half million home-schooled children consistently score better than government trained counterparts, notwithstanding there are some excellent public schools. Indeed, school choice tends to help both public and private school alternatives. Education is what is important, the ability to think and think differently from each other, not government monopoly which can lead to slavery of the mind.

In both the cases cited above, the Virginia and Massachusetts legislatures and virtually all citizens nationwide, would never have imagined that under the Constitution, the federal government would have the power to do what the State legislatures did. If freedoms were restricted and the room for freedom confined, it was only the States that could do it. The federal government had no such power. How could it, since the Bill of Rights is a stricture on the federal government and not on the States?

Fast-forward to the recent Supreme Court ruling in the case of Gonzales v. Raich (previously Raich v. Ashcroft) handed down June 6, 2005. In a split decision, the Court said the activity of a medically ill person growing a half dozen marijuana plants in his own home for private consumption could be regulated by the Congress of the United States *and that the law of the Congress overruled the law of the State of California in this case.* The minor resurgence of federalism in the Rehnquist Court had essentially fizzled at the end of it. Although Justice Sandra Day O'Connor has lacked consistency before, she clearly captured the significance of this case in her written dissent. Were the Court to now deem the mere possession of marijuana within Congress's authority, it "threatens to sweep all of productive human activity into federal regulatory reach." Justice John Paul Stevens, in the majority opinion, wrote with the self-assured and self-righteous sentiment of black-robed dictatorship: "That the regulation ensnares some purely intrastate activity is of no moment."

Sometimes I get depressed. I think Jefferson should have been able to invite his friends over to play billiards, smoke cigars and drink bourbon too! I wouldn't even mind if the kids at Cape Cod had been able to learn more about seashells and the smell of salt sea air than spinning-jennies and social Darwinism. I wouldn't mind if they read the Bible today instead of *Catcher in the Rye*. And quite frankly, it is none of the business of Congress, whether an AIDS victim finds pain relief in home gardening—especially if the sovereign State where the person lives says it is none of their business. America needs to save a little room for freedom nowadays. You never know when you might just miss it, and need some.

Judicial Review and Constitutional Responsibility Article #218
o/a October 20, 2005

The concept of judicial review is an old one in American and British political history. Indeed, our legal system in large measure evolved from English common law. Over 800 years ago, judges in the king's courts began to decide disputes between individuals. Eventually courts decided cases involving the Crown and Parliament. Lord Coke in 1610 held that common law as interpreted through courts (in this case the Court of Common Pleas) might disallow an act of Parliament that was "against common right and reason, or repugnant, or impossible to be performed." The first law professor in the colonies was George Wythe, who taught Thomas Jefferson, John Marshall, and many others of the founding generation. He invoked a similar perspective, that courts should in fact review the acts of the so-called political branches. Many people don't realize how unbridled "democracy" frightened the Founders. In the 11-year period from 1776 until 1787 when the Constitution was drafted, democracy took root in the sovereign States, but without an effective vertical check and balance, in particular without an effective federal judiciary. So legislatures bowed to public pressure and often acted irresponsibly: abrogating debts, expropriating property, restricting liberty and acting arbitrarily. The Constitution was viewed by many of the Founders as a way to stem the democratic lawlessness of the Revolutionary Era.

James Madison, the Father of the Constitution, said that an independent judiciary, which was one of three co-equal branches of government he helped establish (and the only one not political), would serve as "an impenetrable bulwark against every assumption of power in the Legislative or Executive." Alexander Hamilton in *Federalist* 78 wrote: "The complete independence of the courts of justice is peculiarly essential in a limited Constitution. By a limited Constitution, I understand one which contains certain specified exceptions to the legislative authority . . . . Limitations of this kind can be preserved in practice no other way than through the medium of courts of justice, whose duty it must be to declare all acts contrary to the manifest tenor of the Constitution void. Without this, all the reservations of particular rights or privileges would amount to nothing." Hence the power of judicial review was a part of received political thought and the inherited tradition behind Article III (judicial power) of the Constitution, even if it were not absolute and the exact nature of its role entirely anticipated. The first time judicial review was actually used under the Constitution was in Marbury v. Madison in 1803, which codified the principle and set practical precedent that the Supreme Court would be the arbiter in cases involving operation of government according to the law. The branches were co-equal, but courts had the last say.

To some extent, the controversy that currently surrounds judicial review exists not only because the judiciary has become politicized, but also because the other branches of government no longer effectively do their jobs. In the early years of the Republic, the courts weren't very active—and they certainly didn't have to exercise judicial review often. That's because the political branches based their actions on constitutionality also. The Congress actually debated whether it had the authority to enact various proposals! Today the assumption is that Congress can do literally anything. Congressmen cede constitutional responsibility and toss it to the courts. In so doing, Congress contributes to damaging the reputation of the judicial branch. Congress encourages judges to become political—making law instead of merely interpreting it—because Congress fails to do the politically responsible thing, which is to curtail their power according to the limitations imposed by the Constitution. When constitutionally questionable measures got out of Congress in the past, presidents would often veto them. Not today, however. Presidents might exercise their veto power on the grounds of policy, but never on the grounds of constitutionality. Presidents are as bad as Congress therefore, in that, they assume they can do anything—start a war, continue war indefinitely, even spy on Americans and hold citizens without charge. They too have ceded responsibility for upholding the basic law of the land, which is the Constitution. They have thrown it off as surely as Congress has, and like congressmen won't hesitate to seek political advantage by criticizing Supreme Court decisions.

Judicial review by courts is little different from what the other two branches should be doing, which is interpreting the Constitution in the normal course of performing their duties. We ought not to think it irregular, if the President vetoes a bill he believes to be unconstitutional. We ought to hear of Congress occasionally voting down their own measures—not because they fear constitutional scrutiny by the Supreme Court, but because measures fail to meet their own constitutional scrutiny. People ought to expect their congressmen to articulate where and how they derive authority from the Constitution to do the things they propose. Congress and the President need to act more wisely, by first studying the substantive portions of the Constitution. If they would, they could help restore the proper role of judicial review in our land, a role belonging to courts, which nevertheless presupposes review by the other branches.

Tort Reform and the Constitution Article #206
o/a July 28, 2005

Tort law involves wrongful acts, injuries and damages not involving breaches of contract, for which civil actions can be brought. Tort law reform is a matter of political relevance, because litigation costs have ballooned so much and affected the economy and prices people have to pay for goods and services. Since 1930, litigation costs have grown four times faster than the overall economy, and federal class action suits have tripled over the past ten years. Class actions in state courts have risen more than 1,000 percent. The U.S. Chamber of Commerce estimates that the annual equivalent cost of the tort system translates into a 5 percent tax on individual wages. The aggregated cost is 2 ¼ percent of our gross domestic product—and the trend line points to an even higher "tort tax" in our future if nothing gets done. It is little wonder that people have called for tort reform; indeed, legislation that caps malpractice awards and limits attorney fees has been before Congress no fewer than eight times since Republicans took over the House in 1995. The President has called the situation "a national problem that requires a national solution."

But every national problem is not necessarily a problem for the federal government. State legislators, courts, doctors, and their patients are not powerless. At least 36 states have passed damage caps, and all 50 states have passed, or are considering, various tort-reform proposals. The simple matter is that nowhere in the Constitution is there a federal power to set rules that control lawsuits, for example, by in-state plaintiffs against in-state doctors for in-state malpractice. Moreover, as Justice Clarence Thomas has said, "The Constitution does not constrain the size of punitive damage awards." The Constitution guarantees defendants that the *process* followed in determining a punitive award will be reasonable—not that the award itself will be. Republicans and Democrats have tripped all over themselves, albeit they don't lose much sleep, to affix to the Constitution some make-believe authorization for national reform. The Commerce Clause is a "traditional" vehicle of choice, if you figure that anything crossing a state line can be regulated (whether or not it has to do with the operative word commerce). Then again, to invoke the Commerce Clause, Congress is supposed to show that federal action is both "necessary" and "proper" to ensure the free flow of interstate trade. Yikes: substantive federal reforms aren't *necessary* because states are enacting their own reforms! They aren't *proper* either, because they don't square at all with federalism—our system of dual federal-state sovereignty, a vertical check and balance designed by the Founders to promote liberty and limit the scope and concentration of government power. The purpose of tort law is to redress grievances, which is a state-based function and has been throughout the entire history of our Republic. Likewise, using the Fourteenth Amendment‘s Due Process Clause is a distended exercise, with limited applicability through procedural grounds.

One wishes that lawmakers would spend as much energy on making the Constitution work as they do on finding ways to subvert it. The problem of confiscatory state punitive awards can be fixed without trampling on federalism. First, you could take the dollar decision away from the jury—the jury might be instructed to vote yes or no on an award of punitive damages, but the judge would set the amount in accordance with pre-set guidelines. Second, you could limit punitive damages to cases involving actual malice, intentional wrongdoing or gross negligence and thus take them out of garden-variety accidental injuries. Third, states could implement procedural guarantees similar to those available under criminal law, for instance, a higher burden of proof requiring a preponderance of evidence, as well as no double jeopardy (current rules allow punitive awards for the same conduct in multiple lawsuits). Fourth, states should dispense with joint and several-liability that permits plaintiffs to collect all of a damage award from any one of multiple defendants, even if the paying defendant was responsible for a small fraction of the harm. A better rule would be to apportion damages according to the degree of culpability. Fifth, government should pay attorneys' fees when a governmental unit is the losing party in a civil lawsuit. Sixth, contingency fee contracts between private lawyers and government entities should be prohibited. When a private lawyer subcontracts his services to the government, he bears the same responsibility as a government lawyer. He is a public servant beholden to all citizens, including the defendant, and his overriding objective is to seek justice. Imagine a state attorney paid a contingency fee for each indictment, or state troopers paid a bonus for each speeding ticket! Finally, state legislators ought to consider legislation providing that the same legal rules applicable to a private claim by an injured party will also be applicable if the government sues to recover indirect losses related to the same injury. The same rules of evidence, the same standards of responsibility, and the same burden of proof should apply to the sate standing in a plaintiff's shoes as to a plaintiff suing on his own behalf.

Now as hard as it may be to believe, besides these state-based reforms there are actually a couple of useful things the federal government can do too. In the area of tort reform, Congress might preclude local courts from hearing cases unless the defendant engages directly in business activities within the state. Jurisdiction would be triggered if a company purposely directed its product to a state, i.e., exerted control over the decision to sell in a state. That way firms would have an exit option: they could withdraw from a state to avoid the risk of runaway juries and biased judges. Today, some oppressive state tort laws are a threat to out-of-state defendants whose products somehow ended up there. In addition, a new federal choice-of-law rule might apply when a company cannot afford to lose business by exiting from a state. Choice of law is the doctrine that determines which state's laws control litigation when the litigants are from different states. The legal standard could be based upon the state where the manufacturer was located. At any rate, a federal standard in that area would reduce ambiguity and empower manufacturers and customers to make their decisions based upon a clearer understanding of rules. With some mental effort and acuity, politicians can implement constitutional tort reform. Hope that's not asking too much—constitutional reform or the mental acuity.[31]

Natural Right of Property Must be Defended — Article #226
o/a November 18, 2005

Fundamentally governments of, by and for the people come about in order to secure natural rights. That is, people voluntarily combine their efforts and invest some power in government to enhance the people's status in the image and likeness of their Maker—to make themselves more free of the tyranny of earth and the downward tendency of abject necessity and the struggle for survival. God gives you life, true. It's a natural right therefore, but government establishes law (hopefully patterned on divine precepts), as well as enforcement mechanisms, to secure that life better than the law of the jungle would. God also gives you liberty. It's a natural right, but government precludes other human beings from depriving you of that liberty, restricting your movement, limiting options, confining your dreams. God also puts before you a world filled with blessings, and men of course pursue happiness in it. But governments exist to regulate the destructive tendencies inherent in such pursuit, tendencies which might otherwise expunge the happiness of one for the good of another or many; or jeopardize the happiness of many to fulfill the lust of one or a few. The point is that rights precede human government. Government has its purpose, but the onus is on the people to make the most of their own lives—freed, as it were, from the mundane, mortal tasks of fighting off grizzly bears and bands of grisly men. Moreover, if government had no utility at all, I suppose there wouldn't be any—or rather, government of the people would devolve into a kind of law of the jungle on steroids. Perhaps it is possible too, as Jefferson intimated, whenever the people fail in vigilance to keep this republic, either to confine government to its purpose or to limit the exercise of its powers.

The hero of Scotland, Robert the Bruce had a six-foot, six-inch broadsword. He wielded it before the effective independence of his country, which he helped bring about. It was his property, an extension of his physique and his mental will. Our Founders likewise wielded their property to effect American independence. When you think about it, your property too is what you have acquired, which gives you your independence: the roof over your head, the couch you sit on, the car you take to work, every modern convenience—the method and style and quality of *your* life, *your* liberty, and *your* pursuit of happiness. John Locke, the great Enlightenment philosopher characterized property as an extension of self. James Madison opined that property stands on the same footing as the entitlement to speak your mind, to say your prayers or to vote your conscience. Consider the phrase of the Revolution, "No taxation without representation!" What it means is that your property, including wealth may not be taxed except by duly elected representatives—for the same reason that you cannot legitimately be governed, without your consent. The Founders conceived of property far more seriously than we do today. A lot of folks seem positively cavalier about it, as if property were not much to them. Yet it is as plain as the nose on your face. Without it, you are reduced to the animal in the yard, hiding in a hole, hanging on a branch in a tree. Without property, you are naked. The means to tax is therefore a means to destroy; and man deprived of property is a miserable creature. If man or government would confiscate your property *without due process* according to the constitutional government to which we have consented, you are obliged or at least justified, to resist by any and all means—quite literally in self-defense.

In *Kelo v. New London* (2005) the Supreme Court, in yet another example of its supreme arrogance, has assaulted the natural private property right of American citizens. In a blow to home and small business owners, the Court held that governments may use eminent domain to take away homes, so that businesses can make more money off that land—and possibly pay more taxes as a result. The Supreme Court has decided that the property of one can be taken and given to another so that the other may make more money and pay more taxes with it. According to Larry Arnn, president of Hillsdale College, Michigan: "The old man in his childhood home, and the widow in the dwelling where she raised her children, are no longer secure in their abodes." Not only can property taxes do them in (which is another problem), now the government can seize land outright if it can't quite tax them out of it. The Fifth Amendment states: "Nor shall private property be taken for public use without just compensation." There simply is no provision in the Constitution whatsoever for the taking of private land for other private uses. Clearly there are nuances in the matter, because the Bill of Rights constrains the federal government, but eminent domain abuses are by and large abuses by local governments subverted by moneyed special interests. There is no excuse, however, for this green light to abuse given by the Court. If the intent of the Fifth Amendment and others to the Constitution is to be so butchered by the Supreme Court, can the Second be far behind? Still it is the Second that may save the rest. He that hath an ear let him hear.

Power in Context: Article II of the Constitution Article #237
o/a February 24, 2006

I have received bank statements before, which charged fees that turned out to be erroneous. Ditto with credit card companies. Sometimes landlords reference contract language that isn't there, telling you it's 60 days instead of 30, or that your security deposit pays for the owner's repair, etc. Corporate managers and government bureaucrats unknowingly (and occasionally knowingly) enforce policies based on directives or regulations that don't exist or don't apply. Indeed, I served in the Army long enough to know that my best career manager was me, and that my records were almost always better than the Army's about me—that if I wanted to get a record straight, I'd better send the documentation and check back faithfully until they got it right. I've long since concluded, if you don't look out for your own interests, no one else will. And yet there is a comforting tendency to want to depend upon big institutions to keep the records and to just tell us what all the legalese says we're supposed to do. That may be fine for a lifetime gym membership or association with your travel agency, but it doesn't work well with the Constitution. If you want what the Constitution secures, namely freedom and inalienable rights, you have to know what it says and insist upon the enforcement of its letter. Jefferson said, 'Eternal vigilance is the price of freedom.' There's too much at stake, in terms of life, liberty and pursuit of happiness for you, and in terms of money and power for others, to simply leave it up for grabs. Otherwise, a political snake oil salesman will tell you Article II reads one thing, when in fact it reads another. Sort of like what's happening now.

Look at Article II. It's really very short and lays out the executive power and general responsibilities of the president. Section 1 ends with the Oath he takes before entering his office: "I do solemnly swear (or affirm) that I will faithfully execute the Office of President of the United States, and will to the best of my Ability, *preserve, protect and defend the Constitution* of the United States." Section 2 says in part, "The President shall be Commander in Chief" of the armed forces. Section 3 says he'll give a State of the Union address "from time to time" and, among other things "shall take Care that the Laws be faithfully executed." Section 4 says he "shall be removed from Office on Impeachment for, and Conviction of, Treason, Bribery, or other high Crimes and Misdemeanors." Article I deals with the legislative powers, Article III with judicial power. Comparing these three articles (the Constitution has seven, plus Amendments), Article I is by far and away the longer and the most extensive. The president's power as Commander in Chief in Article II is subject to the congressional power to declare war in Article I; as well as subject to congressional power to "make Rules concerning Captures on Land and Water" (there is no executive prerogative here for torture or for secret prisons beyond the reach of law). The president's power as Commander in Chief is subject further to congressional power to make rules for the regulation and discipline of the armed services; to organize, arm and equip them; and to confirm appointment of their officers. In case someone is wondering who might be first among co-equal branches, Article I, Section 8 gives that trump to Congress: the power "To make all Laws which shall be necessary and proper for carrying into Execution the foregoing Powers [to Congress], *and all other Powers vested by this Constitution in the Government of the United States, or in any Department or Office thereof.*"—Ostensibly, to make laws necessary and proper for the execution of the Office of the Presidency and Cabinet. Congress therefore passes a Foreign Intelligence Surveillance Act (FISA) in 1978, which the president is bound to comply with and enforce, or work with Congress to get changed. Otherwise, see Article II, Section 4.

The Founders were suspicious of government power in general, but they were particularly suspicious of Executive power. Executive Power is vested in a President of the United States of America to be sure, but he is subject to a lot of checks and balances. The reason is the Founders founded a Republic and not a dictatorship, a monarchy or one man's personal playpen. They didn't want another King George III or a King George "Dubya" either. The purpose of the Constitution is laid out plainly in its Preamble, something every school child once memorized: "We the people of the United States, in Order to form a more perfect Union, establish Justice, insure domestic Tranquility, provide for the common defence, promote the general Welfare, and secure the Blessings of Liberty to ourselves and our Posterity, do ordain and establish this Constitution for the United States of America." According to which, Ben Franklin said they gave us a Republic: "If you can keep it!"

Separation of Powers Resides with States Article #253
o/a June 23, 2006

When I was a teen-ager in Houston, our Congressman was Bill Archer. He would eventually become chairman of the House Ways and Means Committee before retiring from Congress. I am still grateful to him for his early mentorship and especially, for his clear and unequivocal way of describing the proper relations between state and federal governments. Statesmen can and do contribute vitally to our way of life, as they help transmit cultural and political institutions intact to the next generation, whereas, politicians contribute the very opposite effect. You'd like to have term limits placed on politicians and keep the statesmen. And I suppose the means exists to do so—called elections, these depend on a people who can discern difference, and who care enough to participate. You'll have another opportunity in November, so please get ready. Now back to the subject at hand . . . . A vertical separation of power exists, every bit like the horizontal one between Congress and the President and the Supreme Court. If the separation of powers between Congress and the President is in jeopardy today, which I believe it to be, a separation of powers between the Federal Government and the several States is virtually nonexistent. In practice, States these days amount to so many rubber stamps, dependencies on the largesse and will of the Federal Government. Power resides with Washington, in case you had not perceived it; moreover, the accretion of power continues uninterrupted in that direction since "conservative" Republicans have been in charge.

Notwithstanding, a balance of power ought to result from the dual sovereignty inherent in state and national governments according to American political tradition and the Constitution of our Fathers. While dual sovereignty is tricky business to be sure, it works because the powers ascribed to each level are generally defined and separate in the Constitution: some powers are enumerated and delegated to the national government, while everything else simply isn't. This system of dual-sovereignty is called *federalism*; and it is the most unique aspect in our system of representative government, a theory put to its form and contributed by the Father of the Constitution, James Madison. Federalism is also, arguably, the most important aspect in our system of representative government, in terms of preventing tyranny by the chief executive or indeed by any single branch of the national government. Federalism and dual-sovereignty, understood in this way, are what the most enlightened and thoughtful conservatives have referred to, whenever they spoke of or invoked the term "States Rights" since Reconstruction. Unfortunately, historical scholarship has often lacked rigorous analysis, and has conveyed less understanding. Terms have been shrouded or worse, they have been intentionally de-legitimized by liberal historians and an intellectual class of puppeteers. For those seeking a dictatorship by design—whether consolidated national democracy, or unitary approaches to every problem under heaven, States Rights and the constitutional edifice of federalism are at the heart of what must be destroyed. Enemies of liberty have crosshairs on that target.

States Rights and federalism are routinely conflated with the cause of segregation and other gross violations of civil rights, while this literally mistakes a rubric for the actual substance. It's a really big baby that gets thrown out with the bathwater, in other words! You most certainly may and indeed should, excise legally enforced racial discrimination. But you must do so without removing the very basis for a continued, mutually respectful and covenantal relationship twixt States and the Federal Government on other matters. We have amended the Constitution and may enforce provisions according to the amendments; moreover, I would argue that social evolution has at last caught up with the vision in the Declaration, even if facts haven't in every single case. We must hope that such evolution has not caught up too late, in order to form new political coalitions that will redress the terrible imbalance of power that now exists between the States and Federal Government. Education is, as with so many things, a start. Today, however, if young people come away from a civics class with any appreciation for "checks and balances," it is always for the separation of powers inherent between three co-equal branches of the federal or national government. While extremely important, they learn little to nothing of federalism and have no similar regard for that same concept of "checks and balances" applied vertically. Yet it is the vertical check and balance, which precludes a radical concentration of power in a single person or branch of government. It is the vertical check and balance that forestalls a top-down implementation of tyranny, and which enables States to reach like-minded States for moral and political support, and material assistance to resist Leviathan. In short, in the absence of federalism and the separation of powers it implies, the last vestiges of the American Republic will languish, until restored at length by the people or shorn completely by tyrants.

American Chronology, 1776 to 1798 — Article #254
o/a June 23, 2006

Chronological reasoning is a nearly lost art and skill, as teachers no longer teach important dates and citizens are no longer required to memorize them. It is easy after that to mix things up, easier for manipulators of the mind to lead you down a primrose path. It matters that the Constitution came after the Declaration of Independence. It tells you, for instance, that the Constitution qualifies the Declaration and not the other way around. It matters, because the Declaration was written to throw off an unwritten British constitution, which had devolved into tyranny; whereas, the American Constitution was written down, in full view of the Declaration of Independence, in order to give 'life, liberty and the pursuit of happiness' a practical chance at survival, if these were ever to improve. Democracy was barely in the lexicon; liberty was prized above else. Indeed, the British constitution was almost universally revered by the Founding Fathers, except that, it had been corrupted by king and parliament. They felt that a republican system would be less susceptible to the same kind of experience and concentration of power that led to tyranny, at least if they divided power sufficiently and provided for checks and balances to keep it that way. Moreover, excesses endemic to democratic experiments, both theoretic and in history, gave the Founders pause for thought. They would implement a Republic, albeit, with important democratic provision for electing the representatives. In the early years, however, there were patriots who weren't sure our Republic would survive; and anyway, they were vigilant to watch the signs of their times, in order to discern a direction to the fledgling nation. They were keen observers of precedent, lest their intent go awry and the Constitution be subverted. The Founders were committed to making the republican experiment work to be sure, but if there were a tendency amongst the Founders one way or the other, it was towards monarchy and not to mob rule. The signs of their times even threatened to make reversion to monarchy possible. Fortunately, the Founders and their polity were better republicans than we are.

At the birth of these United States, rebel-patriots and Founders weren't interested in constructing a new constitution; rather, they were keen to shatter the old one. Their political imperative and the actions they took were to effect secession from Great Britain, leading only to "Independence" loosely defined. The principle they invoked to justify the imperative and their actions, is clearly spelled out in the Declaration of Independence. It was merely—and profoundly, that when a long train of abuses shall evince design to reduce the people to despotism, then "it is their right, it is their duty, to throw off such government." The principle has been in place and must ever be, so long as the Republic resembles the Founders' at all. Indeed, just two decades after, Thomas Jefferson and James Madison—that is to say, the author of the Declaration in 1776, as well as chief architect at the Constitutional Convention in 1787—both penned words in defiance to the new government they created! Again thinking chronologically, something by 1798 had forced them to clarify limits on power according to the Constitution. The particulars of this something amounted to a serious foreign policy crisis and ill-advised actions on the part of Federalists holding power at the time. Great Britain and France were at war, and the United States was caught between. "High" Federalists under Adams became increasingly anti-republican, even monarchical in character. The Federalist Congress passed the Alien and Sedition Acts, in violation of the First Amendment, making it a crime to publish criticism of government war policies. In response, Madison and Jefferson wrote the Virginia and Kentucky Resolutions or "Resolves," stating that the Alien and Sedition Acts were unconstitutional and that States need not enforce them. Jefferson wrote Resolves for the Kentucky legislature; Madison wrote his for Virginia. The political climate thus created, both by further Federalist excesses and by republican opposition—including especially these Resolves, led to a popular political backlash against Federalists in the Election of 1800. Jefferson was elected President, and Madison became his Secretary of State. But not before they had clearly reaffirmed the principle of the Declaration of Independence to be in full effect, notwithstanding ratification of the Constitution. In the Kentucky Resolves, Jefferson wrote, "the several States composing the United States of America, are not united on the principles of unlimited submission to their General Government." So whenever tyrants emerge and dare to reign, a quintessential American answer echoes the words of Jefferson and Madison in these great Resolves, written in full view of the Constitution, for rebel-patriots then as now.[32]

Resolves Among America's Great Charters Article #257
o/a July 07, 2006

Considering America's great charters, the historical revisionists have seen to it that we should forget some, while selectively remembering a few lines from others. For instance, the Declaration of Independence is universally celebrated for its recognition based on the faith-based knowledge of our Creator, that "all men are created equal." The Declaration is hardly mentioned, however, for its preponderance of words dedicated to the cause of secession from Great Britain, as well as to the explication of timeless rationale for the just revolution against tyrannical governments, wherever they may be, including theoretically and potentially at least, our own. Of course we give an occasional nod towards the Articles of Confederation in history class, mostly incidental to thanking our extraordinarily lucky stars for the powerful central government we now have under the Constitution. So yes, we do generally recognize a fuzzy "Constitution" as the basis for governmental legitimacy and the legitimate exercise of powers, but we almost entirely forget to mention that it was the Kentucky and Virginia Resolves, which reined in the first series of abuses by the federal government and which asserted the States' role in maintaining constitutional republican government, according to Original Intent.

Indeed, written by Thomas Jefferson and James Madison respectively, the Kentucky and Virginia Resolves lay out an eloquent account of nuts and bolts to ultimate sovereignty, which resides with the People of the several States. They also reinforce divided legislative sovereignty, inherent in our unique system of federalism, which is surprisingly still virtually undisputed by the academy or by courts in principle, if not in practice. Dual or divided sovereignty after all, stems directly from the fact that through the aegis of the Constitution, the People of the several States delegate only certain powers to the national or federal government, and they retain everything else at the level of the States. Hence, the beginning of the restoration of our Republic may be the reinsertion of these Resolves, back into the pantheon of America's great charters. Then we shall return to a Constitution of Rights, as opposed to a Constitution of Powers.

Though the South is most often associated with the doctrine of the Kentucky and Virginia Resolves, in the years after the election of Jefferson and his peaceful political Revolution of 1800, the Northern states recurred to it just as frequently. In 1802, the State of Pennsylvania stopped action by Federal District Judge Peters on behalf of Gideon Olmstead, rendering the Judge's decision "null and void," since the Judge had illegally usurped his power and jurisdiction. In 1808-9, Massachusetts, Delaware and Connecticut employed nullification on the Embargo Act. Indeed, the legislative actions and public protests convinced Congress that continuance of the Embargo was untenable. The doctrine of the Kentucky and Virginia Resolves also animated the Hartford Convention in 1814, as surely as it did South Carolina's Ordinance of Nullification in 1833—a doctrine essentially of state negative aimed at oppressive national laws. In the end, South Carolina's nullification proved successful in prompting Congress to lower its high and disproportionate tariff duties. It is indeed a measure of the loss of freedom in the country as a whole that, since the War Between the States, Northern and Southern, Mid-West and Western States have all witnessed their scope of sovereignty diminish. With the check and balance provided by States gone, the consolidation feared by Anti-Federalists, by Jeffersonian Republicans, by nullifiers in New England and South Carolina, has come to pass. A look at the U.S. Code or a federal appropriations bill proves that Congress, like the British Parliament, claims the authority to legislate on all subjects whatsoever. Moreover, the Supreme Court's claim to be the final arbiter on matters of Constitutionality, is largely acquiesced in—which, if you think about it, doesn't square with the people's position as ultimate sovereigns. In most cases, elections should serve to check tyrannical rulers. The Resolves addressed those situations when/if the General Government assumed powers egregiously violating States' reserved powers, or when/if it passed unjust measures that did not operate equally on all citizens or all sections. In such cases, the added safeguard of a state veto, or nullification, was necessary and could very well be the most efficacious solution. As long as there were statesmen and not just politicians in office, peace was maintained and compromise achieved, the Union held together in bonds of affection, fealty and voluntary submission, rather than by chain links of iron.[33]

War Between the States and Consolidation of Power Article #258
o/a July 08, 2006

Consolidation of power at the national level is what opponents of the Constitution (Anti-Federalists) had feared would happen between 1787 and 1789. Some doubted that a system of dual sovereignty could ever be maintained, because it was such a delicate balancing act, which required high statecraft by men of talent. Hindsight to some extent proves them right, although for over seventy years the States managed to resist serious federal encroachment. The Anti-Federalists accepted the ratification of the Constitution by their home States, so they participated in the political process as strict constructionists and later as Jeffersonian Republicans. They and their ilk were caught up in political realignment during the 1830s. Some joined with Whigs and others with Democrats. Unfortunately, the Second American Party System proved no match for the political stresses that followed the Mexican-American War, over slavery and expansion into the newly acquired territories. Until 1861 and the War Between the States, moreover, the doctrine of nullification or interposition held practical if not universal sway in the Union. Implicitly, States could secede if compromise with the national government failed on a substantive issue they nullified in special convention. If, say, the Supreme Court ruled against the State's position, the State must either decide to tow the line (under protest perhaps), or separate from the Union altogether. Whigs in particular felt that it was a national legislative responsibility to reach a compromise, in order to prevent that kind of situation from arising.

Thomas Jefferson and James Madison envisioned and indeed sanctioned this kind of process taking place, as a vertical check and balance to prevent consolidation of power at the national level. Even though they did not relish the necessity, there was no other way for effective constitutional redress, should the federal government invade reserved powers held by the State. One can argue the problem with trying to maintain dual or divided sovereignty between States and the General Government was the absence of a third party or institution to broker a deal, if it were not a disinterested class of statesmen. William J. Watkins, Jr. has thoughtfully proposed a Constitutional Commission comprised of representatives from all the State legislative sovereigns to operate in that capacity, if such could be enacted by Constitutional amendment. Historically speaking, however, you had a tug of war and test of wills going between two sides; as long as neither side recurred to violence, brinkmanship prevailed and the Union stayed together. Lincoln's 4-year prosecution of total war against the South changed Federal-State relations and altered prevailing calculus. Republicans dotted the "I's" and crossed their "T's" after the fact, as Constitutional amendments followed military occupation. The Thirteenth, Fourteenth and Fifteenth Amendments abolished slavery, defined national rights of citizenship, and enlarged the franchise. The basic political failure in the system, however (i.e., the inability to effectively broker disagreement between the States and Federal Government), was never addressed. Neither was the doctrine of nullification or interposition repudiated officially, though no one dared try it for a long time! More amazing still, and most impressive, secession was never disallowed by Constitutional amendment.

No self-respecting statesman of the day would have suggested that secession under every circumstance was illegal, or for that matter, that the South didn't have one very long and respected trail of precedent dating back to the Revolution on which to base its choice to secede, and to form the Confederacy. That's why the Federal Government never formally prosecuted CSA President Jefferson Davis. "The Union" so called, wasn't fooling anybody. It would take another 100 years to find folks that gullible. After all the bloodshed and devastation, with Constitutional issues central to the conflict, the Constitution's text did not change that much after the War. As amazing, that the South should reintegrate herself, as peacefully and over time, as patriotically, is a precedent of singular status in world history—it just doesn't happen very often that a bloody "civil war" is fought and sides come back together, almost like nothing ever happened. Of course something did happen, and an apotheosis of sorts informed the new Solid South: accepting their home State's destiny, Southerners began to participate like Anti-Federalists before them, as strict constructionists and States Rights advocates. Indeed, the term Conservative was first used extensively in the South after the War Between the States, and while it could refer to a number of things, many chose the label to identify their cause, not so much with the Lost Cause of the Old South, as with the perpetual Promise of the Old Republic. The relevance of this today is that, there is still no Amendment against nullification and interposition, or against secession per se. The Federal Government is less likely to strike with violence against States pursuing a consistent and principled course towards nullification, particularly on issues involving religion and morality that have nothing whatsoever to do with race. Even with the shift in power to the national government because of Northern victory and the accretion of power to the federal government since then, much of what the Framers created remains in place to be rediscovered and reinvigorated. We may yet still use it to remind our fellow countrymen, that the difference twixt slave and free is a political and legal designation that ultimately bears no relation to skin color; rather, slavery results from the consolidation of power into a single sovereign, and this is why the Federal Government must again be checked by sovereign States.[34]

CHAPTER 14

Role of Government

Bill of No Rights   Article #013
March 15, 2001

The following is attributed to Lewis Napper who joined the Libertarian Party in 1995 and ran as a Libertarian for a Mississippi Senate seat in 2000. It parodies the Bill of Rights, the first ten amendments to the Constitution.

> "We, the sensible people of the United States, in an attempt to help everyone get along, restore some semblance of justice, avoid any more riots, keep our nation safe, promote positive behavior, and secure the blessings of debt free liberty to ourselves and our great-great-great-grandchildren, hereby try one more time to ordain and establish some common sense guidelines for the terminally whiny, guilt-ridden, delusional, and other liberal bedwetters.
>
> "We hold these truths to be self-evident: that a whole lot of people are confused by the Bill of Rights and are so dim that they require a Bill of No Rights.
>
> "ARTICLE I: You do not have the right to a new car, big screen TV or any other form of wealth. More power to you if you can legally acquire them, but no one is guaranteeing anything.
>
> "ARTICLE II: You do not have the right to never be offended. This country is based on freedom, and that means freedom for everyone—not just you! You may leave the room, turn the channel, express different opinions, etc., but the world is full of idiots, and probably always will be.

"ARTICLE III: You do not have the right to be free from harm. If you stick a screwdriver in your eye, learn to be more careful; do not expect the manufacturer to make you and all your relatives independently wealthy.

"ARTICLE IV: You do not have the right to free food and housing. Americans are the most charitable people to be found and will gladly help anyone in need, but we are quickly growing weary of subsidizing generation after generation of professional couch potatoes who achieve nothing more than the creation of another generation of professional couch potatoes.

"ARTICLE V: You do not have the right to free health care. That would be nice, but from the looks of public housing, we're just not interested in public health care.

"ARTICLE VI: You do not have the right to physically harm other people. If you kidnap, rape, intentionally maim or kill someone, don't be surprised if the rest of us want to see you fry in the electric chair.

"ARTICLE VII: You do not have the right to the possessions of others. If you rob, cheat or coerce away the goods or services of other citizens, don't be surprised if the rest of us get together and lock you away in a place where you still won't have the right to a big screen color TV or a life of leisure.

"ARTICLE VIII: You don't have the right to demand that our children risk their lives in foreign wars to soothe your aching conscience. We hate oppressive governments and won't lift a finger to stop you from going to fight if you'd like. However, we do not enjoy parenting the entire world and do not want to spend so much of our time battling each and every little tyrant with a military uniform and a funny hat.

"ARTICLE IX: You don't have the right to a job. All of us sure want all of you to have one, and will gladly help you along in hard times, but we expect you to take advantage of the opportunities of education and vocational training laid before you to make yourself useful.

> "ARTICLE X: You do not have the right to happiness. Being an American means that you have the right to pursue happiness—which, by the way, is a lot easier if unencumbered by laws created by those of you who were confused by the Bill of Rights."[35]

Tethered Citizens — Article #035
o/a August 16, 2001

The United States is one of the freest countries on the globe, but unless my sensibilities are entirely out of whack, I assert that this country—the country of Washington, Jefferson, Madison, Randolph, Calhoun, et al—is not nearly free enough. It isn't even as free as we think. Can a man or woman truly live here according to conscience? At one time, we could have answered "almost certainly." Today one's conscience must be conformed in so many ways to so many things. We are not free, except in the most abstract, academic—and ultimately irrelevant—way. Our spirits are dying: death by a thousand pinpricks. Nay worse, a hundred thousand paper cuts from a faceless bureaucracy! Since Eden, there have been so many constraints on man anyway, without the added coercion of the muscular enforcers of state, whether they enforce the will of the few on the many—or the will of the many on the few! I just wish our government were less concerned for my welfare and more concerned for my freedom. I wish it were less concerned for this collective nonentity called "the people" and more concerned for every single individual, made in the image and likeness of God. I wish the government were less concentrated, had less power and authority, and were more respectful of the natural regions and the natural differences that exist amongst us. I don't want to cooperate with everybody else, marching off into a global abyss. I JUST WISH THE GOVERNMENT WOULD LEAVE US ALONE.

Of course, you know what they say about wishing in one hand and picking up horse hockey with the other: one hand is likely to get fuller than the other. I reckon the wish must obtain a will and the necessary resources to in fact change things. God help us. Today the federal government literally employs extortion on the States with the money it taxes from us. To make you wear your seatbelt and do a hundred other things, the feds withhold funds from sovereign States, unless and until those States pass particular laws. They did the same thing after the War Between the

States: permanent military occupation unless the States would approve certain constitutional amendments. The contexts are indeed different, and there were hard historical and practical realities to settle during the Reconstruction. But is another Robert E. Lee or Jeff Davis left anywhere in this unified, chained and tethered house of ours—locked down from the inside out? Is there a governor with backbone anywhere in the country to point out and even put an end to . . . (shall I name it? Are you willing to recognize it?). Tyranny.

Some of you will say, gosh he's gone over the top (again). So you think, "I'm free, right?" Not if you think you ought to be in charge of the money you set aside for retirement, or the age you choose to retire. Not if you think you ought to be able to choose when your child goes to school, for how many weeks he or she should study, as well as what subjects. Walter E. Williams recently reviewed Sheldon Richman's excellent new book, *Tethered Citizens: Time to Repeal the Welfare State* (available at *www.laissezfairebooks.org* and *www.amazon.com*). In the review, he asks "What if you think your child is capable of having a job at age 12, as I was? No dice. The government determines the age at which one can work, and for how long and at what pay." Andrew Jackson joined the American Revolution at the age of 14, and he was a natural soldier. I'm glad nobody told him No dice, Andy. (He probably would have killed somebody on our side). Of course, I'm not advocating enlistment of child soldiers—just pointing out the arbitrariness of well-meaning rules, forced and enforced down every throat in the country—where no one possesses the slightest degree of discretion and no State retains a sovereign prerogative.

Alexis de Tocqueville predicted Americans would face this kind of despotism, to which democracies are prone—more widespread and milder than other forms, degrading men rather than tormenting them. In his masterpiece *Democracy in America*, he writes that our leaders are likely to become as schoolmasters. Our government will try to keep us "in perpetual childhood" and will do this by providing security and necessities, assuming responsibility for our concerns, managing our work. He foresaw government, which "gladly works for ['the people's'] happiness but wants to be the sole agent and judge of it." Williams sums up his review with a very insightful comment, that "Democracy gives an aura of legitimacy to acts that would otherwise be deemed tyranny." Moreover, my fellow tethered citizens, Johann Wolfgang von Goethe observed, there is no one quite as hopelessly enslaved, as the person who thinks he is free but is not!

Implementing America's Principles Articles #068-069
~Part I: Constitutionalism, Rule of Law and Separation of Powers~
October 10, 2002

Recently you and I discussed the theory of America's Founding. Specifically, we reviewed some principles inherent in the Declaration of Independence—principles which, in effect, fueled a successful revolution (and secession) from Great Britain. We'd be remiss, however, if we left it at that. Why? Because the principles we started with aren't the same as what we're left with now, at the beginning of the 21st century. Moreover, a revolution (political or military) is never the same thing as a lasting, much less proper and benign, system of governance. The Declaration of Independence isn't a document designed for governance. It gives us the rationale for becoming who we are and aspire to be; it sets up an idealistic vision for what might come true, what we potentially can accomplish with hard work and God's Blessing. We do not, however, get the American Congress, President or Supreme Court from the Declaration of Independence. Instead, those things come from the Constitution. As in many arenas of life, theory and practice are related but often in tense conflict. In government, how do you really square protection of rights and consent together? How do the people delegate enough power to government to do what it should and, at the same time 'check and balance' it, to preclude government from doing what it should not? Human nature contains a spark of the Divine and that wonderful gift of reason, but it also contains all manner of selfish passion and the downward, destructive tendencies of id and animal.

According to historians Thomas G. West and Douglas A. Jeffrey, the Founders faced the daunting challenge of bringing the practice of American government into line, as it were, with the principles of the Revolution. To that end, they debated and framed the Constitution of the United States of America in Philadelphia, in 1787. The unprecedented success they achieved resulted from six key elements in or about the document they produced and sent to the People for approval: Constitutionalism, Rule of Law, Separation of Powers; Checks and Balances, Representation; and finally, Federalism and Local Self-Government. The first element "Constitutionalism" may sound redundant when talking about the Constitution, but it's not. You see, Americans venerate their Constitution but don't always realize how extraordinary it is to have one in the first place. It is simply a device or technique that can be used, but it isn't the only one. Moreover, America's peculiar *brand* of constitutionalism is something based on written documents (State and Federal). Generically speaking, constitutions don't have to be written at all—Great Britain's still isn't. The theory of America's Founding includes the assertive faith that governments exist to secure rights and that people delegate that job to government, giving to government limited powers—enough and only enough to do the job. A constitution keeps government from going beyond those powers. If ratified by the People in special conventions (the way ours was by the People in each State), a constitution becomes the People's own law, which governs the government even after the government is established. Hence the Constitution is as relevant today as it was in 1789 when it went into effect.

Another important means to insure that government by consent protects rights, is to require that government govern by the *rule of law*. Laws are rules that are general, and they apply to all persons similarly situated (for instance, all citizens). Rule of law also means that no one is above the law, not even one who makes or enforces (or interprets) it. Remember, all men possess equal rights—thus it follows that those who live under the law may participate in making it; and those who make the law must live under the laws they make. To the extent that there may be things a government does that aren't amenable to general rules, i.e., by agencies concerning things which are discretionary, these fall under the executive branch in our system. And even those things must not tend to favor or disfavor particular individuals, or classes, or groups.

Regarding the rule of law, the Founders understood government to include three distinct powers relating to it. These powers are: making laws, enforcing laws, and judging particular violations of law. Placing all three powers in the same hands would, as Madison observed in *Federalist 47*, be the very definition of tyranny. No single authority can be trusted with all three powers—hence the Separation of Powers in the Constitution, which puts each power in a separate, co-equal branch of government. The Founders also felt that separation of powers should help government do its job better. They gave to the legislative, executive and judicial branches different modes of election, different sizes, different tasks and terms in office, all to give to each respective branch the virtues and interests needed to secure rights democratically; and to magnify within each branch its attendant, comparative advantage. These natural advantages were deemed to be deliberation in the legislative branch; energy in the executive;

judgment in the judiciary, whose job was to dispassionately and impartially judge cases *according to the law*. The Founders rejected the more modern view that judges (who do not stand for election) have a law*making* role.

~Part II: Checks and Balances, Representation, Federalism and Local Self-Government~ October 17, 2002

Besides Constitutionalism, Rule of Law and Separation of Powers, all of which we previously discussed, there are three other key elements that explain why America has been so successful in self-governance under the Constitution. They are Checks and Balances, Representation and finally, Federalism and Local Self-Government. Specifically, checks and balances are mechanisms put in place to maintain the separation of powers between the branches of government. There are quite a few in the Constitution. Indeed, to erect three co-equal branches was one thing, but to keep one branch from encroaching on others was another. One of the most important things the Founders did was to forbid Congress from tampering with the fundamental law of the Constitution! Congress might propose an amendment, but changing the Constitution would require the people of the States—and it would be difficult. Another thing the Founders did was to divide the legislative branch into two Houses, the House of Representatives and the Senate. Given their different term lengths, constituencies, sizes and functions, it would be difficult for these two Houses to act unjustly in concert. And while the President was given a veto power over legislation, two-thirds of the members of each House could override his veto. An independent judiciary would be able to review legislation in light of the written Constitution.

The Founders also believed that representation was the best method to ensure that the people remained ultimately in charge. At the same time, representation was a 'check and balance' of sorts on democratic excesses. According to historians Thomas G. West and Douglas A. Jeffrey, "Representation allows the people to have a voice in government by sending elected representatives to do their bidding, while avoiding the need of each and every citizen to vote on every issue considered by government." The latter method would be impractical and would also turn every issue into a campaign, every decision into a popularity snapshot much like a poll. The Framers of the Constitution hoped and theorized that people would also elect the best from amongst themselves to be their representatives;

and these representatives would deliberative carefully, making informed decisions in the common interest with a long view in mind.

The most important device utilized to divide power and to preclude development of national tyranny was *federalism*. States would be the ultimate 'check and balance' on national governmental power. According to the original Constitutional regime, there was no provision per se, for making the national government similarly a ballast to stop potential State tyrannies. This is because political sovereignty was divided or shared out of preexisting State governments—all residual power remained with the States, by virtue of the Ninth and Tenth Amendments to the Constitution, which are part of the original Bill of Rights. The national government received no sanction or authority that was not specifically enumerated (delegated) to it by the people of the States. Hence, the branches were split horizontally as co-equal partners in respective functional orbits that comprise the national government. The States were "vertically" split from the national government, and are likewise co-equal in their orbits with the national government. Today we often use the conceptually confusing term of "federal government," when we are referring to the national government or central government. The *federal* government is really a proper term, however, for the national and State governments collectively, operating in tandem under the Constitution.

The authority of the national government resides in an orbit of things that are national in scope, i.e., foreign policy and national security, general regulation of commerce, etc. James Madison explains in *Federalist 45* and elsewhere, that authority of the States extends to most things. Their orbits, distinct from national matters, comprise the physical and moral environments of the people, things "which, in the ordinary course of affairs, concern the lives, liberties, and properties of the people, and the internal order, improvement, and prosperity of the state." In practice, States historically allowed, encouraged and enabled local self-government. Strong towns and counties in fact predated many of the States. All the Founders also recognized that local and particular interests differ from place to place, and they believed these should be dealt with close to the people. This was not just a matter of efficiency, but also a matter of principle and of propriety. In the original Constitutional regime, indeed in regimes up until the 1970s, State orbits involved all the important matters such as abortion, gun laws, school prayer, and the death penalty. Alexis de Tocqueville observed that local institutions are to liberty what primary schools are to science! It may well be that the emasculation of local and State governments for over thirty years has given to us a generation of moral idiots. Unskilled and unprepared for local self-government, much of the destiny of our lives has been handed to special interests and to a national, liberal ruling elite.

Were the Founders Right? Article #081
o/a March 30, 2003

The Founders gave us a written Constitution, separation of powers, federalism and various public supports to morality, and these were all means to facilitate the goal of good government: the protection of equal rights. But over the course of a century since the Progressive Era, the goal of government has shifted increasingly to producing equality of condition. The change in goal affected government arrangements and practices too, such that, a new administrative or welfare state has supplanted the Republic. The Founders would hardly recognize the controlling leviathan we have unleashed. Indeed, as a matter of logic, the denial of human nature and rejection of natural rights undercut the entire notion of constitutionalism. That notion was to limit the operation of government. *Limited* government has transformed into *unlimited* government to impose the government's new (and hence better) purpose and ever evolving ends. Did you think father really knew best? You poor sot—only Government knows best!

As a practical matter, the separation of powers has been dismantled. Since the 1960s, all three branches have been radically affected. The resulting consolidation of power lacks effective and organized resistance. The mechanics of the Constitution are not working the way the Founders intended. Then again, the people are better "cared for"—and controlled. Was freedom really that valuable to begin with? Perhaps it was overrated. Take the Judiciary, legislating on the pretense of interpreting the Constitution. So what? Okay, grant there is no right to abortion in the Constitution—nobody thinks so. No one argues it from the standpoint of original intent or federalism. But as Justice William Brennan said in 1986, the Framers' Constitution belongs to a "world that is dead and gone." Hence its values must die. Old values can't apply in *modern* America. *Roe v. Wade* in 1973 struck down state laws restricting abortions. The whole matter was arrogated by hubris and naked power to the national level. The Supreme Court decides values for all now, and "life" isn't among the essential panoply. Increasingly, neither is "liberty." How long can it be that we shall "pursue happiness" either, devoid of meaning and standards that do not change? Devoid of meaning and standards that are not ours to decide? Social values used to be decided by *society*. States were those political and social units invested with the broad sovereignty to do that. They still are in fact, but it will take leadership and potentially a showdown to get it right again—to get things back to the way our Founders intended. Judges should not take over local school districts or state prison systems. When they do so, it is gross judicial overreach.

Today the Executive is hamstrung by the multiplicity of little Napoleons: policy-makers in dozens of executive agencies. Under the Framers' Constitution, we had a single executive, the president. He had responsibility, and he was accountable to the people. Today the president is forbidden by law or court order to even control some agency activities. The Chief *Executive* cannot administer his own *executive branch* agencies! Nor can he fire most federal employees. Who's in charge, who's accountable? Well, at least it is a good thing for career bureaucrats. At least the federal bureaucracy can function as a big jobs program for disadvantaged workers. They're people too and deserve our sympathy as fellow human beings—Oklahoma City pointed this out poignantly. But that's not what we're arguing, now is it? We're arguing that the people, bureaucrats included, ought to be following the Constitution of the Founders' intent. The only areas where the president has not been greatly tied down remains foreign policy and the military. Maybe that's why presidents resist so strenuously, even those Constitutional provisions for Congressional authority and oversight. Ever wonder why the Constitution addresses the power to declare war, if such a declaration isn't even necessary?

Then there's the Legislative branch or Congress. Its overreach dwarfs the Supreme Court's or so-called imperial Presidency's. It imposes reporting requirements on executive agencies that are so frequent and detailed, Congress literally asserts itself into the decision making process rightly belonging to the Executive branch. The Congress squeezes bureaucrats better than the president can, by withholding or threatening to withhold funds. Congress issues committee reports with instructions (not laws or orders signed by the president). The instructions steer agencies inside the Executive branch. If executive officials don't play ball, the Congress initiates criminal investigations. With all this administering, the Congress hardly deliberates anymore. What's to deliberate? Used to, the Congress would actually debate whether or not a certain issue fell within its purview. What now can you imagine that does not fall inside the scope of government and that of the Congress? Nothing is out of bounds to the national government. Indeed, administration of the day-to-day lives of Americans has become highly centralized. Not one mile of sewer can be laid anywhere in America without federal permission! State and local governments are reduced to becoming claimants for federal dollars, in effect becoming tools of Washington, D.C. Returning to Constitutional rule of law as the Founders understood it would require Congress to return vast areas of policy-making to the States and localities, and to private citizens.

Earlier Americans were confident that most citizens, acting through self-governing associations like families, churches, and businesses, could take care of their own needs. Maybe they gave us too much credit. But then hope springs eternal, and nothing really prevents us from re-embracing the principles of constitutional government. It remains a viable choice to return to that way of life today. Were the Founders right? Then say so! It is the only way to proceed historically *forward*. The path we're on leads to ancient and medieval tyranny, no matter what the modern twenty-first century devices.[36]

Justice For All Article #207
o/a August 12, 2005

The Pledge of Allegiance ends with a description of the object to which we owe allegiance—namely, a Republic "with liberty and justice for all." Anyone who thinks about it quickly realizes we're pledging ourselves to an ideal, since reality almost always comes up with something short. No nation on the face of the earth, at any time in history, has achieved a state of perfect liberty *and* justice for *all*. Indeed, America—besides the real one—has always existed as an ideal, and striving to reach or become the 'Shining City on a Hill,' i.e., to realize perfection, more often than not, has led to a respectable standard in fact. Reality hasn't been half bad for most people, most of the time!

Discussions about America usually center on Liberty. In that respect, it may be said that Justice generally takes short shrift. Instinctively, we know the two concepts are related, but they aren't exactly the same thing either. Justice might be to lock somebody up and take away his liberty, whereas, somebody's liberty could very well produce injustice to another individual or group. It gets complicated quick. Fortunately, the classic definition of justice advanced by Saint Thomas Aquinas is simple enough. It is simply to render to another his due. From that we derive the notion of rights (entitlements), as well as the notion of right conduct, and the rightness of a given situation. A person's due is what he is entitled to. Your rights therefore are based upon justice, at least as much as they are upon liberty. Moreover, the fact that we are discussing (and must discuss) justice in terms laid down by St. Thomas Aquinas is another example of how American institutions and values are fundamentally Christian in their origin.

Thomas writes that justice is one of four cardinal virtues (the others being temperance, prudence, and fortitude). Justice is the *virtue* of the good citizen, by which one directs his actions to the common good. That means liberty to direct your actions is one thing—the virtue to do it rightly according to justice, however, quite another. In contrast to the other virtues, justice is directed toward the good of others. Justice arguably stands foremost among the cardinal virtues, because the other virtues are directed towards self-perfection, or in the case of fortitude (bravery) especially, are directed towards others in extraordinary circumstances only. Justice directs to the common good those matters that would otherwise, without the concept of justice, concern only private individuals. Anyone who thinks our government isn't value based by definition ought to consider that "We the people of the United States of America" have ordained and established the Constitution for these United States precisely in order to "establish Justice" among other things. Justice is a value-laden term that begs the question what is the common good, which is fairly easy to answer if you're consulting Judeo-Christian tradition. It's more of a challenge, faced with today's multi-cultural and relativist collage of competing moral frameworks.

Social justice, as it were, inevitably involves actions of exchange, obligating parties to fulfill terms of agreement—obligating vendors, for instance, to represent accurately the products they sell, obligating management to honestly administer their corporations. Justice also entails the obligation to ensure that goods are fairly distributed—not necessarily equally, but according to respective economic contributions. Hence the dignity of all honest labor, the idea of fair wages, and the Jeffersonian notion that government and highway robbers ought not to take from the mouth of labor the bread it has earned! Justice, as much as Liberty, lay behind America's traditional commitment to the free market and to free enterprise, since no amount of central planning can efficiently and accurately produce or distribute the things people need or want, like Adam Smith's proverbial "Invisible Hand."

The role of government is to make sure the laws and public institutions of the Republic conform to Liberty and Justice, Justice and Liberty. Government isn't the sole or even primary locus through which individual fulfillment comes—not liberty or justice, certainly not life or happiness. Instead, government is charged with ensuring the *conditions* within which private and family life take place and flourish. Governmental authority is a postulate of the moral order but derives its legitimacy from the people. Government's responsibility and reason for being is to promote the common good or "General Welfare." Laws that contravene the moral order are never binding upon the consciences of free—and just—men and women, who derive their rights from God and who delegate specific powers to government simply to protect those rights.

Trusting Government Article #228
o/a November 25, 2005

Those who trust the government implicitly, at least outside the government's enumerated powers under the Constitution, are certainly bound to be disappointed. They are, quite possibly, bound to be enslaved and probably deserve to be. That's because, as George Washington explained, "Government is not reason; it is not eloquence; it is force. Like fire, it is a dangerous servant and a fearful master." However necessary and protecting, and at times comforting, if people become complacent about such "fire," its tendency is to consume them or their progeny. For as Ronald Reagan said, "Freedom is never more than one generation away from extinction. We didn't pass it to our children in the bloodstream. It must be fought for, protected, and handed on for them to do the same." Those of us who have served in or with the government are all the more skeptical about its intent, and quite sober regarding its frequent and inevitable expediencies. Government at any level is fundamentally no more effective, no more prescient, no more moral—and often very much less so, than the town and county in which you live. Indeed, sometimes the good folks in Middle America tend to mentally transfer or attribute their goodness to Washington, and that's a huge mistake. Beltway bandits may or may not be well intentioned, but their lifestyle, pace, preoccupations and scramble—their function if you will, in political context, in order to be beneficial is predicated on sanity and stability residing at home. The good people of your town should never, ever defer to the government on matters of rights; rather, the federal government ought to and is obliged to defer to the people. The Bill of Rights in fact says so.

Someone living in an affluent and gated community, with armed private security and government security not far behind, may find his or her need for a private weapon incidental or even unimportant. The political class may be unbothered by the United Nations' long-term agenda to outlaw civilian ownership of firearms in all member countries too. If it is good enough for Rwanda, it should be good enough for Vermont and Colorado! Of course most politicians aren't that serious. They figure someone else with horse sense somewhere will cover for their incomprehensibleness. They are often surprised by the lack of interest, much less vigilance on the part of people, which lets them get away with nonsense after election. Take the government's expansion of power under the Patriot Act. We may or may not be in for a long-term War on Terrorism, but the emergency situation per se, which gave rise to the legislation, has clearly abated. The prudent thing to do would be to place more oversight on, as well as to emplace a sunset provision so Congress would be forced to reconsider and to deliberate the need for such measure. Congress ought to debate its renewal, instead of establishing a legacy in perpetuity, of the accumulating accretion of power. The powers were, after all, supposed to be temporary and for a specific purpose. Everyone today still recalls that it was terrorism that gave rise to the Patriot Act and to new governmental powers, yet the powers have been used for law enforcement purposes unrelated to terrorism and no one in the government refutes it. In a political environment where we may reasonably discuss timed withdrawal of troops from Iraq, we ought to be discussing the timed withdrawal of powers that threaten our freedom far more than terrorists do.

Section 213 of the Patriot Act authorizes "delayed notification." People call it "sneak and peek" or "black bag" searches. It steps all over the Fourth Amendment by authorizing government searches without probable cause and without informing you—your home, your car, your business, and your papers. Federal agents simply tell the judge, "It would jeopardize our case if we notified John Doe about searching his home." Notice delayed; constitutional rights denied. Section 215 allows the government to go to a secret court called the Federal Intelligence Surveillance Court and say to the judge, "We want to get some records on John Doe." The secret judge issues an order to collect your details, which could be about firearm purchases, medical history, library books or inter-net browsing, whatever. No reasonable cause is necessary either—only a government agent's claim, that information may be relevant to an 'ongoing anti-terrorism investigation.' I suppose your shoe size is relevant, as well as the box cutter in your toolbox. I hope you didn't get curious and read about militant Islam or American foreign policy. It is easy to link anything in a stupid game of sleuth.

We need to be concentrating on who our enemies are and creating an accurate list of terrorists, suspected terrorists and their associates. We ought to be killing terrorists dead. Instead, the government is using its powers under the Patriot Act as well as other legislation to collect information and to combine and compile it into a mega-computer database covering every single person in the United States. It isn't about terrorists; it isn't even about crime. It is about government control and the bureaucratization of life in America and reducing everyone to personal files that can be studied and ultimately monitored. You see it's the government that doesn't trust you.

Hope for Revolution — Article #351
o/a May 09, 2008

Some weeks ago, I wrote about "occasioning hope." Of course, it is easier said than done. Moreover, it requires a certain object—as in, what to hope *for*. "What we reverence therefore becomes our Hope," I said. In America today, given a fading dream the Founders shared with us: their Republic turned to empire, now arguably in decline—how should we respond in terms of what to hope *for*?

I tell you unequivocally that we should hope for a return to the Constitution. It is as simple and as hard as all that. For the Constitution was the instrument the Founders left us, both to govern and be governed by. Their dream returns the moment we bind ourselves to its strictures. Even the Declaration was not meant to bind us in that manner, since the Declaration declared independence. After the Revolution, our Founders labored and produced the Constitution, in order to give us a government capable of sustaining independence as well as living up to the ideals of the Declaration.

According to constitutional scholar, Dr. Larry P. Arnn, government under the Constitution was justified by an account of the nature of man and his relation to God. Indeed, the biggest reason for the decline of constitutional government in this country may be the decline in a sense of spiritual purpose. Spiritual purpose subordinates Caesar and the state to unalienable rights inhering in individuals, i.e., to the rights of man and woman in God's image. Thus spiritual purpose helps maintain the limited scope and function of government according to the Constitution.

Utility on earth, as well as everyday practical and special interest politics, were subordinate to "the Laws of Nature and of Nature's God" in the Founders' worldview. Those who aspired to lead their Republic, or indeed to live well in freedom, were those who would contemplate the divine order of things and make specific application of it in their lives. Education was entirely separate from any part of the nation-state, and the Constitution contains no language whatsoever to authorize the federal government to have a Department of Education. Indeed, the purpose of education was both intellectual and moral, since the components were deemed connected. How different were their notions of freedom then, and of the good society. How different was their notion of education too, since the Founders looked to a free populace so educated, to maintain their good Republic.

No Founder would have told us to teach Chinese to five year olds or cram science down the students' little throats at any grade, just to ensure your kids get a job and remain competitive in the new world order's global marketplace. Even if you convinced Ben Franklin it was a good idea, he would not have said the federal government had authority under the Constitution to do it or "make it so." Of course, we are far more utilitarian these days, notwithstanding what the Constitution does or does not say; and though I doubt it very much, contemporaries today will say we have so much bigger problems to justify the coercion. They might as well add that we have sufficient problems to throw away integrity and character too, since we clearly lack the stuff to follow the text or written word of the Constitution—even as we pretend government actions retain legitimacy under some magic penumbra.

"Train up the child in the way he should go," Solomon wrote, "and when he is old he will not depart from it." Ronald Reagan added that, "Our leaders must remember that education doesn't begin with some isolated bureaucrat in Washington. It doesn't even begin with State or local officials. Education begins in the home, where it's a parental right and responsibility. Both our public and our private schools exist to aid our families in the instruction of our children, and it's time some people back in Washington stopped acting as if family wishes were only getting in the way."

Not only has government forgot the purpose of education, it has forgotten its own purpose too! The power to hope is the power to see solutions, however. The power to hope is also the power ultimately to change things. Hope is not a plan, but what to hope *for* helps to explain our predicament and points to what must be done. Our statesmen and citizens must return to Original Intent and to a strict interpretation of the Constitution. My hope is on the side of people, because people hope and governments don't. Hope fires the coming political storm and potentially, the backlash. As Sam Adams stated forcefully in 1776: "If ye love wealth better than liberty, the tranquility of servitude better than the animating contest of freedom—go from us in peace. We ask not your counsels or arms. Crouch down and lick the hands, which feed you. May your chains sit lightly upon you, and may posterity forget that ye were our countrymen!" Who would have thought that the hope for a return to the Constitution is hope for a Revolution in our time?

Government Planning the Perfect Life Article #348
o/a May 02, 2008

It occurred to me the other day how nice it would be, to live in that perfect world of holy imagination: where God reigns; and every man, woman and child would know intuitively, without a doubt and without errancy the perfect will of the Father. And if we should know what's right, to think and to do, in that place we would surely want His will to become our own and so freely choose it; and then pray to obtain the power and insight—as we would inevitably His favor gain—to perform the same and make it real, to make all things good concrete in the material world. What a glorious place it would be!

Perhaps a fly buzzing interrupted this daydream, or any number of discomfiting realities. It surely is not the world we live in.

Everyone still wants to live there, however, at least in a place where hard things are decided and perfect will is good enough, and the downside of choices deferred to government is not too low or expensive. In the old days there was a theory of rights, as natural or God-given. Government was a necessary evil, *necessary* nonetheless to secure such rights in the material world—a world the way it is, not hoped for—against all the sundry threats and counterclaims foreign and domestic. This was until FDR changed the universe, after which as he put it in 1932, "rulers were accorded power, and the people consented to that power on consideration that they be accorded certain rights." Rights now emerge from a bargain with government and not as a gift from God. Leaders keep the bargain current moreover, adding new rights and subtracting old ones, keeping the Constitution relevant and *living* in tune with the times.

Instead of having to keep a jealous eye on government, the more power we give it the more rights and benefits accrue back to "the people": Social Security, Medicare, prescription drug benefits, unemployment—and all the promises a presidential candidate is willing to make, such as universal health coverage, the cure of all disease, the end of poverty, and college education for everybody. O ye of little faith! Obama says there's "Change We Can Believe In," if only you'll strike your deal with his unlimited government. Not to be outdone, there's no problem Hillary can't solve based on her experience and hard fighting for you—if only you'll strike your deal with her unlimited government.

And what of the Republican conceit, the stupid idea that a perfect world consists of Washington run like (or for) private business; or better yet, run by war heroes? Not even necessarily a victorious general, but a prisoner of war from a war that ended in defeat—and willing to commit the nation to five more generations of the same, and to commit us to a peculiar brand of honor at the expense of national self-interest. Again strike your deal with unlimited, energetic and manly executive government! Nowhere is there serious consideration in this campaign of what the Founders envisioned as limited or constitutional government. Moreover, as constitutional scholar Dr. Charles Kesler wrote in January, "the Republican dereliction is most troubling, [because] it represents the falling away from the standards of Ronald Reagan's conservatism . . . ." We've come to expect no less from socialists (a.k.a. progressives) in the Democrat party, but none of the would-be emperors wear any clothes. The state is now the full ethical expression of the American people.

Before progressive political assumptions of the modern state displaced the Founders' vision after the New Deal, there was an ascendant view in these United States that government should mainly protect our natural rights to life and liberty, property and contract, etc. Another constitutional scholar, Roger Pilon adds—"leaving us otherwise free to plan and live our lives and responsible for solving our own problems, alone or with others." Which begs the question, does it matter, if I bemoan the fact that cars and trucks displaced the horse and buggy!

For the answer, I turn to men who understood the standards of Ronald Reagan's conservatism, and who indeed helped raise those standards. The late Henry Hazlitt argued that it matters, because of the "cumulative debilitating effects of growing restrictions on human liberty." He points out that "government has nothing to give to anybody that it doesn't first take from somebody else. In other words, all its relief and subsidy schemes are merely ways of robbing Peter to support Paul. Thus, it can be pointed out that the modern Welfare State is merely a complicated arrangement by which nobody pays for the education of his own children, but everybody pays for the education of everybody else's children; by which nobody pays his own medical bills, but everybody pays everybody else's medical bills; by which nobody provides for his own old-age security, but everybody pays for everybody else's old-age security . . . ."

Likewise the great economist and philosopher Ludwig von Mises, in his book *Socialism* written over 35 years ago, reminds us why we should care—if indeed we do still care, about old-fashioned ideas like liberty. He said "no one can find a safe way out for himself if society is sweeping toward destruction," and he implored us to thrust "vigorously into the intellectual battle." Of course, he assumed there might still be one in 2008.

What Would Jefferson Say? No Good Government Here
o/a September 11, 2010 Article #467

As a modern Jeffersonian Republican, my political philosophy can pretty much be summed up by Thomas Jefferson's First Inaugural Address. In that speech, he outlined what he considered to be the sum of good government. Jefferson, Author of the Declaration of Independence and our nation's third president, said that good government consists of these attributes: (1) it is wise and frugal; (2) it keeps men from injuring one another; (3) government otherwise leaves men and women free to their own pursuits of industry and improvement; and (4) government does not take out of the mouth of labor the bread that it has earned. The first two of the attributes have to do with the limited nature of civil government itself, whereas the second two posit an expansive view of the human individual.

Good civil government is first of all wise and frugal. Wise is an adjective purporting wisdom, and wisdom is the right application of knowledge. Scripture says the beginning of wisdom is the fear of God. So how does that apply to civil government? Directly, in that, wise political leaders are humble, recognizing that they are *not* omniscient; good civil magistrates recognize their limitations and govern from a felt sense of humility—they do not profess to know everything. Wise political leaders are cautious, recognizing that though they wield much power, rarely do they achieve the ends which they set out to accomplish. There are sad and unintended consequences to the careless use of power, as with mishandling a loaded gun. Wise political leaders recognize that they too are subject to live under the same laws as they put upon others; and all men and women, including themselves, are subject to fundamental principles of right and wrong and correct behavior.

Frugal is also an adjective meaning thrifty, economical, careful, cautious, prudent, provident, not wasteful, sparing, scrimping; abstemious, abstinent, austere, self-denying, ascetic, monkish, Spartan; parsimonious, miserly, penny-pinching, close-fisted; tightfisted, tight, stingy. Today our present civil government is hardly that and indeed closely resembles the opposite or antonym of the word frugal—our government is *extravagant* and is therefore not a good government on that basis alone! Good civil government secondly, according to Jefferson, keeps men from injuring one another. This too is hardly the case along our southern border with Mexico, and yet this is the fundamental and essential purpose of civil government—to protect life, liberty and property. A Jeffersonian view of humanity recognizes that individual men and woman are sovereign; that they have inalienable rights that are not conferred; not granted by governments or compacts, but bound up in their very nature in who they are—free and responsible and special (according to Scripture *made* in the image of God). The purpose of government is limited and not extensive. It is simply to protect individuals from harm. Civil governments are necessary only because of irresponsible behavior, specifically aggression. If we were angels we would not need civil government. Sovereignty of the state is only an extension of the sovereignty of individuals.

Good civil government, thirdly, leaves men free to their own pursuits of employment and improvement. Civil government is not to direct the actions of individuals, only to keep them from harming others. Sovereignty again is essentially individual and not collective. Today regulations and requirements and the *threat* of legal entanglements, are so pervasive and onerous in relation to just about anything one might try to do. Government literally stands in the way of individual pursuits and dreams contrary to the vision of our Founders. At the same time taxes kill anything you might actually accomplish! Which brings us to Jefferson's Fourth attribute, namely, good civil government does not take out of the mouth of labor the bread that it has earned, i.e., does not steal from the fruits of our labor. Government today steals from Peter to pay Paul and Paulette, and sustains a huge bureaucracy to enforce the terms.

A modern Jeffersonian view of civil government is humble; sees itself as a servant of sovereign individuals and not as their master; recognizes that the fundamental action and authority of civil society is left to free and responsible actions of individuals. Today everything is turned on its head. Instead of individuals having the most responsibility and freedom, civil government controls almost everything. Civil government should be the least of all governments, because remember there are many governments (self, family, church, etc.). Moreover, civil government of the State of Texas should be a far more prevalent factor than, say, the national federal government. Again everything is turned on its head. Mayors every day contend with extensive burdens placed on city government and local schools by a multitude of unconstitutional federal mandates. And oh by the way, the Tenth Amendment of the Constitution is not *merely* a federal issue to be interpreted by the federal government; rather, it is an issue of great consequence for state lawmakers who, among other state officials, *are responsible to defend Texas sovereignty and independence.* This is underscored by the requirement that every office bearer in Texas must swear: to the best of his or her ability to *preserve*, *protect*, and *defend* the Constitution and laws of the U.S. and of this State.

The U.S. Government has grown so large, so powerful and so intrusive, that the States are in very real danger of losing their self-determination and sovereignty. One of the reasons for this growth is the misconception that the federal government itself is the final interpreter or sole arbiter of whether *it* has exercised "the powers not delegated" to it by the Constitution. It is commonly believed the U.S. Supreme Court has the final say concerning whether or not the U.S. has exceeded its constitutional bounds. If this is the case, we find ourselves in a situation akin to Dr. Frankenstein and his monster, where the creature cannot be checked and may in fact overcome its own creator.[37]

States Must Resist Tyranny of Federal Government Article #468
o/a September 11, 2010

As parties to the compact that created and empowered the U.S. Government, States have legal standing to *check* the federal government's use of powers that States did not delegate. Inaction and refusal to comply with an unconstitutional federal mandate is the primary tool that States can employ. An example of *this peaceful, efficient and effective* resistance to federal meddling is the response to The Real ID Act 2005, which requires States to implement certain driver's license and identification card standards and sharing of the same with other States. Most States simply have done nothing, or in fact have passed resolutions opposing it. Neither have they funded the program or implemented it. The Tenth Amendment is very important for state officials to understand because it authoritatively explains that: (1) the States and the people have kept all powers which they did not specifically delegate or specifically give up to form the Union; and (2) U.S. authority at the national federal level is limited, defined, and delegated by the States. The *first* point reminds us that Texas is independent and sovereign and has the wherewithal to take care of herself. The *second* aspect reminds us that the U.S. is not an unlimited and all powerful master but rather, a steward charged by the States with certain duties.

The original Constitution was quickly amended with the "Bill of Rights" (the first Ten Amendments) because there was considerable concern among the Founding Fathers that the original Constitution, without it, might be later misconstrued or misunderstood. The Ninth and Tenth Amendments, in particular, do not add or subtract anything in the way of powers or authority. They do, however, explain to subsequent generations what the Founders explicitly meant by the original Constitution—in military parlance, they communicate the Founders' "intent." The Ninth and Tenth Amendments are simply authoritative declarations which, like a *monument*, mark a boundary for future generations, and like a *fence*, keep some things *on* and some things *off* your property. If Texas is to remain sovereign and independent, Texas officeholders must wisely, peacefully, but immediately endeavor to take care of the State's own affairs and its people and to defend the State and its people against the Federal Government's use of "powers not delegated to the United States."

But what happens if Texas does not preserve local self-government? What happens if the U.S. exercises "the powers not delegated" to it by the Constitution? What if Texas gives up local self-determination either voluntarily or otherwise? What if the U.S. Government overreaches into the affairs of the States and individuals? Is it of any consequence? Article 1, Section 1 of the Texas Constitution indicates that it is of grave consequence: "The maintenance of our free institutions and the perpetuity of the Union depend upon the preservation of the right of local self-government, unimpaired to all the States." 'Houston, I'd say we have a problem!'

In fact, we've had a dual problem for quite some time: (1) the abdication or neglect of self-government by States; and (2) the usurpation of "the powers not delegated" by the U.S. Federal Government. Both acting in tandem make for a perfect storm, in terms of endangering our freedoms and the national Union itself. Patriots are passionate about the Tenth Amendment because it is the cornerstone of our Federal Republic. If we ignore it and fail to line up the other stones in the Constitutional edifice with it, the entire building is in jeopardy of collapsing, and this is very much the way the Founders explained their rationale for building a federal structure with dual State and Federal sovereignty in the first instance. To violate the intent and letter of the Constitution in this regard is illegal, in that it violates the Organic Law of the land. Moreover, it is risky, imprudent and foolish from the basis of history and politics, which the Founders understood extremely well. But this does not need to happen!

If your neighbor begins to build a greenhouse on your property, the neighborly thing to do, is to go talk to your neighbor and point out the problem, i.e., that he has crossed the property line and is on your property. If necessary, you may need to uncover boundary monuments and get out a survey instrument to demonstrate to your neighbor where the boundary line is and how he is encroaching upon your property. This usually solves the problem, especially if it is done in a timely manner. The first point of the illustration is that there is a dual responsibility: one must not encroach, and the other must be diligent enough to identify and defend against such encroachment. This is especially true for a federal republic made up of independent sovereign states. The second point is that vigilance and timely defense is necessary to avoid costly disputes. Even reasonable neighbors are very slow to admit and correct encroachments that are left uncontested for years. Unfortunately, the States have for a long time acquiesced to encroachments on their rights and the rights of the people—often because an unconstitutional federal action appeared to be beneficial.

If Texans are to be free and our Union preserved, then Texas officeholders must wisely, peacefully, incrementally *but immediately* endeavor to restore our State's self-government, which is now impaired by the Federal Government's use of "powers not delegated to the United States." There are two areas where the General Government of the U.S. is presently seeking to unconstitutionally extend its authority: (1) healthcare; and (2) environmental regulation. Other areas of overreach include firearms regulation and legal tender laws. Moreover, the General Government of the U.S. has not merely usurped State and individual rights, but it has also failed to faithfully execute the immigration laws of the United States. All of which means that, as a sovereign, independent State Texas must refuse to comply with, facilitate, or enact unconstitutional federal legislation. We do not fund or budget it. We do not manage or implement it. We do not allow the Federal Government to harass or serve warrants, unless they are for Constitutional laws. This is a tall order but absolutely essential if we are to escape abject tyranny. May God turn us back to Him, and may God save Texas and keep these United States. [38]

CHAPTER 15

TAXES

Taxes Article #006
February 15, 2001

Most Americans know our Founders didn't like taxes very much, but I wish they'd think about it a little more. As financial and bank statements sift in this time of year, I begin to assess the bad news for my family. Will it be a third out of my income this year, or will I contribute half because I wasn't "careful" enough or didn't pay the right CPA? I'm suddenly in touch with deeply American roots and share the same mind that once animated Northerners and Southerners alike, the likes of Sam Adams of Massachusetts or Patrick Henry of Virginia. I'd really like to help with a little Tea Party now if I could: put it in the Potomac—or, better yet, into the White House swimming pool!

GW proposed his $1.3 trillion income tax cut, although I don't think I'll get that much. I hope he delivers it though, even to the so-called rich (meaning those who can afford to pay the taxes). But even if the total amount beats the "targeted" $500 million that Vice President Gore preferred, I think all politicians these days have missed the bull's eye by a mile. The Constitution that called the federal government into existence in 1789 failed to provide that government with the power to levy taxes on income. This was not an oversight; rather, it was common wisdom in that day that individuals had a right to all they earned. Indeed, if a government had power to take earnings, one's position was no different than that of a slave. The power to tax was then and is now the power to destroy. The Founders agreed that some taxation would be necessary, for government to perform its limited functions. Income taxes, however, were the most personal, the most pernicious, and the least to be tolerated—with or without representation.

American society lived and prospered without income taxes for more than 125 years. The reason was philosophical more than anything. Americans simply did not believe they were subordinated to the State, not in terms of what could be confiscated. Governments that historically taxed income had done so on the premise, that the State was supreme and its citizen subordinate. The Declaration of Independence and Constitution changed that premise, and the people restrained government from seizing property or income. Indeed, it took a constitutional amendment to subordinate American citizens and to effectively undo the American Revolution. The Sixteenth Amendment was enacted in 1913 to enable the government to levy income taxes. Today there is no theoretical limit to what percentage the government may take. The government effectively owns your income and "allows" you to keep more or less of it. Since 1943, taxes are also collected automatically through payroll deductions. That measure facilitated the financing of World War II. With the Cold War over now as well, payroll deductions still finance "wars" on poverty, cancer, drugs, you name it. I bet if payroll deductions were stopped and citizens viewed their consolidated tax bills at the end of each year, they'd be a bit more cognizant of what it is they pay and how destructive the burden really is. They might become better for it, more like our ancestors. Then I'd see you at the Tea Party too!

Tax Cuts Forever — Article #059
April 4, 2002

To hear the liberals, you'd think we ought to have to justify tax cuts. What's strange is how anyone could get something so entirely "bass ackwards." It is government spending that ought to (and always) be justified! To hear the media these days, government creates the wealth and parcels it out to the people. If you "spend" money on tax cuts, you waste it. Hello, is anybody out there? I certainly enjoyed my little rebate check—money the government didn't "give" me but merely returned. The fact is that government doesn't create wealth—it can't; it can only confiscate it. Individuals through ingenuity and hard work create the wealth, some of which gets taken from them for taxes. Cutting taxes is merely abstaining from taking as much from producers. As Sheldon Richman explains, "Money never leaves the hands it originates in, because it never goes to Washington in the first place. Thus, all the talk about how much the Bush-plan [gave] the rich is sheer balderdash. [Government] gives nothing to anyone."

Here in America we have become so mired in welfare state thinking, most people approach political issues as though tax revenues are a pot of cash that belongs to the government. Increases in spending are so normal that if someone proposes a smaller increase than planned, it's a budget cut! As Thomas Sowell has pointed out, the historical burden of proof has shifted from politicians to the people, a dangerous situation if you believe as the Founders did, that the power to tax is the power to destroy. Indeed, a government powerful enough to give you everything you want, paid for at taxpayer expense, is a government powerful enough to take everything away from you.

Further, it may be that government is already on the verge of such all-power, because it cannot really be asserted the people have authorized the current tax laws. Richman again: "Tax laws are written in arcane language behind closed doors by a few tenured congressmen and their staffs. Government has myriad devices for mystifying its operations, in order to keep John Q. Citizen at a safe distance. We the people no more authorized the tax-eating monster we live with than we authorized the tornadoes that tore through Arkansas and Mississippi" last year. It is not comforting to contemplate that we may have lapsed into a time before the American Revolution. Is the only apparent effect of the American Revolution that we now spend our Fourth of July differently?

Possibly somewhere in our collective consciousness, the voice of Patrick Henry whispers. If so, there ought to be some resonance with the president's consistent effort to provide tax relief. Whether the economy is jump-started or not is really quite beside the point. I say, "Taxes/taxes: tax cuts now, tax cuts tomorrow, tax cuts forever!" The president has been only partly successful so far, because of domestic political opposition. He still wants to reduce income tax rates; double the child-care tax credit; reduce the marriage penalty; expand charitable deductions; phase out the death tax; and extend the research and experimentation tax credit.

The president is trying to deliver on his campaign promises. As shocking as that is in itself, the irony is that such policy measures by and large, shouldn't need to be justified—for in the absence of compelling justification for government spending, tax money should revert to the people who earn it. If there were a compelling justification today, it might be National Missile Defense, but even that case needs to be explained and "proven." And if the president says he can do both a tax cut and national defense, then I take him at his word. Liberal designs to stop future tax cuts, in order to spend—oh sorry, I mean to "invest"—the money are horse hockey plain and simple. It is high time that we reinstate the burden of proof onto parasitic politicians and their dependents of government largesse—removing it from off the backs of America's breadwinners.

Tea and Taxes Article #392
o/a April 03, 2009

On the night of 16 December 1773, members of the Sons of Liberty dressed up as Mohawk Indians and boarded ships in Boston harbor. A large number of citizens gathered to watch as they broke open hundreds of chests of tea and heaved them overboard into the water. This radical act of protest known as the Boston Tea Party stemmed from the English government's attempt to help one company in dire financial straits off the backs of the people, through higher taxation. Sound familiar? The East India Company was the AIG and Government Motors of the day. Instead of letting the company go under or forcing it to unwind and sell off, the government decided that it was just too big (or too well connected) to fail. So the government subsidized this company through measures that inevitably raised taxes on hardworking Americans. It was the trigger for a Revolution to come, and it meant that things would get much worse for Americans before they finally got better.

Generally that's how the price of freedom gets paid though, i.e., it can be pretty steep up front. Power doesn't let go easily. Ever so often a present generation reaches down deep to find its courage and its character. It chooses not to pay higher taxes but chooses instead to pay in terms of sweat and tears and sometimes blood, so that their children and grandchildren won't have to pay as much of either. Otherwise, the path of least resistance leads to total submission. "Taxation without representation is tyranny." Americans are not easily saddled. Texans never submit to tyranny plain and simple.

Start to ask the questions, whether you are in fact represented therefore at the Federal Reserve, or at big banks, or on boards of directors of failed businesses that now have their hands in your pocket, or at G-20 summits when promises get made to submit to international regulatory regimes. Ask yourself whether Congress can legitimately represent you after failing so miserably at oversight, and then by passing a $500 billion tax bill without reading it. Man "It ain't me—I ain't no fortunate son!"

To tell the truth, I just want to be left alone. But I am cognizant of the price that must be paid, willing as it were to endure hardship to bring about a brighter tomorrow. It is not the endurance of parasites about which I speak, however, nor the press of a hard floor on my forehead, with baby boots of bureaucrats on my back. Liberty is worth all other sacrifice now and forever, and I have enlisted therefore in the Campaign for Liberty, both literally and figuratively. On April 15th the citizens of Bell County gather at Confederate Park in Belton, Texas (4-6 p.m.) for speeches, signs and protest, voter registration and non-partisan organizing efforts. The irony is not lost on the location, given that what we need now more than anything is an army of All-American Rebels to join the cause. Similar tea parties on Tax Day are occurring throughout the state and nation. Those who have decided that we are Taxed Enough Already (TEA) will be there. Those "tea'd off" at decisions being made in Washington with unimaginable consequences for us and for our descendants will be there.

The Congressional Budget Office predicts the government's $3.6 trillion budget will lead to deficits multi-trillions of dollars more than the administration is saying. Folks the gloves are off. A professor of history at Southwest Baptist University writes that as Americans we are entering a period reminiscent of the German people during the 1930s. According to his analysis, we have a socialist regime looking for a pretext to tyranny. The economic crisis provides perfect rationale for a command economy, just as the Great Depression did for smooth talking fascist rogues in Europe. In America the process arguably began years ago with confiscatory tax policies. The methods are thus already in place, but now the philosophical bent of what Grover Norquist calls "the Takings Coalition" is ascendant in national politics, which coincides with an economic emergency.

The combination is more toxic to liberty than all the bad assets in banks. At no time in our history have we been as immediately threatened with extreme taxation. Some nine years ago Ron Paul wrote, "A casual acceptance of the principle behind high taxation, with an income tax and an inheritance tax, is incompatible with a principled belief in a true republic. It is impossible to maintain a high tax system without the sacrifice of liberty and an undermining of property ownership. If kept in place, such a system will undermine prosperity, regardless of how well off we may presently be." The proverbial chickens have come home to roost, but if the people will act quickly and forceful enough like Sons and Daughters of Liberty, then this could be the day and the hour we slap government back down to its constitutional size. The only way to do that ultimately is to puncture its immense moneybag, but in the meantime we should serve notice that it better keep its hands to itself.

Revolt When Taxes Become Confiscatory Article #445
o/a March 12, 2010

Congress passed the health care reform bill that people plainly said they didn't want. The President signed it into law, because he's smarter than you are. Proponents of the massive government take-over of health care and public cooption of private scholarship funding are now complaining about the lack of civility directed towards them. Well the American people owe about as much civility towards Congress and the White House these days as they do to the same mob that stole their property and mugged their kids (same thing only different). There will also come a time when taxes rise to the level of confiscation, when every American taxpayer must decide for him or herself—how far is enough and how far is too far? On what basis rests the fealty of citizens to the nation? Is government always the same thing as the nation, and is the IRS and government bureaucracy the same as good government? These questions should never come up, if the government were confined to purposes for which it was erected.

The average taxpayer is more or less happy to do his part, whenever the government acts constitutionally. The average taxpayer remains true to his legal obligation to pay for government, if it acts in accordance with enumerated powers and responsibilities delegated to it to perform. The hypothetical situation should never arise as to what people would do if the government becomes a tyranny, that is, if the government stayed within its constitutional bounds. Patrick Henry no doubt lacked a certain civility in his day, and so should we. The hypothetical case, however, is relevant because the health care reform bill just passed will dramatically increase taxes and raise national debt. If the government takes 30 percent of your income from you, is that okay? Probably. If the government takes 50 percent of your income from you, is that okay? Possibly. If the government takes 80 percent of your income from you, is that okay? Nay. And most people will refuse, unless they are willing to become as slaves or pawns to

Big Brother government. When taxes become confiscatory, people must revolt. They have a duty to do so.

In American political tradition, revolt will take the form of political action first, civil disobedience second. It may gravitate towards other more extreme forms of resistance, depending upon the action, inaction and counteractions committed by the government. Don't be fooled: the government is not the same as the people and never has been. The government is a representative institution elected and paid for to serve the people. It is not elected and paid for to be our babysitter or minor guardian or Progressive schoolmarm. Its legitimate activities are bound by the strictures of the Constitution. Today unfortunately there is no safe or easy way to resist; and there won't be, should the government fail to get the message politically speaking in 2010 and 2012. Hypothetically there will never be a safe way to resist, *unless or until there is no safe way for the government to confiscate taxes and litigate its citizens*. The conditional phrase, as it were, is reserved for the moment. The point is that a spectrum or sliding scale of populist reaction has been entered into, and quite needlessly. The situation was created, indeed plotted and pulled off by leftist ideologues in the executive branch and morons in Congress.

The president will go down as the worst in our history if judged solely by the health care legislation. Watch closely, however, because his administration plans next to legalize seven million illegal immigrants under so-called comprehensive immigration reform, and this will result in extending health care to them as well. I say again: how far is enough and how far is too far? On what basis rests the fealty of citizens to the nation? Is government always the same thing as the nation, and is the IRS and government bureaucracy the same as good government? The time to avoid the bait is not when hind legs are caught in the mousetrap. When confiscatory taxes threaten your livelihood, future, family and dreams, they are as illegitimate as government that would enact such laws as to require them. Government will make a man do whatever it has the power to coerce. That's why the Founders believed so fervently in withholding power from the federal government. At their urging, states ratified the Constitution and enshrined the principle of limited government, such that, government is illegitimate outside the mandates and allowances of the Constitution.

There is quite simply no legitimate power in the Constitution to mandate that private citizens shall purchase any given product or service, including health insurance. Thus far and no farther, the People must decide and decide quickly! Ironically the cradle of Western democracy, Athens, Greece was shaken by violent clashes starting in March in response to that country's financial collapse and government austerity measures. In that case, the people waited too long to act. They were reduced moreover to the pitiful state of resorting to violence—not in order to restore their Republic or insist upon natural rights of life, liberty and pursuit of happiness. No, rather they resorted to violence merely to clutch at those crumbs of tax-supported handouts and dependent privileges purchased at the cost of confiscatory taxation, self-dignity and freedom.

CHAPTER 16

MILITARY TRIBUTE

Memorial Day
May 16, 2002

Article #062

Sometimes in life, we are privileged to meet outstanding people. If we are really fortunate, we get to work for them. Subordination becomes teamwork. Vision is shared by the entire organization. Success or failure is qualitatively owned, felt personally by every member of the group. In that regard, I have to thank an old boss named WC Garrison. He's an Okie, who made his home in Texas. He happens also to be African-American—which is pretty obvious, so he never wore it on his sleeve. What he wore on his shoulder instead was the rank of full Colonel in the US Army, Infantry. I recall that he always looked sharp and definitely had the gift of gab, but he also possessed the right qualities of leadership behind appearances, as well as considerable intellect and a sincerity of heart. So I'm very pleased to freely adapt comments he wrote some time ago, and to share them with you for the occasion of Memorial Day 2002:

General James A. Garfield, before he became 20th President of the United States, said of veterans who died in battle: "They summed up and perfected, by one supreme act, the highest virtue of men and citizens. For love of country they accepted death, and thus resolved all doubts, and made immortal their patriotism and virtue." Indeed, words such as these are likely to punctuate Memorial Day ceremonies and activities of Americans around the globe. The oratories generally focus audiences on remembrance, to remember the deeds of the dead. And while eloquent speeches provide comfort to some, they also bring out emotions in others, who may have lost a husband, son, mother or daughter, friend or colleague. When all is said, some will never comprehend the message of Memorial

Day: to remember our fallen warriors, and to devote ourselves to those who continue to sacrifice for freedom's sake.

Memorial Day is our chance to remember those men and women, who fought and died for our freedom. Their sacrifice was not for fortune, neither for fame, but for the sacred cause of having and keeping a free country. Our freedom was literally paid for in blood and human suffering. From the snow-laden fields at Valley Forge to the windswept sands of the Middle East, every American generation has given some of its sons and daughters in the cause of freedom. Ordinary people, who were extraordinarily brave, made the ultimate sacrifice by laying down their lives for our great land. So let us remember that freedom isn't free, that its blessings have come to us at the cost of shattered dreams and the suspended hopes of millions. It is entirely fitting and proper that we take a moment to listen to voices far and near in time, to remember our war heroes, to contemplate their sacrifice and to consider their cause. Memorial Day gives us that time, and we must use it to remember.

Remembrance of our military dead should not be the only purpose of Memorial Day, however. Memorial Day should also be about fulfillment, about not letting the sacrifice of previous generations go to waste. To that end, we have a citizen duty to increase our level of devotion to the principles and values that keep our nation free. We have a charge, to make good on the legacy of courage and spirit passed on to us by America's honored dead. Hence, Memorial Day is also about the living. The daily risk of ultimate sacrifice stares our military members in the face every day, as they continue to do the noble work of defending our country and our way of life. Today they fight the nation's War against Terrorism. They redress the injury committed against us. They continue to do us proud.

Memorial Day 2002 finds military members serving in distant, and some hostile lands. Many are doing their part, far away from family and loved ones. Our servicemen and women see duty at airbases, ports, field locations, ships, at regular posts and office buildings. Wherever they are, because they are there and do their duty, we rest easier. Because they are there, we can raise our families and pursue dreams—whether dreams of profit or dreams of achievement. We rest easier knowing these modern-day warriors have inherited the immortal fighting spirit of America's fallen heroes, that their selfless dedication to duty and country continues the proud tradition of service to our Nation.

As we remember the sacrifice of kinsmen and countrymen, let us recall President Abraham Lincoln's words at Gettysburg: "It is for us, the living to be dedicated to the unfinished work which they so nobly advanced." [Note: While Lincoln was thinking about the Union dead and his Civil War aims, one can read these words more inspiringly and apply them here to Confederate dead as well, to the lofty ideals for which they fought. For the truth is that Northerners and Southerners were Americans all]. And as we take one day this year to give homage to those who died so that our nation might live, let us also give thanks to those who live, so that our nation will not die. On May 27, 2002, Americans all: please stop and take a moment to think about the men and women who died for our freedom; and say a prayer asking God to bless the men and women, who now serve in our Nation's armed forces, Active, Guard and Reserve—in the United States' Army, Navy, Air Force, Marine Corps, and Coast Guard. Perhaps Lincoln best summarizes the hope invested in every Memorial Day, that it be "from these honored dead [that] we take increased devotion to that cause for which they gave the last full measure of devotion; that we here highly resolve that these dead shall not have died in vain."

Amazing Sacrifice Article #474
o/a October 30, 2010

Veterans have their day, as it were, every November 11th. The occasion got its start after World War I and was originally called Armistice Day—commemorating the instrument that ended the main hostilities of the Great War, at the 11th hour of the 11th day of the 11th month of 1918, when the Germans signed on to "peace" after four years of bloody carnage and trench warfare. The fact that Veterans Day has its origin in World War I is significant to the topic at hand: the amazing sacrifice of veterans. World War I was so extremely costly and yet achieved little of benefit for either side. Historians will say the end of World War I and the punitive peace that followed, actually laid necessary conditions for the start of World War II and the Holocaust that accompanied the Second Great War.

The Western mind finds it difficult to fathom, let alone to accept meaningless death, or untimely death, particularly the heroic and/or selfless sacrifice of one's own life for the good of others or in the name of a good cause such as one's Country. There needs to be a justifiable purpose for the placement of freemen and freewomen into harm's way, and there must be a formalized memory too of the events that transpire, whenever harm does come their way as it often does. America gives honor to her veterans: to their intent if not always to results in battle, to personal courage and sacrifice, whether unto victory or defeat—and even if and when the political cause of conflict is suspect in hindsight, or the war itself becomes widely regarded as being an utter mistake.

The veteran's sacrifice is sacred by its nature. His example shines because it was the most he could do or give whenever the nation called, and quite often when our collective wellbeing actually depended upon his standing in the breach. On Veterans Day we express our thanks to veterans, and we recognize together the importance of him or her, and by implication the innate importance of every single individual's existence. The loss of life and limb, even the loss of the time of life or of innocence, is part of that amazing sacrifice made by veterans—for when duty called, all gave some and some gave all on behalf of the Nation in Whose God we Trust.

The motives of men and women vary so much when they volunteer and even when they are drafted. Some enlist out of patriotism, others out of a need to prove and search themselves. Some cite more practical things such as a paycheck, or "three hots and a cot." For whatever reason, veterans more often than not are proud to make and proud to have made their sacrifice. Few look upon their service with a sense of regret, or go seeking after pity for the time they spent or the hardships they endured. Their friends' names and faces cause them to regard their own contributions more positively. They honor themselves occasionally, in order to honor them—their experience is always a spotless one where comrades are concerned.

Veterans did what they had to do or felt they were obligated to do, but for those who lived through their experience in uniform, the time they spent in service very often defines them like no other and stamps them with a sense of worth that transcends most other times in their life. Whatever happens to them after (and many veterans go on to do great things), they were nevertheless young and *soldiers*, sailors, marines, airmen and coastguardsmen once! They met or exceeded expectations then and served on quintessential *teams*, all for greater cause than themselves or for a greater good.

An unexpected conclusion presents itself, and that is that from the standpoint of the veteran and his fellow citizen who may not have served in the same capacity, the veteran's service constitutes a period of special risk that he uniquely bore. The risk is often seen as generational, sometimes circumstantial or threat based, but no matter whether the risk was slight or substantial, and however one may choose to explain it—in terms of God or Darwin, whatever happens on the veteran's watch becomes his or her honor to make said sacrifice. The veteran typically doesn't feel sorry for himself, and he doesn't think anyone else should either. The honor therefore that we should bestow this Veterans Day on him is an external counterpart or show of regard for the amazing record of sacrifice by American veterans over the years—most recently through extended Cold War engagement and the indefinite scope and duration of the Global War on Terrorism with its associated multiple deployments. The honor we give moreover reflects the honor they inwardly felt. It is an odd reciprocal relationship really, this reflection, wherein we bask somewhat in their heroism and selflessness, which helps knit generations together; bridge military and civilians; and keep this 'land of the free and the home of the brave' vital and enduring.

Veterans Issues are Everybody's Article #102
July 31, 2003

Some people don't understand what it is military personnel do or even why they would do it. These days, that includes many lawmakers. Few are veterans and, as this exchange between Senators John Glenn and Howard Metzenbaum some years ago makes clear, it can make for a whole different kind of polarization in politics. Senator Metzenbaum apparently asked Senator Glenn, "How can you run for Senate when you've never held a real job?"

Senator Glenn responded with indignation: "I served 23 years in the United States Marine Corps. I served through two wars. I flew 149 missions. My plane was hit by antiaircraft fire on 12 different occasions. I was in the space program. It wasn't my checkbook; it was my Life on the line. It was not a nine to five job, where I took time off to take the daily cash receipts to the bank. I ask you to go with me . . . as I went the other day, to a Veteran's Hospital, and look at those men with their mangled bodies in the eye and tell them they didn't hold a job.

"You go with me to the space program and go as I have gone to the widows and orphans of Ed White and Gus Grissom and Roger Chaffee and you look those kids in the eye and tell them that their dad didn't hold a job. You go with me on Memorial Day and you stand in Arlington National Cemetery, where I have more friends than I'd like to remember and you watch those waving flags. You stand there, and you think about this nation, and you tell me that those people didn't have a job.

"I'll tell you, Howard Metzenbaum, you should be on your knees every day of your life thanking God that there were some men—SOME MEN—who held a job. And they required a dedication to purpose and a love of country and a dedication to duty that was more important than life itself. And their self-sacrifice is what made this country possible. I HAVE HELD A JOB, HOWARD! —What about you?" (For those who don't remember, during W.W.II, Howard Metzenbaum was an attorney representing the Communist Party USA).

Recently we observed the fifty year anniversary of the armistice signing that "ended" the Korean conflict. Soldiers died at a rate of 30 per day for three full years holding that job. Many came home with disabilities or developed problems later. But while veterans have been lately honored and remembered, the government continues to deny concurrent receipt of retirement and disability compensation benefits. For retired veterans, if they have disability compensation, the benefits are deducted from their retirement pay! No other federal employees are treated that way. Civilian employees do not forfeit retirement for disability compensation. The two things are, after all, different matters. Moreover, all veterans wait months for health care due to under-funding and are subjected to the "lurch" when the money dries up and care goes away completely. That's because veterans' benefits aren't fully funded, are discretionary, and require supplemental. Imagine the outcry if we funded Social Security or Medicare that way!

Many veterans are unhappy at $15B for Africa and billions more for open-ended occupation duty, when we don't take care of our own first—those who saved the country and the world once or twice before. Whether we acted too slowly on intelligence (September 11th) or too quickly on intelligence (Iraq), wars and the rumors of war continue. These produce more veterans still, and the nation has had an implicit contract with its veterans since the Civil War to care for them in sickness and old age. When the Nation reaches into its diplomatic pouch to find only the final instrument left for effecting international relations, we require a military force ready and willing to execute violent operations and to achieve at extreme personal cost our Nation's goals and objectives. The goals and objectives come from elected officials. In return for the service of privates and generals, the Nation honors the sacrifice of those who died and tends the sacrifice of those who come home alive. In so doing, we reinforce the essential ideal of selfless service in the military and so benefit generations to come.

Special Category of Hero Article #475
o/a October 31, 2010

Tom Brokaw wrote an introduction to the coffee table book called *Medal of Honor* (2006) containing portraits of Medal winners some years ago. In it he recounts the arbitrary sort of way that veterans may be regarded by their government or fellow citizens depending upon the time in history. Veterans know this better than most, because a distance of inches or time measured in seconds is often the dividing line twixt life and death on the battlefield, or even in training. Timing is everything as they say. Being at the right time and place makes all the difference. Even mistakes, all but inevitable, will figure in to how things turn out. A mistake or shortcoming can evoke guilt in some, ironic gratitude in others. Veterans of the Korean Conflict were, according to Brokaw, "caught in the backwater of World War II." Americans were so preoccupied with their own lives at that point that the bloody conflict received very little public attention. Then as we were consumed by the assassination of President Kennedy and the terrible social and political upheavals that followed in the sixties and seventies, to include bitter divide over the Viet Nam War itself, regard for the veteran and his sacrifice actually receded. It stayed sour to some degree until after the First Gulf War.

There are also family members or friends one may know, who may or may not have been veterans, but who are or were bigger than life characters. The fact that no one knows them makes it no less of the truth. God keeps the full and complete record. History is poorly written, even at its best. Most soldiers, sailors, airmen, marines and coastguardsmen serve and sacrifice nearly anonymously. In a similar way, the politics swirling before, during and after every conflict or engagement, and constant these days throughout every tour of duty, remains a separate reality, unimpressive for the most part, subordinate certainly to the daily tasks and the military missions of all who serve in uniform—with the possible exception of some top brass, who have to answer to the civilian political leadership!

When there is a civil-military dispute, the top brass voice their concern or position to political leaders, but then support and implement whatever decision is duly and legally reached. If disagreements are fundamental or some political embarrassment ensues, top brass may very well have to resign—but this is far preferable, so that the bulk of forces remains insulated from all the furious tempests in teapots that have nothing to do with the proximity of life and death issues in a day's work, or the short and long-term physical wellbeing of men and women defending our nation.

Defense of American's homes and Homeland remains paramount under any circumstance, disagreement or no, just as every man and woman who joins the armed services swears to support and defend the Constitution of the United States of America against all enemies foreign and domestic. The American fighting man or woman is a thinking man or woman too. The special category of hero we cultivate, and sometimes celebrate knows what he is doing, or at least knows in advance what he might do if the training and conditioning kick in. American heroes show forth more moral courage than animal courage. The American soldier who wields his weapon is as deadly, say, as the Hun was in his day—but they are not the same equivalent moral agents, even if sentimentality and an immediate reference to the civilized order must wane until the blood cools and safety will allow it.

American veterans comprise a special category of hero precisely because of who they were going into military service. In a democratic-republic such as ours, the young recruit represents us going in. He or she represents the collective responsibility we share to protect and defend our way of life. So we send our best, and we literally send our hope—out of the city, off the farm, from small towns and neighborhoods they go. Frequently they delay college or their career, and place young family life on hold, or else put it through the lonely hardship of separation. The new recruit represents every citizen, indeed he is a surrogate for the same: to bear the assigned risk; to meet the many challenges, to accomplish the mission, to master skill and craft, to face the enemy. And so, notwithstanding an exquisite execution of violence or the longsuffering execution of mundane duties, the American veteran is heroic, who returns home bringing the same good he brought into service back with him. Indeed, he often packs more of a positive nature and value in his rucksack than what he at first had, in terms of those hallmark signs of military service: maturity, discipline, self-confidence, teamwork, learning and yes, even humanity.

Why Memorials Matter Article #144
o/a May 23, 2004

Secretary of State Colin Powell grew up in a family that annually visited the family cemetery on Memorial Day. Later as a soldier the importance of memorials, of honoring and paying homage to those who have gone before—particularly to those brave fallen, who wore the nation's uniform, deepened for him personally.

Memorials and the meaning of America are, as they are intended, bound up together. So much so that Powell, while Chairman of the Joint Chiefs of Staff, took his Soviet counterpart Gen. Mikhail Moiseyev around D.C. to the memorials, in order to share with him a better understanding of what America is about. At the Jefferson Memorial, Moiseyev was able to read the inscribed passage taken from the Declaration of Independence, "And for the support of this Declaration, . . . we mutually pledge our lives, our fortunes, and our sacred honor"; and the quote from Jefferson at the base of the monument's dome, "I have sworn upon the altar of God eternal hostility against every form of tyranny over the mind of man." The Declaration also says, "We hold these truths to be self-evident, that all men are created equal, that they are endowed by their Creator with certain unalienable Rights," and Powell explained to Moiseyev that Americans of every generation are ready to fight and die for those unalienable rights.

To show the Soviet general the extent of sacrifices Americans are willing to make, Powell took him to the Lincoln Memorial to read immortal words taken from the Gettysburg Address, telling how Americans fought the bloodiest war in our history to have "a new birth of freedom," so that "government of the people, by the people, for the people shall not perish from the earth." And the final words of Lincoln's Second Inaugural: "With malice toward none; with charity for all; with firmness in the right, as God gives us to see the right, let us strive on to finish the work we are in; to bind up the nation's wounds; to care for him who shall have borne the battle, and for his widow, and his orphan . . . ." The two also walked part of the way down the Lincoln Memorial's steps to the place from which Martin Luther King, Jr. delivered his 'I Have a Dream' speech. Powell explained it was there that King challenged his fellow Americans to make the promise of our Founding Fathers come true for all Americans.

Only after that was Powell ready to take Gen. Moiseyev to the Vietnam Veterans Memorial. Powell looked up the name of one of his old college buddies, and they went down together to its location. It was an emotional moment for Powell, and the infantryman in Moiseyev understood and reached out gently to touch the Wall also. Thankfully, our forces no longer face the prospect of war with the Soviet Union. Today, we are cooperating with Russia's evolving democracy and other former foes against 21st-century dangers common to us.

Today's deadly threats come from rogue powers and stateless networks of extremists who have utter contempt for life, liberty and the pursuit of happiness—and for the memorials we dedicate to our dead. What's important, however, is what the monuments and memorials say to us, how much they teach us and remind us about ideas that unite us; about the values that sustain us in times of trial; about the dream that inspires every succeeding generation, which causes ordinary Americans to perform extraordinary acts of service.

This Memorial Day weekend, we will join in celebrating the opening of the National World War II Memorial honoring the great generation of Americans who saved the world from fascist aggression and secured the blessings of liberty for hundreds of millions of people around the world. Today, their descendants are fighting the global war against terrorism, serving and sacrificing in Afghanistan and Iraq and at other outposts on the front lines of freedom. The life of each and every one of them is precious; and each life given in the name of liberty is a life that has not been lost in vain.

In time, lasting memorials will stand where the Twin Towers once etched New York City's skyline, near the west side of the Pentagon, and in the Pennsylvania field where doomed heroes died on September 11, 2001, using their last moments to save the lives of others and most probably the Capitol or the White House—symbols of our living Republic.

All of us live busy lives. We have little time to pause and reflect. But I ask you: Do not hasten through Memorial Day. Take the time to remember the good souls whose memories are a blessing to you and your family. Take your children to our memorial parks and monuments. Teach them the values that lend meaning to our lives and to the life of our nation. Above all, take the time to honor our fellow Americans who have given their last full measure of devotion to our country for the freedoms we cherish.[39]

"The Greatest Generation" Article #116
November 13, 2003

I've been asked to say a few words about the World War II veterans you saw honored here tonight. And I thank you for the honor of being able to do so. I taught American history at West Point for three years—the Second World War was that single most pivotal event of the 20th century, and it shaped the subsequent history of the world and this country. In order to understand the world since 1945, you must study World War II. I would also add, that if you've got an inkling at all about American character, you've probably been informed by the brave men and women, who served this country from 1941 to 1945. Tonight we pause from busy schedules to say "thank you," because those of us here do understand the significance of what occurred and appreciate the magnitude of what this nation offered up on foreign shores to ensure the safety of ourselves and the world. November is that wonderful month, in which we say "Thank you to the Lord in Thanksgiving for His bounty; and thank you to the veterans—and tonight a special thank you to World War II vets—for your service.

I'm a West Point class of 1983 graduate and a combat veteran of the Gulf War. I just retired after 20 years on May 31st this year—and I am awed by what the World War II armies and navies and marine divisions accomplished. I am impressed even more so by *who* the men were—and are, one person at a time. Tom Brokaw referred to their generation as "The Greatest Generation," and I tend to agree. It is interesting that Brokaw characterized the generation based on its veterans. Indeed, most generations come off better looking through the lens of its veterans—none better than World War II.

Tomorrow is Veteran's Day. We pay tribute to all veterans, but I'm glad to see the World War II veterans singled out—today the Cold War is over and we're into another wartime epoch, this one against terrorism. Our veterans of World War II are leaving us in droves every day now, but not before they help us yet again: by reminding us at this juncture of history of their perseverance and commitment and sense of duty, and sacrifice. As a country, we recall the veterans of World War II, in order to put the present into clearer context.

Thirty-six members of this post are World War II veterans—in the immediate area are15 who served in the Army; 2 who served with the Army Air Force; 9 who served on sea with the Navy; and 1 with the

Coast Guard. All received Bronze Stars. These men came of age in the Great Depression, when economic despair was rife in our land. They watched their parents struggle to make ends meet—and many lose their businesses, farms, jobs and hopes. And just as there was a glimmer of economic recovery, war exploded across Europe and Asia. Pearl Harbor made it irrefutably clear that America would be involved, whether she wanted to be or not. So these men were summoned to the parade ground and told to train for war. They left ranches and farms, their jobs on main street America; they gave their place up on assembly lines in factories; they quit school or traded their cap and gown immediately for the uniform. They answered the call to help save the world from the two most powerful and ruthless military machines ever, instruments of conquest in the hands of absolute rulers.

These men faced great odds and a late start (Europe had been at war several years before the United States), but they did not protest. At a time in their lives when their days and nights should have been filled with innocent adventure, love, and the lessons of the workaday world, they were fighting, often hand to hand, in primitive conditions in two theaters of war that spanned a globe: Europe and the Pacific. They were in the air every day, in skies filled with terror, and they went to sea on hostile waters far removed from the shores of their homeland.

The home front too was committed—to free more men for combat. If you were civilian man or woman, you went to work in the laboratories and in the factories, developing new medicines, building ships, planes, and tanks, and raising the families that had been left behind. While at the same time, America's physicists engaged in a secret race to build a new bomb before Germany figured out how to harness the atom.

The World War II generation—and in particular, the veterans of World War II—were a part of historic challenges and achievements of a magnitude the world had never before witnessed. It was an exceptional time, a hard time, but they sacrificed all to give us the world we have today. And without their efforts and sacrifices, our world would be a far different place—worse by virtually any measure. What made the difference were the characteristics of these men: a common mission and common sense—they loved America and believed in America's native values of family, faith and freedom. They believed that these values and corresponding American way of life had to be protected and were worth dying for. They did not lose faith in God or their country. In so many unassuming ways, these men were and continue to be great—self-reliant, grateful for blessings, dedicated to hearth and to peaceful pursuit—even whisked as they were half way around the globe for battles.

Our freedom today is a testament to their sacrifice and service. These men before us will have their World War II memorial in Washington, D.C. The plans are to have it open to the public in April, even before official dedication on Memorial Day 2004. These men before us have their place in the ledgers of history. But no block of marble or elaborate edifice equals their lives of sacrifice and achievement, duty and honor, as monuments to their time—and to us, their posterity. They remain our most proximate and material example of how to live greatly, how to fight the good fight in and out of service. Gentlemen, from me and from those assembled, and on behalf of all generations who follow you—we say, "Well done! Well done!" And may God bless you always and continue to bless America with Americans such as yourselves. [40]

CHAPTER 17

Army Goes Rolling Along

Army Goes Rolling Along Articles #277-278
~Part I~ o/a November 17, 2006

One of the lessons we should have learned over the last three years is the undiminished importance of ground forces, both having enough of them and for utilizing them effectively where they are needed. You can argue all day long about a lot of things, but when a large percentage of your ground forces are engaged, a nation's options are limited elsewhere. George Friedman, writing for the Strategic Forecasting think tank, says North Korea and Russia have taken advantage of that fact with the U.S., and we know Iran has also done so—intentionally exacerbating our problems in Iraq, so they gain a freehand and advantage elsewhere. Ironically, when ground forces are engaged in large numbers, options are limited elsewhere, no matter how big your Navy and your Air Force are. These sister services are needed to support the land force; and further, boots on the ground are what matters at the end of the day. They determine who rules. If you embark to fundamentally remake another nation or society, you must rule and rule for a long time in order to accomplish your goals. You cannot, indeed must not cede sovereignty in short order after you've won it. If your goals are so all encompassing and comprehensive as to aim at erecting democratic institutions where there are none, to rebuild a military whom you have vanquished (twice), to make warring ethnic and sectarian factions live peaceably together, and to transform the Middle East by example—you cannot hope to do so on the cheap, in terms of the numbers of troops or the extreme level of force those troops will have to exert. Of course, your objectives may well come into question, as indeed they should, if you are given to self-analysis or to constructive reassessment.

Historically, a standing army on our soil helped foment the American Revolution, even though we were part of the British Empire and British troops were "here to help." Funny thing about them boots on the ground: if insufficient to quash all resistance, they virtually ensure the unity and persistence of violent opposition aimed at foreign occupiers and the removal of any political fence sitters. Taking a slightly different tack, boots on borders are what nations worry about too, unless you happen to be a very big McDemocracy, and boots on borders mean a lot of friendly undocumented guest workers coming in for 'a better way of life.' Be that as it may, most nations do care about borders. Borders define their space for who they are and where political, ethno-cultural and economic sovereignty lay. Borders define a lot of nations we like and many we don't like. Hypothetically, if we were to put troops in a country bordering on some we dislike, with the express intent of remaking the one we're in before proceeding across its borders to remake others too, we might be in for some complications and a surprise or two. All hypothetical, mind you: far be it from me to suggest decisions have consequences, or that foreign policy mistakes are possible, or that some international idealism is plain stupid. But if this were what you wanted to do, there's really no way to do it without several hundreds of thousands—perhaps millions of troops, as well as a willingness to employ extreme violence, even to risk a broader war.

Nations also recognize that an investment of troops by another nation is practically the most it can do. You don't easily get them out, once men and women are stationed in a place and particularly where they are fighting for very long. The expense of sending, sustaining, reinforcing and rotating troop units is astronomical, the support network immense. Moreover, the impact on a homeland that sends troops is substantial, especially the longer its deployments go. For individuals and families involved, the experience is life changing; for the government it becomes consuming, to the point of setting aside important priorities and allowing serious economic and social problems to grow. For the life and direction of nations, wars involving deployment of troops are historic by their nature. Even when wars like that are necessary, they can never be said to be a good thing. There is death and devastation to be sure, but we are all conditioned to get past that relatively quickly—and some things are admittedly worth that much. But there are also the tragic and largely unknown opportunities lost, as well as the many negative unintended consequences.

Thank God we do have an Army, however. If anyone seriously thinks we'd be free one day without one, then he doesn't understand either the harsh reality behind international relations or the base drive and instincts attendant to human condition that give way only to force. But an Army is a terrible thing to squander. For the United States, the crucial problem is our freedom of action under the current circumstance, whether a freedom to respond or take the initiative to the enemy—the enemy we know or the one on the horizon. For all the early talk of preemption after 9/11, we've virtually given it up, because we've lost that ability with troops. Friedman again: "The military reality on the ground in Iraq severely constrains U.S. options around the world. That, in turn, constrains U.S. diplomacy. Diplomacy without even the distant possibility of military action is impotent . . . . Since the possibility of unilateral action by the United States also does not exist, neither North Korea nor Iran need take the diplomatic initiatives seriously. And they don't . . . . Americans either must dramatically increase the capability of the U.S. Army and Marine Corps or else decrease their commitment in Iraq. If the United States does neither, its ability to control and influence events in other regions will decline."

~Part II~ o/a November 17, 2006

George Friedman, writing for Strategic Forecasting, tells us "The Army is the heart of the matter," i.e., of regaining freedom of action militarily and putting teeth back in American diplomacy. Today's U.S. Army was designed in the 1990s, on the assumption that the need for extended combat operations was a thing of the past. Not only was the Army reduced in size, many key components of combat divisions and critical specialties, such as civil affairs, were shifted to the Army Reserve and National Guard. The administration's expectation for Iraq was that there would be a buildup of forces for several months, a short, intense period of combat operations and a drawdown in forces from a pacified country. The 1990s force was designed just for these kinds of conflicts. The Reserve and National Guard components were mobilized to join and backfill for units deploying to the combat zone. By the end of the year, it was expected, the force would return to peacetime operations. Iraq didn't work out that way. The drawdown never took place because major combat operations were followed by a major insurgency. The expectation of the administration was that the insurgency would be dealt with in a reasonable time, so the Army was not reconfigured for extended warfare.

At any point, proposals for dealing with the fundamental problem—that the force was too small—were rejected, with the thinking that there was no need for a significant overhaul to deal with a problem that would be under control in a matter of months. This expectation turned into hope, the hope into dogma. Thus, the 1990s Army continued to fight a multi-year insurgency with a multidivisional force, while also fighting a second war in Afghanistan and having to stand by for the unexpected.

Having learned from Vietnam that constantly rotating individuals into units for one-year tours undermines unit cohesion, the Army shifted to rotating entire divisions in and out of Iraq after roughly one year. Had the conflict ended in two years, it might have worked fine. But it now has been more than three years and divisions are doing their second tours, mobilizing Reserve and National Guard units as they go. Consider this example: The 1st Cavalry Division is embarked on its second tour to take control of the Baghdad region from the 4th Infantry Division. For the coming year, the 1st Cav is going to be locked down in Iraq, but the 4th ID will not be available for operations elsewhere. Upon arriving back in the United States, they will need to rest, repair and integrate new equipment and integrate new recruits to replace veterans leaving the Army. The 4th ID will not be available to deploy anywhere for many months. In effect, for every division in Iraq, one division is being overhauled. Add to this the weakness in the Reserves and National Guard, and you begin to appreciate the United States' strategic challenge.

Iraq is eating up U.S. geopolitical options by eating up the Army. This is the first major extended ground war the United States has fought in a century without dramatically increasing the size of the Army. World War I, World War II, Korea and Vietnam all brought massive increases in military size, mostly through conscription. The Bush administration did not view Iraq as a potentially multi-year, multi-divisional combat operation. It maintained the force roughly as it started, and now that force is headed towards broke. Indeed, the administration had come to that conclusion prior to the mid-term elections. In October, one sign of a strategy shift was Defense Secretary Donald Rumsfeld, long an opponent of expanding the Army's budget, agreeing to allow the Army to plead its case directly for more money to Congress. In the past, Rumsfeld wanted the Army to find more efficient ways to run counterinsurgency operations, relying more on technology than manpower. That's a good idea and might happen some day, but it didn't happen for this war. It is now pretty late in the game to cut the Army loose for funding—plus, any new funding won't impact the battlefield for a couple of years. But Rumsfeld's move signaled recognition that a basic assumption up to this point was flawed, and this is where he leaves the nation and its Army at the end of his tenure. With its troops and equipment worn down by years of fighting in Iraq and Afghanistan, the Army needs to receive a spike in its share of the Pentagon's budget request when it goes to Congress this year. Significantly, increases to the size of the Army made by Congress since 2001, amounting to 30,000 troops, have become a permanent fixture of the force. Beyond that, the Army is discussing internally whether it should expand by tens of thousands more. Pentagon officials are likely to seek $138 billion, compared to its $112 billion request last year. Army officials say the service was already $50 billion short in equipment when terrorists struck September 11, 2001. The wars in Iraq and Afghanistan require $17 billion in extra spending for 2007 to repair and replace destroyed and worn out vehicles and equipment, and at least $13 billion additional spending for the next five years after that.[41]

CHAPTER 18

Right to Bear Arms

Guns are Good for Health Article #111
o/a October 06, 2003

There are 700,000 physicians in the U.S., and these physicians cause 120,000 accidental deaths per year. That's an accidental death rate of .171 per physician.

Now on the other hand, there are 80 million gun owners in the U.S. and perhaps 1500 accidental gun deaths per year. That's an accidental death rate of .0000188 per gun owner.

Therefore, doctors are approximately 9,000 times more dangerous than gun owners! In fact, I'd recommend if you aren't *really* sick, that you should go to the Temple Gun Club Range and shoot or just stay in bed with your gun. That is a whole lot surer way to recovery than going to a doctor—unless of course, he happens to be a gun owner too.

While I thought that story was funny, there is actually a serious side to the assertion that guns are good public health policy. Oh, the anti-gun movement will convey an impression that firearms in the home are a leading cause of accidental death and injury. In fact, Centers for Disease Control statistics indicate firearms are pretty far down on the list! Deaths and injuries from swimming pools and falls from ladders are a lot more common. There is well-documented evidence too, to show that firearms in the home and carried concealed amount to net health benefits. The National Crime Victimization Survey by the Census Bureau indicates that a minimum of 65,000 crimes are stopped or prevented annually by armed citizens, usually without a shot fired. Thirteen other studies estimate far more crimes are actually thwarted by citizens with their own firearms. Based on that evidence, I think every law abiding gun-owner deserves a break on his life and health insurance simply for owning a gun—more if it's loaded and you're packing!

Seriously, to ignore the data—to focus only on the many fewer deaths caused by firearms, accidental or criminal, is like the physician mentioning only undesirable side effects of a drug that occur, but ignoring the good effects for most people. Imagine how the drug commercials would change—no more dancing through the tulips with clear nasal passages. Instead you'd have a version of Scrooge watching his own funeral procession. Disease would become the acceptable norm, and you couldn't accept the "risk" of being healthy. If that kind of perverse thinking sounds too familiar, it is because politicians actually use it all the time.

General George S. Patton said, "The lowest form of life on earth is a politician. The lowest form of a politician is a liberal." (Actually, he said liberal Democrat, but I'm being as nonpartisan as I can). Anyway, I do agree the lowest form of a politician *is* a liberal. A liberal is someone who holds you up at gunpoint, without giving you the courtesy of letting you know he's doing it. You see the liberal politician doesn't show you his firearm, but it's there: in back of every legal mandate or property seizure; in every tax and every coercive move by the government to take from you what's yours, including future opportunities and potential—all ostensibly for the good of others, but mainly for the good of the political class in the interest of keeping power. When a liberal politician talks about gun control, it isn't about guns but about control. Because he knows the Second Amendment is in place in case he ignores the others. To paraphrase Scripture, 'If you would spoil a strongman's house, you must first bind up the strongman.'

Remember the two young lunatics at Columbine? They broke at least 20 different gun laws that might have landed them in prison for decades, even before the shootings. Liberals will tell you though that we should have passed more laws rather than enforce the ones we've got. Their "logic" so-called is that guns cause crime, and laws—that is, *words on a paper* alone, prevent crime. Yeah, just like pencils cause misspelled words! Like a recipe on the kitchen counter will bake your cake.

The majority of Swiss households contain a fully automatic rifle with ammunition. Firearms are available to nearly every resident of Switzerland, yet the violent crime rate is low. In this country, crime rates are actually lower for regions, such as the Rocky Mountains and North Carolina, and for population groups, such as older males, where gun ownership rates are highest. Concealed carry laws in Texas did not result in shoot-outs at every 4-way stop sign. Of more than 163,000 licensees in Texas in 2002, only three were even arrested in connection with a homicide in a two-year period. Alligator attacks are more common in Florida than crimes committed by citizens licensed to carry concealed weapons. Liberals denounce the gun culture, as if it is a culture of violence when in fact, it is the culture of responsibility and self-reliance and safety. A culture of violence exists alright, but it has more to do with dysfunctional families, drugs and warped media images and the secular pop-culture, than it has to do with Charlton Heston raising his musket high over his head at the NRA Convention.[42]

Guns and Militia   Article #112
o/a October 06, 2003

The Second Amendment to the Constitution—part of the Bill of Rights—states: "A well regulated Militia, being necessary to the security of a free State, the right of the people to keep and bear Arms, shall not be infringed." Some modern liberals try to reinterpret that ancient and well-known right by a semantic sleight of hand. They opine that the ownership of rifles, pistols and shotguns may be restricted and taken away from the public, that unless persons are in the National Guard, they have no Second Amendment protection. Amazingly, that was the position taken by the Deputy U.S. Attorney General William Meteja, representing the Clinton administration before the U.S. Fifth Circuit Court of Appeals in the United States v. Emerson case. Meteja's boss at the time, Janet Reno, had no qualm about that position. And I believe the Clinton administration knew full well that they were deceiving people based upon unfamiliar syntax, though common in the eighteenth and nineteenth centuries.

For instance, here's a free-press clause from the 1842 Rhode Island Constitution: "The liberty of the press being essential to the security of freedom in a state, any person may publish his sentiments of any subject." That provision surely doesn't mean that the right to publish protects only the press. It protects "any person," and one reason among others that it protects any person is that a free press is essential to a free society. Similarly, looking at the two clauses of the Second Amendment, the function of the subordinate clause was not to qualify the right, but instead to show why it must be protected. If the right were not protected, the existence of the militia and the security of the state would be jeopardized. In other words, the second clause, "the right of the people to keep and bear Arms, shall not be infringed," secures the right. The first clause, "A well regulated Militia, being necessary to the security of a free State," justifies the right. And there can be other reasons to justify the right as well.

Fortunately, the Bush Administration has reaffirmed the traditional opinion that law-abiding citizens have an individual right to keep and bear firearms. Like the First and Fourth Amendments, the Second refers explicitly to a right held by the people. The *Emerson* case decision, rendered after Bush's election, was a solid victory for the rights of gun owners. It supported the individual rights interpretation of the Second Amendment. So good is the news, you might not think the Second Amendment needs much emphasis now. Many other things affect people on a day to day basis more, like jobs and health care and education. Surely no one in Texas feels their gun rights are threatened (?). Most households probably have a rifle, shotgun and a pistol already—and enough ammo per small town to hold a small army at bay, much less three stooges in an Al-Qaeda cell. But I have concluded there is something altogether timely about a concern for the Second Amendment.

Here's the situation. While the so-called assault weapon/high cap magazine ban is due to sunset in September 2004, we don't know if congressmen won't try to extend it. While studies show the Brady Act has had no effect on gun homicide, we don't know that congressmen won't turn around and cite the need for more stringent measures in the name of reducing gun crime. That's because while there may be no serious or specific gun control laws pending now that threaten your Second Amendment right, what remains relevant involves the important question of values, a question of philosophy, perspicacity and habits of character in our elective leaders. We are essentially left wondering whether the Second Amendment right and others are going to be guarded and protected and fought for by our elected representatives.

For those who say that I'm trying to press an eighteenth century doctrine into the world of the twenty-first century, you bet I am. I do want to ensure that sacred rights from the Constitution and republican heritage go with us as we tackle this brave new world. Besides, I'm not so old-fashioned really—I like horses, but I have nothing against space travel. And when they finally do invent the phaser on Star Trek or the light saber from Star Wars, I'm going to say they're covered by the Second

Amendment too, on Mars or anywhere else we happen to be! Modern doesn't mean slavish. New doesn't mean that we leave everything else that's precious behind. Moreover, I would argue that the Second Amendment today is extremely relevant, because homeland security in the wake of 9-11 is relevant! It should be regarded as a matter improving our national security, that the populace be armed. The Second Amendment today is relevant also, because the War on Terrorism potentially cuts both ways—the Patriot Acts suggest to me the need for vitality in the Second Amendment. Wars and threats to national security historically increase the size and scope and power of government. The Second Amendment serves as an important deterrent to government tyranny. And while I'm not so concerned with George W. Bush in office, I'd be very concerned if Hillary Clinton wins in 2008.[43]

Guns and Liberty Article #113
o/a October 06, 2003

Perhaps you believe the threat of tyrannical government is slight, or less severe today than when our republic was formed. There is still another important point our Founders understood. Namely, the demand for police or military to defend us increases in proportion to our inability to defend ourselves. That's why disarmed societies adopt police-state tactics. Even if a reduced threat of government tyranny no longer required an armed citizenry, an unarmed citizenry could well create the conditions that lead to tyranny. There is plenty of proof in the last century. Gun control laws and anti-gun attitudes formed a key ingredient in genocides of the 20th Century. They assured that only "authorities" had weaponry. They made it difficult, costly, risky or impossible for civilians to own or use firearms. The Soviet Union, China, Uganda, Cambodia, Guatemala, Rwanda, Ottoman Turkey, and Nazi Germany all had tough gun control laws in place before and during their genocidal periods. Those nations alone murdered 70 million of their own disarmed people.

Talk about repeating history: the Founders had garnered that same lesson from the ancients. They understood that concentrated political power is the most dangerous thing on earth, and they contrived a variety of checks and balances in the Constitution to divide political power—between the separate branches of government, as well as between the federal government and States. The first ten amendments or Bill of Rights were adopted to keep political power from becoming concentrated, by reserving natural or pre-existing rights to the people. Technically speaking, the Constitution doesn't actually bestow upon the people a right to keep and bear arms. The Second Amendment prohibits the government from infringing upon a pre-existing right. The Founders' knew that an armed man must, in a real sense, be regarded as citizen; an unarmed man is subject. English colonists enjoyed the right to keep and bear arms among their inherited rights as freeborn Englishmen. It was George III's attempt to seize the colonial militia's stock of weapons at Lexington and Concord that sparked the American Revolution. I submit to you our Founders took their right to keep and bear arms seriously, well before the Second Amendment. Likewise, they interpreted the king and parliament's move to control firearms as a direct affront to all their rights and liberty.

One of the biggest problems with the English system was that the English constitution was not written or fixed in meaning. Operating on purely common law assumptions, it absorbed precedents leading towards unfettered power. The successful operation of America's written Constitution and the unrivalled political stability of the United States, stems from the Constitution being fixed and relatively difficult to amend. The risk and potential of American decline is entirely, in my view, related to a failure to live *constitutionally*. In the United States, we have allowed the letter and intent of the Constitution to be stretched by the Supreme Court which has given the Constitution a "living" interpretation, and this has reinstated a kind of modern version of colonial-era British common law. We have, in the words of Jefferson, made the Constitution "a blank paper by construction." The solution is to move to recapture the Constitution of original intent, to reestablish it as government's fixed edifice. Key to recapturing the Constitution of our Fathers is the reinvigoration of the Second Amendment. And while that certainly means we need good statesmen and judges to keep its meaning, it also means we ought and must exercise our right to keep and bear arms. Every time you take your son or daughter hunting. Every time you target practice, or break your weapon down to clean it; every time you travel with your firearm and undergo the inconveniences at the airport to do so—you reinforce the Second Amendment and ensure survival of our right to keep and bear arms and pass the torch to another generation.

Why do I tell you this? Because there is a far different course down which this country can slide. Remember I said that our Second Amendment individual right to keep and bear arms existed before the Constitution. The Founders validated that right, and they intended it to guarantee an individual's right to have arms for self-defense and self preservation—something Sam Adams called "the first law of nature." And they also intended firearm ownership and skill in the use of firearms to be general, because the customary American militia necessitated an armed public. The political theory behind that was to stave off tyranny or vindicate liberty when required. Even the position of the Second Amendment in the order of the Bill of Rights underscored its importance. It was the safety valve of the Constitution, affording the means whereby, if parchment barriers proved inadequate, the people could protect their liberties or alter their government. That sounds radical today, but that reasoning was part of William Blackstone's *Commentaries on the Laws of England*, the authoritative source concerning English rights in England and the Colonies during the Revolutionary period and after. Indeed, this inherited right of freeborn Englishmen existed in substantive degree in Great Britain until 1920.[44]

CHAPTER 19

Liberating Labor

Liberating Labor — Articles #295-297
~Part I~ o/a April 20, 2007

The first ten amendments to the Constitution comprise what is known as the Bill of Rights. Historians agree that rights were generally addressed in their order of perceived importance. Hence the First Amendment contains those cherished, primary rights concerning freedom of religion, speech, the press and assembly; the Second contains the right to keep and bear arms and so on. The Bill of Rights also reflects completely the philosophy of the authors of the Constitution, such that, it does not confer positive rights; rather, the guarantee of certain rights takes the form of restrictions on what government may do. Simply stated, individuals are said to already possess certain rights according to natural law, against which the government is forbidden to trespass. Many of the Founders felt the Bill of Rights was actually superfluous, because the Bill of Rights only restated how they intended the Constitution to be read and perceived in the first place. The Bill of Rights spells out what the letter and spirit of the Constitution meant to establish: a regime according to which the most important function of just government is to protect the rights of the people! In hindsight, we ought to be very grateful indeed to those suspicious Anti-Federalists and late converts to ratification of the Constitution, who insisted that we spell some of those rights out in plain language.

Freedom of association is guaranteed by the First Amendment to the Constitution when it states, "Congress shall make no law . . . abridging . . . the right of the people peaceably to assemble." None other than Pope John Paul II explicitly mentioned this historic right of Americans in his *Centesimus Annus*, explaining the principle of freedom of association meant individuals could assemble into whatever peaceful associations they want, and the government is forbidden to interfere. Like the Founders, he found the right utterly consistent with Christian social thought and doctrine. In terms of practical import, it is this principle of free association that is the basis for the legitimacy of political parties and also labor unions. From a religious and political standpoint, the Founders would have supported voluntary unionism and condemned compulsory unionism. Compulsory unionism is a blatant example of how far we've left our country behind, so to speak, as we moved from one Constitutional regime into another after the Progressive Era—codified as it were by the courts during the New Deal. The statute that defines the rules of unionism contrary to First Amendment freedom of association is the National Labor Relations Act (NLRA), enacted in 1935 and amended in 1947 and again in 1959.

According to economist Dr. Charles W. Baird, the word *peaceably* in the First Amendment means that associations we choose to enter may not undertake violence to accomplish their ends; and also, within each association one person may not coerce another. That is to say, "Associations must be based on mutual consent. Coercion always destroys the peace." The fact that the U.S. Constitution guarantees freedom of association, however, does not mean someone may associate with anyone he chooses necessarily—it means someone may choose to associate with anyone else, who also agrees to associate with him! It reminds me of a natural right to emigration, which I've discussed before. You can decide to leave your house, exit your own front door and even cross the street. But you don't have a right to enter someone else's house, force your way in their front door, plop down on their couch and watch TV. Likewise, freedom of association rightly understood has a positive and negative component. Baird again: "We are free to associate with those who will accept us (positive), and we are free to abstain from associations of which we do not approve or that we do not think to be in our interests (negative)." Freedom of association is also the freedom of disassociation, or the freedom not to associate. American courts have erred by failing to recognize this in the case of labor unions. Except in the twenty-two States, including Texas, that have enacted right-to-work laws, workers are forced to pay union dues as a condition of employment. Further insult to injury occurs when the unions take compulsory dues and go support political causes the workers don't even agree with.[45]

~Part II~ o/a April 20, 2007

The concept of voluntary exchange lies at the heart of free market economics. Moreover, the nature of economic analysis rests on a presupposition of exchanges occurring among people who attempt to do the best they can for themselves. Some economic textbooks refer to an assumption of rationality. People are presumed to be rational, and empirical evidence bears out the fact that most people are most of the time—that is to say, while different people have different ideas about the ends they should seek, they will at least try to achieve them as best they can. From a religious standpoint, the ultimate end that man should pursue is a right relationship with God, and Christian theology adds one's fellows to the mix too—i.e., a right relationship with your fellow man and woman. When you do that, you also conceive of voluntary exchange, because that is central to your relationships with others. Politically our Constitution is about erecting the institutions and setting up the checks and balances, deemed necessary by the Founders to maintain freedom. Which of course begs the question, the freedom to do what? To which, part of the answer must be to engage in voluntary exchanges, as well as to pursue the ultimate end of one's religion. Those who view the labor market or any other market from statistical isolation, without reference to political and theological antecedents or supports, may as well believe the world is flat. They will construe wrongly what lies behind the most successful and most humane free market economy the world has ever known.

Freedom and voluntarism are also inextricably linked. You are either a volunteer or you are not. You can't be free to do something and forced to do it at the same time. Your choice entails a right not to make that choice, or to choose something entirely different instead. Voluntary exchange gets to the heart of free market economics, but also to freedom. Hence there is moral dimension and qualitative significance to four criteria that must be simultaneously met, in order for an exchange to be characterized as voluntary: entitlement, consent, escape and no misrepresentation. Take entitlement—literally something to which someone is due, which must include his private property. The seventh commandment, "Thou shalt not steal" implicitly recognizes the existence of private property as an entitlement to be observed by men and governments according to the law of God. In like manner, one's entitlement includes labor services that you are able to perform as a result of your mental and physical abilities, what economists call human capital. In voluntary exchanges, entitlements must be recognized and respected. Workers themselves aren't inputs in production (that would be slavery), only their labor services. You and I own our own labor services; we are entitled to them like our private property. We can thus enter into terms and conditions of employment directly with an employer or through a third party we choose to represent us. Now if a third party you haven't authorized to be your agent agrees to terms of employment you haven't agreed to either, the result is hardly a voluntary exchange. Your labor services would not have been treated as an entitlement, your will would not have been honored; indeed rights attendant to your freedom would be violated.

Likewise the criterion of consent requires that all parties to an exchange must agree to hear the offers being made by others. Consent further requires that offers heard must be freely accepted or not, freely entered in or not. You might decide to hear offers and let the bargaining commence, but at the end of the day all parties to voluntary exchange must consent to whatever bargain emerges. Consent moreover implies an escape criterion. Each party has to be able to turn down offers and walk away, without losing entitlement. According to economist Dr. Charles W. Baird, "A" must be able to walk away from "B" unharmed and without being subject to harassment. Under the National Labor Relations Act (NLRA), however, according to Baird "enterprises may be forced to recognize and bargain with unions." Workers also lose the natural right to sell labor services to willing employers without involving a third party that employers and employees both agree to. Agreements mediated by unions in that way cannot reflect voluntary exchange, and they lack the proper escape mechanism to leave workers unharmed. Of course, no exchange is fully voluntary if any of the parties knowingly and deliberately lie. Voluntary exchange rests to some degree on honesty, or at least on no misrepresentation. Parties must refrain from conveying false information to effect exchange. That is not the same thing as preventing all occurrence of error—though you may try, knowledge is often imperfect; and we live in a world in which different people know different things and assign relevance to different bits of information. "No misrepresentation" doesn't mean you have to tell everything you know either.[46]

~Part III~ o/a April 20, 2007

The most amazing thing about voluntary exchange is that it is mutually beneficial. It is the proverbial win-win situation and not a zero sum game. Individuals will attempt to do the best they can for themselves, and no one else but the individuals in question know how to direct their resources better, including labor services to achieve their goals. Parties to voluntary exchange expect the exchange will prove beneficial to them or they wouldn't enter in. The possibility of error and regret does not impugn voluntary exchange. The possibility of error, when it occurs in fact, is the exception that proves the rule and speaks to life and the human condition. Take it up with God. The long run may prove advantageous, in that, errors and regret are part of the learning and self-correction process that benefits all of society. Moreover, on a qualitative moral basis, the exercise of free choice may be as important as results that accrue; and anyway, no agent besides parties involved can be *legitimate*, or are likely to be as *competent*. Concerning the latter two aspects, economist Dr. Charles W. Baird says, "Only the agent can make choices for himself, and he does not have to do it alone." We all feel inadequate to reach certain decisions by ourselves. "Doctors, lawyers, and clergy are the best examples of experts from whom we seek advice about dealing with other people and ordering our own behavior." There are a myriad of other experts out there as well, from financial advisors to Texas A&M certified tree trimmers—advice services made possible by the mechanism of voluntary exchange.

Other implications of voluntary exchange are also remarkable. For instance, if every person interacts with every other person on the basis of voluntary exchange, the only way for someone to serve his self-interest is to offer others a chance to serve theirs. Voluntary exchange amounts to a direct application of the Golden Rule. Voluntary exchange is reciprocal; therefore according to Baird, it "harnesses self-interest to the service of others" and actually helps build communities. Wealth is acquired by serving the interests of others, and profit motivates the entrepreneurs among us to solve society's pressing problems and to meet its demands. Baird again: "Every problem that emerges in a market is a profit opportunity for an entrepreneur who first notices how to solve it and undertakes the solution. Successful innovations by entrepreneurs elicit imitation." All of us benefit thereby.

Notwithstanding, there are common confusions about labor markets. One such misconception is that workers have inferior bargaining power relative to employers. Another misconception is that employer and employee interests are generally incompatible if not adversarial. Concerning the first common confusion, bargaining power depends on the alternatives that you have, no matter who you are—whether you are an employee or an employer. Depending on time in history (because it changes every decade), as well as the relative health of the economy, employers will face more or less competition from other employers to hire available labor. Similarly, depending on the same things, employees will face more or less competition from other employees to be hired by available capital. The more things you can do and are willing to do, the more qualifications you bring, the more actual and potential resources you have available, etc., the more alternatives you have and hence the greater your bargaining power—no matter which side of the table you're sitting on. In general, technological progress has greatly reduced instances where employers are at great advantage and employees lack alternatives or bargaining power. *Monopsony* power as it is called (literally "one buyer" or one employer) rarely occurs and never lasts in a free economy.

Concerning the second common confusion, employers and employees do indeed have compatible interests most of the time; and teamwork is more than a shibboleth, more than a management ploy. According to Baird, "Any enterprise, however constituted at any point of time, is a package of labor services and capital services that are employed together for the production of goods and services. Both inputs are necessary, and neither is sufficient for such production. Owners of capital and workers—the latter are the owners of labor services—are bound together by contracts by which they work together to serve their customers. In a sense, it is their customers that employ both of them."[47]

CHAPTER 20

DIRTY DOZEN

Dirty Dozen Articles #394-397, 399-400, 402-403, 406, 408-410
~Part I~ o/a April 17, 2009

Two eminent scholars wrote a book last year with a startling and disconcerting thesis. Their argument, that the Constitution is *dead* not just dying, was not even offset by hope or optimism. They did not conclude with a plan for how to fix things, but rather left it up to the People to decide what to do with the information. Thomas Woods, Jr. (Bachelor degree from Harvard, Master and Doctoral degrees from Columbia); and Kevin Gutzman (Doctoral degrees from Texas and Virginia) identified a dozen ways—by no means all of them—that all three branches of the federal government have used to kill the Constitution, essentially removing the restraining elements from federal officials so they can do whatever they want. To the extent that officials do not always act arbitrarily, it is not because they are bound by the strictures of the Constitution any longer; rather, federal officials simply act with political prudence, in terms of what they can reasonably expect to get away with. The Constitution is certainly no obstacle to whatever conceivable federal program they might conjure, and the lawmakers' consideration is typically what their constituents and special interests will bear and bear with a sense of gratitude at the next election. All the lawmakers need are good intentions, or rather the appearance of them. The Constitution is no real object.

One. While the Sedition Act of 1798 attempted to criminalize disloyal speech during the Quasi-War with France, the people were so incensed at the violation of the First, Ninth and Tenth Amendments that a political revolution ensued in 1800 catapulting Thomas Jefferson to the presidency. The Sedition Act expired in 1801, and for more than a century the federal government did not try to pass another anti-sedition law on the books.

That is until the Espionage Act of 1917 and the Sedition Act of 1918. At this point it is worthwhile to observe that a state of war is virtually always injurious to the Republic, because wars and crises serve as occasions for constitutional exception, and for accommodative processes and procedures to adhere that would not otherwise be contemplated or tolerated outside of the justification posed by threat, or by the blind passion of nationalist patriotic fervor. The normal healthy state of a stable free Republic and the desired goal therefore of its leaders is Peace.

With the United States belatedly at war in the Great War (World War I), president Woodrow Wilson by executive order established the Committee on Public Information (CPI), in order to skew communications about the war and to carry out a propaganda mission inside the United States. The Espionage and Sedition Acts essentially ensured that no opposition voices in the media or public would be heard in English or any other language. In Iowa and South Dakota the German language was forbidden in public. Texas banned the teaching of the German language. It is worthwhile to note that laws such as sedition acts will tend to favor and advantage government preferred voices at the expense of others; whereas, the normal operation of the First Amendment with its guarantee of free speech helps ensure that extreme policy advocacy gets countered by thoughtful sober alternatives, or is perhaps muted by the expression of other extremes.

The Espionage Act gave the postmaster general power to remove materials from the mail if he thought they might hamper war effort. The Sedition Act made it illegal to write or speak anything disloyal, profane, scurrilous, or abusive about the government, or the military, or the navy, or the flag. One poor fellow in Montana expressed the opinion that American boys were being drafted and sent to war for the benefit of "Wall Street millionaires." He said it in a town of sixty people, sixty miles from the nearest railway and hundreds of miles from the military. He was nevertheless locked up, until at length acquitted (elected judges do make a difference!).

On the other hand, in *Shaffer v. United States* the U.S. Court of Appeals held that a book the defendant shipped by mail contained language tending to undermine the war effort. This "bad tendency" test put a lot of folks in jail and kept them there. In 1919 after the war, courts heard a number of appeals and tried to add clarity to the standard. Charles Schenck was a socialist, who was put in prison for printing anti-conscription leaflets. Arguments contained in the leaflets were essentially the same used by

Daniel Webster on the floor of Congress during the War of 1812. Of course that was a different war, an earlier time, and constitutional scruples figured more prominently according to the Original Intent.

In *Schenck v. United States* the Supreme Court upheld Schenck's conviction, and Justice Oliver Wendell Holmes delivered the famous opinion: "The question is whether the words used are in such circumstances . . . as to create a clear and present danger." Justice Holmes also used his equally famous analogy about falsely shouting "fire" in a crowded theater and causing panic, asserting that one does not possess that right. For the first time we read in *Schenck* that the First Amendment does not actually mean what it says, and the absolute prohibition on congressional abridgment of the freedom of speech isn't absolute at all. It depends on the circumstances, and the Supreme Court tells us what, how and when. Note also that Holmes's reasoning means congressional abridgment of speech applies even in peacetime—and how different that is from the pre-1917 Constitution.

The Ninth and Tenth Amendments leave power to regulate speech with the states, but now Congress arrogates this power. The crowded theater analogy is a red herring. One is not arrested for speaking or saying "fire" but rather, for causing harm, damage or injury. The example is mostly a property rights issue and not about free speech. If someone *accurately* shouts "fire" in a crowded theater moreover, the truth of the statement may be sufficiently valuable as to compensate for any commotion! The analogy hardly applies at all to criticism of the government. The circumstances of peace and war also merge when wars are no longer declared, when cold wars last for decades, when a war against terror might never end.[48]

~Part II~ o/a April 17, 2009

Two. In 1951 American steelworkers resolved to go on strike. Convinced a work stoppage would imperil the country's war effort in Korea, President Harry Truman ordered his Secretary of Commerce to seize and operate the steel mills! He announced on radio and television that he derived authority for this action simply "as President of the United States and Commander in Chief of the armed forces." Obviously steel company executives and business community were irate, but also the editorial pages of major newspapers seethed. Felix Morley compared Truman's "inherent power" to the divine right of kings. Indeed, there is no law of the United States that gives the president statutory authority to seize private property.

Instead there were a few legal options at his disposal, which would have required more due process than an appearance on TV. For instance, the Taft-Hartley Act enabled the president to impose a cooling off period and negotiations in order to avert strikes dangerous to the nation's health and safety. The Defense Production Act likewise extended the government's power of eminent domain to facilities necessary for national defense, but this required just compensation. Another option relied on a provision in the Selective Service Act of 1948, which allowed the government to operate manufactures to produce goods required by the government—again requiring just compensation to the owner. All this seemed too laborious, however, to the president.

Truman insisted on having inherent executive powers sufficient to seize private property outright. His Assistant Attorney General Holmes Baldridge even claimed that while the legislature was bound by enumerated powers delegated to it, the executive branch was not! The position was untenable, and the press had a field day. In defense of the seizure, the government advanced arguments not heard in English-speaking seats of power since Charles I. The late Chief Justice William Howard Taft had earlier written, "There is no undefined residuum of power which [the president] can exercise because it seems to him to be in the public interest . . . . The grants of executive power are necessarily in general terms in order not to embarrass the Executive within the field of action plainly marked for him, but his jurisdiction must be justified and vindicated by affirmative constitutional or statutory provision, or it does not exist." There may indeed be some theoretical room for stepping outside of limits in the direst emergency, but even this would require political justification after the fact vis-à-vis the Congress or the Court. It cannot be otherwise in a system characterized by checks and balances and by three co-equal branches of the federal government.

President Truman, however, subscribed to an understanding of executive power evolved by activist presidents and based largely on Theodore Roosevelt's tenure and philosophy. He believed the president's power was absolute, absent some provision in the Constitution that denied specific authority. Historically of course, this is the exact opposite of the Original Intent of the Founders. The steel seizure made its way to the Supreme Court in the form of *Youngstown Sheet & Tube Co. v. Sawyer* (1952). In a 6-3 decision the Court overturned the president's seizure of the steel mills. Justice Hugo Black wrote for the majority and argued the president executes and enforces law, whereas the legislature legislates. Truman's seizure amounted to a legislative act. Interestingly, the majority of justices did not deny the president might possess implied or residual powers. Justice Frankfurter also opined that long experience of executive activism might in fact alter the Constitution, i.e., by long-standing experience and not by formal amendment! Accordingly the Constitution is said to be different by virtue of the men who held office, but this would seem contrary to the notion of a government of laws and not of men. Justice Jackson provided a framework for adjudging the president's use of executive power, and he concluded Truman's specific action fell into a weak and constitutionally dubious category.

As political economist and historian Robert Higgs has shown, the Justices viewed the Constitution in this case as an instrument for apportioning power among the several branches, as opposed to a document intended to limit government power overall and to reinforce the federalist construct. They read *Youngstown* as a separation-of-powers case, instead of a seizure-of-property case. They left only vague principles for judging executive behavior, which missed the whole point. The president is not our king. The commentary that surrounds this case reveals a philosophy with legs as it were—incredible relevance over the last eight years, and now more than ever. It reveals the belief of activist presidents and their appointees in the inherent powers of the Executive overriding all congressional prerogatives, reserved powers of the states, and the inalienable rights of people. This is unconstitutional thinking at its worst, even while it belongs to some of the presidents historians teach us to admire the most. The Left took exception to our last president's use of it, but there are others who deserve similar treatment. Our reference should ever be the Constitution and not a particular ideology.[49]

~Part III~ o/a April 17, 2009

Three. According to Woods and Gutzman, the fact that a government decision is beneficial and even morally right, does not make it constitutional. Positive policy outcomes do not ensure proper government action, and in the long run they may undermine the rule of law if adopted contrary to the meaning of the Constitution. Once we substitute a policy preference for decisions based upon sound and rigorous legal reasoning, we allow the government to step outside the bounds of the Constitution and in so doing create powerful precedents for yet more extra-constitutional measures.

This is precisely what happened in the case of *Brown v. Board of Education of Topeka, Kansas* (1954). The popular decision forbade segregation of schools on the basis of race. It overturned the distasteful 'separate but equal' standard handed down in *Plessy v. Ferguson* (1896), but it did so on the basis of declaring that the Fourteenth Amendment's equal protection clause intended public schools to be integrated. The basis was therefore grossly false and historically inaccurate.

The ratifiers of the Fourteenth Amendment would have recognized that the *Brown* decision ran counter to what they intended and clearly made known to posterity. The Fourteenth Amendment was intended to constitutionalize the Civil Rights Act of 1866 and guarantee basic rights to blacks, who had recently been freed from slavery—giving them for instance the right to own land and make and enforce contracts for labor. The Fourteenth Amendment also explicitly overrode the antebellum *Dred Scott v. Sandford* decision, which kept blacks from obtaining U.S. citizenship. At the time the Fourteenth Amendment was proposed, however, 24 of 37 states segregated their schools, and Congress even segregated schools in the District of Columbia. Civil rights legislation after the Fourteenth Amendment never addressed the issue either, and it seems absurd the Fourteenth Amendment would have guaranteed as a right of citizenship desegregation of public schools, when public education wasn't even mandatory everywhere and the most basic emblem of citizenship, i.e. the ballot, was withheld until the Fifteenth Amendment!

Virtually all historians knew the Fourteenth Amendment did not intend to end segregation in schools, and the Supreme Court came to the same conclusion in terms of the history. Justice Frankfurter said, "It is impossible to conclude that the 39th Congress intended that segregation be abolished; impossible also to conclude that they foresaw it might be, under the language they were adopting." Instead of interpreting the law, however, the Court decided to make law. It approached this case from the standpoint of an advocate. The Court therefore set itself above the Constitution and arrogated to itself the power to make law by exercise of its will alone, in direct contravention to Article V, which leaves the authority to States to decide. By rendering the *Brown* decision the way it did, the Court made it one of the most disingenuous in U.S. history. Effects have been among the most pernicious constitutionally speaking, notwithstanding accrued social progress.

In order to justify the *Brown* decision, Justice Frankfurter wrote that the original understanding of the Constitution and the understanding of laws passed by their authors are not binding! Instead, "the effect of changes in men's *feelings* for what is right and just is equally relevant" in determination of the meaning of laws and the Constitution. Moreover, these feelings are to be gauged by polling the nine Justices of the Supreme Court. Chief Justice Earl Warren would place his "human values" before the Constitution, and he deemed Article V processes "petty" by comparison. *The New York Times* called the decision a sociological one rather than a legal one. By almost any standard *Brown* was a legislative act. In terms of separation of powers, the Court did exactly what it roundly criticized the executive branch for in prior cases, i.e., for overstepping constitutional bounds into areas reserved to States or delegated to the Congress. Chief Justice Warren in his written opinion justified the *Brown* decision based on the role of public education in modern American society and not on substantive constitutional grounds.

The bald-faced judicial imperialism continued in a tandem case *Bolling v. Sharpe*. In that decision the Warren Court said the Due Process Clause of the Fifth Amendment banned segregation in the District of Columbia. No matter the Fifth Amendment was drafted by James Madison, a substantial slaveholder and Father of the Constitution who certainly never envisioned such. The *Brown* and *Bolling* case decisions set off waves of political resistance in the country that lasted many years. The decisions also set the stage for complete judicial departure from the Constitution as a document or a regime of governance the Founders may have recognized. The Court's "living" interpretation replaced the Constitution's once fixed meaning until now that it is anyone's guess.[50]

~Part IV~ o/a May 01, 2009

Number *Four* was the outgrowth of *Brown v. Board of Education of Topeka, Kansas* (1954). The Supreme Court arguably decided for a preferred, not to say preferential policy, and this is commonly accepted. The implementation, however, by extra-constitutional means led to bad policy examples built upon that precedent. Worse, it continued the deterioration of constitutional tradition and rule of law. It was the *Brown* decision that led to discriminations in order to end discrimination—the moral equivalent of destroying villages to save them. In *Brown II* (1955) the Supreme Court ruled segregation of state schools must end "with all deliberate speed."

By the two *Brown* decisions the Court became adjunct to Congress and the legislative branch, even a House of Lords lording above the rest. The Civil Rights Act of 1964 for instance gave explicit voice to the representative will of the people. Congress adopted a policy of desegregation and said school assignments would be made without regard to race, but Congress also stated specifically that, "desegregation shall not mean the assignment of students to public schools in order to overcome racial imbalance." Apparently the Supreme Court disagreed and ultimately ordered forced busing fiascoes.

Through a series of cases in the 1960s and 70s, its interpretation and implementation of desegregation became integration instead, and nondiscrimination turned into mandatory discrimination for such "benign" purposes as "remedy for past wrongs." Of course, in English and American legal tradition, an equitable remedy requires that only the malefactor responsible for a plaintiff's injury be punished.

Certainly an equitable remedy never extended to the punishment of any broad class of citizens, much less innocent children. The legal sentiment referred to here was still alive and well during the American Revolution. One of the reasons unrest grew and spread so quickly following the Boston Tea Party is that King and Parliament attempted to punish all residents of Boston and not just the offenders. The Coercive Acts enforced by the Crown were dubbed Intolerable Acts in the Colonies. Chief Justice Warren Burger justified his Intolerable Acts not on the basis of law or the express wish of Congress, but rather "in order to prepare students to live in a pluralistic society"! Besides the blatant social engineering, this kind of judicial policy-making violated American republican political tradition whereby governmental decisions are made by *elected* officials as opposed to courts comprised of appointed judges. Civics 101: legislatures make the law and courts interpret the law.

In 1973 the Supreme Court heard *Keyes v. School District No. One, Denver, Colorado.* The case involved a jurisdiction outside the South, and Denver had always prohibited segregation. As a city it fostered integration before the Supreme Court discovered the word. The Court decided, however, that Denver violated the *Brown* mandate against segregation by not intentionally integrating. Voters had in fact rejected the idea of using busing for that purpose. The only thing the Denver school board did was to assign children to their neighborhood schools. The unintended consequence of forced busing imposed by the Court in Denver, as well as in other cities, ran counter to integration by polarizing cities politically and precipitating white flight, which caused inner cities and associated school districts to become more black. Eventually the Supreme Court abandoned the method without dislodging the precedent in law giving it power. It seems to be the case that power arrogated to government is almost never relinquished, given back as it were to the States respectively, or to the people, whenever a crisis is passed and even when policies implemented by such power are discredited. So it falls to the discretion of future courts and administrations to simply use as much power as they want.[51]

~Part V~ o/a May 02, 2009

Number *Five* is perhaps the most unusual, because it dates back the furthest in its nascent form but has turned into the monstrous yearly habit of pork barrel and the so-called congressional prerogative of spending hundreds of millions of dollars of taxpayers' money on earmarks—those pet, not to say *petty* and self-serving projects that, as it turns out, have very little constitutional basis.

The most famous recent example is the Bridge to Nowhere, when in 2005-2006 we discovered politicians in both parties are complicit in not just scratching each other's backs, but in giving each other Swedish and special massages. Stuck inside of an appropriations bill was the earmark for a bridge in Alaska connecting 9,000 folks in one village to *fifty* (50) folks in another, even though the two villages had a ferry service passing back and forth between them more than a dozen of times each day. The cost of this unnecessary expense was more than $200 million to the federal taxpayer, i.e., to you and me. To add injury to insult as it were, in August 2007 the eight-lane I-35W bridge over the Mississippi River in Minneapolis, Minnesota, collapsed into the river killing scores of people and dumping some fifty vehicles off into the water.

The juxtaposition of these two events brings up a lot of interesting points. For instance, might federal prioritization of funds for bridges been a little smarter? On what basis are such funds, if any, shared? To what degree is responsibility for bridges and such, a local responsibility and to what degree federal? Is it even constitutional for Congress, say, to prioritize projects and redistribute funds for infrastructure if it is in the national interest? Indeed most folks intuitively understand there is such a thing as a "national" interest, even though it is hard to keep something national from disproportionately benefiting a locality. Take the levies in New Orleans for instance! In hindsight, it might have been considered in the national interest to do some serious prophylactic engineering work, in order to save the nation's largest port and area's critical petroleum refining capability.

In the early years of the Republic there were similar issues and questions being raised, because as you can imagine the country didn't even have a basic network of improved roads to pull its wagons on. Congress and the president envisioned national improvements (what we refer to as infrastructure) in order to facilitate trade and commerce in the vast free market economy and unprecedented open market that had been established by the Constitution. Both Jefferson and Madison recognized the need for roads, canal and other projects, as well as the need for a national jurisdiction and means to address them systematically. They nevertheless both concluded that for the federal government to go forward with these public projects, it required an amendment to the Constitution. In similar vein, though more controversial politically, some form of a national bank (functional equivalent of the Federal Reserve) was deemed expedient if not essential for the nation to prosper in peacetime and also finance the prosecution of war. Madison favored provisions for the Bank and spending the government's share of profits for infrastructure, but he vetoed the Bonus Bill containing the provisions because he said it was unconstitutional. His veto message of 1817 is consistent with his constitutional pronouncements in the 1780s and 90s, and it is important to take note of his message if for no other reason than that he is considered to be the Father of the Constitution. He clearly states that Congress has only a few powers, and they are listed in Article I, Section 8 of the Constitution. He says these do not include the power to build roads, bridges or canals. Neither is the power covered in the Necessary and Proper Clause at the end of that section, because internal improvements are not incidental to the exercise of any of the enumerated powers.

Madison likewise did not believe that it was covered in the General Welfare Clause, and he counseled against an overbroad reading of that clause. Instead, he insisted the issue should be addressed by constitutional amendment according to terms outlined in Article V. While constitutional amendment on this point did not follow, for the entire "Middle Period" of American history between the War of 1812 and the War Between the States, Congress debated internal improvements hotly on the basis of which internal improvements were thoroughly "national" in scope or character and hence constitutionally plausible in the opinion of many. This is key to understanding constitutional limits inherent in, say, Henry Clay and the Whig Party's "American System," which conservatives today sometimes criticize but which is still a million miles away from using federal taxpayers' money to fund local parks and museums, much less a bridge to nowhere!

Internal improvements in those days were also light years away from the New Deal roadwork and make-work programs in the 1930s, and the 1956 Federal-Aid Highway Act based upon New Deal precedents. The latter is commonly viewed as a contributor to national security in the Cold War era, in addition to enhancing the nation's transportation infrastructure. The fact that 40,000 miles of roads were seized from 48 states seems hardly worth the notice.[52]

~Part VI~ o/a May 03, 2009

Before discussing Number *Six* there's a point worth making in terms of the broader sweep of history, which perhaps warrants a pause to consider just where we are headed. The point speaks to Original Intent and federalism, but also to a sea change in attitudes amongst the polity—those of us who vote and care enough to participate politically. It may speak to the harmful cumulative effect of inattention in a democracy, and the difficulty of holding government to account or hitting the reset button as it were. In my opinion, it speaks to the way in which freemen and freewomen are turned into vassals by their own government.

To wit, Americans knew that for the federal government to prohibit something like alcohol, it would require an amendment to the Constitution. The Eighteenth Amendment was adopted and ratified therefore to do just that. A policy that worked tolerably well at state level, however, demonstrably did not transfer well to the national level and instead gave rise to organized crime for much the same reason that drug violence is rife today in Mexico. The Eighteenth Amendment was overturned by the Twenty-First, the only constitutional amendment ever to have been repealed. Fast forward: Congress now bans products willy-nilly without the least constraining compunction, and marijuana is an excellent example because of its similarity to alcohol. This is done by the way *without any amendment empowering it to do so*!

Speaking of the harmful cumulative effect of inattention in a democracy, where once the people's money was safe it is now utterly debased. The dollar may give way to an international currency yet, and it will when it is worthless. The dollar used to be based on gold and precious metal, then on confidence and a few shreds of integrity left in the system. Today the value of one dollar is close to a delete function away. The government won't even tell you how many are in the economy. If they did, you might try to calculate what's been done to it. And while you never know where the story will end, in hindsight it is easy to see the first big heist which is Number *Six* in our dirty dozen—the great gold robbery of 1933. Americans hardly read about it or know it happened, and that's another story how history in public classrooms is almost as debased as the dollar.

The U.S. Dollar was defined as roughly one-twentieth of an ounce of gold throughout most of our history. Indeed, gold was the actual money but paper *represented* the specie, being lighter and easier to handle, etc. Assume your raffle ticket is good for a TV—it's only good if you can make the exchange. The point is that paper notes could be redeemed for gold at any time prior to March 1933 when the federal government announced a banking emergency and, in order to cope with it "recalled" all the monetized gold in the U.S. That is to say, if you possessed gold in the bank or a stash of gold coins in the closet, the Government *ordered* you to turn it in. The Trading with the Enemy Act (left over from 1917!) was amended to give the president authority to "investigate, regulate, or prohibit" hoarding of gold. In other words, anyone who kept his gold money was unpatriotic and quite probably an enemy of the New Deal Republic to be dealt with accordingly. Now consider that the confiscation of gold was in the name of a banking and currency management crisis, so most Americans absolutely assumed it would be returned when the emergency abated. The difference between borrowing and theft has a lot to do with whether or not you give it back! People and corporations were given an equivalent amount of paper currency for their gold holdings because of the temporary shortage of gold in the banking system since banks had loaned out too much and held too little in reserve. As soon as the gold was collected, however, the president and Congress passed a joint resolution, which nullified the promise to repay in gold. Payment would henceforth be in whatever the government declared was legal tender.

Democrat Senator Thomas Gore of Oklahoma told Franklin Roosevelt to his face, "Why, that's just plain stealing, isn't it, Mr. President?"

Not only that but it is hardly constitutional. In 1785, even before the Constitution was drafted and some four years before it was ratified, Congress declared the American monetary unit to be the dollar and the Treasury fixed its value to the silver Spanish milled dollar. The power to regulate the dollar in the Constitution is in the same clause as the power to fix weights and measures, i.e., to codify existing standards in order to ensure uniformity. The Constitution did not give politicians or bankers the power to assign arbitrary value to money, any more than Congress can say that one-tenth of a pound now equals a pound or an ounce is the same as a cup. While the value of precious metals does change, the idea behind congressional power to regulate currency is to set the exchange rate of coins and paper in circulation, vis-à-vis some objective standard for predetermined periods of time, and to make it publicly known. The reason they do this is to ensure that an equivalent means exists throughout the country for satisfying payment of debt or purchase of goods.

According to Woods and Gutzman, there are two fundamental reasons why the federal government turned criminal and basically stole from the American people. They are the same reasons we need to begin now reintroducing objective standards and redeemable equivalents in precious metals to our currency: first, "gold severely restricts the ability of government to manipulate the money supply on behalf of the politically well connected"; and second, "Irredeemable paper money . . . gives the government an easier time of financing war and welfare, which can be portrayed as essentially *costless*." The government took us to the cleaners, but it's time to get our money back.[53]

~Part VII~ o/a May 08, 2009

Number *Seven* may be the most important and egregious in terms of what it meant spiritually to the nation. From the standpoint of federalism, it was one of the deepest cuts into the states' exclusive purview ever committed by the Supreme Court. The Court ruling in *Engel v. Vitale* handed down in 1962 banned prayer from public schools. Other studies show the growth of social pathologies dramatically taking off from that date.

In reaching the decision, the Court reinterpreted the First and the Fourteenth Amendments, changing government's extant constitutional relationship vis-à-vis religion. As before, this final verdict is the result of accumulated error and the people with eyes glazed over lulled into submission. For right reasoning we have to start with the most basic fact concerning the Bill of Rights. The first ten Amendments called the Bill of Rights were put there in 1791 entirely to protect the traditional interpretation of individual rights enjoyed by the people, as well as those powers traditionally exercised by state governments *from encroachment by the federal government.* Many of the Founders felt the Bill of Rights superfluous, since they had not given the federal government such authority in the first place. Nevertheless, the Bill of Rights made certain points explicit, for instance the First Amendment, that "Congress *shall make no law* respecting an establishment of religion, or prohibiting the free exercise thereof . . . ." That's because nine of the states had established churches! The others had religious qualifications and requirements of various sorts. Nobody but nobody wanted the federal government to interfere with the prerogatives of the states or people regarding religion.

Of course the Fourteenth Amendment ratified in 1868 strove to give protections to recently freed slaves, by requiring states to provide equal protection of their laws and also due process of law before depriving persons of life, liberty, or property. Only in 1940 in *Cantwell v. Connecticut* did the Supreme Court announce that the Fourteenth Amendment's Due Process Clause made the First Amendment's religion clauses applicable against states. The First Amendment had been in existence for 149 years and the Fourteenth Amendment had been in place 72 years, and this was an entirely new doctrine made out of whole cloth. Indeed, it is called the Doctrine of Incorporation, which has since inverted the entire American federal system. The fox is now in charge of the henhouse, because the federal government began to use the precedent and to make the Fourteenth Amendment a convenient way of subverting the restrictions placed on it by the Bill of Rights. In so doing, the federal government now interprets its own powers instead of abiding by the explicit limits, which were established by the Bill of Rights and intended as such by the Founding Generation.

In 1937 the Court also abandoned attempts to limit violations of the Commerce Clause or enforce the Tenth Amendment vis-à-vis Congress or the president. Given the horrid constitutional situation following the New Deal and World War II, wherein the application of the Bill of Rights is reversed from being a restriction on the federal government to being restrictions on states, it was a matter of time before logic played out in the fateful decision of 1962. According to Woods and Gutzman, "Justice Potter Stewart in dissent noted that he could 'not see how an official religion is established by letting those who want to say a prayer say it.' He went on to note that the inclusion of religious lyrics in 'The Star-Spangled Banner' did not make designation of that hymn as the national anthem an establishment of religion, and that adding 'under God' to the Pledge of Allegiance in 1954 had not made recitation of that oath an establishment, any more than putting 'IN GOD WE TRUST' on American coinage was an establishment." The majority of the people could not see it either, and Americans at large found the decision lamentable. It remains the case, however, that the legitimate amendment process outlined in Article V of the Constitution is far more difficult to enact than the illegitimate Supreme Court arrogation of the amendment process to itself. Though multiple assassins wielded weapons at the Constitution, the Supreme Court leveled a deadly aim through creative destructive "interpretation." No one can say the Constitution is qualitatively what it once was, despite having very few amendments to the text.[54]

~Part VIII~ o/a May 08, 2009

Number *Eight* is the power to draft and to say there is no constitutional power to draft runs counter to some conservatives' patriotic instinct, but then it gets to the heart of what constitutes the American republic and its citizenry, the relationship between them and the extent of power legitimately exercised.

One could argue as William F. Buckley, Jr. did, that if government is entitled to require the people to complete twelve years of schooling then a year or so of labor is perfectly consistent. Indeed, we may well ask ourselves whether the *federal* government (as opposed to state government) has authority to mandate public schooling and the obvious answer is that it does not, albeit almost no one will stand up and say that today. If you concede of the power then ask yourself, why not sixteen years of schooling or even twenty? Why not one year of labor or perhaps ten, at community service and/or in the military? In one of the few instances where a post-Civil War Amendment actually reinforces Original Intent for the majority, the Thirteenth Amendment makes plain that "Neither slavery nor involuntary servitude, except as a punishment for crime whereof the party shall have been duly convicted, shall exist within the

United States, or any place subject to their jurisdiction." The military draft is nothing if not involuntary servitude, but not to worry if you haven't any qualms—because as in so many other instances, the Supreme Court has given its approval and redefined it from being involuntary servitude (one's private perspective) to being an exceedingly wonderful obligation (the Court's pronouncement). Incidentally, the pronoun "their" in the Thirteenth Amendment refers to United States in the plural, exposing again the lie that we became a unitary national democracy as a result of the War Between the States.

There is no article or section contained in the Constitution in which it is written, that the federal government may take children away from parents or parents from their children and compel them to fight the nation's wars. Even in declared wars and even in cases of invasion such as the War of 1812, this was never the case. Today when the presumption has shifted and turned towards such extraordinary power invested in a national government, the country no longer even declares its wars but is constantly at war and no one threatens invasion. The government of these United States was erected to keep a free people free, not to subjugate them and make them serve its own ends of empire building or as a Court might redefine it, extending democracy.

It was Lincoln who first raised "national forces" by means of the draft. The Chief Justice of the Supreme Court at the time rebuked the measure for being unconstitutional on numerous and substantive grounds. The War rendered his opinion very much beside the point as it were, and the Supreme Court did not consider constitutionality of the federal draft again until World War I. Amazingly, the *Selective Draft Law Cases* of 1917 upheld legislation that actually incorporated the National Guard and National Guard Reserve into service of the United States. This effectively converted the states' self-defense organizations into federal agencies! Defendants in the cases had refused to present themselves for the draft ordered by President Woodrow Wilson. Some rural sections of the country rendered enforcement of the draft all but impossible, because of constitutional scruples and an instinct towards freedom—it wasn't cowardice, since armed resistance to the draft was more likely and actually occurred.

The first constitutional precedent for a federal draft the Supreme Court could find was the Conscription Act of 1863—the law so powerfully criticized in Lincoln's day. The law certainly did not follow normal constitutional processes and arguably took place during an existential suspension of the Constitution. The Court finally justified the draft, however, and not surprisingly, according to the post-Civil War Fourteenth Amendment! Chief Justice Edward White wrote that the people had elevated the significance of federal citizenship above that of state citizenship and conveyed with it the power of conscription. Since 1917 the federal government merely assumes it has the power to draft men into the armed forces. Furthermore, there is no legal distinction remaining these days to even exempt women.

Ronald Reagan condemned conscription and said that it "rests on the assumption that your kids belong to the state. If we buy that assumption then it is for the state—not for parents, the community, the religious institutions, or teachers—to decide who shall have what values and who shall do what work, when, where, and how in our society." Exactly. Maybe that's why recent administrations silently reinforce the constitutionally fallacious, and anti-republican precedent. Because even though the draft ended amidst protest in 1973, it gives ambitious chief executives and progressive socialist congress people, particularly in times of crisis, the philosophical wherewithal and basis of unlimited government power over United States citizens. It makes grotesque expansion of government spending programs far easier too. And anyway, if the government can keep you twelve years in school, a few more years of involuntary servitude is really just a continuation of your excellent education.[55]

~Part IX~ o/a July 10, 2009

Number *Nine* involves abuse of the Commerce Clause. Americans may be surprised to learn they have a constitutional duty, according to interpretation by federal courts and the Supreme Court, *to suffer*. The duty to suffer is for the sake of commerce.

To digress a moment, it always bothered me that the government used tax laws, in particular tax *evasion* to target and convict criminals and punish them for other crimes the government could not prove. On an existential and practical level, it may serve the greater good and public welfare and indeed be "just," to put away the likes of Al Capone by expedient means. But it is easy from our vantage point to see how a constitutionally unrestrained government may begin to turn any citizen it wants into a criminal. The process has already begun in fact, and the nature of power makes it entirely likely whenever the government should feel politically threatened. Motivationally, it was *not* the heinous crimes committed by the mafia that mattered to prosecution, so much as the displacement of government authority and its control over the purse.

The same bureaucratic and political motive gives rise to officially sanctioned disinformation, as well as to state-sponsored violence. We may have entered a period beginning in the 1990s where, even absent the admitted Cold War anomalies, power in the central government had grown so great and restraints upon it so ineffectual, that transparency in government operations as well as the trustworthiness of what the government itself was reporting, were compromised and in grave doubt. At such a stage as we are still in, only a severe populist reaction causing political realignment and large-scale replacement of officials, may jolt the system sufficiently to make it amenable to reform and efforts at restoration.

At the Constitutional Convention and in the sixty-three times the word appears in the *Federalist Papers*, "commerce" meant trade. Foreign trade was distinguished from trade or commerce among the several states. The Constitution's Commerce Clause found in Article I, Section 8, Clause 3 grants Congress the power to "regulate Commerce [trade] with foreign Nations, and among the several States, and with the Indian Tribes." Commerce among the several states referred to commerce between one state and another, not commerce inside one state (intrastate) that may be said to have an extenuating effect elsewhere. The point of the Clause was quite frankly to keep one state from setting up and imposing tariffs on goods coming in from another state. The provision is thus largely responsible for the Constitution having enabled setting up a giant free-trade zone throughout the United States, i.e., by preventing states from obstructing the free flow of commerce (So far, so good).

By the twentieth century, however, precedents were compounded to such an extent as to completely undo a distinction between intra and interstate commerce. *Wickard v. Filburn* (1942) thus overlay *Gibbons v. Ogden* (1824), and now a farmer growing wheat on his own land was subject to federal regulation, because while it wasn't interstate commerce per se, it nonetheless *affected* interstate commerce. Had he not grown his own wheat, he might have purchased it from another state! His abstention from purchasing, his *evasion* if you will, brought private activity conducted entirely within a sovereign state under federal jurisdiction.

Given the precedent in *Wickard*, it was an easy hop-skip-and-jump in the case of *Gonzales v. Raich* (2004) for the Supreme Court to say flatly, the federal government may now ban *the use* of substances grown and consumed inside a single state—whether or not they are ever bought or sold, and whether or not there is even a market. The reason is such a substance might "leak" into interstate commerce and affect the overall economy. The suppositional reasoning is far beyond anything envisioned by Founders' Original Intent regarding the Constitution or the Commerce Clause. Indeed, any and everything affects the economy—particularly if one judges effect upon a hypothetical abstention or the leakage of something that isn't even done. One wonders if the hypothetical extends to evasion of taxes on supposed commerce that never occurs, or the commission of crimes you just happened to think about.

Specifically dealing with the question of medical marijuana, though legal in California, the Court favored federal raids and seizure of private property based on the rationale that a leakage for recreational use outside the State of California could disrupt the federal drug prohibition policy, thus making the government's larger regulatory scheme less effective. In one fell swoop the Court set a new enlarged precedent, that federal regulatory regimes trump anything taking place inside states. Not only does the federal government control anything that affects commerce, it now controls anything that affects a regulatory regime. Commerce had morphed a long time ago from *inter*state to *intra*state, but now it involves anything the government says it does. Anything within a state affecting or supposedly affecting a larger federal regulatory scheme is brought within federal control. Moreover, if something is legal in a state today, it can be disallowed whenever the feds want—rendered illegal, simply by erecting a new federal regulatory scheme.

Three states that outlaw medical marijuana (Alabama, Louisiana and Mississippi) filed an amicus brief in protest to the decision in *Gonzales v. Raich*. Alabama's brief on behalf of the three states reads in part that the point is not whether medical marijuana is good or bad or profoundly misguided—rather, "The point is that, as a sovereign member of the federal union, California is entitled to make for itself the tough policy choices that affect its citizens." The federal government may not "displace the States from their traditional role as the enforcers of local criminal law and assume the States' police power to provide for the health, safety, welfare, and morals of their citizens." In point of fact, the federal government says it can. Commerce not only makes us duty bound to suffer as it apparently does for medical marijuana users in California, it makes everyone slave to the central government in Washington, albeit for the greater good of macro-economy as determined by the federal government on your behalf. They've done such a good job too.[56]

~Part X~ o/a July 24, 2009

Number *Ten* is the transformation of the Chief Executive into Prince and the concomitant abuse of power in the exercise of foreign policy. The Constitution had first established a federal structure of government, and the Supreme Court was committed to it *based upon Original Intent* well into the Twentieth century, and even in the area of foreign affairs. Several cases during the 1920s and 1930s, however, upended the constitutional tradition.

At the Constitutional Convention in 1787 the Founders discussed areas in which states might not be as competent to judge or legislate in as, say, Congress. The Virginia Plan proposed by James Madison was actually modified at the Convention over the very question, whether Congress was to be altogether *national* in its scope and reach or whether it remained part of the *federal* construct involving dual sovereignty with states. Today there is little doubt that we have an operative national Congress, but the Founders agreed to a federal Congress instead, with specified powers mainly listed in Article I, Section 8. This was a key point in debates leading to ratification of the Constitution by the people of the several states. The new government would not be able to subvert state and local self-government for which the American Revolution had been fought!

Plain statements by Federalist proponents of the Constitution during ratification debates make clear their intent that treaty power dealt only with external matters and not with matters internal to the states. As if to make the point twice and doubly clear, the Tenth Amendment was added after ratification, i.e., after the language conveying treaty power, to make sure the Federal Government got the message: that it may not make treaties with foreign governments impinging on sovereignty, rights and freedoms inherent in each state. Congress may not, for instance, give a state's territory away to another nation. Congress cannot compromise gun rights, speech rights and freedom of religion in states, as these are not supposed to be subject to negotiation with foreign governments.

The case of *State of Missouri v. Holland* (1920), however, began a radical change to this presumption. Stating a majority opinion for the Supreme Court, Justice Oliver Wendell Holmes practically delimited the federal government's power to make treaties and said the Tenth Amendment did not apply. The case dealt with regulating, a.k.a. *protecting* migratory birds through treaty. Holmes conceded that exclusive federal jurisdiction and power was not there to do it, at least not originally, but it *needed* to be. The policy in question was *right*, even if it were not constitutional. Therefore the Court set a new legal precedent against clear terms in the Constitution. It is worth noting, this is how law may become unconstitutional and ultimately de-legitimized. It is also how revolutions are justified within the bounds of constitutional republican theory.

The development in *State of Missouri v. Holland* came also upon the heels of the Seventeenth Amendment (1913), which transferred the power to elect U.S. Senators from state legislatures to election by popular vote in the several states. The Amendment had the immediate effect of removing political opposition in Congress to incursions on states' reserved powers. As it turns out, the Seventeenth Amendment unintentionally removed an important bulwark shoring up the Tenth Amendment. The Supreme Court took advantage of a unique opportunity, changing the legal precedent and making law that was essentially unconstitutional according to the terms of a previous constitutional regime—creating instead, a new ultra-if not *supra*-national constitutional regime we are still under. Theoretically nothing is beyond the bounds of national treaty making power, subject only to consent of the Senate by two-thirds vote.

The latter stricture too disappeared, and today we make treaties by Executive fiat even without the consent of the Senate. Here is how that happened. The case *United States v. Curtiss-Wright Export Corporation* (1936) dealt with a congressional attempt to delegate broad discretion to the president over the sale and export of arms and munitions to other countries. The Court in that case determined that the federal government through the president had power to undertake executive agreements as a substitute for treaties—binding international agreements not requiring ratification by the Senate! Not only did the case enable the legislative branch to delegate its discretion to another branch of government (something we saw again leading up to the invasion of Iraq), Court opinion reinforced the unhistorical account that sovereignty was unitary and invested with the federal government in the area of foreign affairs. As such it trumped state concerns, so that internal matters are really no objects. The distinction between internal and external was not simply blurred; rather, state internal matters were relegated to an entirely subordinate position. Federalism for all intents and purposes is undone.

On the current basis of Supreme Court opinion, the Constitution could not have erected an unchanging framework of government, since that framework as well as the rights and freedoms attended to by states, are subject to the federal government in the area of foreign affairs through treaty—and now through executive agreement entered into by a single person, the president—either of which can deal literally with anything whatsoever. This is bad news if one believes, as the Founders did, in the sovereign purview and prerogative of each state or in inviolable rights and freedoms. The final blow perhaps came with the case of *United States v. Belmont* (1937) involving Soviet nationalization of assets inside the State of New York. The Supreme Court ruled the state had to yield to an executive agreement that allowed for confiscation, irrespective of the constitutional injunction against taking property without just compensation. An international agreement made by the president simply countermands the policy or determination of any state. It is no wonder how the Supreme Court has begun to quote foreign case law and international standards to set legal and "constitutional" precedent.[57]

~Part XI~ o/a July 31, 2009

Number *Eleven* has to do with presidential war powers; and the extant, counter-constitutional claim that the president has exclusive control over foreign affairs, including the deployment of troops whenever, wherever and however he likes without the consent of Congress.

Original Intent was strong in its prejudice towards the Legislative branch, i.e., to the people's representative body when it came to committing the new Republic to war. No one wanted kingly powers invested in the president, such as the power of committing the nation to war unilaterally. Such power led to potentially ruinous results, with which the people of Great Britain and Europe were all too familiar. Alexander Hamilton, who advocated a strong executive, nevertheless conceded that "the Legislature alone [can place] the nation in a state of war" under the Constitution. John Jay in *Federalist* No. 4 likewise advocated the Constitution, *in contradistinction* to a king's power to prosecute wars unchecked. George Washington specifically disclaimed any executive authority to take the country into war, and so confined his operations against the Indians to defensive measures.

When Japan attacked Pearl Harbor in 1941, the president did not retaliate on his own authority but rather went to Congress for a declaration of war. Indeed, until 1950 it was understood that only Congress could authorize offensive military operations, whereas the president might take immediate defensive measures only without specific authorization. With the exception of the War Between the States, and also what might be termed policing actions (against pirates and criminals, etc.), every president up to and including Franklin Delano Roosevelt followed Original Intent regarding the power to actually prosecute war. In 1950, however, President Truman broke with American tradition by intervening directly and for an extended period in the Korean Conflict. In order to contrive some legal rationale, his administration came up with constitutional theory out of whole cloth, citing a plenary power over the military.

The theory has since evolved and hardened into a constitutionally absurd and grotesque mockery of Original Intent. As explained by John Yoo, while serving as the deputy assistant attorney general for George W. Bush, "The President has the constitutional authority to introduce the U.S. Armed Forces into hostilities when appropriate, with or without specific congressional authorization"—period. In a memo he wrote 25 September 2001, Yoo goes even further, declaring the presidential authority to "retaliate against any person, organization, or State suspected of involvement in terrorist attacks on the United States [and] against foreign States suspected of harboring or supporting such organizations." He states categorically, "The President may deploy military force preemptively against terrorist organizations or the States that harbor or support them, whether or not they can be linked to the specific events of September 11." Moreover, he states that no congressional statute whatsoever can "place any limits on the President's determinations as to any terrorist threat, the amount of military force to be used in response, or the method, timing, and nature of the response. These decisions, under our Constitution, are for the President alone to make. . . . In the exercise of his plenary power to use military force, the President's decisions are for him alone and are *un-reviewable*"! The President is king in other words.

President Bush went so far as to describe himself as the nation's "sole organ" in foreign affairs, inclusive of the power to start and wage war. Conservative columnist George Will refuted this "monarchical doctrine" called executive supremacy, observing that the Constitution's plain language "empowers Congress to ratify treaties, declare war, fund and regulate military forces, and make laws 'necessary and proper' for the execution of all presidential powers." Likewise, the Constitution ascribes a presidential duty to take care that laws passed by Congress are faithfully executed. Similar to Congress and the Courts (two other *co-equal branches of the Federal Government*), there is no indication of a Founders' intent, either in the Constitution or throughout the record of ratification debates, to "vest" in the Chief Executive super-ordinate power, or to give him an array of powers beyond those expressly mentioned in Article II. The President is the Commander-In-Chief of the Armed Forces, not the Commander-In-Chief of the American people or the U.S. Government, or the Commander-In-Chief of these United States of America.[58]

~Part XII~ o/a August 06, 2009

The *Twelfth* is the use and abuse of executive orders and signing statements by the president to usurp the powers of Congress and turn himself into an oracle of law. Of course, selective enforcement of law can amount to the same thing as an executive order, and Andrew Jackson was sometimes famous for this. Except for that grand exception by the self-proclaimed Tribune of the People, and a virtual suspension of the Constitution during the War Between the States, American presidents tended to be conservative and cautious men well into the late nineteenth century.

George Washington set the precedent for Chief Executive in so many ways, to include his point that the president ought not to approve and disapprove various parts of a bill in terms of actual enforcement when and if a bill becomes law. Moreover, he could not simply strike portions out of a bill when he signed it into law. Rather, he had to sign and enforce the whole thing or use his veto to reject the bill *in toto*. With few exceptions, this was how the Chief Executive or President continued to approach his office up until Theodore Roosevelt during the Progressive Era.

An executive order is simply a directive issued by the president. He may issue such directive in pursuit of constitutional objectives and in exercising the powers assigned to him by the Constitution. For instance, he can use an executive order to issue pardons. He can use executive orders to implement policy in line with discretionary authority too. Theodore Roosevelt took things to extreme, however, issuing over a thousand executive orders in nearly two terms. The number represented an exponential increase from his predecessors, but more importantly it represented a qualitative shift in governing philosophy and a departure from the intent of the Founders. "TR" recurred to the Jacksonian notion that the president is the singular and unique representative of the American people, having been elected by all of them. Hence he embodies the people's will as no other branch of government does. Liberal use of the executive order was a steppingstone to liberal use of the presidential signing statement, and George W. Bush is to the presidential signing statement what TR was to the executive order.

A signing statement is a statement issued by the president alongside his approval of a bill. They aren't particularly new, but they were infrequent until very modern times. In the past, they were mostly rhetorical. They might thank a particular group of people for their role in the legislation. They might voice displeasure with a particular aspect of the bill. They might even raise a constitutional question. They were window dressing as it were, largely ceremonial and certainly toothless in terms of legal interpretation and enforcement. John Quincy Adams referred to them as a defacement of public records and archives! From 1789 to 2000, signing statements contained less than 600 outright challenges to the bills signed.

Then George W. Bush issued hundreds of statements by himself, and of more significance they contained over 1,100 specific exceptions to the bills he signed. What's more, he refused to enforce those exceptions he made to the same bills he signed. Remember what George Washington said: the president under the Constitution must sign and enforce the whole bill or reject it entirely. In hindsight that's why George W. Bush used his veto so few times—he apparently didn't think he needed it. Another innovation George W. Bush brought was a kind of reverse non-enforcement thesis that may have made Andrew Jackson a bit squeamish and TR actually blush. Not only would he not enforce select provisions of the law, he would positively enforce his own (read "the people's") will in contravention of specific congressional statutes. According to this approach, the president is more "co-equal" than the other branches; and checks and balances are for the other guy.

According to Phillip Cooper, a professor of public administration, in some eighty-two cases President Bush excepted provisions of bills on the basis of "unitary executive" power vested with him. Seventy-seven times he ignored provisions and did something else, owing to "exclusive power over foreign affairs." In forty-eight instances he referred to the president's "authority to determine and impose national security classifications and withhold information" in order to defy legislation. The statements became such a factor that during the GW Bush years, the Supreme Court began to refer to them in relation to court decisions.

Thomas Jefferson believed in concurrent review, such that all three branches of government should consider a bill's constitutionality. Some of the legislation Bush took exception to may be unconstitutional, but the time for pointing that out is during the legislative process or in preparation of a presidential veto message. The president can veto a bill, not rewrite the thing. The laws are so chock full of holes now, it is hard to know what they are vice what they say. The presidential signing statements are never read aloud but pile up in the *Federal Register*. It takes a technocrat to find them and lawyers to interpret best guess. The Constitution is dead, and we now have what amounts to a corrupt ministerial government of men and not of laws, the same the Founders hated so vehemently and rebelled against in 1776.[59]

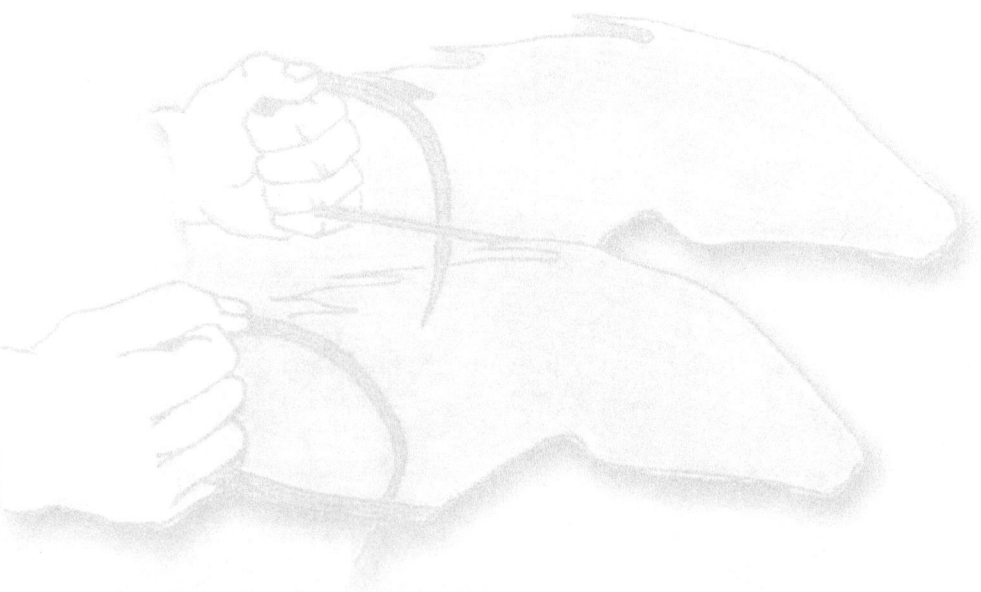

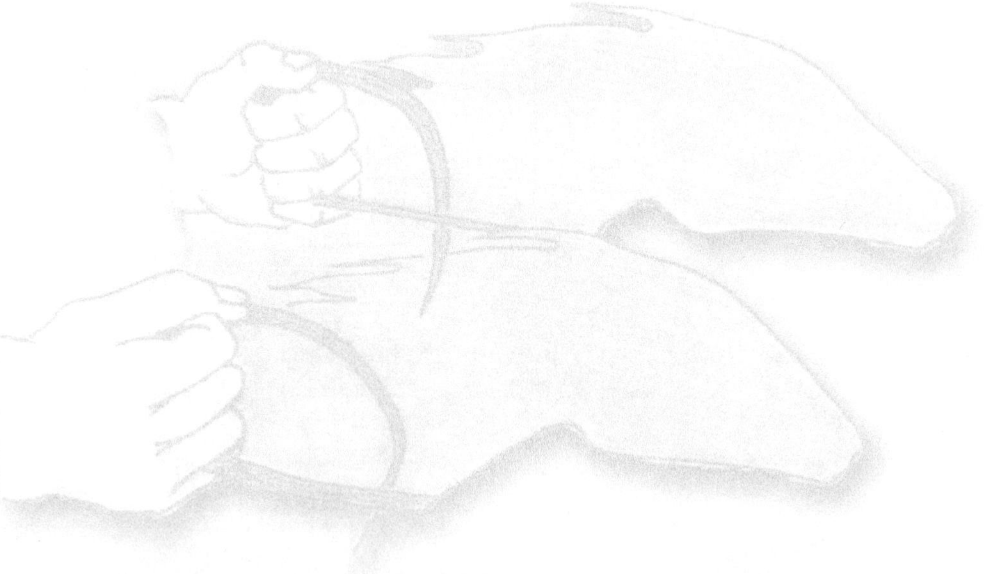

PART THREE: HISTORY

CHAPTER 21

History 101

History
March 22, 2001

Article #014

I'm often amazed at the dire if comical void of knowledge people have about themselves and about their country. I enjoy Jay Leno's late night interviews with less than stellar college students, who don't know much about history (and one wonders what else). But I really do hope the interviewees are drunk, stoned or just joking when the camera shines on them and Jay pops his question. The reason is that the future is by definition a progeny of the past. Collective forgetting today will undoubtedly mess up tomorrow. It isn't necessarily my wish that it were so—it is just the way time works. History is ultimately *His*-story, the chronicle of man and woman made in His image. The "present" (a *gift*) instantly recedes before a future, as yet unknown. The quality of the future, however, is shaped by our knowledge and understanding of the past, to the extent that history informs our choices and actions in the present predicament.

On one level, the past is a database of man's experience. You wouldn't throw away film or news clips from your opponent's old bouts, if you were about to box with him. There are lessons learned and some moves to be avoided. There are techniques to study, trends to identify. Metaphorically, the present is a kind of boxing match. Only lots of people aren't looking at the record, so they get sucker punched daily. I think the government gets far too many licks in, and the reason is simple. History once served as the basis and general framework of knowledge for citizens in this country. For a constitutional republic, history establishes the very legitimacy of our government; original meanings of words in their historical context define constitutional authority, as well as the scope and limits of power.

For instance, liberty was understood in the early Republic as a state of mind and behavior in relation to its deviant opposite, licentiousness. The concept of rights too implied a set of obligations and duties, i.e., restraints. Liberty was, in effect, a capacity to exercise natural rights—a capacity that all people did not even possess. That's why Ben Franklin said of the Founders they'd given us a Republic and qualified as quickly, "If you can keep it!" He probably thought we'd at least remember the Convention. Today Americans speak in Orwellian Newspeak, because they do not know about which they are talking. The Constitution has lost its fixity because of it. The Declaration of Independence is frequently reduced and misconstrued into a partial, pidgin paraphrase of Martin Luther King, Jr.'s beautiful and moving "I Have a Dream" speech. The Bill of Rights has come to mean whatever a judge says it means; freedom means never having to be poor or getting your feelings hurt. The panoply of rights invented since the 1960s, as well as the "penumbra" protections divined by activist judges has significantly altered the meaning of America. But kids and adults know so little about their past, they cannot discern the big stuff—much less the nuances—in terms of the negative change affecting them and limiting their future horizons and potential.

History can help, but only if it can be taught. Parents and community leaders need courage to insist. A lesson from history that bears on the requirement has to do with what the old Whigs called "The Country of Washington." It could also be called "The Country of Lee." It was a nation made up of brave, honest, faithful and courteous individuals, that is, of men and women of *character*, like the Father of Our Country—Americans who would not shirk from their personal or civic duty. Washington and the other Founders knew that liberty would abide, only so long as virtuous character endured. Washington knew his history, and he modeled his personal behavior on classical Roman Virtues (e.g., honor, loyalty, duty) and Judeo-Christian virtues found in the Bible. He expressed and refined the national character in himself and serves as personal role model still, if we pay attention.

From Greece to Rome in the History of Freedom — Article #273
o/a October 13, 2006

It was a momentous step in the progress of nations when the principle that every interest should have the right and the means of asserting itself was adopted by the Athenian constitution. But for those who were beaten in the vote there was no redress. The law did not check the triumph of majorities, or rescue the minority from the dire penalties of having been outnumbered. When the overwhelming influence of Pericles was removed, conflict between classes raged without restraint. The history of Athens provides a classic example of the perils of Democracy. It is bad to be oppressed by a minority; it is worse to be oppressed by a majority. In Athens it followed that the sovereign people had a right to do whatever was within it power, and was bound by no rule of right and wrong but its own judgment of expediency. In this way the emancipated people of Athens became a tyrant. They ruined their city by attempting to conduct war by debate in the marketplace. Like the French Republic centuries later, they put their unsuccessful commanders to death. They treated dependencies with such injustice they lost their maritime empire. They plundered the rich, until the rich conspired with the enemy; and they crowned their guilt by the martyrdom of Socrates.

Rome eclipsed Greece but had to work through many of the same problems. Most of the eminent public men of Rome, like Scipio and Cicero, moreover formed their minds on Grecian models. Romans actually adopted their cultural aesthetics and learning from Greece. The constitutional history of the Roman Republic, however, turned more on endeavors of its aristocracy, who claimed to be the only true Romans. Common families were increasingly impoverished by incessant wars and finally reduced to dependence upon an aristocracy of 2000 wealthy men. After years of struggle, the people who depended on public rations for food were ready to follow any man who promised to obtain for them by revolution what they could not obtain by law. For a time the Senate, representing the threatened order of things, was strong enough to overcome every popular leader that arose, until Julius Caesar (100-44 B.C.) supported by an army he had led in a career of conquest, as well as by famished masses, and admittedly skilled in the imperial arts of governing—converted the Republic into a Monarchy.

Of course the Republic that Caesar overthrew had been anything but a free state. It provided admirable securities for the rights of citizens, but it treated with savage disregard the rights of men; and allowed the free Roman to inflict atrocious wrongs on his children, on debtors and dependents, on prisoners and slaves. Ironically, the Roman Empire rendered greater service to the cause of Liberty than the Roman Republic. The poor got food and circuses; the rich were better protected. The rights of Roman citizens were extended to people in the Provinces. To the imperial epoch belong the better part of Roman literature and nearly the entire Civil Law; and it was the Empire that mitigated slavery, instituted religious toleration, made a beginning of the law of nations, and created a perfect system of the law of property. Eventually the lower class of plebs were admitted to political equality in the year 285, and there followed 150 years of prosperity and glory.

The Empire preserved republican forms until the reign of Diocletian (284-305 A.D.). Notwithstanding, the will of Emperors was horribly uncontrolled, their use of power arbitrary. Individuals and families, associations and dependencies were so much material that the sovereign power consumed for its own purposes. The passengers, as it were, existed for the sake of the ship! Both Greece and Rome destroyed vital elements on which the prosperity of nations rests, and perished by the decay of families and the depopulation of their countries. A generous spirit prefers his country to be poor, weak and of no account, but *free*, rather than powerful, prosperous and enslaved. It is better to be the citizen of a humble commonwealth in the Alps, without the prospect of influence beyond a narrow frontier, than subject to a superb autocracy that overshadows half the world.[60]

CHAPTER 22

THE NEW WORLD

Discovery of Columbia Article #036
October 4, 2001

In 1492, Columbus sailed the ocean blue. And the discovery made all the difference in the world! Even as he sailed, he had a sense of great purpose beyond his own person—beyond the interests of his country even. Columbus had vision, faith and idealism. His crew, however, was rough, experienced, practical, and some were the dregs of society. They didn't have a lot of personal loyalty toward him, even if Columbus did have his mission and charter straight from the King and Queen of Spain. His crew were on the verge of mutiny, when someone cried, "Land, ho!" Columbia was in sight. Columbus was right: the world was round.

An accident gradually displaced the name Columbia for the New World. Even though one finds reference to Columbia centuries after discovery, the favored name became "America," because a mapmaker labeled it such. The pen is indeed mighty (if people read). The Library of Congress recently pledged $10 million to purchase the first map bearing the name "America" published in 1507. A German mapmaker compiled discoveries made in the late 1400s and early 1500s, to update his maps and spread the latest knowledge of geography. One of the early explorers was Amerigo Vespucci, who visited the Western Hemisphere in 1501 and 1502—a decade after Columbus' first trip. But the mapmaker thought Amerigo had been first, so he labeled the new continents after him.

Poor Columbus. He was the instrument of something great, but he didn't get the credit until after he was dead. The Lord works in mysterious ways. Not only that, but Columbus didn't really know where he was when he was alive and kicking. Native Americans are called "Indians" now, because Columbus thought he was somewhere near the coast of India.

That would have been about right, except that he underestimated the size of the world and ran into an unknown and very big roadblock—between Europe and the short trade routes to Asia Columbus thought he would find. This New World meant there was another ocean still to cross, in order to get to Asia. The 1507 map is the first to label a separate Pacific Ocean. The Atlantic Ocean is small by comparison.

Now one presumes the Indians knew they were there, even before Columbus told them. So "discovery" is a relative term. The year 1492 marks Europe's discovery of America, as well as the Indians' discovery of European man. The year 1492 is also significant in world history, because King Ferdinand and Queen Isabella expelled the Muslims and Jews from Spain. This ensured that Europe would be Christian and that Europeans coming to the New World would conquer in the name of country, and in the name of Christ.

Columbus began what became a frantic European race of "discovery" and exploration in the New World. European rivals Spain, Portugal, England and France rushed to obtain a place here. Spain of course had the jump on the rest of Europe, and all the early successes. A northern province owned by Spain, however, would break away—the Netherlands or Dutch would eventually buy Manhattan Island from the Indians and lodge New Amsterdam, which later became New York when the English bought out the Dutch. England was a very late bloomer in the New World, having tried and failed on numerous occasions to start a colony. Finally, the English succeeded at two modest locations: Jamestown, Virginia in 1607; and Plymouth, Massachusetts in 1620. These would begin the North American colonies of England, and nascent North and South of our United States and *American* heritage.

Spain's interest in North America was mainly to keep the English and French at bay. Spain set up a northern buffer zone, a region of forts and missions in the American Southwest to protect its lucrative prize further south. By 1600, Spain was extracting large amounts of gold and silver from mines all over Central and South America, as well as profits from sugar plantations in the Caribbean. Each year Spanish treasure ships ferried the bullion. It was transported by land to the Caribbean coast and put in ships bound for Spain. An expedition from Acapulco also sailed annually to the Philippines, returning with Asian spices and other trade goods. England would play catch-up for more than a century in North America, establishing its empire on a different, but more enduring long-term basis. We know the English turtle won the race, but Columbus deserves his credit.

Founding of New England Article #037
o/a August 30, 2001

In the 17th century, the leading empires of Europe went about carving up the New World. Their motives were varied, some despicable and some quite lofty. If we reduce most of them into categories called God, Gold and Glory, you begin to see what I mean. While Spain most clearly evinced the latter two, and everyone knows the English sought religious freedom, those are gross oversimplifications. Spanish missions served a dual purpose of fortification and care/conversion of the Indian. The Spanish ultimately established legal protection for Indians within its system too, whereas the English kept Indians outside domestic legal protections by establishing frontiers of exclusion. The English did go about establishing New Israel in New England, but they also desired and acquired land and established commerce for profit as much as piety. Moreover, the Puritan dream was sullied some, by Salem's famous panic over witches in 1691-3.

Still it would be hard to find a more beautiful vision, than that which launched New England—and America. Governor John Winthrop captured it in a sermon he delivered aboard his ship *Arbella*. Before his followers could even touch shore, they were thoroughly instructed in "A Modell of Christian Charity" (1630). The model was covenantal, devoted to constructing a community at Massachusetts Bay Colony based upon the word of God:

> Now the only way to . . . provide for our posterity, is to follow the counsel of Micah, 'to do justly, to love mercy, to walk humbly with our God.' For this end, we must be knit together . . . as one man. We must entertain each other in brotherly affection. We must be willing to abridge ourselves of our superfluities, for the supply of others' necessities. We must uphold a familiar commerce together in all meekness, gentleness, patience and liberality. We must delight in each other; make others' conditions our own; rejoice together; mourn together; labor and suffer together, always having before our eyes our commission and community in the

> work, as members of the same body. So shall we keep the unity of the spirit in the bond of peace . . . .

Indeed, Winthrop not only had a way with words—he lived what he preached. He knew what it was to mourn together: his small son Henry drowned in a river within a few days of their arrival. When Winthrop's wife Margaret arrived the following spring, she brought news that two more of their children had died, including the newborn baby daughter he never saw. Winthrop also knew what it was to sacrifice: he paid out his fortune for the colony's provision and re-supply, and he devoted the remainder of his life to the colony's success.

> John Winthrop remained confident that God would see them through. As he wrote in his shipboard sermon: The Lord will be our God, and delight to dwell among us, as His own people, and will command a blessing upon us in all our ways . . . . We shall find that the God of Israel is among us, . . . when He shall make us a praise and glory that men shall say of succeeding plantations, 'the Lord make it like that of New England!' For we must consider that we shall be as a city upon a hill. The eyes of all people are upon us.

And so they were, and so they have remained. Ronald Reagan was the last president to explicitly reference this 'Shining City upon a Hill'—a reference that originally comes from Matthew 5:14, which has come to mean everything good America hopes to be or strives to become.

Americans managed to carry forth the Puritan banner into the 18th century and beyond: the sense of special mission, as well as the work ethic and self-discipline that goes with it. American experience would prove to be exceptional in this regard. Today Europe and England—indeed the rest of the world—look upon us for leadership and example. In large measure, this is because the Puritan vision embraced that role. The Puritan institutions of church, family, and community also evolved along lines that are uniquely *American*. The Puritan Fathers deserve a place of honor in our history, for their idealism and struggle—even if results did not always live up, in their time or ours.

Enlightenment and Great Awakening Article #038
October 11, 2001

Two broad sets of ideas largely determined worldview in 18th century America prior to the American Revolution. While it is true that the Enlightenment more thoroughly influenced the Colonial elite, and the Great Awakening was most influential amongst common people, both found their nexus in America. Both influenced the Declaration of Independence, the Constitution, and the Early Republican period. The phenomenon was not inevitable, since the two sets of ideas were often antagonistic in Europe—particularly during the French Revolution. In America, piety and political philosophy mixed, Reason and Revelation married.

The Enlightenment was centered in Europe but came to the Colonies in books and from the travel of wealthy and influential citizens. It began in the 1690s but had its heyday between 1720 and 1780. Locke, Newton and Blackstone figured prominently in England; Hume and Adam Smith in Scotland; Montesquieu, Rousseau, Voltaire, Descartes in France; and Kant in Germany. Clearly all these folks in the same room would not produce agreement on much. Nevertheless, the Enlightenment held to a central tenet: the power of human reason to understand laws of nature, society, government, etc., and to direct progress in those areas. New assumptions dawned upon man's consciousness: that man had the ability to control his environment; that man possessed immense rational faculty or cognitive ability; that objective Truth existed and that man could approach, if not actually know it completely. The Enlightenment naturally propelled men towards invention and the scientific method. Benjamin Franklin and Thomas Jefferson were leading proponents of Enlightenment ideas and lifestyle in the Colonies and after Independence.

The Great Awakening was centered in America. Indeed, except for the involvement by British evangels in the Colonies, the Great Awakening was an American phenomenon—arguably the first to provide some common experience amongst all Colonies. It began in the 1720s and peaked between 1740 and 1775. The Great Awakening affected most church denominations and helped knit the Eastern seaboard together socially. It witnessed the resurgence of old school Calvinism, so it had doctrinal affinity to earlier Puritanism. But what distinguished the Great Awakening were its new technique of revivalism, and its emphasis on itinerant preaching to backcountry areas and slave communities. This is what brought Christianity to the slaves and to backwoods pioneers. This is what challenged the staid Anglicanism of Virginia and gave rise to the Baptists. Indeed, the challenge posed to established churches by new preachers had the positive effect of reinvigorating faith in old churches too.

When preachers like George Whitefield or Jonathan Edwards came to town or to the countryside, a 20-mile radius might be cleared completely of people. By word of mouth, the news spread and farmers dropped their implements and packed their families into wagons to go hear the Gospel! Thousands heard the Word for the first time; or else, they let it penetrate their hearts fully. America steeled its character, a character of righteousness for the Revolution to come. Although Harvard, William and Mary, and Yale had been founded by Congregationalists before the Great Awakening, Old and "New Lights" of New England, as well as Old and "New Sides" of the Middle Colonies, proceeded to found Princeton (1746), Columbia (1754), Brown (1764), Rutgers (1766), and Dartmouth (1769). They did it to produce clergy, as well as learned men of faith and faithful men of learning.

The Enlightenment and Great Awakening reinforced each other in America. The cooperation between them produced some of America's greatest institutions of higher learning. That's why it is so unfortunate that many universities today incline towards a studied hostility to religion and to the religious impulse. In our Founders' day, we were likely to conclude that man's ability to control his environment (and to properly steward it) depended on his ability to discover and to understand God's laws—His laws of physics and math and history, as much as His law of Love. Truth and the Laws of Nature and God's Law all came together. Men might well reason, and reason well. But God sets the standards we seek and defines Reason "out of the amplitude of His pure affection."

CHAPTER 23

Voicing Unrest/Declaring Freedom

Federalism Key Element in American Tradition Article #093
o/a May 09, 2003

Federalism must be ranked along with Religion and the Constitution itself as a particularly key element of American political tradition. As fixed as the Constitution was and should be in order to serve as parameter and framework for the legitimate exercise of political power in this country, there has always been room for friendly (and sometimes not so friendly) dispute over points requiring interpretation. Indeed, differences of interpretation and understanding about the Bible characterize relations between denominations that nonetheless do find common ground in a broad religious tradition. Similarly, Hamilton and Jefferson found much to disagree about concerning the Constitution's "necessary and proper" clause. Still, Hamiltonians and Jeffersonians found common ground in the federal republican tradition. The point I wish to make is not about differences but about agreement. Federalism in theory is the crux of American republican consensus. To abandon it is to leave the tradition altogether, just as if one's co-religionist suddenly gave up his or her belief in a Higher Being. The nonbeliever might still be able to locate himself in the broad spectrum of world (and Western) philosophies but would certainly be outside Judeo-Christian religious tradition. The "nonbeliever" in dual sovereignty would likewise still find himself in the broad political panoply of Europe but not in American federal, constitutional republican tradition. It is for that reason that I find tremendous justification for the argument that Americans no longer live in their own country, to the extent that government no longer operates by what were the defining characteristics of American federalism. Furthermore, this is an extremely recent development, built upon Progressivism and the New Deal but not completed until after the Great Society. It is this development that has helped to reenergize variant strands of conservatism, including nativist populism and neo-secessionism.

Simply defined, federalism is the division of authority and function between and among the national government and the various state governments. As such, it is at the very heart of our most pressing Constitutional concerns, just as it has frequently been at the center of political controversies before the Civil War and since the New Deal. Historically speaking, the locus of power vis-à-vis states and federal government has *shifted* in practical and juridical terms. In general, the locus of power has shifted over time from the states to the federal government. However, the nationalist liberal insistence on subjugating the states, especially over the last 30 years, has reawakened many Americans to just what is at stake. Indeed, more Americans are paying attention to the Founders' rationale for the original federalist construct. The Founders realized that the potential bureaucrat and potential tyrant would always be around. We cannot eliminate the flaws of human character through fiat, but we may indeed magnify them, if bad ideas or motives gain access to super-ordinate power. Hence, to limit the scope for the generic exercise of power by the federal government is the only guarantee we have that liberty will survive and that the better aspects of human nature will reproduce themselves and grow somewhere in the Union.

Key to understanding the Founders' intent is their fervent faith in the minimalist state and the ultimate sovereignty of the people. The Founding Fathers conceived of government as a necessary evil. If men were angels, wrote Madison, they would have no need of government. Moreover, since no angels were available to rule, government required checks and balances. The Founders did not value government per se; they valued freedom. They did not value what government could do for them, but what they could do for themselves in an environment characterized by ordered liberty. Government was simply needed to *protect* the maximum possible extent of what they valued most, their *liberty*: liberty to pray and to praise, to minister and to enjoy fellowship, to tithe and to serve, to 'work out one's own salvation with fear and trembling,' and to fulfill the purpose of life, *as if there were one*; liberty to love, to wed, to raise children in safety, to nurture, and to pass on a goodly inheritance; liberty to work, to build, to produce, to achieve and to succeed. The word federalism comes from the Latin root *foedus*, which means covenant. The Founding Fathers recognized that the way people think and relate to one another is the most fundamental feature in the whole process of actual governance. Hence federalism was and is more than just a form; it evidences the Founders' most basic assumption concerning human affairs, namely, its grass roots nature. Localities create covenantal relationships with God and with each other, which preclude all *but* a limited role for governments, especially at the national level.

Such is the kind of democracy consistent with republicanism, with federalism, and with the Constitution according to the Founders' vision. It is not the same thing as a national plebiscite. The Founders held a negative view of government that recognized no legitimate power of government to confer, only a delegated power to coerce within the confines of its proper role and limited function. Individuals were prior to society, societies prior to the state, States prior to the federal government; the Lord prior to all creation. Moreover, since the Founders believed in a minimalist state, only specifically enumerated powers were delegated to the central government. The Bill of Rights—including the Tenth Amendment—reinforced the particular form our system of dual or divided sovereignty would take. Natural liberty resided with the people, tempered only by limited powers delegated through the aegis of the States, to the federal government. Under the Constitution, the powers of the federal government, including those of Congress, are *delegated* by the people, *enumerated* in the document, and thus *limited* in scope.

Bill of Rights and the States — Article #095
o/a May 09, 2003

Given the nature of American federalism, the Bill of Rights did not apply to the States per se. Every State already had its own bill of rights when it joined the Union. The first ten amendments to the Constitution were designed by people of the States to curb potential abuse of power by the *federal* government and to expressly limit the power delegated to it. Remember, States had to ratify the Constitution, and it was the Bill of Rights that had been the most important Federalist concession to gain Anti-Federalist support. The people wanted the benefits a stronger central government would accrue, even the stabilization of state economies and the waning of certain democratic excesses to which states were prone. They were skeptical, however, lest the new federal government grow too powerful and threaten the liberty they already enjoyed in their states.

On this basis, if it were *ever* Constitutional in States for children to pray in public schools, then it *remains* Constitutional, barring a change to the Constitution itself. This is true, even if all fifty states changed their *laws* to make it *illegal* to do so. Likewise, if it were *ever* Constitutional for separate State societies to make laws regulating abortion, then it is *ever* Constitutional for them to do so, unless the Constitution is amended or a revolution ensues for that purpose. Punishment that was neither cruel nor unusual under the original Constitution may not become *un*constitutional, simply because the mores of the people change and local laws regulating punishments change. In other words, *people must be Constitutionally able to change their mores back again.* A State must be able to Constitutionally revert to a previously Constitutional position. It is absurd to think that if George Washington were here today, he would be unable to Constitutionally do half the things he could have done when the Constitution read exactly the same. Mind you, I am *not* suggesting that laws might not or should not be different, but laws should not *have* to be different, if Constitutional amendment does not follow temporal changes in the law. It is improper and *un*constitutional for laws to change through the judicial edict of unelected, black-robed politicians. Federal judges do not have the power to suppress a social experiment they decry, whether the social position taken by a given State is old or new. Moreover, it is unconstitutional to dismantle the federalist edifice of government based on dual federal-state sovereignty or to render effective delineation of state sovereignty subject to federal edict.

The Civil War did not change our inherently conservative system of government based on a written constitution and dual sovereignty. The Tribunal of Arms settled two questions that had plagued the country from its inception—slavery and secession. Northern victory meant slavery was abolished; in addition, secession as a legal, *peaceful* alternative was denied within the organic framework of the Constitution. Except for discrete changes, the relationship of restored States to the federal government remained the same as it always had been. The decline of federalism is not the product of the Civil War but the twentieth century—of plebeian democracy, judicial activism, the decline of cultural values, and in particular, government income taxing authority. During the first 125 years of America's existence, only six major federal agencies came into existence. After passage of the income tax Amendment and the Federal Reserve Act in 1913, federal agencies were born at a rate of one a year since then. America launched 88 new agencies in the last 80 years after needing six for the previous 125 years. It is time now for States to become the laboratories of liberty and the cradles of culture they once were and to stop behaving like rubber-stamp administrative entities of the federal government. In fact, an important theoretical point we can draw from the Founding Federalists, including Hamilton, is that sovereign states bear responsibility in the federal system to police the actions of its agent, the federal government, to insure that liberty and property of its citizens are not infringed. The relatively weak individual needs his or her state government to intercede or *interpose* on the individual's behalf. Today that function is all but inoperative, and individuals are left to the mercy of big government. Unfortunately, big governments make for small citizens. States should help political parties rediscover common ground in their discourse. States can, in effect, restore political debate to its proper context by recognizing limits to legitimate federal activity based on the dual nature of sovereignty in American political tradition.

The Flag and the Republic for Which It Stands Article #401
o/a April 17, 2009

The Flag was defined by the Second Continental Congress 14 June 1777 meeting in Philadelphia. The Flag of the United States would have thirteen stripes alternating red and white, and the "union" in the upper left would contain thirteen white stars in a blue field representing the new constellation. Congress subsequently determined that upon the admission of a new State, its own star would be added to the union on the next Fourth of July succeeding admission. Thirteen stripes continue to signify the thirteen original colonies, which became the first states of an independent federal Republic. As you can imagine, the 100th birthday of the Flag in 1877 was quite an occasion considering the nation united had barely survived War Between the States. Indeed, the year 1877 would mark the end of military occupation and "Reconstruction" in the South. To commemorate the Flag's centennial, the U.S. Government requested that it be flown from all public buildings and from that time, unofficial Flag Day celebrations continued each year. In the 1890s it was popular in Philadelphia for schoolchildren to gather at Independence Square or near the Betsy Ross House to celebrate the Flag's birthday. To this day, the Commonwealth of Pennsylvania is the only state where Flag Day is a public holiday, although the day is observed to honor the Flag in all 50 states.

October 12, 1892 was the 400th Anniversary of the discovery of America, so that particular Columbus Day celebration was very much anticipated and planned for. In September that year, a Boston-based youth magazine called *The Youth's Companion* published the first rendition of what would become the Pledge of Allegiance. When Columbus Day rolled around the following month, some 12 million school children across the nation recited the words. Originally the pledge was to "my Flag," but so many immigrants had come and were coming to the country by the late nineteenth/early twentieth century there was justifiable concern that some might mistake the meaning! In 1923 "my Flag" became "the Flag of the United States," and the following year it became "the Flag of the United States of America." Also in 1923 citizens who gathered for the first National Flag Conference in Washington, D.C. not only amended language of the Pledge, but also codified guidelines for "unofficial" proper display and respect for the Flag. Their National Flag Code served as basis for what became public law, adopted by Congress in 1942 and contained in Title 36 of the United States Code. The Pledge was included in that code and so gained official sanction. A year later the Supreme Court ruled that school children could not actually be *forced* to recite the Pledge, although virtually every schoolchild did.

The last change in the Pledge of Allegiance occurred on Flag Day 1954, when the words "under God" were added. President Dwight D. Eisenhower remarked, "In this way we are reaffirming the transcendence of religious faith in America's heritage and future; in this way we shall constantly strengthen those spiritual weapons which forever will be our country's most powerful resource in peace and war." The resultant thirty-one words comprise an individual profession of loyalty and devotion, not only to the Flag but to an American ideal and way of life: *I pledge allegiance to the Flag of the United States of America, and to the Republic for which it stands: one Nation under God, indivisible, with Liberty and Justice for all.*

The insertion of the words "under God" was particularly key and fundamental—and a proper change, although most advocates argued the words were implied from the beginning and generally understood in much the same way as "my Flag" had always meant "the Flag of the United States of America." Notice, however, that while many people will recite the Pledge with a pause after Nation, there is in fact no comma there. The words "under God" modify Nation and qualify the word indivisible. To Boston educators who wrote the word "indivisible" into the first draft appearing in *The Youth's Companion*, it may have meant something more than the words "under God," either implicitly or explicitly. To Southerners, however, the words "under God" mean and have always meant the most. Indeed, it is only if and as the Nation remains a moral compact—sanctioned, blessed, protected, in accordance with Him as it were—that any manmade Union or governmental construct can or should be considered indivisible.

CHAPTER 24

Reflections of Our Early Republic

Wars of 1812 and 2001 Article #039
September 20, 2001

The War of 1812, sometimes called "the Second War of Independence," was fought between the United States and Great Britain 1812-1815. The British struggle against Napoleon's France led to British action against neutral American shipping starting around 1803. The British Navy not only stopped neutral American shipping, they also increasingly boarded ships to seek "deserters"—sometimes impressing American seamen into service for Britain. Economic coercion such as embargoes by Jefferson and Madison failed, as badly as did their attempts to negotiate. The British also incited Indians along the Great Lakes frontier against American settlements. War sentiment grew in the United States, especially in the West and South. It was mostly a matter of national honor that war was finally declared, but military preparedness was not what it should have been. American forays into Canada proved disastrous. Only the small American Navy performed well.

In 1814, with France collapsing, the British launched major attacks against the United States. Washington was occupied—President James Madison and the Congress were forced to flee. It is said the First Family literally left dinner on the table, and British officers sat down to enjoy it. Dolly Madison managed to take some of the White House china, which is fortunate, since the British burned the White House and other public buildings in Washington, DC. British setbacks in Baltimore, on Lake Champlain, and at the Battle of Plattsburg Bay led the British to concentrate on a negotiated settlement rather than to continue the war. Indeed, it was during and after the unsuccessful British bombardment of Fort McHenry at Baltimore, that Francis Scott Key wrote down the words to our national anthem. His amazed and joyful vision of the American flag standing against that smoky sky 'the morning after' in September 1814 was like ours in September 2001. Old Glory stood then, despite the devastation of bombs and rockets; it stands today at the base of what was the World Trade Center in New York, having withstood the devastation of deliberate airplane crashes and the collapse of modern architectural marvels.

The Treaty of Ghent ending the War of 1812 required the return of territory seized by both sides. It was signed in December, prior to the Battle of New Orleans in January 1815. But news of the battle and the peace treaty reached Washington and many people at about the same time. Andrew Jackson's stunning tactical victory looked like it had determined the war's entire outcome. Jackson himself became an overnight sensation and a military hero—with implications beyond the war itself. Moreover, secessionist sentiment had started to influence politics in New England. Madison's stringent embargo hurt the New England economy disproportionately. "Blue light" Federalists were even accused of cavorting with the enemy and signaling British ships. New England delegates, chiefly from Massachusetts, Rhode Island and Connecticut, met in a secret session in Hartford, Connecticut—practically on the eve of victory. They adopted a series of resolutions critical of the War and even voted to nullify pending legislation, should it pass. The Federalist Party collapsed after victory in the War of 1812, discredited in the eyes of the public.

The War of 1812 and the subsequent experience of the Federalist Party established a strong precedent in this country that all political parties would pull together in the event of war. Congress would support the President; the people would support their Congress. In peacetime, political parties debate foreign policy and domestic policy alike. Indeed, it is likely that wars imply certain foreign policy or intelligence or security failures. We may well ask ourselves why others hate us so much. Have we truly followed George Washington's advice not to become too partial to any country at the expense of others—never mind getting into 'entangling alliances'? (I'm grateful, of course, that NATO and other friends abroad have expressed solidarity with America). But are we really the honest broker we claim to be in the Middle East? There will be time for reassessments of foreign policy later—and all the debates a political junkie can handle. To paraphrase Patrick Henry, however, today 'we are not Virginians,' or New Yorkers—or Texans merely. We are Americans. When Americans are killed and war declared, Americans close ranks to vanquish the enemy. Hardship and sacrifice may come. The Nation of Terrorism is no less an enemy than those we've fought before. Then as now, there is no substitute for victory.

The aftermath of the War of 1812 ushered in a great time for America. We finally attained security from serious European threats to independence. Indeed, within a few years, we started a friendship with the British government that blossomed into the special relationship we enjoy today with the British people. The economy started to boom. Domestic politics became more consensus-oriented. The period coinciding with James Monroe's two terms (before the so-called Age of Jackson) is still known as the "Era of Good Feelings." It is up to our generation like generations before, to preserve and defend the greatest Republic in history and the brightest promise for a free and prosperous mankind tomorrow.

Tribune of the People Article #040
October 25, 2001

Towards the end of the Era of Good Feelings, politics started to take on less statesmanlike consensus. The 1820s witnessed the formation of a split in the old Jeffersonian Democratic-Republican party. By 1840, politics in every state was conducted on a new two party basis. Indeed, emergent parties manifested themselves first as rival leadership groups: John Quincy Adams led the faction known as the National Republicans; dissident Democrats aligned with Andrew Jackson. The two camps vied for respective Presidential candidates in 1824, but the electoral votes became divided between four candidates (Jackson, J.Q. Adams and two regional candidates—William Crawford of Georgia and Henry Clay of Kentucky) with no clear majority. Clay threw his support to Adams, despite instructions from his home State to the contrary. When Adams then selected Clay as his Secretary of State, Jackson supporters raised the cry of "corrupt bargain!" Clay even fought a duel (though bloodless) with John Randolph of Roanoke over the matter, in 1826. Clay did agree philosophically with Adams, more than with the other candidates. Both became Whigs during the 1830s. Nevertheless, the charge of "corrupt bargain!" poisoned the political atmosphere and rendered J.Q. Adams's administration lame duck. Jackson swept into power in 1828 after the dirtiest campaign in US history.

Ironically, the acrimony of the campaign and the years that followed is associated with a fundamental political change in our system—from a more republican and elite order to one more thoroughly democratic, which celebrates the common man. Jackson and society in the Age that bears his name (c. 1828-1845) were prone to violence and motivated by prejudice; at the same time, however, they were democratic and egalitarian. The fact that these characteristics flow together in American history, should give pause to those who pursue more direct participation or claim special virtue for majoritarian democracy. Deliberative processes and representative democracy, the protection of minority rights, and the participation by uncommon men—these were more highly prized by the Founding generation. Thomas Jefferson in fact objected to Jackson's bid for the Presidency in 1824. Modern Democrats trace their lineage directly to Jackson; whereas, Jefferson belongs equally to modern Democrats and Republicans. Jefferson would find more philosophic resonance, however, with the modern Republican Party—particularly in the conservative South. Jackson was a radical who characteristically recurred to force, whether it be to the force of personal will, to the force of government, or to the force of arms.

Opponents of Jackson became Whigs. The name sounds strange today, but it was an allusion to the English Whig opponents of the Tories and Crown during America's War for Independence. American Whigs opposed Jackson's concentration of executive authority and said it resembled the use of a royal-like prerogative. Indeed, Jackson used his veto power more than all previous Presidents combined. Jackson chose not to utilize his Cabinet officers in the traditional way, preferring instead to seek advice from a small group of cronies known as the "Kitchen Cabinet." Jackson also ushered in the Spoils system, removing government officeholders wholesale if they worked for previous administrations. Jackson's approach belittled the need for continuity, expertise or predictability in government. Worse still, Jackson selectively refused to enforce laws or court decisions interpreting the law. This led to the infamous Trail of Tears, a forced removal during winter of the peaceful Cherokee tribe. The Supreme Court sided with the Cherokee, but Jackson found it expedient to enforce the will of the People of Georgia. On the other hand, he didn't find it expedient to enforce the will of the People of South Carolina during the Nullification Crisis over high tariffs in 1832. He blasted the very notion of State Sovereignty by backing the Force Act (1833) in Congress.

Jackson liked to call himself the "Tribune of the People"; the President is the only position in government elected by the people at large—so Jackson would mandate popular will and wisdom as only he could see fit. The mishandling of the Nullification Crisis encouraged strident political positions to take root, which dramatically reinforced a developing North-South rift in the country. There would be strong ties between nullifiers of 1832-3 and the secessionist fire-eaters of 1860-1. Democracy helped cause the War Between the States. It infused politics with passion, at the expense of civility, compromise and reason. Bloody civil war broke out in Kansas long before the Lower South seceded. Consider that when you hear modern foreign policy experts declare, that peace is assured if democracy spreads to other nations—the erroneous assumption being that democracies will never fight each other.

Look Away [Yankee] Land Article #041
November 15, 2001

Between 1820 and 1850, fundamental economic and social transformations occurred in these United States of America. Transformations amount to a leaving, and the overall effect was to leave who we were to become something else. Nowhere was this truer than in the North, where most of the qualitative change took place. Like all transformations in a country, change begets a spirit of freshness, hope and high ideals. At the same time, however, it begets anxiety, social stresses, a sense of bewilderment and insecurity. Rapid change always presents a political system with challenges, to contain and to constructively channel the forces at play. Sometimes change begets defensive or reactive movements, which seek to reinvigorate "old times not forgotten." Indeed, we had all these things during the so-called "Middle Period" in American history known to most as the antebellum years—*ante,* because it came *before* the Civil War. The Civil War is still that singular and catastrophic event that defines us as a People more than any other, save the American Revolution itself. It is the only time in our history that the two-party system broke down and could not contain conflicting forces; the only time the Constitution was suspended in key respects; the only time that military occupation supplanted consent of the governed, in order to keep people and States inside "the Union."

For the first time in our Republic's history, we established the precedent (still not actually codified in the Constitution) of a political marriage without provision for divorce. The United States could secede from Great Britain. Vermont could secede out of New Hampshire and New York. The federal government would recognize West Virginia, carved from out of Virginia. Texas could secede from Mexico and join the United States. Texas could not, however, decide to get back out. The irony is that while it is common knowledge the South tried to secede and then lost the War Between the States, it is "horse sense" that explains how in fact the North left the Union first.

Between 1820 and 1850, changes occurred that made parting between North and South likely. The nineteenth century's decade of the 50s is characterized by a worsening political crisis that leads to war. War is, after all, a Tribunal of Arms—a continuation of politics by different means. If two sides have fundamental differences and reject compromise, one side either leaves the room or the two sides fight. If one side won't let the other side leave, then fighting is all but inevitable. What many folks don't realize is that the South simply refused to change the way the majority in the North *wanted* them to change. Southerners preferred to keep and to expand the institution of slavery, rather than to adopt a system of "wage slavery." They rejected factory-driven tempo for white labor and reaffirmed the plantation-driven cotton economy, which made all white men (potentially at least) masters. In the Southern view of the day, capitalists were masters without duties or responsibilities. Southerners pointed out the squalid and unsafe conditions that northern workers endured (few of the protections labor has today existed). Southerners argued the black slave was better off than most workers in the North. Planters provided shelter, clothing, food, time off on weekends, and basic health care to their slaves. Slaves were valuable assets to slaveholders. The Irish and German immigrants who poured into the North enjoyed no such provisions, and labor supply was so great as to be virtually expendable.

Of course, Southerners missed the basic point of the enormity, over which they lorded. Even if a slave were cared for like the finest Arabian steed, a person is not a horse. There is no recorded case of a poor northern worker requesting to become a slave. The prospect of advancement and upward mobility, the sense of a personal, self-directed destiny—for the better or worse that might come—these drove northern workers to survive hardships, which at times were worse than what many slaves encountered.

Religion in the South became more conservative in the antebellum years, as northern attitudes liberalized. Major church denominations broke into northern and southern denominations before the country divided politically into warring camps. The Jeffersonian agrarian model, as well as the Jacksonian creed of the common (white) man rising to great heights—these informed the South's vision of the future, arguably a regionally (if not national) *traditional* vision. Meanwhile, the North urbanized and experienced some early industrialization. The North built its transportation and communications infrastructures for modern, fast-paced transactions. The North invented a modern rat race that we have since perfected almost everywhere, including in the *new* New South. The North embraced the commercial ethos, the market economy, and the materialism (some say greed) that went with it. The term "Almighty Dollar" was coined in the antebellum period, to describe the new god of the North. Meanwhile, the South supplied its cotton to northern textile mills and paid the duties that disproportionately fell on her, which filled the federal coffers—which then paid to build the North's great infrastructure—an advantage that helped it win the War. The aftermath of that War plunged the South into a century of poverty. No blame or regret, however, is worthy. But exactly who left whom, remains a most interesting question.

CHAPTER 25

After the Great Divide

The Deep, Deep South Article #026
o/a June 14, 2001

The other day I ran across a *U.S. News & World Report* piece from 1995. OK, so I'm a little behind in my reading—and you thought your bathroom or coffee table stacks were bad! Well, I found the article interesting if not quite current. Sometimes old news—and old history—is better written, because it is not as politically charged. Over the last couple of years, you've no doubt heard the row over the Confederate Battle Flag symbol. South Carolina removed it from its State House. Georgia reduced its prominence on their State flag. Texas removed plaques honoring Confederate dead, because the horrific symbol were engraved with the inscriptions!—And the NAACP threatens economic boycott wherever the symbol persists or the flag waves. Watch out Brazil: your membership in the Organization of American States could be in jeopardy. The Brazilian nut industry could fall victim to nuts "north of the border."

Jack Epstein had this to report from Americana, Brazil a few years back: "It could have been a soiree of Civil War buffs in Vicksburg or Savannah: Belles in hoop skirts danced the Virginia reel with men in Confederate gray as Rebel flags fluttered and giant speakers blared out "Dixie." Indeed, Scarlett and Rhett would have felt right at home, if only they could speak Portuguese. The occasion was [a] . . . reunion of the Fraternity of American Descendants, whose members meet every spring at an ancestral cemetery to celebrate their Southern roots with song, dance and food. Maintaining Southern ties is a challenge since most of the 100,000 Brazilians with Dixie-born ancestors speak little English and prefer beans and rice to grits and corn bread . . . .

"Brazil's Southern traditions began soon after the Civil War ended. Rather than endure Reconstruction, 40,000 ex-Confederates emigrated south—the biggest political exodus in U.S. history. Roughly half chose the Brazilian wilderness—partly because Brazil (until 1888) still allowed slavery but mainly because Emperor Pedro II, in hopes of building a cotton kingdom, subsidized their trips, exempted them from his draft, guaranteed them freedom of religion, and sold land for 22 cents an acre.

"Some *Confederados*, as they were called, tried to establish plantations along the Amazon. But tropical illnesses and giant cotton-eating ants ended most jungle settlements. Only one colony prospered—a town the settlers named Villa Americana, or 'American Town,' later shorted to Americana. The expatriates produced not only cotton, but also watermelons, peaches and pecans. Today, Americana (population: 200,000) is a thriving textile center, the only city in Brazil with a Confederate flag in its coat of arms.

"The Confederados' descendants are aware that the Confederate flag is viewed by some in the United States as a racist symbol. 'Here it merely represents the history of our ancestors,' said Noemia Pyles, the president of the fraternity and a descendant of a Confederate from Waco, Texas. Among the 1,500 revelers at the reunion was Paulo Roberto dos Santos, 35, a black police officer with a Confederate flag in the brim of his cowboy hat. 'For me,' he said, 'it just represents the cultural roots of my friends.'

"Among the Brazilians placing flowers in the cemetery of the Confederados and their descendants was Rose Lene Vaughan, 47, a pediatrician who visited the graves of her father and grandfather. Like many in the fraternity, she has never been to the land of her ancestors but feels close to it. 'We may not speak English, but we are U.S. Southerners. We will never let our culture die.'"

For everybody's edification, especially Yankees who might be reading good literature—I offer these closing reminders and thoughts. The central symbol of the Confederate Battle Flag is the cross. The colors are red, white and blue. It never flew over a single slave ship—though Old Glory flew on hundreds. I don't think less of the cross because a few have burned it in the past. I don't think less of the national flag, even if it were wrapped (on occasion) around stuff I won't justify. For the puny folks wanting an apology, please hold your breaths till it comes. The Confederate Battle Flag is as American as apple pie. History should also record that during the War Between the States, the American people had two presidents, like it or not.

Constitutional Regime Changes in American History Article #287
o/a March 09, 2007

People don't always consider the constitutional regimes in American history. The fact is the Constitution hasn't always been the same; rather, as organic law of the land it has been implemented in very distinctive ways in different eras. Not all the differences, moreover, are attributable to amendments to the Constitution, which you would expect to happen from time to time. One of the biggest divides between regimes occurred as a result of the War Between the States, miscalled the Civil War. In Kentucky or Kansas it was indeed arguably a civil war, but for the seceding States of the South or CONFEDERATE States of America (CSA) there was practical unanimity and a clear expression of the sovereign will of the people through every representative institution. It was hardly a rebellion, given that the political aim was simply to leave, not overturn the established order. The fiction of a Rebellion, as well as the invention of a supposed political Union without divorce suited the North's design for empire and justified its prosecution of war. Not surprisingly, the Constitutional regime that followed was not the same as it had been.

The locus of power as a practical matter, shifted from States to the General Government. Amendments to the Constitution then codified changes wrought on the battlefield, abolishing slavery and also seeking to confer civil rights and the franchise to four million freed slaves. Confederate president Jefferson Davis was released on bail after two years and never brought to trial. Political secession was never taken up in theory by the Supreme Court nor made unconstitutional by subsequent amendment; indeed, it still resides in the classical liberal worldview and political tradition of our Fathers where it always has been. The practical example of the War Between the States is that its mere attempt is fraught with danger: it pits the political will and power of contending sections more than it weighs constitutional principle or merits in a specific case. (Lesson learned). And yet the change in regime bore consistency—war decides matters rightly or wrongly, but it decides them when and if there's a victor. Notwithstanding military occupation during Reconstruction and the strong-arm tactics to "ratify" post-war amendments, abolition of slavery was almost universally accepted. Nursed and embittered though feelings in the South were, most understood the morally superior development that had taken place in that regard. The "peculiar institution" as slavery was called, became a relic of the Old South; racism as we know, persisted in virulent forms. The constitutional arguments for secession stood scrutiny, regardless. The regime change that occurred was manly nonetheless.

Not so at the next great fault line in constitutional regimes, when Progressives rewrote the Constitution. They contorted the meaning of words, abandoned textual definition and historic precedent; they favored social engineering and government activism, so they legislated from the bench and grew the federal government. While it is true that one may identify secondary "fissures," differences in phase, so to speak, of constitutional regimes (this Court did this and this Court did that), there are really just these two big ones. We've described the one coincident with the War Between the States. The other that occurred is coincident with the Progressive Era, culminating from a constitutional perspective with the New Deal *circa* 1937. We in effect live in the post-Progressive Constitutional regime shaped by what Progressive Justices and theorists did to the law. Conservative political successes in the Executive branch and Congress have done little to alter the condition of this regime. Change to the constitutional regime is preeminently a matter for the Supreme Court and States potentially to effect. The big-government prejudice enshrined by Progressives has been an influential tradition for nearly 100 years, and on key issues, it has been dominant for the past 70 years. There were 72 years from ratification of the Constitution (1789) to the War Between the States (1861), another 72 years from the end of the War (1865) to the New Deal (1937). If timing stays the same, we could be in for a major constitutional regime change in a couple of years—and it would be about time. If and when this happens, pray it is a peaceful transition and the result resembles the Early Republic more than Big Brother.

Progressive Disaster Article #072
o/a December 02, 2002

Today it isn't hard to point out the many good things achieved by Northern victory in the so-called Civil War. It's the safe and oh so politically correct thing to do. The end of the Old South's slave-based civilization is always worth celebrating, no matter how many babies get thrown out with the proverbial bathwater. What the liberal (and also neoconservative) historian fails to mark, more often than not, is the way in which the War Between the States actually gave rise to the Progressive Era and modern liberalism. The Pulitzer Prize winning author Louis Menand, makes the connection is his best-selling book (2001), *The Metaphysical Club*: secession enabled the North to set the terms for national expansion and economic direction. The wartime Congress established the first system of national taxation and national currency. The military defeat of the Confederacy made the Republican party dominant, and the Republicans of that day were champions of business, such that, for more than 30 years a strong central government protected and inordinately promoted industrial capitalism with few checks and balances. The ensuing conditions gave rise to new intellectual assumptions, ways of helping people cope with post-war, "modern" life in America—as well as with a cultural void left in the wake of that terrible War's victory and that terrible War's ruin.

During the Progressive Era which started in the 1890s, Americans turned markedly away from the natural rights theory of the nation's founding. The late nineteenth/early twentieth century social and political Progressive movement was marked by a new emphasis on relativism—the denial of objective truth and a corresponding "practical" doctrine that values can, do and probably *should* change over time. Adherents were found on the political right and left, but the left would shape the twentieth century after Progressivism's logical extremes. Woodrow Wilson, for instance, openly criticized the Declaration of Independence as being outdated, writing condescendingly that "citizens of this country have never got beyond the Declaration of Independence[!]" Imagine that. The idea that human beings have a nature! The idea they are endowed by their Creator with unalienable rights! How utterly primitive. Indeed, the rejection of the theory of natural rights altered common understanding of government's purpose, as well as the government's relationship to "its" people. A new understanding emerged and became the basis for modern liberalism. Today's liberals are starting to call themselves "progressive" again, and the label is logically and historically correct. Rush Limbaugh has argued that modern liberalism became the ascendant majority in the country by 1930. The majority lasted until 1994. Notwithstanding six more years of Clinton after that, liberalism has been fighting for its life from bastions of established power since then.

The election of 2002 validates a new conservative majority, and the liberals are flailing—unable to accept minority status. I recall that when Clarence Thomas was nominated for the Supreme Court, his professed belief in natural rights and natural law was treated as sheer guff. To liberal politicians, Thomas may as well have said the earth were flat. As for me, I'm sure of it! Not really—but if I want to believe it, at least I have that right. Freedom shouldn't mean that dictatorial educators and social engineers and people smarter than me get to program all our brains. Technically maybe they "can," but they don't have that right. If State governments ever say so under the federalist construct again, claiming the sovereignty that's due, i.e., reserved to the people or to the States respectively, a lot of "progressive" notions will no longer stand the test of time or light of day. Free people can say what's acceptable to them, and maybe values *can* change again—maybe even back into *truth*. You see, I've never quite got past the Declaration or the Constitution either.

As historians Thomas G. West and Douglas A. Jeffrey have observed, "If human beings are nothing on their own, it follows that they can do nothing on their own." Rather than the people delegating power to the government, the government empowers all those poor dear people. The Founders thought it should be enough for government to leave people alone and to protect people's rights by requiring others to do likewise. The government of the New Deal in the 1930s presumed all people were needy and helpless instead. So government proceeded to do everything for them, and to pick a few favorites along the way. Today's government worries about the needs and disabilities of racial minorities, homosexuals, the disabled, and women. It steals from Peter to pay Pauline. The denial of human nature leads to a radically different understanding of equality from what the Founders would recognize. Equality is no longer innate in terms of natural rights. Rather, it is something that must be produced by government through unequal treatment. Lyndon B. Johnson said as much in explicit language. The Great Society was all about redistribution, and no wonder. West and Jeffrey again: "Rather than being rightful claims to one's own possessions, rights in the new view are rightful claims to the resources of others. Thus, rather than speak as the Founders did of rights to life, liberty, and the pursuit of happiness, Americans today speak of rights to housing and education and medical care and food stamps."

Moreover, rights to the Founders inhere in individuals; whereas, today rights are often assigned to group membership (blacks, farmers, students, elderly, etc.). Did you catch that? Rights are *assigned* now, not seen as having existed prior to government but as being gifts from the benevolent and "Progressive/Progressives" state. Modern liberals believe it is acceptable to trammel the rights of some citizens to give benefits to others believed by government to be more worthy or needy. Conservatives call that pure "horse hockey." Equal conditions are not what equal rights are all about. Indeed, equal conditions imposed by the government, amounts to a denial of equal rights by definition! The Founders even believed that inheritance and heredity were matters of freedom of association protected by the First Amendment. Communism and socialism deserve the ash heap of history. Did I leave out progressivism? My mistake.

CHAPTER 26

Foundations of American Strength and Pride

History and Knowing Who We Are | Article #196
o/a April 19, 2005

The late and great historian, and Librarian of Congress Daniel Boorstin, said that trying to plan for the future without a sense of the past is like trying to plant cut flowers. It is critically important that we not cut our roots so to speak, and never learn to grow where we are. Unfortunately, you would think modern textbooks are written and published to kill any interest anyone would ever have in history! Most are dreary works, written by committee, often hilariously politically correct. Teachers too often have degrees in education but haven't mastered the subject of history or any other. Moreover, if they don't share a love of the subject, it is hard for students to catch that love. So as with many things, the simple antidote begins at home. Those of you who are parents and grandparents really should be taking children to historic sites, talking about those books in biography and history that you enjoyed, and about those characters in history that mean something to you. Talk about what it was like growing up "in the olden days," and children will pick up amazing amounts of information. More critically, they will develop empathy for those who lived before, and they will start to create impressions in mind and a sense of context they'll need to integrate further knowledge. The secret to teaching history and making it exciting is telling stories. Properly understood, history is a grand narrative—the story of man, literally *his story*.

By learning the history of our parents and grandparents, history comes alive, as it should. Consider that nothing ever really happened in the past, because nobody lived in the past. Jefferson, Adams, Washington weren't standing around saying, "Isn't it fascinating, living in the past?" No, they lived in the present the same as you or I. The difference was it was their present. And just as we don't know how things are going to turn out for us, they didn't either. And nothing ever had to happen the way it did. History could have gone off in any number of different directions in any number of different ways at any point along the way, just as your own life can. You never know. One thing leads to another. Nothing happens in a vacuum. Actions have consequences. It all sounds so self-evident, but it isn't—especially to a young person trying to understand life. That's what I mean by developing historical empathy, which has everything to do with today and so-called "relevant" topics. It is easy to stand on a mountaintop as an historian and find fault with people for why they did this or didn't do that, because we're not involved in it, we're not inside it, we're not confronting what we don't know—as everyone who preceded us always was.

There never was a truly self-made man or self-made woman either. Family, friends, rivals, and competitors—they've all shaped us. And so too have people we've never met, never known, because they lived long before us. They shaped us too—the people who composed the symphonies that move us; the painters, poets and authors who have written the great literature in our language. The laws we live by, the freedoms we enjoy, and the institutions we sometimes take for granted, are all the work of other people who went before us. Ingratitude is a shabby failing, and no less shabby born of ignorance. How can we not want to know about the people who have made it possible for us to live as we live, to have the freedoms we have, to be citizens of the greatest country of all time? It's not just a birthright. It is something others have struggled for, strived for, often suffered for, were often defeated for and died for—for us: Posterity and our generation. If it sounds like ancestor worship, it isn't. A bit of veneration, you bet.

Yet my celebration is tempered knowing full well those who wrote the Declaration of Independence that hot and fateful summer of 1776, weren't superhuman. Every one of the Founding Fathers had his flaws, his failings and weaknesses. Some ardently disliked others among them, and everyone did things in his life he regretted. But the central fact is they could and did rise to the occasion, these imperfect human beings. After all, we are not known only by our failings, by our weaknesses, by our sins (thank God). We are known by being capable of rising to the occasion and exhibiting, not just a sense of direction, but inspiration and incredible strength. The Greeks said that character is destiny, and history has confirmed that for me concerning both men and nations. Almost none of the other nations of the world know when they were born, but we do—we know exactly when we began and why we began and who did it. There's a line in a letter by John Adams to his wife Abigail that illustrates that special measure of character and destiny we are heir to. Writing home to his wife, he paraphrases a line out of the play *Cato*: "We can't guarantee success in this war, but we can do something better. We can deserve it." Now think how different that is from the attitude common today, when all that matters is success, being number one, getting ahead, getting to the top—however you betray or gouge or claw is immaterial. That line Adams wrote is saying that however the Revolutionary War turns out is in the hands of God. We can't control that, but we can control how we behave; and we can *deserve* success. May we always listen to the past and deserve our success, as fully as the Founders deserved theirs.[61]

Yankee Doodle Day Article #404
o/a June 28, 2009

The Fourth of July is the Yankee Doodle Day. For on this day in 1776 the Declaration of Independence passed the Second Continental Congress and our nation became independent from Great Britain. The Declaration is interestingly subtitled, "The Unanimous Declaration of the thirteen united States of America" (that's right, united is not capitalized). Elsewhere in the Declaration, however, it states, "That these United Colonies are, and of Right ought to be, Free and Independent States." In effect the Declaration of Independence is a declaration for the independence of thirteen nations *united* in the cause of Liberty.

The term Yankee Doodle probably dates back to the Seven Years' War—known in the English Colonies as the French and Indian Wars (1689-1763). A popular song amongst regular military units describing Americans, derided them as being disheveled, disorganized and simpleton. Indeed, "doodle" is a derivation from the Low German *dödel* meaning fool. Yankee (sometimes abbreviated Yank) resulted from a corruption of language and the Huron Indian pronunciation of the word English (*l'anglais* in French), which sounded like Yan-gee. The words were set to a popular nursery rhyme, "Lucy Locket." Accordingly "Yankee Doodle went to town a-riding on a pony," and then "He stuck a feather in his cap and called it macaroni." Macaroni in the middle 18th century was a dude, or fashionable person. So the joke was that these American Yankees believed that a feather in the hat was sufficient to make one the height of fashion, a real English Gentleman!

The funniest part about all this is that Americans picked up the tune themselves and started to love it. British and American troops during the Revolutionary War took turns changing lyrics and rubbing it in as it were. During the War Between the States, Southerners added their own lyrics and sang just as proudly, "There was Captain Washington upon a slapping stallion, a-giving orders to his men I guess there was a million." The Great Seal of the Confederacy actually has Washington on a slapping stallion. Southerners had no problem with being a Yankee Doodle, but as for being a Yank or plain Yankee (particularly when the term is prefaced), well that's something different!

The song "Yankee Doodle Boy" or "I'm a Yankee Doodle Dandy," is from a Broadway musical written by George M. Cohan dating back to 1904. The musical concerns the hard knocks of one Little Johnny Jones, a fictional American jockey who rides a horse named Yankee Doodle in the English Derby. The song became a patriotic standard and was performed again in the movie—a biographical film about George M. Cohan called "Yankee Doodle Dandy" and starring James Cagney. Production of the film had just begun when the attack on Pearl Harbor occurred, influencing the film's cast and crew to make an unabashedly uplifting and patriotic film, which they did in spectacular fashion. Release was timed for Memorial Day 1942.

Yankee Doodle these days and forever belongs to these United States. He's an archetype of the American character and a fun-loving, unpretentious one at that. Even foreigners recognize it, although they sometimes mistakenly refer to all Americans simply as "Yanks" or "Yankees," dropping the essential Doodle, ill advisedly in Dixie. On this Fourth of July, as if he needs encouragement and even if he doesn't, "Yankee Doodle keep it up, Yankee Doodle dandy, mind the music and the step, and [let] the girls be handy!" That's what he always does anyway, even when problems mount up as high as the national debt or taxes. He's always smiling and ever amazed at the sights he runs into. The country as it evolved after 1776, in scarcely more than a decade, became a compound republic with dual sovereignties and divided power between the federal government and states, such that, the Constitution drafted in 1787 capitalized the term "United States" as a proper noun for the new nation. Boy that Yankee Doodle Boy is still quite wide-eyed and thoroughly impressed with the fact! One only hopes he finds as many others at tea parties and venues all around, where once he went with Father "down to camp, along with Captain Gooding, and there [they] saw the men and boys, as thick as hasty pudding" all having a Yankee Doodle Day.

Memorial Day Matters Article #451
o/a May 23, 2010

Memorial Day was originally designated as the 30th of May, but starting in 1971 it has been held the last Monday in May creating a convenient 3-day weekend. Memorial Day is observed today as a public holiday dedicated to the memory of the fallen who died in service to their country in wartime. Its origin dates to the terrible War Between the States. The day was actually inaugurated in 1868 as a holiday on which graves of Civil War veterans serving the Union were decorated. The South did not recognize the day as such, but set aside separate days on which to decorate graves belonging to its Confederate veterans. Indeed, organized women's groups in the South had been decorating graves even before the end of the Civil War. Ironically the last Confederate Widow, Alberta S. Martin actually died on Memorial Day, 2004 in Alabama.

The word "memorial" (serving to help people remember some person or event) is ignored too often on Memorial Day by those of us who are the direct beneficiaries of thousands of men and women, who bore the ultimate sacrifice. It is perhaps a hard thing to come to grips with the fact that it is the willing sacrifice of life that has secured for us our blessed freedoms, and continues to do so every day. The least that we should do is to actively remember those who gave their all—our ancestors, family members, neighbors and loved ones who served in uniform and died in service defending and advancing our way of life. Traditionally we are invited each year on Memorial Day to do the following: to visit cemeteries and place flags or flowers on the graves of fallen heroes; to attend memorial services and other public events; to fly the U.S. Flag at half-mast until noon; to observe moments of silence for special reflection and remembrance; to renew pledges of support and aid to the widows and orphans of veterans, as well as to disabled veterans; and to salute the fallen and/or to play Taps in their honor (Taps is a bugle call written during the Civil War, which dates to 1862 and was used by both sides).

Memorial Day of course has its counterpart in other nations, and amongst the Western nations in particular there is a very similar ethos surrounding the honoring of the dead, who died for freedom and the safety of their homeland. One of the most famous poems of remembrance was written by Lieutenant Colonel John McCrae, MD (1872-1918), Canadian Army called "In Flanders Fields" and written in 1915. A beautiful response poem was written by Moina Belle Michael (1869-1944), a native Georgian and American professor, called "We Shall Keep The Faith" written in 1918. Moina Michael became known as the Poppy Lady after she conceived of the idea of using poppies (based on the poem by McCrae) as a symbol of remembrance for those who had served in World War I. A U.S. Postage Stamp was even issued in her honor. Together the two poems do much to bring to mind the importance of Memorial Day, its meaning and why the day matters so much.

John McCrae in his third stanza writes: "To you from failing hands we throw/The torch; be yours to hold it high. /If ye break faith with us who die/We shall not sleep, though poppies grow/ In Flanders fields." Moina Michael writes this rejoinder in the first stanza of her poem: "Oh! You who sleep in Flanders Fields, /Sleep sweet—to rise anew! /We caught the torch you threw/And holding high, we keep the Faith/With All who died." And in the third stanza Moina Michael refers to that one thing all soldiers and those who remember them ask and must reaffirm every Memorial Day and in all the days between, and that is that none of those who died shall have died in vain: "Fear not that ye have died for naught;/We'll teach the lesson that ye wrought/In Flanders Fields." It is up to us from generation to generation to teach the lesson *wrought* as it were, of life and blood and treasure, that so far has kept the Torch of Liberty burning bright in the heart of all true patriots. The lesson reduced to its core is that Freedom isn't free. God bless those who died for it and those who fight for us still.

MLK: What's in the Day? Article #380
o/a November 14, 2008

The Reverend Doctor Martin Luther King, Jr. was born January 15, 1929. He was assassinated in 1968. "MLK Day as it were, is celebrated the third Monday in January close to the time of his birthday. One may ask how such a short life should warrant a federal holiday. Martin Luther King, Jr. never was elected to public office. His life was controversial while he lived it. Moreover, his memory is skewed given that FBI files were sealed under court order until 2027. These records were not accessible to lawmakers, who voted for his holiday in 1983. The measure nevertheless passed with bipartisan support and by large margin before Ronald Reagan signed it into law.

Martin Luther King, Jr. still evokes an ecstatic memory from his admirers, and the man has become something of an icon too. That is to say, the representation of high ideals and idealism is separate and distinct from his actual biography. Of course the same can be said of many others, including Lincoln and Jefferson. Great men are often given a public pass on their blemishes and shortcomings. Historians are or ought to be a bit more circumspect.

The reason for the Day, and celebrating the life of MLK involves the issue of race. Martin Luther King, Jr.'s work was important in achieving a Second Reconstruction so-called, i.e., the end of segregation and the application of rights past state laws based upon the Fourteenth and Fifteenth Amendments.

Martin Luther King, Jr. attended segregated public schools in Georgia. After that he went to Morehouse College in Atlanta and then to Crozer Theological Seminary in Pennsylvania. At Crozer he was elected president of a predominantly white senior class. He then proceeded to Boston University where he earned his Ph. D. in 1955 and met his wife Coretta Scott. They would have two sons and two daughters together.

After educational and professional preparations, King launched himself into the pastorate first in Montgomery, Alabama and then in his native Atlanta, Georgia. At the same time he dedicated himself to political activism throughout the South, in order to end "Jim Crow" discriminatory statutes. As a member of the executive committee of the National Association for the Advancement of Colored People (NAACP) he led the Montgomery bus boycott lasting 382 days. This led to a Supreme Court decision ending bus segregation. During the days of the boycott, King was arrested and subjected to personal abuse, and his home was bombed.

In 1957 he was elected to head the Southern Christian Leadership Conference, from which he provided new leadership for the burgeoning civil rights movement. King employed the teachings and techniques of

Henry David Thoreau and Mahatma Gandhi. His enduring success is largely attributable, however, to skilful adaptation of widely accepted American values, including the rule of law—albeit, through aggressive non-violence; as well as strong appeal to common spiritual beliefs, especially in the South, about God and the moral worth and dignity of man, and to Christian values of forbearance and brotherly love. His historicism was Lincolnesque and so helpful, in that he emphasized the text of the Declaration of Independence, characterizing that document as a promissory note as yet unfulfilled. Thus he appealed to American patriotism, while strongly criticizing social norms regarding race.

In the eleven year period from 1957 to 1968 Martin Luther King, Jr. traveled more than six million miles, gave over twenty-five hundred speeches, wrote five books and numerous articles, consistently preaching against racial hatred and injustice. His activity is largely credited with changing the conscience of America on the subject of race. In 1963 he directed a peaceful march on Washington, D.C. of 250,000 people and delivered perhaps his finest address, "I Have a Dream" from the steps of the Lincoln Memorial. In 1965 he led 30,000 people on a march from Selma, Alabama to Montgomery, where he demanded that black people be allowed to vote without unfair restrictions. The speech televised to a national audience, as well as the Selma march and various protests he orchestrated, stirred general unrest in the South and American cities, leading to the passage of the Civil Rights Act of 1964 and Voting Rights Act of 1965.

In 1964 he became the youngest man to have received the Nobel Peace Prize, turning over that considerable cash prize to the furtherance of civil rights. The iconic ideal he articulated at the Lincoln Memorial is still one of the highest domestic hopes in the land. It has come to define what we mean by a just equality. Speaking of his four little children, he said "I have a dream that . . . one day" they "will live in a nation where they will not be judged by the color of their skin but by the content of their character."

Born on the 4th of July — Article #149
o/a June 27, 2004

Having studied U.S. history in England, I was struck by a consistent puzzlement and amazement there about the American Revolution. Truth be told, the Brits still don't get it. The colonies were probably better off than any other part of the British Empire—wages were 100% higher on average than in the homeland. Proposed taxes by Parliament were to pay for debt incurred during the French and Indian War. The colonies had participated in the war and benefited from British victory. The amounts asked for seemed altogether reasonable. By European and British standards, King George III was certainly no tyrant.

But there's the proverbial rub, because Americans didn't cotton to 'European and British standards' when it came to their rights. They essentially had their own standard. Indeed, Jefferson remarked that a revolution occurred in the American mind before fighting started in 1775. The Declaration of Independence is literally the birth certificate for our Nation, but the United States was forming months and even years before its delivery on July 4th, 1776. Life truly did (and does) begin at conception.

The life of the country was conceived in mind and made up of at least three distinct but complementary elements: political, religious and philosophical. The political component was drawn from the Whig or Country party tradition in English politics. This libertarian and republican perspective was a distinct minority in Great Britain but ascendant in America. One axiom was 'No taxation without actual representation.' Another was that standing armies and police power threatened domestic safety and liberty, absent a compelling security justification. The religious component was Dissenter Protestant in America, not merely Anglican Protestant. Those who were persecuted or felt confined or corrupted by English law and society had fled to America to follow spiritual pursuit. Moreover, a revivalism called the Great Awakening had swept through the colonies for several decades and with it a resurgent Calvinism. The philosophical component of the American mind was drawn from great Enlightenment thinkers, including Locke, Blackstone, Adam Smith and Montesquieu. Americans believed in the power of human reason to understand the laws of nature, society and government, and to direct progress in each area. But whereas the emphasis on reason took an irreligious turn in Europe, especially in France, it generally reinforced faith in America. Americans would associate the Laws of Nature with the Laws of Nature's God. Political science and all the theorizing about social stability and stable government, rested ultimately on patterns that divided power (recognizing human nature and Original Sin); as well as on absolute faith that in God we must trust, because the government is ultimately on His Shoulder.

This past Sunday at the Bell County Expo Center, the 33rd Annual God and Country Concert kicked off a week of patriotic observance in the area. Folks from all over Central Texas came to hear the Sanctuary Choir of First Baptist Church in Belton and the 4th Infantry Division Band, Fort Hood perform. The music and big screen imagery, though modern, would be recognizable to our Founders. The celebration of America's birthday in this manner expressed all the components of the American mind. First, the political: recognition of human equality, waving a flag that stands for freedom, reaffirming the right to end and to resist oppression. Second, the religious: praise and honor due the God of our fathers from Whom we derive natural rights, from Whence our national blessings flow; and the sure knowledge that prayer helps. Lastly, the philosophical: recognition that the People matter, their values and dignity and aspirations are important; the Nation serves the People and thrives, because free people can accomplish anything and meet any challenge whatsoever. One Nation Under God doesn't seem at all contradictory when viewed in the light of history—or in the words of our great hymns and anthems.

A succession of events between 1763 and 1776 led straightway to the American Revolution. It amounted to a series of actions by Great Britain to enforce discipline and control over the colonies, which were punctuated between by reactions from colonists who were of a very different mind. The Sugar Act in 1764, the Stamp and Quartering Acts of 1765, the Declaratory Act (1766), the Townshend Revenue Acts (1767), the Tea Act (1773), the Coercive Acts (1774)—in response the colonists protested, boycotted British goods, drew up resolutions from their own elected Assemblies, sent representatives to England to redress grievances, and ultimately resisted by force of arms. The logic prevails only if we know our mind.

Calling Young Patriots — Article #457
o/a July 04, 2010

When I speak to young people about leadership, I like to draw from my own experiences three points with credibility. First, leadership roles and experiences early on, i.e., in your *youth*—stick with you and make it easier to pick up similar and even greater roles throughout your entire life. Second, although certainly not identical, some leadership skills are transferable from political to military to business and back to political pursuit. My experience today as Chairman of the Central Texas Tea Party is reminiscent of my Teen-Age Republican (TAR) and Young Americans for Freedom (YAF)participation during the Reagan Revolution thirty years ago. Lastly, and borrowing a lesson from history, the big political waves don't come around all that often—when they do, individuals who catch the wave are better off by far and smarter, for having taken part in something historical.

The fact is that everything builds on everything else and there is no "freebie" in life. The process involves an accumulation of study, work, experience and achievements that move or convey you, over time to higher positions and quite possibly, by the grace of God, to your dreams! Everything counts: reading, playing and behaving; studying in high school to make good grades; making good grades in high school in order to get into college; doing well in college or quite possibly at your first job, in order to get to that employment level that starts a ladder of upward mobility; and then taking one position at a time to get to the other; and finally, from one career to another—so that eventually, retirement really does resemble those mythological "Golden Years." Everything you do becomes a vantage point to the next step, and to all else that follows.

Of course what I'm implying is that time and effort spent in youth leadership activities (say, organizing a Young Patriots group) begets other, higher positions of leadership and the skills needed for such positions. As I have stated and written before, there is definitely something going on in the country, including Texas in a reaction to President Obama's relentless progressive agenda. More than at any time since the late 1970s, people have awoken to a sense of danger and a strong desire to do something political. Now I'm going to refrain from saying more about our president or the military's Commander-In-Chief, other than to point out that he is indeed a *civilian* president elected every four years. He has command of the people's military, but Americans have no Commander-In-Chief. The military is subordinate to civilian political leadership and civilians also do not salute their president. Sometimes political leaders forget that Americans are not supposed to take orders from Washington. Rather, Americans are supposed to be left as a free people, at liberty to do things for themselves and families in the ways they personally see fit, with money they have earned.

Historically states created the federal government, not the other way around; and the people of the several states delegated to the federal government enumerated powers but kept everything else to themselves. This past Saturday (26 June) there was a Tenth Amendment Town Hall Meeting held in Temple at which six conservative Texas State legislators, including Ralph Sheffield were present and fielded questions. It was indicative of what you already know if you follow the news carefully, and that is that many states' Attorneys General have filed suit against the Obama health reform bill on *the basis of the Tenth Amendment.*

You need to read the Constitution. If words mean anything, then it is impossible to figure where the federal government discerns a power to make private individuals buy something, much less private health insurance; and then tries to enforce legislation using a taxing agency like the IRS. Every citizen of these United States needs to read and study the Constitution and refuse to let the Constitution be trampled by anyone or by any single branch of the federal government. Before it's all over with, the politics of the tea parties and of conservative groups around the country may even involve civil disobedience—because the principles involved today are as fundamental as what Jim Crow and segregation involved in the 1960s during the civil rights movement. Remember there are different kinds of enslavement and vestiges of the same, as well as tyranny in many guises. The government is not necessarily a benevolent master, and even if it were the American people will not suffer a yoke from any man or institution save Jesus Christ himself.[62]

CHAPTER 27

A Few Good Men

Remembering Washington Article #436
o/a February 04, 2010

The First President George Washington was born 22 February, albeit we'll observe his Birthday on Monday the 15th this year. The day will serve to round out a nice long weekend for many folks, welcome time off during the hardest month of winter. Federal employees too will enjoy the day: time to enjoy with family and friends; time to rest or catch up on projects around the house. The average citizen will enjoy the day the same way, and only hope most Government employees pause long enough to remember the man whom the nation honors with its respite.

Historians now openly talk about the way America has left her Constitution behind. Certainly there is a cumulative case to be drawn, probably starting with the War Between the States. Most accounts of government growth and the accretion of power in Washington, D.C., prominently involve the Progressive Era, and of course the New Deal. Damage was done and also accumulated, but it was not until sometime after World War II when lawmakers actually stopped consulting the Founding Document, when public debates waned concerning the Constitution's relevant meaning to contemporary public policy. Since the 1950s the Government simply uses political mandate to do whatever the Government wants to do.

Regulations and taxes pile up on people in the name of the People, imposed however by Government through a kind of modern *virtual representation*, which the Colonists utterly rejected of Great Britain. Just as the Constitution no longer acts as a parameter on what the Government does, neither can it be said of George Washington that he still informs young people and adults of what constitutes the ideal masculine character or responsible republican citizenship. Washington was a preeminent role model for these things until the middle of the Twentieth Century, when the study of biography receded in education and pop celebrity displaced historic heroes.

Washington might have been King but he chose elective office instead, and then he chose to leave that office after just two terms. He had more than the good judgment to quit while he was ahead! He indeed knew what was most important in his own life: his home Mount Vernon; family and personal obligations; fellowship with friends; reflection, and the study of Scripture. He also knew the nature of power and the temptations attendant to power. He knew the crucial impact that leadership can have, but he valued civil liberties and freedom in society much more. Freedom had been the object of the Revolution, not dynasty or empire.

Washington was esteemed a very wise man, but he eschewed the power to impose his wisdom on everyone else. Washington esteemed the prerogative inherent to liberty, as something more important than either physical wellbeing or scientific certainty in a particular. People run their own lives, some successfully and some not—but it is after all the peoples' lives and theirs to run. Various environments might be comparatively cruel or limited, chimerical or privileged. An asteroid might hit the earth someday, and the sky is always falling or liable to fall to the Chicken Littles amongst us. Still, families are natural institutions that govern even before the Government does. Government didn't give a person life or sanction the marriage between the man and woman who had the baby. Indeed, the Church never asked *nor asks* permission to marry two people. The legal conventions are not always the same as religious ones, albeit for most of our history they have overlapped almost completely, mainly because of the approach to Government the Founders, George Washington included, took.

It bears repeating: It is the *peoples'* lives—and so it should be their private choices that govern in nearly all particulars that pertain. This is true whether the individuals choose wisely or not, whether they are wrong or right; and whether they are brilliant or certifiably stupid, handicapped or studs. Individuals possess a prerogative to live according to their lights, regardless *and irrespective* of circumstances so long as they do not harm anyone else! Individuals possess natural rights according to natural law, and Government must have a compelling interest to intervene and mess with things. If Government does intervene, it does so by exception; further, it should be at the level of the State where a person lives and for some good reason, i.e., to protect others or to promote the general welfare, not necessarily the convenience of society. States are *dual sovereign political entities* alongside the Federal Government in the construct of Washington's Constitution and ours.

Imagine: Washington's Constitution, the Founding Document in light of his and the Founders' worldview—a Restoration of the Republic. This is how I shall be remembering Washington, and how Government better start remembering if I read the Tea Party through to its logical potential conclusion. Remembering Washington means a dedication to the future *and to a very similar project* to that which he faced in his day. As freemen and freewomen we must choose to remember him and the Revolution, as well as the Constitution, which was its crowning achievement. Heroes did and do exist. Sometimes they are celebrities, but most of the time they are people proud to call themselves American, men and women of character and uncompromising determination to be free—free to dream and succeed, free to dream and fail on their own terms and God's. Government is not God. The Constitution as amended, is not subject to the whim of the President or the Congress, not today anymore than it was in Washington's day. It is not subject either to the Supreme Court, in terms of decisions it has made based upon unconstitutional precedents entered in, which break the moral compact and implicit structure of federalism upon which our Union is entirely based. Government has made carrion of the so-called "living" Constitution and given us a Dead Constitution Walking. Political Revolution is in the air, or should we say *brewing*?

Ronald Reagan and the Good Fight Article #147
o/a June 13, 2004

It was a long goodbye, especially these days. The flag flew at half staff reverentially as our nation mourned its busy week for the Great Communicator's passing. Ronald Reagan had spoken optimistically about this nation's inevitable dawns. He said there are many mornings in America to come and not just the one he gave us. And while hopeful, his allusion to better times and tomorrows seem to offer little consolation now. He reminded us that we should believe in new horizons and possibilities, as big as the western sky. Today I profess my faith in the truth of what he said, because of who he proved to be. I am one witness who, notwithstanding sound mind and body, also looks through a glass darkly. Millions will attest, though millions more will forget or have never taken notice. But

I do testify and stake my life and reputation upon this fact: that I saw the Iron Curtain dissipate, like it were a miracle. It fell as surely and inexplicably to mortals as the Wall at Jericho.

Beside the loss felt when a great man and kindly mentor leaves, there is also joy and relief attendant to his departure after a long and fruitful life. We thank God he didn't suffer, and thank Him also for that bright shining moment of clarity before the end, when he looked at Nancy and silently spoke to her: "I love you . . . and it's okay." But loss is felt nonetheless, as nothing can fill the void of a place left by knowledge. Our nation wept, because once he was here and now he is not. Time heals the future. We move on or lapse into sweet forgetfulness. For the meanwhile, we endure the present and purposefully savor the past—even the bitterest dregs. We mourn with Nancy, because we loved him too. He belongs to the Ages indeed, and we are jealous of the Ages and preferred it when he belonged to us!

What a condition is this: temporal and finite humanity, body politic. Grief is so predictable. Reagan was the oldest president when he took the oath of office, so we should have seen it coming. After eight years and a slowing down and longer pauses in his speech than before—he gave us fair warning after all. He entered the sunset of his life with Alzheimer's and told us so to our face! It was a matter of time (as with us all). Yet when the end came, there is a profound welling and outpour of grief. How many of us barely see our parents or some precious loved one nowadays anyway? It is a modern scourge, but if they still be on earth it hardly seems to matter. For their life force emanates, and their spirit bathes us with a comforting sense of presence. The strange connection persists until they are gone. We feel the absence when it comes as something gets torn away, when life removes to another realm. Though we had not seen or thought of them for years, a leaden grief descends upon our hearts. We feel the terrible 'missing' of a separation that we are powerless to change or overcome.

Reagan rose from humble origin and knew personal and professional setbacks along the way. He held firmly to middle class and Middle American values, but he also developed subtle and sophisticated convictions relating to politics and to economics and to faith. He led a socio-political movement that turned back the excesses of modern liberalism in government and will at length bury the malicious lunacy of counterculture and the unconstitutional, judicially imposed secular humanist regime. Reagan inspired a political generation, unlike anyone since Franklin Roosevelt or John F. Kennedy. He followed the leadings of Spirit through his entire life—plying and practicing the craft of Solon, against the odds and despite discouraging opinion polls, until a time of God's choosing. Ronald Reagan was a providential man, who learned his mind and learned to speak his mind; to say something that counts as well as what convinces; to level up the people through elevating messages and righteous sentiment, and unsullied motives. He knew that right words cannot and do not return void.

Reagan was a fighter, who could show flashes of anger and fix his jaw in stubborn resolve. But a good night's sleep or midday nap would fix things, and he never held a grudge. Reagan seemed to have mastered the Christian ideal of hating the sin but loving the sinner. He could separate the error of ways and ideas—knowing full well that ideas do have consequences, from the inherent worth and dignity of people who happen to subscribe to bad ideas. Maybe because he was jocular and forgiving, people underestimated him. If Lincoln were just 'a poor ole country boy' in the courtroom, Reagan was naïve and detached on the political stage or as leader of the Free World. How the media would howl in derision and insult. Reagan's partisan critics were vociferous in their day. I wondered where they all were this week. Reagan outlived quite a few no doubt, others changed their minds about his policies or him personally. Some critics shifted their oblivious remarks to contemporary targets. All were silenced, for those who contended with Reagan were utterly confounded and as a thing of naught. In the sermon Reagan was fond of quoting by John Winthrop, Winthrop makes reference to our land as that 'Shining City on a Hill' in St. Matthew. Winthrop also explains, "We shall find that the God of Israel is among us, when ten of us shall be able to resist a thousand of our enemies, when He shall make us a praise and glory,"—and here I take license and liberty of rephrasing—"that men of succeeding generations shall say, 'The Lord make it like that of Ronald Reagan's America." The vision is living and ever before us. Reagan just handed us the baton.

Leonard Read — Article #004
Jan 25, 2001

Leonard E. Read (1898-1983) was, in my estimation, one of the greatest American philosophers of the twentieth century. He founded the Foundation for Economic Education (FEE) in 1946, the original so-called "think tank" and one dedicated to the classical liberal worldview of our Founding Fathers. Though FEE is based in Irvington-on-Hudson, New York (*www.fee.org*), Texans took to Read's traveling seminars in a very big way. His message about the nature of freedom was thankfully a lot better than New York *picante* sauce and, judging from the recent U.S. Senate race in New York, stuck to our ribs better. I first met Read in 1977 at a seminar in Houston—my Sunday school teacher had told me about it. Read and his coterie of learned people gave talks that hardly comprised a camp meeting, but the seminar amounted to a life changing experience nonetheless.

Leonard Read had a common touch, as well as the ability to translate hard ideas into simple language. For instance, he would quote Edmund Burke but explain it as easy as Will Rogers. One of the ideas he reduced from Burke was this: there are only two forms of human restraint against destructive impulses, external government (the law without) and self-control (the law within). You either impose control on yourself or you get restraint imposed on you by others. Read said that all the modern preoccupation with statutory law was indicative of our loss of self-restraint. Moreover, the further a-field laws become from what's reasonable and just, the more likely it is for good folks to become lawbreakers. The ill-fated Eighteenth Amendment to prohibit liquor proved that point conclusively. Without being too specific and anti-PC, I'll merely suggest that there are an awful lot of modern prohibitionist dictators about, who missed that very important history lesson.

The law without should codify the thou-shalt-nots and prescribe the penalties for infractions—restricting the bad to make good things possible. By confining rules more or less to things not to do, we open an infinite realm of things to do. Ah, the maximum sphere for freedom, potential, achievement and joy! Of course, the "what to do" is informed by that law within, i.e., by self-discipline or obedience to the moral law, which admittedly requires instruction. But this instruction ought to come from parents, teachers, coaches, ministers, and leaders who provide examples of rectitude. Read put it this way, "What a fiasco football would be were the rule book to prescribe the plays! In principle, at least, respectable law for society does not differ from respectable rules in football . . . Yet, in society, most people countenance the unjust along with the just, the unreasonable with the reasonable. They let politicians with their pass-a-law remedies prescribe the plays of life!" Too bad, but pray the fourth quarter's ours!

RIP William F. Buckley, Jr. Article #335
o/a February 22, 2008

An icon of the post-World War II conservative movement in America passed away February 27th at the age of 82. He was in his study at home in Stamford, Connecticut when he died—no doubt writing another erudite, witty piece for *National Review* or maybe his syndicated column "On the Right" for newspapers.

Bill Buckley lived the proverbial life of Riley in many ways, privileged and very rich. His grandfather made millions in oil. His father made millions more through ownership of the Catawba Corporation—providing geological, geophysical, accounting and technical services to his family's oil business. Buckley enjoyed Latin American nursemaids and French governesses. He spoke three languages—Spanish, French and English fluently, and exceedingly well (not to mention Latin). He served in the Army, 1944-6 and then undercover for the CIA in Mexico a year or so after that. He went to Yale and graduated in 1950 with a B.A. degree and honors in political science, economics and history.

Despite his high IQ, he could come across initially a bit like Thurston Howell III on "Gilligan's Island." His quirky mannerisms smacked of an aristocratic conceit, but most people who knew him liked him. He was genuinely compassionate, and a deeply spiritual person. Very conservative and also tolerant, he was devout Roman Catholic, who wed a Protestant from Vancouver, Canada. He and his wife Pat were married for over 56 years until she died last year in April. Bill Buckley's father was of Irish descent, and his mother was a Southerner with Swiss-German ancestry. He was a Renaissance man too: sailor, skier, traveler and adventurer, accomplished pianist and harpsichordist; and loved horses and hunting.

If you ever watched him in debate on the political talk show "Firing Line," which ran 33 years on National Educational Television and PBS, you knew the reason why in America everyone—even bluebloods, have the right to exist and speak out freely. I think that if a redneck or roughneck ever heard him, they figured if they had been so lucky they would like to sound just like that! Buckley made you go to the dictionary a lot, but between trips he made good horse sense. If you happened to disagree—and anyone would at some point over 4 ½ *decades* of writing and political commentary, you nevertheless sure liked the way he said it.

Bill Buckley made an indelible mark on the political history of the 20th Century. He wrote a landmark classic, *God and Man at Yale* in 1951 in which he criticized his alma mater for straying from its original educational mission informed as it should be by Christianity. Indeed, after college he averaged writing one book every year, including spy novels, along with everything else he did. When aggravated by the liberal policies of the first Eisenhower administration, he started the conservative magazine *National Review* in 1955. It became the flagship for a new and rising political movement. The magazine successfully synthesized traditional (paleo-) conservative and classical liberal/libertarian strands of thought. In so doing, Buckley contributed much to what passes for modern conservative thought today; and as importantly, he supplied powerful ideas to a political movement and new coalition that began with Goldwater in the 1960s and ended up with the triumph of Ronald Reagan in 1980.

While he is credited with helping to fuse conservatives and libertarians together on economic grounds and opposition to communism, he was also a figure in the nascent and continuing quarrels within the conservative movement with Objectivists (followers of Ayn Rand) and also with members of the John Birch Society. Moreover, he was critical of George W. Bush on the basis of fiscal irresponsibility and what he increasingly viewed as a misadventure in foreign policy involving war in Iraq.

One of the hallmarks of Bill Buckley was his stylistic method of argument: characteristically charming, humorous, almost always polite and civil in discourse, speaking in terms that were always decent. In a day when there were far fewer choices on TV than we have now, we nevertheless had this sort of person talking to us about politics and about ideas that matter. His style, as well as the content of his speech, contrasted starkly with the loud, obnoxious, in-your-face sort of programs on radio and TV we have today, which spew a so-called conservative line or message without an appreciation for either nuance or complexity, critical thinking or independence of mind.

At his funeral Bill Buckley once said that he wanted to hear Bach, and I'm sure he and Pat will enjoy their concert together. From those of us who continue this side working, in the interval between the two eternities, we offer this blessing to our friend and friend of humanity: May he rest in peace. *In paradisum deducant te Angeli; in tuo adventu suscipiant te martyres, et perducant te in civitatem sanctam Jerusalem. (May the angels conduct you to Paradise; and at your coming may the martyrs receive you, and lead you to the holy city of Jerusalem).* Amen.[63]

Living Memorial: The Case of Henry T. Waskow Article #398
o/a May 01, 2009

More than 65 years ago a much-loved company commander with the 36th Infantry Division was killed in action during World War II. The "old man" was just 25 years old when he died, and his men were visibly moved. On the night of 14 December 1943 they took the body of Captain Henry T. Waskow of Belton, Texas down San Pietro Hill, Italy on the back of a mule. The moment is immortalized in words by the famed war correspondent Ernie Pyle, who witnessed the grim moonlit procession and wrote about it in a column. Pyle's column, as well as circumstances surrounding the battle of San Pietro became the basis for a famous film called "The Story of G.I. Joe," which appeared in movie theaters the summer of 1945. Robert Mitchum played the role of Henry Waskow, who was given a different name at the Army's insistence. Waskow is "Lieutenant Bill Walker" in the film.

Waskow is buried in an Allied cemetery in Italy but a revered marker bears his name on a plot in the North Belton Cemetery. Henry T. Waskow High School and the Henry T. Waskow VFW Post #4008 in Belton are both named after the real G.I. Joe. Waskow is uncommonly "memorialized" therefore, for himself certainly but also as an archetype for every American Infantryman. When we think of him we know for sure that he was brave, had grit and determination, cared for his buddies and the men he led. In death he tells us a lot. In life, one wonders if he would have told us even more by way of deeds or career; or sterling example; or through progeny had he survived the war to marry. Even so, he left us with a note about life with uncommon advice in it on how to live—ironically, it was his last letter home and his official Will and Testament.

Here are some things he mentions. First, all of us should *want to live* but be willing to die for how we want to live. That is to say, notwithstanding the ultimate sacrifice, that sacrifice is a living thing and life involves it. It would be foolhardy to want to die and thus avoid the sacrifice required of us in living right. He says we ought to live in and for this country, *the United States of America* as if we would die for it every day. There's just not a lot of room in that characterization for couch potatoes, dropouts, people who are lackadaisical, oblivious, morose or unconcerned! Henry, or "Snort" (his nickname for accidentally swallowing some corn liquor) would have us care deeply and work hard in all our various capacities and stations—personally, professionally, and as church and community members and citizens of the state and nation.

Second, Waskow says life should be spent in service to others and defense of the oppressed. His personal code is clearly chivalric. He says that he aspired to lead but also to sacrifice for those whom he led. He refers to the men under his charge as "magnificent Americans" and relates how he has striven to be worthy of their trust and the trust the nation placed in him to lead them. He says leadership involves strength, character and courage, and he recommends those who pray to pray for their leaders. In his case, he refers to the several times he asked his family to pray in regard to his capacity as leader, in order to gird him with the needed qualities in abundance: to be a better leader, in order to better serve his men. Notice he did not ask for prayers to relieve him of a single iota of responsibility. "Snort" wants us to be strong, to build and evince character, to show courage in the face of adversity, to lead if and when we are called.

Third, Waskow understands life to be quintessentially a matter of choice. He takes his stand willingly and so accepts whatever consequences come. He interprets his life in a way that is empowering, refusing to regret. After all, he chose his responsibility. Indeed, he expects all freemen and freewomen to do the same, even when choices are hard. His were also hard. He did not start the war, but he volunteered for the Armed Forces. He did not want to die, but he chose to fight and keep his country free and his friends and family safe. He characterizes his choices as a "service to the cause," but he inclusively leaves room for every one of us to choose the same thing—even if our capacities and stations are quite different at work or on the home front. We are all brothers and sisters in arms so to speak, if and when we serve the righteous cause together. "When you remember me," he says, "remember me as a fond admirer of all of you, for I thought so much of you and loved you with all my heart. My wish for all of you is that you get along well together and prosper—not in money—but in happiness, for happiness is something that all the money in the world can't buy. Try to live a life of service—to help someone where you are or whatever you may be—take it from me, you can get happiness out of that, more than anything if life." Waskow must have had a deep and abiding sense of satisfaction even on the day he died, because he died as he chose to live. We remember him this Memorial Day, and hope to honor him by our living.

CHAPTER 28

Evolution: For Better or Worse

Civil War Not an End to Federalism Article #094
o/a May 09, 2003

According to the Tenth Amendment, "the powers not delegated to the United States by the Constitution, nor prohibited by it to the States, are reserved to the States respectively, or to the people." While the Civil War may have altered the federal-state relationship, it did not justify social revolution beyond the terms of peace or actual Constitutional amendment. For instance, the Civil War did not change Natural Law, common American republican heritage (including the right to revolution), Founders' intent, nor most of the original compact. As regards federalism, the most basic mechanism for vertical check-and-balance, it is absolutely crucial to the operation of the Constitution itself as a social, legal or moral compact. American federalism may not be said therefore to have undergone fundamental change on every issue. If anything, the existential fact that the thirty years following Reconstruction were *laissez-faire*, indicates that the federal government gained no super-ordinate role over the States by virtue of the War alone. The existential fact that courts did not apply the Bill of Rights to States until the 1930s—and then only selectively through the Fourteenth Amendment's "due process" clause—indicates the application is of much more recent origin than the Civil War. Courts did not even start to apply the Fourteenth Amendment to activities by private companies and individuals until the 1950s. Indeed, liberal historians *use* the Civil War to exaggerate Constitutional change and an associated "social revolution," in order to validate subsequent changes they approve and to avoid defense of the measures on substantive Constitutional grounds.

Whether for years the federal government neglected a legitimate role of enforcing the intent of the Civil War Constitutional amendments and whether one admits of Southern noncompliance with legitimate mandates on racial issues or not—*these criticisms and shortcomings are beside the point.* The use of the Fourteenth Amendment by the High Court as a subterfuge for attacking perceived social ills in the States is not legitimate and represents a departure from original intent, as well as from the Natural Law that makes the Constitution a moral compact. Whereas one *may* expunge slavery from the system through force of arms, and whereas one *may* establish the legal precedent of federal judicial review, one may not, *in particulars outside the revolutionary instance of change*, alter respective federal and state prerogatives. Moreover, even judicial review must serve the limits and ends of the Constitution itself. Judicial review is legitimate only to the extent that it is consistent with dual sovereignty and the inherently limited scope of federal power and function.

John C. Calhoun's words remain true in this context, regardless of the Civil War's outcome:

> . . . we must view the General Government and those of the States as a whole, each in its proper sphere, sovereign and independent; each perfectly adapted to its respective objects; the States acting separately, representing and protecting the local and peculiar interests; and acting jointly through one General Government, with the weight respectively assigned to each by the Constitution, representing and protecting the interest of the whole; and thus perfecting, by an admirable but simple arrangement, the great principle of representation and responsibility, without which no government can be free or just. To preserve this sacred distribution, as originally settled, . . . [is what upon] in all probability, our liberty depends.

Notwithstanding the particulars of revolutionary change or bona fide Constitutional amendment, the orbits of respective sovereignty between State and Federal levels remain inviolable.

States joined the Union to better insure their viability and self-determination, meaning the ability to engage in voluntary social evolution unimpeded by the vicissitudes and problems encountered under the Articles of Confederation. Further, we know that Texas, having been independent for ten years, obviously joined the Union in 1845 with the same intention. No State ever voluntarily joined the Union to destroy what was unique about itself. States joined to enhance or secure their uniqueness and to improve social conditions voluntarily over time. If anything, joining the national political Union insured societal *independence*. States were *supposed* to govern themselves differently, because their people and their circumstances differed.

Mount Vernon Statement and the Battle for the Republic
o/a February 18, 2010 Article #438

Not far from the home of George Washington, leaders of major conservative organizations signed "the Mount Vernon Statement" on 17 February, the day before their annual Conservative Political Action Conference (CPAC) began in Washington, D.C. The statement was billed in the press as something of a manifesto or list of principles similar in scope to the Sharon Statement of 1960, a statement by conservative intellectuals which gave rise to Goldwater's takeover of the GOP and eventually to Reagan's national triumph in 1980. If the Mount Vernon Statement is like the Sharon Statement, and there are differences, let's hope it doesn't take as long to reach electoral fruition. The country may not have as long to wait.

Among those who signed the statement and indeed helped to orchestrate the event, was former Attorney General Edwin Meese III. Other signatories read like a *Who's Who* of conservative thinkers and activists: Ed Feulner, Jr., president of the Heritage Foundation; Tony Perkins, president of the Family Research Council; Alfred Regnery, publisher; David Keene, president of the American Conservative Union; David McIntosh, co-founder of the Federalist Society; Grover Norquist, president of Americans for Tax Reform; William Wilson, president of Americans for Limited Government; Richard Viguerie of direct mail fame, who also chairs ConservativeHQ.com; and many others. Their coming together is a symbolic gesture of unity to be sure, but it is also a material step towards formation of a new conservative consensus. It is the start of the next phase, as it were, in the history of an impressively resilient and adaptive movement in American politics. The next phase in the life of the conservative movement is turning out to be Constitutional Conservatism. Said another way, the neo-conservatism of the Bush years has given way to neo-federalism, reminiscent of Reagan but more forceful in terms of states rights and separation of powers.

The content of the Mount Vernon Statement is less intellectual than that of the original Sharon Statement. Signers of the Mount Vernon Statement would presumably find most if not all of the Sharon Statement, as true today as when it was written in 1960. Indeed, the Sharon Statement was about "transcendent values" and tenets of American conservatism that change but little over time. That said, national priorities have dramatically shifted in the intervening 50 years, and of course communism is no longer "the greatest single threat to [our] liberties." What the Mount Vernon Statement lacks in detail and sophistication, however, it makes up for in clarity. Moreover, it explicitly announces a declaration of political war, which stakes the future of the conservative movement on "retaking and resolutely defending the high ground of America's founding principles."

Signatories of the Mount Vernon Statement in effect, "recommit [themselves] . . . to the ideas of the American Founding." They contend that, "Through the Constitution, the Founders created an enduring framework of limited government based on the rule of law . . . [and likewise] sought to secure national independence, provide for economic opportunity, establish true religious liberty and maintain a flourishing society of republican self-government." The signatories further assert that it is these very principles most responsible for the unparalleled prosperity and justice of our nation and as such, the principles constitute "our highest [political] achievements." Yet according to the Statement, "Each one . . . is presently under sustained attack"! In an oblique reference to modern progressives and possibly to president Obama himself, the Mount Vernon Statement makes reference to "Some [who] insist that America must change, cast off the old and put on the new," suggesting that those who do, deal in "empty promise or . . . dangerous deception."

The Mount Vernon Statement is helping to draw the battle lines for 2010 and 2012, and quite possibly beyond. No less than the future of the Republic—or its end, will be determined in our own time. The case made by the Mount Vernon Statement is so simple and fundamentally clear, it calls every citizen to witness again the miracle of Constitutional Convention and to either accept or reject its eternal thesis. Either we shall renew our Spirit and advocate for ancient American rights and liberty, or else we shall fail in our role as Posterity to free and brave men and succumb to the lure of command.

The Bounds of Judicial Restraint Article #349
o/a May 02, 2008

For most of American history, the doctrine of judicial restraint inhered in the operation of the U.S. Supreme Court and was deemed by justices to be the proper and legitimate paradigm for long-term stable, republican government under the Constitution. The idea is that rule of law should help shape society, not the rule of judges per se; and the rule of law means it is the American people who must make the law, abide by it, and change the law when/if they want to. Of course, there were always the contrary impulses both to gain power and to "do good," but (with notable exceptions) these did not gain ascendancy in terms of judicial activism until the Warren Court in the 1960s. The appointments of Chief Justice Roberts and Justice Alito have arguably initiated a movement toward tighter reasoning and restraint in Court decisions, but there are also decades of bad precedent to overcome and special interests that enjoy power and prestige afforded by it.

Judicial restraint in part is characterized by judicial review of the Supreme Court, i.e., to decide on the constitutionality of the Acts of Congress and state laws or enactments. The right of judicial review by the Supreme Court is not explicit in the Constitution, given that the three branches of government are co-equals and states are co-equal sovereignties with the federal government. Nevertheless the precedent did take shape in the early years of the Republic with assent and tutelage of the Founding Fathers themselves. Moreover, it was consistent with British Whig tradition. It can be argued that only through an application of restraint, by which the Court decides judiciously what it will hear and in rare cases only, ventures to overturn the acts of Congress or states—will respect for that institution long endure in a democratic body politic. The Court so restrained, refrains from deciding what is best, only what is legal in some circumstances. The Court's energetic nullification of laws would surely diminish politicians' and the people's sense of independent responsibility to enforce constitutional guarantees or to enact wise policy. According to Edith Jones, Chief Judge of the United States Court of Appeals for the Fifth Circuit, "It is the people and their representatives, . . . who bear [ultimate] responsibility for maintaining the constitutional structure of our government" and not the courts.

Four precepts characterize judicial restraint in the American tradition and serve as soft though proper bounds for how it should be exercised. First, avoiding counter-majority decisions, which unnecessarily place the Court at odds with the people and their elected representatives. Legislation should receive full benefit of the presumption of constitutionality. Moreover, avoiding decisions on ultimate constitutional issues is often better, if it preserves the responsibility and authority of the legislative process. Second, judges should appreciate the limits of judicial power—i.e., to understand that such power is not competent to right all wrongs or solve social problems. Judicial power is not a remedy for political mischief, in other words, and the Founders did not enthrone the Judiciary. Third, a restrained judge knows his own prejudices and fallibility and approaches his task of adjudication with humility. This means the judge seeks to tame his own subjectivity, to apply self-control in the exercise of his judgment. Finally, attention must be given to the judicial craft itself, to careful writing and fidelity to the record, to excellence in logic and reasoning. It is of course a professional and ethical duty for judges to do so, but it also involves skills to hone and to practice, and represents a high aim to attain.

The most grievous violation of judicial restraint in American history, as well as the grossest violation of every American legal precedent and professional standard of conduct whatsoever, is the recourse to foreign and international legal sources to interpret the U.S. Constitution! This has only been done in the last few years, a 21st century innovation; and there are now five members of the Supreme Court who subscribe to this device, who indeed should all be impeached. By citing foreign sources, the Court opens itself up directly to foreign influence through amicus briefs from international groups who presume to tell the American people how their government should be run. Another practical problem is the citing of some sources but not other contrary ones, given that the histories and traditions are entirely separate from our own, and can be from each other. Justice Scalia rightly observes the practice of citing foreign sources by U.S. Justices has been result-oriented, essentially citing what the activist judge has decided to say. Small comfort, since even legal rigor outside the bounds of the U.S. Constitution and the sovereign, independent and federal legal tradition of these United States, has no place.[64]

July 4th Worth Conserving Article #025
June 28, 2001

April 19th is a date now associated with Waco and Oklahoma City. What a pity, since it ought to be remembered for the start of the American Revolution at Lexington and Concord. If Americans knew their history better, even a journalist might mention the date in that context occasionally. Between April 1775 and July 1776, however, things went from bad to worse between the Colonies and Great Britain. On July 4th, the final break was made—the Colonies decided to become free and independent. The Declaration of Independence both announced and justified the political action by Continental Congress. The Colonies would secede from Great Britain, owing to the tyranny of King George III and Parliament.

This Fourth of July, these United States of America celebrate 225 years of independence (gads, and I can remember the Bicentennial of 1976 like it were yesterday!). To hear some folks talk, America is a young nation. In some respects it may be—its culture is not as old as China's, for instance. In terms of fundamentally unchanged form of government, however, which is based on the Declaration of Independence and the Constitution—it is in fact the oldest. We were a country before Italy or Germany. We did not kill the Czar's family for dictatorship by the proletariat like in Russia. We are not exactly green or wet behind the ears, when it comes to self-governance! No, I'm not saying we've always done the best job of it. Conservatives, however, who still look to conserve this great Republic for many more years, will find a lot in the Declaration worth conserving and worth the reverence we give it this time of year. The following is an explanation provided by Larry Arnn, past president of the Claremont Institute, who is currently the president of Hillsdale College in Michigan. He helps us appreciate some of the words at the beginning of the Declaration much better.

"*We hold these truths to be self-evident* . . . Humans are rational creatures. We can think, deliberate, and come to reasonable agreements about law and justice. We can also make intelligent decisions for our own lives (even if we don't always do so). A free people is not supervised and regulated in every detail. And no legitimate government can claim to rule on the basis of some special knowledge that it alone possesses, whether a Marxist historical dialectic, a mystical revelation, or the supposed scientific expertise of regulatory bureaucracies.

"*[T]hat all men are created equal* . . . Though we differ in talents, intelligence and other attributes, we are all equally human; neither beasts nor angels. We are entitled to equal protection of our rights, and government may not treat some classes as superior—deserving of special treatment or favors—and others as inferior. Every individual, even the President, must be equal before the law, because he is equal in his rights.

"*[T]hat [we] are endowed by our Creator with certain unalienable rights* . . . Our rights are inherent to us—they are part of our nature—and not created or dispensed by government. A government that gives us rights may also take them away. Our rights come from a Creator, and are defined by the 'laws of nature and nature's God' mentioned in the first paragraph of the Declaration. As government does not create our rights, neither do we create them for ourselves. Our rights come from something higher than us. And so a certain degree of moral decency and self-control, which comes from a respect for nature and nature's God, is necessary to self-government.

"*[T]hat among these are life, liberty, and the pursuit of happiness* . . . We are entitled to the 'pursuit' of happiness, not happiness itself. Government can secure the conditions—peace, security, the rule of law—but we must make a success of our own lives. The pursuit of happiness was used interchangeably by the Founders with the right to property. James Madison wrote, 'As we have a property in our rights, so we have a right to our property.' Life, liberty and property are not the only rights we have; but at the same time not everything is a 'right.' A government that tries to ensure a 'right' to affordable housing, but neglects to protect our lives and liberties, is misguided and dangerous.

"*That to secure these rights governments are instituted among men* . . . Government exists to secure our rights, not to do anything it pleases simply because it seems expedient or desirable. And government exists for the people, not the people for the government. That is why it must be controlled and held accountable. The procedures and institutions set up in the Constitution—elections, separation of powers, and federalism, for example—derive from this principle.

"*[D]eriving their just powers from the consent of the governed* . . . Not unlimited power, but only 'just powers' may legitimately be exercised by government. And the operation of government must continually be monitored. Thus, policy decisions must be made by elected representatives who can be removed if they don't do their jobs. The judiciary was intended by the Founders to have 'neither force nor will,' and should not be a policy-making branch of government, isolated from popular control. Likewise, a vast, un-elected, and anonymous bureaucracy controlling citizens' lives from a remote capital is equally objectionable to government by consent."

Enjoy your picnic, but chew on that!

CHAPTER 29

Perilous Times

Veterans Day and the Ft. Hood Massacre Article #423
o/a November 06, 2009

Veterans Day was formerly called Armistice Day, having been inaugurated in 1918 at the end of World War I. Originally "Veterans Day" honored the veterans of that terrible Great War and was dedicated to the cause of world peace. Commemorations were subsequently enlarged to include veterans from World War II and Korea. Today the day honors all who served our nation while in uniform, though little is mentioned about world peace. In the aftermath of so many wars of the Twentieth and early Twenty-First centuries, including the Cold War and ongoing Global War on Terror, Americans appreciate explicitly the connection between our existence as a free people and country, and the hard work and sacrifice of veterans and their families. American generations each put forward their best and oft-times brightest, America's young men and women—quite literally the promise and future of the nation, in order to bear the burdens and risk of defending and protecting our cherished way of life. Veterans Day in this respect is our first day of Thanksgiving held each year in November.

Last week the constant drone of news noise gave way to breaking news that got people's attention. On 5 November a single shooter at Ft. Hood shot and killed thirteen people in the Soldier Readiness Center and wounded thirty others. Sergeant Kim Munley was the civilian police officer stationed on post, who shot and stopped the gunman and was seriously wounded herself taking that action. The gunman was identified as Major Nidal Malik Hasan, 39, unmarried, a lifelong Muslim and psychiatrist serving in the Army since 1995, who was about to be deployed to the Middle East. He was born in Virginia to parents who emigrated to the

U.S. from Jordan. At a mosque in Silver Spring, Maryland he frequented, however, he identified himself as Palestinian. The Army's investigation will no doubt reveal more about his motive and the mechanics of what happened (two hand-guns, so many rounds of ammunition, etc.), but it is hard to explain tragedy, much less explain it away.

Recently someone impressed with my prior military service and the fact that I was able to live and work around the world asked me, "Do you find people are much the same everywhere . . . aside from their government, culture and laws?" I remember thinking to myself that government, culture and laws are fairly substantial differences (!), but ignoring these, how should one answer? Although the question is difficult and interesting, the short answer has to be "No." Americans need to think about it carefully too, because it means a lot in terms of immigration policy as well as the magnitude of foreign policy objectives that we assign ourselves abroad. This may fly in the face of so much universalistic rhetoric employed by liberal and conservative idealists alike throughout American history—and even contrary to greats, such as Thomas Jefferson if/when he is taken out of context. To the point, however, it is difficult to put a finger on human nature, and those ethno-cultural patterns are not easily separable from a person's given identity and especially from his or her "will-to-action." There is a human *condition* to be sure (finite/sensory) and some would add to this Original Sin, which I would argue is validated by events of the last week.

In addition, there is such a thing as the human spirit, which our better poets have described as indomitable (enduring/reaching/surviving). The seriously wounded and the family members of those slain will evince this human characteristic. Gratefully many will know the inexplicable touch of the Divine Comforter, who comes to hold them and carry them through the searing pain and grief. Finally I must entertain that there is broad common humanity among all people everywhere (related perhaps to common experience and to emotions) and strong gender patterns that cut across ethnic and cultural lines too. What I've found most of the time, however, is that people individually and one-to-one are the most similar they are going to be, whereas family and social constructs take over almost immediately as soon as three or more are gathered together. Crowds and armies are ever quite distinct.

Notwithstanding, the American people have a more individualistic ethos than any other significant group on the planet. Our most common mistake is to presume that everyone is just like us, when in fact they really aren't. I'll be so bold as to say that some people aren't even fit (that is to say, ready) to be free or democratic. That isn't my moral judgment or my wish, just the cold recognition that not everyone will rise to the occasion as it were, or even accept and *value* that responsibility. Free peoples can also be radically different from each other, and contrary to the self-delusion of some who have held office, free people can and do go to war against each other. Someone's lone criminal or terrorist act is to some extent, the free choice of one who thinks quite differently from the rest of us. Of course, we'll probably put a sanitizing label on his behavior, like *Sudden Jihad Syndrome*, and enter the insanity plea on his behalf with or against his will, in order to avoid offending anyone else "just like us."

What it Takes — Article #049
December 13, 2001

Sometimes in our day-to-day rush and familiar surroundings and cultural norms, we forget how truly amazing America is. Folks, who have been away for some time, almost universally feel the need to get back. They need to "recharge," in a sense. You know something's special here, if you consider that millions want to come. Millions more look to America from their homes for guidance, assistance or example.

Ignorant people in the world think we're soft, because they see the plenty and don't understand what it has taken—and what it takes—to have what we have. They don't understand the discipline we live each day, in terms of balancing hard work and family relations, and service to our country and to God. They don't understand our striving to be the best we can be, and I mean in every single capacity God has granted us: mental, physical, spiritual, social and emotional. We strive to be "whole" persons, and we strive to be good. We also strive to win, because we're good. That's actually pretty unique in this world of ours.

Our own countrymen often overlook the value we subconsciously place on "freedom"—the freedom to do things, to go places, to have fun, to start new enterprises. We also generally place emphasis on personal responsibility, on self-reliance, on dignity and yes, even on clean living. It's horse sense really: you reap what you sow. The Taliban is certainly learning that. But they didn't have any American horses. They didn't know Middle America—or New York, for that matter. They sure as "H" didn't know a Texan or they would have known we'd kick their rear end. They thought Americans were weak and cowardly materialists, but I suppose it's easy to mistake the love of freedom for lack of virtue, or the love of peace for cowardice.

It's a shame our attackers didn't read our history (it's a shame a lot of us don't), because then they'd realize what it takes to be American. What it takes, in addition to good education and tons of elbow grease, is one or more wars practically every generation. Now did we really think that the twenty-first century was going to be any different, perhaps more peaceful because of the victory "the greatest generation" won in World War II? Believe it or not, that's a sentiment made by the famous historian Stephen Ambrose, just two days before the attacks on the World Trade Center and Pentagon! I guess the Cold War, Korea, Viet Nam, and the Gulf War were just chopped liver. Anyway, I am very grateful for the World War II generation, certainly the greatest of the twentieth century. But don't think their accomplishment means we've got less to do, because it doesn't.

The principal of Somerville College, Oxford, said to his new arrivals in 1944 that all beginnings are hopeful. So the new century/new millennium probably invites optimism, and optimism is not all bad—indeed, it's essential. But as one of the great Free World leaders during the Cold War—Margaret Thatcher—said, "My generation remembers that we had such faith after World War I that there could never be another world war, we let our defenses down." Do you see a pattern? Again and again, we prove what it takes. The measure in blood, however, depends on our preparedness at the time.

Out of 150 countries in the world, only 72 are free. I'd say the odds are we're in for a few more challenges. History and prudence dictate that we be prepared. Again, Thatcher has the right advice for Americans:

> We must keep our defenses up and we must have equipment of the very latest technology. This is absolutely vital . . . . I believe the first duty of any government is to protect the lives of its citizens . . . . And we do that by having the latest technology in the United States. My friends, you're citizens of

a wonderful country. You've built the greatest country in the world in terms of establishing the rule of law, defending the freedoms of others, and building a most prosperous future for your people. If those who do not have liberty would be guided by your example, what a much better world it would be. In the meantime, . . . [you] must continue to keep up [your] reputation.

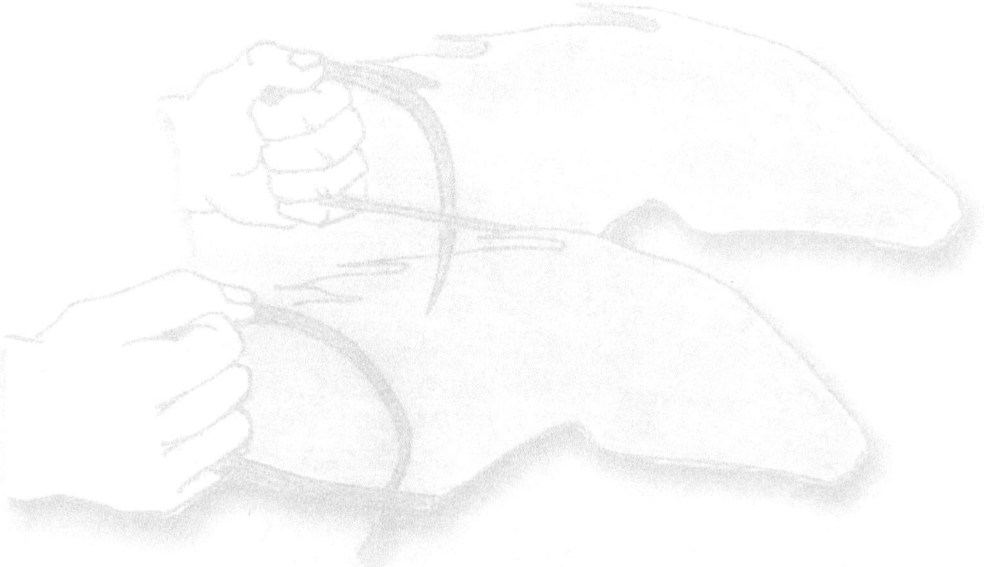

PART FOUR: ECONOMY

CHAPTER 30

MARKET SOCIETY

Free Trade and Prosperity Article #048
o/a November 30, 2001

Many Americans do not thoroughly appreciate the magic of the marketplace, in particular the international marketplace. The unprecedented wealth the United States enjoys is due in large measure to the open economic market established within the borders of the Union by the Founding generation. Even though political and social differences characterize the various States, and laws differ, States may not generally restrict commerce within or between States. Individuals can and do buy and sell with neighbors in other States. Indeed, it is clearly an American ethos that men and women engaged in honest work may enjoy the fruits of their labor without government interference—to include exchanging what they produce for something produced by others, i.e., trade. Early in the nineteenth century, it was settled by courts that no State could erect barriers (tariffs, etc.) to discourage goods and services from moving across State borders. The result has been tremendous economic growth stemming from interstate commerce. Moreover, the United States has generally pursued free trade with other countries as an extension of that same principle. Of all regions, the South has most consistently supported free trade.

Adam Smith, the Father of Economics, proved the efficacy of free trade back in 1776. Today the rule still holds: nations open to trade tend to be most prosperous. The most recent *Economic Freedom of the World* study by James Gwartney and Robert Lawson finds that the most economically open nations from 1980 through 1998 grew five times faster than the most closed. Regions of the world where poverty has been the most intractable, such as sub-Saharan Africa and South Asia, have been the least open to trade and foreign investment. In a way it is like extending the "fall line" inland, if you have free trade. In the old days, areas below the fall line (where rivers became navigable) tended to be wealthier. It was harder to transport and exchange goods in inland areas that were more remote. Trains, highways and air transportation have long since overcome the geographic fall line, but the analytical principle remains useful. Policies now draw the fall lines of the world. Some countries remain perpetual backcountries/perpetual backwaters, by refusing to buy and sell their goods freely with others.

Now I would argue that some commonality of culture is probably preferred and necessary, in order to have the freest kind of exchange or open market. Nevertheless, that case can be (and usually is) overdrawn. Empirically, we started with Canada, and there's nothing like it in the world for free exchange across virtually open borders to the mutual benefit of both countries. US policy since the Eighties has sought to extend a North American free trade zone into Mexico. While a bit more problematic, there's a lot of promise there, since Vincente Fox and the PAN (National Action Party) ended seventy years of corrupt, one-party rule in that country a year ago. Indeed, unless a trading partner is actually hostile, there's every reason to reduce economic barriers—notwithstanding the necessity to maintain *political* sovereignty and socio-cultural self-determination. What I am saying is that Hawaii and Alaska trade with one another but don't infringe on political and social prerogatives of each State—there's a bright line there. The bright line is brighter when you're dealing with countries.

The big caution concerning free trade has to do with potentially hostile trading partners, as well as with national security and strategic imperatives. Here's what I mean. Lenin joked that a capitalist would sell him the very rope he would use to hang him with. Point well-taken: you probably don't wish to sell the means of your destruction to your enemy. Even if the Taliban could afford it, you shouldn't whip up your best strain of botulism and sell it at a premium price. Should we have sold military command and control computers to the former Soviet Union? What about China? In subtler terms, the United States also protects and subsidizes its manufacturing base and some agricultural interests, in order to ensure that we have means to produce basic goods and to fight the nation's wars. Recent events reinforce the need, not only to appreciate the magic of the international marketplace, but also its unfortunate and prudent limits.

Miracle of the Market — Article #127
o/a January 27, 2004

Day in and day out we give little thought to the vast and complex array of economic processes, which if they were to stop or severely malfunction would mean hardship or even disaster for many of us. The supermarkets are daily replenished with wide varieties of fruits, vegetables, meats, canned and packaged goods, dairy products, and many other items. We crowd the shopping malls and find them filled with practically every conceivable commodity we can imagine, with each of them offered in attractive and diverse varieties. Just think of the wide spectrum of shoes and clothes placed at our disposal in those malls as an example of this. And if we do not want the inconveniences and irritations of crowded shopping areas, a growing number of us now do an increasing amount of our shopping over the internet with the mere click of the "mouse."

Even if we wanted to fully understand how all those goods are actually brought to the marketplace for our various wants and desires, virtually none of us would be able to trace through all the intricate ways by which our demands are satisfied. Back in 1958, Leonard Read, the founder of FEE, wrote a famous essay titled "I, Pencil." He outlined a history of manufacturing a simple old-fashioned wooden pencil, from a tree being cut down in a forest and the mining of the graphite in a faraway country to its assembly and finished form so that it might be readily available for purchase by any of us in some neighborhood store. Read's central insight was to remind us that no one individual or even wise and informed group of us possesses all the knowledge or information that has gone into that pencil's manufacture.

Furthermore, it is not necessary for anyone to fully understand the processes involved in making that pencil for it to be available to us and our uses for such a writing instrument. Indeed, if it were required for some mastermind to know all that is needed to know to make all of the goods offered to us every day on the market, the variety of goods available to us would be both fewer in number and poorer in quality.

How are the activities of an increasingly larger group of individuals successfully coordinated, so that all the multitudes of demands and supplies are brought into balance and harmony? The Austrian economist and Nobel Laureate Friedrich Hayek showed how all of the knowledge and information in society can be encapsulated in the price system of the free-market economy. In our roles as both consumers and producers we communicate to one another what we think goods, resources, capital, and labor services are worth to us in their various and competing uses through the prices we are willing to pay for them. These "price signals" serve as the means for all of us to decide and coordinate what we want and are willing to do together with other members of society.

Thus, and indeed quite miraculously, it is not necessary for an "economy czar" to rule over and command us in our everyday market activities to assure that a vast quantity of food gets to the supermarkets or that thousands of different varieties of goods are constantly available in the shopping malls or other stores and businesses throughout the land. Each individual finds his own corner of specialization—guided by those opportunities, expressed in market prices, that seem to offer the greatest likelihood of earning an income that will enable him to buy from others all of the goods he himself desires.

Competition in these voluntary interactions of the market helps us to discover where each of us can best serve our fellow men within the system of division of labor while pursuing our own personal interests. The competitive process tests us through the reward of profits and the penalties of losses. Profits lure us into those production activities that our neighbors, as consumers, want us to do more of. Losses warn us that we have undertaken production actions that those same neighbors think are not worth the costs of our continuing to do them in the same way.

No overseer's whip is needed to prod people to do more of some things and less of others. No paternalistic planner is needed to assure that everything that is wanted is produced and in the most economically cost-efficient way. No restraining regulations and controls are needed to hamper the free choices and actions of the multitudes of millions in society—other than the crucial and general legal rules against murder, theft, and fraud in our dealings with one another.

Mutual agreement and voluntary consent are the bases of these market relationships. It is not the police power of the government, with its use or the threat of violence and force, that compels the cooperation and collaboration of humanity.[65]

Morality of the Market — Article #128
o/a February 02, 2004

In addition to the market's "miracle" of efficiency, there is an important moral element in the functioning of the free-market economy that we sometimes overlook or undervalue. There are none who are only masters and others who are simply servants! In the market society we are all both servants and masters, but without either force or its threat. In our roles as producers—be it as men who hire out our labor for wages, resource owners who rent out or sell our property for a price, or entrepreneurs who direct production for anticipated profits—we serve our fellow men in attempting to make the products and provide the services we think they may be willing and interested in buying from us.

"Service with a smile" and "the customer is always right" are hallmarks of the seller's deference to those to whom they offer their supplies. What motivates such attitudes is the fact that in an open, competitive market no one can compel us to buy from a seller who offers something less attractive or more costly than what some rival of his is presenting to us for our consideration.

And why are we interested in not offending or driving away some potential customer into the arms of our rival suppliers? Because only by successfully making the better and less expensive product can we hope to earn the income that then enables us to re-enter the market, now in the role of consumer and demander of what our neighbors are offering to sell to us.

As consumers, we become the "masters" who those same neighbors attempt to satisfy with newer, better, and cheaper products. Now those whom we have served defer to us. We "command" them, not through the use of force but through the attraction of our demand and the money we offer for the goods they bring to the market. By how much we can "command" the service of others in the market in our role as consumer is directly related to the extent we have been successful in our service to our neighbors as reflected in the money income we have earned from satisfying their wants and desires.

In a free society, no man is required to do work or supply any good he considers morally wrong and ethically questionable. He may earn less from choosing to supply something that is valued less highly in the market, but he cannot be forced to produce anything that God and/or conscience dictates to be wrong.

On the other hand, we cannot prevent others from supplying a good or service we find morally objectionable. The ethics of liberty and the free market require that we use only morally justifiable means to stop our neighbors from demanding and supplying something that offends us. We must use reason, persuasion, and example of a better and more right way to live.

Unfortunately, too many of our fellow men want to preserve or extend a return to a form of a slave society—regardless of the name under which it is presented. Too many want to dictate how others may make a living, or at what price and under what terms they may peacefully and voluntarily interact with their fellow human beings for purposes of mutual material, cultural, and spiritual betterment.

Our task, for those of us who understand and care deeply about human liberty, is to reawaken our fellow men an awareness of the miracle and morality of the market. The task, I know, seems daunting. But it must have seemed that way to our American Founding Fathers when they heralded the truth of the unalienable rights of man for which they fought and then won a revolution, or when advocates of economic freedom first made the case for the free market.

The world was transformed by these ideals of the morality of free men in free markets. What is most important is that each of us understands as best we can the miracle and the morality of the market economy. Too often the friends of freedom allow the advocates of various forms of government regulation, control, and redistribution to set the terms of the debate. Freedom will not win if we do not put those proponents of political paternalism on the defensive.

By that moral right do they claim to tell other men how to peacefully go about their private and market affairs—as long as those men do not use murder, theft, or fraud in their dealings with others? By what ethical norms do those political paternalists declare their right to take that which others have honestly acquired through production and trade, and redistribute it without the voluntary consent of those from whom it has been taken? By what assertion of superior wisdom and knowledge do they presume to know more than the individual minds of all the members of society about how the market should go about the business of manufacturing all the things we want, and matching the demands with the supplies?

Defenders of individual freedom and the market economy have nothing to be ashamed or fearful of in advocating the free society. The American system of limited government, personal liberty, and free enterprise liberated the individual creativity and energies of many millions of people. It provided the greatest opportunity for individual betterment and the highest standard of living ever experienced in human history. It also generated the most charitable and philanthropic society in the world. Therefore, it should be the critics and opponents of this system of individual freedom that should have to justify their continuing calls for reducing our liberty.

It was clear thinking and moral courage that won men liberty in the past. Liberty can triumph again, if each of us is willing but to try. We need to take to heart the words o the free-market Austrian economist and long-time FEE senior adviser, Ludwig von Mises:

> Everyone carries a part of society on his shoulders; no one is relieved of his share of responsibility by others. And no one can find a safe way out for himself if society is sweeping towards destruction . . . What is needed to stop the trend towards socialism and despotism is common sense and moral courage.[66]

Love Yourself and Your Neighbor — Article #152
o/a July 18, 2004

In thinking about what kind of society is good for business and investing, we need to remember two things. First, enlightened self-interest is a powerful and positive force for good in a free society. As Adam Smith said, "It is not from the benevolence of the butcher, the brewer, or the baker, that we expect our dinner, but from their regard to their own interest." In this light, it is a worrisome fact that Americans are becoming increasingly dependent when it comes to making the decisions that most affect their interests—e.g., decisions about caring for their health, educating their children and spending their earnings. If we are to keep America and its economy on the right track, we must find a way to return to our citizens more control over their lives.

Second, love of neighbor is the *most* powerful means of changing things for the good. It was with this in mind that President George W. Bush asked each of us in his 2001 inaugural address "to do small things with great love." Too often we create and depend on grandiose bureaucratic programs to address social problems, and in the meantime allow ourselves to forget about real people. For those of us with faith, it is enough to remember that we are called on by the Lord not to eradicate poverty, but to help our neighbor. For all of us, it should be clear enough by now that bureaucratic programs, such as the 40-year-old War on Poverty, tend to be counterproductive, whereas one-on-one efforts and private and local efforts—what I call lighthouse missions—bear real fruits.

Let me tell you a story to explain what I mean by lighthouse missions: An elderly couple living in a small coastal village approached the lighthouse keeper one day and said, "We are out of oil for our home, and it is cold." He gave them oil. The next day, a young couple petitioned for oil for their lamps so their children could study after dark. He gave them oil as well. But as a result of these and other well-meaning deeds, he ran out of oil, and without the light that it was his duty to provide, two ships crashed on the rocks killing hundreds of sailors.

It is not good or productive to allow ourselves to lose focus on our individual lighthouse missions, no matter how well meaning the thing that distracts us. And the same general principle adheres politically: Our local, state and national governments have lighthouse missions—responsibilities or duties that they are best suited to perform, and on which they should focus. In the case of the national government, these responsibilities are assigned by the Constitution. For instance, it is charged with providing the whole people a defense against foreign threats, for which it is uniquely suited. It is not, on the other hand, tasked with providing individuals with their various unique needs. And when it attempts to do the latter, it usually makes things worse.

We Americans today cede too much power to our elected representatives, and we need to take that power back. Let me give you an example. Our legislators find increasingly creative ways to misappropriate the hard-earned money of American workers: Consider $50,000 procured by Congresswoman Lois Capps to cover the costs of tattoo removal for her constituents in and around Santa Barbara, California. This immoral misuse of the American worker's earnings must be stopped. American taxpayers should determine tax rates, e.g., by demanding of their elected officials that those rates be capped at no more than 25 percent. At that point we can hold our legislators responsible, not for being less wasteful than their colleagues, but for setting the right priorities with limited resources.

But to regain this authority over our own lives in such a way as to be able to keep it—in other words, to remain free—we will need to become individually responsible: helping our neighbors and not demanding special treatment for ourselves. Winston Churchill spoke to the second point: "The inherent vice of capitalism is the unequal sharing of blessings; the inherent virtue of socialism is the equal sharing of misery." A free society mandates that constituents know how to live free and not as slaves to their passions.

Contrasted to Adam Smith's insight that free people in pursuit of their own self-interest will, in the process, fulfill the needs of others, there was a humble carpenter over 2000 years ago who encouraged us to give selflessly of ourselves to others. The economic success of our country depends, in a sense, on our ability to attend simultaneously to both of these ideals.[67]

Capital and Civilization — Article #195
o/a April 18, 2005

Money isn't everything to be sure; and yet, in a complex and developed economy dollars attest to a market-based valuation of the work you do. Unless you've chosen to please your fellow man through volunteer work, prayerful meditation, or some other work outside the scope of the economy, money equates to 'certificates of performance.' I mow your lawn, repair your roof, or teach your kid history. In turn you give me dollars. With these dollars in hand (our so-called certificates of performance), I go to my grocer and ask him to give me a pound of steak and a six-pack of (non-alcoholic) beer that my fellow man produced. The grocer may in effect say, "You're making a claim on something your fellow man produced. You're asking him to serve you—but did you serve him?" I can say, "Well yes, I did." And if the grocer says, "Prove it!" then I show him my certificates of performance—namely, the money my fellow man paid me to mow his lawn. In a free society, income is earned this way: through pleasing and serving one's fellow man. The more you please, so goes the theory, the more you can make. Luciano Pavarotti makes more singing than a bullfrog. Lloyd Conover, who created the antibiotic tetracycline while working for Pfizer Company, does a little better than your average snake oil salesman.

The magic of capitalism is that it not only enriches the few gifted people, but it raises all boats. Sometimes you'll hear an envious person malign the rich and blame the system for the rich man's toys. But when you think about it, it doesn't make a whole lot of sense. The rich under any and every system find a way to afford their distractions, indulgences, and entertainment! The only difference is there are fewer rich in some systems to enjoy these things, but the real point is, that it was the development and marketing of radio and television that made the rich man's entertainment accessible to the common man. The rich never did their own laundry or ironing—are you kidding? If you can afford a butler, you certainly aren't going to beat your own carpets or wax the floor. It was the development and mass production of washing machines, wash and wear clothing, vacuum cleaners and no-wax floors, that spared the common man and the common woman particularly, so much of the drudgery—even if it is still a lot of work! At one time only the rich could afford automobiles, telephones and computers. Now virtually every American can enjoy these goods.

Let's hear it then for capitalism and consider what else it brings. Namely, the output and wealth generated through free enterprise contributes to a more civilized society. For most of mankind's existence, man has had to spend most of his time simply eking out a living. In pre-industrial society and in many places in the world still today, the most optimistic scenario for the ordinary citizen was to meet the physical needs for today. With the rise of capitalism and the concomitant rise in human productivity that yielded economic progress, it was no longer necessary for man to spend his entire day simply providing for minimum physical needs. People were able to satisfy their physical needs with less time, which made it possible for them to have time and resources to develop spiritually and culturally. In other words, the rise of capitalism enabled the gradual extension of civilization to greater numbers of people. More now have time available to read, to become educated in the liberal arts, and to gain knowledge about the world around them. Greater wealth permits the majority of people to attend the arts, afford recreation, contemplate more fulfilling and interesting life activities, and to enjoy culturally enriching activities formerly within the exclusive purview of the very rich.

Adam Smith describes an almost magical relation twixt the market system and a kind of leveling up of civilization that makes everyone better off. Even if you take your stereotypic (and improbable) 'greedy capitalist,' he can't help but serve his fellow man, because profits are generated and linked through a process which not only finds out what human wants are not being met but which also finds the ways to meet them! As Smith explains, "By directing that industry in such a manner as its produce may be of the greatest value, [the entrepreneur] intends only his own gain, and he is in this, as in many other cases, led by an invisible hand to promote an end which was no part of his intention." In the same way, we had an entrepreneur like Thomas Watson, Sr. found IBM and become a leader in the information revolution. From the 1930s onward, IBM was at the forefront developing very profitable machines to handle large amounts of data accurately and rapidly, and this has led to unimaginable progress for human kind. Civilization is, in a way, purchased with and by the capital it takes to pay for the lawnmower, groceries and TV. You have an invisible hand in it, so to speak, with every certificate of performance you earn.[68]

Market Entrepreneurs — Article #389
o/a March 14, 2009

Between the generation of our Founding and World War II, there have been other "greatest" generations too. Perhaps the least appreciated in our time has been that post-Civil War generation of market entrepreneurs, who led America from being a second tier economic power to being the industrial powerhouse of the world. In today's economic downturn, it is perhaps helpful to remember the method that led to the most success before, as well as those ways that did not work in the past. One distinction that needs to be raised immediately is one between *market* entrepreneur and *political* entrepreneur. Businessmen aren't angels and neither are congressmen or plain folk, but competition tends to bring out better performance in people, whereas subsidization from public (tax) money risks funding and perpetuating substandard performance and inefficiencies.

Businessmen will often try to get favors or handouts from the government, because it may be easier than gathering together the necessary venture capital. Very often after that first taste, they return again and again to the same trough rather than wean off the public dole. The market entrepreneur pursues his business privately through private means. The political entrepreneur is in league with government, to the extent that he pursues his business semi-privately but through means that are exclusively or partially public. Then as today, political entrepreneurs are hard to avoid and even harder to get rid of, even though they are a drag on economic vitality and injurious to the wellbeing of the country. Market entrepreneurs go about their business freely and mostly wanting to be left alone, creating wealth and growing the economy. Government gets big off taxing productive market entrepreneurial activities, ironically enabling far too many government payouts to leeches in the business community of a political entrepreneurial bent.

Regulated bailouts could be the worst of all worlds if it institutionalizes business dependency on the government over the long haul and/or results in the permanent bureaucratic management by government of a private sector activity. Some historical examples are instructive. In the 1840s a political entrepreneur approached Congress to help him develop the U.S. steamship route between New York and Liverpool, and to cut into the business of rival English ships. Since the British government subsidized shipping, our man Edward Collins said he would need $3 million of taxpayers' money to construct five vessels and then an annual subsidy of $385,000 to drive passenger fares down low enough to compete.

Playing on congressional fears of British domination in trade, Collins got his money. He only built four ships, but who's counting. While he promised to phase out the annual subsidy, he was soon lobbying for more, and more, and more (up to $850,000 per year). Cornelius Vanderbilt tried to get in on the action too but by offering a cheaper deal, however the Congress had formed a cozy relationship with Collins so it turned him down. Forced to compete entirely, he used privately financed and self-insured vessels, slowed the ships' speed down to save on fuel, and invented a new, cheaper passenger class called *steerage*. A year later, Vanderbilt's operation was flourishing while Collins was even worse off and returned again to Congress asking for higher subsidy. When two of his ships sank because of poor maintenance and running the engines too fast, Collins had to resort to Congress for their replacement value. The Senate finally got wise after looking into the management practices, and no doubt comparing results and bottom line with that of Vanderbilt's operation. Collins lost his subsidy and within a year went bankrupt, enabling Vanderbilt to pick up more of the business privately, at less cost and far better value to customers—not to mention dominance of the seas from an American side.

A decade or so later Congress began subsidizing political entrepreneurs representing transcontinental railroad ventures: the Union Pacific, the Central Pacific, and later the Northern Pacific. The government gave these companies tens of millions of acres of free land and tens of millions of dollars, and because the companies had no incentive to be efficient, the railroads evidenced shoddy construction, as well as circuitous routes and uneven grades. The privately funded railroad called Great Northern, however, was a success that put the others to shame. James J. Hill built his line for durability and efficiency and without government money, taking the shortest distance, lowest grades and least curvature that he could. He also supervised construction and imported the very highest quality Bessemer rails. Although these cost more up front, they also lasted a long time and were more dependable. He took the same approach to his railroad bridges, constructing the solid granite Stone Arch Bridge 2,100 feet long and 82 feet high across the Mississippi River—a Minneapolis landmark for many decades.

Similar stories mark the success of Andrew Carnegie in steel, and John D. Rockefeller in oil. These men were *market* entrepreneurs not "robber barons." They created wealth and propelled the United States to first rank economically in the world. Moreover, so far as generations go, they stood head and shoulders above the risk-averse, sycophantic and slinking *political* entrepreneurs, who pass for so many CEOs and leaders in American business today.[69]

Unfinished Legacy: President Reagan and the Socrates Project
o/a November 27, 2010 Article #478

President Reagan established a proud legacy during his two terms in office, the philosophical hallmarks of which were a reduction in the size of the federal government and empowerment of the private sector of the economy. What is not fully appreciated is that Reagan intended another aspect, which should still be added. Reagan started a process whereby he would overlay this aspect through executive order, at least initially. Unfortunately his attempt to provide a technology strategy and vision did not survive the follow-on George Herbert Walker Bush administration.

The executive order was drafted towards the end of his second term and would have created a government agency somewhat on par with the National Aeronautics and Space Administration (NASA). The agency would have answered directly to the White House and had the mission and the means to enable U.S. government organizations and American companies to work together in a highly coherent and unprecedented fashion. Reagan essentially tried to provide the marketplace, as well as select government planning agencies, with new tools that were possible with the onset of the Information Age.

Reagan was convinced that this additional aspect would ensure not only America's economic survival, but also its preeminence and continued economic superpower status. On the basis of his draft executive order, Michael C. Sekora established a prototype program called the Socrates Project within the U.S. intelligence community. The program was aimed at improving America's economic efficiencies and reducing the frictional components of the marketplace through better information, particularly in those domains relating to technology. The program design was meant specifically to address an apparent decline in U.S. manufacturing and competitiveness worldwide. The Socrates Project's mission was two-fold: to determine the underlying cause of America's declining competitiveness; and to use this determination to propose the subsequent development of means to reverse the economic decline.

To determine the cause of America's declining competitiveness, the Socrates team used all source intelligence to generate a holistic, bird's eye view of competition worldwide. The team's view and understanding went well beyond the inferior data that is still the best available to most university professors, think tank analysts and consultants, in terms of scope and completeness.

What the Socrates team determined was that the source of America's declining competitiveness followed an epochal shift in thinking that took place after World War II. It was not directly related to investment or to patterns of destruction, so much as it was based on the decision-makers' response to post-war political and economic conditions. At the end of World War II decision-makers throughout the U.S. began shifting away from technology-based planning and began adopting economic-based planning instead. Within a few years, the economic-based planning model had become the standard, all-but-unchallenged foundation for decision-making throughout U.S. industry, government and academe. At the same time, much of the rest of the world continued refining and utilizing technology-based models of planning.

In technology-based planning the foundation for decision-making is the acquisition and utilization of technology, where technology is defined as any application of science to accomplish a function, in order to produce a better product or service. Based on targeted information, technology can be manipulated, offensively and defensively in a chess-like way, in order to acquire and maintain competitive advantage. In contrast, economic-based planning models lead to manipulation of funds as the foundation for decision-making. The measure of success based on economic-based thinking, is the efficiency at which one manipulates so-called economic drivers. Economic manipulation, unlike its technological counterpart is unrelated to anything real or tangible and is not even integrally coordinated with the nation's wealth or productive outputs per se.

What was also obvious to the Socrates team from their unique bird's eye view of competition, was that countries like China and India were using technology-based planning to catch up and further, to undercut America's ability to generate or regain competitive advantage. Indeed, they were rapidly transforming themselves into world economic superpowers as our status slipped and the U.S. position was being eclipsed. While we in the U.S. were coming up with increasingly sophisticated economic shell games to maximize profits, China and India were systematically outmaneuvering us in the acquisition and utilization of technology to eliminate our ability to produce products and services that had competitive advantage in foreign markets, and increasingly in our own domestic markets.

With the global bait and switch nearly completed and the United States suffering through its worst recession since the Great Depression, Reagan's initiative with Socrates seems positively prescient. With revitalized conservatism in vogue again since the last election, tea partiers and conservatives in the next Congress would do well, not only to follow the fiscally prudent "Roadmap for America's Future" laid out by Congressman Paul Ryan (R-WI), but to revisit the national strategic level effort required which Ronald Reagan suggested before we got into this mess.

CHAPTER 31

Reflecting on Economic Woes

Economic Outlook Good, But . . . Article #060
o/a March 15, 2002

Let's take a minute to look back at the economic situation the past year or so, and then I want to look ahead to what the rest of 2002 and early next year hold. Despite two serious setbacks since 2000, the view ahead looks pretty good. To understand why, I refer to work done by Dr. David Fand, a leading monetary expert, who teaches at George Mason University in Virginia. Dr. Fand was a student of famed economist and Nobel Prize winner Milton Friedman at the University of Chicago; and he has also served as consultant to the Federal Reserve, to the Secretary of the Treasury, and to the Congressional Joint Economic Committee. His assessment is basically that the U.S. economy is in recovery from a technical recession, continuing its bound back from both the capital spending collapse of mid-2000 and the spending downturn in 2001 that followed September 11th.

While the assessment does not take into account the corporate scandals of 2002 or the war jitters that continue to affect the stock market, his analysis of fundamentals is valid and applicable at the present time. That's because the Bush Administration cracked down on the bad guys in business, and corporate America moved smartly to restore ethics and sound practices on their own. The resort to private and governmental nontoleration worked. The economic impact of ENRON and the other scandals should be minimal, unless liberals turn fear and resentment to political advantage in November and ruin the economy themselves. The year will continue along a path to recovery, owing to good American values, to our high quality labor force, as well as to sound monetary and fiscal policy. The primary caveat Fand offers is this: as the War on Terrorism drags on, there are associated long-term negative economic impacts. Indeed, that's the only thing that could change our fundamentals. Otherwise, the year's spate of high profile scandals is really pretty transitory; and a relatively quick beating of Iraq will just make everyone feel much better, as well as wind up lowering energy prices.

After September 11, 2001 many experts predicted a deep recession or depression. The attacks on the World Trade Center and Pentagon caused substantial property damage and loss of life, as well as severe economic dislocations. Many industries were hit hard directly: airlines, hotels, restaurants and travel. Only after two or three months did these industries start to partially recover. Moreover, as mentioned, an economic slow-down had already started in mid-2000. Excessive capital spending had occurred over several years, and the downturn followed a decline in aggregate demand—particularly, as you will recall, in the high tech sector. No one has yet found a way to repeal the business cycle! The interesting aspect about the 2000 downturn, however, was that it resembled recessions experienced before establishment of the Federal Reserve in 1914, more than it did any of the nine post-World War II recessions prior to 2000. The 2000-2001 downturns were not preceded by inflation or by rising interest rates, so experts got very jittery and expected a hard boom-bust cycle, more akin to the 19th century than to the 20th.

The reasons that dire predictions did not pan out, speak to uncommon strengths in the American economy and to some uncommon luck. First of all, the work habits, optimism, courage and values of the American people—coupled with the fact that we operate in a relatively free market economy—produced remarkably good results. While there has been a trend in the last century towards big government, we still have the smallest government relative to Gross Domestic Product (GDP) among major industrial economies. We have an educated, innovative and hard-working work force—truly unrivalled in the world. Give it freedom to produce, and you produce a miracle! Second, we must also add that our Federal Reserve has done extraordinarily well in its conduct of monetary policy in recent years, starting with Chairman Paul Volcker's brilliant success taming the terrible stagflation period between 1978 and 1982. The success then continued under Chairman Alan Greenspan, who has become something of a folk hero for being so adept at keeping inflation and interest rates under control. Third, we've been very lucky.

The luck came in the area of fiscal policy. The huge budget surplus we built up in recent years has helped us weather the recent storm. But that surplus was hardly the result of prudent policy; rather, it came as a direct result of the divided government we've had since 1994. According to Dr. Fand:

> When the Republicans won the Congress in the 1994 elections, they were able to stop some of President Clinton's spending initiatives. Their veto on his expenditure plans, coupled with an economy still benefiting from the earlier Reagan tax cuts, helped produce a large surplus. If the Democrats had controlled congress there would have been no surplus because they would have increased spending—similarly if the Republicans had controlled the Executive Branch there would have been no surplus because they would have cut taxes. While we were fortunate to have a surplus when this downturn developed, it was in large measure the result of divided government. It was not the result of anybody's policy.

Add to the luck, if you will, the short-term impact (2002-3) of rebuilding and increased military spending tied to the War on Terrorism. Short-term, that spending too will stimulate the economy. Longer term, however, Fand and many economists are less sanguine. Additional expenditures on the military or on personnel and safety equipment will inevitably exact a social cost or "tax" on society that retards long-term economic growth. The reason is that it necessarily reallocates resources to security and away from the production of other marketable goods and services. Budget surpluses are likely to be lower still, because spending on defense and homeland security will probably not be offset by cuts in other programs. To sum up, the economy is on the mend for the time being. If the War on Terrorism drags on and turns into an open-ended commitment to rid the world of evildoers, however, it will cost us blood to be sure. It will also cost us treasure and quite possibly, the prosperity that's become a hallmark for our American way of life.

American Prospects, 2003 Article #077
January 23, 2003

Let's talk about the economic outlook for 2003. Notwithstanding his tremendous popularity, George W. Bush would do well to remember Bill Clinton's snide internal campaign slogan of 1992 ('It's the economy,

Stupid!'), because the potential parallel to 2004 is uncanny. If George W. comes out on top and even more wildly popular after his War with Iraq in 2003, how different is that from the Elder Bush's situation in 1991? His popularity could fade as quickly in one year's time as did his father's. Then he could be running a race between declining popularity and approval ratings and time to the Presidential election. If the economy hits a recession after the war, George W. could be sinking fast by fall of 2004. I guess the trick is timing—and presidents have even been known to tweak economies to their benefit. But it is less than a perfect science! Ronald Reagan took over an economy from Jimmy Carter that was already in a wreck, and Reagan weathered a serious recession early in his first term. The Elder Bush unfortunately had his recession late in his first (and as it turned out *only*) term, which gave the advantage to his challenger who harped on the economy. Since the economy lately has been pretty weak (Christmas sales were down), this President Bush stands a very good prospect of winning a war and following up with an economy in recovery, if not at full steam.

Indeed, the market was down for the third straight year in 2002. If it goes down for a fourth year, it will be the first time since 1929-32. So historical odds have it, that the economy, if measured by the stock market, will be up in 2003. Surely George W. won't repeat his father's terrible mistake and pull back on tax cuts either. This would prove the equivalent of his dad's own "read my lips" miscalculation—believing he could compromise with Congressional opponents on a practical matter and trust they would give him a bye politically. George W. should not believe his tax cut critics—they will definitely skewer him for waffling on a tax cut plan come election time. If anything, he should try to speed up planned tax cuts, to get a boost near-term in the economy. His recently unveiled economic stimulus plan is pretty good in that respect.

It is true, however, wars and economies are tied together. But the argument that you can't buy guns and butter in the present context is a red herring. President Johnson could not turn up the heat on a nearly decade's-old war in Vietnam and have his Great Society cake too, at least not without double-digit inflation. But a short war is doable without the same inflation fallout. Moreover, the economy now is artificially depressed because of war jitters. People are holding back their spending, and the market reflects the uncertainty and unsettled mood. Qualitatively the Bush tax cut approach is different from LBJ's tax spend approach, because Bush would have spending on butter, if you will, come from people with money in their own pockets, not from government spending on social programs on the people's behalf. Unlike the early 80s then, when fundamentals were not sound after two ravaged decades—they are good now, thanks to keeping inflation in check. Thanks also to fortuitous changes in technology, giving us market windfalls and at least a fleeting budget surplus during Clinton's administrations.

Thus I predict, the prospect for the U.S. economy in 2003 is to continue slow improvement. It is even now bounding back from the capital spending collapse of mid-2000, a spending downturn in 2001 following 9-11, and corporate scandals of 2002. Indeed, the latter was the most serious potential peril for the economy, but the Bush Administration fortunately cracked down on the bad guys in business (some 34 have been criminally prosecuted); and corporate America moved smartly to restore ethics and sound practices on their own. The resort to private and governmental non-toleration worked. The economic impact of the scandals has been minimal. Otherwise, the liberals would have turned fear and resentment to political advantage during these last elections, which they were not able to do. Economic news in the year ahead, by all rights should be in keeping with recovery, owing to good ole American values, to our high quality labor force, as well as to sound monetary and fiscal policy. The primary caveat that I would offer is this: as the War on Terrorism drags on (beyond a short War in Iraq), there are associated long-term negative economic consequences—and this is where the guns and butter analogy holds. Indeed, to my mind extended war is the only thing that can change US economic fundamentals. Last year's spate of high profile scandals has already proven to be transitory; a relatively quick beating of Iraq will make everyone feel better and also wind up lowering energy prices. The work habits, optimism, courage and values of the American people—these, coupled with the fact that we operate in a relatively free market economy—produce remarkably good results. These will always win the peace.

Granted while there has been a trend in the last century towards big government, we still have the smallest government relative to Gross Domestic Product (GDP) among major industrial economies. We have an educated, innovative and hard-working work force—truly unrivalled in the world. Give it freedom to produce, and you produce a miracle! I would also add that our Federal Reserve has done extraordinarily well in its conduct of monetary policy, starting with Chairman Paul Volcker's brilliant success taming stagflation and continuing with Chairman Alan Greenspan, who has become something of a folk hero for keeping inflation and interest rates under control. Long term, however, additional expenditures on the military or on personnel and safety equipment will inevitably exact a social cost or "tax" on society that retards long-term economic growth. The reason is Economics 101: it necessarily reallocates resources to security and away from the production of other marketable goods and services. Budget surpluses are likely to be lower too, because spending on defense and homeland security will probably not be offset by cuts in other government programs—even if you or I hope they might be. The economy is on the mend, as I said. But if the War on Terrorism drags on and turns into an open-ended commitment to rid the world of evildoers, it will cost us blood to be sure, and also lots and lots of treasure; and ultimately perhaps, the prosperity that has become the hallmark for our 'American way of life'—the same that the terrorists sought to destroy and couldn't.[70]

On Values and Spending — Article #120
o/a December 08, 2003

In August I attended a Rotary breakfast, and a prominent politician was the featured speaker. I can tell you it was enough to almost spoil breakfast—and Rotary does a pretty good job. I listened to him rattle off every program he was responsible for supporting, including the amounts he's personally added to the budget—to parks, water, transportation and highways, construction, etc. Never mind local taxes go up just to match federal funds—in 20 years, I'm sure you'll see the benefit of all these "investments." Anyway, I added up the money he took credit for, and it literally came to $1 Billion. The politician bragged about blocking every single Bush administration attempt to trim "essential" expenses too. In the next breath, this same politician soundly castigated the president for running an approximately 400 billion dollar budget deficit this coming year! "I'm worried about that—it is a real concern," he said. And I'm sitting there, wondering where the logic just went . . . 'Is anybody out there?' Does anybody connect the dots, as they say—drawing the connection between spending and debt?

By my calculation, if congressmen were as "successful" as this unnamed politician in delivering pork and programs, it would entirely explain our budget shortfall. I agree—we all should be concerned. The 2004 federal budget is going to be 22% larger than the 2001 budget, which belies an average annual growth rate in spending of 7-8%. Even Clinton's budgets increased just 3 to 4% a year. Then again, wars are expensive—and you do trade domestic political capital to hold the line on spending whenever you wage wars. And liberals will always take advantage—as they did during the Reagan years.

I heard the same politician again last week. In a political stump speech, he equated "Central Texas values" with all sorts of entitlement and federal programs: medical care, IMPACT aid, military construction, etc. His spokespeople bragged again about his ability to add more to the federal budget than anybody else—year after year after year. Folks, I have to tell you that my notion of Central Texas values is entirely different. The values I believe in are Jeffersonian and Madisonian—they are Life, Liberty and the Pursuit of Happiness. Life—the sanctity of it from conception to natural death; Liberty—the ability to pursue your dreams, unencumbered by government regulations and obstacles that seek to control and enslave; Pursuit of Happiness—local and State self-determination and the strength of institutions closest to the people: home and family, church and schools. "Things"—no matter how important some are—these should never displace our most cherished values! For instance, you wouldn't vote your pocket book at the expense of human life (yours or someone else's), would you? WOULD YOU? You wouldn't vote for creature comfort or subsidy to your pet cause at the expense of your freedom, would you? WOULD YOU?

I spent 20 years in the military. I joined to do two things: to defeat communism; and to enable my fellow citizens to live in freedom while I bore conformity and risk to help defend the country. I was motivated explicitly by Ronald Reagan's vision, and I consider him to be my political mentor. I was his youth advisor for the State of Texas in 1979 before heading off to West Point and a subsequent Army career. Reagan accomplished important things during the Eighties, winning the Cold War, rolling back tax rates and giving conservatism a good name. But today we have unfinished business to attend to, in order to complete the Reagan Revolution. For while we won the Cold War, we have not won the one involving the culture. We have not restored constitutional government either, by redressing the imbalance that exists now between the state and federal governments. Culture is a local prerogative;

it emanates from families, churches, communities and States. States were meant to be the Union's cradles of culture and laboratories of liberty. They were never intended to be homogeneous provinces or mere appendages of an omnipotent central State. Ronald Reagan wanted and tried to downsize government and empower individuals and States. But the federal government is more of the behemoth today than in 1989. I left the military to find that so-called civil society resembles a military camp more every day, in more ways than most feel comfortable to admit. Not only that, people are willingly trading their freedoms daily—using majoritarian democracy and the power of a consolidated nation-state-empire to fleece various segments of the population, in order to redistribute wealth to others or to purchase a fleeting sense of security at the expense of liberty itself—Liberty most precious and liberty that's worth dying for. Ladies and Gentlemen, I did not serve 20 years and fight two wars—one cold and one hot—to see my country turn into a nation of people who take orders and serve the collective, or live to execute missions assigned to us by superiors. The military is a wonderful institution. Martial values are extraordinarily valuable—essential for a Republic, but only in the context provided for by our magnificent Constitution.

The liberals' redefinition and corruption of values helps explain how some vote for a politician, who delivers a favorite good or service but votes, say, against the ban on partial birth abortion. Ironically, a trade of this sort—which is nothing short of a trade with the devil—isn't even necessary! You can have essential military construction, you can have economic growth and opportunity, you can keep your promises to veterans and ensure Ft. Hood remains vital, etc. all at the same time you vote for a moral society that protects and defends the things that are most important. Of course, you may not get the same wanton spending.

Ted Kennedy says the Bush administration pushed the 400 Billion dollar Medicare package for political advantage, as a way to introduce privatization of Medicare now and as a prelude to privatize Social Security later. Gee, I sure hope so! I'm afraid he may be giving us too much credit though. Perhaps the Administration will use an increased Congressional margin in 2005 to follow up with aggressive roll-back of the welfare state. If so, we need to ensure that margin is provided by States Rights, constitutionalist conservatives—not big spending liberals (or even big spending so-called conservatives)! That's the best face I can put on an ill-advised and unfunded subsidy program like the one passed by Congress that was signed into law this week.

CHAPTER 32

FIX THE TRACK OR EXPECT A CRASH

Reason to Balance the Federal Budget — Article #244
o/a March 17, 2006

The economics and the politics of deficit spending are controversial if not also unclear. As you might guess, liberals tend to fear balancing the budget will lead to slashing pet government programs. Supply-side conservatives, however, fear that balancing the budget provides a ready excuse for politicians to raise your taxes. Those primarily interested in national defense fear balancing the budget at times, because it potentially squeezes defense and intelligence spending. Indeed, some economists now think balancing the budget isn't really very important at all, because inflation can be controlled by effective monetary policy irrespective of the budgetary surplus or deficit. While relative trade-offs, in terms of priority, differ any given year (and I won't hold my breath for a resolution of economic debate) there is independently one very compelling reason why we ought to pursue a balanced federal budget.

Balancing the federal budget begets better government. A permanent deficit relieves politicians of responsibility to say no to any interest group or constituency. If government spending is an open-ended credit card without consequences, politicians will pander to every group and say yes to every request. (Oh yeah, incidentally that's where we are today). If deficits do not matter, the most rational strategy for every bureaucratic agency is to simply ask for more money. Moreover, since resources are artificially delimited through deficit spending, there is little incentive to hold costs down by finding innovative, less costly and more productive ways of doing business. Any spirit of entrepreneurial public management is driven out of the process or given short shrift. Politicians, who would ordinarily face the ire of voters in a constrained environment, because they raised taxes or spent profligately, now hide behind all the free goodies and stuff they bring home to their districts. Arguably it mortgages the kids' future, but what—the-hey: 'taint nothing compared to the reelection campaign two years from now.

Keeping the lid on spending through a balanced federal budget was a major brake on the size of the U.S. government prior to 1929. Moreover, as an historian, I am persuaded the healthiest periods for most countries during peacetime have been when the political leadership was forced to set priorities and balance the budget by controlling spending. When all things are possible, nothing is probable—least of all, a sense of purpose and national direction borne of hard work and persuasion. Over time, lower interest rates and less inflation follow balanced budgets, notwithstanding the ability of the Federal Reserve to compensate for deficits short-term and in generally good economic circumstance. Where spending is no object, there is less structural form for opposition to take, less cause to insist upon accountability either.

When I consider the terrific increase in federal spending that has taken place in the GW Bush years and the associated pandering to special interests, it is all the more sad and astonishing to remember that in 1995 Republicans passed the constitutional amendment for a balanced budget out of the House and were just one vote shy of passing it in the Senate. What a difference one vote does make! Now they've given up and many have given in. The growth of K-Street lobbyists is less indicative of corruption than it is of increased size, scope and power in Washington. If the government didn't do so much, there wouldn't be so much to lobby about. The number of registered lobbying firms in the last six years alone has jumped from 1,701 to 2,060. Lobbyist spending increased 50%, and the number of companies who hire lobbyists increased 58%. Lobbyists in the nation's capital number almost 35,000, double what it was in 2000. The connection between out of control government spending, the rise of lobbyists and the debasement of principled republican government, is palpable. As budget surpluses are squandered and deficits run high, the real price of not balancing the federal budget becomes apparent. Balancing the budget not only makes good fiscal sense, it is a prerequisite to continuance of good government for a reason that, at first may not appear obvious. For want of a nail, the horseshoe was lost; for want of a shoe the horse was lost; for want of that horse, supplies ran low; for want of ammunition, the battle and the war were lost. Today we risk much for want of a reason to balance the federal budget, but if you see the connection, you value a nail and the reason besides.[71]

Economic Patriotism Article #285
o/a March 02, 2007

On February 27th stocks on Wall Street plunged by more than 400 points. It was the single biggest decline since the market re-opened after 9-11 in 2001. In extremely heavy selling, more than 4 billion shares were traded. The market was due for correction, as markets will be from time to time, but the cause of this precipitous decline was something new. Five years ago, China was almost no factor at all in the American economy. The huge falloff at the beginning of 2007, however, is a direct result of news coming out of China. The Hong Kong index dropped nine percent, reverberating and causing the Dow to lose more than three. The fact that stock punters in China have impact in New York is something new and probably something to be concerned about. China and the United States are at odds on economic issues ranging from intellectual property rights to currency valuation. Meanwhile China has become one of the largest holders of American debt; and while the U.S. trade deficit with China continues to balloon, China has become a labor-outsourcing platform for mostly large American businesses. Taken together—the corporate outsourcing of cheap labor abroad and corporate "in-sourcing" to illegal labor at home has set the United States up for quite the dubious long-term comparative advantage! No one argues the fact we are rapidly losing economic sector diversity or self-sufficiency, though horse sense has it that when self-sufficiency goes, self-determination is sure to follow.

The loss of manufacturing jobs in the U.S. economy is one thing, but dependency on the wiles of Chinese communist government is another. Do not forget the Chinese economy is a planned economy, that 100% of the shares in the Chinese stock market are government owned. Moreover, do not mistake the political and international ambitions of the Chinese government or the fact that when we downsized our military and turned it towards Islamist terrorists, China continued to build and modernize theirs, judging us to be their strategic rival and most likely potential enemy. In February they sought to reduce speculation and overproduction in their economy, and the policy change announcements made in China impacted the American stock market. We should ask ourselves what tomorrow brings if trends continue and we are in fact strategic rivals. The only reason the U.S. and Canadian economies could be safely intertwined and open borders allowed, was that we are culturally similar and more importantly, we are unquestioned strategic allies. The reason we could not pursue the same policy towards the old Soviet Union was because they were out to kill us. Mutual advantage in that context strengthens enemies disproportionately; comparative advantage becomes a likely vulnerability. Indeed, our experience vis-à-vis Great Britain in the early years of the Republic was similar. We manifestly rejected unalloyed free trade, in order to build up American manufactures and stay self-sufficient while Great Britain remained a strategic rival and possible threat.

Pat Buchanan has argued for a course correction in trade policy and more "economic patriotism" this day and age. His critics say he's a knee-jerk isolationist, who wants to secede from the world and create a hide-bound economic Fortress America—something impossible, as it would be inadvisable. Notwithstanding, it occurs to me that we do need to start doing what's good for America: not only in terms of foreign policy and security, but in terms of trade policy and the economy. Call it economic patriotism or doing your constitutional duty. Ideology, whether progressive, conservative or something else ought to be informed by what's happening. One size does not fit all, and as Americans we must not buy the internationalist snake oil of inevitability either. We cannot afford blind-leading-blind globalists down the primrose path to self-destruction in the name of free trade or anything else. We live in a world of nation states; we deal with regional economic blocs and with some countries that have huge markets but command economies. Not all these have interests identical with or even friendly to our own. Not all of these offer level playing fields either, for economic competition and investment. Many could care less about the environment or the wages of their workers, much less ours. The point is simply this: every trade agreement needs to be judged on its merits, including second and third order effects, including its portent for the future. Every trade agreement also needs to be reassessed in light of actual experience. Politicians must never be allowed to consign America to disadvantageous or corrupt bargains; and they must not compromise the wellbeing and livelihoods of her people. And if anyone dare say all this means that you care too little for the world, have the courage to answer thus: what is good for America is ultimately good for the world! Because the last time I checked, we were still the last, best hope of mankind, and hopefully, still its beacon of liberty to anyone willing and strong enough to follow our example.

America the Broke Article #311
o/a February 23, 2004

Galveston used to be great when I was a kid, but today the beach has all but washed away. Dubai, UAE is able to restore and expand their coastline by miles, but the U.S. these days seems unable to think or invest as big. Our infrastructure is crumbling and bridges literally collapsing. A major American city gets swept away, and there is no unified cry to rebuild it, little sense of responsibility or concern by any level of government to do so. Billions of federal dollars are thrown at it, but still there is little visible evidence today, in terms of improvement in and around New Orleans. Sometimes I wonder what it is that eclipses a nation, what causes the dynamism to pass away, or a people to cease being great by ceasing to act great. Part of it, of course, is that we are "developed" by definition; and only now have the circumstances and resources converged to enable much of the rest of the world to develop in a similar way. We've heard about Chinese economic growth, about computer geniuses coming out of India. Part of it could be our own doing too, as we squander the wealth we have as if it will always be there, on war and profligate spending. Indeed, we are spending ourselves into oblivion and no longer saving for a rainy day or even to invest in the future. The economy seemed to be good, at least until the August credit crunch. Surprise surprise.

The 2008 Federal Budget will cost taxpayers $2.9 trillion. The third largest expenditure in the budget (after defense and Social Security) is interest on the federal debt! That national debt is debt all of us owe, and it has risen from $5.6 trillion to $8.8 trillion in just seven years. The sleight of hand done mostly by Republicans was increasing spending more than at any time since the New Deal, but doing so without increasing taxes. The latest Congressional report says we spend about $2 billion per week on the wars in Afghanistan and Iraq, all funded by more debt. The approach makes spending politically palatable, but it is tantamount to a gross deceit and fraud committed on the American people (not to mention cynicism of the highest order). That's because currency ends up devalued if you fail to pay down the debt. Anyone who travels abroad has certainly already noticed it. The U.S. has also become vulnerable to foreign holders of our debt—over 44 percent of the national debt is actually owned by foreigners. Inflation will of course offer a way out, but this is precisely part and parcel of the fraud. Politicians can blame the price of oil, even though the price of oil in gold terms has remained constant since 1945. Politicians can also hide the fact, because inflation statistics are so easy to manipulate. There have been many changes to the calculation since 1970. The 1970's calculation would have us at about 8% inflation today, as opposed to the ridiculously low figure reported and trumpeted by our government. As the artificially low figure continues to creep up, however, the government merely asks us to focus on the "Core" Consumer Price Index (CPI), excluding food and energy!

The Emperor simply has no clothes or integrity either, while government misleads the public reporting 2.7% inflation—all the while keeping Social Security cost of living adjustments down, knowing full well the true figure of inflation is much higher. Americans scratch their heads when they have no money left, and health care and education are increasing at double digits. Meanwhile the constitutional system that underpins and supports the American economy is a shamble. Maybe you do not realize the United States now signs international trade agreements with numerous other countries, but we don't call them treaties so that we can avoid the Senate ratification required by the Constitution! That way, you see, you don't get all the scrutiny you would normally have or expect in terms of impact on American wages, job sectors, and quaint old-fashioned ideas like political and territorial sovereignty. Meanwhile the Chinese have already hinted they might be forced to liquidate vast holdings of U.S. treasuries if Washington tries to impose sanctions or press too many reforms. Whether forced to or not, $1.33 trillion in foreign reserves held by China constitutes a political weapon capable of precipitating, quite possibly, recession in our economy or a dollar collapse. Russia, Switzerland and several other countries have already begun to reduce dollar holdings.

Oil: The Long Goodbye Article #346
o/a April 25, 2008

Peak Oil is a self-evident truth, if you aren't a stickler about just when it should happen. Most experts agree that petroleum and fossil fuels are exhaustible resources. They are nonrenewable unless you've got millions of years to spare. Peak Oil is the point in time when the maximum rate of global petroleum production is reached, after which, the rate of production enters its natural decline. In laymen's terms, we start to run out of (cheap) oil. If consumption isn't reduced and/or alternatives discovered and developed in time before the peak—whenever that happens, it is simple economics that prices rise, and an energy crisis will ensue.

As you might imagine, lots of variables intervene. The moment you predict Peak Oil, you've got a laundry list of caveats to make. But let's consider a few that might affect things. Take consumption rates. Do you think those are coming down? Nope. Has the world's population stopped growing? Nope, it more than doubled in the last fifty years. World crude oil demand has increased far above predictions a few years ago, driven by an insatiable need from China and India. China's oil consumption has grown 8 per cent per annum since 2002, and its economy is still experiencing oil shortage. As huge energy consumers impact the market, they will compete for a dwindling, nonrenewable supply and hence drive up energy prices. As many other economies enter a similar stage of economic development, energy needs will skyrocket and add to the pressure.

I'm sure run-of-the-mill monetary inflation is much to blame for price increases at the gas pump, but folks you need to start getting a little more sophisticated (or at least read the big print writing on the wall!). Don't wait for the government to tell you, much less do anything about it. The Bush administration isn't exactly known for its candor with the American people (it's all a state secret, or Executive prerogative); or for that matter competence and being proactive (Katrina, War in Iraq, etc.). Global oil production actually already hit plateau in 2005, when Texas oilman T. Boone Pickens predicted that we probably reached the proverbial Peak Oil point.

Even if you don't buy that, and many experts don't, we're just quibbling over the next ten years and your favorite colored deck chair on the Titanic. At an energy conference in Houston this past month, the Peak Oil prediction was 2015. Nine of the world's twenty-one largest fields show decline, and some fields are beginning to accelerate downward. Even more skeptical observers will concede that discoveries peaked around 1961 and have long since failed to replace the full amount of oil produced. Oil is being depleted in other words, we just can't say how fast; the train is careening, but it may not go off the tracks for a couple more presidential election cycles.

It is important to consider what we're talking about: Peak Oil for *Le Monde*, the World. We already passed it for the United States back in 1970, for North Sea oil production in 1985. In fact, Peak Oil production has been reached in almost every oil-producing country in the world, except three notables: Iraq (may not reach it until 2018); Kuwait (predicted peak in 2013); and Saudi Arabia (predicted peak 2014). Of course, I didn't mention another big oil producer—Iran, because we don't really know, and probably won't get to the supply short of military invasion (which could happen). Moreover, Kuwait and Saudi Arabia and other OPEC countries have every reason to overstate their proven reserves and probably have. If you look at the frantic pace at which Saudi Arabia and the entire Gulf is diversifying economies, one wonders if the United States and other developed countries shouldn't be reducing dependency on Middle East oil at least that fast.

Hurricane Katrina initially wiped out 15% of U.S. refining capacity, which was strained and still is. This resulted in a price spike of 100% as the price of gasoline went from $1.50/gallon to $3.00/gallon in just a few days. When the Iranian revolution occurred in 1979 and crude oil prices doubled, world oil consumption dropped 15% and a worldwide recession lasted until 1982. There isn't much resiliency in the energy supply chain, and domestic storage capacity is less than two months. And we're really talking about a much bigger problem.

Civilization probably won't end short of a big meteor hitting the earth, but if you're going to do anything constructive to mitigate problems our economy will face after the world hits Peak Oil, you need at least ten years to get busy. Suggesting a bigger picture, consider that most farm equipment depends on oil and diesel, what that means to food prices and food availability. Nearly all fertilizers and pesticides are made from oil too, as well as most plastics—used in everything from computers, mobile phones, to pipelines, clothing and carpets. Metal production, such as aluminum, depends on oil; and even things like cosmetics, hair dye, ink, and common painkillers. The construction of a single car takes at least 20 barrels of oil.

It behooves us therefore to have an energy policy, unless your policy is simply to endure economic upheavals. You might want to foster conservation, R&D, transition to alternatives—particularly other liquid fuels (alcohol, esters, vegetable oils, etc.; and liquefied petroleum products from natural gas and coal). You might want to invest in infrastructure too, say, in storage, pipelines, rigs and rail transportation. You should at least want to talk about it. Now I'm not really one to run around like Chicken Little, yelling "The sky is falling, the sky is falling," but oil production really is. Our country faces an immense and unprecedented risk management problem, yet no presidential candidate seriously addresses it. To the Republican candidate, it is probably a state secret like everything else. To Democrats, it just makes their heads hurt. Which leaves our national policy, deliberate or otherwise, essentially to suck it up: the easy oil first, and the economic consequences that follow for failure to prepare for anything else.

Good As Gold Article #382
o/a December 04, 2008

People brace for an extended period of hard economic times. The irony is how few saw the big collapse coming. "Why things were so good only last year," but people should have seen it coming. They really should have. Talk about government and corporate malfeasance on a massive scale. The leading indicators based on government statistics just handed you a tin cup. Economics 101: runaway military and entitlement spending cannot be sustained indefinitely. No duh.

Instead of recognizing that fact and restraining the impulse to spend, spend, spend the U.S. Government has been counterfeiting money value by printing more dollars literally to the tune of trillions. Since the last link to gold was severed in 1971, the dollar lost 92 percent of its value relative to gold. In 1934, twenty dollars bought an ounce of gold. Today the same amount of gold costs you more than eight hundred dollars. There's really no magic about it—gold was a fixed standard that kept politicians honest with the value of people's money. A gold standard simply means having a monetary system in which a certain mass of gold defines the monetary unit (like the dollar) and serves as ultimate medium of redemption. The alternative is a fiat money system, which is what we have now and means that a central banking committee gets to determine growth in the stock of money untied to anything but their wizardry.

Gold is objective, whereas wizards have bad days. The Fed and "under-sight" committees in Congress let a bunch of thieves loot the whole system. They not only tanked the economy but also placed American economic freedom in jeopardy. It gets even better because the Government now gets asked to fix the economy by, guess what, printing more money! If things wind down in Iraq, surely Afghanistan is calling loudly; and if the welfare rolls dwindle a bit, I'm sure national health care and insurance will pick up the slack. The Government provided economic doctors are ordering up more poison for the poison patient—a little more should do the trick. Good luck if you call me in the morning.

Horse Sense 101: If you find yourself at the bottom of a hole, stop digging. If you've got mounting credit card debt, you've got to begin to pay it down. Now it really is too bad we can't use the Government's method, or we'd print the money off in a jiffy. You can't counterfeit—it's a serious offense, but the U.S. Government does it every day. The big boys don't have to, because they have the golden parachutes. The rest lose their savings and investments and tens of thousands more come to depend upon the ever-expanding government welfare state. Come to think of it the wizards may be smarter than we think, at rigging.

Lawrence H. White is F.A. Hayek Professor of Economic History at the University of Missouri-St. Louis. He says the gold standard is no crazy idea. For most of American history we used some semblance of it. When we did use the gold standard, according to Professor White and an extensive economic study done by Arthur Rolnick and Warren Weber, the country experienced higher annual growth rates and also less average inflation. Contrary to popular myth, the U.S. monetary contraction of 1929-33 happened on the Federal Reserve's watch. A weak banking system and befuddled Fed were largely responsible. Other countries on the gold standard, for example Canada, had no banking panic in 1929-33. Indeed, perhaps the most successful former Fed Chairman Alan Greenspan actually recommends controlling the fiat money supply by mimicking the price-level behavior of a gold standard! At a 2001 Congressional hearing, he said: "Mr. Chairman, so long as you have fiat currency, which is a statutory issue, a central bank properly functioning will endeavor to, in many cases, *replicate what a gold standard would itself generate.*" You know, it sort of sparkles like a diamond or at least a very hard quartz. "Oh thank you Honey for the cubic zirconia engagement ring—it is so much better than having the real thing!"

Stupid 101: Paper money backed by paper is better than paper backed by gold. Under a gold standard, market forces automatically tailor the money supply to the economy's demand for money. A price-specie-flow mechanism brings gold from the rest of the world to any single country where demand for money has grown. In lieu of market forces, we can tax the private economy so much and then borrow from foreigners. The amount we can borrow, however, is limited by the total foreign debt and current accounts deficit. Ignoring everything we can continue our marvelous spending spree, but this will inevitably result in higher interest rates and a further devaluation of the dollar meaning the dollar is worth less until it is worthless.

The good news of course is that this kind of a system of government can't last. The sense that 'the end is near' significantly contributes to a growing sense of anxiety for most Americans, especially those who pay the bills. According to Rep. Ron Paul (R-TX), "Generally speaking, there are two controlling forces that determine the nature of government: the people's concern for their economic self-interests and the philosophy of those who hold positions of power and influence in any particular government. Under Soviet communism the workers believed their economic best interests were being served while a few dedicated theoreticians placed themselves in positions of power. Likewise, the intellectual leaders of the American Revolution were few but rallied the colonists to risk all to overthrow a tyrannical king."[72] Hmmm, wonder what he meant by that.

De-Linked At Last? Economy and World Oil Prices Article #183
o/a February 11, 2005

The global oil market defied all forecasts in 2004 with an explosion of demand, prices rising to $55 per barrel from $33 at the beginning of the year, and no detrimental impact on global GDP growth. Saudi Arabia increased production throughout the year to average 9 million barrels per day (b/d), even as prices continued to rise. Industry forecasters everywhere got it wrong in 2004. The International Energy Agency (IEA), for example, forecast in January 2004 that global demand for oil would grow by 1.2 million b/d in 2004. By December, the IEA had changed its forecast for 2004 demand growth to 2.6 million b/d. The irony is that demand growth is usually the easiest and most precise element of the global oil market to predict. Oil supply and prices tend to be much more volatile and less accurately predicted. Over the past 30 years, worldwide oil demand has tended to grow at a steady pace between 1 and 2 percent per year, less than half the rate of global GDP growth. In 2004, oil demand grew at the highest rate since 1976 at 3.3 percent, and closer to the rate of global GDP growth, which was likely over 4.5 percent.

The primary unexpected factor in oil demand growth was China. In December 2003 the IEA projected Chinese oil demand to grow by 320,000 b/d in 2004. Now the IEA estimates that Chinese oil demand grew by 810,000 b/d in 2004, almost triple the country's average demand growth of the previous 9 years, making this surprising demand growth in China the most important factor behind the rise in prices in 2004. Reasons cited for the surge include high GDP growth in China (9.7 percent annual growth in the first half of 2004) combined with a catch-up in electric power generation, the growth of auto sales (replacing bicycles), a surge in air transport after the 2003 SARS-driven slowdown, and a buildup of crude oil inventories (implementation of a strategic reserve similar to the United States). In twenty-five years, if average economic growth rates remain the same between the U.S. and China, China could surpass the United States to become the world's largest economy.

An important question for 2005 and beyond for oil producers, especially Saudi Arabia, is whether the higher growth in oil consumption means the world will require higher oil output on a sustained basis. Saudi Arabia has not experienced a sustained growth in oil output in 25 years, and the Kingdom of Saudi Arabia's oil production capacity today is about where it was in 1981. The demand growth of 2004 tightened supply availability to the point that the world had only 1 million b/d in excess production capacity in mid-2004, and all of that resided in Saudi Arabia. Virtually every producer in the world was producing oil at maximum capacity except Saudi Arabia, which at its peak produced 9.6 million b/d versus its sustainable maximum capacity of 10.5 million b/d. The tightness in supply contributed to the price rise and added a risk premium to the price of oil due to worries of supply cutoffs from, for example, Iraq (oilfield sabotage); Norway (oil workers strike); Nigeria (ethnic violence); and Russia (political turmoil and scandal involving oil giant Yukos). Significant shortfalls did not occur, but prices were sensitive to the bad news.

Saudi Arabia concluded that, for the first time since the 1970s, an overall expansion in production capacity was justified. During the last half of 2004, the Kingdom brought 800,000 b/d of new capacity on line, offsetting declines elsewhere, and brought Saudi production capacity to 11 million b/d at year's end. Saudi Arabia started 2005 with 2 million b/d of excess capacity, and the Oil Minister announced investments to increase capacity up to 15 million b/d. With this and other global production capacity additions (U.S. Gulf of Mexico, Angola, other OPEC countries, and the Caspian), within the next few years the world should return to a condition of around 3 million b/d of excess production capacity, which will bolster market fundamentals and reduce price volatility and risk premium—which probably accounts for $10 per barrel in the price of oil today. Moreover, another surprise in the 2004 oil market needs to be reckoned and cannot be overstated in terms of its importance; namely, the sharp rise in prices did not appear to have much negative impact on the global or U.S. economy! For the first time in a long time, the health of the economy and oil price levels appear de-linked.

High oil prices have coincided with each of the past five recessions in the U.S. going back to 1974, leading many economists to conclude that while high oil prices may not have caused the recessions, they certainly were a major drag on growth in the major global economies. In 2004, however, the U.S. and the world enjoyed high levels of growth despite record high oil prices. In September 2004 as oil prices were rising to record levels, the IMF in its semi-annual World Economic Outlook said, "Over the past year, the global recovery has become increasingly well established, with global GDP growth now projected to average 5 percent in 2004, the highest for nearly three decades." The IMF is projecting global growth in 2005 to be a robust 4.3 percent. For the first time in decades, this growth is occurring while oil prices are high, leading economists to re-think assumptions about the impact of oil prices on the economy.[73]

Unemployment and Social Problems Likely for the Long Haul

o/a April 09, 2010 Article #446

Some economic indicators have thankfully ticked up lately. The stock market rallied some and job losses have slowed. The economy grew a little over two percent in the third quarter last year, the first real increase in two years. Since the Great Recession started officially in 2007, it sure has taken its time. Indeed, every recession since the 1980s has taken longer for us to get out of. Even so, the downturns before 2007 did not result in chronic unemployment or rates of unemployment above 8 percent. So that puts our current recession in a different category for length and for depth. It truly is the worst economy the United States has experienced since the Great Depression. In October 2009 the unemployment rate hit 10 percent, and even Government statistics predict the unemployment rate will remain above 9 percent for four to five more years. No wonder the administration wants 26 year olds to be able to keep their parents' health insurance coverage. They're likely to be living at home anyway.

Unemployment sounds so clinical concerning the economy, a mere statistic. People are involved certainly, but if it is only a temporary phenomenon in life like the flu, well there's arguably no lasting harm done. The fact is that more people are experiencing unemployment and for longer periods of time. The average duration of unemployment has crept up to more than six months, the worst since the Bureau of Labor Statistics started keeping track after World War II. Moreover, the problem is that our recovery isn't looking so good and the turn-around is hardly built on solid ground. Chronic unemployment has already started, and sociologists are observing in white working class neighborhoods the onset of blight, as well as crime, drug and welfare problems resembling black ghettos of some forty years ago. Deputy Managing Editor of *The Atlantic*, Don Peck calls the new jobless reality a "slow-motion social catastrophe."

The economy lacks 10 million jobs now just to get us down to 5 percent, the rate we had when the Great Recession started. Of course, given the natural and not-so-natural immigration growth rate of people who need work, we would have to produce 1.5 million jobs each year just to stay even. That's about 125,000 jobs per month to stay in the hole we're in. What we need is about 600,000 jobs per month, so that we can start to dig out of recession and high unemployment—and it would still take us a couple years to do so! Of course, the problem is we haven't seen that kind of a sustained employment growth rate for more than 30 years and aren't likely to do so very soon. In the intervening years we've also sold out our manufacturing base. New jobs are lower paying, and typically they are in the services industry.

According to economist Edmund Phelps, the innovative potential of the U.S. economy looks limited. Dynamism in the U.S. economy has actually been in decline for the past decade, according to a recent article he wrote with Leo Tilman in *Harvard Business Review*. Phelps also believes the best that we can hope for is an unemployment floor of between 6.5

and 7.5 percent, even after the so-called recovery is complete. In 2014 unemployment will likely remain at 8 percent. This is the same as Obama's inundated high water mark, the level at which he predicted should be our worst.

The impact is that a generation of young people could see their life chances and accomplishments diminished by this recession. Statistics bear out that first jobs have an inordinate impact on career path and lifetime earnings. Extended periods of unemployment or underemployment moreover tend to reduce people's confidence and ambition; raise stress levels; and correspondingly reduce lifespan and good health. America is likely to experience social problems attributable to the Great Recession, more so than usual because young adults today are temperamentally unprepared for what they now face in the job market. Jean Twenge is Associate Professor of Psychology at San Diego State University and author of the book *Generation Me* (2006). After analyzing national survey data, she concludes that many high school graduates in the 2000s have a toxic combination of attitudes. While they value financial success and have very high material expectations, they do not have as intense work ethic as do previous generations. They have high self-esteem and also fully expect their jobs to cater to personal interest and lifestyles, but they lack the instinct to persevere in hard times. They are more likely to quit or change jobs, and also to turn down starter positions and first time opportunities.

For men especially, chronic unemployment acts in ways similar to bereavement. It can leave psychological scars and make married life untenable for them and their spouses. Indeed, it is another troubling aspect about this recession, that male-dominated industries such as construction, finance and manufacturing have been the hardest hit; whereas sectors that disproportionately employ women, such as education and health care, have held up pretty well. Men between the ages of 25 to 54 (prime working age) are experiencing an unemployment rate of *more than 19 percent*, again the highest since the Bureau of Labor Statistics started tracking. It is possible that in 2010 for the first time in American history, women could hold the majority of jobs. For those looking out at Tea Party rallies and observing angry, mostly white men and traditional working-class and Middle Americans protesting, some for the very first time, it is small wonder.[74]

Loss of Manufacturing is the Federal Government's Fault
o/a October 09, 2010 Article #471

Anne Marie Cox of Catholic News Service (CNS) reported on the president during his recent campaign swing through four states. On September 29th President Barack Obama visited a Mid-West family in a Des Moines, Iowa neighborhood and spoke to a group assembled in backyard lawn chairs. The local parish priest, Father Michael Amadeo of the Holy Trinity School, was the last one to pose a question. The priest shared a story about a parishioner. Apparently the 55-year-old father had lost his manufacturing job over one year ago and the family was struggling. The priest asked what the president's economic policies would do in the next year to help people in that circumstance. If anyone were looking for hope, however, they might as well have phoned a call center in India.

President Obama responded that many of the manufacturing jobs simply will not return, because modern factories are so efficient and require fewer workers. Moreover, some jobs are moving overseas where wages are cheaper. His concluding advice was for the unemployed man to keep his skills honed and to be ready when the economy finally turns around again. The president plugged clean energy as a promising business alternative and then left. Not only was the president less than empathetic to the priest's question or the plight of unemployed man, his administration has got its economics all wrong and government policies are sure to drag this recession all the way to Kingdom Come.

The following analysis is taken from Tom Pauken's excellent book, *Bringing America Home* (2010). In it he details those policies behind our nation's marked economic decline. A central reason for huge trade deficits and the shift of economic power from Main Street to Wall Street is a business tax system that gives private-equity moguls incentives to take imprudent risks with the companies they control. In this respect, they have a distinct advantage over owners of U.S. companies who would like to run their businesses in a tried and true conservative fashion or pursue capital accumulation-based strategies, but find that our tax structure "disincentivizes" them. The United States has a corporate income-tax rate of 35 percent. That rate is an economic incentive for financiers to load a company up with high levels of corporate debt in order to avoid taxation. It is a no-brainer—you can write off debt on your taxes, but savings and investments get taxed heavily. No rational businessman would want his company to accumulate significant savings if the interest on those savings is taxed at 35 percent.

American businesses that have their plants and employees in the United States also do not operate on a level playing field with our trading partners or competitors. Every major trading country in the world except for the United States provides a tax advantage for domestic manufacturers. Even as other countries have removed tariffs over the past four decades, they have been careful to put into place value-added taxes or VATs that provide their companies with a significant economic advantage over foreign businesses. Austin business economist David Hartman has developed data on the effects of a border-adjusted VAT. Starting with France in the mid-1960s, European countries began adopting border-adjusted VATs that now average 19 percent. All Organization for Economic Co-operation and Development (OECD) countries, made up of over 30 developed countries—all except the United States, that is—have since adopted VATs or their equivalents averaging 18 percent. As a result, U.S. goods carry the full burden of federal, state, and local taxes, plus an added tax averaging 18 percent when they are shipped to foreign markets. To make matters worse, foreign goods that are shipped into the United States enjoy an 18-percent VAT abatement—yet are subject to none of the taxes imposed on U.S. manufacturers.

It really is small wonder that so many big companies have moved their manufacturing outside the United States. It is more of a wonder why the rest haven't gone! The hollowing out of our manufacturing base and the resultant unemployment and regrettable socio-economic inequalities that have been produced, were predictable. They were caused by the federal government's regressive tax and trade policies. The president shows every indication of perpetuating the same policies of what Doug Ingram has called a design for "exporting prosperity." In the past ten years the United States has lost one-third of its manufacturing jobs. Obama did not start the problem, but Obama's deficits after less than two years in office already exceed President George W. Bush's after eight years. Unemployment is stuck at nearly ten percent and is likely to remain there for two more years. The Democrat Congress, for the first time in recent memory has not even passed a part of the proposed budget out of committee for the fiscal year that already began. In other words, the president honestly can't give much hope to the priest in reply to his question. Either the president doesn't know what to do in the next year, or else his intent is for more of the same that got us in this mess in the first place.

Security Risk to the Bad Economy, Loss of Manufacturing
o/a October 09, 2010 Article #472

America's security ultimately hinges on America's economic prosperity, as well as having a manufacturing base at home. Wars and defense preparedness cost money. The manufacturing base—as well as related technological capacity for discovery, and capability for commercialization and sheer output—is, as it always has been, tied directly to military superiority and to the level of deterrence the United States is able to maintain. In the nineteenth century other countries produced cannonballs "cheaper," but the manufacturing capability at home proved *invaluable* in the War of 1812 and again during the Mexican-American War. The same manufacturing advantage tipped the scale during the War Between the States in favor of the North. No matter what the economics are, it *pays* in terms of security to make the right kinds of stuff. Cotton balls are great but cannonballs make the point more forcefully. Smoke signals work but computers are faster. Cinnamon oil is good, but petroleum oil and gasoline work better in most engines—and dependence on foreign sources of energy, carries associated risks that dependence on cinnamon sticks doesn't.

Manufacturing ultimately helped bring us out of the Great Depression, as well as giving us the wherewithal to win World War II. The "American Century" was defined largely by the second half of the Twentieth Century and made possible by a corresponding "delta" or difference: the fact that the United States enjoyed nearly total lack of destruction on its infrastructure and manufacturing, compared to that of Europe and elsewhere. We thrived then by recruiting the brightest scientists and engineers and putting them to work in our factories and businesses. Application of their talent in industry led to new discovery and more commercial development of technology. The truth is that you can't innovate or make something *better* if you don't at first make something at all. According to Andy Grove, senior adviser to Intel and its former CEO, when you lose millions of manufacturing jobs like the United States has you also break the chain of experience so important in technological evolution.

According to a recent CNN Report based on congressional testimony, there is reason today for serious concern. Whereas the United States for the moment retains its military might, the underpinnings in the manufacturing base have largely gone away. The United States military depends increasingly on parts and products that are no longer made in the USA. Many of them are not as high quality, and there is a problem with sub-standard parts that put the lives of American soldiers at risk. "We have allowed our industrial base to deteriorate for the last two to three decades. As a result, just in national defense terms, our supply lines for strategic parts and materials have been stretched around the world," says Jeff Faux, founding president and distinguished fellow of the Economic Policy Institute. Robert Baugh, executive director of the AFL-CIO adds, "As you watch globalization move the manufacturing base offshore, in essence you are [watching] the defense base [move] offshore . . . , [which] is dangerous."

China's manufacturing sector likewise is close to surpassing that of the United States. The value of goods produced last year by China's factories was $1.6 trillion, compared to $1.7 trillion by U.S. manufacturers. An eclipse of America's economy by China will likely be followed by the eclipse of America's military. This situation represents a bipartisan challenge and policy imperative to begin to do things much more smartly. As Rep. John Tierney, a Democrat from Massachusetts says, "It is critical that we focus on modernizing and improving our industrial base to improve our economy, provide better employment opportunities to Americans, and strengthen national security . . . . We have to start to think strategically about the industrial challenges we face and take aggressive action to fully address them."

Strategically the United States needs far more technology-based thinking and must produce many more opportunities in the manufacturing industries. The fundamental responsibility of government is the security and physical defense of its lands and people, so the health of manufacturing is key and essential to government's prime responsibility. Not every economic calculus the government makes is created equal. We can have the greatest service economy in the world, but the manufacturing sector is necessary to being a great power, much less a superpower. Even the wealth of other nations in Europe and Asia is made possible by their dependency on the preeminence of America's military might, which in turn is (or has been until lately) dependent upon an unparalleled manufacturing base at home in the United States.

CHAPTER 33

Great Myths of the Great Depression

Great Myths of the Great Depression ~Part I~ o/a December 03, 2009 Articles #427-428, 431

Free market capitalism did not cause the Great Depression any more than teeth cause cavities. Instead, poor government policy played a central role in precipitating that disaster and perpetuating dire economic conditions. Today our government, woefully blind to history, pursues a similar theme blaming the unregulated markets on recession and seeking to implement similar solutions, albeit even more costly. Economic problems come and go, but government just keeps getting worse. The accumulation of power in Washington is matched only by the accumulation of national debt. Both are ruinous to the future health of our country, even as the government plans to mandate the purchase of individual health insurance as well as public options. Asked by a reporter recently where the Constitution grants authority to Congress to create such a mandate, Speaker Pelosi said that it wasn't a serious question and simply refused to answer. That's pretty much the approach government took during the Great Depression too.

Congress not only evinces contempt for the Constitution but also for economic fundamentals. Facts by themselves, even without analysis are alarming: the national debt is well over $12 trillion, accumulating at a rate of $3.88 billion per day. The annual budget deficit government actually *plans* for hit the record level this year of $1.4 trillion—roughly 10% of the nation's entire gross domestic product and the highest since World War II. Unless people mobilize politically and change out Congress in 2010, and begin to silence the progressive policies that emanate from there and the White House, this generation will experience what our grandparents and great-grandparents did in the terrible hardships attendant to a Great Depression Two (and potentially World War III to help "get us out" mistakenly or not).

The Great Depression devastated nearly every part of America, even its smallest towns. Between 1929 and 1933 economic production fell by half. Disposable income fell one-third. Stock prices collapsed to one-tenth their value. Unemployment rose until one in every four workers had no job, a rate of 25%. The modern fairy tale taught in schools is that Herbert Hoover pursued *laissez-faire* capitalism. This somehow caused a crash, and it was up to his successor Franklin Delano Roosevelt (peace be upon him) to save the day by giving government an active role in the economy. And Dorothy made it back from the Land of Oz to Kansas.

Of course the Great Depression was not the first serious economic downturn although it turned out to be the longest. It turned out to be *three times longer* than any previous depression, because of government interventions that compounded earlier mistakes. The initial errors in virtually all downturns turn out to be mischief with the money and credit supply. After that, how a government chooses to handle the "bust" determines how quickly the country gets out of depression. The Fed or central bank bloated the money supply by more than 60% during the so-called Roaring Twenties. The expansion of money and credit was very similar to what the American public recently experienced with easy consumer credit and cheap housing loans and for the very same reason. Overexpansion then and now drives interest rates low and stocks way up, until the proverbial bubble bursts. Some mechanics differ, but the processes are remarkably the same. The Fed began to contract money supply at the tail end of the 1920s, and this contraction resulted in recession. The federal government, however, responded in ways that made things far worse and turned recession into the worst depression on record. This is essentially what we risk happening today. Historians are well aware that the stock market crash and Great Depression did not occur in one day. There were rallies and rosy government estimates too, then there were bad days that followed on news coming out of Washington. Indeed, the market more or less rose and fell in synchronization with what the Fed or Congress were doing; and what the government did during the 1930s under the New Deal sealed the economic fate of a decade.

As fate would have it moreover, a Democrat would take over from a Republican at the moment of recession. Roosevelt and the Democrats inherited a bad situation no doubt, but attributed it falsely to "hands off" conservatism of the Hoover administration. Ironically, Hoover actually started the massive spending and bailouts, not unlike president Bush did this go round. Roosevelt raised the ante, not unlike Obama today. As one of Franklin Roosevelt's top aides remarked, "Practically the whole New Deal was extrapolated from programs that Hoover started." The neoconservatives of the Bush administration will be partially responsible for any neo-New Deal or progressive folly that comes out of the Obama administration in four or eight years. The crowning folly for Hoover was his Smoot-Hawley Tariff, passed in June 1930. It virtually closed the American economy to foreign goods and ignited an international trade war, the opposite of what was needed for economic recovery. The act levied specific amounts of money instead of percentages of prices, so that as prices plummeted the effective rate of tariffs actually doubled. This is one lesson the United States and international community seem to have learned and thus far sought assiduously to avoid.[75]

~Part II~ o/a December 03, 2009

Politics not only makes for strange bedfellows, it can make it hard to tell who's wrapped up in sheets next to you. Contrary to the popular myth about Herbert Hoover being this laissez-faire capitalist and Franklin Delano Roosevelt saving the day with New Deal socialism, Hoover actually started interventionist policies that Roosevelt continued and intensified. Not only did Hoover support the disastrous Smoot-Hawley Tariff drying up nearly all overseas goods and investment, he signed the Revenue Act of 1932, which doubled the income tax. FDR came into office on a Democrat Party platform, which called for *less* government spending and regulation. So much for party platforms! Candidates and presidents, candidates and congressmen often bear little resemblance to each other. While *Candidate* Roosevelt pledged to curtail President Hoover's "extravagance" in the face of economic downturn, *President* Roosevelt made tax-and-spending by Hoover look perfectly small fry by comparison.

President Roosevelt adapted a phrase from Henry David Thoreau declaring that, "We have nothing to fear but fear itself." But Americans had genuine reason to fear as FDR in his first hundred days swung hard against the profit order and guaranteed a prolonged depression. He led government seizure of private gold holdings and thereby devalued the dollar by 40 percent. Dramatic devaluation of the dollar, though for different reasons is similar to what we recently experienced and is a telltale sign of economic troubles ahead. Such devaluation is by definition caused by government action. Frustrated and angry at the time, Roosevelt's Director of the Bureau of the Budget, Lewis W. Douglas, resigned after a year in office and warned us about the terrible choice we were making—today as well by a factor of several times. He said the country was making a bad choice going for the New Deal, that to go that direction meant necessarily succumbing to the "despotism of bureaucracy, controlling our every act." The choice meant a sacrifice of freedom. Instead, Douglas reminded us what the proper role of the federal government was: "national defense, maintaining law and order, protecting life and property, preventing dishonesty, and . . . guarding the public against . . . vested special interests." Senator Carter Glass called the government's seizure of gold and its concomitant refusal to redeem paper money in gold as promised, nothing short of "dishonor." Cynically, President Roosevelt exclaimed that "it would be a good time for [a] beer"—and he ended Prohibition to help salve morale.

Between 1933 and 1936 government expenditures rose more than 83 percent, and federal debt grew 73 percent. FDR sold Congress on Social Security in 1935 and a comprehensive minimum wage law in 1938. The minimum wage has kept young, inexperienced and unskilled workers out of the job market, and Social Security continues to provide an unsustainable safety net, which also precludes attainment of real wealth for millions of Americans. Things would be even worse today had everything in the New Deal actually stuck. Roosevelt led passage of the National Industrial Recovery Act, which established the National Recovery Administration (NRA). It almost immediately raised the cost of doing business in America by 40 percent by promulgating over 500 codes for the production and manufacture of almost everything. Black markets grew up spontaneously everywhere to bypass the regulatory lunacy, and fortunately the Supreme Court found the Act unconstitutional. It is unclear whether the Supreme Court would find it unconstitutional again, so "living" has our Constitution become these days.

The Roosevelt administration passed multiple tax hikes and raised the top income tax bracket to 90 percent. Senator Arthur Vandenberg characterized the approach as trying to "lift the lower one-third up [by pulling] the upper two-thirds down." If the overarching objective was economic recovery rather than social engineering or empowering government bureaucrats, these policies were counter-productive. This was also the time when government became a primary employer. Make work projects abounded. Suggestions by employees or subject matter experts to bring efficiency to operations were met with disapproval and summarily dismissed, because the government valued the jobs more than the work per se. Government hiring became a social program in effect. Government hired people to do almost anything, in order to keep people busy ostensibly so they wouldn't do something wrong or feel hopeless. Such tax policies and "job creating" prolonged the depression.

Think about it. As Lawrence Reed writes: "If a thief goes house to house robbing everybody in the neighborhood, then heads off to a nearby shopping mall to spend his ill-gotten loot, it is not assumed that because his spending 'stimulated' the stores at the mall he has thereby performed a national service or provided a general economic benefit. Likewise, when the government hires someone to catalog the many ways of cooking spinach, his tax-supported paycheck cannot be counted as a net increase to the economy because the wealth used to pay him was simply diverted, not created." Money comes from productive citizens, not the tooth fairy or Peter roughed up and robbed to pay Paul.[76]

~ Postscript~ o/a December 04, 2009

Many modern academics are reflexively anti-capitalist. Moreover, whether they are in the humanities or sciences, ethics and honesty are something else reserved for the little guy. Tenured idiots feel they don't need to be particularly honest with the common folk, since they have more important agendas at stake. Professors are no less basely motivated or subject to original sin than the rest of us, and they are altogether more likely to lie about climate change or the truth about historical "consensus" if they don't quite square with the research evidence. Americans, if they are a confident free people, should never give control of their thoughts and opinions to eggheads or government officials. Doing so leads inevitably to manipulation, exploitation, and to eventual enslavement. What we need to do instead is hone our critical thinking skills and weigh things carefully, but always trust oneself more than others. Now if you trust just one thing I'm going to say, however, believe me that, notwithstanding some family member or significant other, *you are the only person in the world who has your best interests in mind!* Government never does.

The New Deal was responsible for prolonging the Great Depression because of the uncertainty created by numerous and conflicting interventions in the economy. One of the leading investors of the day, Lammot du Pont explained in 1937 that the tax situation, the labor situation, the level of inflation or deflation, as well as the legal conditions under which businesses operate were all up in the air. Even Roosevelt's mood swings, whenever he faced political opposition, might generate vindictive executive orders aimed at capping profits or taxing more. FDR's very own Treasury Secretary, Henry Morgenthau, confided to his personal diary: "We have tried spending money. We are spending more than we have ever spent before and it does not work. . . . We have never made good on our promises. . . . I say after eight years of this Administration we have just as much unemployment as when we started . . . and an enormous debt to boot!" It is not frequently admitted by so-called "consensus" historians, but the economic hardship of the Great Depression persisted and even grew worse, and President Roosevelt's political popularity correspondingly declined to such a degree that he may not have won reelection a third time had Pearl Harbor not intervened.

Americans rallied around their president in wartime. Economic conditions also improved, because along with the horrendous destruction and death associated with World War II there came a revival of trade with the Allies. The Fed also changed its monetary policy, and re-inflation of the money supply helped to counteract the high costs of the New Deal. President Truman then came in behind Roosevelt and rhetorically at least, started to encourage business activities and investment. The free market did not cause or prolong the Great Depression, political bungling did—and the same thing is about to happen today. According to Lawrence Reed, "This time we have nothing to fear but myths and misconceptions." We should know and do better, in other words! The financial crisis that has gripped America since 2008 can end in a couple years or take a decade, and it is our choice to make at the polls and/or by applying responsible political pressure on Washington.

From 2001 to 2005 the Fed expanded the money supply at double-digit rates. The dollar lost value, but banks flushed with liquidity lowered interest rates and made riskier loans. When the bubble burst, the culprits of the bad policies recommended those government bailouts! Many of them are now calling for higher taxes and tariffs to supposedly help reduce debt, but also to maintain the ridiculously high level of spending. The same nonsense took a recession in 1930 and turned it into the Great Depression. Not only will future generations be saddled with the bills we have for decades, but we are also still throwing good money after bad. In so doing we are undermining free enterprise and the soundness of our currency. The great economist Ludwig von Mises once observed that, "Government is the only institution that can take a valuable commodity like paper, and make it worthless by applying ink." He was describing inflation and the way government expands the money supply by printing more of it. The value of each monetary unit erodes as the supply of money increases, until the unit (say, the dollar) becomes potentially worthless.

The impact along the way will be prices rising and erosion of savings and investment. Lawrence Reed again: "Our economy looks like a roller coaster because Congresses, Presidents and the agencies they've empowered never cease their monetary mischief. . . . [Politicians blame] each other, scrambling to cover their behinds and score political points in the midst of a crisis, and piling debts upon debts they audaciously label 'stimulus packages.'" Reed then poses some simple questions that begin to address in a very personal way the *culprits* as it were behind the culprits; namely, "Why do so many Americans want to trust [the politicians] with their health care, education, retirement and a host of other aspects of their lives?" Does freedom really mean so little to the people anymore? And do they know so little about past experience that they would walk into a swirling propeller? George Santayana famously wrote, "Those who cannot remember the past are condemned to repeat it." I should say that we have received fair warning.[77]

CHAPTER 34

MONEY AND MELTDOWN

Money and Meltdown Articles #415-420
~Part I~ o/a September 11, 2009

The United States has been in official recession since late 2007, and it is widely agreed that trouble began (or was at least exposed) with a precipitous housing downturn. By the end of 2008, we were experiencing a full-fledged increasingly global meltdown. Stocks now are down by more than a third—which is a nice way of saying that millions of people lost their shirts, as years of savings for retirement or investment have vanished. Over three hundred metropolitan areas in the United States are depressed economically. Texas is the biggest notable exception. The national unemployment average is almost ten percent, but because government has played fast and loose with statistics in order to hide information from the American people, you may be interested in knowing unemployment is really over 16 percent the way it used to be calculated as late as the 1970s.

The economic crisis has exposed some structural problems in the financial system worldwide. Banks in Europe proved no more resilient than in America. China turned out to be dependent on the west, at least for now—and fortunately foreign capital did flood back into the U.S. as the best safe haven available for uncertain times. We can describe it, but the question is what to do. The Great Depression happened too and despite shallow consensus on a few points, historians and economists argue vigorously over why it came about and whether New Deal policies and/or World War II pulled us out—even if they are never quite sure how. Some writers are dubbing the current crisis as the Great Recession. Others compare it to a so-called Long Depression affecting some areas from 1873 to 1896. The irony is that it is hard to expect things to improve unless we have some clue about how we got into the predicament. Unfortunately, there are a lot of very smart people who never did have a clue, giving the government advice and calling shots. Stupid is as stupid does.

Most government solutions tried so far or being contemplated are in fact *interventions* into the economy based upon a false premise that the free market economy failed. It may be countered, however, that it is government intervention that has messed things up so badly in the first instance, namely the Federal Reserve and its manipulation of the money supply and interest rates. The architects of the debacle are planning our recovery, while the competing voice of reason is largely gone missing from argument. Not only is the Fed ignored as a source of trouble by mainstream media, there is also strangely a veritable range of subjects excluded from national dialogue—the Fed and money to name two. Politicians aren't going to save us this time, if they ever did, and one of the most important concepts the sovereign people better learn these days is called the "Austrian" business cycle theory. Austrian refers to the school of economics—and it was the only school to accurately predict the onset of our current crisis.

Thomas E. Woods, Jr., an academic of Austrian economic persuasion argues convincingly in his book, *Meltdown* that the financial crisis was not caused by the free market but by government's intervention in the market. Moreover, the greatest intervention into the economy is America's central bank, the Federal Reserve System. If this is true, the Fed must be looked at. Clearly we need to stop further government interventions likely to aggravate the problem or precipitate economic catastrophe. The government's failure in this regard is being passed off and blamed on everything and everybody else except the government; worse, it is used to justify further increases in government power. Ask yourself where all the excess risk, leverage, debt and housing bubble came from. The answers that one gets like excessive risk-taking or greed beg the question. Liberals (who now prefer to be called Progressives) are not only continuing their attack on the foundations of the Republic by denying the Constitution, they are like termites eating away at the foundations of free market economy, about to take us with them to the basement. They are blaming "unregulated markets" for the financial crisis, having manufactured the crisis through very different means.

More bailouts, regulation and government will only make matters much worse and prolong depressed economic conditions around the country. In November 2008 German chancellor Angela Merkel warned correctly, if Washington's policies create more money and encourage more borrowing, they sow "the seeds of a similar crisis." Nonetheless, by the end of 2008 and thanks to the congressional bailout package, the American people were on the hook for 7.7 trillion dollars more. Then President Obama came into office riding the horse of more bailout, more spending, more debt, and more government regulation to stimulate the economy. He inherited a mess, but he feels duty bound to make it worse. Meanwhile nobody wants to talk about that large furry creature in the living room, whose name is the Fed and which for all intents and purposes is an arm of the federal government.[78]

~Part II~ o/a September 11, 2009

Now and again it crosses my mind, how in the world our representative government can be so silent and so inept. Then again, according to the Center for Responsive Politics the securities and investment industry contributed $53 million to congressional and presidential candidates in the 2008 cycle. That places the industry second behind lawyers. Congressmen who voted for the bailout one year ago happened to receive 54% more in campaign contributions from the banks and securities firms than those who didn't. Americans have notoriously bad memories, and that really is a shame. Of all the things President Obama said he expects of school-aged children in his address to them, critical thinking and historical memory got short shrift. They aren't as important as the many technical and lab problems that need solving. Just so long as the little precious stays patriotic and doesn't drop out, and drinks the stuff the state serves up. Some things are settled, like evolution and money laundering on a grand scale.

The government was going to buy all those bad ("toxic") assets from banks, remember? Well, the approach was abandoned entirely, and a few months later the government said it had to prop up consumer debt, since millions of Americans faced rising credit card rates and reduced access to the credit they needed (*for everyday purchases!*). Not sure where cash for clunkers fit into the overall economic picture. It may have encouraged a few more green cars on the road, our big transition to technology to save the planet. Most the money went to overseas car producers, however. Now health care reform is the rage, and is sold to us not only as a cure for what ails you but also for ballooning deficits! Meanwhile that large furry creature next to Pelosi, whose name is the Fed, claps loudest of all at Obama's speeches.

The Federal Reserve System, a.k.a. the Fed was created by an act of Congress. Its chairman is chosen by government appointment. The organization is endowed with monopoly privilege and is dedicated to the most far-reaching form of centralized economic planning. Instead of planning steel and concrete production quotas, say, as in the old Soviet Union, the Fed plans the money and interest rates. The consequences necessarily reverberate throughout the whole economy. We don't talk about it, because it was the Fed's policy of intervening in the economy to push interest rates lower than the market would set that was the single biggest contributor to the financial crisis. Making cheap credit available encouraged the excessive leverage, speculation, and indebtedness the government now blames on the free market. Manipulating interest rates misled investors about real economic conditions, misdirected capital into unsustainable lines of production, and desynchronized the entire market. The Fed's intervention into the economy gave rise (as it has before) to a boom-bust cycle making us all feel rosy pink and prosperous until the inevitable crash—which of course the free market gets blamed for.

In terms of stakes, however, they couldn't be any higher. As Peer Steinbrück, German finance minister said, as a result of the current crisis America stands to "lose its status as the superpower of the global financial system." Indeed, a lot of people welcome that development, while others don't hope for it but point out the fundamentals are *not* sound for a debt-ridden, over-consuming, under-producing American empire—the fall of which is not inconceivable. International economic crises have a way of upending the geopolitical order, hastening the fall of established powers and the rise of new ones. In *The Post-American World* (2008), Fareed Zakaria argues that modern history's third great power shift is upon us. The rise of the West in the 15th century and the rise of America in the 19th were the previous two. Zakaria says the transition now has less to do with American decline and more to do with "the rise of the rest." That may be so, but America's leadership seems intent on hastening the day.

For far too long American leaders have been anything but representative, and not at all consultative with the American people concerning their doom. One wonders what the government will do when the entitlement crisis hits and the federal government is put on the hook for tens of trillions of more dollars, as millions of baby boomers retire with high expectations. The President says he'll tackle that looming crisis once health care is overhauled. In other words, spend now and then spend again later. The problem is that government lacks all understanding and a modicum of imagination. When they try to print their way out of the gargantuan levels of debt afflicting us over the next decade, they will have debased the U.S. Dollar forever.[79]

~Part III~ o/a September 11, 2009

The financial crisis began when mortgage defaults increased substantially, triggering a chain reaction throughout the financial sector. The standard account explains the mechanics well but not the causes. Housing prices started to fall in the third quarter of 2006. People having trouble making their mortgage could no longer simply sell or refinance. Meanwhile the banks had sold many of their mortgages to other institutions like Fannie Mae, which in turn bundled them together into mortgage-backed securities. The financial system was heavily invested in these mortgage-backed securities, so default on home mortgage loans suddenly threatened a much wider field. One of the associated scandals in all this is that ratings agencies consistently gave AAA ratings to the securities. Institutions and people who thought they were investing prudently, even conservatively, were misled by ratings that had little bearing on actual risk exposure. At least six culprits in terms of causes of the housing crash can be identified.

The first is the Federal National Mortgage Association (Fannie Mae) and Federal Home Loan Mortgage Corporation (Freddie Mac). These large corporations officially known as government-sponsored enterprises (GSEs) buy loans from banks on the secondary market. Fannie and Freddie receive the stream of monthly payments associated but also bear the risk of default. The originating bank has funds to go back into the mortgage market and make new loans. The process spurs mortgage lending and inflates home prices. The process is also artificial, i.e., not market based, because of special privileges and the implicit guarantee of solvency granted by government to Fannie and Freddie. Even so, their role in the economy was small until the 1990s, so the economic distortion was relatively low. By the time the housing bubble burst, however, those agencies had a hand in half of all home mortgages—three-quarters of newer ones. This was caused by the Clinton Administration pressuring these agencies to take on risky loans, in order to increase home ownership among poor and minorities despite bad credit ratings.

Second the Community Reinvestment Act (CRA) also received new life by the Clinton administration. It was a Carter-era law that opened banks up to discrimination suits if they did not lend to minorities in sufficient numbers to suit bureaucrats. The political establishment in the 1990s pressed for lower lending standards, such that, the old credit score frameworks were cast aside. Government used one of the twelve regional Federal Reserve banks, the Boston Fed to spread easy lending criteria by means of a so-called discrimination study. It mattered more that one was minority, than whether one could afford the house. Left-wing groups like ACORN helped to "enforce" the policy. Political pressure caused subprime and adjustable-rate mortgage loans to increase.

The third culprit of the crisis is government's overall stimulus to speculation. Government through the Fed made banks so flush with reserves to lend, that lending innovations like no down payments proliferated. Underwriting standards in general declined, even for high-income borrowers and speculators. Many more people bought houses on a speculative basis than before, betting that prices would continue to rise. Speculative home buying accounted for one-quarter of home purchases at the time the housing bubble popped. When foreclosures skyrocketed, it initially involved this speculative group who had used the flexible, no-money-down mortgages hoping for a quick profitable resell. No money down made walking away easy.

Number four is the tax code, which government blatantly uses for social engineering schemes and incentivizing certain behavior. Hundreds of little programs affecting consumers and developers encouraged people to build and buy homes, channeling artificial demand into the housing sector. The federal government takes 35 percent of the average worker's income in taxes but gives it back *if* one engages in certain activities. It's sort of a public twist on trickle down economic theory. For instance, invest in the stock market through an IRA or 401(k) and shield some money from the taxman. Pay premiums to a health insurance company through an employer and you can deduct it. The biggest deduction by far for most families is the home mortgage interest deduction. Government thereby introduces strong incentive to buy rather than rent, as well as to borrow in order to buy.

Fifth is the Federal Reserve and artificially cheap credit. This had the biggest impact simply because it is so pervasive in its distortion to the economy. An increase in the supply of money and credit starts the economy off on an unsustainable boom. Pushing down interest rates by increasing money supply, the Fed encourages production of longer-term projects, such as construction. This is quite a bit different than stimulus provided by real consumer demand. More and different projects are started than the economy can sustain. When not enough people can afford McMansions, the price each one fetches is far less than anticipated and a bust comes to the real estate market. The Fed started the boom that gave rise to this latest bust, by increasing the money supply through the banking system. In the wake of September 11th and just over a year after the dot-com bust, the Fed sought to reinvigorate the economy through a series of rate cuts culminating in a target federal funds rate of just one percent for a year (June 2003 to June 2004). The supply of money increased dramatically, such that, more dollars were created between 2000 and 2007 than in all the rest of our country's history! The money and credit found its way to the housing market, where lax lending standards made excessive home purchases and speculation in homes seem like smart financial moves. The quasi-government agencies Fannie and Freddie channeled money the Fed was creating into the housing market.

Finally a "too Big to Fail" mentality deserves some blame, as certain actors in financial markets operated in the confidence and even assurance, that they would not be allowed to fail and that the American people would absorb their losses if they got into trouble. Letting major firms in or out of the financial sector go bankrupt, would do more quickly to jolt the financial sector into being prudent, than all the regulatory tinkering and bailout money in the world. It wasn't unregulated markets that caused the current crisis.[80]

~Part IV~ o/a September 11, 2009

Economic news of late has been pretty good or at least encouraging. Stocks are going back up, and first time jobless claims are down from what was expected. There are always little rallies in the midst of bear markets. The Dow rebounded to historic highs during the early period of the Great Depression. Don't be fooled by the rim of a precipice. The bailouts didn't save the economy. They may have made things worse, even if they staved off a day of reckoning. The problem we're in is systemic and no longer a matter of pumping in sufficient stimulus. The Treasury Department formed a new office called the Office of Financial Stability. Legitimized and armed by its Orwellian title, the charter has the federal government seeking ownership in banks. The Federal Reserve System combined private banks with government regulation at its start in 1913, but now we are nationalizing the private banks. Hugo Chavez, Venezuela's president, reportedly said "Bush is to the left of me now . . . Comrade Bush announced he [is buying] shares in private banks!"

Of course this government ownership does not mean any more responsible approach to anything, and it won't reduce risk taking any more than it can stop a mistake. Rather, according to Harvard economist Jeffrey Miron, "Government ownership means that political forces will determine who wins and who loses in the banking sector. The government, for example, will push banks to aid borrowers with poor credit histories, to subsidize politically connected industries, and to lend in the districts of powerful members of Congress." It is more of the same that put us into this financial crisis, only an order of magnitude worse. Unchecked, it will lead to destruction of Middle America. The bailouts thus far have slowed recovery by delaying the de-leveraging process at banks and removing a sense of urgency from financial firms. Other industries have lined up at the door for money and gotten some. The profit and loss system in some respects has been jettisoned for a system of guaranteed profit for business and loss for wage earners. Mismanagement is rewarded with taxpayer funding, and bad managers still get their bonuses.

Government loans to failing financial firms, is terribly ill advised. If one peels away the onion, the government is trying so desperately to keep things expensive! It wants to prop up asset values and keep both stocks and home prices high—as if this will help the holders of those assets. The fall of prices is not the cause of economic problems but rather, a symptom that reflects conditions in the economy. Bubbles need to burst. Instead, the government is intent on propping up bubble prices above what the market will support, and guaranteeing the difference with taxpayer finance. The way an aspiring homeowner must do these days is to drive further into debt for his American dream home, instead of being allowed to pay the low market price it is worth. It is as if the government wants citizens enthralled and burdened with debt just so it can bail them out.

Falling prices, no less than prices rising under normal healthy economic conditions, are simply the market's way of rationally valuing assets, correcting for economic distortions created from whatever source, including the government's past intervention and the rapid expansion of the money supply emanating from the Federal Reserve since 2000.

Unfortunately, the government's effort to pour funds into the economy and keep prices artificially high will touch off a round of inflation. There is likely to be an explosion in consumer prices because of the bailouts. Since late 2008, the Fed created 3 trillion new dollars and added the money to its balance sheet, but this acts as a base for banks to create ten times that much based on the multiplier. In order to avoid the predictable outcome, the Fed may try to contract the money supply but this will give rise to more instability. With the entitlement collapse coming and with it, the insolvency of Social Security and Medicare, the same process will likely play out to the tune of *tens of trillions* of dollars more. Things will then get much worse.

The sooner we allow the market to coordinate production and consumption, the quicker this economy will be allowed to heal. The sooner the government begins to control its appetite for spending and start to reduce budget deficits, as well as the national debt over time, the freer and more prosperous the American people will become. America's central bank, the Federal Reserve, set this particular boom-bust cycle into motion—and it is bigger than anything we've ever seen. Since there is no known shortcut for creating real wealth through government edict, what went up is definitely coming down—one way or another.[81]

~Part V~ o/a September 11, 2009

The U.S. Federal Reserve failed to let the recession of 2000 take its course and decided to create trillions of dollars out of thin air. The recession that year is the only one on record that did not see housing starts decline. The Fed's monetary policy led directly to the housing bubble and onset of our current crisis. The Fed intervened and postponed what it was trying to avoid, making the crash worse when it came. There's a developed country in Asia we ought to pay more attention to, in terms of what works and what doesn't economically. Its people have great work ethic and are highly educated, yet it is mired in economic difficulty and indeed has been for more than a decade and a half. Lesson learned: it matters what the government will or will not do in this type of financial crisis that we are facing. Some policy measures will absolutely prolong a bad economy. Japan empirically proves the free market case and cautions us to stop clowning around.

Historian Thomas Woods, Jr., relates how Japan fed its economic boom during the 1980s with inflationary credit expansion—increasing the money supply through the central banking system while at the same time keeping interest rates artificially low. Japan actually pushed interest rates to zero, thereby obstructing market correction of the malinvestments. When the bust came, it came hard. Then it lasted so long because of what the Japanese government did after that. Namely, the Japanese government resorted to interventionist tools in order to "kick start" their economy and do better than what the market supposedly could. During the 1990s it launched at least ten fiscal stimulus packages worth more than 100 trillion yen, and this ballooned their national debt—exactly what we are doing today to fix our own mess.

To get banks lending again, Japan pumped money into the banking system at the rate of nearly 300% per year for three years, but this led to a 4.5% *decrease* every year in bank loans. Public works programs were extensive but did not broadly stimulate the economy. Ironically, we are following a very bad example of what not to do and pursuing failed Keynesian interventionist policies, instead of recurring to American experience and best American instinct. In 1920-21 the U.S. and Japan both faced recession too. Japan opted to intervene and suffered seven years of industrial stagnation because of it. Meanwhile the United States allowed its economy to readjust by keeping government spending and taxation low and reducing public debt. The result was recovery. Unfortunately the Fed began to pursue an inflationary policy for the rest of the decade, thus setting up another boom-bust cycle—that one resulting in the Great Depression. Instead of a quick liquidation and return to prosperity, Presidents Hoover and Franklin Roosevelt pursued policies to prop up prices and wages.

A lot of people attribute World War II to the eventual recovery, but the U.S. recovery coincided with abandonment of New Deal programs in the 1940s. A new, New Deal these days is certain to prolong economic difficulties. If war and spending on munitions really makes a country wealthy, the U.S. and Japan can do the following to help each other out. Have their respective fleets meet in the Pacific and evacuate naval personnel (to avoid the loss of life normally incident to war). Then sink the two fleets plain and simple. Both countries can celebrate how much wealthier they've become by devoting labor, steel and a million other diverted inputs to the production of things that get destroyed, things civilians can't use, and things that lay at the bottom of the ocean. Then just repeat the process. Although facetious, the example points to a central fallacy entertained by the current U.S. administration: the idea that spending alone, regardless of what for, gives rise to prosperity.

Neither does consumer spending drive an economy, if the spending doesn't make any sense. And that's what we're talking about: economic nonsense made out of distortions to the economy fueled by reckless credit expansion in which profit, loss and value become virtually impossible to judge. Distortions result because the government acquires its resources through seizure, unlike the private sector, which acquires them through voluntary means. Even when the government gives one something, it is akin to an assault because the action still lacks voluntary means, as well as market feedback. If it is money, the government had to have taken it from someone else directly, or else from everyone indirectly by printing it and devaluing people's assets. The purpose of production in the free market is to satisfy real consumer demands, but politically motivated or arbitrary diversions of resources cannot accomplish that purpose.

Investment adviser Peter Schiff compares an artificial boom in the economy to a circus coming to town. Say the circus arrives and its employees and the public, who come to visit the circus, begin to patronize the restaurant across the street. This may go on day after day, night after night for weeks. The restaurant owner may conclude the situation is permanent. If he adds on an addition, doubles his kitchen staff or opens up another location entirely, he will have tragically miscalculated when the big tent folds. Extending cheap credit to him afterwards misses the point and makes matters worse. His expanded restaurant will become a bubble activity that works only under the most phony of conditions. Moreover in an artificial boom created by the Fed, you may as well send in the clowns and watch them do the kabuki—because *all* firms and businesses, and the whole economy are affected.[82]

~Part VI~ o/a September 14, 2009

It is time we address some fundamental issues about money. First, money didn't originate with government. It originated amongst people who needed a way to exchange their goods indirectly, instead of through direct barter all the time. One could make a hat and want a basketball, and trading a hat for a basketball might even work, but one quickly finds that having a practical medium will make the myriad of exchanges so much easier. So money is that medium of exchange that gives rise to complex economies. Historically it has been many things, including seashells, berries, gold and silver. Interestingly, only with a pre-existing or inherited array of barter prices (relative sense of assessed value unique to the given society) are people able to substitute money for barter. Money moreover is a useful commodity in its own right and must be, to function effectively as a medium. While paper per se might be close to worthless, the paper money replaces or substitutes for a preexisting commodity money through government fiat and legal tender laws. In our case, Federal Reserve Notes replaced gold and silver, but even then the paper money was redeemable for a given weight of the actual commodity for most of our history. Indeed, a successful paper system will always insist on the paper money being redeemable in its commodity version. Only in this way can the money retain its assessed value and confidence be assured.

Secondly, precious metals work well as money because they are durable, inherently valuable, and easily divisible. Gold is so valuable that most daily transactions people make would be in silver coins—copper for smaller transactions. Private bank notes or checks would represent the same thing. That is, if our paper were tied to its original commodity version! The U.S. government, however, severed that connection, not surprisingly because it favors the ability to increase money without restraint. In so doing, the dollar has lost 95% of its value. Under a commodity standard, if the government needs money it would have to resort to borrowing or taxation. These are obvious and transparent to the people. By de-linking the paper money supply from gold and silver, the government prints money and so skirts political and fiscal accountability through the means of inflation.

Third, as the great economist Joseph Schumpeter said, only the gold standard is compatible with freedom precisely because it places restriction on the government's ability to expand credit unabated and hence, places natural limit on the government's ability to seize power. Schumpeter considered gold to be a kind of economic check and balance, more effective than the political sort, because he knew if we lost having our paper currency tied to the commodity then government would be able to deceive all political checks and balances. The Federal Reserve Act of 1913 was special interest legislation at its worst, conceived to favor the class of bankers and politicians. This favoritism comes at the direct expense of the people. The Fed controls the money supply and also moves interest rates up or down. It operates as a lender too (nice when you control interest rates), and it can purchase literally any kind of asset it wants; albeit, the Fed normally buys up government bonds—hence underwriting the government's design on unrestricted power, indeed *with a profit motive to do so*!

Fourth it is the Federal Reserve System, which is exclusively responsible for price inflation—by definition this is true, because only the Fed can increase the money supply. Moreover, inflation is the Fed's great game not only giving rise to boom and bust, but also producing profits for a favored few by exploiting the broader society. When the government inflates the money supply, new money enters the economy at discrete points. The earliest recipients include politically favored constituencies, i.e., banks and firms with government contracts—actually, wherever the government spends its money. These parties receive the money before inflation pushes prices upward. In effect the economy doesn't know how much the money supply has been increased, so prices haven't yet adjusted. Of course, by the time the new money makes its way through the economy, prices will have risen—but not until the privileged firms make purchases at the previously existing price level and silently loot those they buy from. When the average person gets his new money, through higher wages or lower borrowing costs, the prices have already risen. The value of his money was diluted before it reached him.

To continue along these same lines, consider that the money in your possession is actually compensation for a good or service you provided. If you buy a dozen apples, you do so with proceeds from a good or service you provided in the past. Indeed, you can only buy apples or anything else, because you provided someone else something they needed. However, in the case of a privileged business firm or bank with new money courtesy of the Fed, it comes out of thin air and not from the sale of a previous good or service. So when they spend new money, they actually take from the existing stock of goods without providing anything in exchange. They are benefited as it were, at the expense of the rest of society. As economic historian Thomas E. Woods, Jr., puts it, "The analogous case under a system of barter would be one in which, instead of trading my bread for your orange juice, I just take your orange juice!"[83]

CONCLUSION

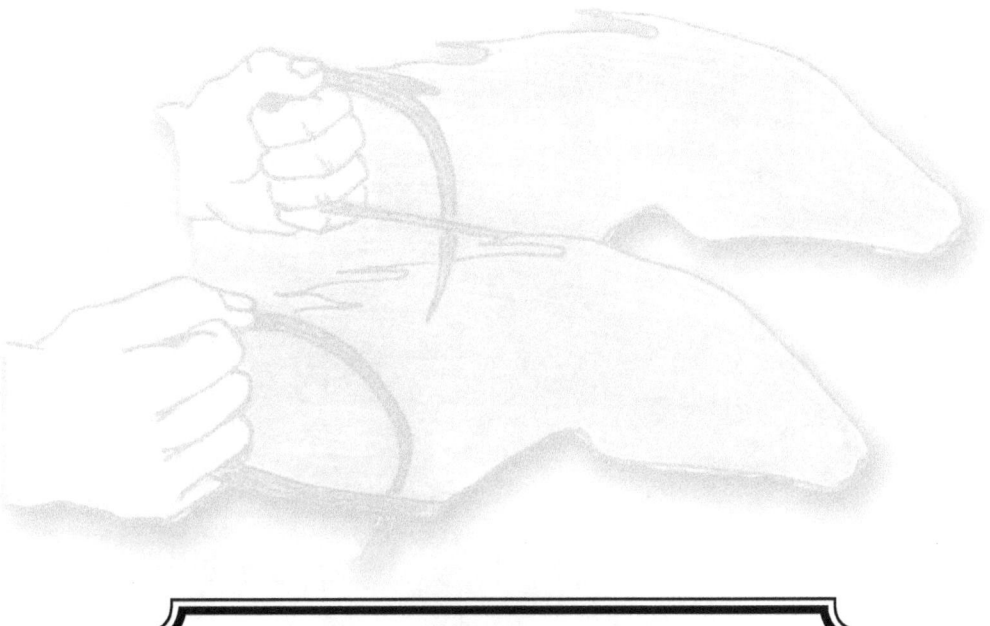

CHAPTER 35

HORSE SENSE FOR THE TWENTY-FIRST CENTURY

Horse Sense for the Twenty-First Century Article #222
o/a November 03, 2005

Newt Gingrich, American historian and former House Speaker, writes in his recent book, *Winning the Future* (2005): "Since the 1960s, the conservative majority has been intimidated, manipulated, and bullied by the liberal minority. The liberal elites who dominate academia, the courts, the press, and much of the government bureaucracy share an essentially European secular-socialist value system." Amen, Brother. The liberal elites are low down and disagreeable rascals. They disagree with everything I'm about to say, things which more or less define you and me as conservatives and red-blooded Americans. To wit, we should be allowed to say "one nation under God" in the Pledge of Allegiance—and yep, you guessed it: I do believe in God and I'm extremely proud to be an American (plus I'm at least that proud to be Texan). A Texan is quite simply twice as blessed! I genuinely think able-bodied folk on welfare should be required to work or else get kicked off; and men who assault pregnant women and kill the unborn child should be prosecuted for assault and murder—and receive death by hanging. The United States should put her own interests first and cooperation with international organizations second, and only when it's in our interests first. Did I say that I'm proud to be an American? There are too many foreigners in our country already, but if they're legal immigrants then they ought to be taught about American values. Everybody must learn English, period (good punctuation). English is the American language, but the English also speak it, sort of. Personal injury lawyers should be (well, you fill in the blank)—"encouraged" to get a real job and never ever get more than 15 percent of any award! They're generally a sorry lot anyway, worse than bank robbers or politicians. And for redneck sophisticates all, let's think about the future for ten seconds—maybe we ought to start using our technology and science towards developing us some clean, renewable energy that protects the environment for tree huggers; protects the economy for greedy capitalists; and gets us away from this ridiculous and downright dangerous dependence on Middle Eastern oil. God I'm proud to be an American!

All of which leads me to this serious point, involving 'We the People' and the goals we choose to pursue collectively through government. You see I figure you might agree with me, that what we want is an America that's free, safe and prosperous. Our children and grandchildren deserve that much to inherit. The fact there are obstructionist yahoos out there who preclude this, means that we've got work, argument, struggle and even a fight or two, to make our opinions known until they stick in Washington. But it is hardly the first time we the People have faced such a challenge. One of my favorite historical examples is the 1790s, when Thomas Jefferson and James Madison founded a political party to wrest power from the aristocratic Federalists. In 1800 they won a decisive victory and within fifteen years the Federalists all but disappeared. One of the boldest acts of the Jeffersonian-Republicans was to abolish old judgeships and to assert the right of the people to correct the Supreme Court if it misinterpreted the Constitution. That is a fight that desperately needs to be renewed. Indeed, it is a fight we see playing out in front of us—in the president's nominations for the Supreme Court and in Senate battles to confirm his nominations. Judicial philosophy was never more important than today, because liberal judicial philosophy no longer adheres to the Constitution at all, but rather reflects the so-called present man's wisdom over Judeo-Christian tradition—positing a relativist, "living" meaning to words shorn from actual text, from historical context, and worst of all from Original Intent of the Founders.

Let us plainly state the case: we've got serious challenges facing us as a nation, as well as a liberal elite squarely in the way of progress. These things must be done in spite of them, over them, under them, around them—or run straight through in a joust: First, we've got to commit to defending America against its enemies, dramatically improving our intelligence capabilities, and planning and picking jobs for the military carefully; Second, we must reestablish as a central tenet, that rights come from our Creator and that an America that has driven God out of the public arena is an America in decay and headed for defeat; Third, we need to insist on patriotic immigration policies and an education based upon classic American history and the wisdom of the Founding Fathers—whether taught at home or in public schools; Fourth, we've got to transform domestic institutions, harnessing modern science and technology to continue to create quality jobs and wealth for Americans, ensuring America leads the world economy; and finally, we should end the vestige of obsolete New Deal socialism, by establishing a much better deal and far more freedom through personal Social Security accounts, portable personal pension accounts and personal health savings accounts—so the wealth we create during our working lives is wealth that we control and can pass on to our heirs. Newt Gingrich calls the agenda his '21st Century Contract with America.' I call it good horse sense.

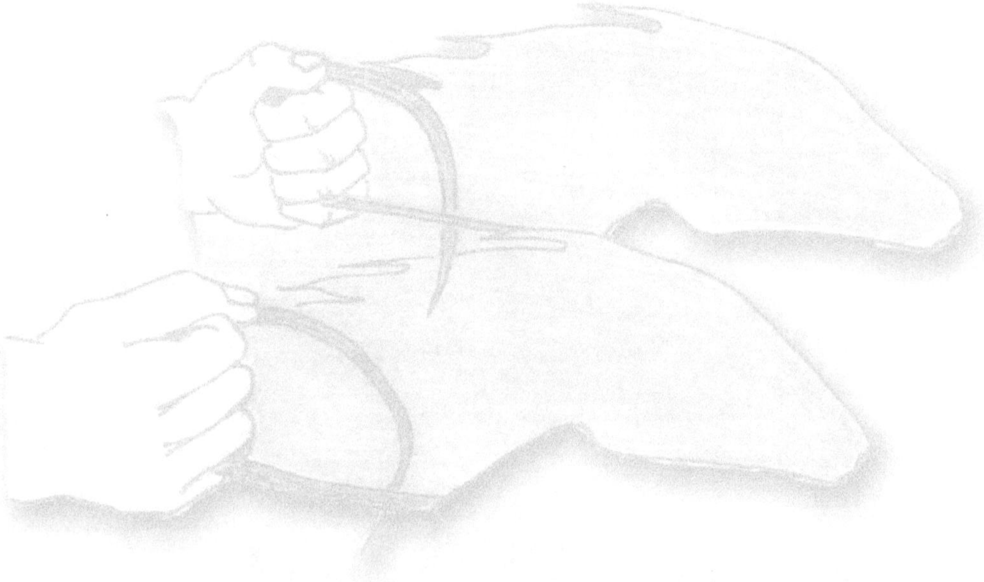

APPENDICES

APPENDIX A

Abuses by King John caused a revolt by nobles who compelled him to execute this recognition of rights for both noblemen and ordinary Englishmen. It established the principle that no one, including the king or a lawmaker, is above the law.

THE MAGNA CARTA[84]

(The Great Charter)

Preamble: John, by the grace of God, king of England, lord of Ireland, duke of Normandy and Aquitaine, and count of Anjou, to the archbishop, bishops, abbots, earls, barons, justiciaries, foresters, sheriffs, stewards, servants, and to all his bailiffs and liege subjects, greetings. Know that, having regard to God and for the salvation of our soul, and those of all our ancestors and heirs, and unto the honor of God and the advancement of his holy Church and for the rectifying of our realm, we have granted as underwritten by advice of our venerable fathers, Stephen, archbishop of Canterbury, primate of all England and cardinal of the holy Roman Church, Henry, archbishop of Dublin, William of London, Peter of Winchester, Jocelyn of Bath and Glastonbury, Hugh of Lincoln, Walter of Worcester, William of Coventry, Benedict of Rochester, bishops; of Master Pandulf, subdeacon and member of the household of our lord the Pope, of brother Aymeric (master of the Knights of the Temple in England), and of the illustrious men William Marshal, earl of Pembroke, William, earl of Salisbury, William, earl of Warenne, William, earl of Arundel, Alan of Galloway (constable of Scotland), Waren Fitz Gerold, Peter Fitz Herbert, Hubert De Burgh (seneschal of Poitou), Hugh de Neville, Matthew Fitz Herbert, Thomas Basset, Alan Basset, Philip d'Aubigny, Robert of Roppesley, John Marshal, John Fitz Hugh, and others, our liegemen.

1. In the first place we have granted to God, and by this our present charter confirmed for us and our heirs forever that the English Church shall be free, and shall have her rights entire, and her liberties inviolate; and we will that it be thus observed; which is apparent from this that the freedom of elections, which is reckoned most important and very essential to the English Church, we, of our pure and unconstrained will, did grant, and did by our charter confirm and did

obtain the ratification of the same from our lord, Pope Innocent III, before the quarrel arose between us and our barons: and this we will observe, and our will is that it be observed in good faith by our heirs forever. We have also granted to all freemen of our kingdom, for us and our heirs forever, all the underwritten liberties, to be had and held by them and their heirs, of us and our heirs forever.

2. If any of our earls or barons, or others holding of us in chief by military service shall have died, and at the time of his death his heir shall be full of age and owe "relief", he shall have his inheritance by the old relief, to wit, the heir or heirs of an earl, for the whole barony of an earl by £100; the heir or heirs of a baron, £100 for a whole barony; the heir or heirs of a knight, 100s, at most, and whoever owes less let him give less, according to the ancient custom of fees.

3. If, however, the heir of any one of the aforesaid has been under age and in wardship, let him have his inheritance without relief and without fine when he comes of age.

4. The guardian of the land of an heir who is thus under age, shall take from the land of the heir nothing but reasonable produce, reasonable customs, and reasonable services, and that without destruction or waste of men or goods; and if we have committed the wardship of the lands of any such minor to the sheriff, or to any other who is responsible to us for its issues, and he has made destruction or waster of what he holds in wardship, we will take of him amends, and the land shall be committed to two lawful and discreet men of that fee, who shall be responsible for the issues to us or to him to whom we shall assign them; and if we have given or sold the wardship of any such land to anyone and he has therein made destruction or waste, he shall lose that wardship, and it shall be transferred to two lawful and discreet men of that fief, who shall be responsible to us in like manner as aforesaid.

5. The guardian, moreover, so long as he has the wardship of the land, shall keep up the houses, parks, fishponds, stanks, mills, and other things pertaining to the land, out of the issues of the same land; and he shall restore to the heir, when he has come to full age, all his land, stocked with ploughs and wainage, according as the season of husbandry shall require, and the issues of the land can reasonable bear.

6. Heirs shall be married without disparagement, yet so that before the marriage takes place the nearest in blood to that heir shall have notice.

7. A widow, after the death of her husband, shall forthwith and without difficulty have her marriage portion and inheritance; nor shall she give anything for her dower, or for her marriage portion, or for the inheritance which her husband and she held on the day of the death of that husband; and she may remain in the house of her husband for forty days after his death, within which time her dower shall be assigned to her.

8. No widow shall be compelled to marry, so long as she prefers to live without a husband; provided always that she gives security not to marry without our consent, if she holds of us, or without the consent of the lord of whom she holds, if she holds of another.

9. Neither we nor our bailiffs will seize any land or rent for any debt, as long as the chattels of the debtor are sufficient to repay the debt; nor shall the sureties of the debtor be distrained so long as the principal debtor is able to satisfy the debt; and if the principal debtor shall fail to pay the debt, having nothing wherewith to pay it, then the sureties shall answer for the debt; and let them have the lands and rents of the debtor, if they desire them, until they are indemnified for the debt which they have paid for him, unless the principal debtor can show proof that he is discharged thereof as against the said sureties.

10. If one who has borrowed from the Jews any sum, great or small, die before that loan be repaid, the debt shall not bear interest while the heir is under age, of whomsoever he may hold; and if the debt fall into our hands, we will not take anything except the principal sum contained in the bond.

11. And if anyone die indebted to the Jews, his wife shall have her dower and pay nothing of that debt; and if any children of the deceased are left under age, necessaries shall be provided for them in keeping with the holding of the deceased; and out of the residue the debt shall be paid, reserving, however, service due to feudal lords; in like manner let it be done touching debts due to others than Jews.

12. No scutage not aid shall be imposed on our kingdom, unless by common counsel of our kingdom, except for ransoming our person, for making our eldest son a knight, and for once marrying our eldest daughter; and for these there shall not be levied more than a reasonable aid. In like manner it shall be done concerning aids from the city of London.

13. And the city of London shall have all it ancient liberties and free customs, as well by land as by water; furthermore, we decree and grant that all other cities, boroughs, towns, and ports shall have all their liberties and free customs.

14. And for obtaining the common counsel of the kingdom anent the assessing of an aid (except in the three cases aforesaid) or of a scutage, we will cause to be summoned the archbishops, bishops, abbots, earls, and greater barons, severally by our letters; and we will moveover cause to be summoned generally, through our sheriffs and bailiffs, and others who hold of us in chief, for a fixed date, namely, after the expiry of at least forty days, and at a fixed place; and in all letters of such summons we will specify the reason of the summons. And when the summons has thus been made, the business shall proceed on the day appointed, according to the counsel of such as are present, although not all who were summoned have come.

15. We will not for the future grant to anyone license to take an aid from his own free tenants, except to ransom his person, to make his eldest son a knight, and once to marry his eldest daughter; and on each of these occasions there shall be levied only a reasonable aid.

16. No one shall be distrained for performance of greater service for a knight's fee, or for any other free tenement, than is due therefrom.

17. Common pleas shall not follow our court, but shall be held in some fixed place.

18. Inquests of novel disseisin, of mort d'ancestor, and of darrein presentment shall not be held elsewhere than in their own county courts, and that in manner following; We, or, if we should be out of the realm, our chief justiciar, will send two justiciaries through every county four times a year, who shall alone with four knights of the county chosen by the county, hold the said assizes in the county court, on the day and in the place of meeting of that court.

19. And if any of the said assizes cannot be taken on the day of the county court, let there remain of the knights and freeholders, who were present at the county court on that day, as many as may be required for the efficient making of judgments, according as the business be more or less.

20. A freeman shall not be amerced for a slight offense, except in accordance with the degree of the offense; and for a grave offense he shall be amerced in accordance with the gravity of the offense, yet saving always his "contentment";

and a merchant in the same way, saving his "merchandise"; and a villein shall be amerced in the same way, saving his "wainage" if they have fallen into our mercy: and none of the aforesaid amercements shall be imposed except by the oath of honest men of the neighborhood.

21. Earls and barons shall not be amerced except through their peers, and only in accordance with the degree of the offense.

22. A clerk shall not be amerced in respect of his lay holding except after the manner of the others aforesaid; further, he shall not be amerced in accordance with the extent of his ecclesiastical benefice.

23. No village or individual shall be compelled to make bridges at river banks, except those who from of old were legally bound to do so.

24. No sheriff, constable, coroners, or others of our bailiffs, shall hold pleas of our Crown.

25. All counties, hundred, wapentakes, and trithings (except our demesne manors) shall remain at the old rents, and without any additional payment.

26. If anyone holding of us a lay fief shall die, and our sheriff or bailiff shall exhibit our letters patent of summons for a debt which the deceased owed us, it shall be lawful for our sheriff or bailiff to attach and enroll the chattels of the deceased, found upon the lay fief, to the value of that debt, at the sight of law worthy men, provided always that nothing whatever be thence removed until the debt which is evident shall be fully paid to us; and the residue shall be left to the executors to fulfill the will of the deceased; and if there be nothing due from him to us, all the chattels shall go to the deceased, saving to his wife and children their reasonable shares.

27. If any freeman shall die intestate, his chattels shall be distributed by the hands of his nearest kinsfolk and friends, under supervision of the Church, saving to every one the debts which the deceased owed to him.

28. No constable or other bailiff of ours shall take corn or other provisions from anyone without immediately tendering money therefor, unless he can have postponement thereof by permission of the seller.

29. No constable shall compel any knight to give money in lieu of castle-guard, when he is willing to perform it in his own person, or (if he himself cannot do it from any reasonable cause) then by another responsible man. Further, if we

have led or sent him upon military service, he shall be relieved from guard in proportion to the time during which he has been on service because of us.

30. No sheriff or bailiff of ours, or other person, shall take the horses or carts of any freeman for transport duty, against the will of the said freeman.

31. Neither we nor our bailiffs shall take, for our castles or for any other work of ours, wood which is not ours, against the will of the owner of that wood.

32. We will not retain beyond one year and one day, the lands those who have been convicted of felony, and the lands shall thereafter be handed over to the lords of the fiefs.

33. All kydells for the future shall be removed altogether from Thames and Medway, and throughout all England, except upon the seashore.

34. The writ which is called praecipe shall not for the future be issued to anyone, regarding any tenement whereby a freeman may lose his court.

35. Let there be one measure of wine throughout our whole realm; and one measure of ale; and one measure of corn, to wit, "the London quarter"; and one width of cloth (whether dyed, or russet, or "halberget"), to wit, two ells within the selvedges; of weights also let it be as of measures.

36. Nothing in future shall be given or taken for a writ of inquisition of life or limbs, but freely it shall be granted, and never denied.

37. If anyone holds of us by fee-farm, either by socage or by burage, or of any other land by knight's service, we will not (by reason of that fee-farm, socage, or burgage), have the wardship of the heir, or of such land of his as if of the fief of that other; nor shall we have wardship of that fee-farm, socage, or burgage, unless such fee-farm owes knight's service. We will not by reason of any small serjeancy which anyone may hold of us by the service of rendering to us knives, arrows, or the like, have wardship of his heir or of the land which he holds of another lord by knight's service.

38. No bailiff for the future shall, upon his own unsupported complaint, put anyone to his "law", without credible witnesses brought for this purposes.

39. No freemen shall be taken or imprisoned or disseised or exiled or in any way destroyed, nor will we go upon him nor send upon him, except by the lawful judgment of his peers or by the law of the land.

40. To no one will we sell, to no one will we refuse or delay, right or justice.

41. All merchants shall have safe and secure exit from England, and entry to England, with the right to tarry there and to move about as well by land as by water, for buying and selling by the ancient and right customs, quit from all evil tolls, except (in time of war) such merchants as are of the land at war with us. And if such are found in our land at the beginning of the war, they shall be detained, without injury to their bodies or goods, until information be received by us, or by our chief justiciar, how the merchants of our land found in the land at war with us are treated; and if our men are safe there, the others shall be safe in our land.

42. It shall be lawful in future for anyone (excepting always those imprisoned or outlawed in accordance with the law of the kingdom, and natives of any country at war with us, and merchants, who shall be treated as if above provided) to leave our kingdom and to return, safe and secure by land and water, except for a short period in time of war, on grounds of public policy—reserving always the allegiance due to us.

43. If anyone holding of some escheat (such as the honor of Wallingford, Nottingham, Boulogne, Lancaster, or of other escheats which are in our hands and are baronies) shall die, his heir shall give no other relief, and perform no other service to us than he would have done to the baron if that barony had been in the baron's hand; and we shall hold it in the same manner in which the baron held it.

44. Men who dwell without the forest need not henceforth come before our justiciaries of the forest upon a general summons, unless they are in plea, or sureties of one or more, who are attached for the forest.

45. We will appoint as justices, constables, sheriffs, or bailiffs only such as know the law of the realm and mean to observe it well.

46. All barons who have founded abbeys, concerning which they hold charters from the kings of England, or of which they have long continued possession, shall have the wardship of them, when vacant, as they ought to have.

47. All forests that have been made such in our time shall forthwith be disafforsted; and a similar course shall be followed with regard to river banks that have been placed "in defense" by us in our time.

48. All evil customs connected with forests and warrens, foresters and warreners, sheriffs and their officers, river banks and their wardens, shall immediately by inquired into in each county by twelve sworn knights of the same county chosen by the honest men of the same county, and shall, within forty days of the said inquest, be utterly abolished, so as never to be restored, provided always that we previously have intimation thereof, or our justiciar, if we should not be in England.

49. We will immediately restore all hostages and charters delivered to us by Englishmen, as sureties of the peace of faithful service.

50. We will entirely remove from their bailiwicks, the relations of Gerard of Athee (so that in future they shall have no bailiwick in England); namely, Engelard of Cigogne, Peter, Guy, and Andrew of Chanceaux, Guy of Cigogne, Geoffrey of Martigny with his brothers, Philip Mark with his brothers and his nephew Geoffrey, and the whole brood of the same.

51. As soon as peace is restored, we will banish from the kingdom all foreign born knights, crossbowmen, serjeants, and mercenary soldiers who have come with horses and arms to the kingdom's hurt.

52. If anyone has been dispossessed or removed by us, without the legal judgment of his peers, from his lands, castles, franchises, or from his right, we will immediately restore them to him; and if a dispute arise over this, then let it be decided by the five and twenty barons of whom mention is made below in the clause for securing the peace. Moreover, for all those possessions, from which anyone has, without the lawful judgment of his peers, been disseised or removed, by our father, King Henry, or by our brother, King Richard, and which we retain in our hand (or which as possessed by others, to whom we are bound to warrant them) we shall have respite until the usual term of crusaders; excepting those things about which a plea has been raised, or an inquest made by our order, before our taking of the cross; but as soon as we return from the expedition, we will immediately grant full justice therein.

53. We shall have, moreover, the same respite and in the same manner in rendering justice concerning the disafforestation or retention of those forests which Henry our father and Richard our broter afforested, and concerning the

wardship of lands which are of the fief of another (namely, such wardships as we have hitherto had by reason of a fief which anyone held of us by knight's service), and concerning abbeys founded on other fiefs than our own, in which the lord of the fee claims to have right; and when we have returned, or if we desist from our expedition, we will immediately grant full justice to all who complain of such things.

54. No one shall be arrested or imprisoned upon the appeal of a woman, for the death of any other than her husband.

55. All fines made with us unjustly and against the law of the land, and all amercements, imposed unjustly and against the law of the land, shall be entirely remitted, or else it shall be done concerning them according to the decision of the five and twenty barons whom mention is made below in the clause for securing the pease, or according to the judgment of the majority of the same, along with the aforesaid Stephen, archbishop of Canterbury, if he can be present, and such others as he may wish to bring with him for this purpose, and if he cannot be present the business shall nevertheless proceed without him, provided always that if any one or more of the aforesaid five and twenty barons are in a similar suit, they shall be removed as far as concerns this particular judgment, others being substituted in their places after having been selected by the rest of the same five and twenty for this purpose only, and after having been sworn.

56. If we have disseised or removed Welshmen from lands or liberties, or other things, without the legal judgment of their peers in England or in Wales, they shall be immediately restored to them; and if a dispute arise over this, then let it be decided in the marches by the judgment of their peers; for the tenements in England according to the law of England, for tenements in Wales according to the law of Wales, and for tenements in the marches according to the law of the marches. Welshmen shall do the same to us and ours.

57. Further, for all those possessions from which any Welshman has, without the lawful judgment of his peers, been disseised or removed by King Henry our father, or King Richard our brother, and which we retain in our hand (or which are possessed by others, and which we ought to warrant), we will have respite until the usual term of crusaders; excepting those things about which a plea has been raised or an inquest made by our order before we took the cross; but as soon as we return (or if perchance we desist from our expedition), we will immediately grant full justice in accordance with the laws of the Welsh and in relation to the foresaid regions.

58. We will immediately give up the son of Llywelyn and all the hostages of Wales, and the charters delivered to us as security for the peace.

59. We will do towards Alexander, king of Scots, concerning the return of his sisters and his hostages, and concerning his franchises, and his right, in the same manner as we shall do towards our owher barons of England, unless it ought to be otherwise according to the charters which we hold from William his father, formerly king of Scots; and this shall be according to the judgment of his peers in our court.

60. Moreover, all these aforesaid customs and liberties, the observances of which we have granted in our kingdom as far as pertains to us towards our men, shall be observed b all of our kingdom, as well clergy as laymen, as far as pertains to them towards their men.

61. Since, moveover, for God and the amendment of our kingdom and for the better allaying of the quarrel that has arisen between us and our barons, we have granted all these concessions, desirous that they should enjoy them in complete and firm endurance forever, we give and grant to them the underwritten security, namely, that the barons choose five and twenty barons of the kingdom, whomsoever they will, who shall be bound with all their might, to observe and hold, and cause to be observed, the peace and liberties we have granted and confirmed to them by this our present Charter, so that if we, or our justiciar, or our bailiffs or any one of our officers, shall in anything be at fault towards anyone, or shall have broken any one of the articles of this peace or of this security, and the offense be notified to four barons of the foresaid five and twenty, the said four barons shall repair to us (or our justiciar, if we are out of the realm) and, laying the transgression before us, petition to have that transgression redressed without delay. And if we shall not have corrected the transgression (or, in the event of our being out of the realm, if our justiciar shall not have corrected it) within forty days, reckoning from the time it has been intimated to us (or to our justiciar, if we should be out of the realm), the four barons aforesaid shall refer that matter to the rest of the five and twenty barons, and those five and twenty barons shall, together with the community of the whole realm, distrain and distress us in all possible ways, namely, by seizing our castles, lands, possessions, and in any other way they can, until redress has been obtained as they deem fit, saving harmless our own person, and the persons of our queen and children; and when redress has been obtained, they shall resume their old relations towards us. And let whoever in the country desires it, swear to obey the orders of the said five and twenty barons for the execution of all the aforesaid matters, and along with them, to molest us to the utmost of his power; and we publicly and freely grant leave to

everyone who wishes to swear, and we shall never forbid anyone to swear. All those, moveover, in the land who of themselves and of their own accord are unwilling to swear to the twenty five to help them in constraining and molesting us, we shall by our command compel the same to swear to the effect foresaid. And if any one of the five and twenty barons shall have died or departed from the land, or be incapacitated in any other manner which would prevent the foresaid provisions being carried out, those of the said twenty five barons who are left shall choose another in his place according to their own judgment, and he shall be sworn in the same way as the others. Further, in all matters, the execution of which is entrusted, to these twenty five barons, if perchance these twenty five are present and disagree about anything, or if some of them, after being summoned, are unwilling or unable to be present, that which the majority of those present ordain or command shall be held as fixed and established, exactly as if the whole twenty five had concurred in this; and the said twenty five shall swear that they will faithfully observe all that is aforesaid, and cause it to be observed with all their might. And we shall procure nothing from anyone, directly or indirectly, whereby any part of these concessions and liberties might be revoked or diminished; and if any such things has been procured, let it be void and null, and we shall never use it personally or by another.

62. And all the will, hatreds, and bitterness that have arisen between us and our men, clergy and lay, from the date of the quarrel, we have completely remitted and pardoned to everyone. Moreover, all trespasses occasioned by the said quarrel, from Easter in the sixteenth year of our reign till the restoration of peace, we have fully remitted to all, both clergy and laymen, and completely forgiven, as far as pertains to us. And on this head, we have caused to be made for them letters testimonial patent of the lord Stephen, archbishop of Canterbury, of the lord Henry, archbishop of Dublin, of the bishops aforesaid, and of Master Pandulf as touching this security and the concessions aforesaid.

63. Wherefore we will and firmly order that the English Church be free, and that the men in our kingdom have and hold all the aforesaid liberties, rights, and concessions, well and peaceably, freely and quietly, fully and wholly, for themselves and their heirs, of us and our heirs, in all respects and in all places forever, as is aforesaid. An oath, moreover, has been taken, as well on our part as on the art of the barons, that all these conditions aforesaid shall be kept in good faith and without evil intent.

Given under our hand—the above named and many others being witnesses—in the meadow which is called Runnymede, between Windsor and Staines, on the fifteenth day of June, in the seventeenth year of our reign.

[1] Source Note—Gerald Murphy (The Cleveland Free-Net—aa300): This is but one of three different translations found of the Magna Carta; it was originally done in Latin.. It was in force for only a few months, when it was violated by the king. Just over a year later, with no resolution to the war, the king died, being succeeded by his 9-year old son, Henry III. The Charter (Carta) was reissued again, with some revisions, in 1216, 1217 and 1225. The version presented here is the one that preceeded all of the others; nearly all of it's provisions were soon superceded by other laws, and none of it is effective today.

The two other versions, professed to be the original, as well. The basic intent of each is the same.

APPENDIX B

FEDERALIST PAPERS[85]

The Federalist Papers : No. 4

The Same Subject Continued:
Concerning Dangers From Foreign Force and Influence
For the Independent Journal.
JOHN JAY

To the People of the State of New York:

MY LAST paper assigned several reasons why the safety of the people would be best secured by union against the danger it may be exposed to by JUST causes of war given to other nations; and those reasons show that such causes would not only be more rarely given, but would also be more easily accommodated, by a national government than either by the State governments or the proposed little confederacies.

But the safety of the people of America against dangers from FOREIGN force depends not only on their forbearing to give JUST causes of war to other nations, but also on their placing and continuing themselves in such a situation as not to INVITE hostility or insult; for it need not be observed that there are PRETENDED as well as just causes of war.

It is too true, however disgraceful it may be to human nature, that nations in general will make war whenever they have a prospect of getting anything by it; nay, absolute monarchs will often make war when their nations are to get nothing by it, but for the purposes and objects merely personal, such as thirst for military glory, revenge for personal affronts, ambition, or private compacts to aggrandize or support their particular families or partisans. These and a variety of other motives, which affect only the mind of the sovereign, often lead him to engage in wars not sanctified by justice or the voice and interests of his people. But, independent of these inducements to war, which are more prevalent in absolute monarchies, but which well deserve our attention, there are others which affect nations as often as kings; and some of them will on examination be found to grow out of our relative situation and circumstances.

With France and with Britain we are rivals in the fisheries, and can supply their markets cheaper than they can themselves, notwithstanding any efforts to prevent it by bounties on their own or duties on foreign fish.

With them and with most other European nations we are rivals in navigation and the carrying trade; and we shall deceive ourselves if we suppose that any of them will rejoice to see it flourish; for, as our carrying trade cannot increase without in some degree diminishing theirs, it is more their interest, and will be more their policy, to restrain than to promote it.

In the trade to China and India, we interfere with more than one nation, inasmuch as it enables us to partake in advantages which they had in a manner monopolized, and as we thereby supply ourselves with commodities which we used to purchase from them.

The extension of our own commerce in our own vessels cannot give pleasure to any nations who possess territories on or near this continent, because the cheapness and excellence of our productions, added to the circumstance of vicinity, and the enterprise and address of our merchants and navigators, will give us a greater share in the advantages which those territories afford, than consists with the wishes or policy of their respective sovereigns.

Spain thinks it convenient to shut the Mississippi against us on the one side, and Britain excludes us from the Saint Lawrence on the other; nor will either of them permit the other waters which are between them and us to become the means of mutual intercourse and traffic.

From these and such like considerations, which might, if consistent with prudence, be more amplified and detailed, it is easy to see that jealousies and uneasinesses may gradually slide into the minds and cabinets of other nations, and that we are not to expect that they should regard our advancement in union, in power and consequence by land and by sea, with an eye of indifference and composure.

The people of America are aware that inducements to war may arise out of these circumstances, as well as from others not so obvious at present, and that whenever such inducements may find fit time and opportunity for operation, pretenses to color and justify them will not be wanting. Wisely, therefore, do they consider union and a good national government as necessary to put and keep them in SUCH A SITUATION as, instead of INVITING war, will tend to repress and discourage it. That situation consists in the best possible state of defense, and necessarily depends on the government, the arms, and the resources of the country.

As the safety of the whole is the interest of the whole, and cannot be provided for without government, either one or more or many, let us inquire whether one good government is not, relative to the object in question, more competent than any other given number whatever.

One government can collect and avail itself of the talents and experience of the ablest men, in whatever part of the Union they may be found. It can move on uniform principles of policy. It can harmonize, assimilate, and protect the several parts and members, and extend the benefit of its foresight and precautions to each. In the formation of treaties, it will regard the interest of the whole, and the particular interests of the parts as connected with that of the whole. It can apply the resources and power of the whole to the defense of any particular part, and that more easily and expeditiously than State governments or separate confederacies can possibly do, for want of concert and unity of system. It can place the militia under one plan of discipline, and, by putting their officers in a proper line of subordination to the Chief Magistrate, will, as it were, consolidate them into one corps, and thereby render them more efficient than if divided into thirteen or into three or four distinct independent companies.

What would the militia of Britain be if the English militia obeyed the government of England, if the Scotch militia obeyed the government of Scotland, and if the Welsh militia obeyed the government of Wales? Suppose an invasion; would those three governments (if they agreed at all) be able, with all their respective forces, to operate against the enemy so effectually as the single government of Great Britain would?

We have heard much of the fleets of Britain, and the time may come, if we are wise, when the fleets of America may engage attention. But if one national government, had not so regulated the navigation of Britain as to make it a nursery for seamen—if one national government had not called forth all the national means and materials for forming fleets, their prowess and their thunder would never have been celebrated. Let England have its navigation and fleet—let Scotland have its navigation and fleet—let Wales have its navigation and fleet—let Ireland have its navigation and fleet—let those four of the constituent parts of the British empire be under four independent governments, and it is easy to perceive how soon they would each dwindle into comparative insignificance.

Apply these facts to our own case. Leave America divided into thirteen or, if you please, into three or four independent governments—what armies could they raise and pay—what fleets could they ever hope to have? If one was attacked, would the others fly to its succor, and spend their blood and money in its defense? Would there be no danger of their being flattered into neutrality by its specious promises, or seduced by a too great fondness for peace to decline hazarding their tranquillity and present safety for the sake of neighbors, of whom perhaps they have been jealous, and whose importance they are content to see diminished? Although such conduct would not be wise, it would, nevertheless, be natural. The history of the states of Greece, and of other countries, abounds with such instances, and it is not improbable that what has so often happened would, under similar circumstances, happen again.

But admit that they might be willing to help the invaded State or confederacy. How, and when, and in what proportion shall aids of men and money be afforded? Who shall command the allied armies, and from which of them shall he receive his orders? Who shall settle the terms of peace, and in case of disputes what umpire shall decide between them and compel acquiescence? Various difficulties and inconveniences would be inseparable from such a situation; whereas one government, watching over the general and common interests, and combining and directing the powers and resources of the whole, would be free from all these embarrassments, and conduce far more to the safety of the people.

But whatever may be our situation, whether firmly united under one national government, or split into a number of confederacies, certain it is, that foreign nations will know and view it exactly as it is; and they will act toward us accordingly. If they see that our national government is efficient and well administered, our trade prudently regulated, our militia properly organized and disciplined, our resources and finances discreetly managed, our credit re-established, our people free, contented, and united, they will be much more disposed to cultivate our friendship than provoke our resentment. If, on the other hand, they find us either destitute of an effectual government (each State doing right or wrong, as to its rulers may seem convenient), or split into three or four independent and probably discordant republics or confederacies, one inclining to Britain, another to France, and a third to Spain, and perhaps played off against each other by the three, what a poor, pitiful figure will America make in their eyes! How liable would she become not only to their contempt but to their outrage, and how soon would dear-bought experience proclaim that when a people or family so divide, it never fails to be against themselves.

PUBLIUS.

The Federalist Papers : No. 28

The Same Subject Continued
(The Idea of Restraining the Legislative Authority in Regard to the Common Defense Considered)
For the Independent Journal.
ALEXANDER HAMILTON

To the People of the State of New York:

THAT there may happen cases in which the national government may be necessitated to resort to force, cannot be denied. Our own experience has corroborated the lessons taught by the examples of other nations; that emergencies of this sort will sometimes arise in all societies, however constituted; that seditions and insurrections are, unhappily, maladies as inseparable from the body politic as tumors and eruptions from the natural body; that the idea of governing at all times by the simple force of law (which we have been told is the only admissible principle of republican government), has no place but in the reveries of those political doctors whose sagacity disdains the admonitions of experimental instruction.

Should such emergencies at any time happen under the national government, there could be no remedy but force. The means to be employed must be proportioned to the extent of the mischief. If it should be a slight commotion in a small part of a State, the militia of the residue would be adequate to its suppression; and the national presumption is that they would be ready to do their duty. An insurrection, whatever may be its immediate cause, eventually endangers all government. Regard to the public peace, if not to the rights of the Union, would engage the citizens to whom the contagion had not communicated itself to oppose the insurgents; and if the general government should be found in practice conducive to the prosperity and felicity of the people, it were irrational to believe that they would be disinclined to its support.

If, on the contrary, the insurrection should pervade a whole State, or a principal part of it, the employment of a different kind of force might become unavoidable. It appears that Massachusetts found it necessary to raise troops for repressing the disorders within that State; that Pennsylvania, from the mere apprehension of commotions among a part of her citizens, has thought proper to have recourse to the same measure. Suppose the State of New York had been inclined to re-establish her lost jurisdiction over the inhabitants of Vermont, could she have hoped for success in such an enterprise from the efforts of the militia alone? Would she not have been compelled to raise and to maintain a more regular force for the execution of her design? If it must then be admitted that the necessity of recurring to a force different from the militia, in cases of this extraordinary nature, is applicable to the State governments themselves, why should the possibility, that the national government might be under a like necessity, in similar extremities, be made an objection to its existence? Is it not surprising that men who declare an attachment to the Union in the abstract, should urge as an objection to the proposed *Constitution* what applies with tenfold weight to the plan for which they contend; and what, as far as it has any foundation in truth, is an inevitable consequence of civil society upon an enlarged scale? Who would not prefer that possibility to the unceasing agitations and frequent revolutions which are the continual scourges of petty republics?

Let us pursue this examination in another light. Suppose, in lieu of one general system, two, or three, or even four Confederacies were to be formed, would not the same difficulty oppose itself to the operations of either of these Confederacies? Would not each of them be exposed to the same casualties; and when these happened, be obliged to have recourse to the same expedients for upholding its authority which are objected to in a government for all the States? Would the militia, in this supposition, be more ready or more able to support the federal authority than in the case of a general union? All candid and intelligent men must, upon due consideration, acknowledge that the principle of the objection is equally applicable to either of the two cases; and that whether we have one government for all the States, or different governments for different parcels of them, or even if there should be an entire separation of the States, there might sometimes be a necessity to make use of a force constituted differently from the militia, to preserve the peace of the community and to maintain the just authority of the laws against those violent invasions of them which amount to insurrections and rebellions.

Independent of all other reasonings upon the subject, it is a full answer to those who require a more peremptory provision against military establishments in time of peace, to say that the whole power of the proposed government is to be in the hands of the representatives of the people. This is the essential, and, after all, only efficacious security for the rights and privileges of the people, which is attainable in civil society.*1*

If the representatives of the people betray their constituents, there is then no resource left but in the exertion of that original right of self-defense which is paramount to all positive forms of government, and which against the usurpations of the national rulers, may be exerted with infinitely better prospect of success than against those of the rulers of an individual state. In a single state, if the persons intrusted with supreme power become usurpers, the different parcels, subdivisions, or districts of which it consists, having no distinct government in each, can take no regular measures for defense. The citizens must rush tumultuously to arms, without concert, without system, without resource; except in their courage and despair. The usurpers, clothed with the forms of legal authority, can too often crush the opposition in embryo. The smaller the extent of the territory, the more difficult will it be for the people to form a regular or systematic plan of opposition, and the more easy will it be to defeat their early efforts. Intelligence can be more speedily obtained of their preparations and movements, and the military force in the possession of the usurpers can be more rapidly directed against the part where the opposition has begun. In this situation there must be a peculiar coincidence of circumstances to insure success to the popular resistance.

The obstacles to usurpation and the facilities of resistance increase with the increased extent of the state, provided the citizens understand their rights and are disposed to defend them. The natural strength of the people in a large community, in proportion to the artificial strength of the government, is greater than in a small, and of course more competent to a struggle with the attempts of the government to establish a tyranny. But in a confederacy the people, without exaggeration, may be said to be entirely the masters of their own fate. Power being almost always the rival of power, the general government will at all times stand ready to check the usurpations of the state governments, and these will have the same disposition towards the general government. The people, by throwing themselves into either scale, will infallibly make it preponderate. If their rights are invaded by either, they can make use of the other as the instrument of redress. How wise will it be in them by cherishing the union to preserve to themselves an advantage which can never be too highly prized!

It may safely be received as an axiom in our political system, that the State governments will, in all possible contingencies, afford complete security against invasions of the public liberty by the national authority. Projects of usurpation cannot be masked under pretenses so likely to escape the penetration of select bodies of men, as of the people at large. The legislatures will have better means of information. They can discover the danger at a distance; and possessing all the organs of civil power, and the confidence of the people, they can at once adopt a regular plan of opposition, in which they can combine all the resources of the community. They can readily communicate with each other in the different States, and unite their common forces for the protection of their common liberty.

The great extent of the country is a further security. We have already experienced its utility against the attacks of a foreign power. And it would have precisely the same effect against the enterprises of ambitious rulers in the national councils. If the federal army should be able to quell the resistance of one State, the distant States would have it in their power to make head with fresh forces. The advantages obtained in one place must be abandoned to subdue the opposition in others; and the moment the part which had been reduced to submission was left to itself, its efforts would be renewed, and its resistance revive.

We should recollect that the extent of the military force must, at all events, be regulated by the resources of the country. For a long time to come, it will not be possible to maintain a large army; and as the means of doing this increase, the population and natural strength of the community will proportionably increase. When will the time arrive that the federal government can raise and maintain an army capable of erecting a despotism over the great body of the people of an immense empire, who are in a situation, through the medium of their State governments, to take measures for their own defense, with all the celerity, regularity, and system of independent nations? The apprehension may be considered as a disease, for which there can be found no cure in the resources of argument and reasoning.

PUBLIUS.

1 Its full efficacy will be examined hereafter.

The Federalist Papers : No. 39

The Conformity of the Plan to Republican Principles
For the Independent Journal.
JAMES MADISON

To the People of the State of New York:

THE last paper having concluded the observations which were meant to introduce a candid survey of the plan of government reported by the convention, we now proceed to the execution of that part of our undertaking.

The first question that offers itself is, whether the general form and aspect of the government be strictly republican. It is evident that no other form would be reconcilable with the genius of the people of America; with the fundamental principles of the Revolution; or with that honorable determination which animates every votary of freedom, to rest all our political experiments on the capacity of mankind for self-government. If the plan of the convention, therefore, be found to depart from the republican character, its advocates must abandon it as no longer defensible.

What, then, are the distinctive characters of the republican form? Were an answer to this question to be sought, not by recurring to principles, but in the application of the term by political writers, to the constitution of different States, no satisfactory one would ever be found. Holland, in which no particle of the supreme authority is derived from the people, has passed almost universally under the denomination of a republic. The same title has been bestowed on Venice, where absolute power over the great body of the people is exercised, in the most absolute manner, by a small body of hereditary nobles. Poland, which is a mixture of aristocracy and of monarchy in their worst forms, has been dignified with the same appellation. The government of England, which has one republican branch only, combined with an hereditary aristocracy and monarchy, has, with equal impropriety, been frequently placed on the list of republics. These examples, which are nearly as dissimilar to each other as to a genuine republic, show the extreme inaccuracy with which the term has been used in political disquisitions.

If we resort for a criterion to the different principles on which different forms of government are established, we may define a republic to be, or at least may bestow that name on, a government which derives all its powers directly or indirectly from the great body of the people, and is administered by persons holding their offices during pleasure, for a limited period, or during good behavior. It is ESSENTIAL to such a government that it be derived from the great body of the society, not from an inconsiderable proportion, or a favored class of it; otherwise a handful of tyrannical nobles, exercising their oppressions by a delegation of their powers, might aspire to the rank of republicans, and claim for their government the honorable title of republic. It is SUFFICIENT for such a government that the persons administering it be appointed, either directly or indirectly, by the people; and that they hold their appointments by either of the tenures just specified; otherwise every government in the United States, as well as every other popular government that has been or can be well organized or well executed, would be degraded from the republican character. According to the constitution of every State in the Union, some or other of the officers of government are appointed indirectly only by the people. According to most of them, the chief magistrate himself is so appointed. And according to one, this mode of appointment is extended to one of the co-ordinate branches of the legislature. According to all the constitutions, also, the tenure of the highest offices is extended to a definite period, and in many instances, both within the legislative and executive departments, to a period of years. According to the provisions of most of the constitutions, again, as well as according to the most respectable and received opinions on the subject, the members of the judiciary department are to retain their offices by the firm tenure of good behavior.

On comparing the Constitution planned by the convention with the standard here fixed, we perceive at once that it is, in the most rigid sense, conformable to it. The House of Representatives, like that of one branch at least of all the State legislatures, is elected immediately by the great body of the people. The Senate, like the present Congress, and the Senate of Maryland, derives its appointment indirectly from the people. The President is indirectly derived from the choice of the people, according to the example in most of the States. Even the judges, with all other officers of the Union, will, as in the several States, be the choice, though a remote choice, of the people themselves, the duration of the appointments is equally conformable to the republican standard, and to the model of State constitutions The House of Representatives is periodically elective, as in all the States; and for the period of two years, as in the State of South Carolina. The Senate is elective, for the period of six years; which is but one year more than the period of the Senate of Maryland, and but two more than that of the Senates of New York and Virginia. The President is to continue in office for the period of four years; as in New York and Delaware, the chief magistrate is elected for three years, and in South Carolina for two years. In the other States the election is annual. In several of the States, however, no constitutional provision is made for the impeachment of the chief magistrate. And in Delaware and Virginia he is not impeachable till out of office. The President of the United States is impeachable at any time during his continuance in office. The tenure by which the judges are to hold their places, is, as it unquestionably ought to be, that of good behavior. The tenure of the ministerial offices generally, will be a subject of legal regulation, conformably to the reason of the case and the example of the State constitutions.

Could any further proof be required of the republican complexion of this system, the most decisive one might be found in its absolute prohibition of titles of nobility, both under the federal and the State governments; and in its express guaranty of the republican form to each of the latter.

"But it was not sufficient," say the adversaries of the proposed Constitution, "for the convention to adhere to the republican form. They ought, with equal care, to have preserved the FEDERAL form, which regards the Union as a

CONFEDERACY of sovereign states; instead of which, they have framed a NATIONAL government, which regards the Union as a CONSOLIDATION of the States." And it is asked by what authority this bold and radical innovation was undertaken? The handle which has been made of this objection requires that it should be examined with some precision.

Without inquiring into the accuracy of the distinction on which the objection is founded, it will be necessary to a just estimate of its force, first, to ascertain the real character of the government in question; secondly, to inquire how far the convention were authorized to propose such a government; and thirdly, how far the duty they owed to their country could supply any defect of regular authority.

First. In order to ascertain the real character of the government, it may be considered in relation to the foundation on which it is to be established; to the sources from which its ordinary powers are to be drawn; to the operation of those powers; to the extent of them; and to the authority by which future changes in the government are to be introduced.

On examining the first relation, it appears, on one hand, that the Constitution is to be founded on the assent and ratification of the people of America, given by deputies elected for the special purpose; but, on the other, that this assent and ratification is to be given by the people, not as individuals composing one entire nation, but as composing the distinct and independent States to which they respectively belong. It is to be the assent and ratification of the several States, derived from the supreme authority in each State, the authority of the people themselves. The act, therefore, establishing the Constitution, will not be a NATIONAL, but a FEDERAL act.

That it will be a federal and not a national act, as these terms are understood by the objectors; the act of the people, as forming so many independent States, not as forming one aggregate nation, is obvious from this single consideration, that it is to result neither from the decision of a MAJORITY of the people of the Union, nor from that of a MAJORITY of the States. It must result from the UNANIMOUS assent of the several States that are parties to it, differing no otherwise from their ordinary assent than in its being expressed, not by the legislative authority, but by that of the people themselves. Were the people regarded in this transaction as forming one nation, the will of the majority of the whole people of the United States would bind the minority, in the same manner as the majority in each State must bind the minority; and the will of the majority must be determined either by a comparison of the individual votes, or by considering the will of the majority of the States as evidence of the will of a majority of the people of the United States. Neither of these rules have been adopted. Each State, in ratifying the Constitution, is considered as a sovereign body, independent of all others, and only to be bound by its own voluntary act. In this relation, then, the new Constitution will, if established, be a FEDERAL, and not a NATIONAL constitution.

The next relation is, to the sources from which the ordinary powers of government are to be derived. The House of Representatives will derive its powers from the people of America; and the people will be represented in the same proportion, and on the same principle, as they are in the legislature of a particular State. So far the government is NATIONAL, not FEDERAL. The Senate, on the other hand, will derive its powers from the States, as political and coequal societies; and these will be represented on the principle of equality in the Senate, as they now are in the existing Congress. So far the government is FEDERAL, not NATIONAL. The executive power will be derived from a very compound source. The immediate election of the President is to be made by the States in their political characters. The votes allotted to them are in a compound ratio, which considers them partly as distinct and coequal societies, partly as unequal members of the same society. The eventual election, again, is to be made by that branch of the legislature which consists of the national representatives; but in this particular act they are to be thrown into the form of individual delegations, from so many distinct and coequal bodies politic. From this aspect of the government it appears to be of a mixed character, presenting at least as many FEDERAL as NATIONAL features.

The difference between a federal and national government, as it relates to the OPERATION OF THE GOVERNMENT, is supposed to consist in this, that in the former the powers operate on the political bodies composing the Confederacy, in their political capacities; in the latter, on the individual citizens composing the nation, in their individual capacities. On trying the Constitution by this criterion, it falls under the NATIONAL, not the FEDERAL character; though perhaps not so completely as has been understood. In several cases, and particularly in the trial of controversies to which States may be parties, they must be viewed and proceeded against in their collective and political capacities only. So far the national countenance of the government on this side seems to be disfigured by a few federal features. But this blemish is perhaps unavoidable in any plan; and the operation of the government on the people, in their individual capacities, in its ordinary and most essential proceedings, may, on the whole, designate it, in this relation, a NATIONAL government.

But if the government be national with regard to the OPERATION of its powers, it changes its aspect again when we contemplate it in relation to the EXTENT of its powers. The idea of a national government involves in it, not only an authority over the individual citizens, but an indefinite supremacy over all persons and things, so far as they are objects of lawful government. Among a people consolidated into one nation, this supremacy is completely vested in the national legislature. Among communities united for particular purposes, it is vested partly in the general and partly in the municipal legislatures. In the former case, all local authorities are subordinate to the supreme; and may be controlled, directed, or abolished by it at pleasure. In the latter, the local or municipal authorities form distinct and independent portions of the supremacy, no more subject, within their respective spheres, to the general authority, than the general authority is subject to them, within its own sphere. In this relation, then, the proposed government cannot be deemed a NATIONAL one; since its jurisdiction extends to certain enumerated objects only, and leaves to the several States a residuary and inviolable sovereignty over all other objects. It is true that in controversies relating to the boundary between the two jurisdictions, the tribunal which is ultimately to decide, is to be established under the general government. But this does not change the principle of the case. The decision is to be impartially made, according to the rules of the Constitution; and all the usual and most effectual precautions are taken to secure this impartiality. Some such tribunal is clearly essential to prevent an appeal to the sword and a dissolution of the compact; and that it ought to be established under the general rather than under the local governments, or, to speak more properly, that it could be safely established under the first alone, is a position not likely to be combated.

If we try the Constitution by its last relation to the authority by which amendments are to be made, we find it neither wholly NATIONAL nor wholly FEDERAL. Were it wholly national, the supreme and ultimate authority would reside in the MAJORITY of the people of the Union; and this authority would be competent at all times, like that of a majority of every national society, to alter or abolish its established government. Were it wholly federal, on the other hand, the concurrence of each State in the Union would be essential to every alteration that would be binding on all. The mode provided by the plan of the convention is not founded on either of these principles. In requiring more than a majority, and principles. In requiring more than a majority, and particularly in computing the proportion by STATES, not by CITIZENS, it departs from the NATIONAL and advances towards the FEDERAL character; in rendering the concurrence of less than the whole number of States sufficient, it loses again the FEDERAL and partakes of the NATIONAL character.

The proposed Constitution, therefore, is, in strictness, neither a national nor a federal Constitution, but a composition of both. In its foundation it is federal, not national; in the sources from which the ordinary powers of the government are drawn, it is partly federal and partly national; in the operation of these powers, it is national, not federal; in the extent of them, again, it is federal, not national; and, finally, in the authoritative mode of introducing amendments, it is neither wholly federal nor wholly national.

PUBLIUS.

The Federalist Papers : No. 45

The Alleged Danger From the Powers of the Union to the State Governments Considered

For the Independent Journal.

JAMES MADISON

To the People of the State of New York:

HAVING shown that no one of the powers transferred to the federal government is unnecessary or improper, the next question to be considered is, whether the whole mass of them will be dangerous to the portion of authority left in the several States. The adversaries to the plan of the convention, instead of considering in the first place what degree of power was absolutely necessary for the purposes of the federal government, have exhausted themselves in a secondary inquiry into the possible consequences of the proposed degree of power to the governments of the particular States. But if the Union, as has been shown, be essential to the security of the people of America against foreign danger; if it be essential to their security against contentions and wars among the different States; if it be essential to guard them against those violent and oppressive factions which embitter the blessings of liberty, and against those military establishments which must gradually poison its very fountain; if, in a word, the Union be essential to the happiness of the people of America, is it not preposterous, to urge as an objection to a government, without which the objects of the Union cannot be attained, that such a government may derogate from the importance of the governments of the individual States? Was, then, the American Revolution effected, was the American Confederacy formed, was the precious blood of thousands spilt, and the hard-earned substance of millions lavished, not that the people of America should enjoy peace, liberty, and safety, but that the government of the individual States, that particular municipal establishments, might enjoy a certain extent of power, and be arrayed with certain dignities and attributes of sovereignty? We have heard of the impious doctrine in the Old World, that the people were made for kings, not kings for the people. Is the same doctrine to be revived in the New, in another shape that the solid happiness of the people is to be sacrificed to the views of political institutions of a different form?

It is too early for politicians to presume on our forgetting that the public good, the real welfare of the great body of the people, is the supreme object to be pursued; and that no form of government whatever has any other value than as it may be fitted for the attainment of this object. Were the plan of the convention adverse to the public happiness, my voice would be, Reject the plan. Were the Union itself inconsistent with the public happiness, it would be, Abolish the Union. In like manner, as far as the sovereignty of the States cannot be reconciled to the happiness of the people, the voice of every good citizen must be, Let the former be sacrificed to the latter. How far the sacrifice is necessary, has been shown. How far the unsacrificed residue will be endangered, is the question before us. Several important considerations have been touched in the course of these papers, which discountenance the supposition that the operation of the federal government will by degrees prove fatal to the State governments. The more I revolve the subject, the more fully I am persuaded that the balance is much more likely to be disturbed by the preponderancy of the last than of the first scale.

We have seen, in all the examples of ancient and modern confederacies, the strongest tendency continually betraying itself in the members, to despoil the general government of its authorities, with a very ineffectual capacity in the latter to defend itself against the encroachments. Although, in most of these examples, the system has been so dissimilar from that under consideration as greatly to weaken any inference concerning the latter from the fate of the former, yet, as the States will retain, under the proposed Constitution, a very extensive portion of active sovereignty, the inference ought not to be wholly disregarded. In the Achaean league it is probable that the federal head had a degree and species of power, which gave it a considerable likeness to the government framed by the convention. The Lycian Confederacy, as far as its principles and form are transmitted, must have borne a still greater analogy to it. Yet history does not inform us that either of them ever degenerated, or tended to degenerate, into one consolidated government. On the contrary, we know that the ruin of one of them proceeded from the incapacity of the federal authority to prevent the dissensions, and finally the disunion, of the subordinate authorities. These cases are the more worthy of our attention, as the external causes by which the component parts were pressed together were much more numerous and powerful than in our case; and consequently less powerful ligaments within would be sufficient to bind the members to the head, and to each other.

In the feudal system, we have seen a similar propensity exemplified. Notwithstanding the want of proper sympathy in every instance between the local sovereigns and the people, and the sympathy in some instances between the general sovereign and the latter, it usually happened that the local sovereigns prevailed in the rivalship for encroachments. Had no external dangers enforced internal harmony and subordination, and particularly, had the local sovereigns possessed the affections of the people, the great kingdoms in Europe would at this time consist of as many independent princes as there were formerly feudatory barons. The State government will have the advantage of the Federal government, whether we compare them in respect to the immediate dependence of the one on the other; to the weight of personal influence which each side will possess; to the powers respectively vested in them; to the predilection and probable support of the people; to the disposition and faculty of resisting and frustrating the measures of each other. The State governments may be regarded as constituent and essential parts of the federal government; whilst the latter is nowise essential to the operation or organization of the former. Without the intervention of the State legislatures, the President of the United States cannot be elected at all. They must in all cases have a great share in his appointment, and will, perhaps, in most cases, of themselves determine it. The Senate will be elected absolutely and exclusively by the State legislatures. Even the House of Representatives, though drawn immediately from the people, will be chosen very much under the influence of that class of men, whose influence over the people obtains for themselves an election into the State legislatures. Thus, each of the principal branches of the federal government will owe its existence more or less to the favor of the State governments, and must consequently feel a dependence, which is much more likely to beget a disposition too obsequious than too overbearing towards them.

On the other side, the component parts of the State governments will in no instance be indebted for their appointment to the direct agency of the federal government, and very little, if at all, to the local influence of its members. The number of individuals employed under the Constitution of the United States will be much smaller than the number employed under the particular States. There will consequently be less of personal influence on the side of the former than of the latter. The members of the legislative, executive, and judiciary departments of thirteen and more States, the justices of peace, officers of militia, ministerial officers of justice, with all the county, corporation, and town officers, for three millions and more of people, intermixed, and having particular acquaintance with every class and circle of people, must exceed, beyond all proportion, both in number and influence, those of every description who will be employed in the administration of the federal system. Compare the members of the three great departments of the thirteen States, excluding from the judiciary department the justices of peace, with the members of the corresponding departments of the single government of the Union; compare the militia officers of three millions of people with the military and marine officers of any establishment which is within the compass of probability, or, I may add, of possibility, and in this view alone, we may pronounce the advantage of the States to be decisive. If the federal government is to have collectors of revenue, the State governments will have theirs also. And as those of the former will be principally on the seacoast, and not very numerous, whilst those of the latter will be spread over the face of the country, and will be very numerous, the advantage in this view also lies on the same side.

It is true, that the Confederacy is to possess, and may exercise, the power of collecting internal as well as external taxes throughout the States; but it is probable that this power will not be resorted to, except for supplemental purposes of revenue; that an option will then be given to the States to supply their quotas by previous collections of their own; and that the eventual collection, under the immediate authority of the Union, will generally be made by the officers, and according to the rules, appointed by the several States. Indeed it is extremely probable, that in other instances, particularly in the organization of the judicial power, the officers of the States will be clothed with the correspondent authority of the Union. Should it happen, however, that separate collectors of internal revenue should be appointed under the federal government, the influence of the whole number would not bear a comparison with that of the multitude of State officers in the opposite scale. Within every district to which a federal collector would be allotted, there would not be less than thirty or forty, or even more, officers of different descriptions, and many of them persons of character and weight, whose influence would lie on the side of the State. The powers delegated by the proposed Constitution to the federal government are few and defined. Those which are to remain in the State governments are numerous and indefinite. The former will be exercised principally on external objects, as war, peace, negotiation, and foreign commerce; with which last the power of taxation will, for the most part, be connected.

The powers reserved to the several States will extend to all the objects which, in the ordinary course of affairs, concern the lives, liberties, and properties of the people, and the internal order, improvement, and prosperity of the State. The operations of the federal government will be most extensive and important in times of war and danger; those of the State governments, in times of peace and security. As the former periods will probably bear a small proportion to the latter, the State governments will here enjoy another advantage over the federal government. The more adequate, indeed, the federal powers may be rendered to the national defense, the less frequent will be those scenes of danger which might favor their ascendancy over the governments of the particular States. If the new Constitution be examined with accuracy and candor, it will be found that the change which it proposes consists much less in the addition of NEW POWERS to the Union, than in the invigoration of its ORIGINAL POWERS. The regulation of commerce, it is true, is a new power; but that seems to be an addition which few oppose, and from which no apprehensions are entertained. The powers relating to war and peace, armies and fleets, treaties and finance, with the other more considerable powers, are all vested in the existing Congress by the articles of Confederation. The proposed change does not enlarge these powers; it only substitutes a more effectual mode of administering them.

The change relating to taxation may be regarded as the most important; and yet the present Congress have as complete authority to REQUIRE of the States indefinite supplies of money for the common defense and general welfare, as the future Congress will have to require them of individual citizens; and the latter will be no more bound than the States themselves have been, to pay the quotas respectively taxed on them. Had the States complied punctually with the articles of Confederation, or could their compliance have been enforced by as peaceable means as may be used with success towards single persons, our past experience is very far from countenancing an opinion, that the State governments would have lost their constitutional powers, and have gradually undergone an entire consolidation. To maintain that such an event would have ensued, would be to say at once, that the existence of the State governments is incompatible with any system whatever that accomplishes the essental purposes of the Union.

PUBLIUS.

The Federalist Papers : No. 47

The Particular Structure of the New Government and the Distribution of Power Among Its Different Parts

From the New York Packet. Friday, February 1, 1788.

JAMES MADISON

To the People of the State of New York:

HAVING reviewed the general form of the proposed government and the general mass of power allotted to it, I proceed to examine the particular structure of this government, and the distribution of this mass of power among its constituent parts. One of the principal objections inculcated by the more respectable adversaries to the Constitution, is its supposed violation of the political maxim, that the legislative, executive, and judiciary departments ought to be separate and distinct. In the structure of the federal government, no regard, it is said, seems to have been paid to this essential precaution in favor of liberty. The several departments of power are distributed and blended in such a manner as at once to destroy all symmetry and beauty of form, and to expose some of the essential parts of the edifice to the danger of being crushed by the disproportionate weight of other parts. No political truth is certainly of greater intrinsic value, or is stamped with the authority of more enlightened patrons of liberty, than that on which the objection is founded.

The accumulation of all powers, legislative, executive, and judiciary, in the same hands, whether of one, a few, or many, and whether hereditary, selfappointed, or elective, may justly be pronounced the very definition of tyranny. Were the federal Constitution, therefore, really chargeable with the accumulation of power, or with a mixture of powers, having a dangerous tendency to such an accumulation, no further arguments would be necessary to inspire a universal reprobation of the system. I persuade myself, however, that it will be made apparent to every one, that the charge cannot be supported, and that the maxim on which it relies has been totally misconceived and misapplied. In order to form correct ideas on this important subject, it will be proper to investigate the sense in which the preservation of liberty requires that the three great departments of power should be separate and distinct. The oracle who is always consulted and cited on this subject is the celebrated Montesquieu. If he be not the author of this invaluable precept in the science of politics, he has the merit at least of displaying and recommending it most effectually to the attention of mankind. Let us endeavor, in the first place, to ascertain his meaning on this point. The British Constitution was to Montesquieu what Homer has been to the didactic writers on epic poetry. As the latter have considered the work of the immortal bard as the perfect model from which the principles and rules of the epic art were to be drawn, and by which all similar works were to be judged, so this great political critic appears to have viewed the Constitution of England as the standard, or to use his own expression, as the mirror of political liberty; and to have delivered, in the form of elementary truths, the several characteristic principles of that particular system. That we may be sure, then, not to mistake his meaning in this case, let us recur to the source from which the maxim was drawn.

On the slightest view of the British Constitution, we must perceive that the legislative, executive, and judiciary departments are by no means totally separate and distinct from each other. The executive magistrate forms an integral part of the legislative authority. He alone has the prerogative of making treaties with foreign sovereigns, which, when made, have, under certain limitations, the force of legislative acts. All the members of the judiciary department are appointed by him, can be removed by him on the address of the two Houses of Parliament, and form, when he pleases to consult them, one of his constitutional councils. One branch of the legislative department forms also a great constitutional council to the executive chief, as, on another hand, it is the sole depositary of judicial power in cases of impeachment, and is invested with the supreme appellate jurisdiction in all other cases. The judges, again, are so far connected with the legislative department as often to attend and participate in its deliberations, though not admitted to a legislative vote. From these facts, by which Montesquieu was guided, it may clearly be inferred that, in saying "There can be no liberty where the legislative and executive powers are united in the same person, or body of magistrates," or, "if the power of judging be not separated from the legislative and executive powers," he did not mean that these departments ought to have no PARTIAL AGENCY in, or no CONTROL over, the acts of each other. His meaning, as his own words import, and still more conclusively as illustrated by the example in his eye, can amount to no more than this, that where the WHOLE power of one department is exercised by the same hands which possess the WHOLE power of another department, the fundamental principles of a free constitution are subverted. This would have been the case in the constitution examined by him, if the king, who is the sole executive magistrate, had possessed also the complete legislative power, or the supreme administration of justice; or if the entire legislative body had possessed the supreme judiciary, or the supreme executive authority.

This, however, is not among the vices of that constitution. The magistrate in whom the whole executive power resides cannot of himself make a law, though he can put a negative on every law; nor administer justice in person, though he has the appointment of those who do administer it. The judges can exercise no executive prerogative, though they are shoots from the executive stock; nor any legislative function, though they may be advised with by the legislative councils. The entire legislature can perform no judiciary act, though by the joint act of two of its branches the judges may be removed from their offices, and though one of its branches is possessed of the judicial power in the last resort. The entire legislature, again, can exercise no executive prerogative, though one of its branches constitutes the supreme executive magistracy, and another, on the impeachment of a third, can try and condemn all the subordinate officers in the executive department. The reasons on which Montesquieu grounds his maxim are a further demonstration of his meaning. "When the legislative and executive powers are united in the same person or body," says he, "there can be no liberty, because apprehensions may arise lest THE SAME monarch or senate should

ENACT tyrannical laws to EXECUTE them in a tyrannical manner." Again: "Were the power of judging joined with the legislative, the life and liberty of the subject would be exposed to arbitrary control, for THE JUDGE would then be THE LEGISLATOR. Were it joined to the executive power, THE JUDGE might behave with all the violence of AN OPPRESSOR." Some of these reasons are more fully explained in other passages; but briefly stated as they are here, they sufficiently establish the meaning which we have put on this celebrated maxim of this celebrated author.

If we look into the constitutions of the several States, we find that, notwithstanding the emphatical and, in some instances, the unqualified terms in which this axiom has been laid down, there is not a single instance in which the several departments of power have been kept absolutely separate and distinct. New Hampshire, whose constitution was the last formed, seems to have been fully aware of the impossibility and inexpediency of avoiding any mixture whatever of these departments, and has qualified the doctrine by declaring "that the legislative, executive, and judiciary powers ought to be kept as separate from, and independent of, each other AS THE NATURE OF A FREE GOVERNMENT WILL ADMIT; OR AS IS CONSISTENT WITH THAT CHAIN OF CONNECTION THAT BINDS THE WHOLE FABRIC OF THE CONSTITUTION IN ONE INDISSOLUBLE BOND OF UNITY AND AMITY." Her constitution accordingly mixes these departments in several respects. The Senate, which is a branch of the legislative department, is also a judicial tribunal for the trial of impeachments. The President, who is the head of the executive department, is the presiding member also of the Senate; and, besides an equal vote in all cases, has a casting vote in case of a tie. The executive head is himself eventually elective every year by the legislative department, and his council is every year chosen by and from the members of the same department. Several of the officers of state are also appointed by the legislature. And the members of the judiciary department are appointed by the executive department. The constitution of Massachusetts has observed a sufficient though less pointed caution, in expressing this fundamental article of liberty. It declares "that the legislative department shall never exercise the executive and judicial powers, or either of them; the executive shall never exercise the legislative and judicial powers, or either of them; the judicial shall never exercise the legislative and executive powers, or either of them." This declaration corresponds precisely with the doctrine of Montesquieu, as it has been explained, and is not in a single point violated by the plan of the convention. It goes no farther than to prohibit any one of the entire departments from exercising the powers of another department. In the very Constitution to which it is prefixed, a partial mixture of powers has been admitted. The executive magistrate has a qualified negative on the legislative body, and the Senate, which is a part of the legislature, is a court of impeachment for members both of the executive and judiciary departments. The members of the judiciary department, again, are appointable by the executive department, and removable by the same authority on the address of the two legislative branches. Lastly, a number of the officers of government are annually appointed by the legislative department.

As the appointment to offices, particularly executive offices, is in its nature an executive function, the compilers of the Constitution have, in this last point at least, violated the rule established by themselves. I pass over the constitutions of Rhode Island and Connecticut, because they were formed prior to the Revolution, and even before the principle under examination had become an object of political attention. The constitution of New York contains no declaration on this subject; but appears very clearly to have been framed with an eye to the danger of improperly blending the different departments. It gives, nevertheless, to the executive magistrate, a partial control over the legislative department; and, what is more, gives a like control to the judiciary department; and even blends the executive and judiciary departments in the exercise of this control. In its council of appointment members of the legislative are associated with the executive authority, in the appointment of officers, both executive and judiciary. And its court for the trial of impeachments and correction of errors is to consist of one branch of the legislature and the principal members of the judiciary department.

The constitution of New Jersey has blended the different powers of government more than any of the preceding. The governor, who is the executive magistrate, is appointed by the legislature; is chancellor and ordinary, or surrogate of the State; is a member of the Supreme Court of Appeals, and president, with a casting vote, of one of the legislative branches. The same legislative branch acts again as executive council of the governor, and with him constitutes the Court of Appeals. The members of the judiciary department are appointed by the legislative department and removable by one branch of it, on the impeachment of the other. According to the constitution of Pennsylvania, the president, who is the head of the executive department, is annually elected by a vote in which the legislative department predominates. In conjunction with an executive council, he appoints the members of the judiciary department, and forms a court of impeachment for trial of all officers, judiciary as well as executive. The judges of the Supreme Court and justices of the peace seem also to be removable by the legislature; and the executive power of pardoning in certain cases, to be referred to the same department. The members of the executive counoil are made EX-OFFICIO justices of peace throughout the State. In Delaware, the chief executive magistrate is annually elected by the legislative department. The speakers of the two legislative branches are vice-presidents in the executive department. The executive chief, with six others, appointed, three by each of the legislative branches constitutes the Supreme Court of Appeals; he is joined with the legislative department in the appointment of the other judges. Throughout the States, it appears that the members of the legislature may at the same time be justices of the peace; in this State, the members of one branch of it are EX-OFFICIO justices of the peace; as are also the members of the executive council. The principal officers of the executive department are appointed by the legislative; and one branch of the latter forms a court of impeachments. All officers may be removed on address of the legislature.

Maryland has adopted the maxim in the most unqualified terms; declaring that the legislative, executive, and judicial powers of government ought to be forever separate and distinct from each other. Her constitution, notwithstanding, makes the executive magistrate appointable by the legislative department; and the members of the judiciary by the executive department. The language of Virginia is still more pointed on this subject. Her constitution declares, "that the legislative, executive, and judiciary departments shall be separate and distinct; so that neither exercise the powers properly belonging to the other; nor shall any person exercise the powers of more than one of them at the same time, except that the justices of county courts shall be eligible to either House of Assembly." Yet we find not only this express exception, with respect to the members of the irferior courts, but that the chief magistrate, with his executive council, are appointable by the legislature; that two members of the latter are triennially displaced at the pleasure of the legislature; and that all the principal offices, both executive and judiciary, are filled by the same department. The executive prerogative of pardon, also, is in one case vested in the legislative department.

The constitution of North Carolina, which declares "that the legislative, executive, and supreme judicial powers of government ought to be forever separate and distinct from each other," refers, at the same time, to the legislative department, the appointment not only of the executive chief, but all the principal officers within both that and the judiciary department. In South Carolina, the constitution makes the executive magistracy eligible by the legislative department. It gives to the latter, also, the appointment of the members of the judiciary department, including even justices of the peace and sheriffs; and the appointment of officers in the executive department, down to captains in the army and navy of the State. In the constitution of Georgia, where it is declared "that the legislative, executive, and judiciary departments shall be separate and distinct, so that neither exercise the powers properly belonging to the other," we find that the executive department is to be filled by appointments of the legislature; and the executive prerogative of pardon to be finally exercised by the same authority. Even justices of the peace are to be appointed by the legislature. In citing these cases, in which the legislative, executive, and judiciary departments have not been kept totally separate and distinct, I wish not to be regarded as an advocate for the particular organizations of the several State governments. I am fully aware that among the many excellent principles which they exemplify, they carry strong marks of the haste, and still stronger of the inexperience, under which they were framed. It is but too obvious that in some instances the fundamental principle under consideration has been violated by too great a mixture, and even an actual consolidation, of the different powers; and that in no instance has a competent provision been made for maintaining in practice the separation delineated on paper. What I have wished to evince is, that the charge brought against the proposed Constitution, of violating the sacred maxim of free government, is warranted neither by the real meaning annexed to that maxim by its author, nor by the sense in which it has hitherto been understood in America. This interesting subject will be resumed in the ensuing paper.

PUBLIUS.

The Federalist Papers : No. 51

The Structure of the Government Must Furnish the Proper Checks and Balances Between the Different Departments

From the New York Packet. Friday, February 8, 1788.
ALEXANDER HAMILTON or JAMES MADISON

To the People of the State of New York:

TO WHAT expedient, then, shall we finally resort, for maintaining in practice the necessary partition of power among the several departments, as laid down in the Constitution? The only answer that can be given is, that as all these exterior provisions are found to be inadequate, the defect must be supplied, by so contriving the interior structure of the government as that its several constituent parts may, by their mutual relations, be the means of keeping each other in their proper places. Without presuming to undertake a full development of this important idea, I will hazard a few general observations, which may perhaps place it in a clearer light, and enable us to form a more correct judgment of the principles and structure of the government planned by the convention.

In order to lay a due foundation for that separate and distinct exercise of the different powers of government, which to a certain extent is admitted on all hands to be essential to the preservation of liberty, it is evident that each department should have a will of its own; and consequently should be so constituted that the members of each should have as little agency as possible in the appointment of the members of the others. Were this principle rigorously adhered to, it would require that all the appointments for the supreme executive, legislative, and judiciary magistracies should be drawn from the same fountain of authority, the people, through channels having no communication whatever with one another. Perhaps such a plan of constructing the several departments would be less difficult in practice than it may in contemplation appear. Some difficulties, however, and some additional expense would attend the execution of it. Some deviations, therefore, from the principle must be admitted. In the constitution of the judiciary department in particular, it might be inexpedient to insist rigorously on the principle: first, because peculiar qualifications being essential in the members, the primary consideration ought to be to select that mode of choice which best secures these qualifications; secondly, because the permanent tenure by which the appointments are held in that department, must soon destroy all sense of dependence on the authority conferring them.

It is equally evident, that the members of each department should be as little dependent as possible on those of the others, for the emoluments annexed to their offices. Were the executive magistrate, or the judges, not independent of the legislature in this particular, their independence in every other would be merely nominal. But the great security against a gradual concentration of the several powers in the same department, consists in giving to those who administer each department the necessary constitutional means and personal motives to resist encroachments of the others. The provision for defense must in this, as in all other cases, be made commensurate to the danger of attack. Ambition must be made to counteract ambition. The interest of the man must be connected with the constitutional rights of the place. It may be a reflection on human nature, that such devices should be necessary to control the abuses of government. But what is government itself, but the greatest of all reflections on human nature? If men were angels, no government would be necessary. If angels were to govern men, neither external nor internal controls on government would be necessary. In framing a government which is to be administered by men over men, the great difficulty lies in this: you must first enable the government to control the governed; and in the next place oblige it to control itself.

A dependence on the people is, no doubt, the primary control on the government; but experience has taught mankind the necessity of auxiliary precautions. This policy of supplying, by opposite and rival interests, the defect of better motives, might be traced through the whole system of human affairs, private as well as public. We see it particularly displayed in all the subordinate distributions of power, where the constant aim is to divide and arrange the several offices in such a manner as that each may be a check on the other that the private interest of every individual may be a sentinel over the public rights. These inventions of prudence cannot be less requisite in the distribution of the supreme powers of the State. But it is not possible to give to each department an equal power of self-defense. In republican government, the legislative authority necessarily predominates. The remedy for this inconveniency is to divide the legislature into different branches; and to render them, by different modes of election and different principles of action, as little connected with each other as the nature of their common functions and their common dependence on the society will admit. It may even be necessary to guard against dangerous encroachments by still further precautions. As the weight of the legislative authority requires that it should be thus divided, the weakness of the executive may require, on the other hand, that it should be fortified.

An absolute negative on the legislature appears, at first view, to be the natural defense with which the executive magistrate should be armed. But perhaps it would be neither altogether safe nor alone sufficient. On ordinary occasions it might not be exerted with the requisite firmness, and on extraordinary occasions it might be perfidiously abused. May not this defect of an absolute negative be supplied by some qualified connection between this weaker department and the weaker branch of the stronger department, by which the latter may be led to support the constitutional rights of the former, without being too much detached from the rights of its own department? If the principles on which these observations are founded be just, as I persuade myself they are, and they be applied as a criterion to the several State constitutions, and to the federal Constitution it will be found that if the latter does not perfectly correspond with them, the former are infinitely less able to bear such a test.

There are, moreover, two considerations particularly applicable to the federal system of America, which place that system in a very interesting point of view. First. In a single republic, all the power surrendered by the people is submitted to the administration of a single government; and the usurpations are guarded against by a division of the government into distinct and separate departments. In the compound republic of America, the power surrendered by the people is first divided between two distinct governments, and then the portion allotted to each subdivided among distinct and separate departments. Hence a double security arises to the rights of the people. The different governments will control each other, at the same time that each will be controlled by itself. Second. It is of great importance in a republic not only to guard the society against the oppression of its rulers, but to guard one part of the society against the injustice of the other part. Different interests necessarily exist in different classes of citizens. If a majority be united by a common interest, the rights of the minority will be insecure.

There are but two methods of providing against this evil: the one by creating a will in the community independent of the majority that is, of the society itself; the other, by comprehending in the society so many separate descriptions of citizens as will render an unjust combination of a majority of the whole very improbable, if not impracticable. The first method prevails in all governments possessing an hereditary or self-appointed authority. This, at best, is but a precarious security; because a power independent of the society may as well espouse the unjust views of the major, as the rightful interests of the minor party, and may possibly be turned against both parties. The second method will be exemplified in the federal republic of the United States. Whilst all authority in it will be derived from and dependent on the society, the society itself will be broken into so many parts, interests, and classes of citizens, that the rights of individuals, or of the minority, will be in little danger from interested combinations of the majority.

In a free government the security for civil rights must be the same as that for religious rights. It consists in the one case in the multiplicity of interests, and in the other in the multiplicity of sects. The degree of security in both cases will depend on the number of interests and sects; and this may be presumed to depend on the extent of country and number of people comprehended under the same government. This view of the subject must particularly recommend a proper federal system to all the sincere and considerate friends of republican government, since it shows that in exact proportion as the territory of the Union may be formed into more circumscribed Confederacies, or States oppressive combinations of a majority will be facilitated: the best security, under the republican forms, for the rights of every class of citizens, will be diminished: and consequently the stability and independence of some member of the government, the only other security, must be proportionately increased. Justice is the end of government. It is the end of civil society. It ever has been and ever will be pursued until it be obtained, or until liberty be lost in the pursuit. In a society under the forms of which the stronger faction can readily unite and oppress the weaker, anarchy may as truly be said to reign as in a state of nature, where the weaker individual is not secured against the violence of the stronger; and as, in the latter state, even the stronger individuals are prompted, by the uncertainty of their condition, to submit to a government which may protect the weak as well as themselves; so, in the former state, will the more powerful factions or parties be gradnally induced, by a like motive, to wish for a government which will protect all parties, the weaker as well as the more powerful.

It can be little doubted that if the State of Rhode Island was separated from the Confederacy and left to itself, the insecurity of rights under the popular form of government within such narrow limits would be displayed by such reiterated oppressions of factious majorities that some power altogether independent of the people would soon be called for by the voice of the very factions whose misrule had proved the necessity of it. In the extended republic of the United States, and among the great variety of interests, parties, and sects which it embraces, a coalition of a majority of the whole society could seldom take place on any other principles than those of justice and the general good; whilst there being thus less danger to a minor from the will of a major party, there must be less pretext, also, to provide for the security of the former, by introducing into the government a will not dependent on the latter, or, in other words, a will independent of the society itself. It is no less certain than it is important, notwithstanding the contrary opinions which have been entertained, that the larger the society, provided it lie within a practical sphere, the more duly capable it will be of self-government. And happily for the REPUBLICAN CAUSE, the practicable sphere may be carried to a very great extent, by a judicious modification and mixture of the FEDERAL PRINCIPLE.

PUBLIUS.

The Federalist Papers : No. 54

The Apportionment of Members Among the States

From the New York Packet. Tuesday, February 12, 1788.
ALEXANDER HAMILTON or JAMES MADISON

To the People of the State of New York:

THE next view which I shall take of the House of Representatives relates to the appointment of its members to the several States which is to be determined by the same rule with that of direct taxes.

It is not contended that the number of people in each State ought not to be the standard for regulating the proportion of those who are to represent the people of each State. The establishment of the same rule for the appointment of taxes, will probably be as little contested; though the rule itself in this case, is by no means founded on the same principle. In the former case, the rule is understood to refer to the personal rights of the people, with which it has a natural and universal connection. In the latter, it has reference to the proportion of wealth, of which it is in no case a precise measure, and in ordinary cases a very unfit one. But notwithstanding the imperfection of the rule as applied to the relative wealth and contributions of the States, it is evidently the least objectionable among the practicable rules, and had too recently obtained the general sanction of America, not to have found a ready preference with the convention.

All this is admitted, it will perhaps be said; but does it follow, from an admission of numbers for the measure of representation, or of slaves combined with free citizens as a ratio of taxation, that slaves ought to be included in the numerical rule of representation? Slaves are considered as property, not as persons. They ought therefore to be comprehended in estimates of taxation which are founded on property, and to be excluded from representation which is regulated by a census of persons. This is the objection, as I understand it, stated in its full force. I shall be equally candid in stating the reasoning which may be offered on the opposite side. "We subscribe to the doctrine," might one of our Southern brethren observe, "that representation relates more immediately to persons, and taxation more immediately to property, and we join in the application of this distinction to the case of our slaves. But we must deny the fact, that slaves are considered merely as property, and in no respect whatever as persons. The true state of the case is, that they partake of both these qualities: being considered by our laws, in some respects, as persons, and in other respects as property.

In being compelled to labor, not for himself, but for a master; in being vendible by one master to another master; and in being subject at all times to be restrained in his liberty and chastised in his body, by the capricious will of another, the slave may appear to be degraded from the human rank, and classed with those irrational animals which fall under the legal denomination of property. In being protected, on the other hand, in his life and in his limbs, against the violence of all others, even the master of his labor and his liberty; and in being punishable himself for all violence committed against others, the slave is no less evidently regarded by the law as a member of the society, not as a part of the irrational creation; as a moral person, not as a mere article of property.

The federal Constitution, therefore, decides with great propriety on the case of our slaves, when it views them in the mixed character of persons and of property. This is in fact their true character. It is the character bestowed on them by the laws under which they live; and it will not be denied, that these are the proper criterion; because it is only under the pretext that the laws have transformed the negroes into subjects of property, that a place is disputed them in the computation of numbers; and it is admitted, that if the laws were to restore the rights which have been taken away, the negroes could no longer be refused an equal share of representation with the other inhabitants. "This question may be placed in another light. It is agreed on all sides, that numbers are the best scale of wealth and taxation, as they are the only proper scale of representation. Would the convention have been impartial or consistent, if they had rejected the slaves from the list of inhabitants, when the shares of representation were to be calculated, and inserted them on the lists when the tariff of contributions was to be adjusted? Could it be reasonably expected, that the Southern States would concur in a system, which considered their slaves in some degree as men, when burdens were to be imposed, but refused to consider them in the same light, when advantages were to be conferred? Might not some surprise also be expressed, that those who reproach the Southern States with the barbarous policy of considering as property a part of their human brethren, should themselves contend, that the government to which all the States are to be parties, ought to consider this unfortunate race more completely in the unnatural light of property, than the very laws of which they complain? "It may be replied, perhaps, that slaves are not included in the estimate of representatives in any of the States possessing them. They neither vote themselves nor increase the votes of their masters. Upon what principle, then, ought they to be taken into the federal estimate of representation?

In rejecting them altogether, the Constitution would, in this respect, have followed the very laws which have been appealed to as the proper guide. "This objection is repelled by a single observation. It is a fundamental principle of the proposed Constitution, that as the aggregate number of representatives allotted to the several States is to be determined by a federal rule, founded on the aggregate number of inhabitants, so the right of choosing this allotted number in each State is to be exercised by such part of the inhabitants as the State itself may designate. The qualifications on which the right of suffrage depend are not, perhaps, the same in any two States. In some of the States the difference is very material.

In every State, a certain proportion of inhabitants are deprived of this right by the constitution of the State, who will be included in the census by which the federal Constitution apportions the representatives. In this point of view the Southern States might retort the complaint, by insisting that the principle laid down by the convention required that no regard should be had to the policy of particular States towards their own inhabitants; and consequently, that the slaves, as inhabitants, should have been admitted into the census according to their full number, in like manner with other inhabitants, who, by the policy of other States, are not admitted to all the rights of citizens. A rigorous adherence, however, to this principle, is waived by those who would be gainers by it. All that they ask is that equal moderation be shown on the other side. Let the case of the slaves be considered, as it is in truth, a peculiar one. Let the compromising expedient of the Constitution be mutually adopted, which regards them as inhabitants, but as debased by servitude below the equal level of free inhabitants, which regards the SLAVE as divested of two fifths of the MAN. "After all, may not another ground be taken on which this article of the Constitution will admit of a still more ready defense? We have hitherto proceeded on the idea that representation related to persons only, and not at all to property. But is it a just idea? Government is instituted no less for protection of the property, than of the persons, of individuals. The one as well as the other, therefore, may be considered as represented by those who are charged with the government.

Upon this principle it is, that in several of the States, and particularly in the State of New York, one branch of the government is intended more especially to be the guardian of property, and is accordingly elected by that part of the society which is most interested in this object of government. In the federal Constitution, this policy does not prevail. The rights of property are committed into the same hands with the personal rights. Some attention ought, therefore, to be paid to property in the choice of those hands. "For another reason, the votes allowed in the federal legislature to the people of each State, ought to bear some proportion to the comparative wealth of the States. States have not, like individuals, an influence over each other, arising from superior advantages of fortune. If the law allows an opulent citizen but a single vote in the choice of his representative, the respect and consequence which he derives from his fortunate situation very frequently guide the votes of others to the objects of his choice; and through this imperceptible channel the rights of property are conveyed into the public representation. A State possesses no such influence over other States. It is not probable that the richest State in the Confederacy will ever influence the choice of a single representative in any other State. Nor will the representatives of the larger and richer States possess any other advantage in the federal legislature, over the representatives of other States, than what may result from their superior number alone. As far, therefore, as their superior wealth and weight may justly entitle them to any advantage, it ought to be secured to them by a superior share of representation.

The new Constitution is, in this respect, materially different from the existing Confederation, as well as from that of the United Netherlands, and other similar confederacies. In each of the latter, the efficacy of the federal resolutions depends on the subsequent and voluntary resolutions of the states composing the union. Hence the states, though possessing an equal vote in the public councils, have an unequal influence, corresponding with the unequal importance of these subsequent and voluntary resolutions. Under the proposed Constitution, the federal acts will take effect without the necessary intervention of the individual

States. They will depend merely on the majority of votes in the federal legislature, and consequently each vote, whether proceeding from a larger or smaller State, or a State more or less wealthy or powerful, will have an equal weight and efficacy: in the same manner as the votes individually given in a State legislature, by the representatives of unequal counties or other districts, have each a precise equality of value and effect; or if there be any difference in the case, it proceeds from the difference in the personal character of the individual representative, rather than from any regard to the extent of the district from which he comes. "Such is the reasoning which an advocate for the Southern interests might employ on this subject; and although it may appear to be a little strained in some points, yet, on the whole, I must confess that it fully reconciles me to the scale of representation which the convention have established. In one respect, the establishment of a common measure for representation and taxation will have a very salutary effect. As the accuracy of the census to be obtained by the Congress will necessarily depend, in a considerable degree on the disposition, if not on the co-operation, of the States, it is of great importance that the States should feel as little bias as possible, to swell or to reduce the amount of their numbers. Were their share of representation alone to be governed by this rule, they would have an interest in exaggerating their inhabitants. Were the rule to decide their share of taxation alone, a contrary temptation would prevail. By extending the rule to both objects, the States will have opposite interests, which will control and balance each other, and produce the requisite impartiality.

PUBLIUS.

The Federalist Papers : No. 78

The Judiciary Department
From McLEAN'S Edition, New York.
ALEXANDER HAMILTON

To the People of the State of New York:

WE PROCEED now to an examination of the judiciary department of the proposed government.

In unfolding the defects of the existing Confederation, the utility and necessity of a federal judicature have been clearly pointed out. It is the less necessary to recapitulate the considerations there urged, as the propriety of the institution in the abstract is not disputed; the only questions which have been raised being relative to the manner of constituting it, and to its extent. To these points, therefore, our observations shall be confined.

The manner of constituting it seems to embrace these several objects: 1st. The mode of appointing the judges. 2d. The tenure by which they are to hold their places. 3d. The partition of the judiciary authority between different courts, and their relations to each other.

First. As to the mode of appointing the judges; this is the same with that of appointing the officers of the Union in general, and has been so fully discussed in the two last numbers, that nothing can be said here which would not be useless repetition.

Second. As to the tenure by which the judges are to hold their places; this chiefly concerns their duration in office; the provisions for their support; the precautions for their responsibility.

According to the plan of the convention, all judges who may be appointed by the United States are to hold their offices DURING GOOD BEHAVIOR; which is conformable to the most approved of the State constitutions and among the rest, to that of this State. Its propriety having been drawn into question by the adversaries of that plan, is no light symptom of the rage for objection, which disorders their imaginations and judgments. The standard of good behavior for the continuance in office of the judicial magistracy, is certainly one of the most valuable of the modern improvements in the practice of government. In a monarchy it is an excellent barrier to the despotism of the prince; in a republic it is a no less excellent barrier to the encroachments and oppressions of the representative body. And it is the best expedient which can be devised in any government, to secure a steady, upright, and impartial administration of the laws.

Whoever attentively considers the different departments of power must perceive, that, in a government in which they are separated from each other, the judiciary, from the nature of its functions, will always be the least dangerous to the political rights of the Constitution; because it will be least in a capacity to annoy or injure them. The Executive not only dispenses the honors, but holds the sword of the community. The legislature not only commands the purse, but prescribes the rules by which the duties and rights of every citizen are to be regulated. The judiciary, on the contrary, has no influence over either the sword or the purse; no direction either of the strength or of the wealth of the society; and can take no active resolution whatever. It may truly be said to have neither FORCE nor WILL, but merely judgment; and must ultimately depend upon the aid of the executive arm even for the efficacy of its judgments.

This simple view of the matter suggests several important consequences. It proves incontestably, that the judiciary is beyond comparison the weakest of the three departments of power*1*; that it can never attack with success either of the other two; and that all possible care is requisite to enable it to defend itself against their attacks. It equally proves, that though individual oppression may now and then proceed from the courts of justice, the general liberty of the people can never be endangered from that quarter; I mean so long as the judiciary remains truly distinct from both the legislature and the Executive. For I agree, that "there is no liberty, if the power of judging be not separated from the legislative and executive powers." *2* And it proves, in the last place, that as liberty can have nothing to fear from the judiciary alone, but would have every thing to fear from its union with either of the other departments; that as all the effects of such a union must ensue from a dependence of the former on the latter, notwithstanding a nominal and apparent separation; that as, from the natural feebleness of the judiciary, it is in continual jeopardy of being overpowered, awed, or influenced by its co-ordinate branches; and that as nothing can contribute so much to its firmness and independence as permanency in office, this quality may therefore be justly regarded as an indispensable ingredient in its constitution, and, in a great measure, as the citadel of the public justice and the public security.

The complete independence of the courts of justice is peculiarly essential in a limited Constitution. By a limited Constitution, I understand one which contains certain specified exceptions to the legislative authority; such, for instance, as that it shall pass no bills of attainder, no ex-post-facto laws, and the like. Limitations of this kind can be preserved in practice no other way than through the medium of courts of justice, whose duty it must be to declare all acts contrary to the manifest tenor of the Constitution void. Without this, all the reservations of particular rights or privileges would amount to nothing.

Some perplexity respecting the rights of the courts to pronounce legislative acts void, because contrary to the Constitution, has arisen from an imagination that the doctrine would imply a superiority of the judiciary to the legislative power. It is urged that the authority which can declare the acts of another void, must necessarily be superior to the one whose acts may be declared void. As this doctrine is of great importance in all the American constitutions, a brief discussion of the ground on which it rests cannot be unacceptable.

There is no position which depends on clearer principles, than that every act of a delegated authority, contrary to the tenor of the commission under which it is exercised, is void. No legislative act, therefore, contrary to the Constitution, can be valid. To deny this, would be to affirm, that the deputy is greater than his principal; that the servant is above his master; that the representatives of the people are superior to the people themselves; that men acting by virtue of powers, may do not only what their powers do not authorize, but what they forbid.

If it be said that the legislative body are themselves the constitutional judges of their own powers, and that the construction they put upon them is conclusive upon the other departments, it may be answered, that this cannot be the natural presumption, where it is not to be collected from any particular provisions in the Constitution. It is not otherwise to be supposed, that the Constitution could intend to enable the representatives of the people to substitute their WILL to that of their constituents. It is far more rational to suppose, that the courts were designed to be an intermediate body between the people and the legislature, in order, among other things, to keep the latter within the limits assigned to their authority. The interpretation of the laws is the proper and peculiar province of the courts. A constitution is, in fact, and must be regarded by the judges, as a fundamental law. It therefore belongs to them to ascertain its meaning, as well as the meaning of any particular act proceeding from the legislative body. If there should happen to be an irreconcilable variance between the two, that which has the superior obligation and validity ought, of course, to be preferred; or, in other words, the Constitution ought to be preferred to the statute, the intention of the people to the intention of their agents.

Nor does this conclusion by any means suppose a superiority of the judicial to the legislative power. It only supposes that the power of the people is superior to both; and that where the will of the legislature, declared in its statutes, stands in opposition to that of the people, declared in the Constitution, the judges ought to be governed by the latter rather than the former. They ought to regulate their decisions by the fundamental laws, rather than by those which are not fundamental.

This exercise of judicial discretion, in determining between two contradictory laws, is exemplified in a familiar instance. It not uncommonly happens, that there are two statutes existing at one time, clashing in whole or in part with each other, and neither of them containing any repealing clause or expression. In such a case, it is the province of the courts to liquidate and fix their meaning and operation. So far as they can, by any fair construction, be reconciled to each other, reason and law conspire to dictate that this should be done; where this is impracticable, it becomes a matter of necessity to give effect to one, in exclusion of the other. The rule which has obtained in the courts for determining their relative validity is, that the last in order of time shall be preferred to the first. But this is a mere rule of construction, not derived from any positive law, but from the nature and reason of the thing. It is a rule not enjoined upon the courts by legislative provision, but adopted by themselves, as consonant to truth and propriety, for the direction of their conduct as interpreters of the law. They thought it reasonable, that between the interfering acts of an EQUAL authority, that which was the last indication of its will should have the preference.

But in regard to the interfering acts of a superior and subordinate authority, of an original and derivative power, the nature and reason of the thing indicate the converse of that rule as proper to be followed. They teach us that the prior act of a superior ought to be preferred to the subsequent act of an inferior and subordinate authority; and that accordingly, whenever a particular statute contravenes the Constitution, it will be the duty of the judicial tribunals to adhere to the latter and disregard the former.

It can be of no weight to say that the courts, on the pretense of a repugnancy, may substitute their own pleasure to the constitutional intentions of the legislature. This might as well happen in the case of two contradictory statutes; or it might as well happen in every adjudication upon any single statute. The courts must declare the sense of the law; and if they should be disposed to exercise WILL instead of JUDGMENT, the consequence would equally be the substitution of their pleasure to that of the legislative body. The observation, if it prove any thing, would prove that there ought to be no judges distinct from that body.

If, then, the courts of justice are to be considered as the bulwarks of a limited Constitution against legislative encroachments, this consideration will afford a strong argument for the permanent tenure of judicial offices, since nothing will contribute so much as this to that independent spirit in the judges which must be essential to the faithful performance of so arduous a duty.

This independence of the judges is equally requisite to guard the Constitution and the rights of individuals from the effects of those ill humors, which the arts of designing men, or the influence of particular conjunctures, sometimes disseminate among the people themselves, and which, though they speedily give place to better information, and more deliberate reflection, have a tendency, in the meantime, to occasion dangerous innovations in the government, and serious oppressions of the minor party in the community. Though I trust the friends of the proposed Constitution will never concur with its enemies,*3* in questioning that fundamental principle of republican government, which admits the right of the people to alter or abolish the established Constitution, whenever they find it inconsistent with their happiness, yet it is not to be inferred from this principle, that the representatives of the people, whenever a momentary inclination happens to lay hold of a majority of their constituents, incompatible with the provisions in the existing Constitution, would, on that account, be justifiable in a violation of those provisions; or that the courts would be under a greater obligation to connive at infractions in this shape, than when they had proceeded wholly from the cabals of the representative body. Until the people have, by some solemn and authoritative act, annulled or changed the established form, it is binding upon themselves collectively, as well as individually; and no presumption, or even knowledge, of their sentiments, can warrant their representatives in a departure from it, prior to such an act. But it is easy to see, that it would require an uncommon portion of fortitude in the judges to do their duty as faithful guardians of the Constitution, where legislative invasions of it had been instigated by the major voice of the community.

But it is not with a view to infractions of the Constitution only, that the independence of the judges may be an essential safeguard against the effects of occasional ill humors in the society. These sometimes extend no farther than to the injury of the private rights of particular classes of citizens, by unjust and partial laws. Here also the firmness of the judicial magistracy is of vast importance in mitigating the severity and confining the operation of such laws. It not only serves to moderate the immediate mischiefs of those which may have been passed, but it operates as a check upon the legislative body in passing them; who, perceiving that obstacles to the success of iniquitous intention are to be expected from the scruples of the courts, are in a manner compelled, by the very motives of the injustice they meditate, to qualify their attempts. This is a circumstance calculated to have more influence upon the character of our governments, than but few may be aware of. The benefits of the integrity and moderation of the judiciary have already been felt in more States than one; and though they may have displeased those whose sinister expectations they may have disappointed, they must have commanded the esteem and applause of all the virtuous and disinterested. Considerate men, of every description, ought to prize whatever will tend to beget or fortify that temper in the courts: as no man can be sure that he may not be to-morrow the victim of a spirit of injustice, by which he may be a gainer to-day. And every man must now feel, that the inevitable tendency of such a spirit is to sap the foundations of public and private confidence, and to introduce in its stead universal distrust and distress.

That inflexible and uniform adherence to the rights of the Constitution, and of individuals, which we perceive to be indispensable in the courts of justice, can certainly not be expected from judges who hold their offices by a temporary commission. Periodical appointments, however regulated, or by whomsoever made, would, in some way or other, be fatal to their necessary independence. If the power of making them was committed either to the Executive or legislature, there would be danger of an improper complaisance to the branch which possessed it; if to both, there would be an unwillingness to hazard the displeasure of either; if to the people, or to persons chosen by them for the special purpose, there would be too great a disposition to consult popularity, to justify a reliance that nothing would be consulted but the Constitution and the laws.

There is yet a further and a weightier reason for the permanency of the judicial offices, which is deducible from the nature of the qualifications they require. It has been frequently remarked, with great propriety, that a voluminous code of laws is one of the inconveniences necessarily connected with the advantages of a free government. To avoid an arbitrary discretion in the courts, it is indispensable that they should be bound down by strict rules and precedents, which serve to define and point out their duty in every particular case that comes before them; and it will readily be conceived from the variety of controversies which grow out of the folly and wickedness of mankind, that the records of those precedents must unavoidably swell to a very considerable bulk, and must demand long and laborious study to acquire a competent knowledge of them. Hence it is, that there can be but few men in the society who will have sufficient skill in the laws to qualify them for the stations of judges. And making the proper deductions for the ordinary depravity of human nature, the number must be still smaller of those who unite the requisite integrity with the requisite knowledge. These considerations apprise us, that the government can have no great option between fit character; and that a temporary duration in office, which would naturally discourage such characters from quitting a lucrative line of practice to accept a seat on the bench, would have a tendency to throw the administration of justice into hands less able, and less well qualified, to conduct it with utility and dignity. In the present circumstances of this country, and in those in which it is likely to be for a long time to come, the disadvantages on this score would be greater than they may at first sight appear; but it must be confessed, that they are far inferior to those which present themselves under the other aspects of the subject.

Upon the whole, there can be no room to doubt that the convention acted wisely in copying from the models of those constitutions which have established GOOD BEHAVIOR as the tenure of their judicial offices, in point of duration; and that so far from being blamable on this account, their plan would have been inexcusably defective, if it had wanted this important feature of good government. The experience of Great Britain affords an illustrious comment on the excellence of the institution.

PUBLIUS.

1 The celebrated Montesquieu, speaking of them, says: "Of the three powers above mentioned, the judiciary is next to nothing." "Spirit of Laws." vol. i., page 186.

2 Idem, page 181.

3 Vide "Protest of the Minority of the Convention of Pennsylvania," Martin's Speech, etc.

APPENDIX C

DECLARATION OF INDEPENDENCE[86]

IN CONGRESS, 4 July 1776
The Unanimous Declaration of the thirteen united States of America

When, in the course of human events, it becomes necessary for one people to dissolve the political bonds which have connected them with another, and to assume among the powers of the earth, the separate and equal station to which the laws of nature and of nature's God entitle them, a decent respect to the opinions of mankind requires that they should declare the causes which impel them to the separation.

We hold these truths to be self-evident, that all men are created equal, that they are endowed by their Creator with certain unalienable rights, that among these are life, liberty and the pursuit of happiness. That to secure these rights, governments are instituted among men, deriving their just powers from the consent of the governed. That whenever any form of government becomes destructive to these ends, it is the right of the people to alter or to abolish it, and to institute new government, laying its foundation on such principles and organizing its powers in such form, as to them shall seem most likely to effect their safety and happiness. Prudence, indeed, will dictate that governments long established should not be changed for light and transient causes; and accordingly all experience hath shown that mankind are more disposed to suffer, while evils are sufferable, than to right themselves by abolishing the forms to which they are accustomed. But when a long train of abuses and usurpations, pursuing invariably the same object evinces a design to reduce them under absolute despotism, it is their right, it is their duty, to throw off such government, and to provide new guards for their future security.—Such has been the patient sufferance of these colonies; and such is now the necessity which constrains them to alter their former systems of government. The history of the present King of Great Britain is a history of repeated injuries and usurpations, all having in direct Declaration of Independence 2 object the establishment of an absolute tyranny over these states. To prove this, let facts be submitted to a candid world.

> He has refused his assent to laws, the most wholesome and necessary for the public good.
>
> He has forbidden his governors to pass laws of immediate and pressing importance, unless suspended in their operation till his assent should be obtained; and when so suspended, he has utterly neglected to attend to them.
>
> He has refused to pass other laws for the accommodation of large districts of people, unless those people would relinquish the right of representation in the legislature, a right inestimable to them and formidable to tyrants only.
>
> He has called together legislative bodies at places unusual, uncomfortable, and distant from the depository of their public records, for the sole purpose of fatiguing them into compliance with his measures.
>
> He has dissolved representative houses repeatedly, for opposing with manly firmness his invasions on the rights of the people.
>
> He has refused for a long time, after such dissolutions, to cause others to be elected; whereby the legislative powers, incapable of annihilation, have returned to the people at large for their exercise; the state remaining in the meantime exposed to all the dangers of invasion from without, and convulsions within.
>
> He has endeavored to prevent the population of these states; for that purpose obstructing the laws for naturalization of foreigners; refusing to pass others to encourage their migration hither, and raising the conditions of new appropriations of lands.
>
> He has obstructed the administration of justice, by refusing his assent to laws for establishing judiciary powers.
>
> He has made judges dependent on his will alone, for the tenure of their offices, and the amount and payment of their salaries.
>
> He has erected a multitude of new offices, and sent hither swarms of officers to harass our people, and eat out their substance.

He has kept among us, in times of peace, standing armies without the consent of our legislature.

He has affected to render the military independent of and superior to civil power.

He has combined with others to subject us to a jurisdiction foreign to our constitution, and unacknowledged by our laws; giving his assent to their acts of pretended legislation:

For quartering large bodies of armed troops among us:

For protecting them, by mock trial, from punishment for any murders which they should commit on the inhabitants of these states:

For cutting off our trade with all parts of the world:

For imposing taxes on us without our consent:

For depriving us in many cases, of the benefits of trial by jury:

For transporting us beyond seas to be tried for pretended offenses:

For abolishing the free system of English laws in a neighboring province, establishing therein an arbitrary government, and enlarging its boundaries so as to render it at once an example and fit instrument for introducing the same absolute rule in these colonies:

For taking away our charters, abolishing our most valuable laws, and altering fundamentally the forms of our governments:

For suspending our own legislatures, and declaring themselves invested with power to legislate for us in all cases whatsoever.

He has abdicated government here, by declaring us out of his protection and waging war against us.

He has plundered our seas, ravaged our coasts, burned our towns, and destroyed the lives of our people.

He is at this time transporting large armies of foreign mercenaries to complete the works of death, desolation and tyranny, already begun with circumstances of cruelty and

> perfidy scarcely paralleled in the most barbarous ages, and totally unworthy the head of a civilized nation.
>
> He has constrained our fellow citizens taken captive on the high seas to bear arms against their country, to become the executioners of their friends and brethren, or to fall themselves by their hands.
>
> He has excited domestic insurrections amongst us, and has endeavored to bring on the inhabitants of our frontiers, the merciless Indian savages, whose known rule of warfare, is undistinguished destruction of all ages, sexes and conditions.

In every stage of these oppressions we have petitioned for redress in the most humble terms: our repeated petitions have been answered only by repeated injury. A prince, whose character is thus marked by every act which may define a tyrant, is unfit to be the ruler of a free people.

Nor have we been wanting in attention to our British brethren. We have warned them from time to time of attempts by their legislature to extend an unwarrantable jurisdiction over us. We have reminded them of the circumstances of our emigration and settlement here. We have appealed to their native justice and magnanimity, and we have conjured them by the ties of our common kindred to disavow these usurpations, which, would inevitably interrupt our connections and correspondence. We must, therefore, acquiesce in the necessity, which denounces our separation, and hold them, as we hold the rest of mankind, enemies in war, in peace friends.

We, therefore, the representatives of the United States of America, in General Congress, assembled, appealing to the Supreme Judge of the world for the rectitude of our intentions, do, in the name, and by the authority of the good people of these colonies, solemnly publish and declare, that these united colonies are, and of right ought to be free and independent states; that they are absolved from all allegiance to the British Crown, and that all political connection between them and the state of Great Britain, is and ought to be totally dissolved; and that as free and independent states, they have full power to levy war, conclude peace, contract alliances, establish commerce, and to do all other acts and things which independent states may of right do. And for the support of this declaration, with a firm reliance on the protection of Divine Providence, we mutually pledge to each other our lives, our fortunes and our sacred honor.

Georgia:
- Button Gwinnett
- Lyman Hall
- George Walton

North Carolina:
- William Hooper
- Joseph Hewes
- John Penn

South Carolina:
- Edward Rutledge
- Thomas Heyward, Jr.
- Thomas Lynch, Jr.
- Arthur Middleton

Massachusetts:
- John Hancock
- Samuel Adams
- John Adams
- Robert Treat Paine
- Elbridge Gerry

Maryland:
- Samuel Chase
- William Paca
- Thomas Stone
- Charles Carroll of Carrollton

Virginia:
- George Wythe
- Richard Henry Lee
- Thomas Jefferson
- Benjamin Harrison
- Thomas Nelson, Jr.
- Francis Lightfoot Lee
- Carter Braxton

Pennsylvania:
- Robert Morris
- Benjamin Rush
- Benjamin Franklin
- John Morton
- George Clymer
- James Smith
- George Taylor
- James Wilson
- George Ross

Delaware:
- Caesar Rodney
- George Read
- Thomas McKean

New York:
- William Floyd
- Philip Livingston
- Francis Lewis
- Lewis Morris

New Jersey:
- Richard Stockton
- John Witherspoon
- Francis Hopkinson
- John Hart
- Abraham Clark

New Hampshire:
- Josiah Bartlett
- William Whipple
- Matthew Thornton

Rhode Island:
- Stephen Hopkins
- William Ellery

Connecticut:
- Roger Sherman
- Samuel Huntington
- William Williams
- Oliver Wolcott[b]

---

[b] The colonies and signatures for the Declaration of Independence are not listed in the same order as the original document. All are represented.

APPENDIX D

THE CONSTITUTION OF THE UNITED STATES[87]

Preamble

We the People of the United States, in Order to form a more perfect Union, establish Justice, insure domestic Tranquility, provide for the common defence, promote the general Welfare, and secure the Blessings of Liberty to ourselves and our Posterity, do ordain and establish this Constitution for the United States of America.

Article. I.—The Legislative Branch

Section 1—The Legislature
All legislative Powers herein granted shall be vested in a Congress of the United States, which shall consist of a Senate and House of Representatives.

Section 2—The House
The House of Representatives shall be composed of Members chosen every second Year by the People of the several States, and the Electors in each State shall have the Qualifications requisite for Electors of the most numerous Branch of the State Legislature.

No Person shall be a Representative who shall not have attained to the Age of twenty five Years, and been seven Years a Citizen of the United States, and who shall not, when elected, be an Inhabitant of that State in which he shall be chosen.

Representatives and direct Taxes shall be apportioned among the several States which may be included within this Union, according to their respective Numbers, which shall be determined by adding to the whole Number of free Persons, including those bound to Service for a Term of Years, and excluding Indians not taxed, three fifths of all other Persons [*Modified by Amendment XIV*]. The actual Enumeration shall be made within three Years after the first Meeting of the Congress of the United States, and within every subsequent Term of ten Years, in such Manner as they shall by Law direct. The Number of Representatives shall not exceed one for every thirty Thousand, but each State shall have at Least one Representative; and until such enumeration shall be made, the State of New Hampshire shall be entitled to chuse three, Massachusetts eight, Rhode-Island and Providence Plantations one, Connecticut five, New-York six, New Jersey four, Pennsylvania eight, Delaware one, Maryland six, Virginia ten, North Carolina five, South Carolina five, and Georgia three.

When vacancies happen in the Representation from any State, the Executive Authority thereof shall issue Writs of Election to fill such Vacancies.

The House of Representatives shall chuse their Speaker and other Officers; and shall have the sole Power of Impeachment.

Section. 3—The Senate

The Senate of the United States shall be composed of two Senators from each State, *chosen by the Legislature thereof* [*Modified by Amendment XVII*], for six Years; and each Senator shall have one Vote.

Immediately after they shall be assembled in Consequence of the first Election, they shall be divided as equally as may be into three Classes. The Seats of the Senators of the first Class shall be vacated at the Expiration of the second Year, of the second Class at the Expiration of the fourth Year, and of the third Class at the Expiration of the sixth Year, so that one third may be chosen every second Year; *and if Vacancies happen by Resignation, or otherwise, during the Recess of the Legislature of any State, the Executive thereof may make temporary Appointments until the next Meeting of the Legislature, which shall then fill such Vacancies* [*Modified by Amendment XVII*].

No Person shall be a Senator who shall not have attained to the Age of thirty Years, and been nine Years a Citizen of the United States, and who shall not, when elected, be an Inhabitant of that State for which he shall be chosen.

The Vice President of the United States shall be President of the Senate, but shall have no Vote, unless they be equally divided.

The Senate shall chuse their other Officers, and also a President pro tempore, in the Absence of the Vice President, or when he shall exercise the Office of President of the United States.

The Senate shall have the sole Power to try all Impeachments. When sitting for that Purpose, they shall be on Oath or Affirmation. When the President of the United States is tried, the Chief Justice shall preside: And no Person shall be convicted without the Concurrence of two thirds of the Members present.

Judgment in Cases of Impeachment shall not extend further than to removal from Office, and disqualification to hold and enjoy any Office of honor, Trust or Profit under the United States: but the Party convicted shall nevertheless be liable and subject to Indictment, Trial, Judgment and Punishment, according to Law.

Section. 4—Elections, Meetings
The Times, Places and Manner of holding Elections for Senators and Representatives, shall be prescribed in each State by the Legislature thereof; but the Congress may at any time by Law make or alter such Regulations, except as to the Places of chusing Senators.

The Congress shall assemble at least once in every Year, *and such Meeting shall be on the first Monday in December* [*Modified by Amendment XX*], unless they shall by Law appoint a different Day.

Section. 5—Membership, Rules, Journals, Adjournment
Each House shall be the Judge of the Elections, Returns and Qualifications of its own Members, and a Majority of each shall constitute a Quorum to do Business; but a smaller Number may adjourn from day to day, and may be authorized to compel the Attendance of absent Members, in such Manner, and under such Penalties as each House may provide.

Each House may determine the Rules of its Proceedings, punish its Members for disorderly Behaviour, and, with the Concurrence of two thirds, expel a Member.

Each House shall keep a Journal of its Proceedings, and from time to time publish the same, excepting such Parts as may in their Judgment require Secrecy; and the Yeas and Nays of the Members of either House on any question shall, at the Desire of one fifth of those Present, be entered on the Journal.

Neither House, during the Session of Congress, shall, without the Consent of the other, adjourn for more than three days, nor to any other Place than that in which the two Houses shall be sitting.

Section. 6—Compensation
The Senators and Representatives shall receive a Compensation for their Services, to be ascertained by Law, and paid out of the Treasury of the United States. They shall in all Cases, except Treason, Felony and Breach of the Peace, be privileged from Arrest during their Attendance at the Session of their respective Houses, and in going to and returning from the same; and for any Speech or Debate in either House, they shall not be questioned in any other Place.

No Senator or Representative shall, during the Time for which he was elected, be appointed to any civil Office under the Authority of the United States, which shall have been created, or the Emoluments whereof shall have been encreased during such time; and no Person holding any Office under the United States, shall be a Member of either House during his Continuance in Office.

Section. 7—Revenue Bills, Legislative Process, Presidential Veto
All Bills for raising Revenue shall originate in the House of Representatives; but the Senate may propose or concur with Amendments as on other Bills.

Every Bill which shall have passed the House of Representatives and the Senate, shall, before it become a Law, be presented to the President of the United States;[2] If he approve he shall sign it, but if not he shall return it, with his Objections to that House in which it shall have originated, who shall enter the Objections at large on their Journal, and proceed to reconsider it. If after such Reconsideration two thirds of that House shall agree to pass the Bill, it shall be sent, together with the Objections, to the other House, by which it shall likewise be reconsidered, and if approved by two thirds of that House, it shall become a Law. But in all such Cases the Votes of both Houses shall be determined by yeas and Nays, and the Names of the Persons voting for and against the Bill shall be entered on the Journal of each House respectively. If any Bill shall not be returned by the President within ten Days (Sundays excepted) after it shall have been presented to him, the Same shall be a Law, in like Manner as if he had signed it, unless the Congress by their Adjournment prevent its Return, in which Case it shall not be a Law.

Every Order, Resolution, or Vote to which the Concurrence of the Senate and House of Representatives may be necessary (except on a question of Adjournment) shall be presented to the President of the United States; and before the Same shall take Effect, shall be approved by him, or being disapproved by him, shall be repassed by two thirds of the Senate and House of Representatives, according to the Rules and Limitations prescribed in the Case of a Bill.

Section. 8—Powers of Congress
The Congress shall have Power To lay and collect Taxes, Duties, Imposts and Excises, to pay the Debts and provide for the common Defence and general Welfare of the United States; but all Duties, Imposts and Excises shall be uniform throughout the United States;

To borrow Money on the credit of the United States;
To regulate Commerce with foreign Nations, and among the several States, and with the Indian Tribes;

To establish an uniform Rule of Naturalization, and uniform Laws on the subject of Bankruptcies throughout the United States;

To coin Money, regulate the Value thereof, and of foreign Coin, and fix the Standard of Weights and Measures;

To provide for the Punishment of counterfeiting the Securities and current Coin of the United States;

To establish Post Offices and post Roads;

To promote the Progress of Science and useful Arts, by securing for limited Times to Authors and Inventors the exclusive Right to their respective Writings and Discoveries;

To constitute Tribunals inferior to the supreme Court;

To define and punish Piracies and Felonies committed on the high Seas, and Offences against the Law of Nations;

To declare War, grant Letters of Marque and Reprisal, and make Rules concerning Captures on Land and Water;

To raise and support Armies, but no Appropriation of Money to that Use shall be for a longer Term than two Years;

To provide and maintain a Navy;

To make Rules for the Government and Regulation of the land and naval Forces;

To provide for calling forth the Militia to execute the Laws of the Union, suppress Insurrections and repel Invasions;

To provide for organizing, arming, and disciplining, the Militia, and for governing such Part of them as may be employed in the Service of the United States, reserving to the States respectively, the Appointment of the Officers, and the Authority of training the Militia according to the discipline prescribed by Congress;

To exercise exclusive Legislation in all Cases whatsoever, over such District (not exceeding ten Miles square) as may, by Cession of particular States, and the Acceptance of Congress, become the Seat of the Government of the United States, and to exercise like Authority over all Places purchased by the Consent of the Legislature of the State in which the Same shall be, for the Erection of Forts, Magazines, Arsenals, dock-Yards, and other needful Buildings;—And

To make all Laws which shall be necessary and proper for carrying into Execution the foregoing Powers, and all other Powers vested by this Constitution in the Government of the United States, or in any Department or Officer thereof.

Section. 9—Limits on Congress
The Migration or Importation of such Persons as any of the States now existing shall think proper to admit, shall not be prohibited by the Congress prior to the Year one thousand eight hundred and eight, but a Tax or duty may be imposed on such Importation, not exceeding ten dollars for each Person.

The Privilege of the Writ of Habeas Corpus shall not be suspended, unless when in Cases of Rebellion or Invasion the public Safety may require it.

No Bill of Attainder or ex post facto Law shall be passed.

No Capitation, or other direct, Tax shall be laid, unless in Proportion to the Census or Enumeration herein before directed to be taken.

No Tax or Duty shall be laid on Articles exported from any State.

No Preference shall be given by any Regulation of Commerce or Revenue to the Ports of one State over those of another; nor shall Vessels bound to, or from, one State, be obliged to enter, clear, or pay Duties in another.

No Money shall be drawn from the Treasury, but in Consequence of Appropriations made by Law; and a regular Statement and Account of the Receipts and Expenditures of all public Money shall be published from time to time.

No Title of Nobility shall be granted by the United States: And no Person holding any Office of Profit or Trust under them, shall, without the Consent of the Congress, accept of any present, Emolument, Office, or Title, of any kind whatever, from any King, Prince, or foreign State.

Section. 10—Powers prohibited of States
No State shall enter into any Treaty, Alliance, or Confederation; grant Letters of Marque and Reprisal; coin Money; emit Bills of Credit; make any Thing but gold and silver Coin a Tender in Payment of Debts; pass any Bill of Attainder, ex post facto Law, or Law impairing the Obligation of Contracts, or grant any Title of Nobility.

No State shall, without the Consent of the Congress, lay any Imposts or Duties on Imports or Exports, except what may be absolutely necessary for executing it's inspection Laws; and the net Produce of all Duties and Imposts, laid by any State on Imports or Exports, shall be for the Use of the Treasury of the United States; and all such Laws shall be subject to the Revision and Controul of the Congress.

No State shall, without the Consent of Congress, lay any Duty of Tonnage, keep Troops, or Ships of War in time of Peace, enter into any Agreement or Compact with another State, or with a foreign Power, or engage in War, unless actually invaded, or in such imminent Danger as will not admit of delay.

Article. II.

Section. 1—The President
The executive Power shall be vested in a President of the United States of America. He shall hold his Office during the Term of four Years, and, together with the Vice President, chosen for the same Term, be elected, as follows:

Each State shall appoint, in such Manner as the Legislature thereof may direct, a Number of Electors, equal to the whole Number of Senators and Representatives to which the State may be entitled in the Congress: but no Senator or Representative, or Person holding an Office of Trust or Profit under the United States, shall be appointed an Elector.

The Electors shall meet in their respective States, and vote by Ballot for two Persons, of whom one at least shall not be an Inhabitant of the same State with themselves. And they shall make a List of all the Persons voted for, and of the Number of Votes for each; which List they shall sign and certify, and transmit sealed to the Seat of the Government of the United States, directed to the President of the Senate. The President of the Senate shall, in the Presence of the Senate and House of Representatives, open all the Certificates, and the Votes shall then be counted. The Person having the greatest Number of Votes shall be the President, if such Number be a Majority of the whole Number of Electors appointed; and if there be more than one who have such Majority, and have an equal Number of Votes, then the House of Representatives shall immediately chuse by Ballot one of them for President; and if no Person have a Majority, then from the five highest on the List the said House shall in like Manner chuse the President. But in chusing the President, the Votes shall be taken by States, the Representation from each State having one Vote; a quorum for this Purpose shall consist of a Member or Members from two thirds of the States, and a Majority of all the States shall be necessary to a Choice. In every Case, after the Choice of the President, the Person having the greatest Number of Votes of the Electors shall be the Vice President. But if there should remain two or more who have equal Votes, the Senate shall chuse from them by Ballot the Vice President [*Modified by Amendment XII*].

The Congress may determine the Time of chusing the Electors, and the Day on which they shall give their Votes; which Day shall be the same throughout the United States.

No Person except a natural born Citizen, or a Citizen of the United States, at the time of the Adoption of this Constitution, shall be eligible to the Office of President; neither shall any Person be eligible to that Office who shall not have attained to the Age of thirty five Years, and been fourteen Years a Resident within the United States.

In Case of the Removal of the President from Office, or of his Death, Resignation, or Inability to discharge the Powers and Duties of the said Office, the Same shall devolve on the Vice President, and the Congress may by Law provide for the Case of Removal, Death, Resignation or Inability, both of the President and Vice President, declaring what Officer shall then act as President, and such Officer shall act accordingly, until the Disability be removed, or a President shall be elected [*Modified by Amendment XXV*].

The President shall, at stated Times, receive for his Services, a Compensation, which shall neither be increased nor diminished during the Period for which he shall have been elected, and he shall not receive within that Period any other Emolument from the United States, or any of them.

Before he enter on the Execution of his Office, he shall take the following Oath or Affirmation:—"I do solemnly swear (or affirm) that I will faithfully execute the Office of President of the United States, and will to the best of my Ability, preserve, protect and defend the Constitution of the United States."

Section. 2—Civilian Power over Military, Cabinet, Pardon Power, Appointments

The President shall be Commander in Chief of the Army and Navy of the United States, and of the Militia of the several States, when called into the actual Service of the United States; he may require the Opinion, in writing, of the principal Officer in each of the executive Departments, upon any Subject relating to the Duties of their respective Offices, and he shall have Power to grant Reprieves and Pardons for Offences against the United States, except in Cases of Impeachment.

He shall have Power, by and with the Advice and Consent of the Senate, to make Treaties, provided two thirds of the Senators present concur; and he shall nominate, and by and with the Advice and Consent of the Senate, shall appoint Ambassadors, other public Ministers and Consuls, Judges of the supreme Court, and all other Officers of the United States, whose Appointments are not herein otherwise provided for, and which shall be established by Law: but the Congress may by Law vest the Appointment of such inferior Officers, as they think proper, in the President alone, in the Courts of Law, or in the Heads of Departments.

The President shall have Power to fill up all Vacancies that may happen during the Recess of the Senate, by granting Commissions which shall expire at the End of their next Session.

Section. 3—State of the Union, Convening Congress

He shall from time to time give to the Congress Information of the State of the Union, and recommend to their Consideration such Measures as he shall judge necessary and expedient; he may, on extraordinary Occasions, convene both Houses, or either of them, and in Case of Disagreement between them, with Respect to the Time of Adjournment, he may adjourn them to such Time as he shall think proper; he shall receive Ambassadors and other public Ministers; he shall take Care that the Laws be faithfully executed, and shall Commission all the Officers of the United States.

Section. 4—Disqualification
The President, Vice President and all civil Officers of the United States, shall be removed from Office on Impeachment for, and Conviction of, Treason, Bribery, or other high Crimes and Misdemeanors.

Article. III.

Section. 1—Judicial powers
The judicial Power of the United States shall be vested in one supreme Court, and in such inferior Courts as the Congress may from time to time ordain and establish. The Judges, both of the supreme and inferior Courts, shall hold their Offices during good Behaviour, and shall, at stated Times, receive for their Services a Compensation, which shall not be diminished during their Continuance in Office.

Section. 2—Trial by Jury, Original Jurisdiction, Jury Trials
The judicial Power shall extend to all Cases, in Law and Equity, arising under this Constitution, the Laws of the United States, and Treaties made, or which shall be made, under their Authority;—to all Cases affecting Ambassadors, other public Ministers and Consuls;—to all Cases of admiralty and maritime Jurisdiction;—to Controversies to which the United States shall be a Party;—to Controversies between two or more States;—between a State and Citizens of another State [*Modified by Amendment XI*];—between Citizens of different States;—between Citizens of the same State claiming Lands under Grants of different States, and between a State, or the Citizens thereof, and foreign States, Citizens or Subjects.

In all Cases affecting Ambassadors, other public Ministers and Consuls, and those in which a State shall be Party, the supreme Court shall have original Jurisdiction. In all the other Cases before mentioned, the supreme Court shall have appellate Jurisdiction, both as to Law and Fact, with such Exceptions, and under such Regulations as the Congress shall make.

The Trial of all Crimes, except in Cases of Impeachment, shall be by Jury; and such Trial shall be held in the State where the said Crimes shall have been committed; but when not committed within any State, the Trial shall be at such Place or Places as the Congress may by Law have directed.

Section. 3—Treason
Treason against the United States shall consist only in levying War against them, or in adhering to their Enemies, giving them Aid and Comfort. No Person shall

be convicted of Treason unless on the Testimony of two Witnesses to the same overt Act, or on Confession in open Court.

The Congress shall have Power to declare the Punishment of Treason, but no Attainder of Treason shall work Corruption of Blood, or Forfeiture except during the Life of the Person attainted.

Article. IV.

Section. 1—Each State to Honor all others
Full Faith and Credit shall be given in each State to the public Acts, Records, and judicial Proceedings of every other State. And the Congress may by general Laws prescribe the Manner in which such Acts, Records and Proceedings shall be proved, and the Effect thereof.

Section. 2—State citizens, Extradition
The Citizens of each State shall be entitled to all Privileges and Immunities of Citizens in the several States.

A Person charged in any State with Treason, Felony, or other Crime, who shall flee from Justice, and be found in another State, shall on Demand of the executive Authority of the State from which he fled, be delivered up, to be removed to the State having Jurisdiction of the Crime.

No Person held to Service or Labour in one State, under the Laws thereof, escaping into another, shall, in Consequence of any Law or Regulation therein, be discharged from such Service or Labour, but shall be delivered up on Claim of the Party to whom such Service or Labour may be due [*Modified by Amendment XIII*].

Section. 3—New States
New States may be admitted by the Congress into this Union; but no new State shall be formed or erected within the Jurisdiction of any other State; nor any State be formed by the Junction of two or more States, or Parts of States, without the Consent of the Legislatures of the States concerned as well as of the Congress.

The Congress shall have Power to dispose of and make all needful Rules and Regulations respecting the Territory or other Property belonging to the United States; and nothing in this Constitution shall be so construed as to Prejudice any Claims of the United States, or of any particular State.

Section. 4—Republican government
The United States shall guarantee to every State in this Union a Republican Form of Government, and shall protect each of them against Invasion; and on Application of the Legislature, or of the Executive (when the Legislature cannot be convened), against domestic Violence.

Article. V.

The Congress, whenever two thirds of both Houses shall deem it necessary, shall propose Amendments to this Constitution, or, on the Application of the Legislatures of two thirds of the several States, shall call a Convention for proposing Amendments, which, in either Case, shall be valid to all Intents and Purposes, as Part of this Constitution, when ratified by the Legislatures of three fourths of the several States, or by Conventions in three fourths thereof, as the one or the other Mode of Ratification may be proposed by the Congress; Provided that no Amendment which may be made prior to the Year One thousand eight hundred and eight shall in any Manner affect the first and fourth Clauses in the Ninth Section of the first Article; *and that no State, without its Consent, shall be deprived of its equal Suffrage in the Senate* [*Possibly abrogated by Amendment XVII*].

Article. VI.

All Debts contracted and Engagements entered into, before the Adoption of this Constitution, shall be as valid against the United States under this Constitution, as under the Confederation.

This Constitution, and the Laws of the United States which shall be made in Pursuance thereof; and all Treaties made, or which shall be made, under the Authority of the United States, shall be the supreme Law of the Land; and the Judges in every State shall be bound thereby, any Thing in the Constitution or Laws of any State to the Contrary notwithstanding.

The Senators and Representatives before mentioned, and the Members of the several State Legislatures, and all executive and judicial Officers, both of the United States and of the several States, shall be bound by Oath or Affirmation, to support this Constitution; but no religious Test shall ever be required as a Qualification to any Office or public Trust under the United States.

Article. VII.

The Ratification of the Conventions of nine States, shall be sufficient for the Establishment of this Constitution between the States so ratifying the Same.

Done in Convention by the Unanimous Consent of the States present the Seventeenth Day of September in the Year of our Lord one thousand seven hundred and Eighty seven and of the Independence of the United States of America the Twelfth In witness whereof We have hereunto subscribed our Names.

Go. Washington—President and deputy from Virginia
New Hampshire—John Langdon, Nicholas Gilman
Massachusetts—Nathaniel Gorham, Rufus King
Connecticut—Wm Saml Johnson, Roger Sherman
New York—Alexander Hamilton
New Jersey—Wil Livingston, David Brearley, Wm Paterson, Jona. Dayton
Pensylvania—B Franklin, Thomas Mifflin, Robt Morris, Geo. Clymer, Thos FitzSimons,
Jared Ingersoll, James Wilson, Gouv Morris
Delaware—Geo. Read, Gunning Bedford jun, John Dickinson, Richard Bassett, Jaco. Broom
Maryland—James McHenry, Dan of St Tho Jenifer, Danl Carroll
Virginia—John Blair, James Madison Jr.
North Carolina—Wm Blount, Richd Dobbs Spaight, Hu Williamson
South Carolina—J. Rutledge, Charles Cotesworth Pinckney, Charles Pinckney, Pierce Butler
Georgia—William Few, Abr Baldwin

The Word, "the," being interlined between the seventh and eighth Lines of the first Page, The Word "Thirty" being partly written on an Erazure in the fifteenth Line of the first Page, The Words "is tried" being interlined between the thirty second and thirty third Lines of the first Page and the Word "the" being interlined between the forty third and forty fourth Lines of the second Page.

Attest William Jackson
Secretary

The Amendments

Note: The following are the Amendments to the Constitution. The first ten Amendments collectively are commonly known as the Bill of Rights.

Amendment 1—Freedom of Religion, Press, Expression. Ratified 12/15/1791.
Congress shall make no law respecting an establishment of religion, or prohibiting the free exercise thereof; or abridging the freedom of speech, or of the press; or the right of the people peaceably to assemble, and to petition the Government for a redress of grievances.

Amendment 2—Right to Bear Arms. Ratified 12/15/1791.
A well regulated Militia, being necessary to the security of a free State, the right of the people to keep and bear Arms, shall not be infringed.

Amendment 3—Quartering of Soldiers. Ratified 12/15/1791.
No Soldier shall, in time of peace be quartered in any house, without the consent of the Owner, nor in time of war, but in a manner to be prescribed by law.

Amendment 4—Search and Seizure. Ratified 12/15/1791.
The right of the people to be secure in their persons, houses, papers, and effects, against unreasonable searches and seizures, shall not be violated, and no Warrants shall issue, but upon probable cause, supported by Oath or affirmation, and particularly describing the place to be searched, and the persons or things to be seized.

Amendment 5—Trial and Punishment, Compensation for Takings. Ratified12/15/1791.
No person shall be held to answer for a capital, or otherwise infamous crime, unless on presentment or indictment of a Grand Jury, except in cases arising in the land or naval forces, or in the Militia, when in actual service in time of War or public danger; nor shall any person be subject for the same offense to be twice put in jeopardy of life or limb; nor shall be compelled in any criminal case to be a witness against himself, nor be deprived of life, liberty, or property, without due process of law; nor shall private property be taken for public use, without just compensation.

Amendment 6—Right to Speedy Trial, Confrontation of Witnesses. Ratified12/15/1791.
In all criminal prosecutions, the accused shall enjoy the right to a speedy and public trial, by an impartial jury of the State and district wherein the crime shall have been committed, which district shall have been previously ascertained by law, and

to be informed of the nature and cause of the accusation; to be confronted with the witnesses against him; to have compulsory process for obtaining witnesses in his favor, and to have the Assistance of Counsel for his defence.

Amendment 7—Trial by Jury in Civil Cases. Ratified 12/15/1791.
In Suits at common law, where the value in controversy shall exceed twenty dollars, the right of trial by jury shall be preserved, and no fact tried by a jury, shall be otherwise reexamined in any Court of the United States, than according to the rules of the common law.

Amendment 8—Cruel and Unusual Punishment. Ratified 12/15/1791.
Excessive bail shall not be required, nor excessive fines imposed, nor cruel and unusual punishments inflicted.

Amendment 9—Construction of Constitution. Ratified 12/15/1791.
The enumeration in the Constitution, of certain rights, shall not be construed to deny or disparage others retained by the people.

Amendment 10—Powers of the States and People. Ratified 12/15/1791.
The powers not delegated to the United States by the Constitution, nor prohibited by it to the States, are reserved to the States respectively, or to the people.
Amendment 11—Judicial Limits. Ratified 2/7/1795.
The Judicial power of the United States shall not be construed to extend to any suit in law or equity, commenced or prosecuted against one of the United States by Citizens of another State, or by Citizens or Subjects of any Foreign State.

Amendment 12—Choosing the President, Vice-President. Ratified 6/15/1804.
The Electors shall meet in their respective states, and vote by ballot for President and Vice-President, one of whom, at least, shall not be an inhabitant of the same state with themselves; they shall name in their ballots the person voted for as President, and indistinct ballots the person voted for as Vice-President, and they shall make distinct lists of all persons voted for as President, and of all persons voted for as Vice-President and of the number of votes for each, which lists they shall sign and certify, and transmit sealed to the seat of the government of the United States, directed to the President of the Senate; The President of the Senate shall, in the presence of the Senate and House of Representatives, open all the certificates and the votes shall then be counted; The person having the greatest Number of votes for President, shall be the President, if such number be a majority of the whole number of Electors appointed; and if no person have such majority, then from the persons having the highest numbers not exceeding three on the list of those voted for as President, the House of Representatives shall

choose immediately, by ballot, the President. But in choosing the President, the votes shall be taken by states, the representation from each state having one vote; a quorum for this purpose shall consist of a member or members from two-thirds of the states, and a majority of all the states shall be necessary to a choice. And if the House of Representatives shall not choose a President whenever the right of choice shall devolve upon them, before the fourth day of March next following, then the Vice-President shall act as President, as in the case of the death or other constitutional disability of the President. The person having the greatest number of votes as Vice-President, shall be the Vice-President, if such number be a majority of the whole number of Electors appointed, and if no person have a majority, then from the two highest numbers on the list, the Senate shall choose the Vice-President; a quorum for the purpose shall consist of two-thirds of the whole number of Senators, and a majority of the whole number shall be necessary to a choice. But no person constitutionally ineligible to the office of President shall be eligible to that of Vice-President of the United States.

Amendment 13—Slavery Abolished. Ratified 12/6/1865.
1. Neither slavery nor involuntary servitude, except as a punishment for crime whereof the party shall have been duly convicted, shall exist within the United States, or any place subject to their jurisdiction.

2. Congress shall have power to enforce this article by appropriate legislation.

Amendment 14—Citizenship Rights. Ratified 7/9/1868.
1. All persons born or naturalized in the United States, and subject to the jurisdiction thereof, are citizens of the United States and of the State wherein they reside. No State shall make or enforce any law which shall abridge the privileges or immunities of citizens of the United States; nor shall any State deprive any person of life, liberty, or property, without due process of law; nor deny to any person within its jurisdiction the equal protection of the laws.

2. Representatives shall be apportioned among the several States according to their respective numbers, counting the whole number of persons in each State, excluding Indians not taxed. But when the right to vote at any election for the choice of electors for President and Vice-President of the United States, Representatives in Congress, the Executive and Judicial officers of a State, or the members of the Legislature thereof, is denied to any of the male inhabitants of such State, being twenty-one years of age, and citizens of the United States, or in any way abridged, except for participation in rebellion, or other crime, the basis of representation therein shall be reduced in the proportion which the number of such male citizens

shall bear to the whole number of male citizens twenty-one years of age in such State.

3. No person shall be a Senator or Representative in Congress, or elector of President and Vice-President, or hold any office, civil or military, under the United States, or under any State, who, having previously taken an oath, as a member of Congress, or as an officer of the United States, or as a member of any State legislature, or as an executive or judicial officer of any State, to support the Constitution of the United States, shall have engaged in insurrection or rebellion against the same, or given aid or comfort to the enemies thereof. But Congress may by a vote of two-thirds of each House, remove such disability.

4. The validity of the public debt of the United States, authorized by law, including debts incurred for payment of pensions and bounties for services in suppressing insurrection or rebellion, shall not be questioned. But neither the United States nor any State shall assume or pay any debt or obligation incurred in aid of insurrection or rebellion against the United States, or any claim for the loss or emancipation of any slave; but all such debts, obligations and claims shall be held illegal and void.

5. The Congress shall have power to enforce, by appropriate legislation, the provisions of this article.

Amendment 15—Race No Bar to Vote. Ratified 2/3/1870.
1. The right of citizens of the United States to vote shall not be denied or abridged by the United States or by any State on account of race, color, or previous condition of servitude.

2. The Congress shall have power to enforce this article by appropriate legislation.

Amendment 16—Status of Income Tax Clarified. Ratified 2/3/1913.
The Congress shall have power to lay and collect taxes on incomes, from whatever source derived, without apportionment among the several States, and without regard to any census or enumeration.

Amendment 17—Senators Elected by Popular Vote. Ratified 4/8/1913.
The Senate of the United States shall be composed of two Senators from each State, elected by the people thereof, for six years; and each Senator shall have one vote. The electors in each State shall have the qualifications requisite for electors of the most numerous branch of the State legislatures. When vacancies happen in

the representation of any State in the Senate, the executive authority of such State shall issue writs of election to fill such vacancies: Provided, That the legislature of any State may empower the executive thereof to make temporary appointments until the people fill the vacancies by election as the legislature may direct. This amendment shall not be so construed as to affect the election or term of any Senator chosen before it becomes valid as part of the Constitution.

Amendment 18—Liquor Abolished. Ratified 1/16/1919. Repealed by Amendment 21,12/5/1933.
1. After one year from the ratification of this article the manufacture, sale, or transportation of intoxicating liquors within, the importation thereof into, or the exportation thereof from the United States and all territory subject to the jurisdiction thereof for beverage purposes is hereby prohibited.

2. The Congress and the several States shall have concurrent power to enforce this article by appropriate legislation.

3. This article shall be inoperative unless it shall have been ratified as an amendment to the Constitution by the legislatures of the several States, as provided in the Constitution, within seven years from the date of the submission hereof to the States by the Congress.

Amendment 19—Women's Suffrage. Ratified 8/18/1920.
The right of citizens of the United States to vote shall not be denied or abridged by the United States or by any State on account of sex. Congress shall have power to enforce this article by appropriate legislation.

Amendment 20—Presidential, Congressional Terms. Ratified 1/23/1933.
1. The terms of the President and Vice President shall end at noon on the 20th day of January, and the terms of Senators and Representatives at noon on the 3d day of January, of the years in which such terms would have ended if this article had not been ratified; and the terms of their successors shall then begin.

2. The Congress shall assemble at least once in every year, and such meeting shall begin at noon on the 3d day of January, unless they shall by law appoint a different day.

3. If, at the time fixed for the beginning of the term of the President, the President elect shall have died, the Vice President elect shall become President. If a President shall not have been chosen before the time fixed for the beginning of his term, or if the President elect shall have failed to qualify, then the Vice President elect

shall act as President until a President shall have qualified; and the Congress may by law provide for the case wherein neither a President elect nor a Vice President elect shall have qualified, declaring who shall then act as President, or the manner in which one who is to act shall be selected, and such person shall act accordingly until a President or Vice President shall have qualified.

4. The Congress may by law provide for the case of the death of any of the persons from whom the House of Representatives may choose a President whenever the right of choice shall have devolved upon them, and for the case of the death of any of the persons from whom the Senate may choose a Vice President whenever the right of choice shall have devolved upon them.

5. Sections 1 and 2 shall take effect on the 15th day of October following the ratification of this article.

6. This article shall be inoperative unless it shall have been ratified as an amendment to the Constitution by the legislatures of three-fourths of the several States within seven years from the date of its submission.

Amendment 21—Amendment 18 Repealed. Ratified 12/5/1933.
1. The eighteenth article of amendment to the Constitution of the United States is hereby repealed.
2. The transportation or importation into any State, Territory, or possession of the United States for delivery or use therein of intoxicating liquors, in violation of the laws thereof, is hereby prohibited.

3. The article shall be inoperative unless it shall have been ratified as an amendment to the Constitution by conventions in the several States, as provided in the Constitution, within seven years from the date of the submission hereof to the States by the Congress.

Amendment 22—Presidential Term Limits. Ratified 2/27/1951.
1. No person shall be elected to the office of the President more than twice, and no person who has held the office of President, or acted as President, for more than two years of a term to which some other person was elected President shall be elected to the office of the President more than once. But this Article shall not apply to any person holding the office of President, when this Article was proposed by the Congress, and shall not prevent any person who may be holding the office of President, or acting as President, during the term within which this Article becomes operative from holding the office of President or acting as President during the remainder of such term.

2. This article shall be inoperative unless it shall have been ratified as an amendment to the Constitution by the legislatures of three-fourths of the several States within seven years from the date of its submission to the States by the Congress.

Amendment 23—Presidential Vote for District of Columbia. Ratified 3/29/1961.
1. The District constituting the seat of Government of the United States shall appoint in such manner as the Congress may direct: A number of electors of President and Vice President equal to the whole number of Senators and Representatives in Congress to which the District would be entitled if it were a State, but in no event more than the least populous State; they shall be in addition to those appointed by the States, but they shall be considered, for the purposes of the election of President and Vice President, to be electors appointed by a State; and they shall meet in the District and perform such duties as provided by the twelfth article of amendment.

2. The Congress shall have power to enforce this article by appropriate legislation.

Amendment 24—Poll Tax Barred. Ratified 1/23/1964.
1. The right of citizens of the United States to vote in any primary or other election for President or Vice President, for electors for President or Vice President, or for Senator or Representative in Congress, shall not be denied or abridged by the United States or any State by reason of failure to pay any poll tax or other tax.

2. The Congress shall have power to enforce this article by appropriate legislation.

Amendment 25—Presidential Disability and Succession. Ratified 2/10/1967.
1. In case of the removal of the President from office or of his death or resignation, the Vice President shall become President.

2. Whenever there is a vacancy in the office of the Vice President, the President shall nominate a Vice President who shall take office upon confirmation by a majority vote of both Houses of Congress.

3. Whenever the President transmits to the President pro tempore of the Senate and the Speaker of the House of Representatives his written declaration that he is unable to discharge the powers and duties of his office, and until he transmits

to them a written declaration to the contrary, such powers and duties shall be discharged by the Vice President as Acting President.

4. Whenever the Vice President and a majority of either the principal officers of the executive departments or of such other body as Congress may by law provide, transmit to the President pro tempore of the Senate and the Speaker of the House of Representatives their written declaration that the President is unable to discharge the powers and duties of his office, the Vice President shall immediately assume the powers and duties of the office as Acting President.

Thereafter, when the President transmits to the President pro tempore of the Senate and the Speaker of the House of Representatives his written declaration that no inability exists, he shall resume the powers and duties of his office unless the Vice President and a majority of either the principal officers of the executive department or of such other body as Congress may by law provide, transmit within four days to the President pro tempore of the Senate and the Speaker of the House of Representatives their written declaration that the President is unable to discharge the powers and duties of his office. Thereupon Congress shall decide the issue, assembling within forty eight hours for that purpose if not in session. If the Congress, within twenty one days after receipt of the latter written declaration, or, if Congress is not in session, within twenty one days after Congress is required to assemble, determines by two thirds vote of both Houses that the President is unable to discharge the powers and duties of his office, the Vice President shall continue to discharge the same as Acting President; otherwise, the President shall resume the powers and duties of his office.

Amendment 26—Voting Age Set to 18 Years. Ratified 7/1/1971.
1. The right of citizens of the United States, who are eighteen years of age or older, to vote shall not be denied or abridged by the United States or by any State on account of age.

2. The Congress shall have power to enforce this article by appropriate legislation.

Amendment 27—Limiting Congressional Pay Increases. Ratified 5/7/1992.
No law, varying the compensation for the services of the Senators and Representatives, shall take effect, until an election of Representatives shall have intervened.

APPENDIX E

THE VIRGINIA AND KENTUCKY RESOLUTIONS

The Kentucky Resolutions of 1798[88]

In the House of Representatives,
November 10*th*, 1798.

I. Resolved, that the several states composing the United States of America, are not united on the principle of unlimited submission to their General Government; but that by compact under the style and title of a Constitution for the United States and of amendments thereto, they constituted a General Government for special purposes, delegated to that Government certain definite powers, reserving each state to itself, the residuary mass of right to their own self Government; and that whensoever the General Government assumes undelegated powers, its acts are unauthoritative, void, and of no force: That to this compact each state acceded as a state, and is an integral party, its co-states forming as to itself, the other party: That the Government created by this compact was not made the exclusive or final *judge* of the extent of the powers delegated to itself; since that would have made its discretion, and not the constitution, the measure of its powers; but that as in all other cases of compact among parties having no common Judge, each party has an equal right to judge for itself, as well of infractions as of the mode and measure of redress.

II. Resolved, that the Constitution of the United States having delegated to Congress a power to punish treason, counterfeiting the securities and current coin of the United States, piracies and felonies committed on the High Seas, and offences against the laws of nations, and no other crimes whatever, and it being true as a general principle, and one of the amendments to the Constitution having also declared, "that the powers not delegated to the United States by the Constitution, nor prohibited by it to the states, are reserved to the states respectively, or to the people," therefore also the same act of Congress passed on the 14th day of July, 1798, and entitled "An act in addition to the act entitled an act for the punishment of certain crimes against the United States;" as also the act passed by them on the 27th day of June, 1798, entitled "An act to punish frauds committed on the Bank of the United States" (and all other their acts which assume to create, define, or punish crimes other than those enumerated in the constitution) are altogether void and of no force, and that the power to create, define, and punish such other crimes is reserved, and of right appertains solely and exclusively to the respective states, each within its own Territory.

III. Resolved, that it is true as a general principle, and is also expressly declared by one of the amendments to the Constitution that "the powers not delegated to the United States by the Constitution, nor prohibited by it to the states, are reserved to the states respectively or to the people;" and that no power over the freedom of religion, freedom of speech, or freedom of the press being delegated to the United States by the Constitution, nor prohibited by it to the states, all lawful powers respecting the same did of right remain, and were reserved to the states, or to the people: That thus was manifested their determination to retain to themselves the right of judging how far the licentiousness of speech and of the press may be abridged without lessening their useful freedom, and how far those abuses which cannot be separated from their use, should be tolerated rather than the use be destroyed; and thus also they guarded against all abridgement by the United States of the freedom of religious opinions*[1]* and exercises, and retained to themselves the right of protecting the same, as this state by a Law passed on the general demand of its Citizens, had already protected them from all human restraint or interference: And that in addition to this general principle and express declaration, another and more special provision has been made by one of the amendments to the Constitution which expressly declares, that "Congress shall make no law respecting an Establishment of religion, or prohibiting the free exercise thereof, or abridging the freedom of speech, or of the press," thereby guarding in the same sentence, and under the same words, the freedom of religion, of speech, and of the press, insomuch, that whatever violates either, throws down the sanctuary which covers the others, and that libels, falsehoods, and defamation, equally with heresy and false religion, are withheld from the cognizance of federal tribunals. That therefore the act of the Congress of the United States passed on the 14th day of July 1798, entitled "An act in addition to the act for the punishment of certain crimes against the United States," which does abridge the freedom of the press, is not law, but is altogether void and of no effect.*[2]*

IV. Resolved, that alien friends are under the jurisdiction and protection of the laws of the state wherein they are; that no power over them has been delegated to the United States, nor prohibited to the individual states distinct from their power over citizens; and it being true as a general principle, and one of the amendments to the Constitution having also declared, that "the powers not delegated to the United States by the Constitution nor prohibited by it to the states are reserved to the states respectively or to the people," the act of the Congress of the United States passed on the 22d day of June, 1798, entitled "An act concerning aliens," which assumes power over alien friends not delegated by the Constitution, is not law, but is altogether void and of no force.

V. Resolved, that in addition to the general principle as well as the express declaration, that powers not delegated are reserved, another and more special provision inserted in the Constitution from abundant caution has declared, "that the *migration* or importation of such persons as any of the states now existing shall think proper to admit, shall not be prohibited by the Congress prior to the year 1808." That this Commonwealth does admit the migration of alien friends described as the subject of the said act concerning aliens; that a provision against prohibiting their migration, is a provision against all acts equivalent thereto, or it would be nugatory; that to remove them when migrated is equivalent to a prohibition of their migration, and is therefore contrary to the said provision of the Constitution, and void.

VI. Resolved, that the imprisonment of a person under the protection of the Laws of this Commonwealth on his failure to obey the simple *order* of the President to depart out of the United States, as is undertaken by the said act entitled "An act concerning Aliens," is contrary to the Constitution, one amendment to which has provided, that "no person shall be deprived of liberty without due process of law," and that another having provided "that in all criminal prosecutions, the accused shall enjoy the right to a public trial by an impartial jury, to be informed of the nature and cause of the accusation, to be confronted with the witnesses against him, to have compulsory process for obtaining witnesses in his favour, and to have the assistance of counsel for his defence," the same act undertaking to authorize the President to remove a person out of the United States who is under the protection of the Law, on his own suspicion, without accusation, without jury, without public trial, without confrontation of the witnesses against him, without having witnesses in his favour, without defence, without counsel, is contrary to these provisions also of the Constitution, is therefore not law but utterly void and of no force.

That transferring the power of judging any person who is under the protection of the laws, from the Courts to the President of the United States, as is undertaken by the same act concerning Aliens, is against the article of the Constitution which provides, that "the judicial power of the United States shall be vested in Courts, the Judges of which shall hold their offices during good behaviour," and that the said act is void for that reason also; and it is further to be noted, that this transfer of Judiciary power is to that magistrate of the General Government who already possesses all the Executive, and a qualified negative in all the Legislative powers.

VII. Resolved, that the construction applied by the General Government (as is evinced*[3]* by sundry of their proceedings) to those parts of the Constitution of the United States which delegate to Congress a power to lay and collect taxes, duties, imposts, and excises; to pay the debts, and provide for the common defence, and general welfare of the United States, and to make all laws which shall be necessary and proper for carrying into execution the powers vested by the Constitution in the Government of the United States, or any department thereof, goes to the destruction of all the limits prescribed to their power by the Constitution—That words meant by that instrument to be subsiduary only to the execution of the limited powers, ought not to be so construed as themselves to give unlimited powers, nor a part so to be taken, as to destroy the whole residue of the instrument: That the proceedings of the General Government under colour of these articles, will be a fit and necessary subject for revisal and correction at a time of greater tranquility, while those specified in the preceding resolutions call for immediate redress.

VIII. Resolved, that the preceding Resolutions be transmitted to the Senators and Representatives in Congress from this Commonwealth, who are hereby enjoined to present the same to their respective Houses, and to use their best endeavours to procure at the next session of Congress, a repeal of the aforesaid unconstitutional and obnoxious acts.

IX. Resolved lastly, that the Governor of this Commonwealth be, and is hereby authorised and requested to communicate the preceding Resolutions to the Legislatures of the several States, to assure them that this Commonwealth considers Union for specified National purposes, and particularly for those specified in their late Federal Compact, to be friendly to the peace, happiness, and prosperity of all the states: that faithful to that compact, according to the plain intent and meaning in which it was understood and acceded to by the several parties, it is sincerely anxious for its preservation: that it does also believe, that to take from the states all the powers of self government, and transfer them to a general and consolidated Government, without regard to the special delegations and reservations solemnly agreed to in that compact, is not for the peace, happiness, or prosperity of these states: And that therefore, this Commonwealth is determined, as it doubts not its Co-states are, tamely*[4]* to submit to undelegated & consequently unlimited powers in no man or body of men on earth: that if the acts before specified should stand, these conclusions would flow from them; that the General Government may place any act they think proper on the list of crimes & punish it themselves, whether enumerated or not enumerated by the Constitution as cognizable by them: that they may transfer its cognizance to the President or any other person, who may himself be the accuser, counsel, judge, and jury, whose *suspicions* may be the evidence, his order the sentence, his officer the executioner, and his breast the sole record of the transaction: that a very numerous and valuable description of the inhabitants of these states, being by this precedent reduced as outlaws to the absolute dominion of one man and the barrier of the Constitution thus swept away from us all, no rampart now remains against the passions and the power of a majority of Congress, to protect from a like exportation or other more*[5]* grievous punishment the minority of the same body, the Legislatures, Judges, Governors, & Counsellors of the states, nor their other peaceable inhabitants who may venture to reclaim the constitutional rights & liberties of the states & people, or who for other causes, good or bad, may be obnoxious to the views or marked by the suspicions of the President, or be thought dangerous to his or their elections or other interests public or personal: that the friendless alien has indeed been selected as the safest subject of a first experiment: but the citizen will soon follow, or rather has already followed; for, already has a Sedition Act marked him as its prey: that these and successive acts of the same character, unless arrested at the threshold, may tend to*[6]* drive these states into revolution and blood, and will furnish new calumnies against Republican Governments, and new pretexts for those who wish it to be believed, that man cannot be governed but by a rod of iron: that it would be a dangerous delusion were a confidence in the men of our choice to silence our fears for the safety of our rights: that confidence is every where the parent of despotism: free government is founded in jealousy and not in confidence; it is jealousy and not confidence which prescribes limited Constitutions to bind down those whom we are obliged to trust with power: that our Constitution has accordingly fixed the limits to which and no further our confidence may go; and let the honest advocate of confidence read the Alien and Sedition Acts, and say if the Constitution has not been wise in fixing limits to the Government it created, and whether we should be wise in destroying those limits? Let him say what the Government is if it be not a tyranny, which the men of our choice have conferred on the President, and the President of our choice has assented to and accepted over the friendly strangers, to whom the mild spirit of our Country and its laws had pledged hospitality and protection: that the men of our choice have more respected the bare suspicions of the President than the solid rights of innocence, the claims of justification, the sacred force of truth, and the forms & substance of law and justice. In questions of power then let no more be heard of confidence in man, but bind him down from mischief by the chains of the Constitution.

That this Commonwealth does therefore call on its Co-states for an expression of their sentiments on the acts concerning Aliens, and for the punishment of certain crimes herein before specified, plainly declaring whether these acts are or are not authorised by the Federal Compact? And it doubts not that their sense will be so announced as to prove their attachment unaltered to limited Government, whether general or particular, and that the rights and liberties of their Co-states will be exposed to no dangers by remaining embarked on a common bottom with their own: That they will concur with this Commonwealth in considering the said acts as so palpably against the Constitution as to amount to an undisguised declaration, that the Compact is not meant to be the measure of the powers of the General Government, but that it will proceed in the exercise over these states of all powers whatsoever: That they will view this as seizing the rights of the states and consolidating them in the hands of the General Government with a power assumed to bind the states (not merely in cases made federal) but in all cases whatsoever, by laws made, not with their consent, but by others against their consent: That this would be to surrender the form of Government we have chosen, and to live under one deriving its powers from its own will, and not from our authority; and that the Co-states recurring to their natural right in cases not made federal, will concur in declaring these acts void and of no force, and will each unite with this Commonwealth in requesting their repeal at the next session of Congress.

EDMUND BULLOCK, *S. H. R.*
JOHN CAMPBELL, *S. S. P. T.*

Passed in the House of Representatives, Nov. 10, 1798.
Attest,

THO'S. TODD, *C. H. R.*

In SENATE, *Nov. 13th, 1798—unanimously concurred in.*
Attest,

B. THURSTON, *C. S.*

Approved, November 16th, 1798.

JAMES GARRARD
Governor of Kentucky.

By THE GOVERNOR,

HARRY TOULMIN,
Secretary of State.

*[1]*Evans, No. 48494: "principles."

*[2]*Evans, No. 48494: "force."

*[3]*Evans, No. 48494: "evident."

*[4]*Word lacking in Evans, No. 48494, and in the resolutions as printed in *Kentucky Gazette*, 14 Nov. 1798.

*[5]*Word lacking in Evans, No. 48494.

*[6]*In place of the preceding three words Evans, No. 48494, has "necessarily." [89]

The Virginia Resolutions of 1798 [90]

Friday, December 21*st*, 1798.

RESOLVED, That the General Assembly of Virginia, doth unequivocably express a firm resolution to maintain and defend the *Constitution of the United States*, and the Constitution of this State, against every aggression either foreign or domestic, and that they will support the government of the United States in all measures warranted by the former.

That this assembly most solemnly declares a warm attachment to the Union of the States, to maintain which it pledges all its powers; and that for this end, it is their duty to watch over and oppose every infraction of those principles which constitute the only basis of that Union, because a faithful observance of them, can alone secure it's existence and the public happiness.

That this Assembly doth explicitly and peremptorily declare, that it views the powers of the federal government, as resulting from the compact, to which the states are parties; as limited by the plain sense and intention of the instrument constituting the compact; as no further valid that they are authorized by the grants enumerated in that compact; and that in case of a deliberate, palpable, and dangerous exercise of other powers, not granted by the said compact, the states who are parties thereto, have the right, and are in duty bound, to interpose for arresting the progress of the evil, and for maintaining within their respective limits, the authorities, rights and liberties appertaining to them.

That the General Assembly doth also express its deep regret, that a spirit has in sundry instances, been manifested by the federal government, to enlarge its powers by forced constructions of the constitutional charter which defines them; and that implications have appeared of a design to expound certain general phrases (which having been copied from the very limited grant of power, in the former articles of confederation were the less liable to be misconstrued) so as to destroy the meaning and effect, of the particular enumeration which necessarily explains and limits the general phrases; and so as to consolidate the states by degrees, into one sovereignty, the obvious tendency and inevitable consequence of which would be, to transform the present republican system of the United States, into an absolute, or at best a mixed monarchy.

That the General Assembly doth particularly protest against the palpable and alarming infractions of the *Constitution*, in the two late cases of the "*Alien* and *Sedition Acts*" passed at the last session of Congress; the first of which exercises a power no where delegated to the federal government, and which by uniting legislative and judicial powers to those of executive, subverts the general principles of free government; as well as the particular organization, and positive provisions of the federal constitution; and the other of which acts, exercises in like manner, a power not delegated by the constitution, but on the contrary, expressly and positively forbidden by one of the amendments thererto; a power, which more than any other, ought to produce universal alarm, because it is levelled against that right of freely examining public characters and measures, and of free communication among the people thereon, which has ever been justly deemed, the only effectual guardian of every other right.

That this state having by its Convention, which ratified the federal *Constitution*, expressly declared, that among other essential rights, "the Liberty of Conscience and of the Press cannot be cancelled, abridged, restrained, or modified by any authority of the United States," and from its extreme anxiety to guard these rights from every possible attack of sophistry or ambition, having with other states, recommended an amendment for that purpose, which amendment was, in due time, annexed to the *Constitution*; it would mark a reproachable inconsistency, and criminal degeneracy, if an indifference were now shewn, to the most palpable violation of one of the Rights, thus declared and secured; and to the establishment of a precedent which may be fatal to the other.

That the good people of this commonwealth, having ever felt, and continuing to feel, the most sincere affection for their brethren of the other states; the truest anxiety for establishing and perpetuating the union of all; and the most scrupulous fidelity to that constitution, which is the pledge of mutual friendship, and the instrument of mutual happiness; the General Assembly doth solemenly appeal to the like dispositions of the other states, in confidence that they will concur with

this commonwealth in declaring, as it does hereby declare, that the acts aforesaid, are unconstitutional; and that the necessary and proper measures will be taken by each, for co-operating with this state, in maintaining the Authorities, Rights, and Liberties, referred to the States respectively, or to the people.
That the Governor be desired, to transmit a copy of the foregoing Resolutions to the executive authority of each of the other states, with a request that the same may be communicated to the Legislature thereof; and that a copy be furnished to each of the Senators and Representatives representing this state in the Congress of the United States.

Agreed to by the Senate, December 24, 1798.

The Kentucky Resolutions of 1799[91]

Resolutions In General Assembly,
November 14*th*, 1799.

THE representatives of the good people of this commonwealth in general assembly convened, having maturely considered the answers of sundry states in the Union, to their resolutions passed at the last session, respecting certain unconstitutional laws of Congress, commonly called the *alien* and *sedition laws*, would be faithless indeed to themselves, and to those they represent, were they silently to acquiesce in principles and doctrines attempted to be maintained in all those answers, that of Virginia only excepted. To again enter the field of argument, and attempt more fully or forcibly to expose the unconstitutionality of those obnoxious laws, would, it is apprehended be as unnecessary as unavailing.

We cannot however but lament, that in the discussion of those interesting subjects, by sundry of the legislatures of our sister states, unfounded suggestions, and uncandid insinuations, derogatory of the true character and principles of the good people of this commonwealth, have been substituted in place of fair reasoning and sound argument. Our opinions of those alarming measures of the general government, together with our reasons for those opinions, were detailed with decency and with temper, and submitted to the discussion and judgment of our fellow citizens throughout the Union. Whether the decency and temper have been observed in the answers of most of those states who have denied or attempted to obviate the great truths contained in those resolutions, we have now only to submit to a candid world. Faithful to the true principles of the federal union, unconscious of any designs to disturb the harmony of that Union, and anxious only to escape the fangs of despotism, the good people of this commonwealth are regardless of censure or calumniation.

Least however the silence of this commonwealth should be construed into an acquiescence in the doctrines and principles advanced and attempted to be maintained by the said answers, or least those of our fellow citizens throughout the Union, who so widely differ from us on those important subjects, should be deluded by the expectation, that we shall be deterred from what we conceive our duty; or shrink from the principles contained in those resolutions: therefore.

RESOLVED, That this commonwealth considers the federal union, upon the terms and for the purposes specified in the late compact, as conducive to the liberty and happiness of the several states: That it does now unequivocally declare its attachment to the Union, and to that compact, agreeable to its obvious and real intention, and will be among the last to seek its dissolution: That if those who administer the general government be permitted to transgress the limits fixed by that compact, by a total disregard to the special delegations of power therein contained, annihilation of the state governments, and the erection upon their ruins, of a general consolidated government, will be the inevitable consequence: That the principle and construction contended for by sundry of the state legislatures, that the general government is the exclusive judge of the extent of the powers delegated to it, stop nothing short of despotism; since the discretion of those who adminster the government, and not the constitution, would be the measure of their powers: That the several states who formed that instrument, being sovereign and independent, have the unquestionable right to judge of its infraction; and that a nullification, by those sovereignties, of all unauthorized acts done under colour of that instrument, is the rightful remedy: That this commonwealth does upon the most deliberate reconsideration declare, that the said *alien* and *sedition laws*, are in their opinion, palpable violations of the said constitution; and however cheerfully it may be disposed to surrender its opinion to a majority of its sister states in matters of ordinary or doubtful policy; yet, in momentous regulations like the present, which so vitally wound the best rights of the citizen, it would consider a silent acquiesecence as highly criminal: That although this commonwealth as a party to the federal compact; will bow to the laws of the Union, yet it does at the same time declare, that it will not now, nor ever hereafter, cease to oppose in a constitutional manner, every attempt from what quarter soever offered, to violate that compact:

AND FINALLY, in order that no pretexts or arguments may be drawn from a supposed acquiescence on the part of this commonwealth in the constitutionality of those laws, and be thereby used as precedents for similar future violations of federal compact; this commonwealth does now enter against them, its SOLEMN PROTEST.

Approved December 3rd, 1799.

INDEX

A

B

C

D

E

F

G

H

I

J

K

L

M

N

O

P

Q

R

S

T

U

V

W

Y

COLUMN CITATIONS

1 Article #138 is based on a CATO Institute briefing paper by fiscal policy analyst Veronique de Rugy, 3 March 2004.

2 Article #131-These remarks are excerpted from a stump speech by Wesley Allen Riddle at *The Florentine* Candidates' Forum, Andice Community Center, Andice, TX, 21 February 2004.

3 Article #259 is loosely based on William J. Watkins, Jr., *Reclaiming the American Revolution* (Palgrave Macmillan, 2004), chapters 4-6.

4 Ibid., 71 (Article #260).

5 Article #286 is loosely based on Richard A. Epstein's book, *How Progressives Rewrote the Constitution* (Cato Institute, 2006).

6 Ibid., 77 (Article #288).

7 Article #292 draws on details from book by J. William Middendorf II, *A Glorious Disaster: Barry Goldwater's Presidential Campaign and the Origins of the Conservative Movement* (2006).

8 Article #339 is loosely based on *George Washington and Benedict Arnold: A Tale of Two Patriots* by Dave R. Palmer (2006).

9 Article #344 based on Dave R. Palmer's book *George Washington and Benedict Arnold: A Tale of Two Patriots*, chapter 24 (2006).

10 Articles #321 is based on Osvaldo Schenone and Samuel Gregg, *A Theory of Corruption: The Theology and Economics of Sin* (Acton Institute, 2003).

11 Ibid., 99 (Article #322).

12 Ibid., 100 (Article #323).

13 Article #130 is excerpted from remarks made by Wesley Allen Riddle to teachers and students at Ellison High School Leadership Academy conference called "Leadership in Action" at Ellison High School in Killeen, Texas on January 31, 2004.

14 Article #333 is loosely based on chapter 10 of Steve Laffey's book, *Primary Mistake* (2007).

15 Article #366 is loosely based on reports by George Friedman, Chief Intelligence Officer of Strategic Forecasting (STRATFOR) in September 2008.

[16] Article #371 is loosely based on an editorial by John Samples, director of the Center for Representative Government at the Cato Institute, in *The Baltimore Sun* (8 January 2008).

[17] Article #372 is loosely based on an article in *The American Conservative* (October 2008) by Claes Ryn, professor of politics at Catholic University of America and chairman of NHI.

[18] Article #449 is loosely based on remarks by Paul Ryan (R-WI) in January 2010.

[19] Article #407 is from remarks to the Central Texas Conservatives, Temple, TX, 25 May 2009.

[20] Article #405 is based on remarks to the Friends of Wes Riddle Picnic at the Overlook Pavilion by Lake Belton, TX, 7 June 2009.

[21] Articles #459 is loosely based on an essay by David Horowitz. (2010)

[22] Ibid., 170 (Article #460).

[23] Ibid., 172 (Article #461).

[24] Article #151 is abridged and adapted from a speech by U.S. Congressman Ron Paul (R-TX, Dist. 14) before the U.S. House of Representatives, 11 February 2004.

[25] Article #143 is abridged and excerpted from a speech by U.S. Congressman Ron Paul (R-TX, Dist. 14) to the Foundation for Economic Education (FEE) in Irvington-on-Hudson, New York in February 2004.

[26] Article #193 borrows ideas and research from Randy Barnett's book, *Restoring the Lost Constitution—The Presumption of Liberty* (Princeton University, 2004).

[27] Article #194 is based on a speech by Dr. Richard Pipes, professor emeritus of history at Harvard, to the Foundation for Economic Education in Irvington, NY, October 2004

[28] Article #197 is based on remarks he made to Friends of Wes Riddle during their annual Picnic, Frank's Pavilion by Lake Belton, TX, 21 May 2005.

[29] Ibid., 239 (Article #198).

[30] Article #212 is largely excerpted from an address at a Hillsdale College Seminar by Stephen Markman, former Assistant Attorney General of the United States under President Reagan, currently a Justice of the Michigan Supreme Court, 29 April 2003.

[31] Article #206 is based on an essay by senior fellow in constitutional studies at Cato Institute, Robert A. Levy, published in *The Freeman* (May 2005).

[32] Article #254 is loosely based on a study of the Kentucky and Virginia Resolutions by William J. Watkins, Jr., *Reclaiming the American Revolution* (Palgrave Macmillan, 2004).

[33] Article #257 is loosely based on William J. Watkins, Jr., *Reclaiming the American Revolution* (Palgrave Macmillan, 2004), chapters 4-6.

[34] Ibid., 259 (Article #258).

[35] Lewis Napper, *Bill of No Rights* (1993). Retrieved July 10, 2011. Lew's Wesbiste Tawas Bay Michigan. *http://www.lrudel.com/bill.htm.*

[36] Article #081 is based on work by Claremont Institute historians Thomas West and Douglas Jeffrey.

[37] Article #467 is condensed from remarks made by State Rep. Elect David Simpson to Republican Club of Austin, 7 September 2010.

[38] Ibid., 279 (Article #468).

[39] Article #144 is based on an essay by Secretary of State Colin Powell and published in *USA Weekend* (May, 2002).

[40] Article #116-Much of this piece is paraphrased from Tom Brokaw's book, *The Greatest Generation* (Random House, 2004). These remarks delivered to Belton American Legion Post#55, in tribute of local World War II veterans, 10 November 2003.

[41] Article #278 is condensed from STRATFOR Geopolitical Intelligence Report by George Friedman. Army budget figures are from Thom Shanker and David Cloud of the *New York Times*, October 2006.

[42] Article #111 is taken from remarks he delivered at the Senior Fellowship Center to the Temple Gun Club, 6 October 2003.

[43] Ibid., 304 (Article #112).

[44] Ibid., 306 (Article #113).

[45] Article #295 is loosely based on a monograph by Charles W. Baird called *Liberating Labor* (Acton Institute, 2002).

[46] Ibid., 310 (Article 296).

[47] Ibid., 311 (Article 297).

[48] Article #394 is based on the book by Woods and Gutzman, *Who Killed the Constitution?* (2008).

[49] Ibid., 315 (Article #395).

[50] Ibid., 317(Article #396).

[51] Ibid., 319 (Article #397).

[52] Ibid., 320 (Article #399).

[53] Ibid., 322 (Article #400).

[54] Ibid., 324 (Article #402).

[55] Ibid., 325 (Article #403).

[56] Ibid., 327 (Article #406).

[57] Ibid., 329 (Article #408).

[58] Ibid., 331 (Article #409).

59 Ibid., 333 (Article #410).

60 Article #273 is largely abridged and condensed from an address by Lord Acton to the Bridgnorth Institute in England on 26 Feb 1877.

61 Article #196 is based on remarks by popular historian David McCullough at a Hillsdale College National Leadership Seminar, Phoenix, AZ, 15 February 2005.

62 Article #457 is based on remarks to the Southwest Youth Leadership Conference held at Central Texas College in Killeen, TX, 28 June 2010.

63 Article #335- Latin phrase is a benediction from the memorial for Buckley by Father Robert A. Sirico, 4 April 2008.

64 Article #349 is loosely based on address to the Ashbrook Center for Public Affiairs at Ashland University, Ohio, by Judge Edith Jones for Constitution Day, 17 September 2007.

65 Article #127 is excerpted from an essay by Dr. Richard Ebeling, president of the Foundation for Economic Education, *www.fee.org* (2003).

66 Ibid., 396 (Article #128).

67 Article #152 is abridged from a speech by Foster S. Friess delivered at Hillsdale College in Michigan, upon receiving that college's Adam Smith Award, 11 May 2002.

68 Article #195 is based on remarks by Walter E. Williams, professor of economics at George Mason University, to a seminar at Hillsdale College, Hillsdale, Michigan in February 2005.

69 Article #389 is based on a lecture by Burton W. Folsom, Jr.: "The Myth of the Robber Barons."

70 Article #077 is based on remarks made to the Temple Lion's Club (noon group), 8 January 2003.

71 Article #244 is loosely based on Newt Gingrich's *Winning the Future* (Washington, DC: Regnery Publishing, Inc., 2005), chapter 11.

72 Ron Paul, "Why Are Americans So Angry?" U.S. House of Representatives, 29 June 2006.

73 Article #183 is excerpted and adapted from a report on the Saudi Economy by Brad Bourland, Chief Economist for Saudi American Bank (SAMBA), February 2005.

74 Article #446 is loosely based on essay by Don Peck in *The Atlantic* magazine (March 2010).

75 Articles #427 is based on essay of the same title, *Great Myths of the Great Depression*, by Lawrence W. Reed and published jointly by the Mackinac Center for Public Policy and Foundation for Economic Education, 2008.

76 Ibid., 431 (Article #428).

77 Ibid., 433 (Article #431).

[78] Articles #415 is loosely based on the book by Thomas E. Woods, Jr., *Meltdown* (2009).

[79] Ibid., 437 (Article #416).

[80] Ibid., 438 (Article #417).

[81] Ibid., 440 (Article #418).

[82] Ibid., 442 (Article #419).

[83] Ibid., 444 (Article #420).

[84] Archbishop Stephen Langton and the Barons. *The Magna Carta* (1215). Retrieved July 10, 2011 from the *Constitution Society.* Prepared by Nancy Troutman (The Cleveland Free- Net - aa345). Distributed by the Cybercasting Services Division of the National Public Telecomputing Network (NPTN). *http://www.constitution.org/eng/magnacar.htm.*

[85] Hamilton, Alexander, John Jay, and James Madison. *The Federalist Papers* (1781-1789). Retrieved July 10, 2011 from Yale Law Library, Avalon Project: *Documents in Law, History and Diplomacy. http://avalon.law.yale.edu/subject_menus/fed.asp.*

[86] Jefferson, Thomas et al. *Declaration of Independence* (1776), Retrieved July 10, 2011 from the The U.S. National Archives and Records Administration, The Charters of Freedom. *http://www.archives.gov/exhibits/charters/declaration_transcript.html.*

[87] Madison, James et al. *The Constitution of the United States* (1787). Retrieved July 10, 2011 from USConstitution.net and Constitution.org. *http://www.usconstitution.net/const.html* and *http://www.constitution.org/us_doi.htm*, respectively.

[88] Jefferson, Thomas. *The Kentucky Resolutions of 1798*, from *The Papers of Thomas Jefferson, Volume 30: 1 January 1798 to 31 January 1799.* Princeton University Press, 2003, 550-56. Retrieved July 10, 2011. *http://www.princeton.edu/~tjpapers/kyres/kyadopted.html.*

[89] Madison, James. *The Virginia Resolutions of 1798.* Retrieved July 10, 2011. Yale Law Library, Avalon Project: *Documents in Law, History and Diplomacy. http://www.constitution.org/cons/virg1798.htm.*

[90] Jefferson, Thomas. *The Kentucky Resolutions of 1799.* Retrieved July 10, 2011. Yale Law Library, Avalon Project: *Documents in Law, History and Diplomacy. http://www.constitution.org/cons/kent1799.htm.*

www.ingramcontent.com/pod-product-compliance
Lightning Source LLC
LaVergne TN
LVHW091651070526
838199LV00050B/2141
* 9 7 9 8 8 9 0 3 1 8 0 6 0 *